AN MMY MONOGRAPH

Publications of

THE INSTITUTE OF MENTAL MEASUREMENTS

Edited by Oscar Krisen Buros

EDUCATIONAL, PSYCHOLOGICAL, AND PERSONALITY TESTS OF 1933 AND 1934

EDUCATIONAL, PSYCHOLOGICAL, AND PERSONALITY TESTS OF 1933, 1934, AND 1935

EDUCATIONAL, PSYCHOLOGICAL, AND PERSONALITY TESTS OF 1936

THE NINETEEN THIRTY-EIGHT MENTAL MEASUREMENTS YEARBOOK

THE NINETEEN FORTY MENTAL MEASUREMENTS YEARBOOK

THE THIRD MENTAL MEASUREMENTS YEARBOOK

THE FOURTH MENTAL MEASUREMENTS YEARBOOK

THE FIFTH MENTAL MEASUREMENTS YEARBOOK

TESTS IN PRINT

THE SIXTH MENTAL MEASUREMENTS YEARBOOK

READING TESTS AND REVIEWS

PERSONALITY TESTS AND REVIEWS

THE SEVENTH MENTAL MEASUREMENTS YEARBOOK

TESTS IN PRINT II

ENGLISH TESTS AND REVIEWS

FOREIGN LANGUAGE TESTS AND REVIEWS

INTELLIGENCE TESTS AND REVIEWS

MATHEMATICS TESTS AND REVIEWS

PERSONALITY TESTS AND REVIEWS II

READING TESTS AND REVIEWS II

SCIENCE TESTS AND REVIEWS

SOCIAL STUDIES TESTS AND REVIEWS

VOCATIONAL TESTS AND REVIEWS

ENGLISH

TESTS AND REVIEWS

EDITORIAL ASSOCIATE

JOAN STEIN PASZAMANT

EDITORIAL ASSISTANT

SANDRA BOXER DISCENZA

PRODUCTION AND SECRETARIAL

MARY ANNE MILLER BECKER

DORIS GREENE MCCAN

BARBARA RUIS MARTKO

MARY T. MOONEY

NATALIE J. ROSENTHAL TURTON

ENGLISH

TESTS AND REVIEWS

A Monograph
Consisting of the English Sections of the
SEVEN MENTAL MEASUREMENTS YEARBOOKS (1938–72)
and
TESTS IN PRINT II (1974)

Edited by
OSCAR KRISEN BUROS
Director, The Institute of Mental Measurements

THE GRYPHON PRESS
HIGHLAND PARK · NEW JERSEY
1975

DESIGNED BY LUELLA BUROS

COPYRIGHT 1975 BY OSCAR KRISEN BUROS, PUBLISHED BY THE GRYPHON PRESS,
220 MONTGOMERY STREET, HIGHLAND PARK, NEW JERSEY 08904. No part of this publication may
be reproduced in any form, nor may any of the contents be used in an informational storage,
retrieval, or transmission system without the prior written permission of the publisher.

LC 75-8109, ISBN 910674-15-9

MANUFACTURED BY QUINN & BODEN COMPANY, INC., RAHWAY, NEW JERSEY
PRINTED IN THE UNITED STATES OF AMERICA

To
Hannah and Al

TABLE OF CONTENTS

MMY TEST REVIEWERS

Janet G. Afflerbach	5:232	Paul B. Diederich	1:972, 1:976
John C. Almack	1:1159, 2:1310, 2:1315		2:1300, 7:196, 7:220
Nicholas Anastasiow	7:205	John S. Diekhoff	3:129, 3:146, 4:183
J. Douglas Ayers	6:253		4:187, 4:196, 5:206, 5:211
Walter Barnes	1:969A	Jerome E. Doppelt	5:237
Roland L. Beck	2:1272, 2:1278	Vincent R. D'Oyley	7:208, 7:213
Harold H. Bixler	3:158, 3:162	Walter N. Durost	4:170
	3:164, 4:198, 4:204, 4:211	Ralph D. Dutch	7:185
Hillel Black	6:292	Reginald Edwards	5:192
Fred H. Borgen	7:231, 7:232	Leonard S. Feldt	5:176, 6:249
M. Alan Brimer	5:174, 5:182		6:256, 7:200, 7:208, 7:214
	5:183, 6:271, 7:207	James A. Fitzgerald	5:230
M. Eustace Broom	2:1310	Robert Fitzpatrick	7:231
Miriam M. Bryan	6:277, 6:280	C. M. Fleming	4:215
Paul S. Burnham	3:161, 3:169	Thomas G. Foran	1:1159
Nancy W. Burton	7:222	Charles Fox	2:1275
John B. Carroll	7:201	Ann L. Gebhardt	2:1296, 2:1307
Robert S. Cathcart	5:221	J. Raymond Gerberich	3:127, 5:175, 6:266
Henry Chauncey	6:263	H. H. Giles	1:969A, 2:1296, 2:1304
Ruth D. Churchill	3:136	Marvin D. Glock	6:268
William E. Coffman	6:293, 7:209	Keith Goltry	2:1273, 2:1282
John Cohen	3:135	Neil Gourlay	5:187
Walter W. Cook	2:1311, 2:1312	Harry A. Greene	2:1274
Edgar Dale	3:160, 3:161		2:1292, 3:126, 3:133
John C. Daniels	5:182	Walter S. Guiler	4:202, 4:203
Charlotte Croon Davis	3:122, 3:125	R. Gulliford	7:194
	3:128, 4:153, 4:154	Chester W. Harris	3:139
	4:175, 4:178, 5:207, 6:276, 6:287		3:140, 3:143, 4:155
Frederick B. Davis	4:178	David P. Harris	7:186, 7:200
Frank P. DeLay	2:1269, 2:1290	A. N. Hieronymus	5:233, 6:292
Clarence Derrick	4:166, 4:167, 5:174	Jean Hoard	2:1274, 2:1285
	6:250, 6:275, 7:189, 7:201	Thomas D. Horn	7:229, 7:230
Joseph C. Dewey	2:1311	Robert W. Howard	2:1269.1, 2:1278

PREFACE

IT IS my considered belief that most standardized tests are poorly constructed, of questionable or unknown validity, pretentious in their claims, and likely to be misused more often than not. This conviction began to form 48 to 50 years ago when I was taking courses in testing at the University of Minnesota. I vividly recall presenting a paper entitled "Common Fallacies in the Use of Standardized Tests" in an advanced educational psychology class taught by Professor W. S. Miller, a paper in which I criticized some of the views of my instructors. Shortly thereafter, I had the good fortune to read a book which was a landmark in the consumer movement—*Your Money's Worth* by Stuart Chase and F. J. Schlink. It was this book which led to the founding of Consumers' Research, Inc., an organization which tests and evaluates commonly used commercial products. This book and the establishment of Consumers' Research stimulated me to begin thinking about a test users' research organization to evaluate tests.

After failing to secure financial support for the initiation of a test users' research organization, I scaled down my objectives to the establishment of a cooperative test reviewing service which would report on and evaluate standardized tests used in education, industry, and psychology. One hundred thirty-three specialists in a wide variety of disciplines cooperated by contributing "frankly critical reviews" for *The 1938 Mental Measurements Yearbook* (also called *The First Yearbook*). Later yearbooks (each volume supplementing earlier volumes) were published in 1941, 1949, 1953, 1959, 1965, and 1972.

The objectives of the *Mental Measurements Yearbooks* (MMY's) have remained essentially the same since they were first presented in detail in *The 1940 Mental Measurements Yearbook* (also called *The Second Yearbook*): (*a*) to provide information about tests published as separates throughout the English-speaking world; (*b*) to present frankly critical test reviews written by testing and subject specialists representing various viewpoints; (*c*) to provide extensive bibliographies of verified references on the construction, use, and validity of specific tests; (*d*) to make readily available the critical portions of test reviews appearing in professional journals; and (*e*) to present fairly exhaustive listings of new and revised books on testing along with evaluative excerpts from representative reviews in professional journals.

As important as the above objectives are, I place even greater importance on these less tangible objectives: (*f*) to impel test authors and publishers to publish better tests and to provide test users with detailed information on the validity and limitations of these tests; (*g*) to inculcate in test users a keener awareness of the values and limitations of standardized tests; (*h*) to stimulate contributing reviewers to think through more carefully their own beliefs and values relevant to testing; (*i*) to suggest to test users better methods of appraising tests in light of their own particular needs; and (*j*) to impress upon test users the need to suspect all tests unaccompanied by detailed data on their construction, validity, uses, and limitations—

even when products of distinguished authors and reputable publishers.

As the number of published tests and, especially, the related literature increased tremendously over the years, the MMY's became increasingly more encyclopedic in scope. Many test users, however, are interested in only one or two areas of testing. To meet their needs, we announced in 1941 plans for publishing monographs in English, foreign languages, intelligence, mathematics, personality, reading, science, social studies, and vocations. Unfortunately, we were too optimistic; it was over a quarter of a century before we were able to finance the publication of the first monograph, *Reading Tests and Reviews* (RTR I), published in 1968.

The next monograph, *Personality Tests and Reviews* (PTR I), was published in 1970. The core of these two monographs, RTR I and PTR I, consists of a reprinting of the reading and personality sections, respectively, of the first six MMY's and a new section listing both in print and out of print tests in the area represented by the monograph.

Despite the use of a large amount of reprinted material, the preparation and publication of these two monographs turned out to be very costly. Since sales later proved insufficient to finance similar monographs in other areas, we temporarily abandoned our plans for additional monographs.

Following the publication of *The Seventh Yearbook* in early 1972, we began devoting all of our time to the completion of *Tests in Print II: An Index to Tests, Test Reviews, and the Literature on Specific Tests* (TIP II). In mid-1974, while TIP II was in press, it suddenly occurred to me that up-to-date monographs could be prepared at a manageable cost by reprinting a given section of TIP II along with the corresponding sections of the seven MMY's. As a consequence, we are now publishing monographs in nine areas: second monographs in personality and reading, and first monographs in English, foreign languages, intelligence, mathematics, science, social studies, and vocations. Hopefully, the publication of these monographs will make our material available to many test users who might otherwise not consult the MMY's and TIP II. Broadening the readership of our test reviews will bring us closer to achieving our objectives.

This monograph, *English Tests and Reviews,* reflects the changing state of the art over 50 years of English testing. Except for the development of college accreditation and advanced placement tests, little progress has been made in providing better standardized English tests. A comparison of English tests reviewed in recent years with those in the 2nd and 3rd MMY's shows, with the above exceptions, that a wider range of objectives was being covered 20 to 30 years ago. Considering the extensive use of English tests—especially as parts of achievement batteries at elementary and secondary school levels—and the influence of testing on the learning process, it is important that we have the best possible tests. To achieve this goal, specialists in English education should give more attention to the development, use, and validation of standardized tests in English. It would be especially helpful if professional journals in education would give more adequate coverage to English testing. In addition to more articles on testing, the journals might regularly print reviews of tests, including the "closed" tests of organizations such as the CEEB. If each journal reviewed three to five English tests per year, the critical coverage provided by the MMY's would be greatly complemented.

It has been particularly hectic preparing nine MMY monographs simultaneously. Fortunately, I have been assisted by a dedicated staff. Although other people worked for shorter periods of time, there are seven whom I would like to name for special recognition: Mary Anne Miller Becker, Sandra Boxer Discenza, Doris Greene McCan, Barbara Ruis Martko, Mary T. Mooney, Joan Stein Paszamant, and Natalie J. Rosenthal Turton. I am greatly indebted to my staff colleagues for their assistance in producing these nine derivative monographs.

We plan to publish *The Eighth Mental Measurements Yearbook* in 1977, followed by *Tests in Print III* in 1978. The English sections of these volumes will supplement and update the material in this monograph.

OSCAR KRISEN BUROS

Highland Park, New Jersey
February 24, 1975

INTRODUCTION

FOR THE past 40 years we have been providing test users in education, industry, and psychology with a series of publications designed to assist them in the selection and use of tests which best meet their needs. We maintained an annual production schedule for our first four volumes (1935–38); since then, however, the intervals between books have been quite irregular with publication dates 1941, 1949, 1953, 1959, 1961, 1965, 1968, 1970, 1972, and 1974. Our publications through 1974 include three test bibliographies, seven *Mental Measurements Yearbooks,* two monographs, and two *Tests in Print.*[1] Nine derivative monographs—this volume and eight others—are being published in 1975. A brief description of our first fourteen publications follows.

FIRST THREE PUBLICATIONS

Although the earliest three publications are noncritical bibliographies, the original intent had been to prepare an annual critical review of new tests for journal publication. It soon became apparent, however, that this was far beyond the capacity of a single individual. A more modest goal was substituted, the publication of an annual bibliography of tests, as described in the Introduction to the first one:

To locate the standard tests recently published in specific areas is a laborious task. The usual bibliographic aids for locating periodical, monograph, and book publications are of little value in locating standard tests. New tests are being published so rapidly that the test technicians themselves find it difficult to locate the test titles of the past year without an inordinate amount of searching. For these reasons, the writer has undertaken the task of preparing a bibliography of psychological, achievement, character, and personality tests published in 1933 and 1934. This bibliography will be the first of a series to be published annually by the School of Education, Rutgers University.[2]

This 44-page bibliography lists 257 tests that were new, revised, or supplemented in 1933 and 1934. Many of these tests, usually revised editions, are still in print today.

Similar test bibliographies[3] were published in 1936 and 1937. During this time, attempts were being made to obtain a grant to initiate a

[1] The first fourteen publications (1935–1974), edited by Oscar K. Buros and now published by The Gryphon Press, are listed from the most recent to the oldest:
a) Tests in Print II: An Index to Tests, Test Reviews, and the Literature on Specific Tests, December 1974. Pp. xxxix, 1107. $70.
b) The Seventh Mental Measurements Yearbook, Vols. I and II, 1972. Pp. xl, 935; vi, 937–1986. $70 per set.
c) Personality Tests and Reviews: Including an Index to The Mental Measurements Yearbooks, 1970. Pp. xxxi, 1659. $45. For reviews, *see* 7:B120.
d) Reading Tests and Reviews: Including a Classified Index to The Mental Measurements Yearbooks, 1968. Pp. xxii, 520. $20. For reviews, *see* 7:B121.
e) The Sixth Mental Measurements Yearbook, 1965. Pp. xxxvii, 1714. $45. (Reprinted 1971) For reviews, *see* 7:B122.
f) Tests in Print: A Comprehensive Bibliography of Tests for Use in Education, Psychology, and Industry, 1961. Pp. xxix, 479. $15. (Reprinted 1974) For reviews, *see* 6:B105.
g) The Fifth Mental Measurements Yearbook, 1959. Pp. xxix, 1292. $35. (Reprinted 1961) For reviews, *see* 6:B104.
h) The Fourth Mental Measurements Yearbook, 1953. Pp. xxv, 1163. $30. (Reprinted 1974) For reviews, *see* 5:B84.
i) The Third Mental Measurements Yearbook, 1949. Pp. xv, 1047. $25. (Reprinted 1974) For reviews, *see* 4:B71.
j) The Nineteen Forty Mental Measurements Yearbook, 1941. Pp. xxv, 674. $20. (Reissued 1972) For reviews, *see* 3:788 and 4:B70.
k) The Nineteen Thirty Eight Mental Measurements Yearbook, 1938. Pp. xv, 415. $17.50. (Reissued 1972) For reviews, *see* 2:B858.
l) Educational, Psychological, and Personality Tests of 1936: Including a Bibliography and Book Review Digest of Measurement Books and Monographs of 1933–36, 1937. Pp. 141. Out of print. For reviews, *see* 1:B326.
m) Educational, Psychological, and Personality Tests of 1933, 1934, and 1935, 1936. Pp. 83. Out of print. For reviews, *see* 36:B46.
n) Educational, Psychological, and Personality Tests of 1933 and 1934, 1935. Pp. 44. Out of print. For a review, *see* 36:B45.

[2] *Educational, Psychological, and Personality Tests of 1933 and 1934,* p. 5.
[3] *Educational, Psychological, and Personality Tests of 1933, 1934, and 1935.*
Educational, Psychological, and Personality Tests of 1936.

research organization which would serve as a bureau of standards for the evaluation of educational and psychological tests. It was only after we despaired of raising such funds that we decided to set up a test reviewing service.

THE SEVEN MMY'S

Since tests, unlike books, were rarely reviewed in professional journals, it was a revolutionary step forward when we published *The 1938 Mental Measurements Yearbook* 37 years ago. In his Foreword, Clarence E. Partch's comments reflect our excitement and mood in those early days:

The publication of *The 1938 Mental Measurements Yearbook of the School of Education, Rutgers University* is likely to prove a landmark of considerable importance in the history of tests and measurements. Heretofore, despite the obvious need of test users for frank evaluations of tests by competent reviewers, few standardized tests have been critically appraised in the professional journals and textbooks for students of education and psychology. Now, for the first time, a large number of frankly evaluative reviews by able test technicians, subject-matter specialists, and psychologists are available to assist test users in making more discriminating selections from among the hundreds of tests on the market.[4]

Except for a few test authors and publishers who objected to unfavorable reviews, *The 1938 Yearbook* (also referred to as *The First Yearbook*) was enthusiastically acclaimed in this country and abroad. It took some time, however, before most of the protesting publishers were able to accept unfavorable test reviews with equanimity.

Before *The 1938 Yearbook* was off the press, we began sending out invitations to review tests for a 1939 yearbook. Unfortunately, because of financing and production problems, we were unable to maintain our annual production schedule. It took us over two years to publish the next volume, *The 1940 Mental Measurements Yearbook*.

Much enlarged and greatly improved over its predecessor, *The 1940 Yearbook* (also referred to as *The Second Yearbook*) has been the prototype for all later yearbooks. In addition to the increased number of tests, reviews, and references, there were many qualitative changes: (*a*) The objectives which have characterized all MMY's were presented in detail for the first time. (*b*) The format was standardized. (*c*) The classification of tests was

changed from 40 specific categories to 12 broad categories. (*d*) The practice of including very short reviews of 100 words or less was discontinued. (*e*) The review coverage was extended to old tests and to tests previously reviewed as well as new tests. (*f*) The instructions given to reviewers concerning the preparation of their test reviews were presented. (*g*) The reactions of test authors and publishers—most of them objecting strenuously to unfavorable reviews—were reprinted for the first and last time.

In the Preface of *The 1940 Yearbook* we announced that the yearbooks would be published every two years. Because of World War II, however, *The Third Mental Measurements Yearbook* was not published until 1949. Except for its larger size and more thorough preparation, *The Third Yearbook*—like all later yearbooks—is very similar in its coverage, format, indexing, and organization to *The 1940 Yearbook*. There were, however, several improvements: (*a*) The "Classified Index of Tests," an expanded table of contents, was introduced. (*b*) Stars and asterisks were used preceding test titles to indicate, respectively, tests listed in a yearbook for the first time and tests revised or supplemented since last listed. (*c*) Asterisks were used at the end of a reference to indicate that the reference had been examined personally for accuracy and relevance. (*d*) Whenever possible, the abstract in *Psychological Abstracts* was cited for each reference. (*e*) Two improvements were made in the name index. Previously authors of references for specific tests had been indexed merely by citing the test for which the reference appears. After locating the test, one then had to search through the references to find those by that author. The new index eliminated this searching by citing each reference both to the test number and the reference number. Secondly, the index was converted into an "analytic index" in which *"test," "rev," "exc," "bk,"* and *"ref"* were used to indicate whether a citation referred to authorship of a test, review, excerpted review, book, or reference. These five features have been included in all later yearbooks.

In *The Fourth Mental Measurements Yearbook,* published in 1953, our review coverage was extended for the first time to many tests restricted to testing programs administered by organizations such as the College Entrance Ex-

---

4 *The 1938 Mental Measurements Yearbook,* p. xi.

amination Board. Six years later, in 1959, *The Fifth Yearbook* was published. Upon the completion of that volume, we were concerned that some cutbacks would be necessary to stem the phenomenal growth of production costs, as well as the ever increasing length of each MMY. As a result, we decided to discontinue specific test bibliographies and almost all reviews of foreign tests. The appreciative reviews *The Fifth Yearbook* received, however, especially those mentioning the value of the specific bibliographies to students of testing, caused us to reconsider. Consequently, despite the expanding literature on specific tests, we decided to continue all features of the earlier volumes. As a result, it took us six years to publish in 1965 *The Sixth Mental Measurements Yearbook,* a 1,751-page volume, approximately one-third larger than the previous yearbook. In addition to its more extensive coverage, *The Sixth Yearbook* presents a comprehensive listing of all tests in print as of mid-1964. The latest yearbook to date, *The Seventh Yearbook,* was published in 1972. This massive two-volume work of 2,032 pages may well be considered the zenith of the MMY's.

Like all other volumes published since 1938, *The Seventh Yearbook* supplements rather than supplants earlier yearbooks. For complete coverage, therefore, a reader must have access to all seven MMY's. A person using only the latest, *The Seventh Yearbook,* will miss a tremendous amount of valuable information in the six earlier volumes. Although the more recent yearbooks—especially the last three—are of greatest value, the third and fourth yearbooks also contain much useful information on many in print tests. Even though the first two yearbooks are mainly of historical interest, they also include some critical information on currently used tests. Our faith in the value of the first four MMY's, published between 1938 and 1953, is attested to by our reissuing of the first and second yearbooks in 1972 and reprinting of the third and fourth in 1974. Consequently, all seven yearbooks are now in print.

EARLIER MMY MONOGRAPHS

It is with amusement and wonder that we look back at some of the dreams of our youth. *The 1940 Mental Measurements Yearbook* was the first yearbook published by my wife and myself. In those depression days, money was scarce but printing was cheap and penny post-cards could be used for advertising. Borrowed capital of $3,500 was sufficient to launch us into book publishing. Even before our first book was off the press we were planning to publish not only a new MMY every two years, but also a series of derivative monographs. Our plans were confidently announced in the Preface of *The 1940 Yearbook* thus:

In order to make the material in the yearbooks more easily accessible to individuals who are interested in only a small part of each volume, a new series of monographs is being planned. If the first two or three monographs prove successful, others will eventually be prepared to cover tests in each of the following fields: business education, English and reading, fine arts, foreign languages, health and physical education, home economics, industrial arts, intelligence, mathematics, sciences, social studies, and vocational aptitudes. The first publication in each field will include: a comprehensive bibliography of all standard tests in print in that area; a reprinting, in part or in full, of all reviews of these tests which have appeared in previous yearbooks or in the journal literature; new reviews written especially for the monograph (to be, in turn, reprinted, in part or in full, in the following yearbook); and an extensive list of references on the construction, validation, use, and limitations of the tests. Separates in each field will be issued every four, six, or eight years depending upon the frequency of test publication. These monographs will range in size from fifty to two hundred pages. This new series will make it possible for an individual to purchase, at a nominal cost, every four, six, or eight years a monograph devoted solely to the tests and reviews of most interest to him.[5]

However, the publishing of the MMY's alone, even at intervals of 4 to 8 years, proved to be so time consuming and difficult that initiating the monograph series had to be continually postponed. But the dreams were never abandoned.

In 1968, 27 years after the monograph series was initially announced, the first monograph, *Reading Tests and Reviews* (RTR I), was published. This 542-page volume consists of a comprehensive bibliography of reading tests as of May 1968 and a reprinting of the reading sections of the first six MMY's. A second monograph, *Personality Tests and Reviews* (PTR I), was published two years later. This 1,695-page volume lists all personality tests as of June 1969 and provides a reprinting of the personality sections of the first six MMY's. The preparation of these two monographs turned out to be too costly and time consuming to justify working on monographs in other areas.

[5] *The 1940 Mental Measurements Yearbook,* p. xx.

TIP I AND TIP II

In 1961, we published the ninth volume in the MMY series: *Tests in Print: A Comprehensive Bibliography of Tests for Use in Education, Psychology, and Industry.* The objectives and nature of *Tests in Print* (hereafter called *Tests in Print I* or TIP I) are described in its Introduction as follows:

The objectives of *Tests in Print* are threefold: first, to present a comprehensive bibliography of tests—achievement, aptitude, intelligence, personality, and certain sensory-motor skills—published as separates and currently available in English-speaking countries; second, to serve as a classified index and supplement to the volumes of the *Mental Measurements Yearbook* series published to date; third, to give a wider distribution to the excellent recommendations for improving test manuals made by committees of the American Psychological Association, the American Educational Research Association, and the National Council on Measurements Used in Education.[6]

TIP I lists 2,967 tests—2,126 in print and 841 out of print as of early 1961, and also serves as a master index to the contents of the first five MMY's. Originally, we had planned to publish a new edition of TIP shortly after the publication of each new MMY, but poor sales of TIP I caused these plans to be abandoned. *The Sixth Yearbook,* in effect, served as a new edition of *Tests in Print* by referring to the tests in TIP I which were still in print as of mid-1964. Surprisingly, however, sales of the 1961 *Tests in Print* began to pick up after publication of *The Sixth Yearbook* in 1965. This unexpected upturn encouraged us to begin devoting all of our time to the preparation of a new edition of TIP immediately after approving the last proofs for *The Seventh Yearbook.*

Tests in Print II: An Index to Tests, Test Reviews, and the Literature on Specific Tests (TIP II) was published in December 1974. Like the 1961 volume, *Tests in Print II* presents: (*a*) a comprehensive bibliography of all known tests published as separates for use with English-speaking subjects; (*b*) a classified index to the contents of the test sections of the seven *Mental Measurements Yearbooks* published to date; and (*c*) a reprinting of the 1974 APA-AERA-NCME *Standards for Educational and Psychological Tests.*

In addition, TIP II introduces the following new features: (*d*) comprehensive bibliographies through 1971 on the construction, use,

6 *Tests in Print,* p. xv.

and validity of specific tests; (*e*) a classified list of tests which have gone out of print since TIP I; (*f*) a cumulative name index for each test with references; (*g*) a title index covering in print and out of print tests, as well as inverted, series, and superseded titles in the MMY's and monographs; (*h*) an analytic name index covering all authors of tests, reviews, excerpts, and references in the MMY's and monographs; (*i*) a publishers directory with a complete listing of each publisher's test titles; (*j*) a classified scanning index which describes the population for which each test is intended; (*k*) identification of foreign tests and journals by presenting the country of origin in brackets immediately after a test entry or journal title; (*l*) inclusions of factual statements implying criticism such as "1971 tests identical with tests copyrighted 1961 except for format," and "no manual"; (*m*) listing of test titles at the foot of each page to permit immediate identification of pages consisting only of references or names; and (*n*) directions on how to use the book and an expanded table of contents printed on the endpages to greatly facilitate its use.

TIP II contains 2,467 in print test entries, 16.0 percent more than in TIP I. Table 1 presents a breakdown of the number of tests and new references in TIP II by classification. Personality—the area in which we know the least about testing—has, as it did in 1961, the greatest number of tests. Although the percentage of personality tests is 17.9, 44.9 percent of the TIP II references are for personality tests. Three categories—intelligence, personality, and

TABLE 1
TESTS AND NEW REFERENCES IN TESTS IN PRINT II

Classification	Tests		References	
	Number	Percent	Number	Percent
Achievement Batteries	50	2.0	438	2.6
English	131	5.3	220	1.3
Fine Arts	35	1.4	229	1.4
Foreign Languages	105	4.3	81	.5
Intelligence	274	11.1	4,039	24.4
Mathematics	168	6.8	166	1.0
Miscellaneous	291	11.8	866	5.2
Multi-Aptitude	26	1.1	235	1.4
Personality	441	17.9	7,443	44.9
Reading	248	10.1	837	5.1
Science	97	3.9	72	.4
Sensory-Motor	62	2.5	382	2.3
Social Studies	85	3.4	49	.3
Speech and Hearing	79	3.2	216	1.3
Vocations	375	15.2	1,301	7.8
Total	2,467	100.0	16,574	99.9

vocations—make up 44.2 percent of tests and 77.1 percent of the references in TIP II.

ENGLISH TESTS AND REVIEWS

This volume's subtitle, *A Monograph Consisting of the English Sections of the Seven Mental Measurements Yearbooks (1938–72) and Tests in Print II (1974)*, succinctly describes its contents. In addition to the 20-page reprint from TIP II and the 324-page section of reprints from the seven MMY's, *English Tests and Reviews* (ETR) includes a publishers directory, title index, name index, and an English scanning index. The TIP II scanning index is reprinted in full also.

TIP II TESTS REPRINT

The section of this volume reprinted from *Tests in Print II,* TIP II Tests, contains a bibliography of in print English tests, references for specific tests, cumulative name indexes for specific tests with references, and lists of tests which have gone out of print since appearing in TIP I. (The out of print tests are listed alphabetically at the ends of the subsections: general, literature, spelling, and vocabulary.) The first three of these categories will be described in more detail.

ENGLISH TESTS

The TIP II reprint section lists 131 English tests in print as of early 1974—28.0 percent fewer tests than were listed 14 years ago in TIP I (Table 2).

Although there was a drop in the number of tests in all categories, the decrease was largest in literature (45.9 percent) and in spelling (43.3 percent). Although 63.7 percent of the English tests listed in the 1961 TIP I are now out of print, some tests being currently sold

TABLE 2

IN PRINT ENGLISH TESTS
IN TIP II AND TIP I

Classification	TIP II		TIP I	
	Number	Percent	Number	Percent
General	74	56.5	89	48.9
Literature	20	15.3	37	20.3
Spelling	17	13.0	30	16.5
Vocabulary	20	15.3	26	14.3
Total	131	100.1	182	100.0

have not been revised since published 20, 30, 40, and in two instances, 50 years ago. Of the 131 in print English tests, 9.2 percent (12 tests) are new since the 7th MMY; 26.7 percent (35 tests), revised or supplemented.

Unlike the long test entries in the *Mental Measurements Yearbooks,* the TIP II entries in this volume are short entries supplying the following information:

a) TITLE. Test titles are printed in boldface type. Secondary or series titles are set off from main titles by a colon. Titles are always presented exactly as reported in the test materials. Stars precede titles of tests listed for the first time in TIP II; asterisks precede titles of tests which have been revised or supplemented since last listed.

b) TEST POPULATION. The grade, chronological age, or semester range, or the employment category is usually given. Commas are used to indicate separate grade levels. "Grades 1.5–2.5, 2–3, 4–12, 13–17" means that there are four test booklets: a booklet for the middle of the first grade through the middle of the second grade, a booklet for the beginning of the second grade through the end of the third grade, a booklet for grades 4 through 12 inclusive, and a booklet for undergraduate and graduate students in colleges and universities. "First, second semester" means that there are two test booklets: one covering the work of the first semester, the other covering the work of the second semester. "1, 2 semesters" indicates that the second booklet covers the work of the two semesters. "Ages 10-2 to 11-11" means ages 10 years 2 months to 11 years 11 months and "Grades 4-6 to 5-9" means the sixth month in the fourth grade through the ninth month in the fifth grade. "High school and college" denotes a single test booklet for both levels; "High school, college" denotes two test booklets, one for high school and one for college.

c) COPYRIGHT DATE. The range of copyright dates (or publication dates if not copyrighted) includes the various forms, accessories, and editions of a test. When the publication date differs from the copyright date, both dates are given; e.g., "1971, c1965–68" means that the test materials were copyrighted between 1965 and 1968 but were not published until 1971. Publication or copyright dates enclosed in brackets do not appear on the test materials but were obtained from other sources.

d) ACRONYM. An acronym is given for many tests. Following the alphabetical sequence of test titles in the Index of Titles, there is an alphabetical listing of acronyms for tests with 10 or more references.

e) SPECIAL COMMENTS. Some entries contain special notations, such as: "for research use only"; "revision of the *ABC Test*"; "tests administered monthly at centers throughout the United States"; "subtests available as separates"; and "verbal creativity." "For research use only" should be interpreted to mean that the *only* use of the test should be in research designed to assess its usefulness; contrary to what the implications seem to be, "for research use only" does not mean that a test has any use, whatsoever, as a research instrument. Tests used in research studies should have demonstrated validity before being selected as research tools. A statement such as "verbal creativity" is intended to further describe what the test claims to measure.

f) PART SCORES. The number and description of part scores is presented.

g) FACTUAL STATEMENTS IMPLYING CRITICISM. Some of the test entries include factual statements which imply criticism of the test, such as "1970 test identical with test copyrighted 1960" and "no manual."

h) AUTHOR. For most tests, all authors are reported. In the case of tests which appear in a new form each year, only authors of the most recent forms are listed. Names are reported exactly as printed on test materials. Names of editors are generally not reported.

i) PUBLISHER. The name of the publisher or distributor is reported for each test. Foreign publishers are identified by listing the country in brackets immediately following the name of the publisher. The Publishers Directory and Index must be consulted for a publisher's address.

j) FOREIGN ADAPTATIONS. Revisions and adaptations of tests for foreign use are listed in parentheses following the description of the original edition.

k) CLOSING ASTERISK. An asterisk following the publisher's name indicates that the entry was prepared from a first-hand examination of the test materials.

l) SUBLISTINGS. Levels, editions, subtests, or parts of a test which are available in separate booklets are sometimes presented as sublistings with titles set in small capitals. Sub-sublistings are indented with titles set in italic type.

m) CROSS REFERENCES. Except for tests being listed for the first time, a test entry includes a second paragraph with cross references to relevant material which may be found in the MMY reprint sections in this volume, or, in some instances (such as reviews of testing programs), to material in other sections of the MMY's. These cross references may be to "additional information" reported in longer entries, or to reviews, excerpts, and references for specific tests.

REFERENCES

The specific test bibliographies in this monograph contain 782 references on the construction, use, and validity of specific tests—569 of these references for tests currently in print. Of the references for in print tests, 18.5 percent are for the last six years reported on, 1966–71. Relatively little research and writing is being done on standardized tests in English—currently about 15 references per year.

Only nine of the in print tests have generated bibliographies of 10 or more references: *Cooperative English Tests,* 300 references; *College Board Achievement Test in English Composition,* 37; *Iowa Placement Examinations: English Training,* 26; *New Purdue Placement Test in English,* 21; *Sequential Tests of Educational Progress: Writing,* 16; *Iowa Placement Examinations: English Aptitude,* 15; *Moray House English Tests,* 14; *Purdue High School English Test,* 12; and *California Achievement Tests: Language,* 10. The first test mentioned, *Cooperative English Tests,* has more references than the combined total for all other in print English tests.

These specific test bibliographies cover not only the literature of the English-speaking world, but also the literature in English published in non-English-speaking countries. Our goal has been to include all published material—articles, books, chapters, and research monographs—as well as unpublished theses. We do not list as references research reports prepared for internal organizational use, prepublication reports, ERIC material, or abstracts of documents which are reproduced only on receipt of a purchase order (e.g., JSAS manuscripts). Secondary sources (e.g., *Psychological Abstracts*) may provide leads, but if the original publication cannot be located and examined, the reference is not used. We do, however, rely on secondary sources (primarily *Dissertation Abstracts International*) for unpublished theses. Except for doctoral dissertations abstracted in DAI, in recent years all thesis entries have been checked for accuracy by the degree-granting institutions.

References for a given test immediately follow the test entry. They are numbered consecutively for each test as they appear in the first through the seventh MMY and TIP II. References which appeared in earlier volumes are referred to but not repeated; e.g., "85–142. See 5:179." means references 85–142 can be found following test 179 in the section "Fifth MMY Reviews" in this volume.

References are arranged in chronological order by year of publication and alphabetically by authors within years. No references later than 1971 have been included. Supplementary bibliographies will be provided in the forthcoming 8th MMY for those tests which are listed again in that volume; the bibliographies for other tests will be brought up to date in *Tests in Print III,* scheduled for publication after the 8th MMY.

CUMULATIVE NAME INDEXES

A cumulative name index has been provided for every in print test having references to facilitate the search for an author's writings relevant to that test. To simplify indexing, forenames were reduced to initials. Authors not consistent in reporting their names may be listed under two or more citations. On the other hand, a given name may represent two or more persons. In all cases, however, the references present names exactly as they appear in the publication referenced.

TABLE 3

Reviews, Excerpts, and References
for the 292 English Tests
in This Volume

Reprint	Tests	Rev's	Exc's	Ref's
TIP II	131			220
7th MMY	55	41	1	31
6th MMY	99	49	2	145
5th MMY	69	50		95
4th MMY	71	38		112
3rd MMY	57	47	1	120
2nd MMY	60	56	4	58
1st MMY	26	10		1
Total	292 [1]	291	8	782

[1] The total number of different tests in all publications is 292—131 in print and 161 out of print.

MMY REVIEWS REPRINT

This chapter is a reprinting of the English test sections of the seven *Mental Measurements Yearbooks* presented in their order of publication: 1st MMY (1938, 11 pages), 2nd MMY (1941, 44 pages), 3rd MMY (1949, 40 pages), 4th MMY (1953, 42 pages), 5th MMY (1959, 53 pages), 6th MMY (1965, 77 pages), and 7th MMY (1972, 57 pages). This chapter brings together in a single well-indexed volume a tremendous amount of information on English testing covering the past 50 years and more.

Included in this chapter are 291 original test reviews written by 134 specialists, 8 excerpted test reviews, and 562 references on the construction, use, and validity of specific tests (Table 3). Of the 299 reviews and excerpts, 44.8 percent are for tests currently in print, although not always the most recent editions. Of the 782 references in this monograph, 72.8 percent are for tests in print.

The contributing reviewers represent a wide range of interests and viewpoints. Every effort was made to select reviewers who would be considered highly competent by a sizable group of test users. Our practice of publishing multiple reviews of given tests makes it possible to give representation to differing viewpoints among reviewers. The test reviews in a given yearbook are not limited to new and revised tests; old tests, especially those generating considerable research and writing, are frequently reviewed in successive yearbooks.

In order to make sure that persons invited to review would know what was expected of them, a sheet entitled "Suggestions to MMY Reviewers" was enclosed with each letter of invitation. The suggestions follow:

1. Reviews should be written with the following major objectives in mind:
a) To provide test users with carefully prepared appraisals of tests for their guidance in selecting and using tests.
b) To stimulate progress toward higher professional standards in the construction of tests by commending good work, by censuring poor work, and by suggesting improvements.
c) To impel test authors and publishers to present more detailed information on the construction, validity, reliability, uses, and possible misuses of their tests.

2. Reviews should be concise, the average review running from 600 to 1,200 words in length. The average length of the reviews written by one person generally should not exceed 1,000 words. Except for reviews of achievement batteries, multi-factor batteries, and tests for which a literature review is made, longer reviews should be prepared only with the approval of the Editor.

3. Reviews should be frankly critical, with both strengths and weaknesses pointed out in a judicious manner. Descriptive comments should be kept to the minimum necessary to support the critical portions of the review. Criticism should be as specific as possible; implied criticisms meaningful only to testing specialists should be avoided. Reviews should be written primarily for the rank and file of test users. An indication of the relative importance and value of a test with respect to competing tests should be presented whenever possible. If a reviewer considers a competing test better than the one being reviewed, the competing test should be specifically named.

4. If a test manual gives insufficient, contradictory, or ambiguous information regarding the construction, validity, and use of a test, reviewers are urged to write directly to authors and publishers for further information. Test authors and publishers should, however, be held responsible for presenting adequate data in test manuals—failure to do so should be pointed out. For comments made by reviewers based upon unpublished information received personally from test authors or publishers, the source of the unpublished information should be clearly indicated.

5. Reviewers will be furnished with the test entries which will precede their reviews. Information presented in the entry should not be repeated in reviews unless needed for evaluative purposes.

6. The use of sideheads is optional with reviewers.

7. Each review should conclude with a paragraph presenting a concise summary of the reviewer's overall evaluation of the test. The summary should be as explicit as possible. Is it the best of its kind? Is it recommended for use? If other tests are better, which of the competing tests is best?

8. A separate review should be prepared for each test. Each review should begin on a new sheet. The test and forms reviewed should be clearly indicated. Your name, title, position, and address should precede each review, e.g.: John Doe, Professor of Education and Psychology, University of Maryland, College Park, Maryland. The review should begin a new paragraph immediately after the address.

9. All reviews should be typed double spaced and in triplicate. Two copies of each review should be submitted to the Editor; one copy should be retained by the reviewer.

10. If for any reason a reviewer thinks he is not in a position to write a frankly critical review in a scholarly and unbiased manner, he should request the Editor to substitute other tests for review.

11. Reviewers may not invite others to collaborate with them in writing reviews unless permission is secured from the Editor.

12. Most tests will be reviewed by two or more persons in order to secure better representation of various viewpoints. Noncritical content which excessively overlaps similar materials presented by another reviewer may be deleted. Reviews will be carefully edited, but no important changes will be made without the consent of the reviewer. Galley proofs (unaccompanied by copy) will be submitted to reviewers for checking.

13. The Editor reserves the right to reject any review which does not meet the minimum standards of the MMY series.

14. Each reviewer will receive a complimentary copy of *The Seventh Mental Measurements Yearbook.*

The long test entries in the section Seventh MMY Reviews contain all the information in the short TIP II entries plus the following:

a) INDIVIDUAL OR GROUP TEST. All tests are group tests unless otherwise indicated.

b) FORMS, PARTS, AND LEVELS. All available forms, parts, and levels are listed with copyright dates.

c) PAGES. The number of pages on which print occurs is reported for test booklets, manuals, technical reports, profiles, and other nonapparatus accessories.

d) FACTUAL STATEMENTS IMPLYING CRITICISM. Much more so than short entries, the long entries include factual statements implying criticism of the following type: "no data on reliability," "no data on validity," "no norms," "norms for grade 5 only," "no description of the normative population," "no norms for difference scores," "test copyrighted in 1970 identical with test copyrighted in 1960," and "statistical data based on earlier forms."

e) MACHINE SCORABLE ANSWER SHEETS. All types of machine scorable answer sheets available for use with a specific test are reported: Digitek (OpScan Test Scoring and Document Scanning System), IBM 805 (IBM Test Scoring Machine), IBM 1230 (IBM Optical Mark Reader), MRC (MRC Scoring and Reporting Service), NCS (NCS Scoring and Reporting Service), and NCS Sentry/70, and a few other answer sheets less widely used.

f) COST. Price information is reported for test packages (usually 20 to 35 tests), answer sheets, all other accessories, and specimen sets. The statement "$5.20 per 35 tests" means that all accessories are included unless separate prices are given for accessories. The statement also means 35 tests of one level, one edition, or one part unless stated otherwise. Quantity discounts and special discounts are not reported. Specimen set prices include copies of each level and part—but not all forms—unless otherwise indicated. Since 1970 prices are reported, the latest catalog of a test publisher should be consulted for current prices.

g) SCORING AND REPORTING SERVICES. Scoring and reporting services provided by publishers are reported along with information on costs. Special computerized scoring and interpretation services are sometimes given in separate entries immediately following the test entry.

h) TIME. The number of minutes of actual working time allowed examinees and the approximate length of time needed for administering a test are provided whenever obtainable. The latter figure is always enclosed in parentheses. Thus, "50(60) minutes" indicates that the examinees are allowed 50 minutes of working time and that a total of 60 minutes is needed to administer the test. When the time necessary to administer a test has been obtained through correspondence with the test publisher or author, the time is enclosed in brackets.

RUNNING HEADS AND FEET

To use this volume most efficiently, it is important to take advantage of the information given at the top and bottom of each page in the test and review sections. Both test entry and page numbers are given in the running heads. However, since all citations in the indexes and cross references are to entry numbers, these numbers, found next to the outside margins on facing pages, can be used as guide numbers in locating a particular test. The entry number on the left-hand page corresponds to the test embodying the first line of type on that page; the entry number on the right-hand page refers to the test containing the last line of type on that page. The test titles corresponding to these guide numbers are given in the running feet at the bottom of the page. Thus, the reader can quickly identify the first and last test discussed on each pair of facing pages.

The first reprint section, from *Tests in Print II,* has guide numbers in the range 51 to 182; the second reprint section, from the seven MMY's, has the successive ranges: 1:957 to 1:1162, 2:1267 to 2:1322, 3:114 to 3:170, 4:148 to 4:218, 5:173 to 5:241, 6:248 to 6:343, and 7:184 to 7:238. The digit preceding the colon in the guide number corresponds to the number of the yearbook being reprinted. The numbers following the colon are the test entry numbers within that yearbook.

TIP II SCANNING INDEX

The complete TIP II Scanning Index, a classified listing of all tests in TIP II, has been reprinted to provide readers with an overview of tests available in areas other than English. The 2,467 tests are divided into the categories delineated in Table 1 of this Introduction. Since the English section of the TIP II Scanning Index will be of most interest to readers of this monograph, we have reprinted that section (entitled English Scanning Index) at the end of this volume for convenient reference. This end-of-the-book index is especially useful for locating tests suitable for a given population, since descriptions of these populations are reported immediately following the test titles.

PUBLISHERS DIRECTORY AND INDEX

Instead of giving only the entry numbers of the tests of a given publisher, as in our earlier publications, this Publishers Directory and Index gives both test titles and entry numbers. Stars denote the 22 publishers with test catalogs listing 10 or more tests (not necessarily English tests).

All addresses have been checked by the publishers as of late 1973. However, with such a large number of publishers (including many author-publishers), some address changes must be expected.

The directory lists 47 publishers of English tests, 46.8 percent of which publish only one English test. Their geographical distribution covers 5 foreign countries: Great Britain, 5 publishers; Canada, 3; Australia, 1; India, 1; and South Africa, 1.

INDEX OF TITLES

This cumulative title index includes (*a*) English tests in print as separates as of February 1, 1974; (*b*) out of print or status unknown English tests; and (*c*) tests reclassified since last listed in the English sections of the seven *Mental Measurements Yearbooks.*

Citations are to test entry numbers, not to pages. Numbers without colons refer to in print tests listed in the first reprint section (TIP II Tests) in this volume; numbers with colons refer to tests out of print, status unknown, or reclassified since last listed with English tests. Unless preceded by the word "consult," all numbers containing colons refer to tests in this volume. To obtain the latest information on a test no longer classified with English tests, the reader is directed to consult TIP II. For example, "Arizona Articulation Proficiency Scale, 6:307a; reclassified, *consult* T2:2065" indicates that the test was last listed as an English test in the *Sixth Yearbook,* but for the latest information, test 2065 in TIP II must be consulted. Superseded titles are listed with cross references to the current title. Tests which are part of a series are listed under their individual titles and also their series titles.

INDEX OF NAMES

This cumulative index is an analytical index distinguishing between authorship of a test, test review, excerpted review, or reference dealing with a specific test. Furthermore, the index indicates whether the relevant test is in print or out of print. Numbers with colons refer to out of print or status unknown tests. Unless preceded by the word "consult," all numbers containing colons refer to tests in this volume.

Forenames have been reduced to initials to lower the cost of indexing. Since authors are not always consistent in how they list their names, two or more listings may refer to the same person. On the other hand, the use of initials sometimes results in one name representing two or more persons. Reference to the cited material in the text will resolve these difficulties in almost all cases.

Except for test authors, the use of the Index of Names is a two-step process. For example, if the name index reports *"rev, 113"* for H. Black, the reader must look at the cross reference for test 113 in the TIP II Tests section of this volume to learn where Black's review may be found in the yearbook reprints. Similarly, if the name index reports *"ref, 69"* for F. B. Davis, the reader must look at the Cumulative Name Index for test 69 to learn where in this volume Davis' reference or references on that test may be found. The Cumulative Name Index for test 69 indicates that Davis is the author of 8 references for this test, each cited by number, so the reader can quickly locate them in the list of references following the test entry.

ENGLISH

TESTS AND REVIEWS

ENGLISH – TIP II

[51]

*Advanced Placement Examination in English. High school students desiring credit for college level courses or admission to advanced courses; 1954–73; replaces separate tests in English composition and literature; available to secondary schools for annual administration on specified days in May; inactive forms are available to colleges for local administration in the *Testing Academic Achievement* program; program administered for the College Entrance Examination Board by Educational Testing Service. * For the testing program entry, see 1045.

For additional information concerning earlier forms, see 7:184 (1 reference); for a review by Robert C. Pooley of an earlier form of the English composition test, see 5:205; for a review by John S. Diekhoff of an earlier form of the literature test, see 5:211. For reviews of the testing program, see 7:662 (2 reviews).

REFERENCES THROUGH 1971
1. See 7:184.
2. THOMAS, CLEVELAND A. "English Composition for Advanced Placement Students." *Col Board R* 38:33–6 sp '59. *
3. NEILSON, JOAN BUTLER. *Predicting Success in the English Advanced Placement Program in Utah Public Schools.* Master's thesis, University of Utah (Salt Lake City, Utah), 1965.

CUMULATIVE NAME INDEX
Diekhoff, J. S.: *rev*, 5:211   Smith, E. H.: 1
Neilson, J. B.: 3   Thomas, C. A.: 2
Pooley, R. C.: *rev*, 5:205

[52]

American School Achievement Tests: Part 3, Language and Spelling. Grades 4–6, 7–9; 1941–63; 2 scores: language, spelling; forms copyrighted 1955–57 are identical with forms copyrighted 1941–43 except for format; Willis E. Pratt, Robert V. Young, and Clara E. Cockerille (manuals); Bobbs-Merrill Co., Inc. * For the complete battery entry, see 4.

For additional information, see 6:248 (1 reference); for reviews by M. A. Brimer and Clarence Derrick, see 5:174. For reviews of the complete battery, see 6:2 (2 reviews), 5:1 (2 reviews), 4:1 (1 review), and 3:1 (2 reviews).

REFERENCES THROUGH 1971
1. See 6:248.

CUMULATIVE NAME INDEX
Brimer, M. A.: *rev*, 5:174   Groff, P. J.: 1
Derrick, C.: *rev*, 5:174

[53]

Analytical Survey Test in English Fundamentals.
Grades 9–13; 1932–57; formerly called *Diagnostic Survey Test in English Fundamentals*; 8 scores: spelling, capitalization, punctuation, sentence organization, sentence structure, grammatical usage, grammatical terminology, total; J. Helen Campbell and Walter Scribner Guiler; Bobbs-Merrill Co., Inc. *

For additional information and reviews by Leonard S. Feldt and Roger A. Richards, see 6:249 (2 references).

REFERENCES THROUGH 1971

1–2. See 6:249.
3. GUILER, W. S., AND CAMPBELL, J. HELEN. "Remedial English at the College Level." *J Am Assn Col Reg* 18:246–55 Ap '43. *
4. GUILER, WALTER SCRIBNER. "Disabilities of College Freshmen in Sentence Structure." *Sch R* 54:480–7 O '46. * (*PA* 21:601)
5. KOSTYSHAK, THEODORE. *An Analytical Study of the Guiler-Campbell English Test.* Master's thesis, Miami University (Oxford, Ohio), 1953.

CUMULATIVE NAME INDEX

Campbell, J. H.: 3   Kostyshak, T.: 5
Feldt, L. S.: *rev*, 6:249   Richards, R. A.: *rev*, 6:249
Guiler, W. S.: 1–4

[54]

Barrett-Ryan English Test. Grades 7–13; 1926–61; E. R. Barrett, Teresa M. Ryan, M. W. Sanders (Forms 1, 2, 3), H. E. Schrammel (Forms 1948, 1954, manual), and E. R. Wood (manual); Bureau of Educational Measurements. *

For additional information and a review by Clarence Derrick, see 6:250 (2 references); for a review by J. Raymond Gerberich, see 5:175.

REFERENCES THROUGH 1971

1–2. See 6:250.
3. WOOD, SUSAN. *An Evaluation of Published English Tests,* pp. 9–12. Madison, Wis.: Wisconsin Department of Public Instruction, 1967. Pp. 91. *

CUMULATIVE NAME INDEX

Anderson, M. R.: 1   Groff, P. J.: 2
Derrick, C.: *rev*, 6:250   Stegman, E. J.: 1
Gerberich, J. R.: *rev*, 5:175   Wood, S.: 3

[55]

★**Berry-Talbott Language Test: Comprehension of Grammar.** Ages 5–8; 1966; BTLT; experimental; "to *explore* the child's ability to make up and to use rules of grammar and syntax" using nonsense words; 8 scores: plural noun, past tense, third person singular, possessive singular-plural, derived adjective, adjective: comparative-superlative, diminutive-derived word, progressive-derived word; Mildred F. Berry and Ruth Talbott; Berry Language Tests. *

[56]

Bristol Achievement Tests: English Language.
Ages 8-0 to 9-11, 9-0 to 10-11, 10-0 to 11-11, 11-0 to 12-11, 12-0 to 13-11; 1969; 6 scores: word meaning, paragraph meaning, sentence organisation, organisation of ideas, spelling and punctuation, total; Alan Brimer and Herbert Gross; Thomas Nelson & Sons Ltd. [England]. * For the complete battery entry, see 5.

For additional information and a review by Ralph D. Dutch, see 7:185. For reviews of the complete battery, see 7:4 (2 reviews).

[57]

Business English Test: The Dailey Vocational Tests. Grades 8–12 and adults; 1964–65; BET; John T. Dailey and Kenneth B. Hoyt (manual); Houghton Mifflin Co. * For the complete battery entry, see 2105.

For additional information, see 7:976c. For reviews

of the complete battery, see 7:976 (2 reviews, 2 excerpts)

[58]

*****CLEP General Examinations: English Composition.** 1–2 years of college or equivalent; 1964–73; for college accreditation of nontraditional study, advanced placement, or assessment of educational attainment; a retired subtest of the *College-Level Examination Program General Examinations* published as a separate for local administration through the *Testing Academic Achievement* program (see 1061); program administered for the College Entrance Examination Board by Educational Testing Service. * For the testing program entry, see 1050.

For additional information concerning earlier forms, see 7:8b. For reviews of the testing program, see 7:664 (3 reviews).

REFERENCES THROUGH 1971

1. BURKETT, EVA. "Composition Tests for Screening Prospective Teachers." *Col Comp & Commun* 22(5):355–62 D '71. *

CUMULATIVE NAME INDEX

Burkett, E.: 1

[59]

*****CLEP Subject Examination in English Composition.** 1 year or equivalent; 1965–73; for college accreditation of nontraditional study, advanced placement, or assessment of educational achievement; tests administered monthly at centers throughout the United States; program administered for the College Entrance Examination Board by Educational Testing Service. * For the testing program entry, see 1050.

For additional information and a review by David P. Harris, see 7:186. For reviews of the testing program, see 7:664 (3 reviews).

[60]

★**CLEP Subject Examination in Freshman English.** 1 year or equivalent; 1973; for college accreditation of nontraditional study, advanced placement, or assessment of educational achievement; tests administered monthly at centers throughout the United States; program administered for the College Entrance Examination Board by Educational Testing Service. * For the testing program entry, see 1050.

For reviews of the testing program, see 7:664 (3 reviews).

[61]

*****California Achievement Tests: Language.** 1933–72; earlier editions called *Progressive Language Tests;* 2 editions; Ernest W. Tiegs and Willis W. Clark; CTB/McGraw-Hill. * For the complete battery entry, see 7.

a) 1957 EDITION WITH 1963 NORMS. Grades 1–2, 2.5–4.5, 4–6, 7–9, 9–14; 1933–63; test booklet title is *California Language Test;* 4 scores: mechanics of English, spelling, total, handwriting; 1963 tests identical with tests copyrighted 1957 except for profile.

b) 1970 EDITION. Grades 1.5–2.5, 2.5–4.5, 4–6, 6–9, 9–12; 1933–72; 4 or 5 scores: auding (grades 1.5–2.5 only), mechanics, usage and structure, total, spelling.

For additional information concerning the 1970 edition, see 7:187 (2 references); for a review by Richard E. Schutz of the 1957 edition, see 6:251 (1 reference); for reviews by Constance M. McCullough and Winifred L. Post, see 5:177 (3 references); for reviews by Gerald V. Lannholm and Robert C. Pooley of an earlier edition, see 4:151; for reviews by Harry A. Greene and J. Paul Leonard, see 2:1292. For reviews of the complete battery, see 6:3 (2 reviews), 5:2 (1 review), 4:2 (3 reviews), 3:15 (1 review), 2:1193 (2 reviews), and 1:876 (1 review, 1 excerpt).

REFERENCES THROUGH 1971

1–3. See 5:177.
4. See 6:251.
5–6. See 7:187.
7. McGuire, Carson. "Sex Role and Community Variability in Test Performances." *J Ed Psychol* 52:61–73 Ap '61. * (*PA* 38:3207)
8. Katz, Stanley S. "Selection and Evaluation of Students in Medical Technology Degree Programs." *Am J Med Technol* 30:51–63 Ja '64. *
9. Winston, Wilma Essex. *A Correlation Between Language Achievement and Musical Aptitude of Thirty Sixth Grade Pupils at Booker T. Washington School, East Gadsden, Alabama.* Master's thesis, Alabama A & M College (Normal, Ala.), 1967.
10. Wood, Susan. *An Evaluation of Published English Tests,* pp. 13–7. Madison, Wis.: Wisconsin Department of Public Instruction, 1967. Pp. 91. *

CUMULATIVE NAME INDEX

Conquest, G. R.: 1
Greene, H. A.: *rev,* 2:1292
Groff, P. J.: 4
Katz, S. S.: 8
Lannholm, G. V.: *rev,* 4:151
Leonard, J. P.: *rev,* 2:1292
McCullough, C. M.: *rev,* 5:177
McGuire, C.: 7
Palate, E. L.: 6
Pooley, R. C.: *rev,* 4:151
Post, W. L.: *rev,* 5:177
Reid, T. J.: 1
Sangster, C. H.: 2
Schutz, R. E.: *rev,* 6:251
Sopchak, A. L.: 3
Turner, D.: 5
Winston, W. E.: 9
Wood, S.: 10

[62]

*Canadian Achievement Test in English. Grade 10; 1961–68; CATE; a test in the *Canadian Test Battery, Grade 10;* Ontario Institute for Studies in Education; distributed by Guidance Centre [Canada]. * For the complete battery entry, see 1046.

For additional information and a review by Bernard Spolsky, see 6:252 (2 references).

REFERENCES THROUGH 1971

1–2. See 6:252.

CUMULATIVE NAME INDEX

D'Oyley, V. R.: 1–2   Spolsky, B.: *rev,* 6:252

[63]

*Canadian English Achievement Test. Grades 8.5–9.0; 1959–68; CEAT; a test in the *Canadian Test Battery, Grades 8–9;* 3 or 4 scores; the reading subtest is also listed separately; Ontario Institute for Studies in Education; distributed by Guidance Centre [Canada]. * For the complete battery entry, see 1047.
a) PART 1, READING COMPREHENSION.
b) PART 2, MECHANICS OF EXPRESSION. 2 scores in grade 8 (separate scores are obtained for the first 60 and the last 60 items).
c) PART 3, EFFECTIVENESS OF EXPRESSION. Items selected from early forms of the *Cooperative English Tests.*

For additional information and reviews by J. Douglas Ayers and Bernard Spolsky, see 6:253 (2 references).

REFERENCES THROUGH 1971

1–2. See 6:253.

CUMULATIVE NAME INDEX

Ayers, J. D.: *rev,* 6:253   Spolsky, B.: *rev,* 6:253
D'Oyley, V. R.: 1–2

[63A]

★Canadian English Language Achievement Test. Candidates for college entrance; 1968–73; CELAT; test administered annually in April and December at centers established by the publisher; parallel edition for French language available; Service for Admission to College and University [Canada]. * For the testing program entry, see 1060.

REFERENCES THROUGH 1971

1. D'Oyley, Vincent R., and Scott, Douglas M. "Objective Testing and the Evaluation of English: Some Comments." *Engl Q* (Canada) 3(1):87–93 sp '70. *
2. D'Oyley, Vincent R. "Development of the SACU Tests." *Sch Guid Worker* (Canada) 26(4):12–6 Mr–Ap '71. *
3. Elley, W. B. "SACU English Language Achievement and Verbal Aptitude Tests." *Interchange* (Canada) 2(3):83–6 '71. * (*PA* 48:5618)
4. Elliott, H. A. "SACU and the SACU Tests: Past, Present, and Future." *Sch Guid Worker* (Canada) 26(4):6–11 Mr–Ap '71. *
5. Holmes, Mark. "The Relationship Between SACU Test Scores and Other Criteria of High School Academic Performance." *Sch Guid Worker* (Canada) 26(4):25–30 Mr–Ap '71. *

CUMULATIVE NAME INDEX

D'Oyley, V. R.: 1–2
Elley, W. B.: 3
Elliott, H. A.: 4
Holmes, M.: 5
Scott, D. M.: 1

[64]

*College Board Achievement Test in English Composition. Candidates for college entrance; 1943–73; test administered on specified dates at centers established by the publisher; inactive forms, entitled *College Placement Tests in English Composition,* are available to colleges for local administration; program administered for the College Entrance Examination Board by Educational Testing Service. * For the testing program entry, see 1048.

For additional information, see 7:188 (10 references); for reviews by Charlotte Croon Davis, Robert C. Pooley, and Holland Roberts of earlier forms, see 6:287 (6 references); see also 5:204 (14 references); for a review by Charlotte Croon Davis (with Frederick B. Davis), see 4:178 (6 references). For reviews of the testing program, see 6:760 (2 reviews).

REFERENCES THROUGH 1971

1–6. See 4:178.
7–20. See 5:204.
21–26. See 6:287.
27–36. See 7:188.
37. Muhlenkamp, Ann F. "Prediction of State Board Scores in a Baccalaureate Program." *Nursing Outl* 19(1):57 Ja '71. *

CUMULATIVE NAME INDEX

Barth, C. A.: 32
Black, D. B.: 21
Bobbitt, J. M.: 7
Clark, E. W.: 27
College Entrance Examination Board: 11, 17, 28
Davis, C. C.: *rev,* 4:178, 6:287
Davis, F. B.: *rev,* 4:178
Davis, S. E.: 3
Dyer, H. S.: 8, 13
Eley, E. G.: 14
Elledge, S.: 35
Evenson, A. B.: 19
Farmer, P.: 23
Fels, W. C.: 6
Fishman, J. A.: 18
French, J. W.: 7, 20, 24, 29
Halladay, R. E.: 33
Huddleston, E. M.: 5
Ivanoff, J. M.: 30
King, R. G.: 13
Ludlow, H. G.: 36
McCall, J. N.: 10
Malloy, J. P.: 30
Marshall, J. J.: 34
Miller, P. M.: 12
Morgan, J. M.: 36
Muhlenkamp, A. F.: 37
Newman, S. H.: 7
Noyes, E. S.: 1, 26
Olsen, M. A.: 9
Palmer, O.: 22
Pearson, R.: 15
Peixotto, H. E.: 4
Pooley, R. C.: *rev,* 6:287
Pugh, R. C.: 36
Roberts, H.: *rev,* 6:287
Rose, J. R.: 30
Shostak, J.: 31
Smith, D. E.: 19
Stoke, S. M.: 2
Swineford, F.: 16
Weaver, L. J.: 2
Webb, S. C.: 10

[65]

College English Placement Test. College entrants; 1969; CEPT; Oscar M. Haugh and James I. Brown; Houghton Mifflin Co. *

For additional information and reviews by Clarence Derrick and Osmond E. Palmer, see 7:189.

REFERENCES THROUGH 1971

1. Novak, Mary Lou Bayer. *The English Language Proficiency of Secondary Student Teachers in Selected Nebraska Colleges and Universities.* Doctor's thesis, University of Nebraska (Lincoln, Neb.), 1970. (*DAI* 31:4016A)
2. Neal, L. Ramon, and Ellis, W. Geiger. "College English Placement Test: A Review." *J Ed Meas* 8(3):228–30 f '71. *

[66]
College English Test: National Achievement Tests. Grades 12–13; 1937–43; 7 scores: punctuation, capitalization, language usage, sentence structure, modifiers, miscellaneous principles, total; 1942 form identical with test copyrighted 1937 except for minor changes; A. C. Jordan; Psychometric Affiliates. *

For additional information and a review by Osmond E. Palmer, see 5:178; for reviews by Constance M. McCullough and Robert W. Howard, see 2:1269.1.

[67]
*College Placement Tests in English Composition. Entering college freshmen; 1962–72, c1958–72; reprintings of inactive 1966 and 1967 forms of *College Board Achievement Test in English Composition;* tests available to colleges for local administration; 2 tests: 1-hour version, shortened version entitled *College Placement Test in English Composition (Forty Minute Version)*; program administered for the College Entrance Examination Board by Educational Testing Service. * For the testing program entry, see 1051.

For additional information and a review by John C. Sherwood, see 7:190 (3 references). For a review of the testing program, see 7:665. For reference to reviews of the *College Board Achievement Test in English Composition,* see 64.

REFERENCES THROUGH 1971
1–3. See 7:190.

[68]
*Comprehensive Tests of Basic Skills: Language. Grades 2.5–4, 4–6, 6–8, 8–12; 1968–71; 4 scores: mechanics, expression, spelling, total; CTB/McGraw-Hill. * For the complete battery entry, see 11.

For additional information, see 7:191. For reviews of the complete battery, see 7:9 (2 reviews, 3 excerpts).

[69]
Cooperative English Tests. Grades 9–12, 13–14; 1940–60; CET; 6 scores: reading comprehension (vocabulary, level, speed, total), English expression, total; subtests available as separates; revision by Clarence Derrick, David P. Harris, and Biron Walker; Cooperative Tests and Services. *

For additional information, reviews by Leonard S. Feldt and Margaret F. Lorimer, and an excerpted review by Laurence Siegel, see 6:256 (52 references); see also 5:179 (58 references) and 4:155 (53 references); for reviews by J. Paul Leonard, Edward S. Noyes, and Robert C. Pooley of an earlier edition, see 3:120 (29 references); see also 2:1276 (1 reference). For reviews of the expression subtest, see 6:258 (2 reviews); the reading subtest, see 6:806 (2 reviews); and an earlier edition of the reading subtest, see 3:497 (2 reviews).

REFERENCES THROUGH 1971
1–2. See 2:1276.
3–31. See 3:120.
32–84. See 4:155.
85–142. See 5:179.
143–194. See 6:256.
195. GLADFELTER, M. E. "The Value of the Cooperative English Test in Prediction in College." *Sch & Soc* 44:383–4 S 10 '36. * (PA 11:460)

196. DRAKE, LEWIS E., AND HENMON, V. A. C. "The Prediction of Scholarship in the College of Letters and Science at the University of Wisconsin." *Sch & Soc* 45:191–4 F 6 '37. * (PA 11:2441)
197. MANNING, FRANK LEROY. "How Accurately Can We Predict Success in College?" *J Am Assn Col Reg* 14:35–8 O '38. * (PA 13:4365)
198. DOUGLASS, LOWELL N. "A Study of Certain Factors Influencing Academic Achievement With Special Reference to the Health Factor." *J Exp Ed* 7:235–44 Mr '39. * (PA 13:5911)
199. ARSENIAN, SETH. "Own Estimate and Objective Measurement." *J Ed Psychol* 33:291–302 Ap '42. * (PA 17:934)
200. McCLANAHAN, WALTER R., AND MORGAN, DAVID H. "Use of Standard Tests in Counseling Engineering Students in College." *J Ed Psychol* 39:491–501 D '48. * (PA 23:3448)
201. RAUSCH, OSCAR P. "The Effects of Individual Variability on Achievement." *J Ed Psychol* 39:469–78 D '48. * (PA 23:3450)
202. BERGERON, WILBUR LEE. *An Analysis of the Relationship Between Selected Characteristics and Academic Success of Freshmen at the University of Arkansas.* Doctor's thesis, University of Arkansas (Fayetteville, Ark.), 1953. (DA 13:505)
203. JARVIS, JOHN ASA. *Student Survival Factors in the Stout Institute: A Statistical Study of High School Records, Entrance Test Scores, College Course Grades and Other Measures With Relation to Survival in and Graduation by a College of Teacher Training Type-Male Students, Industrial Arts Division, Four Years, 1947–51.* Doctor's thesis, University of Minnesota (Minneapolis, Minn.), 1953. (DA 13:700)
204. SMITH, ALLAN B. *The Prediction of Scholastic Success for Freshman Entrants to the University of Connecticut 1933–1951.* Doctor's thesis, University of Connecticut (Storrs, Conn.), 1953. (DA 13:1121)
205. HENDRICKS, RICHARD. *Relationships Among Tests of Intelligibility, Word-Reception, and Other Measures of Symbolic Formulation.* Doctor's thesis, Ohio State University (Columbus, Ohio), 1956. (DA 16:2239)
206. JONES, TOM M. *Comparisons of Test Scores of High School Graduates of 1954 Who Go to College With Those Who Do Not Go, and a Study of Certain Factors Associated With Going to College.* Doctor's thesis, University of Arkansas (Fayetteville, Ark.), 1956. (DA 16:1373)
207. PEPPARD, PAULA LAFORGE, AND VOTAW, DAVID F., SR. "Objective Methods of Detecting Needs for Remedial Work in Writing." *J Ed Res* 49:537–41 Mr '56. * (PA 31:5148)
208. SHEA, ELLEN MARIE. *The Prognostic Value of Admissions Procedures in a State Teachers College.* Doctor's thesis, University of Connecticut (Storrs, Conn.), 1957. (DA 17:2503)
209. ENGELBRECHT, GLADYS M. *Scholastic Success of Students Changing School or College Within the University of Connecticut.* Doctor's thesis, University of Connecticut (Storrs, Conn.), 1958. (DA 19:986)
210. KING, EDWARD S., AND KING, DONALD B. "English Usage and Spelling in Law School: An Experiment and Possible Solution." *J Legal Ed* 11(2):253–6 '58. *
211. KRATTIGER, JOHN TRUBERT. *An Evaluation of the Freshman Testing Program of Southeastern State College of Oklahoma.* Doctor's thesis, University of Oklahoma (Norman, Okla.), 1958. (DA 19:718)
212. FLETCHER, JUNIOR EUGENE. *A Study of the Relationships Between Ability to Use Context as an Aid in Reading and Other Verbal Abilities.* Doctor's thesis, University of Washington (Seattle, Wash.), 1959. (DA 20:2675)
213. FRADENBURG, LEO GLENN. *An Investigation of the Correlation Between Pre-Course Test Results and Academic Success in the Air Force Squadron Officer School for Prediction Purposes.* Doctor's thesis, Purdue University (Lafayette, Ind.), 1959. (DA 20:3193)
214. KITTELL, JACK E. "Relationship of Language Scores to Residence Classifications of College Freshmen." *J Ed Res* 52:190–3 Ja '59. * (PA 34:12104)
215. KUNHART, WILLIAM E., AND OLSEN, LIONEL R. "An Analysis of Test Scores and Grades for Predicting Success of College Students in English Composition." *J Ed Res* 53:79 O '59. *
216. PAERATAKUL, CHAWAL. "Differences in Performance on the Doctoral Admission Examinations at Indiana University by Thai Students, Foreign Non-Thai Students, and American Students." *B Sch Ed Ind Univ* 35(3):41–64 My '59. * (PA 34:6571)
217. GOWAN, J. C., AND DIBLE, ISABEL. "Age Effects on the Test Scores of Women Teaching Candidates." *Calif J Ed Res* 11:37–8 Ja '60. * (PA 34:8417)
218. HILL, EDWIN S. *An Analysis of the Results of Special Training in Listening Compared to Special Training in Reading Skills.* Doctor's thesis, Indiana University (Bloomington, Ind.), 1961. (DA 22:3093)
219. BALLANTYNE, ROBERT HUBBARD. *An Analysis of Criteria for Selecting Freshmen Students for an Honors Program at Washington State University.* Doctor's thesis, Washington State University (Pullman, Wash.), 1962. (DA 23:2439)
220. BASHAW, W. L. "The Prediction of Grades of First-Time Florida Freshmen at the Florida State University." *Fla J Ed Res* 4:27–36 Ja '62. *

221. DeHart, Arla Lando, Jr. *Possible Selective Admissions Criteria for the California Public Junior College.* Doctor's thesis, Stanford University (Stanford, Calif.), 1962. (*DA* 22:4233)

222. Medlin, Yancey Leonard. *An Analysis of Some Aspects of the English Proficiency of White Secondary School Teacher Candidates in North Carolina, 1959–1961.* Doctor's thesis, University of North Carolina (Chapel Hill, N.C.), 1962. (*DA* 24:1495)

223. Babbott, Edward French. *The Differential Effectiveness of Eight 9th Grade Variables in Predicting Success in Three 10th Grade Academic Subjects at Summit High School: A Study in Differential Prediction.* Doctor's thesis, New York University (New York, N.Y.), 1963. (*DA* 25:993)

224. Cieutat, Victor J. "Individual Differences in Verbal Learning." *Percept & Motor Skills* 17:275–8 Ag '63. * (*PA* 38:7320)

225. Hermsen, Leon Paul. *A Comparative Study of the Background Data, Academic Achievement and the Persistence of Students Electing Business Teacher Education With Those in Other Subject Fields at Wisconsin State College, Whitewater.* Doctor's thesis, University of Wisconsin (Madison, Wis.), 1963. (*DA* 24:1492)

226. Lehmkuhl, Carlton Burdell. *Test Performance Relationships Among Occupational Patterns of Educational Administration Program Graduates.* Doctor's thesis, University of Minnesota (Minneapolis, Minn.), 1963. (*DA* 24:4510)

227. Taulbee, George C., Sr. *Construction and Validation of a Scale for Predicting Graduation From a College of Optometry.* Doctor's thesis, University of Houston (Houston, Tex.), 1963. (*DA* 24:387)

228. Torres, Leonard. *A Study of the Relationship Between Selected Variables and the Achievement of Industrial Arts Students at Long Beach State College.* Doctor's research study No. 1, Colorado State College (Greeley, Colo.), 1963. (*DA* 25:316)

229. Williams, Robert A. *An Assessment of the Success of C Average High School Graduates in Grand Rapids Junior College.* Doctor's thesis, Michigan State University (East Lansing, Mich.), 1963. (*DA* 25:317)

230. Zimmerman, William George, Jr. *An Analysis of Selected Aspects of the Master of Education Program at the University of Miami.* Doctor's thesis, University of Miami (Coral Gables, Fla.), 1963. (*DA* 28:95A)

231. Anderson, A. W. "Reading and English Scores of a Group of Foreign Students Entering the University of Western Australia in 1964." *Austral J Higher Ed* 2:84–90 N '64. *

232. Boe, Erling E. "The Prediction of Academic Performance of Engineering Students." *Ed & Psychol Meas* 24:377–83 su '64. * (*PA* 39:5975)

233. Brown, Frederick G., and Dubois, Thomas E. "Correlates of Academic Success for High-Ability Freshman Men." *Personnel & Guid J* 42:603–7 F '64. * (*PA* 39:5820)

234. Chase, Clinton I.; Ludlow, H. Glenn; and Pugh, Richard C. *Predicting Success for Master's Degree Students in Education.* Indiana Studies in Prediction No. 5. Bloomington, Ind.: Bureau of Educational Studies and Testing, Indiana University, 1964. Pp. v, 25. *

235. Chase, Clinton I.; Ludlow, H. Glenn; Pugh, Richard C.; and Pomeroy, Martha C. *Predicting Success for Advanced Graduate Students in Education.* Indiana Studies in Prediction No. 4. Bloomington, Ind.: Bureau of Educational Studies and Testing, Indiana University, 1964. Pp. v, 18. *

236. Cooper, Carl J. "Some Relationships Between Paired-Associates Learning and Foreign-Language Aptitude." *J Ed Psychol* 55:132–8 Je '64. * (*PA* 39:5823)

237. Engen, Harold Bernard. *Differential Prediction of Academic Success and Attrition-Survival of Entering Freshmen at the University of South Dakota.* Doctor's thesis, State University of South Dakota (Vermillion, S.D.), 1964. (*DA* 25:2847)

238. Hughes, Donald L. *A Study to Predict the Academic Success of Low Achieving High School Students at Brigham Young University With Selected Tests.* Master's thesis, Brigham Young University (Provo, Utah), 1964.

239. Schreck, Thomas C. "Selected Factors Related to Academic Success in College." *Ed & Psychol R* (India) 4:71–6 Ap '64. *

240. Space, Margaret Niven. *A Study of Individual Predictability Based on Intra-Individual Variability on Certain Achievement Measures.* Doctor's thesis, University of Minnesota (Minneapolis, Minn.), 1964. (*DA* 26:879)

241. Webb, Sam C. "The Psychological Components of Scores for Two Tests of Report Writing Ability." *Ed & Psychol Meas* 24:31–46 sp '64. * (*PA* 39:1770)

242. Chaudhry, Ghulam Mohammed, and Kayani, Mohammed Rashid. "A Comparative Study of the DAT Verbal Reasoning, ACE Psychological Examination and Cooperative English Comprehension Tests as Predictors of Academic Success in the Institute of Education and Research, University of the Panjab." *B Ed & Res* (Pakistan) 4(2):1–21 '65. *

243. Davis, Luther Edward, Jr. *A Study of Selected Traits of St. Petersburg Junior College Students and Their Value in Predicting Academic Success in Certain Courses of Study at the Senior College Level.* Doctor's thesis, Auburn University (Auburn, Ala.), 1965. (*DA* 26:791)

244. Jungeblut, Ann. "A Note on the 1960 Revision of the Cooperative English Test." *Ed Rec B* 88:64–6 Jl '65. *

245. Kimball, Webster H. *Persistence and Success Prediction in Accounting.* Master's thesis, California State College (Long Beach, Calif.), 1965.

246. Leutenegger, Ralph R.; Mueller, Theodore H.; and Wershow, Irving R. "Auditory Factors in Foreign Language Acquisition." *Mod Lang J* 49:22–31 Ja '65. *

247. Stone, Donald Bradford. *Predicting Student Retention and Withdrawal in a Selected State University College of New York.* Doctor's thesis, Cornell University (Ithaca, N.Y.), 1965. (*DA* 26:5184)

248. Taylor, Jean. *An Examination of the Relationships Between Test Scores and Grades in Eleventh Grade English Groups at Hillcrest High School.* Master's thesis, University of Utah (Salt Lake City, Utah), 1965.

249. Troy, Elizabeth McGoldrick. *A Study of the Predictive Value of Eleven Variables Used at King's College to Determine General Scholastic Achievement of Two Hundred Forty-Three Entering Students.* Master's thesis, Marywood College (Scranton, Pa.), 1965.

250. Wenberg, Burness G., and Ingersoll, Ralph W. "Medical Dietetics: Part 2, The Development of Evaluative Techniques." *J Am Dietetic Assn* 47:298–300 O '65. *

251. Wyeth, Ezra R. "Evaluation of the Effectiveness of the Leadership Training Program in the Area of the Deaf at San Fernando Valley State College." *Am Ann Deaf* 110:479–82 S '65. * (*PA* 40:5848)

252. Bretnall, Doris, and Davis, Frederick B. "The Effect of the Conventional Correction for Chance on Distributions of Scores From Form B of the 1960 Edition of the Cooperative English Tests." *Ed Rec B* 90:55–7 Jl '66. *

253. Campbell, John P. "Comparison of Criterion Clusters Obtained by Analyzing the Homogeneity of a Set of Regression Equations and the Matrix of Intercorrelations." *Ed & Psychol Meas* 26:405–17 su '66. * (*PA* 40:12757)

254. Cunningham, William. *A Thirteen-Year Retrospective Study of Standardized Test Data.* Doctor's thesis, Western Reserve University (Cleveland, Ohio), 1966. (*DA* 27:3305A)

255. Gross, Nathan. *English Grades as a Function of Intellectual Ability, Performance, and the Congruency of Teacher-Pupil Perceptions of Interpersonal Values.* Doctor's thesis, Harvard University (Cambridge, Mass.), 1966. (*DA* 28:123A)

256. Jex, Frank B. *Predicting Academic Success Beyond High School.* Salt Lake City, Utah: University of Utah Bookstore, 1966. Pp. vi, 41. *

257. Schofield, William, and Merwin, Jack C. "The Use of Scholastic Aptitude, Personality, and Interest Test Data in the Selection of Medical Students." *J Med Ed* 41:502–9 Je '66. *

258. Schroeder, Pearl. "Relative Spelling Ability as a Predictor of the Academic Performance of Superior Ability College Freshmen." *J Ed Res* 59:427–8 My–Je '66. * (*PA* 40:11463)

259. Smith, William Charles. *A Factor Analytic Study of the "Test of Sound Reasoning."* Doctor's thesis, University of Missouri (Kansas City, Mo.), 1966. (*DA* 28:408A)

260. Stallings, William Marion. *A Study of Non-Intellective Factors in the Prediction of Academic Success for Master's Degree Level Students in the School of Education, Indiana University.* Doctor's thesis, Indiana University (Bloomington, Ind.), 1966. (*DA* 27:3324A)

261. Tucker, Harmon. *A Statistical Study to Determine the Relationship Between Scores of the Cooperative English Test and the Aptitude Sections of the Graduate Record Examinations.* Master's thesis, Stetson University (DeLand, Fla.), 1966.

262. Barnett, Thomas Marvin. *The Predictive Validities, as Measured by Multiple Correlation, of Two Batteries Using Academic Achievement as Criterion.* Doctor's thesis, North Texas State University (Denton, Tex.), 1967. (*DA* 28:2006A)

263. Ingram, John Allen. *Factors Affecting the Success of Transfer Students at Drake University.* Doctor's thesis, Iowa State University (Ames, Iowa), 1967. (*DA* 28:1341A)

264. Lohnes, Paul R., and McIntire, Paul H. "Classification Validities of a Statewide 10th Grade Test Program." *Personnel & Guid J* 45:561–7 F '67. *

265. Pickle, John H. *Analysis of the Relation of Entrance Examination Scores and Marks Earned in Eight Semesters by Graduates of the College of Education.* Doctor's thesis, University of Arkansas (Fayetteville, Ark.), 1967. (*DA* 28:405A)

266. Walters, Nancy Rockhill. *Predictive Characteristics of Depauw University Freshman Dropouts Over a Three Year Period.* Doctor's thesis, Indiana University (Bloomington, Ind.), 1967. (*DA* 28:3471A)

267. Wood, Susan. *An Evaluation of Published English Tests,* pp. 19–21. Madison, Wis.: Wisconsin Department of Public Instruction, 1967. Pp. 91. *

268. Brown, Thomas O. *The Urban University Student. Selected Factors Related to Continuation and Withdrawal.* Doctor's thesis, Kent State University (Kent, Ohio), 1968. (*DA* 29:4318A)

269. Colgan, Richard Thomas. *A Longitudinal Study of the Relationship of Teacher Judgment Versus Objective Test Data With Respect to College Success.* Doctor's thesis, Southern Illinois University (Carbondale, Ill.), 1968. (*DA* 29:3413B)

270. Conklin, R. C., and Ogston, D. G. "Prediction of

Cooperative English Tests

Academic Success for Freshmen at the University of Calgary." *Alberta J Ed Res* (Canada) 14:185–92 S '68. * (*PA* 44:4244)

271. COY, MICHAEL. *Factorial Study of Variables Related to College Grade Point Average.* Master's thesis, Humboldt State College (Arcata, Calif.), 1968.

272. DALY, JOSEPH L., AND STAHMANN, ROBERT F. "The Effect of Time Limits on a University Placement Test." *J Ed Res* 62:103–4 N '68. *

273. HEDLEY, CAROLYN NEAL. "Learning Relationship Differences and Curriculum Choice." *Improving Col & Univ Teach* 16:268–72 au '68. *

274. JOHNSON, RICHARD W.; KEOCHAKIAN, SIMON V.; MORNINGSTAR, MONA; AND SOUTHWORTH, J. ALFRED. "Validation of Freshman Orientation Test Battery." *Ed & Psychol Meas* 28:437–40 su '68. * (*PA* 42:19274)

275. McGEE, JIM ED. *Selected Factors Associated With Success or Failure on the Junior English Examination at the University of Arkansas.* Doctor's thesis, University of Arkansas (Fayetteville, Ark.), 1968. (*DA* 29:99A)

276. MILLER, RICHARD HADDEN. *A Descriptive Study of the Relationship Between Potential and Performance of Freshman Students at the University of South Dakota.* Doctor's thesis, University of South Dakota (Vermillion, S.D.), 1968. (*DA* 29:2612A)

277. MUNDAY, LEO. "Correlations Between ACT and Other Predictors of Academic Success in College." *Col & Univ* 44:67–76 f '68. *

278. VAN DERSLICE, JOHN FREDERICK. *The Educational, Social, and Economic Background of Engineering and Technical Students Analyzed for the Purpose of Establishing Profiles for Use in Counseling.* Doctor's thesis, Utah State University (Logan, Utah), 1968. (*DA* 29:1431A)

279. WILSON, ANAISE VICTORIANNE. *A Study of the Relationship of Selected Factors to the Academic Achievement of College Freshmen in the School of Education of Tuskegee Institute.* Doctor's thesis, New York University (New York, N.Y.), 1968. (*DAI* 30:144A)

280. DAVIS, J. MICHAEL. *The Relationship of Selection Factors in the Cuban Teacher Retraining Program to the Effective Classroom Performance of Cuban Teachers.* Doctor's thesis, University of Miami (Coral Gables, Fla.), 1969. (*DAI* 30:3222A)

281. ELTING, ROBERT A., AND BUTTERFIELD, MARY. "Academic Performance of Cuban-Teacher Students at the University of Miami." *Col & Univ* 44(3):263–7 sp '69. *

282. EVANS, JAMES D. "The Relationships of Three Personality Scales to Grade Point Average and Verbal Ability in College Freshmen." *J Ed Res* 63(3):121–5 N '69. * (*PA* 46:5658)

283. FOLLMAN, JOHN. "Factor Analysis of Three Critical Thinking Tests, One Logical Reasoning Test, and One English Test." *Yearb Nat Read Conf* 18:154–60 '69. *

284. FOLLMAN, JOHN COSGROVE. *A Factor Analytic Study of Three Critical Thinking Tests, One English Test, and One Logical Reasoning Test.* Doctor's thesis, Indiana University (Bloomington, Ind.), 1969. (*DAI* 30:1015A)

285. GEORGE, WARREN EDWIN. *Significant Predictors for College Achievement in Specified Areas of Music Education and Identification of Potential Graduates.* Doctor's thesis, University of Kansas (Lawrence, Kan.), 1969. (*DAI* 30:3040A)

286. HUCKABEE, MALCOM W. "Personality and Academic Aptitude Correlates of Cognitive Control Principles." *South J Ed Res* 3(1):1–9 Ja '69. *

287. HUSEMOLLER, KENNETH E. *The Prediction of Freshmen Academic Success at Eastern New Mexico University, Roswell, by Means of Selected Demographic and Standardized Tests Data.* Doctor's thesis, Colorado State College (Greeley, Colo.), 1969. (*DAI* 30:1467A)

288. MILLER, RICHARD H. "Students Show a Preparation Increase but No Increase in Grades Was Shown." *Col & Univ* 45(1):28–30 f '69. *

289. POSTON, WILLIAM KENNETH, JR. *Educational Administrator Job Performance and Training Program Admission Criteria.* Doctor's thesis, Arizona State University (Tempe, Ariz.), 1969. (*DAI* 30:532A)

290. PREAS, NANCY BUSH. *A Study of the Relationship Between Selected Variables and Academic Achievement in a Community College.* Doctor's thesis, North Carolina State University (Raleigh, N.C.), 1969. (*DAI* 30:5245A)

291. WENBERG, BURNESS S; INGERSOLL, RALPH W.; AND DOHNER, CHARLES W. "Evaluation of Dietetic Interns." *J Am Dietetic Assn* 54(4):297–301 Ap '69. *

292. WILLIAMS, VERNON. *A Multi-Predictive Measure to Predict Success at Two Levels in Freshman College Mathematics.* Doctor's thesis, Oklahoma State University (Stillwater, Okla.), 1969. (*DAI* 31:4026A)

293. ELTING, ROBERT ARTHUR. *The Prediction of Freshman Year Academic Performance of Foreign Students From Pre-Admission Data.* Doctor's thesis, New York University (New York, N.Y.), 1970. (*DAI* 31:5697A)

294. FOLLMAN, JOHN. "Correlational and Factor Analysis of Critical Thinking, Logical Reasoning, and English Total Test Scores." *Fla J Ed Res* 12(1):91–4 Ja '70. *

295. FOLLMAN, JOHN; BROWN, LAURENCE; AND BURG, ELDON. "Factor Analysis of Critical Thinking, Logical Reasoning, and English Subtests." *J Exp Ed* 38(4):11–6 su '70. *

296. JANSEN, DAVID G.; ROBB, GEORGE P.; AND BONK, EDWARD C. "Characteristics of High-Rated and Low-Rated Master's Degree Candidates in Counseling and Guidance." *Counselor Ed & Sup* 9(3):162–70 sp '70. * (*PA* 46:5559)

297. LAUTZ, ROBERT; MacLEAN, G. DONALD; VAUGHAN, ANDREW T.; AND OLIVER, THOMAS C. "Characteristics of Successful Students Following Academic Suspension." *Col & Univ* 45(2):192–202 w '70. *

298. LIBBY, WILLIAM L., JR. "Reaction Time and Remote Association in Talented Male Adolescents." *Develop Psychol* 3(3):285–97 N '70. * (*PA* 45:4001)

299. RUSSELL, WENDELL PHILLIPS. *Intellectual and Non-Intellectual Factors Affecting the Attrition Rate of Students Entering Virginia Union University in 1965.* Doctor's thesis, University of Virginia (Charlottesville, Va.), 1970. (*DAI* 31:4474A)

300. MAZUR, JAMES MATTHEW. *A Study of Predictive Validity of Standardized Tests Used for Placement of Vocational Students at Rockingham Community College.* Master's thesis, North Carolina State University (Raleigh, N.C.), 1971.

301. SMITH, RICHARD LEE. *A Factor-Analytic Study of Critical Reading/Thinking, Influenceability, and Related Factors.* Doctor's thesis, University of Maine (Orono, Me.), 1971. (*DAI* 32:6229A)

CUMULATIVE NAME INDEX

Cooperative English Tests

[70]

Cooperative Primary Tests: Writing Skills. Grades 2.5–3; 1965–67; 3 scores: spelling, capitalization-punctuation-usage, total; Cooperative Tests and Services. * For the complete battery entry, see 12.

For reviews of the complete battery, see 7:10 (2 excerpts).

[71]

*****Cotswold Junior English Ability Test.** Ages 8.5–9.5, 9.5–10.5; 1949–70; 2 levels; tests A, B, and E are out of print; C. M. Fleming; Robert Gibson & Sons, Glasgow, Ltd. [Scotland].

a) JUNIOR ENGLISH C AND D. Ages 8.5–9.5; 1967–70, c1954–57.

b) JUNIOR ENGLISH F. Ages 9.5–10.5; 1968–70, c1961.

For additional information and reviews by M. A. Brimer and John C. Daniels of earlier forms, see 5:182.

[72]

*****Cotswold Measurement of Ability: English.** Ages 10–12; 1947–69; C. M. Fleming; Robert Gibson & Sons, Glasgow, Ltd. [Scotland]. *

For additional information and reviews by M. A. Brimer and S. C. Richardson of earlier forms, see 5:183.

[73]

English Expression: Cooperative English Tests. Grades 9–12, 13–14; 1940–60; this subtest of the *Cooperative English Tests* is a revision of the subtests *Effectiveness of Expression* and *Mechanics of Expression* in earlier editions of the battery; revision by Clarence Derrick, David P. Harris, and Biron Walker; Cooperative Tests and Services. * For the complete battery entry, see 69.

For additional information and reviews by John C. Sherwood and John M. Stalnaker, see 6:258; for a review by Chester W. Harris of an earlier edition, see 4:155. For reviews of the complete battery, see 6:256 (2 reviews, 1 excerpt) and 3:120 (3 reviews).

[74]

English IX–XII: Achievement Examinations for Secondary Schools. Grades 9, 10, 11, 12; 1951–54; Form 4 ('54) of a series of tests, currently (1973) entitled *Language Arts: Minnesota High School Achievement Examinations* (see 90), issued annually for May testing; 4 levels; Bobbs-Merrill Co., Inc. *

a) ENGLISH IX. Grade 9; Carl Towley.

b) ENGLISH X. Grade 10; Ina Engburg.

c) ENGLISH XI. Grade 11; Winifred Murray.

d) ENGLISH XII. Grade 12; Ina Engburg.

For additional information concerning later and earlier forms, see 90, 7:197, 6:268 (1 review), 5:185, and 5:186 (1 review).

REFERENCES THROUGH 1971

1. GROFF, PATRICK J. "Parts of Speech in Standardized English Tests." Sch R 69:457–60 w '61. *

CUMULATIVE NAME INDEX

Groff, P. J.: 1

[75]

*****English Progress Tests.** Various ages 7-3 to 15-6; 1952–72; 13 tests; tests B, C, D, and F are out of print; published for the National Foundation for Educational Research in England and Wales; Ginn & Co. Ltd. [England]. *

a) ENGLISH PROGRESS TEST A. Ages 8-0 to 9-0; 1952–60; A. F. Watts.

b) ENGLISH PROGRESS TEST E. Ages 12-0 to 13-0; 1956; M. A. Brimer and A. F. Watts.

c) ENGLISH PROGRESS TEST G. Ages 13-0 to 15-6; 1962; test by S. M. Unwin.

d) ENGLISH PROGRESS TEST A2. Ages 7-3 to 8-11; 1962-66; test by Betsy Barnard.

e) ENGLISH PROGRESS TEST B2. Ages 8-6 to 10-0; 1959-60; manual by Valerie C. Land.

f) ENGLISH PROGRESS TEST C2. Ages 9-6 to 11-0; 1961; Valerie Land.

g) ENGLISH PROGRESS TEST D2. Ages 10-6 to 12-0; 1963-64; Jennifer Henchman.

h) ENGLISH PROGRESS TEST E2. Ages 11-0 to 13-0; 1962-72; test by S. M. Unwin.

i) ENGLISH PROGRESS TEST F2. Ages 12-0 to 13-6; 1963-72; test by Jennifer Henchman and Elsa Hendry.

j) ENGLISH PROGRESS TEST B3. Ages 8-0 to 9-6; 1970-72.

k) ENGLISH PROGRESS TEST C3. Ages 9-0 to 10-9; 1970-72.

l) ENGLISH PROGRESS TEST D3. Ages 10-0 to 11-8; 1970-72.

m) ENGLISH PROGRESS TEST F3. Ages 12-0 to 13-6; 1969.

For additional information, see 7:192; for reviews by Neil Gourlay and Stanley Nisbet of Tests A–F, see 5:187.

[76]

English Test FG. Ages 12–13; 1952; formerly called *English Test 2*; G. A. V. Morgan; published for the National Foundation for Educational Research in England and Wales; Ginn & Co. Ltd. [England]. *

For additional information and reviews by Reginald Edwards, S. C. Richardson, and Cleveland A. Thomas, see 5:192.

[77]

English Test: Municipal Tests: National Achievement Tests. Grades 3–6, 6–8; 1938–56; subtest of *Municipal Battery;* 5 scores: language usage-words, language usage-sentences, punctuation and capitalization, expressing ideas, total; 1952–56 tests identical with tests copyrighted 1938–39; Robert K. Speer and Samuel Smith; Psychometric Affiliates. *

For additional information, see 5:190. For reviews of the complete battery, see 5:18 (1 review), 4:20 (1 review), and 2:1191 (2 reviews).

REFERENCES THROUGH 1971
1. GROFF, PATRICK J. "Parts of Speech in Standardized English Tests." Sch R 69:457-60 w '61. *

CUMULATIVE NAME INDEX
Groff, P. J.: 1

[78]

English Test: National Achievement Tests. Grades 3–8, 7–12; 1936–57; 2 levels; Robert K. Speer and Samuel Smith; Psychometric Affiliates. *

a) GRADES 3–8. 1936–38; 7 scores: capitalization, punctuation, language usage (sentences), language usage (words), expressing ideas, letter writing, total.

b) GRADES 7–12. 1936–57; 7 scores: word usage, punctuation, vocabulary, language usage (sentences), expressing ideas, expressing feeling, total; 1952 test identical with test copyrighted 1938.

For additional information, see 5:191; for a review by Winifred L. Post, see 4:162; for a review by Harry A. Greene, see 3:126.

REFERENCES THROUGH 1971
1. GROFF, PATRICK J. "Parts of Speech in Standardized English Tests." Sch R 69:457-60 w '61. *

CUMULATIVE NAME INDEX
Greene, H. A.: *rev*, 3:126   Post, W. L.: *rev*, 4:162
Groff, P. J.: 1

[79]

English Tests (Adv.). Ages 12–13; 1954–67; 5 tests; distribution restricted to directors of education; published for the National Foundation for Educational Research in England and Wales; Ginn & Co. Ltd. [England]. *

a) ENGLISH TEST (ADV.) 1. 1954–55; G. A. V. Morgan.

b) ENGLISH TEST (ADV.) 2. 1957. *Out of print.*

c) ENGLISH TEST (ADV.) 3. 1958.

d) ENGLISH TEST (ADV.) 4. 1960.

e) ENGLISH TEST (ADV.) 5. 1962–67.

For additional information and a review by Stanley Nisbet, see 7:193; for a review by A. E. G. Pilliner of Tests 1–4, see 6:262.

[80]

*****English Tests 14–20 and 22.** Ages 10–11; 1951–71; new test published annually except for 1970; tests 1 and 3–13 are out of print; distribution restricted to directors of education; published for the National Foundation for Educational Research in England and Wales; Ginn & Co. Ltd. [England]. *

a) ENGLISH TEST 14. 1963–64.

b) ENGLISH TEST 15. 1964–65.

c) ENGLISH TEST 16. 1965–66.

d) ENGLISH TEST 17. 1966–67.

e) ENGLISH TEST 18. 1967–68.

f) ENGLISH TEST 19. 1968–69.

g) ENGLISH TEST 20. 1969–70.

h) ENGLISH TEST 22. 1971.

For additional information and a review by R. Gulliford of tests 13–20, see 7:194; for reviews by Stanley Nisbet and H. J. Sants of earlier tests, see 6:264 (1 reference).

REFERENCES THROUGH 1971
1. See 6:264.

CUMULATIVE NAME INDEX
Butcher, H. J.: 1   Nisbet, S.: *rev*, 6:264
Gulliford, R.: *rev*, 7:194   Sants, H. J.: *rev*, 6:264
Moreton, C. A.: 1

[81]

Essentials of English Tests, Revised Edition. Grades 7–13; 1939–61; 6 scores: spelling, grammatical usage, word usage, sentence structure, punctuation and capitalization, total; 1961 forms identical with forms copyrighted 1939 and 1940 except for revisions in 12 items; 1961 manual essentially the same as a 1944 manual except for wording changes; original edition by Dora V. Smith and Constance M. McCullough, revision by Carolyne Green; American Guidance Service, Inc. *

For additional information and a review by J. Raymond Gerberich, see 6:266; for reviews by Charlotte W. Croon and Gerald V. Lannholm and an excerpted review by William J. Jones, see 3:128.

REFERENCES THROUGH 1971
1. WOOD, SUSAN. *An Evaluation of Published English Tests,* pp. 27-9. Madison, Wis.: Wisconsin Department of Public Instruction, 1967. Pp. 91. *

CUMULATIVE NAME INDEX
Croon, C. W.: *rev*, 3:128   Lannholm, G. V.: *rev*, 3:128
Gerberich, J. R.: *rev*, 6:266   Wood, S.: 1
Jones, W. J.: *exc*, 3:128

[82]

★**Functional Grammar Test.** High school and college; 1970; FGT; Joyce E. Lackey; Psychometric Affiliates. *

[83]

*****Grammar and Usage Test Series.** Grades 7–9, 10–12; 1950–70; 2 levels; no manual; Perfection Form Co. *

a) JUNIOR HIGH SCHOOL SERIES. Grades 7–9; formerly called *Objective Tests in English;* 6 tests.
  1) *Plurals and Possessives.*
  2) *Punctuation.*
  3) *Parts of Speech.*
  4) *Pronoun Usage.*
  5) *Word Usage.*
  6) *Final Examination.*
b) SENIOR HIGH SCHOOL SERIES. Grades 10–12; formerly called *Objective Test in Grammar;* 7 tests.
  1) *Plurals and Possessives.*
  2) *Punctuation.*
  3) *Parts of Speech.*
  4) *Pronoun Usage.*
  5) *Verbals.*
  6) *Word Usage.*
  7) *Final Examination.*
For additional information concerning the earlier tests, see 4:171 and 4:172.

[84]

Grammar, Usage, and Structure Test and Vocabulary Test. College entrants; 1963–68; William A. McCartney; the Author. *
For additional information, see 7:195.

[85]

Hoyum-Sanders English Tests. I, 2 semesters in grades 2–4, 5–6, 7–8; 1962–64; first published 1962–63 in the Every Pupil Scholarship Test series; 3 tests; Vera Davis Hoyum and M. W. Sanders; Bureau of Educational Measurements. *
a) HOYUM-SANDERS ELEMENTARY ENGLISH TEST. I, 2 semesters in grades 2–4.
b) HOYUM-SANDERS INTERMEDIATE ENGLISH TEST. I, 2 semesters in grades 5–6.
c) HOYUM-SANDERS JUNIOR HIGH SCHOOL ENGLISH TEST. I, 2 semesters in grades 7–8.
For additional information and a review by Paul B. Diederich, see 7:196.

[86]

Iowa Placement Examinations: English Aptitude. Grades 12–13; 1925–26; test by M. F. Carpenter and G. D. Stoddard; Bureau of Educational Research and Service. *
For additional information and reviews by Clarence Derrick and W. C. Kvaraceus, see 4:166 (5 references); for a review by Robert C. Pooley, see 3:115 (9 references).

REFERENCES THROUGH 1971
1–9. See 3:115.
10–14. See 4:166.
15. HAMMOND, H. P., AND STODDARD, GEORGE DINSMORE. "A Study of Placement Examinations." *Univ Iowa Studies Ed* 4(7):1–59 '28. * (*PA* 3:2069)

CUMULATIVE NAME INDEX
Derrick, C.: *rev,* 4:166
Edmonson, L. D.: 12
Gerberich, J. R.: 7
Hammond, H. P.: 15
Hansen, G. W.: 10
Kvaraceus, W. C.: *rev,* 4:166
Langlie, T. A.: 2–3, 5
Larsen, H. P.: 11
Leaf, C. T.: 9
Miller, L. W.: 8
O'Brien, C. C.: 14
Pooley, R. C.: *rev,* 3:115
Stalnaker, J. M.: 6
Stoddard, G. D.: 1, 4, 15
Topetzes, N. J.: 14
Uhrbrock, R. S.: 13
Wittenborn, J. R.: 11

[87]

Iowa Placement Examinations: English Training. Grades 12–13; 1925–44; 2 editions; test by M. F. Carpenter, G. D. Stoddard, L. W. Miller (*b*), and D. B. Stuit (*b*); Bureau of Educational Research and Service. *

a) SERIES ET-1, REVISED. 1925–26.
b) NEW SERIES ET-2, REVISED. 1925–44.
For additional information and reviews by Clarence Derrick and W. C. Kvaraceus, see 4:167 (5 references); for a review by Robert C. Pooley, see 3:131 (15 references).

REFERENCES THROUGH 1971
1–15. See 3:131.
16–20. See 4:167.
21. HAMMOND, H. P., AND STODDARD, GEORGE DINSMORE. "A Study of Placement Examinations." *Univ Iowa Studies Ed* 4(7):1–59 '28. * (*PA* 3:2069)
22. NELSON, M. J. "Some Data From Freshman Tests." *Sch & Soc* 31:772–4 Je 7 '30. * (*PA* 4:3694)
23. GARNETT, WILLIAM LESLIE. "A Study of Status and Improvement of College Freshmen in Certain Skills of English Composition." *J Exp Ed* 6:29–34 S '37. * (*PA* 12:2108)
24. LONG, JOHN MARSHALL. *The Prediction of College Success From a Battery of Tests and From High School Achievement.* Doctor's thesis, University of Virginia (Charlottesville, Va.), 1960. (*DA* 21:1100)
25. CRANE, WILLIAM J. "Screening Devices for Occupational Therapy Majors." *Am J Occup Ther* 16:131–2 My–Je '62. * (*PA* 37:4078)
26. LONG, JOHN M. "Sex Differences in Academic Prediction Based on Scholastic, Personality and Interest Factors." *J Exp Ed* 32:239–48 sp '64. * (*PA* 39:6058)

CUMULATIVE NAME INDEX
Adams, M.: 14
Adams, W. M.: 15
Barnette, W. L.: 11
Crane, W. J.: 25
Derrick, C.: *rev,* 4:167
Donnelly, M. C.: 12
Freeman, K. H.: 19
Garnett, W. L.: 23
Gerberich, J. R.: 7
Giesecke, G. E.: 17
Hammond, H. P.: 21
Hansen, G. W.: 16
Kvaraceus, W. C.: *rev,* 4:167
Langlie, T. A.: 2–3, 5
Larsen, R. P.: 17–8
Long, J. M.: 24, 26
Merrill, R. A.: 10
Miller, L. W.: 8
Nelson, M. J.: 22
Pankaskie, M.: 13
Pooley, R. C.: *rev,* 3:131
Root, A. R.: 9
Stalnaker, J. M.: 6
Stoddard, G. D.: 1, 4, 21
Stuit, D. B.: 12
Uhrbrock, R. S.: 20
Wittenborn, J. R.: 17–8

[88]

*The Iowa Tests of Educational Development: Test 3, Correctness and Appropriateness of Expression. Grades 9–12; 1942–67; Forms X-4 and Y-4; more recent Forms X5 and Y5 are not available as separates; prepared under the direction of E. F. Lindquist and Leonard S. Feldt; Science Research Associates, Inc. * For the complete battery entry, see 20.
For additional information concerning earlier forms, see 6:267 (1 reference). For reviews of the complete battery, see 6:14 (2 reviews), 5:17 (2 reviews), 4:17 (1 review), and 3:12 (3 reviews).

REFERENCES THROUGH 1971
1. See 6:267.

CUMULATIVE NAME INDEX
Groff, P. J.: 1

[89]

★Language Arts Diagnostic Probes. Grades 3–9; 1970; also called SALI (Systems Approach to Language Instruction); **2** tests; Stella B. Warner; American Testing Co. *
a) LANGUAGE ARTS DIAGNOSTIC PROBE I: PROBES INTO CAPITALIZATION. SALI I; 3 scores: Probe 40 (8 skills), 41 (9 skills), 42 (9 skills).
b) LANGUAGE ARTS DIAGNOSTIC PROBE II: PROBES INTO PUNCTUATION. SALI II; 2 scores: Probes 43 (17 skills), 44 (8 skills).

[90]

Language Arts: Minnesota High School Achievement Examinations. Grades 7, 8, 9, 10, 11, 12; 1951–70; a new, revised, or previously inactive form issued each May; Achievement Examinations for Secondary Schools, High School Achievement Examinations, and

Midwest High School Achievement Examinations have also been used as series titles; Form GJ Rev ('70, some tests for grade 10 have 1973 copyright) used in 1970 and 1973 testings; Form 4 ('54), entitled *English IX–XII: Achievement Examinations for Secondary Schools,* is available from another publisher (see 74); 6 levels; edited by V. L. Lohmann; American Guidance Service, Inc. *

a) LANGUAGE ARTS GRADE 7. 1962–70.
b) LANGUAGE ARTS GRADE 8. 1962–70.
c) LANGUAGE ARTS GRADE 9. 1951–70.
d) LANGUAGE ARTS GRADE 10. 1951–70.
e) LANGUAGE ARTS GRADE 11. 1951–70.
f) LANGUAGE ARTS GRADE 12. 1951–70.

For additional information, see 7:197; for a review by Marvin D. Glock of Forms E (1962) and F (1963), see 6:268; see also 5:185; for a review by Roger A. Richards of Form A (1955) and Form B (1957), see 5:186.

[91]

Language Arts Tests: Content Evaluation Series. Grades 7–9; 1969; 3 tests in 1 booklet; Elsa Graser (a), Leonard Freyman (b), and Ruth Reeves (c); Houghton Mifflin Co. *

a) LANGUAGE ABILITY TEST: CONTENT EVALUATION SERIES.
b) COMPOSITION TEST: CONTENT EVALUATION SERIES.
c) LITERATURE TEST: CONTENT EVALUATION SERIES.

For additional information and reviews by Joan J. Michael and Blaine R. Worthen, see 7:198.

[92]

Language Perception Test. Business and industry; 1959–63; Richardson, Bellows, Henry & Co., Inc. *
For additional information, see 6:269.

[93-4]

*Language Usage: Differential Aptitude Tests. Grades 8–12 and adults; 1947–73; 2 editions; George K. Bennett, Harold G. Seashore, and Alexander G. Wesman; Psychological Corporation. * For the complete battery entry, see 1069.

a) FORM A. 1947–59; 2 scores: spelling, sentences. *Out of print.*
b) FORM T. 1947–73; revision of Form M ('62).

For reviews of the complete battery, see 7:673 (1 review, 1 excerpt), 6:767 (2 reviews), 5:605 (2 reviews), 4:711 (3 reviews), and 3:620 (1 excerpt).

REFERENCES THROUGH 1971
1. BOURNE, ROBERT K., AND ROTHNEY, JOHN W. M. "Assessments of Counselees Writing Skills by Tests and Essays." *Voc Guid Q* 9:21–4 au '60. *
2. WOOD, SUSAN. *An Evaluation of Published English Tests,* pp. 23–5. Madison, Wis.: Wisconsin Department of Public Instruction, 1967. Pp. 91. *

CUMULATIVE NAME INDEX
Bourne, R. K.: 1   Wood, S.: 2
Rothney, J. W. M.: 1

[95]

Moray House English Tests. Ages 8.5–10.5, 10–12, 12–14; 1935–70; 3 levels; Godfrey Thomson Unit, University of Edinburgh; University of London Press Ltd. [England]. *

a) MORAY HOUSE JUNIOR ENGLISH TEST. Ages 8.5–10.5; 1952–70.
b) MORAY HOUSE ENGLISH TEST. Ages 10–12; 1935–69.
c) MORAY HOUSE ENGLISH TEST (ADV.). Ages 12–14; 1947–58.

For additional information, see 7:202 (1 reference); for a review by M. Alan Brimer, see 6:271 (7 references).

REFERENCES THROUGH 1971
1–7. See 6:271.
8. See 7:202.
9. DOCKRELL, W. B. "The Relationship Between Socio-Economic Status, Intelligence and Attainment in Some Scottish Primary Schools." *Indian Psychol B* 4:1–6 Ja '59. * (*PA* 37:4715)
10. LEWIS, D. G. "Differences in Attainment Between Primary-Schools in Mixed-Language Areas: Their Dependence on Intelligence and Linguistic Background." *Brit J Ed Psychol* 30:63–70 F '60. *
11. MANLEY, D. R. "Mental Ability in Jamaica: (An Examination of the Performance of Children in the Jamaican Common Entrance Examination, 1959)." *Social & Econ Studies* (Jamaica) 12:51–71 Mr '63. * (*PA* 38:767)
12. HALLWORTH, H. J. "Personality Ratings of Adolescents: A Study in a Comprehensive School." *Brit J Ed Psychol* 34:171–7 Je '64. * (*PA* 39:3180)
13. HOROBIN, GORDON; OLDMAN, DAVID; AND BYTHEWAY, BILL. "The Social Differentiation of Ability." *Sociology* 1:113–29 My '67. *
14. NISBET, J. D., AND ENTWISTLE, N. J. "Intelligence and Family Size, 1949–1965." *Brit J Ed Psychol* 37:188–93 Je '67. * (*PA* 41:15274)

CUMULATIVE NAME INDEX
Armstrong, H. G.: 5   Lewis, D. G.: 10
Brimer, M. A.: *rev,* 6:271   MacNamara, J.: 8
Buchan, J.: 7   Manley, D. R.: 11
Bytheway, B.: 13   Mukherjee, L.: 6
Dockrell, W. B.: 9   Nisbet, J.: 7
Emmett, W. G.: 3, 4   Nisbet, J. D.: 14
Entwistle, N. J.: 14   Oldman, D.: 13
Hallworth, H. J.: 12   Peel, E. A.: 5
Horobin, G.: 13   Pilliner, A. E. G.: 2
Lambert, C. M.: 1   Wilmut, F. S.: 3

[96]

*National Teacher Examinations: English Language and Literature. College seniors and teachers; 1940–73; an inactive form (1966) entitled *Teacher Education Examination Program: English Language and Literature* is available to colleges for local administration; another inactive form (1968) entitled *Specialty Examinations: English Language and Literature* is available to school systems for local use as part of the program entitled *School Personnel Research and Evaluation Services;* Educational Testing Service. * For the testing program entry, see 869.

For additional information concerning earlier forms, see 7:203 (1 reference); for a review by Holland Roberts, see 6:259. For reviews of the testing program, see 7:582 (2 reviews), 6:700 (1 review), 5:538 (3 reviews), and 4:802 (1 review).

REFERENCES THROUGH 1971
1. See 7:203.

CUMULATIVE NAME INDEX
Medlin, Y. L.: 1   Roberts, H.: *rev,* 6:259

[97]

Nationwide English Composition Examination. Grades 4–12; 1959–63; no manual; [Donald R. Honz]; Educational Stimuli. *
For additional information, see 6:290.

[98]

Nationwide English Grammar Examination. Grades 4–12; 1957–63; no manual; [Donald R. Honz]; Educational Stimuli. *
For additional information, see 6:272.

[99]

The New Purdue Placement Test in English. Grades 11–16; 1931–55; revision of *The Purdue Placement Test in English;* 8 scores: punctuation, grammar, sentence structure, reading (study), reading (pleasure), vocabulary, spelling, total; G. S. Wykoff, J. H. McKee, and H. H. Remmers; Houghton Mifflin Co. *
For additional information and reviews by Gerald V.

Lannholm and M. J. Wantman, see 5:199 (5 references); see also 4:173 (9 references).

REFERENCES THROUGH 1971

1-9. See 4:173.
10-14. See 5:199.
15. PERRY, ROBERT D. *Prediction Equations for Success in College Mathematics.* Contribution to Education No. 122. Nashville, Tenn.: George Peabody College for Teachers, 1934. Pp. xiii, 58. * (*PA* 8:3277)
16. READ, CECIL B. "The Prediction of Scholastic Success in a Municipal University." *Sch & Soc* 48:187-8 Ag 6 '38. * (*PA* 12:6645)
17. DOUGLASS, LOWELL N. "A Study of Certain Factors Influencing Academic Achievement With Special Reference to the Health Factor." *J Exp Ed* 7:235-44 Mr '39. * (*PA* 13:5911)
18. SPOERL, DOROTHY TILDEN. "The Academic and Verbal Adjustment of College Age Bilingual Students." *J Genetic Psychol* 64:139-57 Mr '44. * (*PA* 18:2275)
19. ADAMS, SAM, AND GARRETT, H. L. "Scholastic Background as Related to Success in College Physics." *J Ed Res* 47:545-9 Mr '54. * (*PA* 28:7951)
20. LEBOLD, WILLIAM KERNS. *A Longitudinal Study of Purdue Engineering Students.* Doctor's thesis, Purdue University (Lafayette, Ind.), 1957. (*DA* 17:2057)
21. SPAHR, BETTE JEANNE WEINTZ. *A Study of the Correlation Between Scores on the Purdue Placement Test in English and Success in Graduate Education Programs at Purdue University.* Master's thesis, Purdue University (Lafayette, Ind.), 1960.

CUMULATIVE NAME INDEX

Adams, S.: 19	Lawrence, W. A.: 2
Baker, P. C.: 12	LeBold, W. K.: 20
Belman, H. S.: 7, 9	Lott, H. V.: 3
Bonner, L. W.: 14	Perry, R. D.: 15
Brown, J. I.: 5	Pred, G. D.: 8
Douglass, L. N.: 17	Quaid, T. D. D.: 1
Dungan, E. W.: 13	Read, C. B.: 16
Elliott, D. N.: 6	Remmers, H. H.: 6
Evans, R. N.: 7, 9	Severance, K. M.: 11
Gage, N. L.: 6	Spahr, B. J. W.: 21
Garrett, H. L.: 19	Spoerl, D. T.: 18
Johnson, A. P.: 19	Varnado, G. R.: 4
Lannholm, G. V.: *rev,* 5:199	Wantman, M. J.: *rev,* 5:199

[100]

*Objective Tests in Constructive English. Grades 7, 8, 9, 10-12; 1955-64; 1964 tests identical with tests copyrighted 1955 except for format and directions; no manual; Gunnar Horn; Perfection Form Co. *

[101]

*Objective Tests in Punctuation. Grades 7, 8, 9, 10-12; 1955-64; 1964 tests identical with tests copyrighted 1955 except for format and directions; no manual; Gunnar Horn; Perfection Form Co. *

[102]

Pacific Tests of English Attainment and Skills: Pacific Test Series. Job applicants in Papua and New Guinea; 1933-68; PTEAS; 3 tests; I. G. Ord; Australian Council for Educational Research [Australia]. *
a) PACIFIC READING COMPREHENSION TEST. 1933-68; PRCT; adaptation of Part 3 of *A.C.E.R. Silent Reading Test,* Forms A and B.
b) PACIFIC WORD KNOWLEDGE TEST. 1933-68; PWKT.
c) PACIFIC WORD FORMATION TEST. 1968; PWFT.
For additional information, see 7:204.

[103]

Picture Story Language Test. Ages 7-17; 1965; PSLT; developmental scale for written language; 5 scores: productivity (total words, total sentences, words per sentence), syntax, abstract-concrete; Helmer R. Myklebust; Grune & Stratton, Inc. *
For additional information, reviews by Nicholas Anastasiow and William H. Perkins, and excerpted reviews by C. H. Ammons and Joseph M. Wepman, see 7:205 (5 references).

REFERENCES THROUGH 1971

1-5. See 7:205.
6. MYKLEBUST, HELMER R.; BANNOCHIE, MARGARET N.; AND KILLEN, JAMES R. Chap. 9, "Learning Disabilities and Cognitive Processes," pp. 213-51. In *Progress in Learning Disabilities, Vol. 2.* Edited by Helmer R. Myklebust. New York: Grune & Stratton, Inc., 1971. Pp. ix, 404. *

CUMULATIVE NAME INDEX

Ammons, C. H.: *exc,* 7:205	Mason, C. W.: 2
Anastasiow, N.: *rev,* 7:205	Moore, A. B.: 3
Anderson, R. P.: 5	Myklebust, H. R.: 1, 6
Bannochie, M. N.: 6	O'Toole, T. J.: 4
Bell, D. B.: 5	Perkins, W. H.: *rev,* 7:205
Killen, J. R.: 6	Wepman, J. M.: *exc,* 7:205
Lewis, F. D.: 5	

[104]

Pressey Diagnostic Tests in English Composition. Grades 7-12; 1923-24; 4 tests; Bobbs-Merrill Co., Inc. *
a) CAPITALIZATION. S. L. Pressey, E. V. Bowers, and Blythe Pearce.
b) PUNCTUATION. S. L. Pressey, Helen Ruhlen, and Blythe Pearce.
c) GRAMMAR. F. R. Conkling, S. L. Pressey, and L. C. Pressey.
d) SENTENCE STRUCTURE. F. R. Conkling, S. L. Pressey, and L. C. Pressey.
For additional information and reviews by Harry A. Greene and Jean Hoard, see 2:1274.

REFERENCES THROUGH 1971

1. PRESSEY, SIDNEY L. "Measurement of Progress in English in the Upper Grades." *Ann Conf Ed Meas* 8:35-45 '21. *
2. CAVINS, L. V. "An Experiment With Standardized Tests in a State Teachers' Examination." *J Ed Res* 14:206-12 O '26. * (*PA* 1:489)
3. DEAN, CECIL H. "Report of Diagnostic Tests in English Composition Given in Schenley High School." *Pittsburgh Sch* 1:8-14 N-D '26. *
4. WILLING, MATTHEW H. "Valid Diagnosis in High School Composition." *Teach Col Contrib Ed* 230:1-64 '26. *
5. BELL, J. CARLETON. Chap. 15, "Attainments of High School Pupils in the Pressey Diagnostic Tests in English Composition," pp. 87-96. In *Contributions to Education, Vol. 2.* Edited by J. Carleton Bell and Ambrose L. Suhrie. Yonkers, N.Y.: World Book Co., 1928. Pp. xi, 425. * (*PA* 2:2313)
6. LYONS, ELVA ANNE. "Objective Measurements in English." *Ed Res B* (Los Angeles City Schools) 9:481-9 N 19 '30. *
7. WERNER, OSCAR H. Chap. 2, "The Influence of the Study of Modern Foreign Languages on the Development of Desirable Abilities in English," pp. 97-145. (*PA* 4:2847) In *Studies in Modern Language Teaching.* By E. W. Bagster-Collins and Others. New York: Macmillan Co., 1930. Pp. xxxi, 491. *

CUMULATIVE NAME INDEX

Bell, J. C.: 5	Lyons, E. A.: 6
Cavins, L. V.: 2	Pressey, S. L.: 1
Dean, C. H.: 3	Werner, O. H.: 7
Greene, H. A.: *rev,* 2:1274	Willing, M. H.: 4
Hoard, J.: *rev,* 2:1274	

[105]

The Purdue High School English Test. Grades 9-12; 1931-62; abbreviated modification of *New Purdue Placement Test in English* which is also available; all items selected from the earlier test; 6 scores: grammar, punctuation, effective expression, vocabulary, spelling, total; H. H. Remmers, R. D. Franklin, G. S. Wykoff, and J. H. McKee; Houghton Mifflin Co. *
For additional information and reviews by Charlotte Croon Davis and Benjamin Rosner, see 6:276.

REFERENCES THROUGH 1971

1. BONNER, LEON WILLIAM. *Factors Associated With the Academic Achievement of Freshmen Students at a Southern Agricultural College.* Doctor's thesis, Pennsylvania State University (University Park, Pa.), 1956. (*DA* 17:266)
2. PALACIOS, JOHN RAYMOND. *A Validation Study of Selected Tests for Possible Use in Admission to Professional Education Sequences at Purdue University.* Doctor's thesis, Purdue University (Lafayette, Ind.), 1959. (*DA* 20:2679)
3. BATES, CHARLES O. *A Study of Creative Potential as Found in Elementary Student Teachers.* Doctor's thesis, Ball State Teachers College (Muncie, Ind.), 1963. (*DA* 24:4561)

4. FOURNET, FRANCIS GARY, JR. *A Study of Various Factors Related to Success in College General Mathematics.* Doctor's thesis, Louisiana State University (Baton Rouge, La.), 1963. (*DA* 24:5239)

5. BLACK, HUBERT PERRY. *The Predictive Value of Selected Factors for Achievement of Lee College Freshmen.* Doctor's thesis, University of Tennessee (Knoxville, Tenn.), 1965. (*DA* 27:618A)

6. LEEP, ALBERT GENE. *Selected Pre-Service Measures as Predictors of First Year Teaching Performance of Elementary Teachers.* Doctor's thesis, Ball State Teachers College (Muncie, Ind.), 1965. (*DA* 26:3163)

7. WOOD, SUSAN. *An Evaluation of Published English Tests,* pp. 57–9. Madison, Wis.: Wisconsin Department of Public Instruction, 1967. Pp. 91. *

8. MEDLER, BYRON WAYNE. *A Comparative Study of Selected Variables Between Students Completing the Elementary Education Curriculum and Those Students Who Left the Elementary Education Curriculum Due to Academic Disqualification or Change of Major.* Doctor's thesis, Ball State University (Muncie, Ind.), 1968. (*DA* 29:3503A)

9. MUNDAY, LEO. "Correlations Between ACT and Other Predictors of Academic Success in College." *Col & Univ* 44:67–76 f '68. *

10. SHALLCROSS, MARCIA KEEL. *Predicting Success in Written Communications in Business by Using the New Purdue Placement Test in English.* Master's thesis, San Diego State College (San Diego, Calif.), 1968.

11. CHERRY, ADA LOU. *A Comparison of Selected Characteristics of Graduated Students and Academically Disqualified Students Who Were Admitted With Warning to Ball State University Autumns, 1963 and 1964.* Doctor's thesis, Ball State University (Muncie, Ind.), 1969. (*DAI* 30:4217A)

12. CHIMONIDES, STELIOS GEORGIOU. *Some Relationships Associated With Academic Success in Graduate Work at a Midwestern University.* Master's thesis, Western Michigan University (Kalamazoo, Mich.), 1969. (*Masters Abstracts* 7:200)

CUMULATIVE NAME INDEX

Bates, C. O.: 3
Black, H. P.: 5
Bonner, L. W.: 1
Cherry, A. L.: 11
Chimonides, S. G.: 12
Davis, C. C.: *rev,* 6:276
Fournet, F. G.: 4
Leep, A. G.: 6
Medler, B. W.: 8
Munday, L.: 9
Palacios, J. R.: 2
Rosner, B.: *rev,* 6:276
Shallcross, M. K.: 10
Wood, S.: 7

[106]

RBH Spelling Test and Word Meaning Test. Business and industry; 1957–63; Richardson, Bellows, Henry & Co., Inc. *

For additional information, see 6:324.

[107]

RBH Test of Language Skills. Business and industry; 1949–63; Richardson, Bellows, Henry & Co., Inc. *

For additional information, see 6:285.

[108-9]

SRA Achievement Series: Language Arts. Grades 2–4, 4–9; 1954–69; Forms C and D; more recent Forms E and F are not available as separates; 4 scores: capitalization and punctuation, grammatical usage, spelling, total; Louis P. Thorpe, D. Welty Lefever, and Robert A. Naslund; Science Research Associates, Inc. * For the complete battery entry, see 29.

a) HAND SCORED EDITION. Grades 2–4; 1955–68; test booklet title is *How Should We Say This? Out of print.*

b) MULTILEVEL EDITION. Grades 4–9; 1963–69.

For additional information, see 7:206; for a review by Miriam M. Bryan of earlier forms, see 6:277 (1 reference); for reviews by Constance M. McCullough and Winifred L. Post, see 5:200. For reviews of the complete battery, see 7:18 (2 reviews), 6:21 (1 review), and 5:21 (2 reviews).

REFERENCES THROUGH 1971

1. See 6:277.
2. WOOD, SUSAN. *An Evaluation of Published English Tests,* pp. 65–8. Madison, Wis.: Wisconsin Department of Public Instruction, 1967. Pp. 91. *

CUMULATIVE NAME INDEX

Bryan, M. M.: *rev,* 6:277
Groff, P. J.: 1
McCullough, C. M.: *rev,* 5:200
Post, W. L.: *rev,* 5:200
Wood, S.: 2

[110]

The Schonell Diagnostic English Tests. Ages 9.5–16; 1940; 5 scores: English usage, capital letters and punctuation, vocabulary, sentence structure, composition; F. Eleanor Schonell; Oliver & Boyd [Scotland]. *

For additional information and reviews by John Cohen and Robert H. Thouless, see 3:135.

REFERENCES THROUGH 1971

1. SCHONELL, FLORENCE ELEANOR. *An Experimental Study of Diagnostic Tests in English.* Master's thesis, University of London (London, England), 1941.

CUMULATIVE NAME INDEX

Cohen, J.: *rev,* 3:135
Schonell, F. E.: 1
Thouless, R. H.: *rev,* 3:135

[111]

***Senior English Test.** Technical college entrants; 1963–71; 1971 manual essentially the same as 1964 manual except for deletion of 3 paragraphs and inclusion of 1963 norms formerly published separately; distribution restricted to colleges of further education; published for the National Foundation for Educational Research in England and Wales; Ginn & Co. Ltd. [England]. *

For additional information and reviews by M. A. Brimer and David A. Walker, see 7:207.

[112]

★Sequential Tests of Educational Progress, Series 2: English Expression. Grades 4–6, 7–9, 10–12, 13–14; 1969–72; Cooperative Tests and Services. * For the complete battery entry, see 35.

For reviews of the original edition of the complete battery, see 6:25 (2 reviews) and 5:24 (2 reviews, 1 excerpt).

[113]

***Sequential Tests of Educational Progress: Writing.** Grades 4–6, 7–9, 10–12, 13–14 (except b); 1956–72; 2 editions; Cooperative Tests and Services. * For the complete battery entry, see 35.

a) ORIGINAL SERIES: WRITING [70 MINUTE TESTS]. Grades 4–6, 7–9, 10–12, 13–14; 1956–63; Braille and large type editions (grades 4–12) are available from American Printing House for the Blind, Inc.

b) SERIES 2: MECHANICS OF WRITING [40 MINUTE TESTS]. Grades 4–6, 7–9, 10–12; 1956–72; 3 scores: spelling, capitalization and punctuation, total.

For additional information, reviews by Hillel Black and Albert N. Hieronymus, and an excerpted review by Dean A. Allen of a, see 6:292 (3 references); for reviews by Charlotte Croon Davis, John M. Stalnaker, and Louis C. Zahner, see 5:207. For reviews of the original edition of the complete battery, see 6:25 (2 reviews) and 5:24 (2 reviews, 1 excerpt).

REFERENCES THROUGH 1971

1–3. See 6:292.
4. MICHAEL, WILLIAM B.; CATHCART, ROBERT; AND ZIMMERMAN, WAYNE S. "Linguistic Factors in Various Measures of Communication Skills for College Students With Implications for Predictive Validity." *Ed & Psychol Meas* 24:363–7 su '64. * (*PA* 39:3192)
5. CHASE, CLINTON I. *The University Freshman Dropout.* Indiana University, Monograph of the Bureau of Educational Studies and Testing, Indiana Studies in Prediction, No. 6. Bloomington, Ind.: the Bureau, 1965. Pp. 36. *
6. ELLIOTT, MERLE H., AND BADAL, ALDEN W. "Achievement and Racial Composition of Schools." *Calif J Ed Res* 16:158–66 S '65. * (*PA* 40:1478)
7. WHEELER, FRED. "An Experimental Study of Means to Improve Writing." *J Sec Ed* 40:331–5 N '65. *

8. Madaus, George F., and Rippey, Robert M. "Zeroing in on the STEP Writing Test: What Does It Tell a Teacher?" *J Ed Meas* 3:19–25 sp '66. *

9. Phelps, Arthur M. *Predicting First Semester Grades in the Junior College Two-Year Terminal Vocational-Technical Programs.* Master's thesis, Stetson University (DeLand, Fla.), 1966.

10. Pierson, Howard. *Peer and Teacher Correction: A Comparison of the Effects of Two Methods of Teaching Composition in Grade Nine English Classes.* Doctor's thesis, New York University (New York, N.Y.), 1967. (*DA* 28:1350A)

11. Tenopyr, Mary L. "Social Intelligence and Academic Success." *Ed & Psychol Meas* 27:961–5 w '67. * (*PA* 42:9509)

12. Wood, Susan. *An Evaluation of Published English Tests,* pp. 73–8. Madison, Wis.: Wisconsin Department of Public Instruction, 1967. Pp. 91. *

13. Wilson, Anaise Victorianne. *A Study of the Relationship of Selected Factors to the Academic Achievement of College Freshmen in the School of Education of Tuskegee Institute.* Doctor's thesis, New York University (New York, N.Y.), 1968. (*DAI* 30:144A)

14. Rippey, Robert M. "A Comparison of Five Different Scoring Functions for Confidence Tests." *J Ed Meas* 7(3):165–70 f '70. *

15. Hall, Lucien T., Jr. "The Prediction of Success in Each of Six Four-Year Selections of Secondary Mathematics Courses." *Sch Sci & Math* 71(8):693–6 N '71. *

16. Shaver, James P., and Nuhn, Dee. "The Effectiveness of Tutoring Underachievers in Reading and Writing." *J Ed Res* 65(3):107–12 N.'71. * (*PA* 48:1878)

CUMULATIVE NAME INDEX

Allen, D. A.: *exc,* 6:292
Badal, A. W.: 6
Black, H.: *rev,* 6:292
Cathcart, R.: 3–4
Chase, C. I.: 5
Davis, C. C.: *rev,* 5:207
Elliott, M. H.: 6
Endler, N. S.: 2
Groff, P. J.: 1
Hall, L. T.: 15
Hieronymus, A. N.: *rev,* 6:292
Madaus, G. F.: 8
Michael, W. B.: 3–4
Milfs, M.: 3
Nuhn, D.: 16
Phelps, A. M.: 9
Pierson, H.: 10
Rippey, R. M.: 8, 14
Shaver, J. P.: 16
Stalnaker, J. M.: *rev,* 5:207
Steinberg, D.: 2
Tenopyr, M. L.: 11
Wheeler, F.: 7
Wilson, A. V.: 13
Wood, S.: 12
Zahner, L. C.: *rev,* 5:207
Zimmerman, W. S.: 3–4

[114]

Stanford Achievement Test: High School English and Spelling Tests. Grades 9–12; 1965–66; catalog uses the title *Stanford High School English and Spelling Tests;* subtest of *Stanford Achievement Test: High School Basic Battery;* Eric F. Gardner, Jack Merwin, Robert Callis, and Richard Madden; Harcourt Brace Jovanovich, Inc. * For the complete battery entry, see 37.

For additional information and reviews by Vincent R. D'Oyley and Leonard S. Feldt, see 7:208. For reviews of the complete battery, see 7:27 (2 reviews).

[115]

Stanford Achievement Test, 1964 Edition: Spelling and Language Tests. Grades 4.0–5.4, 5.5–6.9, 7.0–9.9; 1940–68; catalog uses the title *Stanford Language Tests;* same as spelling and language subtests of *Stanford Achievement Test;* not available as a separate in the 1973 edition of the battery; 2 scores: spelling, language; Braille editions are available from American Printing House for the Blind, Inc.; Truman L. Kelley, Richard Madden, Eric F. Gardner, and Herbert C. Rudman; Harcourt Brace Jovanovich, Inc. * For the complete battery entry, see 36.

For additional information and reviews by William E. Coffman and Carleton B. Shay, see 7:209. For reviews of the complete battery, see 7:25 (1 excerpt), 6:26 (1 review, 1 excerpt), 5:25 (1 review), 4:25 (2 reviews), and 3:18 (2 reviews).

REFERENCES THROUGH 1971

1. Willing, Matthew H. "Valid Diagnosis in High School Composition." *Teach Col Contrib Ed* 230:1–64 '26. *

CUMULATIVE NAME INDEX

Coffman, W. E.: *rev,* 7:209
Shay, C. B.: *rev,* 7:209
Willing, M. H.: 1

[116]

Survey Tests of English Usage. Grades 9–13; 1947–49; title on some forms is *Achievement Test of English Usage;* L. J. O'Rourke; O'Rourke Publications. *

For additional information and a review by Holland Roberts, see 6:281 (1 reference).

REFERENCES THROUGH 1971

1. See 6:281.

CUMULATIVE NAME INDEX

Groff, P. J.: 1
Roberts, H.: *rev,* 6:281

[117]

Teacher Education Examination Program: English Language and Literature. College seniors preparing to teach secondary school; 1957–72; reprinting of inactive 1966 form of *National Teacher Examinations: English Language and Literature;* test available to colleges for local administration; Educational Testing Service. * For the testing program entry, see 898.

For additional information concerning an earlier form, see 6:260. For a review of the testing program, see 5:543. For reference to a review of the *National Teacher Examinations: English Language and Literature,* see 96.

[118]

A Test of English Usage. English-speaking high school and college students and adults; 1963–64; A. Edwin Harper, Jr., and Rhea S. Das; Manasayan [India]. *

For additional information, see 6:284.

[119]

Tests of Academic Progress: Composition. Grades 9–12; 1964–66; Dale P. Scannell and Oscar M. Haugh; Houghton Mifflin Co. * For the complete battery entry, see 44.

For additional information and reviews by Ellis Batten Page and Osmond E. Palmer, see 7:210 (1 reference). For a review of the complete battery, see 7:31.

REFERENCES THROUGH 1971

1. See 7:210.

CUMULATIVE NAME INDEX

Goolsby, T. M.: 1
Page, E. B.: *rev,* 7:210
Palmer, O. E.: *rev,* 7:210

[120]

Tests of Basic Experiences: Language. Prekgn-kgn, kgn–grade 1; 1970–72; Margaret H. Moss; CTB/McGraw-Hill. * For the complete battery entry, see 47.

For additional information, see 7:211 (1 reference). For a review of the complete battery, see 7:33.

REFERENCES THROUGH 1971

1. See 7:211.
2. Compton, Mary Elizabeth. *A Study of the Relationship Between Oral Language Facility and Reading Achievement of Selected First-Grade Children.* Doctor's thesis, University of North Carolina (Chapel Hill, N.C.), 1971. (*DAI* 32:6848A)

CUMULATIVE NAME INDEX

Compton, M. E.: 2
Moss, M. H.: 1

[121]

Tressler English Minimum Essentials Test, Revised Edition. Grades 8–12; 1932–56; 8 scores: grammatical correctness, vocabulary, punctuation and capitalization, the sentence and its parts, sentence sense, inflection and accent, spelling, total; 1954 test identical with test copyrighted 1941 except for changes in 4 items; 1955 manual identical with sheet copyrighted 1941 except for minor changes; J. C. Tressler; Bobbs-Merrill Co., Inc. *

For additional information and reviews by Osmond E. Palmer and Roger A. Richards, see 6:286 (1 reference).

REFERENCES THROUGH 1971
1. See 6:286.

CUMULATIVE NAME INDEX
Groff, P. J.: 1   Richards, R. A.: *rev,* 6:286
Palmer, O. E.: *rev,* 6:286

[122]

Walton-Sanders English Test. 1, 2 semesters in grades 9–13; 1962–64; first published 1962–63 in the Every Pupil Scholarship Test series; Charles E. Walton and M. W. Sanders; Bureau of Educational Measurements. *

For additional information, see 7:212.

[123]

Watson English Usage and Appreciation Test, Fourth Edition. Grades 4–8; 1966; G. Milton Watson; Book Society of Canada Ltd. [Canada]. *

For additional information and a review by Vincent R. D'Oyley, see 7:213.

[124]

Writing Skills Test. Grades 9–12; 1961, c1960–61; Macklin Thomas; Science Research Associates, Inc. *

For additional information and reviews by William E. Coffman and Osmond E. Palmer, see 6:293.

[125]

Writing Test: McGraw-Hill Basic Skills System. Grades 11–14; 1970; also called *MHBSS Writing Test;* although designed for use with the MHBSS instructional program, the test may be used independently; 4 scores: language mechanics, sentence patterns, paragraph patterns, total; Alton L. Raygor; McGraw-Hill Book Co., Inc. *

For additional information and a review by Leonard S. Feldt, see 7:214.

[Out of Print Since TIP I]

A.C.E.R. English Usage Tests, 5:173 (1 review)
Ability for English (Language): Fife Tests of Ability, Test 1, 3:114 (1 reference)
Barrett-Ryan-Schrammel English Test, 5:176 (5 reviews, 1 reference)
Basic Language Skills: Iowa Every-Pupil Tests of Basic Skills, Test C, 4:150
Clapp-Young English Test, 3:117 (1 review)
College Entrance Examination Board Writing Sample, 6:289 (1 review, 2 references)
College Placement Test in English, 4:153 (1 review)
College Preparatory Test in English, 4:154 (1 review)
Columbia Research Bureau English Test, 2:1270 (2 reviews)
Cooperative English Test: Usage, Spelling, and Vocabulary, 6:255 (10 reviews, 16 references)
Coordinated Scales of Attainment: English, 5:180
Correct English Usage Test, 4:156
Correctness and Effectiveness of Expression, 5:181 (1 review); now available only as a subtest of *Tests of General Educational Development,* 48
Cross English Test, 2:1272 (2 reviews, 3 references)
Eaton Diagnostic-Accomplishment Tests in English, T:421
Eleventh Year English Fundamentals: Manchester Semester-End Achievement Tests, T:422, 36:639
English: Every Pupil Scholarship Test, 6:257 (1 reference)
English: Northumberland Standardised Tests (1925 Series), T:428
English Survey Test: Ohio Scholarship Tests: Ohio Senior Survey Tests, 5:188 (2 reviews, 1 reference)

English Test (Four-Year Course): Affiliation Testing Program for Catholic Secondary Schools, 6:263 (1 review)
English: Thanet Mental Tests, 2:1279 (1 review)
English Usage: Every Pupil Test, 6:265 (1 review, 2 references)
Greene-Stapp Language Abilities Test, 5:195 (2 reviews, 1 reference)
Hoyum-Schrammel English Essentials Tests, 5:196 (2 reviews)
Iowa Grammar Information Test, 4:164 (1 review)
Iowa Language Abilities Test, 4:165 (1 review)
Iowa Primary Language Test, T:446, 36:642
Kentucky English Test, 3:132 (1 review, 1 reference); revised edition was available only as a part of *Kentucky Classification Battery,* 4:301 (1 review, 4 references)
Kirby Grammar Test, T:448
Language Battery: National Institute for Personnel Research High Level Battery, T:450; revised edition now available only as a subtest of *High Level Battery: Test A/75,* 1075
Language Battery: National Institute for Personnel Research Normal Battery, T:451; now available only as a subtest of *National Institute for Personnel Research Normal Battery,* 1085
Language Essentials Tests, 3:133 (1 review)
Linguistic Awareness Test, 2:1287
Mechanics of Written English, 7:199
Metropolitan Achievement Tests: High School Language Tests, 7:200 (2 reviews)
Missouri College English Test, 7:201 (2 reviews, 1 reference)
Nelson's High School English Test, 2:1290 (2 reviews)
Ninth Year English Fundamentals: Manchester Semester-End Achievement Tests, T:459, 36:644
Novelty Grammar Tests (status unknown), 6:273
Pribble-Dallmann Diagnostic Tests in Elementary Language Skills, 6:274 (2 reviews)
Pribble-McCrory Diagnostic Tests in Practical English Grammar, 6:275 (1 review)
Public School Achievement Tests: Grammar, T:439; *Language Usage,* T:453
Rinsland-Beck Natural Test of English Usage, 2:1293 (2 reviews, 1 excerpt, 3 references)
Scholastic Achievement Series: English-Spelling, 6:278 (2 reviews, 1 reference)
Sequential Tests of Educational Progress: Essay Test, 6:291 (3 reviews, 3 references)
Survey of Language Achievement: California Survey Series, 6:280 (1 review)
T.C. English Test, 6:282
Tenth Year English Fundamentals: Manchester Semester-End Achievement Tests, T:475, 36:646
Test of Creative Writing Aptitude and Ability, T:484
Test of English Usage, 6:283 (2 reviews)
Tests of Language Usage: Cooperative Inter-American Tests, 4:176 (1 review, 3 references)
Twelfth Year English Fundamentals: Manchester Semester-End Achievement Tests, 36:647; for revision, see *Senior English Fundamentals: Manchester Semester-End Achievement Tests,* T:472
20th Century Test for English—9th Grade, 4:159; *10th Grade,* 4:160

LITERATURE

[126]

*American Literature Anthology Tests. High school; 1959–70; revisions of the *Objective Tests in*

Tressler English Minimum Essentials Test

American Anthology by Carl H. Larson and the *Alternate Objective Tests in American Anthology* by Dorothy A. Mason; 7 tests; no manual; Perfection Form Co. *

a) COLONIAL TIMES AND MAKING OF A NATION.
b) FLOWERING OF THE EAST.
c) THE GENIUS OF NEW ENGLAND.
d) CIVIL WAR AND THE WESTWARD MOVEMENT.
e) GROWTH OF REALISM.
f) MODERN AMERICAN LITERATURE.
g) FINAL TEST.

For additional information concerning the earlier tests, see 7:223.

[127]

★CLEP Subject Examination in American Literature. 1 year or equivalent; 1971–73, c1970–73; for college accreditation of nontraditional study, advanced placement, or assessment of educational achievement; tests administered monthly at centers throughout the United States; program administered for the College Entrance Examination Board by Educational Testing Service. * For the testing program entry, see 1050.

[128]

*CLEP Subject Examination in Analysis and Interpretation of Literature. 1 year or equivalent; 1964–73; for college accreditation of nontraditional study, advanced placement, or assessment of educational achievement; tests administered monthly at centers throughout the United States; program administered for the College Entrance Examination Board by Educational Testing Service. * For the testing program entry, see 1050.

For additional information concerning an earlier form, see 7:215. For reviews of the testing program, see 7:664 (3 reviews).

[129]

*CLEP Subject Examination in English Literature. 1 year or equivalent; 1970–73; for college accreditation of nontraditional study, advanced placement, or assessment of educational achievement; tests administered monthly at centers throughout the United States; program administered for the College Entrance Examination Board by Educational Testing Service. * For the testing program entry, see 1050.

For additional information, see 7:216. For reviews of the testing program, see 7:664 (3 reviews).

[130]

*College Board Achievement Test in Literature. Candidates for college entrance; 1968–73; test administered on specified dates at centers established by the publisher; inactive forms, entitled *College Placement Test in Literature,* are available to colleges for local administration; program administered for the College Entrance Examination Board by Educational Testing Service. * For the testing program entry, see 1048.

For additional information, see 7:217 (2 references). For reviews of the testing program, see 6:760 (2 reviews).

REFERENCES THROUGH 1971
1–2. See 7:217.

CUMULATIVE NAME INDEX
Elledge, S.: 2   Purves, A. C.: 1

[131]

*College Placement Test in Literature. Entering college freshmen; 1968–72; reprinting of inactive 1968 form of *College Board Achievement Test in Literature;*

test available to colleges for local administration; program administered for the College Entrance Examination Board by Educational Testing Service. * For the testing program entry, see 1051.

For additional information, see 7:218. For a review of the testing program, see 7:665.

[132]

★Cooperative Literature Tests. Grades 9–12; 1972–73; CLT; 19 tests: The Bridge of San Luis Rey, Great Expectations, Hamlet, Huckleberry Finn, Julius Caesar, Macbeth, The Merchant of Venice, Moby Dick, The Odyssey, Oedipus the King, The Old Man and the Sea, Our Town, Pride and Prejudice, Pygmalion, The Red Badge of, Courage, The Return of the Native, The Scarlet Letter, Silas Marner, A Tale of Two Cities; Cooperative Tests and Services. *

[133]

*English Literature Anthology Tests. High school; 1959–70; slight revisions of the *Objective Tests in English Anthology* by Carl H. Larson and the *Alternate Objective Tests in English Anthology* by Dorothy A. Mason; 9 tests; no manual; Perfection Form Co. *

a) BEGINNINGS OF ENGLISH LITERATURE. 1959–70.
b) THE EIGHTEENTH CENTURY. 1959–70.
c) THE ELIZABETHAN PERIOD. 1959–70.
d) THE ENGLISH NOVEL. 1964–70.
e) THE PURITAN PERIOD. 1959–70.
f) THE ROMANTIC PERIOD. 1959–70.
g) THE TWENTIETH CENTURY. 1959–70.
h) THE VICTORIAN PERIOD. 1959–70.
i) FINAL EXAMINATION. 1959–70.

For additional information concerning the earlier tests, see 7:224.

[134]

English Tests for Outside Reading. Grades 9–10, 11–12; 1939; 100 tests on specific literary works; Henrietta Silliman; the Author. *

For additional information, see 2:1301.

[135]

*The Graduate Record Examinations Advanced Literature in English Test. Graduate school candidates; 1939–73; Educational Testing Service. * For the testing program entry, see 1053.

For additional information concerning earlier forms, see 7:219 (1 reference); for a review by Robert C. Pooley, see 5:215. For reviews of the testing program, see 7:667 (1 review) and 5:601 (1 review).

REFERENCES THROUGH 1971
1. See 7:219.

CUMULATIVE NAME INDEX
Lannholm, G. V.: 1   Pooley, R. C.: *rev,* 5:215
Marco, G. L.: 1   Schrader, W. B.: 1

[136]

Hollingsworth-Sanders Junior High School Literature Test. 1, 2 semesters in grades 7–8; 1962–64; first published 1962–63 in the Every Pupil Scholarship Test series; Leon Hollingsworth and M. W. Sanders; Bureau of Educational Measurements. *

For additional information and a review by Paul B. Diederich, see 7:220.

[137]

Hoskins-Sanders Literature Test. 1, 2 semesters grades 9–13; 1962–64; first published 1962–63 in the Every Pupil Scholarship Test series; Thomas Hoskins and M. W. Sanders; Bureau of Educational Measurements. *

For additional information and a review by Alan C. Purves, see 7:221.

[138]

*The Iowa Tests of Educational Development: Test 7, Ability to Interpret Literary Materials. Grades 9–12; 1942–67; Forms X-4 and Y-4; more recent Forms X5 and Y5 are not available as separates; prepared under the direction of E. F. Lindquist and Leonard S. Feldt; Science Research Associates, Inc. * For the complete battery entry, see 20.

For additional information concerning earlier forms, see 6:300 (1 reference). For reviews of the complete battery, see 6:14 (2 reviews), 5:17 (2 reviews), 4:17 (1 review), and 3:12 (3 reviews).

REFERENCES THROUGH 1971
1. See 6:300.
2. WEISGERBER, CHARLES A. "Accuracy in Judging Emotional Expressions as Related to Understanding of Literature." *J Social Psychol* 46:253–8 N '57. * (*PA* 34:2619)
3. TRELA, THADDEUS M. "Comparing Achievement on Tests of General and Critical Reading." *J Read Specialist* 6:140–2 My '67. * (*PA* 41:14190)

CUMULATIVE NAME INDEX
Trela, T. M.: 1, 3   Weisgerber, C. A.: 2

[139]

Literature Test: National Achievement Tests. Grades 7–12; 1937–57; 5 scores: recognizing effects, recognizing qualities, analyzing moods, miscellaneous facts, total; 1944 and 1954 tests identical with tests copyrighted 1937 and 1939, respectively; Robert K. Speer and Samuel Smith; Psychometric Affiliates. *

For additional information, see 5:219; for reviews by H. H. Giles and Robert C. Pooley, see 2:1304.

[140]

*Literature Tests/Objective. High school; 1929–71; 2 series; no manual; Perfection Form Co. *
a) 50-QUESTION SERIES. 1950–71; 284 tests on specific literary works; formerly called *Book Review Tests*.
b) 100-QUESTION SERIES. 1929–70; 174 tests on specific literary works; formerly called *Objective Tests in English*.

For additional information concerning earlier editions, see 6:295 and 6:304.

[141]

A Look at Literature: The NCTE Cooperative Test of Critical Reading and Appreciation. Grades 4–6; 1968–69; 3 scores: Parts 1 (selections read aloud by examiner while read silently by examinee), 2 (selections read silently by examinee), total; developed and sponsored jointly by Research Foundation of the National Council of Teachers of English and Educational Testing Service; Cooperative Tests and Services. *

For additional information and reviews by Nancy W. Burton and Walter J. Moore, see 7:222.

[142]

★Poetry Test/Objective. Grades 7–9, 10–12; 1968; no manual; Perfection Form Co. *

[143]

Tests of Academic Progress: Literature. Grades 9–12; 1964–66; Dale P. Scannell and Oscar M. Haugh; Houghton Mifflin Co. * For the complete battery entry, see 44.

For additional information and reviews by Robert C. Pooley, Alan C. Purves, and John C. Sherwood, see

7:225 (1 reference). For a review of the complete battery, see 7:31.

REFERENCES THROUGH 1971
1. See 7:225.

CUMULATIVE NAME INDEX
Goolsby, T. M.: 1   Purves, A. C.: *rev*, 7:225
Pooley, R. C.: *rev*, 7:225   Sherwood, J. C.: *rev*, 7:225

[144]

*The Undergraduate Program Field Tests: Literature Tests. College; 1969–73; formerly called *The Undergraduate Record Examinations: Literature Tests;* tests available to colleges for local administration; 2 tests: field, modular; Educational Testing Service. * For the testing program entry, see 1062.
a) LITERATURE TEST.
b) EUROPEAN AND AMERICAN LITERATURE TEST: A MODULAR TEST DESIGNED TO COMPLEMENT THE TWO-HOUR LITERATURE TEST.

For additional information, see 7:226. For reviews of the testing program, see 7:671 (2 reviews).

REFERENCES THROUGH 1971
1. SCHNITZEN, JOSEPH P., AND COX, JOHN A. "Concurrent Validity of a Literature Test in Relation to Selection of Persons for Graduate Study in English." *Ed & Psychol Meas* 31(2):485–9 su '71. *

CUMULATIVE NAME INDEX
Cox, J. A.: 1   Schnitzen, J. P.: 1

[145]

★World Literature Anthology Tests. High school; 1964–70; revision of *Objective Tests in World Anthology* by Dorothy A. Mason; 5 tests; no manual; Perfection Form Co. *
a) CLASSICAL LITERATURE.
b) EUROPEAN LITERATURE.
c) ORIENTAL LITERATURE.
d) RUSSIAN LITERATURE.
e) FINAL TEST.

[Out of Print Since TIP I]

American and English Literature: Every Pupil Test, 1:968
American Literature: Every Pupil Scholarship Test, 5:208
American Literature: Every Pupil Test, 6:294
Awareness Test in 20th Century Literature, 4:182 (2 reviews)
Barrett-Ryan Literature Test, 3:139 (1 review)
Carroll Prose Appreciation Test, 3:140 (1 review, 4 references)
Catholic Book Tests, 6:296
Center-Durost Literature Acquaintance Test, 5:210 (1 review, 1 reference)
Cooperative Literary Comprehension and Appreciation Test, 4:184 (1 review, 4 references)
Davis-Roahen-Schrammel American Literature Test, 6:297 (2 reviews)
Eaton Book-Report System, 1:972 (1 review)
Eaton Literature Tests, T:496
Elementary Literature: Every Pupil Scholarship Test, 5:218; for a later edition, see *Literature: Every Pupil Scholarship Test,* 6:301
English Literature: Every Pupil Test, 6:298
Interpretation of Literary Materials, 5:216; now available only as a subtest of *Tests of General Educational Development,* 48
Literature Appreciation Tests, 4:190 (1 review)
Literature: Every Pupil Scholarship Test, 6:301
New Eaton Literature Tests, 1:978
Objective Tests in American Literature, T:512

SPELLING

[146]

Buckingham Extension of the Ayres Spelling Scale. Grades 2–9; [1918?]; B. R. Buckingham; Bobbs-Merrill Co., Inc. *

REFERENCES THROUGH 1971

1. Otis, Arthur S. "The Reliability of Spelling Scales, Involving a 'Deviation Formula' for Correlation." *Sch & Soc* 4:676–83, 716–22, 750–6, 793–6 O 28, N 4, 11, 18 '16. *
2. Franzen, Raymond. "The Geography of Intelligence." *J Ed Psychol* 15:499–512 N '24. *
3. Garrison, S. C., and Ryan, Florence. "Age-Grade-Sex Percentile Norms for Some Educational Tests." *Peabody J Ed* 1:191–200 Ja '24. *
4. Gates, Arthur I., and LaSalle, Jessie. "A Study of Writing Ability and Its Relation to Other Abilities Based on Repeated Tests During a Period of 20 Months." *J Ed Psychol* 15:205–16 Ap '24. *
5. Symonds, Percival M. "The Accuracy of Certain Standard Tests for School Classification." *J Ed Res* 9:315–29 Ap '24. *
6. Trabue, Marion Rex. *Measuring Results in Education,* pp. 128–43. New York: American Book Co., 1924. Pp. 492. *
7. Omwake, Katharine T. "The Relation of Abstract Intelligence to Ability to Spell." *Pub Personnel Studies* 3:197–201 Jl '25. *
8. Sifferd, Calvin S. "A Survey of Spelling Ability." *El Sch J* 47:340–6 F '47. *
9. Doyle, Andrew M. "A Study of Spelling Achievement." *Cath Ed R* 48:171–4 Mr '50. *

CUMULATIVE NAME INDEX

[147]

★**Correct Spelling.** Grades 10–13; 1967; "cognition of symbolic units" and "clerical aptitude"; Ralph Hoepfner and J. P. Guilford; Sheridan Psychological Services, Inc. *

[148]

Group Diagnostic Spelling Test. Grades 9–13; 1958; Thomas G. Kemp; Reading Laboratory and Clinic. *
For additional information, see 6:319.

[149]

The Iowa Spelling Scales. Grades 2, 3, 5, 6, 7, 8; 1921–45; no manual; Ernest J. Ashbaugh; Bureau of Educational Research and Service. *

REFERENCES THROUGH 1971

1. Ashbaugh, Ernest J. *The Iowa Spelling Scales: Their Derivation, Uses, and Limitations.* Bloomington, Ill.: Public School Publishing Co., 1922. Pp. 144. *
2. Tidyman, W. F. "The Iowa Spelling Scales: A Review." *J Ed Res* 7:163–4 F '23. *

CUMULATIVE NAME INDEX

[150]

Kansas Spelling Tests. 1, 2 semesters in grades 3, 4–6, 7–8; 1962–64; first published 1962–63 in the Every Pupil Scholarship Test series; 3 tests; Connie Moritz, Alice Robinson, Mary T. Williams, and M. W. Sanders; Bureau of Educational Measurements. *
a) KANSAS ELEMENTARY SPELLING TEST. 1, 2 semesters in grade 3.
b) KANSAS INTERMEDIATE SPELLING TEST. 1, 2 semesters in grades 4–6.
c) KANSAS JUNIOR HIGH SCHOOL SPELLING TEST. 1, 2 semesters in grades 7–8.
For additional information, see 7:227.

[151]

Kelvin Measurement of Spelling Ability. Ages 7–12; 1933; C. M. Fleming; Robert Gibson & Sons, Glasgow, Ltd. [Scotland]. *
For additional information, see 1:1160.

[152]

Lincoln Diagnostic Spelling Tests. Grades 2–4 or 2–5, 4–8, 8–12 or 9–12; 1941–62; 2 editions; A. L. Lincoln.
a) EDUCATIONAL RECORDS BUREAU EDITION. Grades 2–4 or 2–5, 4–8, 8–12; 1941–62; 3 levels; Educational Records Bureau. *
1) *Lincoln Primary Spelling Test.* Grades 2–4 in independent schools or 2–5 in public schools; 1960–62.
2) *Lincoln Intermediate Spelling Test.* Grades 4–8; 1941–62; three of the 1949 forms identical with tests published 1947–48.
3) *Lincoln Diagnostic Spelling Test.* Grades 8–12; 1941–62; 1949 test identical with test copyrighted 1941.
b) BOBBS-MERRILL COMPANY EDITION. Grades 9–12; 1949–56; 1956 tests same as Forms 1, 2 of *Lincoln Diagnostic Spelling Test* published 1941 and 1942; Bobbs-Merrill Co., Inc. *
For additional information and a review by Gus P. Plessas, see 6:320 (6 references); for reviews by Walter Scribner Guiler and George Spache of the tests for grades 4–12, see 4:202–3.

REFERENCES THROUGH 1971

1–6. See 6:320.
7. Townsend, Agatha. "An Investigation of Certain Relationships of Spelling With Reading and Academic Aptitude." *J Ed Res* 40:465–71 F '47. * (*PA* 21:3763)
8. Newton, Bertha M. "A Study of Certain Factors Related to Achievement in Spelling." *Alberta J Ed Res* (Canada) 7:202–8 D '61. * (*PA* 36:5KL02N)
9. Babbott, Edward French. *The Differential Effectiveness of Eight 9th Grade Variables in Predicting Success in Three 10th Grade Academic Subjects at Summit High School: A Study in Differential Prediction.* Doctor's thesis, New York University (New York, N.Y.), 1963. (*DA* 25:993)

CUMULATIVE NAME INDEX

[153]

N.B. Spelling Tests. Standards 1–3, 3–5, 6–8, 8–10 for English pupils and 3–5, 6–8, 9–10 for Afrikaans pupils; [1962–64]; Human Sciences Research Council [South Africa]. *
For additional information, see 7:228.

[154]

Nationwide Spelling Examination. Grades 4–12; 1959–63; no manual; [Donald R. Honz]; Educational Stimuli. *

For additional information, see 6:321.

[155]

The New Iowa Spelling Scale. Grades 2–8; 1954; master word list with difficulty values by grades from which teacher may compile tests; Harry A. Greene; Bureau of Educational Research and Service. *

For additional information, see 6:322 (1 reference).

REFERENCES THROUGH 1971

1. See 6:322.

CUMULATIVE NAME INDEX

Groff, P. J.: 1

[156]

Sanders-Fletcher Spelling Test. 1, 2 semesters in grades 9–13; 1962–64; first published 1962–63 in the Every Pupil Scholarship Test series; Gwen Fletcher and M. W. Sanders; Bureau of Educational Measurements. *

For additional information and a review by Thomas D. Horn, see 7:229.

[157]

Spelling: Differential Aptitude Tests. Grades 8–12 and adults; 1947–73; revision of the spelling subtest of Form B of the DAT *Language Usage* (1947), later called Form M of the DAT *Language Usage—Spelling* (1962); George K. Bennett, Harold G. Seashore, and Alexander G. Wesman; Psychological Corporation. * For the complete battery entry, see 1069.

For reviews of the complete battery, see 7:673 (1 review, 1 excerpt), 6:767 (2 reviews), 5:605 (2 reviews), 4:711 (3 reviews), and 3:620 (1 excerpt).

REFERENCES THROUGH 1971

1. VINEYARD, EDWIN E., AND MASSEY, HAROLD W. "The Interrelationship of Certain Linguistic Skills and Their Relationship With Scholastic Achievement When Intelligence Is Ruled Constant." *J Ed Psychol* 48:279–86 My '57. * (*PA* 33:2200)
2. RICHMAN, JAY T. *A Comparison of the Phonetic Structure of a Basal Vocabulary List and the Spelling Section of the Differential Aptitude Test.* Master's thesis, Utah State University (Logan, Utah), 1965.

CUMULATIVE NAME INDEX

Massey, H. W.: 1   Vineyard, E. E.: 1
Richman, J. T.: 2

[158]

Spelling Errors Test. Grades 2–4, 5–6, 7–8; 1948–55; George Spache; Reading Laboratory and Clinic. *

For additional information, see 5:228 (1 reference).

REFERENCES THROUGH 1971

1. See 5:228.

CUMULATIVE NAME INDEX

Lampard, D. M.: 1

[159]

Spelling Test for Clerical Workers: [Personnel Research Institute Clerical Battery]. Stenographic applicants and high school; 1947; Jay L. Otis, David J. Chesler, and Irene Salmi; Personnel Research Institute. * For the complete battery entry, see 2140.

For additional information and a review by Harold H. Bixler, see 4:211. For reviews of the complete battery, see 4:729 (2 reviews).

REFERENCES THROUGH 1971

1. STAPLES, JOHN DIXON. *An Experimental Study to Identify the Basic Abilities Needed to Detect Typescript Errors With*

Implications for the Improvement of Instruction in Typewriting. Doctor's thesis, University of North Dakota (Grand Forks, N.D.), 1965. (*DA* 27:1693A)

CUMULATIVE NAME INDEX

Bixler, H. H.: *rev*, 4:211   Staples, J. D.: 1

[160]

Spelling Test: McGraw-Hill Basic Skills System. Grades 11–14; 1970; also called *MHBSS Spelling Test;* although designed for use with the MHBSS instructional program, the test may be used independently; Alton L. Raygor; McGraw-Hill Book Co., Inc. *

For additional information and reviews by Thomas D. Horn and Albert H. Yee, see 7:230.

[161]

Spelling Test: National Achievement Tests. Grades 3–4, 5–8, 7–9, 10–12; 1936–57; 1956–57 tests identical with tests copyrighted 1939; Robert K. Speer and Samuel Smith; Psychometric Affiliates. *

For additional information and a review by James A. Fitzgerald, see 5:230; for a review by W. J. Osburn, see 1:1161.

[162]

Traxler High School Spelling Test. Grades 9–12; 1937–55; 1955 tests same as tests published 1937–40; Arthur E. Traxler; Bobbs-Merrill Co., Inc. *

For additional information and a review by Gus P. Plessas, see 6:326; for a review by Henry D. Rinsland, see 4:212.

[Out of Print Since TIP I]

A.C.E.R. Spelling Test, 2:1309 (1 review)
A.C.E.R. Spelling Test (Form C), 5:222 (2 reviews)
Ayer Standardized Spelling Test, 6:317 (2 reviews); see also 4:198 (1 reference)
Coordinated Scales of Attainment: Spelling, 5:223
Davis-Schrammel Spelling Test, 4:199 (3 reviews)
Gates-Russell Spelling Diagnostic Tests, 6:318 (3 reviews); see also 4:200 (1 reference)
Graded Word Spelling Test, 5:224 (1 review)
Iowa Dictation Exercise and Spelling Test, T:539
Kansas Spelling Test, 3:153 (2 reviews)
Morrison-McCall Spelling Scale, 4:205 (1 review, 2 references)
New Standard High School Spelling Scale, 4:206
Rich-Engelson Spelling Test, 4:207 (1 review)
Spelling and Vocabulary: Every Pupil Test, 6:323
Spelling: Every Pupil Scholarship Test, 6:325
Spelling: Public School Achievement Tests, T:554
Spelling: Seven Plus Assessment: Northumberland Series, 4:210
Wellesley Spelling Scale, 5:232 (3 reviews, 1 reference)

VOCABULARY

[163]

A.C.E.R. Word Knowledge Test—Adult Form B. Ages 18 and over; 1933–60; identical with part 1 of *A.C.E.R. Silent Reading Tests,* Form B for grades 3–8 except for directions; manual by T. M. Whitford; Australian Council for Educational Research [Australia]. *

For additional information, see 6:327 (1 reference).

REFERENCES THROUGH 1971

1. See 6:327.

CUMULATIVE NAME INDEX

Bucklow, M.: 1   Doughty, P.: 1

[164]

American Literacy Test. Adults; 1962; vocabulary; John J. McCarty; Psychometric Affiliates. *

For additional information and a review by Victor H. Noll, see 6:328.

[165]

Bruce Vocabulary Inventory. Business and industry; 1959–67; Martin M. Bruce; Martin M. Bruce, Ph.D., Publishers. *

For additional information and reviews by Fred H. Borgen and Robert Fitzpatrick, see 7:231.

[166]

*The Iowa Tests of Educational Development: Test 8, General Vocabulary. Grades 9–12; 1942–67; Forms X-4 and Y-4; more recent Forms X5 and Y5 are not available as separates; prepared under the direction of E. F. Lindquist and Leonard S. Feldt; Science Research Associates, Inc. * For the complete battery entry, see 20.

For additional information concerning earlier forms, see 6:332. For reviews of the complete battery, see 6:14 (2 reviews), 5:17 (2 reviews), 4:17 (1 review), and 3:12 (3 reviews).

[167]

Johnson O'Connor English Vocabulary Worksamples. Ages 9–14, 15 and over, "high vocabulary students and adults"; 1934–62; 3 levels; Johnson O'Connor and others; Human Engineering Laboratory Inc. *

a) INTERMEDIATE FORM WORKSAMPLE 176. Ages 9–14.

b) WORKSAMPLE 95. Ages 15 and over; all but 3–7 items of Forms AD, BC, and CC are revisions of items from *The Inglis Tests of English Vocabulary*.

c) ADVANCED FORM WORKSAMPLE 180. "High vocabulary students and adults."

For additional information, see 6:333 (5 references).

REFERENCES THROUGH 1971

1–5. See 6:333.
6. DODGE, ARTHUR F. "Occupational Ability Patterns." *Teach Col Contrib Ed* 658:1–97 '35. * (*PA* 9:5877)
7. GUTHRIE, GEORGE M., AND ZEKTICK, IDA N. "Predicting Performance in the Peace Corps." *J Social Psychol* 71:11–21 F '67. * (*PA* 41:6319)

CUMULATIVE NAME INDEX

Achard, F. H.: 2	Gelman, B.: 3
Clarke, F. H.: 2	Guthrie, G. M.: 7
Dodge, A. F.: 6	O'Connor, J.: 1
Filley, M. E.: 1	Uhrbrock, R. S.: 5
Fisher, F.: 4	Zektick, I. N.: 7

[168]

Johnson O'Connor Vocabulary Tests. Professionals; 1937–58; 6 tests; no manual; [Johnson O'Connor and staff]; Human Engineering Laboratory Inc. *

a) JOHNSON O'CONNOR VOCABULARY OF MATHEMATICS. 1945–56.

b) JOHNSON O'CONNOR VOCABULARY OF ARCHITECTURE. 1946–56.

c) JOHNSON O'CONNOR VOCABULARY OF MUSIC. 1945–56.

d) JOHNSON O'CONNOR VOCABULARY OF PHYSICS. 1937–58.

e) JOHNSON O'CONNOR VOCABULARY OF RADIO AND PHYSICS. 1952–56.

f) JOHNSON O'CONNOR VOCABULARY OF SPORTS. 1953–56.

For additional information, see 6:334.

[169]

Nationwide English Vocabulary Examination. Grades 4–12; 1959–63; [Donald R. Honz]; Educational Stimuli. *

For additional information, see 6:335.

[170]

Purdue Industrial Supervisors Word-Meaning Test. Supervisors; 1952; Joseph Tiffin and Donald A. Long; University Book Store. *

For additional information and reviews by Jerome E. Doppelt and Bernadine Meyer, see 5:237 (2 references).

REFERENCES THROUGH 1971

1–2. See 5:237.
3. GRUENFELD, LEOPOLD WILHELM. *Selection of Executives for a Training Program.* Doctor's thesis, Purdue University (Lafayette, Ind.), 1960. (*DA* 21:1247)
4. KIRCHNER, WAYNE; HANSON, RICHARD; AND BENSON, DALE. "Selecting Foremen With Psychological Tests." *Personnel Adm* 23:27–30 N–D '60. *
5. GRUENFELD, LEOPOLD W. "Selection of Executives for a Training Program." *Personnel Psychol* 14:421–31 w '61. * (*PA* 37:3922)

CUMULATIVE NAME INDEX

Benson, D.: 4	Kirchner, W.: 4
Doppelt, J. E.: *rev,* 5:237	Long, D. A.: 1
Gruenfeld, L. W.: 3, 5	Meyer, B.: *rev,* 5:237
Hanson, R.: 4	Sawyer, J.: 2

[171]

RBH Vocabulary Test. Applicants for clerical and stenographic positions; 1948–63; Richardson, Bellows, Henry & Co., Inc. *

For additional information and a review by Fred H. Borgen, see 7:232.

[172]

Sanders-Fletcher Vocabulary Test. 1, 2 semesters in grades 9–13; 1938–64; first published 1938 in the Every Pupil Scholarship Test series; Gwen Fletcher and M. W. Sanders; Bureau of Educational Measurements. *

For additional information, see 7:233.

[173]

Survey Test of Vocabulary. Grades 3–12; 1931–65; 1940 test identical with test copyrighted 1931; no manual; L. J. O'Rourke; O'Rourke Publications. *

For additional information, see 7:234; see also 5:239 (3 references); for reviews by Verner M. Sims and Clifford Woody, see 3:167 (1 reference).

REFERENCES THROUGH 1971

1. See 3:167.
2–4. See 5:239.
5. POND, FREDERICK L. "Influence of Reading Abilities on School Success in Grade IX." *Sch R* 48:437–44 Je '40. *
6. BURTON, MARY. "The Hearing and Reading Comprehension of Vocabulary Among High-School Seniors." *Sch R* 52:47–50 Ja '44. * (*PA* 18:1862)

CUMULATIVE NAME INDEX

Burton, M.: 6	Stead, W. H.: 2
Janus, S.: 3	War Manpower Commission,
Littleton, I. T.: 4	Division of Occupational
Pond, F. L.: 5	Analysis, Staff: 1
Sims, V. M.: *rev,* 3:167	Woody, C.: *rev,* 3:167

[174]

A Test of Active Vocabulary. Grades 9–12; 1961; Paul W. Lehmann; Educational Publications. *

For additional information, see 6:338.

[175]

★Vocabulary Survey Test. Grades kgn–1; 1971; oral vocabulary; 3 scores: part 1 (nouns, mathematical terms), part 2 (place relationship terms, verbs, adjectives, pronouns, mathematical concepts), total; Marion Monroe, John C. Manning, and Joseph M. Wepman; Scott, Foresman & Co. *

[176]

Vocabulary Test for High School Students and College Freshmen. Grades 9–13; 1964; Arthur E. Traxler; Bobbs-Merrill Co., Inc. *

For additional information, a review by George P. Winship, Jr., and an excerpted review by Joan Bollenbacher, see 7:235 (1 reference).

REFERENCES THROUGH 1971

1. See 7:235.

CUMULATIVE NAME INDEX

Bollenbacher, J.: *exc*, 7:235   Winship, G. P.: *rev*, 7:235
Traxler, A. E.: 1

[177]

Vocabulary Test: McGraw-Hill Basic Skills System. Grades 11–14; 1970; also called *MHBSS Vocabulary Test;* although designed for use with the MHBSS instructional program, the test may be used independently; Alton L. Raygor; McGraw-Hill Book Co., Inc. *

For additional information and a review by George P. Winship, Jr., see 7:236.

[178]

Vocabulary Test: National Achievement Tests. Grades 3–8, 7–12; 1939–57; 1951–57 tests identical with tests copyrighted 1939; Robert K. Speer and Samuel Smith; Psychometric Affiliates. *

For additional information, see 5:241; for a review by Clifford Woody, see 3:168.

[179]

Wide Range Vocabulary Test. Ages 8 and over; 1937–45; C. R. Atwell and F. L. Wells; Psychological Corporation. *

For additional information and a review by Paul S. Burnham, see 3:169 (1 reference).

REFERENCES THROUGH 1971

1. See 3:169.
2. KNEHR, CHARLES A. "Psychological Assessment of Differential Impairment in Cerebral Organic Conditions and Schizophrenics." *J Psychol* 54:165–89 Jl '62. * (*PA* 37:3695)
3. REGER, ROGER. "Brief Tests of Intelligence and Academic Achievement." *Psychol Rep* 11:82 Ag '62. * (*PA* 37:5654)
4. JOHNSTON, JAMES ORRIN. *Relationships Between Intelligence and Personality Variables.* Doctor's thesis, Oklahoma State University (Stillwater, Okla.), 1965. (*DA* 27:315B)
5. RICHARDS, JAMES M., JR. "Can Computers Write College Admissions Tests?" *ACT Res Rep* 15:1–11 O '66. * (*PA* 41:2242)

CUMULATIVE NAME INDEX

Atwell, C. R.: 1   Reger, R.: 3
Burnham, P. S.: *rev*, 3:169   Richards, J. M.: 5
Johnston, J. O.: 4   Wells, F. L.: 1
Knehr, C. A.: 2

[180]

Word Clue Tests. Grades 7–13 and adults; 1962–65; designed primarily for use with instructional booklets in the Word Clues series; 2 tests; Stanford E. Taylor, Helen Frackenpohl, and Arthur S. McDonald; Educational Developmental Laboratories, Inc. *
a) WORD CLUE TEST.
b) WORD CLUE APPRAISAL.
For additional information, see 7:237.

[181]

Word Dexterity Test. Grades 7–16; 1942–50; Shailer Peterson; the Author. *

For additional information, see 4:218; see also 3:170 (2 references).

REFERENCES THROUGH 1971

1–2. See 3:170.

CUMULATIVE NAME INDEX

Peterson, S.: 2   Peterson, S. A.: 1

[182]

Word Understanding. Grades 6–12; 1969; R. Hoepfner, M. Hendricks, and R. H. Silverman; Monitor. *
For additional information, see 7:238.

[Out of Print Since TIP I]

College Vocabulary Test (status unknown), T:562
Cooperative Vocabulary Test, 4:213 (2 reviews, 4 references)
Durost-Center Word Mastery Test, 6:330 (2 reviews)
English Vocabulary Tests for High School and College Students, T:565
Gulick Vocabulary Survey, 6:331 (1 review, 1 reference)
Holborn Vocabulary Test for Young Children, 4:215 (1 review, 1 reference)
Inglis Tests of English Vocabulary, 5:234 (1 review, 10 references)
Kansas Vocabulary Test, 3:164 (1 review)
Lower Extension of the Inglis Tests of English Vocabulary, T:571, 35:225 (1 reference)
Michigan Vocabulary Profile Test, 4:216 (7 reviews, 1 excerpt, 15 references)
New Standard Vocabulary Test, 6:336 (2 reviews)
Quick-Scoring Vocabulary Test: Dominion Tests, 6:337 (1 review)
Schrammel-Wharton Vocabulary Test, 2:1321 (1 review)
Sentence Vocabulary Scale, T:577
Vocabulary: Every Pupil Scholarship Test, 6:339
Vocabulary Test [Management Service Co.] (status unknown), 6:340
Vocabulary Test—GT, 6:342 (1 review, 6 references)

ENGLISH — FIRST MMY

Reviews by *John C. Almack, Walter Barnes, Paul B. Diederich, Thomas G. Foran, H. H. Giles, Carleton C. Jones, W. J. Osburn, Henry D. Rinsland, John M. Stalnaker, Charles S. Thomas, and John H. Thompson.*

ENGLISH, GENERAL

[957]

"Dingwall" Test in English Usage. Ages 9–10, 10–12; p1938; 1 form; 2 levels; 2 booklets at each level; 25(30) minutes per booklet; Educational Institute of Scotland; University of London Press, Ltd.
a) PUPILS AGES 9–10, PUPIL'S BOOKLET I: CONTAINING PARTS 1–4. 3*d.* per test; 2*s.* per 12 tests; 3*s.*6*d.* per 25 tests; 10*s.* per 100 tests.
b) PUPILS AGES 9–10, PUPIL'S BOOKLET II: CONTAINING PARTS 5–9. 3*d.* per test; 2*s.*6*d.* per 12 tests; 4*s.*6*d.* per 25 tests; 15*s.* per 100 tests.
c) PUPILS AGES 10–12, PUPIL'S BOOKLET I: CONTAINING PARTS 1–4. 3*d.* per test; 2*s.* per 12 tests; 3*s.*6*d.* per 25 tests; 10*s.* per 100 tests.
d) PUPILS AGES 10–12, PUPIL'S BOOKLET II: CONTAINING PARTS 5–9. 3*d.* per test; 2*s.* per 12 tests; 3*s.*6*d.* per 25 tests; 10*s.* per 100 tests.

[958]

English Placement Test for Iowa Universities and Colleges, Form D. Grade 13; c1937; a new form is scheduled for publication each September; 40(50) minutes; 3½¢ per test plus transportation (Form D is out of print but Form E will be available for use in September 1938); Committee on State-Wide Placement, Iowa Colleges Conference on English; J. Raymond Derby, chairman, Iowa State College, Ames, Iowa.

[959]

English: Thanet Mental Tests. Age 11; p1937; 1 form; 3*d.* per test; 3*s.*6*d.* per 25 tests; 10*s.* per 100 tests; 1*s.* per handbook; 1*s.*6*d.* per specimen set (including the arithmetic and the school aptitude tests in the Thanet Mental Tests series); 45(50) minutes; W. P. Alexander; University of London Press, Ltd.

ENGLISH LANGUAGE USAGE

[960]

College English Test: National Achievement Tests. For freshmen at entrance; c1937; 1 form; $2.50 per 25 tests; 100 or more, 7½¢ per test; 5¢ per specimen set; nontimed (45–60) minutes; A. C. Jordan; Acorn Publishing Co.

[961]

Cooperative English Test (Usage, Spelling, and Vocabulary): Form 1937. Grades 9–14; c1937; 4 earlier forms of Series 1; 4 earlier forms of Series 2; 80(85) minutes; this series replaces *Cooperative English Tests: Series 1* and *Cooperative English Test, Series 2;* lithotyped; 6¢ per test, 10 to 99 copies; 5½¢ per test, 100 or more; 25¢ per specimen set (Form 1937); 10¢ per sample test (Form 1937); S. A. Leonard, H. M. Willing, V. A. C. Henmon, M. F. Carpenter, E. F. Lindquist, W. W. Cook, D. G. Paterson, F. S. Beers, and G. Spaulding; Cooperative Test Service.

John M. Stalnaker, Princeton University. [*Review of Form 1937.*] The objective tests labelled English are perhaps a poorer measure of what their name suggests than are the objective tests in any other field. The Cooperative English Test, one of the best of the standardized objective tests called English, leaves much to be desired. Its nine authors have restricted themselves to the topics of usage, spelling, and vocabulary. It is only right, therefore, to consider the test as one not of what is commonly called English, but of a restricted part of the field; users of the test should be cognizant of this restriction.

The usage test consists of three separately-timed parts. In the first part the pupil is directed to proofread two themes, making corrections in accordance with rather extensive instructions (one page in length). The selection of the twenty-five errors included in the passages is based on the usage report of the National Council of Teachers of English. The themes, even when the required corrections are made, will be unacceptable to many teachers. In the second part on usage, the pupil is presented with a series of problems, each of which requires him to make certain changes in a given sentence. The types of errors that were covered in the first part are also covered here. Both of these sections may be expected to be dropped from the future forms of the test since they are not in their present form adaptable to the scoring machine. In the third part on usage, the subject merely checks the best sentence in each of a series of four sentences. Correlations among the three parts on usage are not given, but they should be high if the scores are functions of the ability being tested rather than of

Cooperative English Test

the form in which the questions happen to be asked.

Spelling ability is measured by requiring the subject to select the one of four given words which is misspelled or to indicate that all four words are correct. No information is given on the relationship between the scores on this test and the scores on a spelling test of the dictation type, which has frequently been used as a criterion of spelling ability. Early studies suggested that spelling ability was somewhat dissociated from other abilities in English. Is the score on this ten-minute spelling test highly enough related to the scores on the other sections, and indicative of an important enough ability, to justify counting it as approximately one-third of the total score in English?

The final section is a typical synonym vocabulary test of the multiple-choice type.

An ingenious system of Scaled Scores is described in the manual, although the use of these scores as a basis for studies of growth, as is suggested, is not permissible without considerably more information than is supplied. It might be a grave mistake to have teachers of English point their efforts toward developing in their pupils growth in English, as measured by differences in scores on comparable forms of this English test. Appreciable "growth" might be found to be the result of the practice effect from having taken the test before. Undoubtedly the test is responsive to special training which the pupils might be given for the sole purpose of increasing their scores without changing materially their underlying ability. But the chief limitation of the test is the limitation of all objective tests called English which have thus far appeared, and that is that what they measure is not what the expert in English means by ability in English. It is to be hoped that test-makers' statements of what can be measured by objective forms will not in time come to dictate what should be taught.

The *Cooperative English Test,* once its limitations are appreciated and its results interpreted accordingly, may be of value to the teachers of English in the secondary school. It will be of more value when the results of the valuable experimentation which has undoubtedly gone into its development are given. A condensed report of the results, whether favorable or unfavorable to the test, would constitute a valuable

addition to the information now generally available.

Charles S. Thomas, Harvard University. [*Review of Form 1937.*] The *Cooperative English Test,* testing language conventions in such areas as capitalization, punctuation, grammatical forms, and sentence recognition, interestingly and ingeniously provides exercises on which the student is to reveal his knowledge and skill in the recognition and correction of errors in English usage.

The choice of items is excellent. None of them are so elementary as to be merely puerile; none of them lie in doubtful or controversial sectors. Moreover, there is such a wide and a varied range that even the abler students will meet problems in language conventions that will prove genuinely challenging and keep the number of perfect scores severely restricted.

One section of the test is designed to measure discrimination in rhetorical expression rather than strict mechanical forms. Specific emphasis which, falling upon the principle of coherence within the sentence, pathologically directs attention to such faulty and illogical construction as this: "When settling down to an afternoon nap, flies are very disturbing to me."

The section on spelling employs the somewhat questionable device of presenting incorrect forms along with correct forms. The "Directions" for this section seem to me unfortunately phrased: "In each of the following lines of words, select the word that is misspelled and put its number in the parenthesis at the right. If you think all the words in the line are correctly spelled, put a zero (o) in the parenthesis at the right of that line." The one taking the test has to correct the first interpretation that he makes after reading this initial sentence.

The vocabulary section is a valuable feature of the test. Great care and discrimination were evidently expended in the choice of individual items, but, as so often happens in the making of vocabulary lists, words that are of little use to the student are somewhat too freely admitted. The casual reader, with no knowledge of French or Latin, as he glances at the word *indign,* for example, may find it a bit puzzling to select the correct synonym from among the multiple-choice array: *disgraceful, idle, independent, abused, cold.* And even though he knows the meaning, what modern writer would wish to use a word that is now obsolete? But, although I should wish to delete this particular word—along with others—I have real admiration for the test as a whole.

John H. Thompson, Ohio State University. [*Review of Form 1937.*] When considering the merits of this test, one should bear in mind its possible usefulness not only as a measuring device but also as a teaching instrument. If the authors state its purpose to be similar to that of the comparable 1936 form, namely, "to measure ability in English composition by ability to detect or correct errors and difficulties in expression in composition by others," one may doubt whether the test achieves a valid purpose.

Part I, Section 1 of this test asks students to edit two brief compositions. While the ability to edit and revise compositions by others may give some measure of ability in composition, teachers and test makers are not *wholly* justified in assuming that skill in finding and correcting mistakes means ability to compose, since the word *composition* means the selection, arrangement, and organization of materials for a particular purpose. It is the student's own purpose and activity designed to achieve this purpose which the test does not measure.

Recognizing this fact the teacher may be justified in using the test to supplement knowledge of the student's abilities after close observation of student performance in written and oral work and after reports made by other teachers are carefully noted. In content the test emphasizes items which are known to cause difficulty in high school and college composition, and in manner is easily comprehensible by pupils, broad enough in scope to give an adequate estimate of the abilities which it does measure, and simple to administer and score.

In manner of construction, however, there is much to be desired. While Sections 1 and 2 of Part I require thinking of a valuable kind in the revising and correcting of materials, Section 3 of the same part is more likely to confuse the student and thus to assist, at least partially, in blocking attempts made by the teacher and student to achieve the ends of teaching and learning in composition. The directions preceding this section read as follows: "Read each of the following groups of sentences carefully; then decide which sentence in each

group is better than the other sentences in that group, and put the number of this best sentence in the parentheses at the right of the group." In a total of eighty sentences, only twenty are correctly constructed. If the work of the teacher of English is to help the student learn what is right, clear, and coherent, why place before him sixty examples of the wrong ways to put words, phrases, and clauses together. Could not the purposes of measurement be achieved by reversing the proportions thus minimizing the effect of confusion before the student has learned how skillfully to construct sentences? And if he has developed this ability to express himself clearly in properly made sentences, is there any point in placing before him poorly made sentences just to see whether or not he can recognize them?

Approaching Part II, one notes that, out of fifty four-word groups, slightly less than twenty-five per cent of all the words are misspelled, the student being asked to indicate which one of the four words in each group is wrongly spelled. Teachers know that calling attention to words misspelled by other people often causes one to mispell a word which formerly has been written correctly. If the ability to spell must be measured by such a test as this one instead of by careful observation of individual difficulties in written composition, it is all to the good that so few incorrect words are placed before the pupil.

Part III, dealing with vocabulary, tests the ability to recognize words out of context. Is not the real test of one's knowledge of words dependent upon their relationship with other words in the sentence even as the ability to get the meaning of a sentence depends upon its relationship with other sentences within a paragraph?

Since ability to edit does not mean ability to compose; since so many of all the items in this test put before the testee incorrect examples far out of proportion to the correct examples; and since only one section of the test—Section 2, Part I—requires performance in a real learning situation, the writer feels that the test is invalid and that it is only moderately useful either as a teaching device or as a means of supplementing knowledge of students gained by observation by all teachers of their actual speech and writing.

Cooperative English Test

[962]
English No. 4, Grammar and Style: Midland Attainment Tests. Ages 6–14; p1938; 1 form; 2d. per test; 1s.6d. per 12 tests; 2s.9d. per 25 tests; 8s.6d. per 100 tests; 6d. per manual; 1s.3d. per specimen set (including English tests Nos. 1, 2, and 5 in the same series); 20(25) minutes; R. B. Cattell; University of London Press, Ltd.

[963]
English Test: National Achievement Tests. Grades 3–8, 7–12; c1936–37; 1 form; 2 levels; 5¢ per specimen set; nontimed (45–60) minutes; R. K. Speer and S. Smith; Acorn Publishing Co.
a) GRADES 3–8. $1.35 per 25 tests; 100 or more, 4¢ per test.
b) GRADES 7–12. $1.75 per 25 tests; 100 or more, 5½¢ per test.

[964]
English Usage: Every Pupil Test, December 1937 and April 1938. Grades 3–6, 7–9, 10–12; p1937–38; 3 levels; a new form is scheduled for publication each December and April; 2¢ per test; 1¢ per key; specimen set free; 40(45) minutes; grades 3–6: teachers of Trumbull County (Ohio) under the direction of J. C. Berg and W. H. Knight; grades 7–9, 10–12: teachers of Fairfield County (Ohio) under the direction of R. M. Eyman; Ohio Scholarship Tests.

[965]
Iowa Every-Pupil Test in English Correctness: Ninth Annual Iowa Every-Pupil High School Testing Program. p1937; a new form is scheduled for publication each May; 4¢ per test; 5¢ per key; 10¢ per summary report of norms; 50(55) minutes; M. F. Carpenter; edited by [E. F. Lindquist]; distributed by the Bureau of Educational Research and Service.

[966]
Kentucky English Test: A General Achievement Test for High School Students and College Freshmen. c1937; 1 form; worklimit (45–50) minutes; $3.50 per 100 tests; 10¢ per specimen set; E. J. Asher and T. E. McMullin; Kentucky Cooperative Testing Service.

Henry D. Rinsland, University of Oklahoma. Thirteen different kinds of information about English and grammar are included in the 140 multiple-choice items. The correlation of the test with college freshmen English grades is .73 ($N = 69$). The coefficient of reliability for college freshmen is .96 ($N = 143$); for ninth grade it is .95 ($N = 100$). Decile scores and standard deviations are given for grades nine to college freshmen, N varying from 526 for grade nine to 1500 for grade twelve.

The section of the test measuring grammatical knowledge and nomenclature is probably valid statistically, curricularly, and psychologically. Serious doubt as to the psychological and statistical validity of the usage could be raised, as usage demands composition and there is no "composing" in the test. Beck and Rinsland question any usage test in which there is

no writing, as a response in writing is not the same response as selecting one of five forms already given, and the correlation between these two types of responses is very low for any diagnostic value.

[967]
Wisconsin Language Usage Test: Form 1937. Grades 9–12; c1937; a new form is scheduled for publication each spring; less than 100 copies, 5¢ per test; 100 or more, 4¢ per test; 10¢ per specimen test; 50(55) minutes; Bureau of Records and Guidance, School of Education, University of Wisconsin and the Department of English of the University of Wisconsin; E. M. Hale Co.

ENGLISH LITERATURE

[968]
American and English Literature: Every Pupil Test, December 1937 and April 1938. Grades 9–12; p1937–38; a new form is scheduled for publication each December and April; 2¢ per test; 1¢ per key; specimen set free; 40(45) minutes; F. H. Prouty; Ohio Scholarship Tests.

[969]
Awareness Test of 20th Century Literature. High school, college, and candidates for teaching positions in English; c1937; 1 form; 8¢ per test, 10 to 24 copies; $1.50 per 25 tests; sample copies free to teachers upon request; 45(50) minutes; edited by H. H. Bixler; E. R. Smith; Turner E. Smith and Co.

[969A]
Cooperative Current Literature and Arts Test for High School Classes: Form 1937. c1937; a new form is scheduled for publication each May 1; 40(45) minutes; lithotyped; 6¢ per test, 10 to 99 copies; 5½¢ per test, 100 or more; 25¢ per specimen set (Form 1937); 10¢ per sample test (Form 1937); A. C. Eurich, E. C. Wilson, and G. A. Hill, with the editorial collaboration of A. N. Christensen, R. Faulkner, A. Pepinsky, and E. W. Weaver; Cooperative Test Service.

Walter Barnes, New York University. This is a pioneer attempt to measure high school students' "awareness of recent developments in the fields of art, music, and literature." One hundred items are included, each item followed by five "possible answers," from which the student is to select the one "best." Section A: the Movies, consists of 30 items; B: Plays, 10 items; C: Books, 25 items; D: Music and Radio, 20 items; E: Art, 15 items.

I would question, first of all, the relative proportion allotted to these fields. Thirty of the items are concerned with the movies, and nineteen of the items (in Section "D") are concerned with the radio. Almost half the items in an instrument designed to measure students' awareness of *art, music,* and *literature* devoted to the *movies* and the *radio!* Granted that the movies and the radio are media through which students receive impressions and experiences in music and literature; granted, further, that they are the most popular, the most convenient, and, in some respects, the most effective media; there is nevertheless an assumption false and even vicious in the proportion. I will here venture the prophecy that when rated by this test many students who are most thoroughly informed and deeply appreciative of *significant* and *contributive* recent "developments" in art, music, and literature will rank with the dullards. The test puts a premium upon mere knowledge of "what is going on" and "being talked about," of what is being popularized and publicized in the field of the arts; it implies that those who go to the movies and listen to the radio most frequently and who have a fund of that curious knowledge about movie folks and their doings and "who advertises what at what hour" on the radio are those who are most aware of recent developments in literature, in music, in art. It just doesn't make sense. The proportions are askew, lop-sided; they place undue emphasis upon superficialities and trivialities.

This last statement is confirmed by analysis of many of the specific items. More than half the thirty items in Section A (the Movies) are of the who-played-in-what variety. At least one-fourth of the items in Section C (Books) concern books whose merit and significance are negligible. Several of the items in Section D (Music and Radio) relate to the hours or the sponsors of certain broadcasts. And these are questions to test awareness of recent "developments" (presumably important ones) in the Arts!

The items in Section B (Plays) and in Section E (Art) all relate to matters of genuine consequence. Unfortunately, however, some of those in Section E are subjective or ambiguous. Item 93, for example, which begins: "The modern artist believes." Obviously, "*the* modern artist" doesn't exist: modern artists have various and quite varying beliefs. Or item 95: "the most successful of the recent magazines," etc. One must interpret what is meant by "successful."

In spite of these grave weaknesses, this test is to be commended because it opens up a new and a difficult field. We should know what our high school students pay attention to and are aware of in these areas of contemporary life, and this instrument will provide us with information. A wiser apportionment of the items to the various arts and a clearer recognition of what is significant and what is puerile will affect notable improvements in the 1938 and later forms of the test.

H. H. Giles, Ohio State University. The purpose of this test, to measure the student's awareness of recent development in the arts, is a worthy one. It cannot be denied that interest in the arts and focus on the present are two essentials of education which take into account the real interests and needs of children. The inclusion of much material on the news and the radio is a sign that the authors of the tests realize the great importance of these reproductive agents in the lives of children today.

The questions asked show a commendable understanding of basic ideas with regard to modern painting and industrial design. It is particularly valuable to have this emphasis given by the questions relating to industrial design in a society where that design is of such very great importance and so little discussed and understood.

The directions for giving the test are clear and helpful. The absence of Scaled Scores is probably all to the good since it will enforce handling of the results by the teacher and children concerned on a basis of the meaning of those results in the particular situation where the test is given. It is probably not important anyhow to know what the average of "right" answers would be for several thousand children. It would be a very real value to know the relative number of correct answers given by pupils as compared by those given by faculty in the same school.

From these remarks it will be plain that this criticism is written from the point of view of one who conceives the principal function of testing to be its usefulness as an educative device. To make the position still more clear, it may be added that in the opinion of this critic, any testing device which implies an absolute standard of judgment or a static concept of development as being at any point completely measurable, is based on completely false assumptions.

Along with complimentary remarks on the

inclusion of such a test in the general program of the American Council on Education, and of the authors for their informed and discriminating questions, it may be well to include some suggestions with regard to other possibilities than those explored herein.

First of all there should be some elimination of ambiguity. For example, in section E on art, page 7, question 85 includes more than one answer which could be given by a competent worker in the field. The same is true of question 90 in the same section on the same page.

It might be valuable, in fact it would seem essential, to include some questions which would indicate the extent to which pupils have participated in modern art movements by the work of their own hands or by individual and group efforts to do something about the situation of the arts in their communities.

Consonant with this emphasis on participation would be the inclusion of more questions related to ideas which are fundamentally and powerfully operating in the world of the arts. An example of such an idea question is that in section E on art listed as No. 93 on page 8. Carrying this notion a little further, it might be well to include some questions which call for interpretation of general trends, such as the increasing use of music as not only an accompaniment but central motive in moving pictures, the success of poetic drama on the New York stage, the increasing amount of war material in the newsreels.

In connection with the questions on the movies one wonders in passing why the identification of sponsors should be the focus of such questions as 72 on page 6 and 79 on page 7. What does the identification of these sponsors have to do with literature and the arts? It would also seem to be of value to include some questions related to the terms and, perhaps, a few more with regard to sculpture and the home arts.

Understanding that the formulation of the questions is designed to stimulate discussion it is possible to accept such descriptions as "moving and worthy," "most important," and "successful." However, to children making careful answers based on the assumptions implied, the definitions of these terms would be necessary.

On the whole the test undoubtedly is a good beginning in the direction of discovering the amount to which children are aware of recent developments in the fields of the arts. This discovery could certainly be used in many highly important ways for cooperative planning of curriculum by pupils and teachers.

[970]

Cooperative Literary Acquaintance Test: Form 1937. Grades 9–14; c1937; 4 earlier forms; a new form is scheduled for publication each May 1; 40(45) minutes, Form 1937; 45(50) minutes, Forms 1933–1936; lithotyped; 5¢ per test, 10 to 99 copies; 4½¢ per test, 100 or more; 25¢ per specimen set (Form 1934); 10¢ per sample test (Form 1934); F. S. Beers, D. G. Paterson, and G. B. Shepley; Cooperative Test Service.

Carleton C. Jones, University of Chicago. [*Review of Form 1937.*] According to the publishers, the *Cooperative Literary Acquaintance Test* for 1937 was constructed "to fill the need for a measure of an individual's acquaintance with the field of literature," and "makes no direct attempt to measure appreciation or the more subtle phases of understanding." Inspection of the instrument makes it obvious that by "acquaintance with literature" is meant simply "information about literature." But today, English teachers are coming more and more generally to feel that the acquisition of literary information, as such, constitutes an educational objective of relatively minor importance. In view of this fact, therefore, one is inclined to question whether or not there is any real justification for the continued multiplication of instruments of this sort. Probably a much more important contribution could be made through the development of instruments that would get at certain other somewhat less tangible objectives which teachers of English at the present time hold to be generally more significant.

Furthermore, analysis of the test discloses the fact that the field of literature with which the student is expected to be "acquainted" is a very limited one indeed. For the most part, the test samples only that restricted body of subject matter which has long constituted the stock-in-trade of the traditional course in school literature. The conventional materials of English literature comprise nearly 50% of the items; American literature totals another 25%; while the richness of foreign literatures is virtually neglected: French, German, Italian, Spanish, Russian, and Scandinavian literatures together make up only about 10% of the items. Within national groups, also, the limitations of sampling are acute. English literature is represented by only 35 authors; American literature by only 18; and the six foreign literatures mentioned above by only 7.

Another limitation of sampling is evident in the matter of literary periods. Apparently the student is not expected to know anything about modern literature, the modern period (1900 on) being represented by less than 5% of the items of the test. On the other hand, he is expected to know a great deal about the literature of the period between 1800 and 1900. This period is represented by nearly 45% of the items of the test. Other periods are represented as follows: 1700–1800, 10% of the items; 1600–1700, 5%; 1500–1600, 10%; and 1000–1500, 10%. This distribution may, of course, reflect the relative emphasis given to these periods by traditional literature courses, but it is very much to be doubted that it constitutes a sampling of these periods in terms of their present-day importance.

A further limitation of sampling is evident in the matter of literary types. Poetry, probably the least consequential of all literary types so far as modern living is concerned, bulks largest in the test, with items constituting about 40% of the total. Drama has something over 20% of the items—perhaps a fair distribution, except that one-third of these pertain to Shakespeare alone. The novel has items amounting to only 13% of the total; the essay, 6%; the short story, 3%; and the biography, 2%. Yet of these four types, three—the novel, the short story, and the essay (if we include magazine articles in this category)—probably constitute, in almost equal proportions, the bulk of modern reading. And biography certainly would not fall far behind.

In addition to these obvious discrepancies in sampling and distribution, numerous other aspects of the test are likewise open to serious question. For example: (1) Out of 150 items, 37 call for the identification of short quotations, not more than five or six of which really have quotable significance. (2) A considerable number of the items of the test can be answered correctly by judicious guessing without the student's actually possessing the information called for. (3) The test form makes no provision for any diagnostic interpretation of student responses. And (4) a very great deal of the information called for in the test is totally inconsequential, even in terms of "general culture."

John H. Thompson, Ohio State University. [*Review of Form 1937.*] The title of this test is significant in that it does not indicate any claim on the part of those who constructed it that appreciation may be measured by their work. By asking the student to choose from five suggestions each in a total of one hundred and fifty items, one may determine students' acquaintance with the best in literature from the Bible to relatively recent writings, and with the works of authors in many countries. The test embraces matters of techniques, the literary importance of a given piece, the identification and estimate of the qualities of literary characters, the recognition of quotations, the chief event, theme, or subject matter of a product, and the time of its writing. Assuming the use of the typical collection of materials for the four-year high school, and granting that students' knowledge of literature indicates possible appreciation for it, one may say that the test is valuable for its purpose.

Contemplating the use of such a test as this one, teachers should recall that (1) knowledge of literature *may* be just as closely related to depreciation of it as it is to appreciation for it; (2) acquaintance with the best in literature is, for most teachers dealing with the average of present-day literary tastes in high school, only a goal toward which they strive with their students; (3) similar tests, constructed by individual teachers for particular classes and based upon materials chosen to meet the needs and tastes of those classes, may give a better measure of growth toward the goal of acquaintance with the best in literature.

Those teachers preparing students for traditional college-entrance examinations requiring only knowledge of the most excellent in literature should find this work helpful, even though it does not give one a true indication of students' real feeling toward books and the people in them.

[971]

Cooperative Literary Comprehension Test, Form 1937. Grades 9–14; c1937; 2 earlier forms; a new 40-minute form is scheduled for publication each May 1; 45(50) minutes; lithotyped; 5¢ per test, 10 to 99 copies; 4½¢ per test, 100 or more; 25¢ per specimen set (Form 1935); 10¢ per sample test (Form 1935);

M. F. Carpenter and E. F. Lindquist; Cooperative Test Service.

Charles Swain Thomas, Harvard University. The makers, whether or not they had De Quincey in mind, have thought of poetry and literary prose not as media for matters denotative, but rather as media for matters connotative. The appreciative reading of such literary selections implies a recognition of values in imagery, symbolism, melody, nuances, and aesthetic, sensory, and emotional reactions. Accurately to test all these by any objective measure is an impossible task, but this particular instrument does make a real conquest in a limited sector. The sector is perforce an intellectual one, and real literature displays emotional and aesthetic effects. Granted the difficulty of their task, those who have made this test deserve praise for the procedures which are here set up. Even though most of the items necessarily deal with barricades that stand at the gateways to the domain of literature, it is doubtless true that only those who reveal most expertness in gaining entrance through these gates, can later come to a sympathetic appreciation of the worth and treasure of enclosed literary acres.

John H. Thompson, Ohio State University. The builders of this test ask the student to choose from five suggested responses in each of ninety items concerned with six brief poems and eight short prose selections the one response which best completes the meaning of the statement. For example: "La Mancha's Knight" was (1) Don Quixote, (2) Roland, (3) Cervantes, (4) the Cid, (5) Sir Lancelot.

Supposedly the test is one of literary comprehension. By means of the multiple-choice question, one may determine pupils' abilities to *recognize,* and therefore, it is assumed, to comprehend specific phases of the literary selection. But by this means one is not able to determine pupils' reactions to the piece as a whole. It is suggested (1) comprehension means this ability to grasp and react to a poem, essay, or story as a unit; (2) that it means also the capacity to apply the idea, theme, or point of a literary product to meaningful life experiences of the reader; and (3) that a one- or two-sentence summary plus an equal amount of writing indicating reasons for liking or disliking a poem

or story, etc., accomplishes more effectively the avowed purpose of this test.

[972]
Eaton Book-Report System. High school; c1934–37; $1 per 100 book-report sheets of any one form; $1.25 per 100 book-report record cards for permanent cumulative records; H. T. Eaton; Palmer Co.
a) FORM A, FOR NOVELS, DRAMAS, ETC. c1934.
b) FORM B, FOR SHORT STORIES, ESSAYS, ETC. c1934.
c) FORM C, THE BOOK REVIEW. c1936.
d) FORM D, THE PHOTOPLAY REVIEW. c1936.
e) FORM E, BIOGRAPHY. c1937.
f) FORM F, TRAVEL. c1937.
g) EATON BOOK REPORT RECORD CARDS. c1934.

Paul B. Diederich, University of Chicago. The publisher's catalog quotes the comment of a Massachusetts teacher: "The *Eaton Book-Report System* makes the country safe for book-reports." Would that the same could be said for the reading of books. We fail to see how the habit of reading is assisted or confirmed by turning in a report on each book read, giving in forty words or less a few facts about the author, mentioning when, where and how long the action of the book takes place, making a list of all the important places mentioned in the book, giving the names of the major and minor characters and identifying each, summarizing the plot in seventy-five words or less, and giving an opinion of the book in not more than sixty words covering four of the following points: character drawing, setting, tone and atmosphere, plot, romanticism and realism, style, author's purpose, personality, etc. These responses are guided by dehydrated models of the author's own composition. The ulterior purpose of this autopsy is revealed in the publisher's catalog: "No more yearly or semi-yearly reports on the same books unless the teacher approves of the second reading and is willing to give credit for it." Obviously we have here another example of the cat-and-mouse school of evaluation: a device to compel the reading of one book a month, calculated to make the pupil hate it. When there is sufficient rapport between teacher and pupil to stimulate reading for fun, no such accounting is necessary; when there is not, it is futile. We recommend instead a simple record of author, title, and comment, plus a semi-annual checklist for magazine reading, and a short newspaper questionnaire. These yield all the information on reading interests that we really need.

Cooperative Literary Comprehension Test

[973]

English No. 5, Knowledge of Literature: Midland Attainment Tests. Ages 6–14; p1938; 1 form; 3*d.* per test; 2*s.*6*d.* per 12 tests; 4*s.*6*d.* per 25 tests; 15*s.* per 100 tests; 6*d.* per manual; 1*s.*3*d.* per specimen set (including English tests Nos. 1, 2, and 4 in the same series); 15(20) minutes; R. B. Cattell; University of London Press, Ltd.

[974]

English: Understanding and Appreciation of Poetry, State High School Tests for Indiana, 1936–1937 Edition. First, second semesters: grades 9–12; p1936–37; 2 levels; a new first-semester form is scheduled for publication each December; a new second-semester form is scheduled for publication each March; mimeographed; 3¢ per test; 15¢ per sample test; 40(45) minutes; G. S. Wykoff; edited by H. H. Remmers; Division of Educational Reference.

[975]

Iowa Every-Pupil Test in Reading Comprehension in Literature: Ninth Annual Iowa Every-Pupil High School Testing Program. p1937; a new form is scheduled for publication each May; 4¢ per test; 5¢ per key; 10¢ per summary report of norms; 60(65) minutes; M. F. Carpenter and W. R. Wood; edited by [E. F. Lindquist]; distributed by the Bureau of Educational Research and Service.

[976]

Literature Appreciation Tests. High school; c1936–37; $1 per 25 tests; sample copies free to teachers upon request; (40) minutes; edited by H. H. Bixler; Turner E. Smith and Co.

a) AS YOU LIKE IT. c1936; E. R. Smith.
b) HOUSE OF SEVEN GABLES. c1936; H. D. Roberts.
c) MACBETH. c1936; M. J. J. Wrinn.
d) MERCHANT OF VENICE. c1936; E. R. Smith.
e) SILAS MARNER. c1936; L. B. Cook.
f) TREASURE ISLAND. c1936; L. B. Cook.
g) A MIDSUMMER NIGHT'S DREAM. c1937; S. Royster.
h) EVANGELINE. c1937; E. D. Stovall.
i) IDYLLS OF THE KING. c1937; L. B. Cook.
j) THE COURTSHIP OF MILES STANDISH. c1937; E. D. Stovall.

Paul B. Diederich, University of Chicago. These tests yield a searching analysis of what the pupil has remembered from the usual clinical study of a book in literature courses. A quaint feature of the series is that each test consists of exactly 100 items, each of which is given one point, so that the total score can be entered readily into the teacher's bookkeeping system. This total score is broken up into such components as the following on *A Midsummer Night's Dream:* understanding of the play (memory of details), recognition of situations (identification of quotations), identification of characters, familiarity with the poetry of the play (completing quotations), interpretation of meaning (of unusual words), identification of soliloquy (who said it?), appreciation of meaning (this selection illustrates Shakespeare's:

power of analysis; appreciation of external nature; lack of unity; humor), and interpretation of motives (who is trying to do what in short quotations— calling mainly upon memory of these quotations).

Such tests represent pretty accurately what is done to a book in 98% or better of our high school English courses. They explain why the habit of reading declines steadily throughout the senior high school period in every community surveyed by the American Library Association, and why the average American adult reads less than one book a year. They make the reading of books so difficult, so unnatural, and so unrelated to pupils' concerns that it is no wonder that pupils lose interest in reading. We recommend these tests as good, thorough tests of what teachers are now doing. One way to increase their effectiveness would be to brand their scores on pupils' quivering backsides.

[977]

Literature Test: National Achievement Tests. Grades 7–12; c19[36]–37; 1 form; $2 per 25 tests; 100 or more, 6½¢ per test; 5¢ per specimen set; nontimed (40–60) minutes; R. K. Speer and S. Smith; Acorn Publishing Co.

[978]

New Eaton Literature Tests. High school; c1937; 5 to 99 copies, 2½¢ per test; 100 to 999, 2¢ per test; 1000 or more, $18 per 1000; (40–50) minutes; H. T. Eaton; Palmer Co.

a) COLERIDGE'S "THE RIME OF THE ANCIENT MARINER."
b) DICKENS' "A TALE OF TWO CITIES."
c) SCOTT'S "IVANHOE."
d) SCOTT'S "LADY OF THE LAKE."
e) SHAKESPEARE'S "JULIUS CAESAR."
f) SHAKESPEARE'S "MACBETH."
g) ELIOT'S "SILAS MARNER."
h) SHAKESPEARE'S "MERCHANT OF VENICE."

[979]

Rigg Poetry Test. High school and college; p1937; 2 forms (D and C); 5¢ per test; 10¢ per scoring key and directions; 15¢ per specimen set; 40(45) minutes; Melvin G. Rigg; School of Education, Oklahoma Agricultural and Mechanical College.

ENGLISH VOCABULARY

[980]

English No. 2, Vocabulary: Midland Attainment Tests. Ages 6–14; p1938; 1 form; 2*d.* per test; 1*s.*6*d.* per 12 tests; 2*s.*9*d.* per 25 tests; 8*s.*6*d.* per 100 tests; 6*d.* per manual; 1*s.*3*d.* per specimen set (including English tests Nos. 1, 4, and 5 in the same series); 5(10) minutes; R. B. Cattell; University of London Press, Ltd.

[981]

English Recognition Vocabulary Test. Grades 7–16 and adults; c1937; 1 form; $3.50 per 100 tests; 50¢ per manual; R. H. Seashore and L. D. Eckerson; published by R. H. Seashore, Department of Psychology, Northwestern University, Evanston, Ill.

[982]
Wide Range Vocabulary Test. Grades 3–16; c1937; 1 form; 75¢ per 25 tests; $2.50 per 100; 15¢ per specimen set; C. R. Atwell and F. L. Wells; Psychological Corporation.

SPELLING

[1158]
Buffalo Spelling Scale. Grades 2–8; c1934; 2 forms; 15¢ per specimen set (no materials needed for pupils); A. J. Williams; Public School Publishing Co.

Henry D. Rinsland, University of Oklahoma. The words are selected from the *Buckingham Extension of the Ayres Spelling Scale.* The words are dictated in sentences; such as *"See the little boy."* The words in italics are the spelling words. There is an overlapping of words for several grades with eleven sentences for grade two, two additional sentences for grade three, up to a total of 24 sentences, including 100 words, for the eighth grade.

Norms are in forms of grade scores from a *G* of 1.2 for one correctly spelled word, to a *G* of 11.4 for 95 correctly spelled words.

This is a good test on an old list whose curriculum validity is seriously questioned in the light of new vocabulary research. Neither the coefficient of reliability nor the error of a score is given.

[1159]
Gates-Russell Spelling Diagnosis Tests. Grades 2–6; c1937; 1 form; individual; 5¢ per test booklet; 60¢ per manual; 60¢ per specimen set; A. I. Gates and D. H. Russell; Bureau of Publications.

John C. Almack, Stanford University. The *Gates-Russell Spelling Diagnosis Tests* consist of a single form of nine parts or sections: (1) oral spelling, (2) pronunciation, (3) giving letters for letter sounds, (4) spelling one syllable, (5) spelling two syllables, (6) word reversals, (7) spelling attack, (8) auditory discrimination, and (9) combined study methods. It is accompanied by a handbook for teachers. The handbook discusses spelling disability, why children fail in spelling, types of diagnosis, an individual program, case studies, and remedial work.

The source of material in the test is not indicated, nor are any data given which enables one to judge the validity and the reliability of the test. There are norms for each section on a grade-score basis, grades 1 to 6.

Errors are classified by *type* as additions, insertions, omissions, substitutions, transpositions, and phonetic errors. The remedial activities are classified as activities with letters, with words, with sentences, and miscellaneous. There is no evidence that the remedies are specific; the disability is not connected with a definite remedy. The inference is clear that *repetition* is the chief ingredient of each remedy; and next to repetition rates *motivation,* which is defined in the handbook (p. 38) as "changed attitudes and the habit of verifying doubtful words."

Speaking technically, this is not a *diagnostic test;* it is more truly a *method of discovering some of the errors* children make in a list of nine word activities. Nor are the remedial steps and measures true and specific remedies; they are a list of varied devices one may use in teaching spelling. Like patent medicines, the virtues of such panaceas are in doubt, and scarcely to be prescribed until definite value has been proved. While other studies of spelling are cited in the handbook, they are few in number and do not cover the subject.

Thomas G. Foran, Catholic University of America. The *Gates-Russell Spelling Diagnosis Tests* consist of nine tests: spelling words orally, word pronunciation, giving letters for letter sounds, spelling one syllable, spelling two syllables, word reversals, word attack, auditory discrimination, and study methods. Fifteen supplementary tests are listed but do not form part of the main battery. Grade scores are furnished for use with the nine basic tests. The tests are conveniently arranged in a four-page booklet. The manual contains a brief discussion of educational diagnosis and a valuable statement of the nature of the fundamental difficulties encountered by children retarded in spelling. Precise directions for the administration of the tests are provided and several case studies are presented as illustrations of the uses of the tests and the subtleties of diagnosis. The manual also contains some suggestions for remedial instruction in spelling.

The usefulness of such a diagnostic test is too obvious to require proof. The test itself is based on the extensive studies contributed by Gates and his students during the past fifteen years.

Its more immediate background is the excellent study by Russell [*see* reference above]. From comparisons of methods used by normal and retarded spellers, Russell identified the most significant factors associated with retardation. Russell's monograph deserves the careful study of all interested in the psychology and teaching of spelling for the results are important in regard to the teaching of spelling to children with normal ability as well as in understanding the difficulties that beset the minority. By means of the test, accurate diagnosis should lead directly to effective remedial teaching and in this connection, the devices suggested in the manual will be helpful.

The emphasis throughout the tests is directed towards the child's apprehension of the words to be learned. It has been recognized that disability in spelling is often caused by inadequate methods of word perception and analysis. The tests deal with such functions in several ways, thus furnishing a more valid instrument of diagnosis than any hitherto available.

Both the monograph and the tests are important contributions of immediate value to those concerned with the learning of this subject. The careful study conducted by Russell is one of the most valuable in its field.

[1160]
Kelvin Measurement of Spelling Ability. Grades 7–12; 1 form; 2s.6d. per 20 tests; 3d. per specimen set; quantity discounts; C. M. Fleming; Robert Gibson and Sons (Glasgow), Ltd.

[1161]
Spelling Test: National Achievement Tests. Grades 3–8, 5–6, 7–9, 10–12; c1936–37; 4 levels; 1 form; 15¢ per spelling list with class record; 50¢ per 25 pupils' sheets; 5¢ per specimen set; nontimed (15–25) minutes; R. K. Speer and S. Smith; Acorn Publishing Co.

W. J. Osburn, University of Washington. [*Review of Spelling Test.*] The term *National Achievement Test* includes tests in a variety of subjects, but this review will apply only in spelling. The authors claim that their tests apply not only to traditional elements but especially the pupils' progress in fundamental abilities, appreciations, attitudes, judgments, and methods of thinking. It is also stated that "with rare exceptions every test has new elements that no other test has treated so effectively." Some of these claims are not entirely borne out so far as spelling is concerned.

The spelling test covers grades three to twelve inclusive. The words have been selected with care. Each word is to be pronounced, used once in a sentence, and then pronounced again. This plan capitalizes a technique that is known to be very useful. Unfortunately, the authors have not allowed enough space for the sentences. Many of them are too short. The main purpose of such sentences is to supply a meaningful context. Some sentences will not do for this purpose. For example, the sentence, "He will appoint you," will not contribute materially to the meaning of the word "appoint." In like manner, "we expect him," is inadequate for the word "expect" and "He gets a good salary" will hardly define the meaning of the word "salary." Spelling tests half as long containing meaningful sentences would be much better from the standpoint of the teacher.

[1162]
Traxler High School Spelling Test. Grades 9–12; p1937; 2 forms; 2¢ per test blank; 10¢ per specimen set; (20) minutes; mimeographed; A. E. Traxler; Educational Records Bureau.

REPRINTED FROM *The Second Mental Measurements Yearbook*

ENGLISH—SECOND MMY

Reviews by John C. Almack, Roland L. Beck, M. E. Broom, Walter W. Cook, Frank P. De Lay, Joseph C. Dewey, Paul B. Diederich, Charles Fox, Ann L. Gebhardt, H. H. Giles, Keith Goltry, Harry A. Greene, Jean Hoard, Robert W. Howard, Violet Hughes, Carleton C. Jones, G. Frederic Kuder, Lou LaBrant, Herbert A. Landry, J. Paul Leonard, Constance M. McCullough, Jeanette McPherrin, Edward S. Noyes, Jacob S. Orleans, Robert C. Pooley, Henry D. Rinsland, David H. Russell, Rachel Salisbury, L. K. Shumaker, C. Ebblewhite Smith, Robert K. Speer, John M. Stalnaker, Edward A. Tenney, Charles Swain Thomas, Arthur E. Traxler, G. M. Wilson, J. Wayne Wrightstone, and Louis C. Zahner.

GRAMMAR AND USAGE

[1267]

Barrett-Ryan-Schrammel English Test. Grades 9-16; 1938; 2 forms; $1.10 per 25; 15¢ per specimen set; 2¢ per machine-scorable answer sheet; 40(50) minutes; E. R. Barrett, Teresa M. Ryan, and H. E. Schrammel; Yonkers, N. Y.: World Book Co., (London: George G. Harrap & Co., Ltd.)

G. Frederic Kuder, Examiner, Board of Examinations, The University of Chicago. Part I contains 30 points on sentence structure and diction, the student being required to judge whether each selected word or phrase in the passage presented is correctly used. The same technique is used in Part II for 35 words selected from a continuous passage, the errors being grammatical in this case. In addition to judging whether an item is right or wrong the student is required to indicate what the correct construction would be for the wrong items. Part III calls for judgments as to the correctness of 50 instances of punctuation selected from a continuous passage.

Requiring the student to identify errors in context is a highly commendable characteristic of the test. Whether it is justifiable to allot one-third of the points to punctuation in a test of this sort is doubtful. No reasons are given for the distribution of points used. It may be that the authors have found that the particular weighting used is most effective for predicting freshman composition grades. Certainly the validities obtained sound like the answer to a test builder's dream. Correlations of .73, .74, .73, and .75 were obtained for three groups of first-semester college freshmen and one group of first-semester college sophomores numbering respectively 88, 76, 93, and 51, between test scores obtained at the beginning of a semester and marks in English composition obtained at the end of the semester. To what extent similar correlations will be found in other institutions will depend largely, probably, upon the nature of the measure of achievement used.

The reliabilities reported appear to be satisfactory although final judgment on this point must be suspended since no data concerning the nature of the groups from which the reliabilities were obtained are given except for the number of subjects used. Correlations of .88 and .89 between different forms, and Spearman-Brown reliabilities of .94, .91, and .91 for Forms A, B, and C, respectively, were obtained.

Although the authors state that the test may be used for diagnostic purposes, to what extent the scores on the separate parts may be so used is open to question since reliabilities for the parts are not reported. Norms are not given for the parts.

The authors appear to have been successful

in avoiding trivialities which tend to creep into English tests. The material used apparently covers a wide range both as to types of errors represented and difficulties of specific questions.

Robert C. Pooley, Associate Professor in the Teaching of English, The University of Wisconsin. A test of English grammar and usage in three forms, prepared with a detachable answer sheet which is quickly scored by means of a perforated key. The test is reported to have coefficients of reliability between odd and even items of single forms from .91 to .94; the probable error of a score ranges from 3.1 to 3.3. Exact directions for administering and scoring are furnished and norms based on the scores of 31,937 high school students and 7472 college freshmen are supplied. The test is well constructed, easily administered and scored, and its results are capable of useful interpretation.

Each form contains three parts. Part I is a test of sentence structure and diction, formed by underlining words in a running narrative. The student is required to indicate whether the underlined word is right or wrong in its setting. It is a test, of course, of skill in proofreading, but proofreading under extraordinary conditions where each error is heavily underscored. What relationship this skill in proofreading bears to the ability to correct one's own manuscript is not revealed by the authors of the test. Recent studies seem to agree that the relationship is slight. Nevertheless, until better devices are discovered, this one will have to serve if pupils must be tested.

Part II is a combined test of correctness and grammatical knowledge. Each sentence in a running narrative contains one underlined word which must be marked right or wrong. At the same time, one of three grammatical explanations for the form of the word must be selected to explain the reason for marking it right or wrong. Part III is a long and dull exercise on punctuation.

This test should delight a great number of teachers. It tests what they know and what they teach. It belongs to a world in which a comma is of greater importance than a child, and where a grammatical form, duly labeled with a reason, is venerated. Undoubtedly it tests grammar as it is taught in the schools, and to some extent reveals weaknesses in the student's command of cultivated usage. But it is not, and should not be called a test of English. We may rejoice that English cannot be enmeshed in a test of three parts, scored with a perforated card.

Charles Swain Thomas, Associate Professor of Education, Emeritus, Harvard University. The *Barrett-Ryan-Schrammel English Test* is a simple, practical test that makes a direct appeal to all English teachers—those who have had special training in statistical methods and those who have not.

The test is designed to give an objective measure of a student's degree of mastery of the mechanics of English.

Part I, Sentence Structure and Diction, is provided with these specific directions:

In the following paragraphs some expressions are underlined. (The expression may be a word or a group of words.) If the expression is rightly used and rightly placed, make a heavy mark like this in the space between the dots under R on the Answer Sheet. If the expression is either wrongly used or wrongly placed, make a heavy mark in the space under W on the Answer Sheet, as shown in the sample. (See the sample answer on the Answer Sheet.)

Sample. Even though you don't succeed at first,
a
you had ought to try again. . . . .
b

This is followed by a page of composition sprinkled with errors commonly made by high-school and college students. Here are the opening sentences:

In the senior class were six of us boys
who ranked high in scholarship and who . . . . . .
1
wanted to go to college. Five of us could
not of gone even for one year without we . . . . . .
2   3
worked not only for our living expenses but . . . . . .
4
also for our tuition and books. Wishing to . . . . . .
4   5
get work, it was our plan to write to several
colleges and asking what our chances were . . . . . .
6
for employment. Having received encourag- . . . . . .
7
ing letters from one of the colleges, three of
us decided to attend that college. The other . . . . . .
8
two preferred to remain at home rather than
working to pay their way. . . . . . .
9

In Part II—Grammatical Forms, we have this set of directions.

In each numbered portion of the story below there is an underlined word. Some of these underlined words are right and some are wrong. If the word is right, make a mark under R on the Answer Sheet. If the word is wrong, as shown in the sample below, make a mark under W. (See the mark under W on the Answer Sheet.) Then look at the three items numbered 1, 2, and 3, one of which names the correct form to be used. Only one of these items is the right explanation. Choose the right one, and make a mark on the Answer Sheet under the number of that item.

There follows a composition, freely interlarded with mistakes such as these which are underlined—and which the students are asked to correct.

1. Before school closed in June us girls were making plans to spend part of our vacation camping out.

2. 1. possessive case, to modify girls
2. nominative case, subject of were making
3. objective case, in apposition with girls

3. It was left to Jane and I to get a chaperon, for we must have one. After much

4. 1. nominative case, subject of get
2. objective case, object of was left
3. objective case, object of to

5. deliberation as to whom of our teachers would like to spend two weeks in camp, Jane suggested

6. 1. objective case, to agree teachers
2. nominative case, subject of would like
3. objective case, object of to

7. that we have Miss Lee, who we agreed was our favorite teacher. The group was satisfied with

8. 1. objective case, object of agreed
2. nominative case, subject of was
3. objective case, to agree with Miss Lee

9. our choice. It was either Jane or I who was to ask her whether she would consent to go. Then

10. 1. objective case, object of was
2. objective case, to agree with Jane
3. nominative case, in the predicate with was

11. we decided both would ask her. Jane and myself went to her classroom. We found her still busy.

12. 1. objective case, after and
2. nominative case (I), subject of went
3. pronoun ending in self, after and

To facilitate the scoring, the publishers provide a stencil. The whole procedure is simple and practical.

Barrett-Ryan-Schrammel English Test

Indeed, the whole test is extremely sensible. The items chosen are carefully selected—selected largely because the errors made are of frequent occurrence and can be corrected only by drills. The test itself is one of these drills.

[1268]

Basic Language Skills: Iowa Every-Pupil Tests of Basic Skills, Test C. Grades 3-5, 6-8; 1940; Form L, 2 levels; 30¢ per manual; 12¢ per booklet of norms; 40¢ per 25 record cards; single specimen set free; H. F. Spitzer in collaboration with Ernest Horn, Maude McBroom, H. A. Greene, and E. F. Lindquist with the assistance of the faculty of the University Experimental Schools, State University of Iowa; Boston, Mass.: Houghton Mifflin Co.
a) ELEMENTARY BATTERY. Grades 3-5. $1.15 per 25; 51(60) minutes.
b) ADVANCED BATTERY. Grades 6-8. $1.25 per 25; 58(70) minutes.

For reviews by William A. Brownell, J. Murray Lee, and Charles W. Odell of an earlier form of the complete battery, see 872.

[1269]

Cleveland English Composition and Grammar Test. Grades 7-12; 1931-32; 2 forms; 50¢ per 25; single specimen set free; Clarence Stratton, William L. Connor, and Frank A. Redmond; Boston, Mass.: Houghton Mifflin Co.

Frank P. De Lay, Department of English, New Trier Township High School, Winnetka, Illinois. It is not only the lazy teacher who appreciates a test so mechanically constructed that it is quickly and easily corrected. The time of the good teacher is greatly over-filled with work, and an efficiently constructed test such as the Cleveland is a boon. The thing that impresses me most about this test, in addition to its mechanical makeup, is the fact that so much of its space is given to functional grammar. The grammar of recognition, in which the student merely identifies numerous grammatical forms, is largely wasted on the high school student; but he certainly can use that grammar which points out ways of varying his sentence structure, or of being correct by showing the logic of correctness. My only criticism of the test is that Part I merely tests the ability of the student to name a grammatical form, and that Part II does not contain the serious errors most often found in student compositions, but rather deals with finer points in usage the seriousness of which may be debatable in the light of recent studies. The other parts, especially Part VII, really test the student's ability *to use language.*

[1269.1]

College English Test: National Achievement Test. Grades 12-13; 1937; 1 form; $2.50 per 25; 5¢ per specimen set; nontimed (45-60) minutes; A. C. Jordan; Rockville Centre, N. Y.: Acorn Publishing Co.

REFERENCES

1 MARCKWARDT, ALBERT H., AND WALCOTT, FRED G. *Facts about Current English Usage:* Including a Discussion of Current Usage in Grammar from "Current English Usage" by Sterling A. Leonard. National Council of Teachers of English, English Monograph No. 7. New York and London: D. Appleton-Century Co., Inc., 1938. Pp. ix, 144. $0.90; 4s. 6d. Paper.

Constance M. McCullough, Assistant Professor of Education, Western Reserve University. This 120-item test, one of the comprehensive battery entitled National Achievement Tests, is evidently designed for college English placement programs or for prospective college entrants. The advertisement reads, "Every high school student who expects to enter college should take this test." Not a timed test, it is advertised as requiring from 45 to 60 minutes.

Part I, Punctuation, consists of 40 items which the student is to punctuate by inserting the necessary marks and enclosing each of them in parentheses. In the 22 items of Part II, Capitalization, the student is to indicate the need for capitalization by underlining the words which should begin with capital letters. Part III, Language Usage, contains 20 items of 4 sentences each. For each item, the student is to write in the margin the letter preceding the sentence which he thinks is best written. Each item deals with a single type of language error. Part IV, Sentence Structure, offers 20 items of 4 sentences each, to which the student is to make similar responses in the margin. With few exceptions, each item exemplifies one type of error. The types concern pronoun reference, verbosity, tense sequence, placement of modifiers and clauses, subordination and coordination of ideas, and the case of the relative pronoun. Part V, Modifiers, comprises 8 sets of 4 sentences which illustrate the proper and improper placement of modifiers. The student is to respond to this section as he did to the preceding two. Part VI, Miscellaneous Principles, is a matching section of 10 items, which requires the identification of structural and grammatical errors and the recognition of the technical terms appropriate to them. The student is to write after each sentence the letter referring to the principle which applies to the error. The only norm reported for the *College English Test*—which is apparently still in the process of standardization—is an undefined median score. The reliability coefficient, estimated from the correlation between scores on the odd- and even-numbered items and based upon an unidentified population, is .88. The validity of the test proceeds from consultation of "numerous city and state courses of study, widely used textbooks and the judgment of more than one hundred fifty experienced administrators. The tests were further evaluated and criticized by many classroom teachers."

The teacher's directions, class record, scoring key, and "norms" appear with convenient compactness on the two sides of a single sheet.

It is curious, in view of all the available studies of frequency of use and frequency of error, that the author should have chosen textbooks, courses of study, and the judgment of school administrators for the validation of his test items. This type of validation is probably responsible for many of the unusual emphases observable in the test. Perhaps there are those who would agree that three of six parts of an English test should be devoted to matters of sentence structure, that there should be half as many items on grammatical usage as on punctuation, that about one-third of all the items on structural errors should involve the placement of modifiers. But surely few would advocate having three items on the case of the relative pronoun, with only one on the use of the adjective for the adverb; none of the twenty-eight items of sentence structure, exclusive of the technical section, concern parallel construction or the use of the adverbial for the noun clause.

There are peculiar inconsistencies throughout the test. Item 9 in the punctuation section demands a correction in capitalization. The divorce, by the way, of punctuation and capitalization makes it possible for the student to derive clues to the correction of items in the one from items in the other. The principle tested in Item 14 of the language usage section is violated in the very next item and, according to the Marckwardt-Walcott report [1] on current usage, is no longer an issue. Another item in the language usage section appears to be a matter of verbosity better placed in the sentence structure section. An item on the case of the relative pronoun and another involving the use of *says* for *said*, both of which have sister items in the language usage section, appear in the sentence structure section. Three items in this section deal with the placement of modifiers, although the next section is devoted to similar items. It is not clear on what basis the author selected the items on verb form, subject and verb agreement, and sentence structure for the section on miscellaneous principles, which requires a knowledge of technical terms for correct response. While the directions for this section state that the ten sentences are incorrect, one of the optional "principles" listed in the section is, "Sentence is correct as it stands." Marginal spaces for responses are provided for all parts of the test even though the student uses them in only four of the parts. Some students may find this situation confusing.

A high reliability coefficient may be achieved on an English test if niceties and uncommon usages are included. The score on such a test, however, makes a rather doubtful index of a student's actual language ability and encourages teachers to emphasize in their teaching the niceties at the expense of the fundamentals. It is a plausible conjecture that most people have lived entire lifetimes without being called upon to punctuate "LLD" and "I Sam IX 13."

Although there are several items in Parts I and II to which more than one response could be correct, the key provides only one answer for each item. In the capitalization section some responses are highly disputable. Many teachers will consider certain answers in the key utterly wrong. I refer especially to Items 7, 21, and 22.

For both survey and diagnostic purposes, test users will find a number of carefully validated and well constructed tests in this field.

Robert W. Howard, Department of Examinations, The Chicago City Junior Colleges, Chicago, Illinois. This test is a short, easily administered test designed for entering freshmen. Its six parts measure skills in punctuation, capitalization, language usage, sentence structure, modifiers, and miscellaneous principles. The first two parts seem difficult to score since they require corrections within the text. The remaining four parts, however, are easily scored by the strip method. With a little revision, the entire test could be adapted to machine scoring.

The parts devoted to language usage, sentence structure, and modifiers require the student to choose the best sentence from groups of four. The student who selects the correct

sentence from each ingeniously arranged group undoubtedly has a feeling for what is right in English prose. Whether he carries out this feeling in his own writing remains to be proved. The last section, requiring the matching of principles with sentences illustrative of common errors, raises the question of whether the student may not know right from wrong in matters of grammar without possessing the ability to identify the rule governing his performance.

[1270]
Columbia Research Bureau English Test. Grades 11-16; 1925-26; 2 forms; $1.50 per 25; 20¢ per specimen set; 105 (120) minutes; Harrison R. Steeves, Allan Abbott, and Ben D. Wood; Yonkers, N. Y.: World Book Co.

L. K. Shumaker, Director of the Education Clinic, University of Oregon. This test is compact and easy to handle not only by the pupil who has limited desk space at which to work, but also for the teacher whose files must be kept restricted. Part I, Spelling, does not appeal to me because the pupil is asked to choose a correct spelling from a noncontextual setting; the number of words appears to be too small; the incorrect spellings tend to confuse even rather good spellers. Part II, Mechanical Accuracy in Composition, does not make use of contextual setting and the device of copyediting has not been employed to get the best results possible. The test seems to be too short. It is probably rather hard to score. Part III, Vocabulary, fails to use contextual settings which would tend to sharpen the pupil's power to discriminate, in my opinion. Part IV, Literary Knowledge, ought to be particularly useful to teachers who are attempting to estimate the preparation of pupils in the field of literature. It is long enough and sufficiently diversified to give a fair cross section of ready knowledge of a purely factual nature. It does not seem to me to indicate much about literary discrimination, unless this trait is concomitant with factual knowledge about literature.

The time limit feature is both an asset and a liability. As an asset, the time limit makes it possible to plan carefully for the use of the test in a busy program; as a liability, it tends to restrict the sampling of the work of those unable to finish the test and therefore handicaps the teacher who wishes to use the test papers themselves for diagnostic purposes. The chief value I see in the *Columbia Research Bureau English Test* is that it is a useful kind of achievement test in terms of facts retained, for students who have completed some study of literature at the secondary level; and perhaps even at the end of a course in the history of English literature at the college level. Whether or not I should use this test would depend entirely upon the purpose to which I wished to put it. I should never select it as a "language aptitude test"; only as a special type of achievement test.

Louis C. Zahner, Head of the Department of English, Groton School, Groton, Massachusetts. This test is a measure of achievement in a small, limited, elementary area of English studies. It is confined entirely to the more mechanical aspects of English. Familiar testing techniques are used, and the test is thus laid open to criticisms that also are familiar. Composition receives attention only in proofreading tests for recognition of errors in such mechanical elements as spelling, punctuation, reference, grammatical form, and elementary sentence-structure. Vocabulary is given only a test in synonym-matching. Literary knowledge is tested only by multiple-choice items based entirely on factual detail.

Even within this limited area of mechanical matters, serious questions are raised as to just exactly what is being tested. Operationally described, the spelling test is a measure of the pupil's ability to recognize the one correct spelling out of four given versions of the word. Whether performance in this is a measure of his ability to spell the word correctly in his own composition is uncertain. Similarly, even in its limited area of testing mechanical accuracy, the composition test, demanding as it does merely proofreading, is not necessarily even a measure of the pupil's ability to write mechanically accurate composition. It is certainly not a test of his ability to select and to arrange materials gathered from his reading and from his firsthand experience; to develop his ideas in a clear, logically planned essay. The vocabulary test, similarly, measures the pupil's reading-recognition of a word, and his ability to recognize one of its synonyms when it is given to him. It is not a measure of the pupil's ability to select and to use the word in his own writing and speech in a situation in which the use of that word and not another would not only be correct but would also exactly convey the meanings and effects

he wishes to convey. Nor is it a test of the ability of the student fully to comprehend the meanings and effects of the word when he reads it in a context. The literary knowledge section, likewise, tests the pupil's familiarity with some of the factual content of traditional works and his ability to remember a book he has read well enough to identify a fact connected with it. It does not test his assimilation of what he has read; nor does it test his ability to interpret and to criticize literature; nor does it test his ability to see relationships that hold between different books he has read and between literature and his experience with life.

Within these limits, the test is adequate. It might, for instance, be a reasonably accurate instrument for detecting pupils who are close to illiteracy; a pupil making an extremely low score on this test would probably be a poor risk for specialization in the field of English in school or college. A low-scoring pupil would very likely be deficient in his use of English. But it by no means follows that a high-scoring pupil would have special aptitude in English, or would of necessity be a better risk for specialization in the field. Successful work in English demands many things that are not covered by this test.

In the manual of directions, however, the publishers make almost unlimited claims. Among those implicitly or explicitly made are these: that the test measures the entire field of requisites in English studies, and that it will, by itself, furnish a measure of achievement in this entire field; that it will be found useful by supervisors in standardizing the English work in their schools; that college administrators can safely use it in selecting students for admission without any other tests or examinations in English, and in placement and guidance of their students; that its results should be used by teachers in adjusting their teaching and in establishing standards for the teaching of English.

To make such claims for a test limited to the mechanics of composition and the recall of factual details of books is completely to disregard the most important aims and objectives of English studies. That these objectives do not yield results amenable to present techniques of objective testing is not evidence of the unimportance of the objectives, nor is it evidence of the unreality of the results they

Columbia Research Bureau English Test

can yield and are in fact yielding. It is rather an indication of the handicaps under which objective tests labor in this field. These handicaps can possibly be overcome. Already much progress has been made here and there. Extravagant claims made for objective tests in their present stage of development, however, will not only do harm to the teaching of English, but will also retard the development of adequate tests. To make such claims is completely to misunderstand and to underestimate the growing demands put upon English studies today, and the progress being made in meeting these demands. A test of a limited part of the field of English studies is not a test of the whole field, and no talk about reliability and validity, no figures of correlations and norms, will make it so.

[1271]

Cooperative English Test: Usage, Spelling, and Vocabulary. Grades 9-16; 1932-39; 4 editions; 25¢ per specimen set of any one edition; Form P: Sterling A. Leonard, M. H. Willing, V. A. C. Henmon, M. F. Carpenter, E. F. Lindquist, W. W. Cook, D. G. Paterson, F. S. Beers, Charles Swain Thomas, and Geraldine Spaulding with the assistance of Henry S. Dyer and Robert L. McCaul; Form PM: M. F. Carpenter, E. F. Lindquist, W. W. Cook, D. G. Paterson, F. S. Beers, Geraldine Spaulding with the editorial assistance of H. A. Domincovich, Constance M. McCullough, and Natalie D. Starr; New York: Cooperative Test Service.
a) SERIES 1, FORMS 1932 AND 1936. Forms 1933, 1934, and 1935 are out of print; 6¢ per test, 10 to 99 copies; 95(105) minutes.
b) SERIES 2, FORMS 1932 AND 1936. Forms 1933, 1934, and 1935 are out of print; 6¢ per test, 10 to 99 copies; 75(80) minutes.
c) FORMS 1937, O, AND P. 1937-39; 6¢ per test, 10 to 99 copies; 80(85) minutes.
d) FORMS OM AND PM. 1938-39; 8¢ per test, 10 to 99 copies; 1½¢ per machine-scorable answer sheet; 70(75) minutes.

REFERENCES

1 THORNDIKE, E. L. *A Teacher's Word Book.* New York: Bureau of Publications, Teachers College, Columbia University, 1921. Pp. 134. $0.80.
2 HORN, ERNEST. *A Basic Writing Vocabulary*: 10,000 Words Most Commonly Used in Writing. State University of Iowa, Monographs in Education, Series 1, No. 4. Iowa City, Iowa: the University, 1926. Pp. 225. Cloth, $2.25; paper, $1.75.
3 HORN, ERNEST, AND ASHBAUGH, ERNEST J. *Fundamentals of Spelling*: For Grades 1-8, Incorporating the Findings of a Tabular Analysis of 5,100,000 Words of Ordinary Writing. Philadelphia, Pa.: J. B. Lippincott Co., 1928. Pp. xxvii, 148. $0.60.
4 BECK, R. L. *The Reliability and Validity of a National Test of English Composition for High School Seniors and College Freshmen.* Unpublished doctor's thesis, University of Oklahoma, 1932. Pp. 173.
5 BECK, ROLAND L. "A Natural Test of English Usage." *J Exp Ed* 1:280-6 Mr '33.
6 GLADFELTER, M. E. "The Value of the Cooperative English Test in Prediction for Success in College." *Sch and Soc* 44:383-4 S 19 '36.
7 DRAKE, LEWIS E., AND HENMON, V. A. C. "The Prediction of Scholarship in the College of Letters and Science at the University of Wisconsin." *Sch and Soc* 45:191-4 F 6 '37.
8 STUIT, DEWEY B., AND JURGENSEN, CLIFFORD E. "The Effect of Method of Presentation on Spelling Scores." *J Exp Ed* 5:271-3 Mr '37.
9 PATERSON, DONALD G.; SCHNEIDLER, GWENDOLEN G.; AND WILLIAMSON, EDMUND G. *Student Guidance Techniques*, pp. 116-20. New York: McGraw-Hill Book Co., Inc., 1938. Pp.

Columbia Research Bureau English Test

xviii, 316. $3.00. (London: McGraw-Hill Publishing Co., Ltd., 18s.)
10 HANNA, JOSEPH V. "A Comparison of Cooperative Test Scores and High School Grades as Measures for Predicting Achievement in College." *J Appl Psychol* 23:289-97 Ap '39.
11 McCULLOUGH, CONSTANCE M., AND FLANAGAN, JOHN C. "The Validity of the Machine-Scorable Cooperative English Test." *J Exp Ed* 7:229-234 Mr '39.

Carleton C. Jones, Department of English, State Teachers College, Indiana, Pennsylvania. [Review of Forms P and PM.] In setting out critically to review an educational test labeled "English," the reviewer has really to answer just one question—a question which the test publishers themselves should already have answered—namely: *Does the instrument yield a valid measure of a student's ability to speak or write the English language?* If a test does not yield such a measure, it merits no consideration whatsoever; for, in the final analysis, the sole defensible objective of English instruction is the development of the student's powers of linguistic expression. We teach spelling, grammar, punctuation, capitalization, and all the rest, not because they are important in themselves, but because they are integral to the total process of composition. Any evaluation instrument, therefore, which undertakes to investigate student achievement in these matters must do so in such a way that the test results will bear a known relationship to functional usage. And this relationship should always be clearly indicated by experimental data published in conjunction with the test itself. In other words, every test issued in the English field should be accompanied by correlation tables indicating the exact relationship existing between test scores and the actual performance of students in practical composition situations.

In theory, at least, the original authors of the *Cooperative English Test* were in agreement with this reviewer that their test, as a test of usage, should yield evidence of a student's ability actually to express himself in the medium of language. They wrote, when the series was first inaugurated, that the purpose of the test was "to measure ability in English composition"; but they immediately made the unwarranted assumption that such ability could be measured by probing a student's ability "to detect or correct errors and difficulties in expression in composition by others"—an assumption which this reviewer, for one, feels has never been adequately established. But it is on this assumption, nevertheless, that the *Cooperative English Test* is still predicated, despite the fact that the authors apparently have made no effort to establish the validity of their procedure since 1928, when they reported "a substantial correlation with final marks in Freshman English at the University of Wisconsin and elsewhere." Today, of course, there is a general and justifiable skepticism concerning anything, the validity of which has been established on the basis of a correlation with teachers' marks!

An analysis of the *Cooperative English Test,* therefore, leaves this reviewer with one fundamental doubt concerning each of the several parts of the instrument: We doubt, first, that ability to detect and correct errors in English usage in someone else's writing, or ability to select the most appropriate of several alternative constructions for any given sentence can be taken as very conclusive evidence of a student's ability to write grammatically in his own compositional enterprises. We doubt, also, that ability to select the best of four sentences, each expressing the same general idea in a different way, or ability to recast sentences according to a prescribed pattern constitutes too sound an index of a student's ability, on his own part, to compose acceptable sentences. We doubt, furthermore, that the discovery of 30 or 40 misspelled words in a list of 250 can be taken as much of an indication of what a student would normally do in avoiding spelling defections in his own writing. And finally, we doubt that a student's score on the kind of vocabulary test used in this instrument would indicate anything concerning the vocabulary which that student himself would employ in connection with his own efforts at composition; really, the test would seem to give evidence of a student's *reading* vocabulary, rather than of his *compositional* vocabulary.

However, if the test user is willing to accept the basic assumption on which the instrument has been constructed, the *Cooperative English Test* is perhaps as good a test of its sort as is commercially available. The format is good. The items appear to have been carefully constructed. The content has been arrived at on the basis of a careful scientific study. A satisfactory degree of objectivity has been maintained throughout. Reliability of component parts is unusually high. Detailed national norms are available each year as new forms are issued. But the test user needs to be aware that whatever "ability" the test actually measures, it probably is not—certainly is not of necessity—the ability which the English specialist means when he refers to "ability in English."

Jeanette McPherrin, Director of Admissions, Scripps College. This test is divided into subtests of usage, spelling, and vocabulary. The part of the test devoted to usage is really a test of punctuation, points of grammar, and the ability to recognize a simple, direct style in writing. The punctuation items are too simple and too often repeated for students of high school and college level—for example, the numerous uses of contractions. The grammar items are very restricted in number and certain simple points are tested again and again —for example, the difference between the words *their* and *there.* The third section of the usage subtest is composed entirely of multiple-choice items requiring the examinee to discriminate between good and bad sentence structure. None of the items in this section tests the examinee's ability to use concise, grammatical English in writing.

In Part II, devoted to spelling, the words are well chosen for the most part, but a multiple-choice arrangement makes this a test of the ability to recognize misspelled words, rather than a test of the ability to spell. The test manual fails to indicate the correlation between scores on this part of the test and scores made by groups spelling the same words from dictation.

Part III, devoted to vocabulary, would seem to be the best part of the test, although a few of the words have little importance in lifelike situations and would have been learned only by chance—for example, *neap, pomaceous, tarantella.* Parts II and III of the test cannot be described as functional, since the words do not appear in sentences.

The distribution of emphasis among the various parts of the test constitutes one of its greatest weaknesses. Of the possible 267 raw-score points, 117 are given to the usage section of the test (in my opinion the poorest section), and of these 117, almost two-thirds are directly or indirectly concerned with punctuation.

In the first two sections of Part I, the examinee is not penalized for adding irrelevant or even incorrect punctuation. In the third section of Part I, no correction is made for guessing. The same correction is made for guessing in Parts II and III, although the examinee may guess with more chance of success in Part II than in Part III.

The statement in the manual that the choice of test items was based on curriculum surveys, textbook analyses, and consultation with specialists does not constitute a proof of acceptable selection, since no specific titles of surveys and texts or names of specialists are given. The manual offers no evidence of validity beyond a statement that the test has been "tried out on large groups" to choose for retention items that discriminate between good and bad students. The desirability of this type of discrimination is in itself questionable.

The booklet of norms gives reliability coefficients for the total test and for the separate parts of the test, but it does not give coefficients for single grades nor describe the groups of students tested to provide data for the building of coefficients. In giving percentile norms for three types of high schools, the test authors are making a move in the right direction, but still the numbers upon which the norms are based are too large and the various types of schools are not described in sufficient detail to make the norms valuable for comparison with individuals or small groups.

The scoring of the test is complicated by the fact that the raw scores must be converted first into "scaled scores" and then into percentile ranks. The authors claim that scaled scores make possible the comparison of different types of tests without conversion of raw scores into percentiles or "other cumbersome measures." Why the scaled scores are considered less cumbersome than percentile ranks is not clear. Scaled scores are based on the accomplishment of an "average child" who has attended an "average school" and taken the "usual amount" of a subject. These hypothetical averages are meaningless because incapable of definition.

Louis C. Zahner, Head of the Department of English, Groton School, Groton, Massachusetts. [Review of Form P.] This test undertakes, according to its subtitle, to test "Usage, Spelling, and Vocabulary." The word "usage" has a wide and ill-defined range of meanings. Exactly what is meant here by "usage" is not entirely clear. A teacher looking for a test of usage in the sense in which Leonard used the

word in his study of modern usage will not find it in this test, which is perhaps more accurately described as a test in the mechanics of composition. This comment upon the title of the test does not imply that the test is intended to cover more ground than it does cover. The authors make no extravagant claims for it. In the admirable handbook describing the purpose, content, and interpretation of the Cooperative Test Service Tests, there is a clear and fair statement of what this test can be expected to show, how results can safely be interpreted, and what action can safely be taken upon the basis of these results. The claims are modest, and teachers and principals are warned against reading into tests results interpretations they will not fully bear. Any teacher who uses this test with an understanding of its limitations as described by its authors and publishers is on firm ground. This test, furthermore, bears sure marks of forward-looking experiment in the field of the construction of objective tests in English.

The mechanics of composition are tested in Part I, Sections 1 and 2, and in Part II (Spelling). The first and last of these are tests of the proofreading type, raising the old question as to how well proofreading tests measure the ability to write correctly. There is no conclusive evidence either way. Probably such a test would be a good measure of this ability for some pupils and not for others. Here a teacher is driven back to examination of a pupil's original work. An objective proofreading test might be useful as a check upon the teacher's more subjective judgment. This question is fully understood by the authors of this test, who claim only that these items are "probably of value in getting a picture of what a class will do in actual composition." Part I, Section 2, is an ingenious departure from the straight proofreading type of test that deserves further exploration and development. This form of item, however, is limited in the number of elements it can test, and will therefore not be likely to take much of the load now carried by the proofreading type.

Part I, Section 3, calls for the choice of one "best" sentence out of four given sentences. This section could have been more carefully and consistently constructed. The "best" sentence in some of the groups is demonstrably the best by virtue of being the only one free from grammatical blunders. In other groups, however, the "best" sentences would be best only for certain rhetorical effects, while one or another of the discarded sentences might be better for other rhetorical effects. An intelligent choice would require an interpretation of a full context in which the sentence is to be placed. In still other groups the "best" sentence and the discarded sentences simply make different statements. The "best" sentence would be best only if it made the statement the writer wished to make. Here again full context would be necessary for intelligent choice. The danger of this section as it stands is that it may lead some teachers and pupils to believe that sentence-making is simply a matter of applying a priori rules without any necessity of giving attention to the precise meanings and effects the sentence is intended to convey, and without any realization of the importance of the context in determining these meanings and effects. It is dangerous to imply that any sentence is good, let alone "best," apart from the total situation in which it is being used.

The same criticism can be brought against Part III, a vocabulary test of the synonym-matching type that deals with single words out of context. The effective use of language in straight thinking, in reading for full comprehension of meanings, in clear and logical writing and speaking, requires so much more that a bowing acquaintance with a list of synonyms that the claims made for vocabulary tests as measures of general power over language are subject to grave question. In this field the type of item being developed in the verbal section of the *Scholastic Aptitude Test* of the College Entrance Examination Board is unquestionably better.

It is unfortunate that in this particular section the authors themselves have used language so loosely. Most of their supposed synonyms are indeed synonyms. But there are too many items in which the right response is not a synonym at all, but something entirely different. *Drug,* for example, is not a synonym for *insulin,* but a class that includes *insulin. Three dramas* is not a synonym for *trilogy,* but a member of the class *trilogy.* The distinction between synonyms and class-words is one of the fundamentals in the study of words and language, involving as it does both the theory of symbols and the principles of classification. Is it too much to ask that authors of tests in English should set themselves rigorous standards in their use of words? "If gold ruste, what shal iren do?" If the teaching and testing of language is to prosper, test-makers must work from sound principles of language, their subject matter, as well as from sound principles of testing and measuring.

Henry D. Rinsland, Director of the Bureau of Educational Research and Professor of School Measurements, The University of Oklahoma. [Review of Form PM.] The English test is in 3 parts: (*a*) English usage, including grammar and diction of 75 items, punctuation of 60 items, capitalization of 30 items, and sentence structure of 15 items; (*b*) spelling, consists of 45 items; (*c*) vocabulary of 100 words.

The objective test labeled *usage* departs far from securing a natural or normal response which any one gives when he uses English in a written form. The sample illustrates what the student is to do; it also illustrates the psychological validity of the test, that is, the performance measured. The sample given is:

$$\text{That} \begin{Bmatrix} 1 \text{ aren't} \\ 2 \text{ ain't} \\ 3 \text{ isn't} \end{Bmatrix} \text{right.}$$

The student is required to choose the correct form. Now this is just what no one does when he writes; it isn't exactly what any one does when he edits; it is just what some one does when he takes an artificial, unnatural English usage test of this type. It is true that occasionally when one thinks of right and wrong forms, such as the nominative or the objective case of six personal pronouns, that he does do a sort of choosing. It is obvious from the research of Roland L. Beck [4, 5] on the validity of the *Rinsland-Beck Natural Test of English Usage* that the present *Cooperative English Test* has sacrificed validity for an objective and machine scoring device. Perhaps this is one reason why the *Cooperative English Test,* administered during the school year 1934-35, correlated only .50 with school marks when the scores of the psychological examinations were rendered constant. Further, the titles and the subtitles of the usage test are misleading, as there is no grammatical term mentioned in the 75 items, but merely usage. One could make perfect on this test without any knowledge of grammar if he only recognized correct usage of words and phrases. This reviewer cannot understand why the Cooperative group have omitted the measurement of grammar, that is, grammatical terminology and rules of grammar, nor why they have not chosen a more valid measure of English usage, even though it does not lend itself to rapidity of scoring—desirable as the latter is. Certainly in the writings of the authors whose names appear on the title page, none have suggested that validity be sacrificed for objectivity and speed of scoring.

The second part is spelling. This test consists of a presentation of four different words. The student is to find the misspelled word and mark it, or if none are misspelled, to check the phrase *none*. Forty-five sets of four words each are given. From the published studies of the validity of different objective forms, the right or wrong spelling form is about as good as any, except dictation. Dictating 45 words to be spelled may take more time than reading 180 words. Since no description of the sources of these words is furnished with the 1939 edition, one finds a reference to validity on page 17 of *Cooperative Achievement Tests:* A Handbook Describing Their Purpose, Content and Interpretation. The spelling words were chosen from the first five thousand most frequently used words in the Ernest Horn list, *A Basic Writing Vocabulary*.[2] The question arises whether or not the first five thousand most frequently used words represent the proper group for sampling the spelling of students in grades 7-12. Almost all elementary textbooks in spelling in grades 2-8 have approximately four thousand words. Horn's textbook[3] has approximately this number.

The vocabulary test is in the form of multiple choice; a word being given with five choices, only one of which corresponds in meaning as,

1 resistant
      1–1 confusing
      1–2 conjunctive
      1–3 systematical
      1–4 assisting
      1–5 opposing

No statement of the validity of the 1939 vocabulary test is found, however in the 1936 handbook (p. 16) is the information that the words of the vocabulary series are chosen from the E. L. Thorndike, *Teacher's Word Book*.[1] The words chosen come from the first

ten thousand most frequently used words. The reviewer agrees with the authors of the test that the synonym form of five choices presents a broader understanding for the meaning of words than any other objective form. A test of 100 words seems to be a very meager sampling of a reading vocabulary of somewhere around twenty or thirty thousand words, although with the synonym form the complete knowledge runs somewhere from 100 words to 500. However, at least 16 additional groups of words could be added to the last page of the test, as page 15 has available space.

The test can be scored by hand, using perforated sheets, or by the *International Test Scoring Machine*. This is probably the most efficient scoring device available. Norms are in terms of percentages of students (percentiles) attaining and exceeding scaled scores. Scaled scores seem to offer a linear scale which will increase in usefulness as teachers and administrative officers understand it. The reliability of the 1938 test shows the coefficient of reliability of the total English test to be above .98, and the standard errors of measurement of the revised series is approximately six points in terms of raw score. This fluctuation out of a possible 260 points indicates an exceedingly stable score for each individual student. Because this English test is in a series of other subjects with comparable norms, the use and value of such a test is superior in many respects to an independent test of higher validity not in such a series with comparable norms.

L. K. Shumaker, Director of the Education Clinic, University of Oregon. [Review of Form P.] There are certain elements which commend this test at once upon first inspection. It has been prepared under reliable auspices. Without this guarantee, anyone using the test would have to do over again all the laborious work of inquiring into the why's and wherefore's of the original test construction. Then the presentation of test material in contextual form is good. The cross-out-and-write-in feature of Section 2 is good because this form of copy-editing is one way to get discriminative judgment without the use of grammatical terminology. Section 3 does not appeal to me so much because of the limited context and the possibility of debate concerning separate items in the key. Part II should be a fair test of spelling; although I have found that very frequently individuals of a good deal of ability do not give a very sound indication of their capacity to spell if they are asked to recognize correctly spelled words in settings of. misspelled words. Part III would be stronger in my opinion, if the choices were presented in contextual settings. I can foresee quite a bit of hand labor in scoring the test; and this is always a drawback. I should expect this test to be quite effective in separating low from high ability pupils. The norms furnished ought to make the test very useful to teachers who have limited numbers of pupils at different school levels.

The time limit feature of the Cooperative test would enable a busy teacher to estimate how best to fit the test into a full program. On the other hand, time limits in tests of this type deprive them to some extent of their "power testing" quality. A poor student, unable to finish the test, would not give as good a basis for the teacher to make a fair diagnosis of the kind of difficulties which should be removed (if they can be!) to enable this weak student better to meet the competition of stronger ones.

For reviews by John M. Stalnaker, Charles Swain Thomas, and John H. Thompson, see 961.

[1272]
Cross English Test. Grades 9-13; 1923-26; 3 forms; $1.20 per 25; 20¢ per specimen set; 45(50) minutes; E. A. Cross; Yonkers, N. Y.: World Book Co.

REFERENCES

1 HARVEY, NATHAN A. "The Cross English Test." *Am Schoolmaster.* 18:85-6 F '25.
2 FOLEY, LOUIS. "A Test Case." *Engl J* 17:387-94 My '28.
3 EDDS, JESS H., AND McCALL, W. MORRISON "Predicting the Scholastic Success of College Freshmen." *J Ed Res* 27:127-30 O '33.

Roland L. Beck, Professor of Education and Director of the Demonstration School, Central State College, Edmond, Oklahoma. The *Cross English Test* is composed of eight parts: spelling, pronunciation, recognizing a sentence, punctuation, verb forms, pronoun forms, idiomatic expressions, and miscellaneous faulty expressions.

Part I, Spelling, is an alternative form of spelling test with one of the two words misspelled. The validity and psychology of such a test of spelling is, at least, questionable. There is not sufficient evidence to show that such a form does not help to form incorrect spelling habits to recommend its use. Further-

more, the ability to spell a word correctly is not the same as the ability to select the word which is spelled correctly.

Part II, Pronunciation, is also an alternative form of objective test. This part is subject to, at least, part of the criticism mentioned for Part I. The guessing element is also maximum in both parts—that is, there are fifty chances in one hundred that a student may guess the answer without knowing it.

Part III, Recognizing a Sentence, also involves two choices. Certainly, the student needs to be able to know how to write in terms of sentences which are not faulty. Here, again, the ability to use complete and correct sentences is highly desirable. The guessing element is present, as well as the assumption that a student's ability to recognize complete, faulty, or correct sentences in a printed test is the same as the ability to write complete and correct sentences in his own composition.

Part IV, Punctuation, is proofreading which does not measure a student's ability to punctuate his own writing.

Part V, Verb Forms; Part VI, Pronoun Forms; Part VII, Idiomatic Expressions; and Part VIII, Miscellaneous Faulty Expressions —all use the alternate-response or multiple-choice form of recognition. Except for Items 4 and 7 of Part V, guessing is at its maximum; the psychology of this is questionable. For example, in Sentence 4 of Part V, Verb Forms, a boy might say, "I have never 'et' such good pears before." Every student has his own vocabulary of errors. For this reason, if a student is not allowed to supply the missing word in a sentence completion form, one would not be able to know for sure what he would use in his own writing.

The test as a whole is objective, but one should not wonder why many teachers of English prefer to grade subjective tests rather than to place faith in tests of an objective nature, merely because they are objective.

The content of the test is good—that is, if the test really measured a student's ability to use the English forms in his own writing which the test evidently intends to measure, it would be an excellent test.

Edward S. Noyes, Chairman, Board of Admissions and Associate Professor of English, Yale University. Each form of this test deals with composition in the fields of spelling, grammar, pronunciation, etc. Each is divided as follows, the number of items being given in parentheses: Part I, Spelling (32); II, Pronunciation (32); III, Recognizing a Sentence (in five groups totalling 40 items); IV, Punctuation (15); V, Verb Forms (16); VI, Pronoun Forms (12); VII, Idiomatic Expressions (10); VIII, Miscellaneous Faulty Expressions (15). Collation indicates accurate pairing of Forms A and C, in number, kind, and difficulty of items.

Tests of this kind cannot reproduce the conditions under which a student normally exercises the skill being tested. The section devoted to spelling, for instance, has 32 items, each consisting of a word spelled once wrongly and once correctly. The examinee's task is to check the correct spelling. A pupil may be able to recognize the correct spelling of a word on the printed page, by contrast with the incorrect spelling, without being able, in free composition, to spell that same word correctly. Similarly, a student's score on the section on pronunciation might indicate his degree of familiarity with diacritical marks rather than his ability to pronounce the test words correctly in ordinary speech.

These tests assume the inviolable authority of dictionary and grammar-book. They assume that a sentence must be either correct or faulty by itself, as judged by rigid grammatical rules, without consideration of its possible context. Such assumptions are now under fire by a growing number of teachers of English who prefer what might be called a functional approach to grammar and who do not believe that a living and growing language can be treated in a stereotyped fashion. A good deal of water has flowed over the dam since 1923, when these tests were apparently constructed.

On the other hand, even the modern functionalist would scarcely find fault with most of the items in the *Cross English Test* on the ground that they deal with dubious questions of grammatical rules. The errors which they require students to correct are generally so gross as to be unmistakable. According to the manual, these tests were "designed primarily for high school seniors and college freshmen." The present reviewer has been a reader of college entrance examinations for over twenty years, but has only infrequently met on such examinations errors as palpable as "might of" for "might have," "suspicion" as a verb, for

"suspect," or "leave me" for "allow me"—to mention three which are stressed in Forms A and C of the Cross tests. Either he has been dealing with a select group of students, or there has been a general improvement of students at this level. Unless scoring is to be done by the pupils themselves, a key seems hardly necessary.

Occasionally, it is true, there is a question whether an "error" actually exists. The directions in Group B of Part III state: "Place a figure 1 in the parentheses before each expression which should be written as one sentence and a figure 2 before each which should be written as two sentences." Among the items, however, there is at least one expression which, according to the key, should be written as two sentences, but which, according to acceptable modern usage, could be kept as a single sentence if a comma were changed to a colon. In Group D, again, one "faulty" sentence could as easily be corrected by the insertion of a semicolon as by making it into two separate sentences. Such cases are, however, rare.

The time allowance for the test is forty-five minutes, which seems ample. Whether or not the number of items in each part is large enough to measure accurately a student's skill in the field tested is a matter which cannot be decided a priori; it must be left to the judgment and the statistics of those who have administered the tests.

[1273]

Davis-Schrammel Elementary English Test. Grades 4-8; 1934; 2 forms; 50¢ per 25; 15¢ per specimen set; 20(25) minutes; Vera Davis and H. E. Schrammel; Emporia, Kan.: Bureau of Educational Measurements, Kansas State Teachers College.

Keith Goltry, Head of the Department of Education, Parsons College. This test is available in two forms, with percentile norms for both midyear and end-of-year testing in grades 4-8 inclusive. Each form consists of the following parts: punctuation, 20 items; capitalization, 10 items; sentence recognition, 10 items; and language usage (words and forms of words), 50 items. Norms are not available for the separate parts. The test has been developed in connection with the Nation-wide Every Pupil Scholarship Testing Program and is intended solely for survey purposes.

The items of the test are a good representative sample of the items stressed in elementary school textbooks of English. As such, of course, it is a test of the pupil's ability to use textbook English, not acceptable colloquial English. The proofreading test on punctuation, capitalization, and sentence recognition is an acceptable measure of pupils' abilities and much less open to the charge of invalidity than is the multiple-response test of language usage.

The norms, based as they are on large numbers of pupils in a nation-wide survey, possess the so-called characteristic of universality as well as one could ask for. But despite the fact that the test has 90 items, the range of scores is not great and improvement from grade to grade of median scores is only 3 to 7 points, while the semi-interquartile range of scores within each grade varies from 5.5 to 7.5. The reliability of the test is only .87 for all five grades combined, and the average reliability for a single grade is only .77.

Rachel Salisbury, Director of the Junior High School Department, State Teachers College, Platteville, Wisconsin. Each form contains 90 items, printed in two parts on two sides of a single sheet, so that manipulatory problems are reduced to a minimum. The type is large and readable. Part I contains items regarding punctuation, capitalization, and sentence recognition (40 items). Part II is devoted to language usage (50 items).

Part I is true-false, the child being asked to judge whether a sentence is correctly printed or not. Apostrophes are included among the punctuation items. Some of the items seem debatable. Children may well disagree about the comma after an introductory adverbial clause; and "July 1933 was a long, hot month" is accepted by many publishers while it is condemned by many teachers. Probably the example of single quotation marks within doubles should not be included in an elementary test at all. Under Sentence Recognition there are no examples of the run-together sentence; one appears under Punctuation.

Part II is multiple-choice, and includes principal parts of verbs, agreement of subject and verb, homonymns, contractions, double negatives, reflexives, agreement and case of pronouns, split infinitives, comparatives, potential mode, and faulty use of connectives, prepositions, adjectives, and adverbs. Some of the examples seem to labor the point. For example, "For captain they elected me, who (is, are, am) the largest." No grade school child would say

such a sentence; he would use *because*. In "(Who, Whom) shall we ask?" the first form is quite regularly accepted in conversation. Such an item as "All of the boys brought (their, his) skates" is pure test waste; no child would use the singular, for all oral pressure is toward the plural pronoun.

It is easy, of course, to criticize the selection of items in a list of 40. But this reviewer wonders why split infinitives are included when the principal parts of *do* and *go* are omitted; and why the test omits the double subject, such as "(He, Him) and (I, me) never stay for the game," while it includes the less resented "They sang (like, as though) they enjoyed it," and the regularly accepted "You (have, have got) a good bicycle." Most of the "really trulies" are included, however; and the test should discriminate effectively among students who have studied the textbooks.

The test has a reliability coefficient of .87 for a five-grade range (grades 4-8) and an average of .77 for the separate grades. As for validity, "the items were carefully selected from a number of leading elementary school textbooks of English," and the selected items were checked by the subjective judgments of competent teachers and supervisors of English. No statistical evaluation is presented. The use of textbooks as criteria naturally accounts for the inclusion of the debatable or recently accepted items cited above; for it is well known that textbooks continue to present puristic forms long after the dictionaries have acknowledged changes in language. A good language test should be as free as possible of debatable items.

Grade norms, based upon over 16,000 cases in 21 states, give a reliable scale for grade placement, by midyear and end-of-year scores. The raw scores are translated into percentiles, the 50th percentile being the norm for a given grade. There is a useful table for translating percentile ranks into school marks. A class record sheet and a strip key accompany the test.

The Davis-Schrammel test should be an inexpensive and effective instrument for diagnostic use, for ability grouping, and for measuring progress in classes that base their work upon standard textbooks in language.

[1274]

Diagnostic Tests in English Composition. Grades 7-12; 1923; 4 forms, 4 parts; 15¢ per specimen set; S. L. Pressey, L. C. Pressey, F. R. Conkling, E. V.

ENGLISH TESTS AND REVIEWS

Bowers, Helen Ruhlen, and Blythe Pearce; Bloomington, Ill.: Public School Publishing Co.
a) CAPITALIZATION. 75¢ per 100; nontimed, (10) minutes.
b) PUNCTUATION. 75¢ per 100; nontimed, (15) minutes.
c) GRAMMAR. $1.50 per 100; nontimed, (20) minutes.
d) SENTENCE STRUCTURE. $1.50 per 100; nontimed, (17) minutes.

Harry A. Greene, Director of the Bureau of Educational Research and Service and Professor of Education, The State University of Iowa. Four general areas of language skill are sampled by brief four-page tests: Test A, Capitalization; Test B, Punctuation; Test C, Grammar; Test D, Sentence Structure. Each test is available in four practically equal forms.

Test A comprises 28 proofreading exercises sampling a number of important capitalization skills. The spread of items fails to cover a number of variants of socially useful skills emphasized today in the upper grades and high school. Reliability seems to be secured by multiplying the responses to certain types of skills many times within each item.

Test B is made up of 30 proofreading items on punctuation. Here again the sampling is limited in the range of skills and usages tested.

Test C is composed of 30 four-response multiple-choice exercises described as measuring grammar, but much more probably measuring simple usage. Each exercise is made up of four statements, three of which contain correct usages and one of which is incorrect. The usages presented as correct are usually but not always related to the usage error in the incorrect statement. The exercises are grouped to conform to certain grammatical rules governing the usages, but no measure of the knowledge of the rule is involved.

Test D is designed to measure sentence structure. The 24 items comprising this test are four-response multiple-choice exercises similar to those used in Test C. The test is partly a measure of sentence sense, that is, the ability to discriminate fragments from sentences, and partly a measure of the ability to discriminate between sentences of differing levels of quality of structure.

Recent evidence on the best testing techniques for measuring the mechanical aspects of language indicates that the forms used in these tests are not the most effective. Certainly they are far from economical in terms of scoring time when compared with modern quick-scoring techniques. Little or no evidence on

the actual validation process is given by the authors although the items are selected on the basis of data showing the socially useful skills as identified by the authors prior to making the tests. Reliability indices are also not given for the tests. Only grade medians are presented as norms. Grade distributions and percentile tables are not given. The very slight grade growths in the skills measured by these tests as shown by the tables of grade norms are further limitations on the interpretation of the tests. The practical possibilities of the tests are increased somewhat through the use of analytical tabulation sheets which aid in identifying for each pupil the items and skills in which weakness is revealed.

The use of the word *diagnostic* in the title of any language test is doubtless just as optimistic today as it was at the time these tests were made. Language expression is complicated by so many interrelated factors that diagnosis in the strict sense is very difficult if not impossible to secure. At best, these tests, sampling briefly into only four areas of expressional skills, provide an extremely sketchy and vague diagnostic picture of language ability. There are many other tests which are markedly superior for this purpose.

Jean Hoard, Teacher of English in the University High School, The University of Wisconsin. This is a series of tests of English grammar and usage in four forms. The tests provide a teacher of English with the information necessary to evaluate the ability of her students to use correctly the fundamentals of English composition.

Directions for administering the tests are clear; the record sheet accompanying each test enables the teacher to have an individual picture of the strength and weakness of each of her students. Most of the tests are well constructed, and their results should provide useful measurements of student knowledge and ability.

Test A is arranged to give the teacher and the students analytic information about the knowledge of good usage in capitalization. All sentences in the test are correct except that they lack all capitalization. The problem set before the student is to underline each letter that should be a capital. This test demands skill in proofreading, and requires a knowledge of the correct use of capital letters. The sen-

Diagnostic Tests in English Composition

tences used for testing this knowledge cover a wide area of usage and are well balanced.

Test B is a test of correctness in punctuation. It should contain actual errors from student themes, topics, and informal letters in addition to those gathered from magazines, periodicals, and business letters. For the most part, this test is a dull exercise; some of the errors listed are too far-fetched. Sentences 15, 28, 29, and 30 illustrate this point; they do not represent the typical errors made by the average student.

There is no relationship between this test and the ability of students to punctuate their own sentences accurately.

Test C is a better test because it presents errors made in the written work of students. It tests a student's ability to recognize common mistakes in grammar and contains twenty problems of four sentences each. Only one out of the four is wrong and the student must place a check before that one. This test would be more valid if provision were made to underline the error and to insert the correct usage. As it stands the test does not check student knowledge and it does encourage guesswork. To illustrate: a student may place his check correctly because the sentence doesn't sound or look right; he doesn't know the reason for doing it, nor does he possess the grammatical knowledge necessary to effect the change. Therefore, there is no tie-up between this test and the ability to avoid making similar errors the next time a student writes a theme.

Test D seeks to have students recognize common errors in sentence structure. It contains actual sentences from the written work of students. Only one sentence in each group is not well expressed, and a check is to be placed before the poor sentence. Provision should be made to show why the sentence is poor, and to test the student's ability to correct it. Without such provision, the test loses its effectiveness and evidences no valid proof of knowledge.

All four tests in this series are to be used in testing the composition skill of students from the seventh through the twelfth grades. I would like to have a division made in the tests, so that the materials pertaining to the junior high school could be given separately. The first part of each test is too easy for the upper level students and causes carelessness in their proofreading. By the time the upper level

is challenged, the lower level is entirely out of its depth; they either give up trying to solve the problem or else they resort to guessing. Either case destroys the validity of the test's purpose; it encourages bad habits and it definitely fails to present a true picture of student knowledge.

[1275]

"Dingwall" Test in English Usage. Ages 9-10; 10-12; 1937; 1 form, 2 levels, 2 booklets at each level; 25(30) minutes per booklet; 1s. 3d. per specimen set; Educational Institute of Scotland; London: University of London Press, Ltd.
a) PUPILS AGES 9-10, PUPIL'S BOOKLET I: CONTAINING PARTS 1-4. 3d. per test, 2s. per 12; 3s. 6d. per 25.
b) PUPILS AGES 9-10, PUPIL'S BOOKLET II: CONTAINING PARTS 5-9. 3d. per test; 2s. 6d. per 12; 4s. 6d. per 25.
c) PUPILS AGES 10-12, PUPIL'S BOOKLET I: CONTAINING PARTS 1-4. 3d. per test; 2s. per 12; 3s. 6d. per 25.
d) PUPILS AGES 10-12, PUPIL'S BOOKLET II: CONTAINING PARTS 5-9. 3d. per test; 2s. per 12; 3s. 6d. per 25.

Charles Fox, formerly Director of Training, University of Cambridge. This test is issued by the Educational Institute of Scotland and is intended for pupils from 9 to 12 years of age. There are 2 forms of the test; one for pupils 9-10 years in which the instructions are read by the examiner, and the other for those from 10-12 in which the instructions are printed in the test booklets. A table of *tentative* norms for each age group is given.

The present reviewer tried the tests on a group of 70 boys aged 10-11 years and obtained the same total mark as that given in the manual, but with considerable variations in the different subtests; so that it would be unwise to draw any conclusions from the separate parts of the test.

There are a few expressions which are not in accordance with English usage, though they are familiar to Scottish pupils, e.g., "message boy" and "score out" instead of "messenger boy" and "cross out." And, if "I take my breakfast" means "I eat it," very few English boys would use the expression, nor do they use the word "forenoon." Though these locutions make little difference to the results, they are unfortunate in a test intended for general use.

The various parts of the test are concerned with those elementary parts of grammar which every pupil of the ages tested should be familiar with; and many teachers would prefer to construct their own examples instead of the trivial ones given. If they wish to compare their pupils with others they would desire definitive norms instead of tentative ones. In a test of English usage it is desirable to select some, at least, of the examples from acknowledged literary sources instead of inventing them *ad hoc* as the latter tend to have an air of artificiality. There is no lack of English classical or modern writers from which to make a suitable choice for the ages concerned, and these are more appropriate than the stilted sentences given in the test.

[1276]

Effectiveness of Expression Test: Cooperative English Test, Tests B1 and B2. Grades 7-12, 11-16; 1940; 2 levels, Form Q; 5¢ per test, 10 to 99 copies; 1½¢ per machine-scorable answer sheet; 25¢ per specimen set; 40(45) minutes; Geraldine Spaulding with the editorial assistance of Dudley H. Cloud, H. A. Domincovich, E. F. Lindquist, Robert C. Pooley, Marion C. Sheridan, and George Summey, Jr.; New York: Cooperative Test Service.
a) TEST B1, LOWER LEVEL. Grades 7-12.
b) TEST B2, UPPER LEVEL. Grades 11-16.

REFERENCES

1 Cooperative Test Service. *The Cooperative English Expression Tests*: Information Concerning Their Construction, Interpretation, and Use. New York: Cooperative Test Service, 1940. Pp. 4. Gratis. Paper.
2 TRAXLER, ARTHUR. "The Cooperative English Test, Form Q: Correlations with School Marks and Intercorrelations," pp. 42-50. In *1940 Achievement Testing Program in Independent Schools and Supplementary Studies*. Educational Records Bureau Staff. Educational Records Bulletin, No. 30. New York: the Bureau. June 1940. Pp. xii, 76. $1.50. Paper, lithotyped.

[1277]

English Classification Test for High Schools and Colleges: Form X. 1940; 1 form; $1.25 per 25; 10¢ per specimen set; nontimed (90-120) minutes; R. D. Scott, A. A. Reed, and Ruth E. Pike; Lincoln, Neb.: University Extension Division, University of Nebraska.

[1278]

English Placement Test: Form F. Entering college freshmen; 1935-39; 1 form; 5¢ per test; 15¢ per key; nontimed (90) minutes; L. K. Shumaker; Eugene, Ore.: the Author, Friendly Hall, University of Oregon.

REFERENCES

1 SHUMAKER, L. KENNETH. "The Prediction of Success in English Composition," pp. 72-9. In *Research in Higher Education*. United States Department of Interior, Office of Education, Bulletin 1931, No. 12. Washington, D. C.: Government Printing Office, 1932. Pp. vi, 133. $0.15. Paper.
2 SHUMAKER, LAWRENCE K. *A Predictive Measure for Estimating Success in English Composition at the College Level*. Unpublished master's thesis, University of Oregon, 1932. Pp. 65.

Roland L. Beck, Professor of Education and Director of the Demonstration School, Central State College, Edmond, Oklahoma. [Review of Form D.] The *English Placement Test* is divided into four parts—namely, Part I, Words; Part II, Grammar; Part III, Punctuation; and Part IV, Usage.

Part I, Words, is a good objective test in spelling and vocabulary. The device used in this part is much better than selecting the misspelled word in a series of five, or the selection of the correctly spelled word in a series of five.

The use of either method mentioned would permit machine scoring. Teachers and college professors need to realize that ease in scoring tests is not the only important criteria in measurement. Measurement and grading, especially in English, probably never will be validly done if only a machine is used. This part serves very satisfactorily the measurement of spelling and vocabulary.

Part II, Grammar, is a proofreading test of the knowledge of grammar. The numbering of the italicized words is an improved device in proofreading. If the purpose of this part is to measure the ability of a student to do proofreading, then the only question that remains is "Should ability to do proofreading be a part of an English placement test?" Certainly, this part does not measure a student's habitual grammatical usage, but his ability to recognize grammatical errors in someone else's composition.

Part III, Punctuation, is an improved form of proofreading. Attention of the student is called to the necessity for punctuation at specific places in or between the sentences. The form might be improved some by eliminating words, to be supplied by the student, which are associated with, or make necessary, the punctuation. Although, one might question that the test measures a student's ability to punctuate his own composition; nevertheless, a student who would make a good score on this part would have considerable knowledge of punctuation.

Part IV, Usage, is more a form of recognition than of completion. Credit is given if a student can recognize errors in a printed test. This is not proof that a student would or would not use the correct form.

The test as a whole does measure abilities which college freshmen will need in their English classes. However, a student might have the ability to use very good English and still not make a high score on this test. The principal criteria which the test fails to meet is that it measures a student's ability to compose. The test does measure very satisfactorily ability in spelling and vocabulary and the recognition of correct usage in someone else's writing.

Robert W. Howard, Department of Examinations, The Chicago City Junior Colleges, Chicago, Illinois. [Review of Form D.] This test is divided into four parts: words, grammar, punctuation, and usage. The one hundred items in each part make percentages easy for the classroom teacher, and one man's guess is as good as another's in the matter of proportions.

Part I requires the student to recall the correct word to complete a sentence. The clues are the initial letter of the word and parenthetical italicized synonyms or definitive words and phrases. Three pages of the test and 23 minutes of time are required for the testing of 100 words. Since the student must write the recalled word in the indicated space and spell it correctly, he is tested not only in vocabulary but also in spelling. After the guessing game, comes a spelling contest! What are we testing?

In the grammar test, the student is asked to indicate whether certain italicized words are used correctly in a contextual background. An effort has been made, first, to show words as they appear in natural reading conditions, and, second, to present the student with interesting material. Although the aim is admirable, the effect is often the opposite, since the attention of the student is centered only on the italicized and numbered words or phrases, and he will not be interested in any case.

Similarly, in Part III the student is asked to punctuate two pages of material reprinted from a popular magazine, with the author's own punctuation the criterion for the correct marks, while in Part IV he is asked to exercise judgment in usage. In each case he is told to consider certain numbered spaces or italicized words. The usage test includes items which might easily be reclassified as spelling or grammar.

The manual of instructions accompanying the test indicate that in 1937-1938 it was used successfully for placement and diagnosis in thirty northwestern colleges and normal schools. Any English test containing 400 items should serve to distribute students satisfactorily enough for purposes of placement. There are tests of linguistic abilities, however, investigating a wider variety of field, which should provide a more satisfactory basis for diagnosis and remedial instruction.

[1279]

English: Thanet Mental Tests. Age 11; 1937; 1 form; 3s. 6d per 25; 1s. per handbook; 1s. 6d. per specimen set, including the arithmetic and school aptitude tests in the same series; 45(50) minutes; W. P. Alexander; London: University of London Press, Ltd.

C. Ebblewhite Smith, Lecturer in the Department of Higher Degrees and Research, Institute of Education, University of London. This test is to be used in conjunction with the *School Aptitude Test* and the *Arithmetic Test* in the series Thanet Mental Tests. It is designed to test the minumum essentials of English expected of a child about to enter an English secondary school. The test is in three parts.

(1) Reading Comprehension. This part, though short, is well designed involving a minimum of intelligence and a maximum of reading ability.

(2) Test of Punctuation and Use of Capitals. The form of this test is satisfactory but here again the test is too short. It is always a dangerous policy when scoring to subtract marks for errors. For example, it is questionable whether a child who inserts the question mark after the quotation marks should lose a mark when the child who omits it altogether is not similarly penalized.

(3) Spelling. I thought the type of spelling test which gave the correctly spelled word among four misspelled alternatives was universally condemned but here it appears again. Educationally the method is not sound. On what basis were the words chosen?

Children are allowed to hand in their papers when they have finished. This always creates some measure of confusion in the class and anxious souls are worried when others are obviously ahead of them.

The norm for 10-year-old boys is 37 marks; for 11-year-old boys, 40 marks; and for 12-year-old boys, 43 marks. These differences are so small as to be comparable with the standard error of the test. Admittedly it is difficult to prepare a minimum essentials test in English but surely a test could be prepared that would have more than three marks between those who pass the test and those who are one whole year behind standard!

[1280]

Entrance and Classification Examination for Teachers Colleges: English Test, 1939 Edition. 1933-39; 2 forms; 8¢ per test; 3¢ per machine-scorable answer sheet; 30¢ per specimen set; 100(110) minutes; Normal, Ill.: Teachers College Personnel Association (c/o C. F. Malmberg).

REFERENCES

1 HEILMAN, J. D. *Report of the Cooperative Testing Program of the Teachers College Personnel Association.* Greeley, Colo.: Colorado State Teachers College, February 1932. Pp. 65. $0.50. Paper, mimeographed.

2 HEILMAN, J. D. *Report on the 1932–33 Testing Program of the Teachers College Personnel Association.* Greeley, Colo.: Colorado State Teachers College, February 1933. Pp. 71. $0.50. Paper, mimeographed.

3 HEILMAN, J. D. *Report on the 1933-34 Testing Program of the Teachers College Personnel Association.* Greeley, Colo.: Colorado State Teachers College, February 1934. Pp. ii, 83. $0.50. Paper, mimeographed.

4 HEILMAN, J. D. *Report on the 1934–35 Testing Program of the Teachers College Personnel Association.* Greeley, Colo.: Colorado State Teachers College, February 1935. Pp. iii, 74. $0.50. Paper, mimeographed.

5 HEILMAN, J. D. *The 1936 Report on the Cooperative Testing Program of the Teachers College Personnel Association.* Greeley, Colo.: Colorado State College of Education, February 1936. Pp. iii, 87. $0.50. Paper, mimeographed.

6 HEILMAN, J. D. *The 1937 Report on the Cooperative Testing Program of the Teachers College Personnel Association.* Greeley, Colo.: Colorado State College of Education, February 1937. Pp. ii, 102. $0.50. Paper, mimeographed.

7 HEILMAN, J. D. *The 1938 Report on the Cooperative Testing Program of the Teachers College Personnel Association.* Greeley, Colo.: Colorado State College of Education, February 1938. Pp. iii, 71. $0.50. Paper, mimeographed.

8 HEILMAN, J. D. *The 1939 Report on the Cooperative Testing Program of the Teachers College Personnel Association.* Greeley, Colo.: Colorado State College of Education, February 1939. Pp. iii, 44. $0.50. Paper, mimeographed.

9 CONGDON, NORA A. *The 1940 Report on the Cooperative Testing Program of the Teachers College Personnel Association.* Greeley, Colo.: Colorado State College of Education, February 1940. Pp. 32. $0.25. Paper, lithotyped.

[1281]

Essentials of English Tests. Grades 7-13; 1939; 1 form; $1 per 25; 25¢ per specimen set; 45(50) minutes; Dora V. Smith and Constance M. McCullough; Minneapolis, Minn.: Educational Test Bureau, Inc.

[1282]

Gregory Diagnostic Tests in Language. Grades 4-9; 1935; 2 forms; $2.50 per 100; 10¢ per specimen set; nontimed (20-40) minutes; Helen Gregory and C. A. Gregory; Cincinnati, Ohio: C. A. Gregory Co.

Keith Goltry, Head of the Department of Education, Parsons College. This test consists of two forms of 156 two-response items. It is designed to measure the pupil's ability to recognize correct forms in common every-day language expressions. Each item consists of a sentence involving the use of some word or phrase which is not correct according to some standard of usage. In each case the questionable word or words and the so-called correct form are given, and the task of the pupil is to choose the one he believes to be correct. The scoring key is convenient and interpretation of results easy. For convenience in diagnosis the items are divided into 20 groups, each group including expressions involving similar grammatical constructions.

No evidence is presented in the manual as to the validity of the test. No doubt it is, as are most such tests, rather a poor measure of actual ability to speak in accordance with commonly accepted standards of usage. The items involve the most common of questioned usages, but recognition of acceptable forms is no guarantee that such forms are used in speech. In a number of items the form which is marked incorrect by the key is quite ac-

ceptable, at least in colloquial usage, though the test leans less toward the purist view of language than do many courses of study, textbooks, and teachers of English. Such items can of course be ignored in diagnosing pupil difficulties, and interpretation of total scores is probably not seriously altered unless the course of study is unusually generous in recognizing colloquial usage.

No evidence is presented as to what is sometimes termed universality of the norms. It even seems a bit strange that crude scores, sigma scores, and months of chronological age all should happen to increase from one level to another by such regular increments as are shown in the manual. Throughout the range of scores for third- to eleventh-grade pupils, with few exceptions, an increase of one in total score equals an increase of one in sigma score and the equivalent age increment is three months.

J. Paul Leonard, Associate Professor of Education, Stanford University. The authors of the Gregory test recommend it for either diagnostic or survey purposes in everyday language expressions, stressing the fact that the test is comprehensive and able to show language deficiencies which need remedial work. To do this they have prepared two forms, A and B, each form consisting of 156 common language expressions divided into the following 20 groups under three major headings: Pronouns—55 sentences divided into 9 groups of items running from 4 to 9 sentences in each group; Verbs—60 sentences divided into 6 groups of items running from 7 to 16 sentences in each group; Miscellaneous constructions—41 sentences divided into 5 groups of items running from 6 to 12 sentences in each group.

The sections in the pronoun group deal with: compound subjects in the nominative case, the pronoun subject of a comparative clause in the nominative case, the complement of a copulative verb in the nominative case, use of objective case when pronoun is object of a preposition; correct use of compound personal pronouns; objective form with infinitive; possessive form with gerund; use of direct and indirect object, and correct form following indefinites.

The sections in the verb groups deal with tense forms of present, past, and past participial forms, verbs with contractions and with indefinite pronouns, and other common miscellaneous verb usages.

The miscellaneous constructions deal with the use of adverbs; plural, singular, and possessive nouns; prepositions, conjunctions, and adjectives.

All the items in the tests are in complete sentences and for each sentence two possible forms are given. The pupil is to check the one he considers correct, the score being the total of all correct items, or the total for each group may be used as a separate score.

The user of the test is given no indication of the validity or reliability of the test. He is to be content with the statement that "Great care has been taken to select sentences which are in common use and which will illustrate frequently misused constructions." There is no good reason for the number of items in each group and in some of the most difficult usages only four sentences are used whereas in the easier usages eight sentences are used. The sentences are all short and do not give a fair picture of average composition. The material is the same for grades 4-9, but by no means should considerable of the material be taught in these lower grades. A test measuring language proficiency over a range of these six years of study is ill adjusted to the lower grades. The test manual describes each section in terms of a grammatical principle rather than in terms of usage.

The test scores may be converted into "raw scores," "crude scores," "equivalent sigma scores," "age norms," and "grade norms." For these numerous statistical devices not one bit of data are given. The user has to take everything on faith, even the authors' statement that "language achievement, as measured by this test, increases approximately four points per year, or one point for each additional three months of age."

The test deals with common daily usages, is clear and simple for pupils in the upper grades to understand, and for the upper elementary or junior high school years the test could be used as a substitute for exercises which the teacher might make herself. Any good teacher with a few hours of careful study can prepare a test as good as this one and probably better suited to her immediate teaching. The statistical impedimenta of the test are misleading to a teacher who takes them seriously as a measure of growth in language power.

[1283]

Judging the Effectiveness of Written Composition: Test 3.8. Grades 9-12; 1938; and experimental form; 5¢ per test; 1¢ per machine-scorable answer sheet; $1.50 per set of stencils for machine scoring; nontimed (40) minutes; Chicago, Ill.: Evaluation in the Eight Year Study, Progressive Education Association.

REFERENCES

A Descriptive Summary of Evaluation Instruments in the Field of English. Chicago, Ill.: Evaluation in the Eight Year Study, Progressive Education Association, March 1939. Pp. 10. Paper, mimeographed. Out of print.

[1284]

Kentucky English Test: A General Achievement Test for High School Students and College Freshmen [1939 Revision]. Grades 9-13; 1937-39; 2 forms; $3.50 per 100; 10¢ per specimen set; nontimed (25-85) minutes; E. J. Asher and T. E. McMullen; Lexington, Ky.: Kentucky Cooperative Testing Service, University of Kentucky.

REFERENCES

1 ASHER, ESTON J. "The Reliability and Validity of the Kentucky General Scholastic and Kentucky English Tests." Ky Personnel B 21:1-2 S '38.

For a review by Henry D. Rinsland of an earlier form, see 966.

[1285]

Leonard Diagnostic Test in Punctuation and Capitalization. Grades 5-12; 1930-31; 2 forms; 90¢ per 25; 20¢ per specimen set; nontimed (20-40) minutes; J. Paul Leonard; Yonkers, N. Y.: World Book Co.

REFERENCES

1 LEONARD, J. PAUL. "The Use of Practice Exercises in Teaching Punctuation and Capitalization." J Ed Res 21:186-90 Mr '30.
2 LEONARD, JOHN PAUL. The Use of Practice Exercises in the Teaching of Capitalization and Punctuation. Columbia University, Teachers College, Contributions to Education, No. 372. New York: Bureau of Publications, the College, 1930. Pp. vii, 78. $1.50.

Jean Hoard, Teacher of English in the University High School, The University of Wisconsin. There are two forms to this test which covers a wide area of punctuation and capitalization difficulties. The test is well constructed, and shows a careful study of the needs of students in this field of writing fundamentals. The sentence problems are chosen well and are challenging as they increase in problem difficulty. The instructions for giving the test are clear, and the directions are easy to follow. It is one of the most satisfactory tests that has come to my attention.

Form A contains 52 sentences, all of which are correct, except that they lack some of the necessary punctuation marks and capital letters; these are to be supplied by the student. Not only is this a test of skill in proofreading, but also an exercise for testing a student's ability to correct errors similar to his own.

The test reveals to a student how much, or how little he knows, and likewise informs the teacher about the remedial work to be done. The test is of value, because the types of errors contained in it are common to all students.

Form B is like Form A and contains the same number of problems; they are more difficult, and accurate knowledge is necessary to solve them. The sentences are challenging and should produce interesting results.

Both of these tests present sentence problems that demand knowledge and judgment from the student; they are valuable as a check-up on classroom teaching and student learning.

[1286]

Mechanics of Expression: Cooperative English Test, Test A. Grades 7-16; 1940; Form Q; 5¢ per test, 10 to 99 copies; 1½¢ per machine-scorable answer sheet; 25¢ per specimen set; 40(45) minutes; Geraldine Spaulding and W. W. Cook with the editorial assistance of Dudley H. Cloud, H. A. Domincovich, E. F. Lindquist, Robert C. Pooley, Marion C. Sheridan, and George Summey, Jr.; New York: Cooperative Test Service.

REFERENCES

1 Cooperative Test Service. *The Cooperative English Expression Tests*: Information Concerning Their Construction, Interpretation, and Use. New York: Cooperative Test Service, 1940. Pp. 4. Gratis. Paper.
2 TRAXLER, ARTHUR. "The Cooperative English Test, Form Q: Correlations with School Marks and Intercorrelations," pp. 42-50. In *1940 Achievement Testing Program in Independent Schools and Supplementary Studies*. Educational Records Bureau Staff. Educational Records Bulletin, No. 30. New York: the Bureau, June 1940. Pp. xii, 76. $1.50. Paper, lithotyped.

[1287]

Linguistic Awareness Test. High school; 1938; 1 form; $1.25 per 25; sample copy free; 45(50) minutes; Elmer R. Smith; Atlanta, Ga.: Turner E. Smith & Co.

[1288]

Literary Information Test: American Literature: Test 3.5. Grades 9-12; 1937; 1 form; 5¢ per test; 1¢ per mimeographed key; nontimed (90) minutes; Chicago, Ill.: Evaluation in the Eight Year Study, Progressive Education Association.

REFERENCES

1 *A Descriptive Summary of Evaluation Instruments in the Field of English.* Chicago, Ill.: Evaluation in the Eight Year Study, Progressive Education Association, March 1939. Pp. 10. Paper, mimeographed. Out of print.

[1289]

Literary Information Test: English Literature: Test 3.4. Grades 9-12; 1939; 1 form; 5¢ per test; 2½¢ per set of machine-scorable answer sheets; 1¢ per mimeographed key; $1.50 per set of stencils for machine scoring; nontimed (90) minutes; Chicago, Ill.: Evaluation in the Eight Year Study, Progressive Education Association.

REFERENCES

1 *A Descriptive Summary of Evaluation Instruments in the Field of English.* Chicago, Ill.: Evaluation in the Eight Year Study, Progressive Education Association, March 1939. Pp. 10. Paper, mimeographed. Out of print.

[1290]

Nelson's High School English Test. Grades 7-12; 1931-32; 2 forms; $1.65 per 25, including 25 answer booklets; 75¢ per 25 answer booklets; single speci-

men set free; 40(50) minutes; M. J. Nelson; Boston, Mass.: Houghton Mifflin Co.

Frank P. De Lay, Department of English, New Trier Township High School, Winnetka, Illinois. The self-correcting nature of this test will make it most desirable to the busy teacher, if the student is made to understand clearly what he is to do. Students, through inattention to instructions, often do work incorrectly; and this test requires most careful explanation, especially in Part IV. However, training in the accurate following of directions is a thing greatly needed in our work, and a test such as this may afford as a by-product an example of the importance of such accuracy.

The fact that the Nelson test contains a large number of questions in each section makes it a more accurate test. The sections on word usage, sentence structure, and punctuation are functional, and can be used to the end of improving the ability of the student in writing accurate and effective sentences. The section on grammar does not meet with my personal favor because it is for the purpose of testing the student's ability to *name* the various grammatical elements in a sentence; but it does not deal in involved grammatical constructions, and all of the elements it seeks to identify should be included in the student's information for all are needed in the most simple explanation of sentence construction.

The *Cleveland English Composition and Grammar Test* and *Nelson's High School English Test* make a good pair, both for diagnostic and remedial work; however, if one of the two must be selected, I prefer the Nelson test.

Jacob S. Orleans, Associate Professor of Education, The College of the City of New York. This test is offered to serve four purposes, two administrative (grouping and prediction), and two instructional. In view of the fact that the test is entirely of the recognition type it is questionable that the analysis of the results can be accepted at their face value for teaching or remedial purposes as far as the student's *use* of language and of the mechanics of language are concerned. The test covers four phases of the mechanics of English (language usage, sentence structure, grammar, and punctuation) with 196 items in all. The information provided by the authors indicates a sound basis for content validity. The statements made concerning statistical validity may be questioned in view of the fact that, apart from grades eight and nine, a point of test score represents about a month and one-half of achievement for the test as a whole. In the case of the individual parts a single point represents on the average from two and one-half months to seven months of achievement.

The reliability coefficients are high, approximately .90 for the entire test. However, the coefficients were computed for populations covering a range of four years. No data are given on the reliability of scores on the entire test for a single-year group. It is doubtful that the separate divisions are, for most grades and for most parts of the test, reliable enough even for group measurement. No reliability data are available for the separate parts.

The test has the very marked advantage of saving much time and effort in the scoring of the papers, since it uses the Clapp-Young self-marking technique. However, in the case of part four in particular the method of indicating the answers is rather complicated. It may lead to errors on the part of the examinee in indicating the answer when he does mean to note the correct answer. The type size is rather small, especially for the junior high school grades.

Norms are provided for apparently representative groups for the end of the school year in the form of percentile ranks of scores for each of grades seven to twelve for each part of the test as well as the total scores. Comparisons in terms of grade levels are hardly feasible except for total score because of the very small differences in norms between grades.

The tenth percentile score for the seventh grade is 85 points. As is to be expected many of the items (approximately a third) are answered correctly by almost all of even the poorest pupils. This condition is bound to hold true for a test in language usage and the mechanics of English if it is to be valid, from the standpoint of content, for learning purposes. If the test is to be used only for administrative purposes, content validity is of significance only in so far as it produces accuracy in the interpretation of scores for administrative purposes. The effect of trying to cover both learning and administrative purposes is a much longer test (at the easier levels) than is needed for administrative purposes, and a consequent reduction of the dis-

criminative power of the test. That is, despite the length of the test (the total score is 226 points) only 12 points represent the two years from the end of grade 10 to the end of grade 12. The entire range of five years of achievement (grades 7 to 12) is represented by 45 points or only one-fifth of the entire range of possible scores.

This test would hardly seem to serve better the need for an analytical achievement test in English than is already provided for by other available tests.

[1291]

Pressey English Tests for Grades 5 to 8. 1923-38; an abbreviated adaptation of *Diagnostic Tests in English Composition*; 3 forms; $2 per 100; 15¢ per specimen set; 30(40) minutes; S. L. Pressey and others; Bloomington, Ill.: Public School Publishing Co.

Ed Res B 19:60 Ja 17 '40. J. Wayne Wrightstone. * The tests probably measure capitalization, good usage, punctuation, and sentence structure as validly as such factors can be measured in a test of recognition of language errors. Many questions have been raised about the validity of testing such language skills in a so-called new type objective test. The assumption that the proficiency in skills which pupils use in oral and written language may not correlate highly with recognition of errors in the test situations, is unquestioned by the authors. For those who are willing to make a similar assumption these tests do provide one index of the ability of pupils to recognize errors in selected language skills.

Teach Col J 10:72 Ja '39. Mary Reid McBeth. The new adaptation of the Pressey tests is well planned to give definite and detailed information concerning each pupil's knowledge of the essentials of capitalization, punctuation, word usage, and sentence structure. * All of the material is practical, and a maximum of diagnosis is done in a minimum of time and space. Directions for administering and for taking the test are simple and concise, and the scoring key is efficiently arranged. A particularly excellent and useful feature of the Pressey tests is the accompanying *Diagnostic Record Chart* with correlated scale and concise summary of the rules covered by the test *

[1292]

Progressive Language Tests. Grades 1-3, 4-6, 7-9, 9-13; 1933-39; 4 levels; identical to the language tests in the battery *Progressive Achievement Tests*; 2¢ per machine-scorable answer sheet; 15¢ per speci-

men set of any one level; Ernest W. Tiegs and Willis W. Clark; Los Angeles, Calif.: California Test Bureau.
a) PRIMARY. Grades 1-3; 1933-38; 3 forms; 50¢ per 25.
b) ELEMENTARY. Grades 4-6; 1933-37; 3 forms; 50¢ per 25; *Machine Scoring Edition*: 1933-39; 2 forms; 5¢ per test.
c) INTERMEDIATE. Grades 7-9; 1933-37; 3 forms; 50¢ per 25; *Machine Scoring Edition*: 1933-39; 2 forms; 5¢ per test.
d) ADVANCED. Grades 9-13; 1933-37; 3 forms; 75¢ per 25; *Machine Scoring Edition*: 1933-37; 2 forms; 5¢ per test.

Harry A. Greene, Director of the Bureau of Educational Research and Service and Professor of Education, The State University of Iowa. These tests are identical in content with the language sections of the battery *Progressive Achievement Tests.* Capitalization, punctuation, usage and sentence sense, spelling, and handwriting are measured at different levels of difficulty in the three tests comprising the series. The test content itself is compressed on the two inside pages of a four page folder for the elementary and intermediate tests. The advanced test requires three pages. A diagnostic profile chart and an analysis of learning difficulties represented by the items in the test occupy the first page of the folder. It is apparent that the analysis of skills is more valuable as a teaching aid than the profile chart due to the obviously inadequate sampling provided in each of the parts of the test. The spelling tests and the grammar test (in the advanced examination) are the only subtests composed of as many as thirty items.

The tests are described by the authors as "diagnostic tests keyed to the curriculum." The entire series of tests comprising the Progressive achievement battery is not extensive enough to function as a reliable diagnostic instrument, so it is apparent that the brevity of these language tests and the inadequate sampling of language skills they afford could not furnish a reliable diagnostic measure in written expression. While it is true that the capitalization and punctuation skills sampled may be those of high social significance, it is doubtful if ten or fifteen reactions in these fields constitute a sufficiently reliable sampling to provide meaningful results.

The evidence presented on the validity of the tests is not particularly conclusive. The use of the term *diagnostic* in connection with any brief four-page (or even longer) test is optimistic. The complexity of language expression is so great that brief cross-sections of

isolated areas of skill can scarcely be taken as diagnostic evidence. The sampling of items covered in these tests would indicate a very narrow and limited curriculum.

The reliability coefficients reported for the elementary or intermediate tests are adequate, but they are based upon talent ranging over two or three school grades. Thus, a reliability coefficient of .92 for the elementary examination based on a three-grade range is not too convincing. Furthermore, the reliabilities reported are based on odd-even correlations stepped up by formula rather than the intercorrelation of the two forms of the test. No data of the extent of the population involved in the reliability computations are given.

Convincing norms based upon more than one hundred thousand cases are provided for both the elementary and intermediate tests. Grade and percentile norms based upon fifteen hundred cases are given for the advanced tests. Grades and percentile norms, taking into account differences in mental level, accompany the elementary and the intermediate tests.

Machine-scored editions of the intermediate and the advanced tests are available. The importance of this procedure in the case of such brief tests is not apparent. Furthermore, the numerous changes in the administration of the tests, and the somewhat unusual procedures in recording the answers on the separate answer sheets introduce factors which should necessitate separate norms for the machine-scored and the hand-scored tests.

J. Paul Leonard, Associate Professor of Education, Stanford University. All three batteries of the *Progressive Language Tests* are designed to diagnose for individual pupils their language proficiency. The items which the tests measure are the "skills and abilities which are included in the objectives of education" and are "based upon the results of scientific studies," selected from skills "which represent the essential elements of the basic skills now being taught . . . in recent courses of study." Just what courses or objectives or studies were used is not told the reader.

The test makers claim further that the tests will produce "a diagnostic profile which reveals graphically the pupil's actual achievement in relation to normal achievement for his particular grade placement" and reveal "which pupils are achieving satisfactorily," thus enabling the teacher to determine "the particular type of remedial work necessary for those who are experiencing one or more of the different types of learning difficulty." In these claims the makers place themselves in a position of criticism by modern students of language growth who believe the determination of general minimum language essentials to be a myth and the determination of satisfactory language growth by resort to norms based upon average achievement to be a fallacious method of diagnosis.

All three batteries of the test deal with capitalization, punctuation, words and sentences, spelling and handwriting. The authors claim that "while the basic elements of these skills are the same on all levels, the increasing difficulty and complexity of the materials of instruction require a corresponding increase in tool mastery." They claim, therefore, to have increased the difficulty of these items in the three batteries and "selected test situations which reveal the extent to which tool mastery is adequate to the demands put upon it." If any language test could do these things adequately, curriculum workers would flock to it. The intermediate battery adds a section on parts of speech, while the advanced battery adds a section on grammar, to the basic four sections in all three batteries. Norms for the elementary and intermediate batteries are based upon 100,000 cases and for the advanced battery upon 1500 cases.

These tests offer a meagre survey of a few language uses and in the manual tend to overemphasize by far the validity and diagnostic value of the tests. The number of items to cover the different usages are entirely too small. For instance, in the elementary battery 33 sentences are used to cover 17 different groups of language usage (counting such things as tense, good usage, case, and commas as one group); the intermediate battery used 36 sentences to cover 26 different groups and the advanced battery 80 sentences to cover 28 different groups. The advanced battery is the only one having enough items to warrant any reasonable claim to having diagnostic values. The tests may be fairly useful for general survey purposes but seem to be of very little value for individual diagnostic purposes. They are not nearly so diagnostic as the *Gregory Diagnostic Tests in Language* in the items covered by both tests.

For reviews by D. Welty Lefever, C. W. Odell, and Hugh B. Wood of the complete battery, see 876 and 1193.

[1293]

Rinsland-Beck Natural Test of English Usage. Grades 9-13; 1934-39; 2 forms; $1.50 per 25; 10¢ per teacher's handbook; 50¢ per specimen set; Henry D. Rinsland and Roland L. Beck; Bloomington, Ill.: Public School Publishing Co.
a) TEST I [MECHANICS]. 45(50) minutes.
b) TEST II [GRAMMAR]. 30(35) minutes.
c) TEST III [RHETORIC]. 45(50) minutes.

REFERENCES

1 BECK, R. L. *The Reliability and Validity of a Natural Test of English Composition for High School Seniors and College Freshmen.* Unpublished doctor's thesis, University of Oklahoma, 1932. Pp. 173.
2 BECK, ROLAND L. "A Natural Test of English Usage." *J Exp Ed* 1:280-6 Mr '33.
3 BECK, ROLAND L. "Predicting Success in College English." *Col Engl* 1:541-2 Mr '40.

John M. Stalnaker, Consultant Examiner, College Entrance Examination Board and Associate Professor of Psychology, Princeton University. These tests are designed to measure the ability to use language needed by high school seniors and college students. Three tests are offered: one in mechanics, one in grammar, and one in rhetoric. The tests are timed so that almost all pupils complete them.

The tests are of the recall rather than the more popular recognition type: the pupil does not check one of several given answers but must supply the correct answer himself. Test III, in particular, requires the actual writing of complete sentences by the pupil. It is a hopeful sign to find on the market a test labeled "English" which requires some actual writing. Such tests, of course, are not easily scored when compared with the modern machine-scoring procedures. Because numerous judgments must be made, the authors advise that persons scoring the tests should have a knowledge of English. It is claimed, however, that the entire test can be scored with a high degree of objectivity. If the test does provide a dependable measure of the ability to use language, the increased time required and the increased cost of scoring will be justified. Certain important skills and abilities may never lend themselves to measurement in a short time or to techniques which permit rapid and cheap scoring. It is to be hoped that they will not be sacrificed in favor of less important abilities measured more cheaply.

In general the three tests are too easy and do not give as wide a range of scores as is desirable. A perfect score on the combined three tests is 223 points. The lower quartile for high-school seniors is 143 points and the upper quartile is 175.

The manual describes how the tests have been developed, and discusses the reliability and validity of the tests. Percentile norms are given. A diagnostic record chart is available for each test. The items of the test are classified according to the item of English which is being tested.

Charles Swain Thomas, Associate Professor of Education, Emeritus, Harvard University. The first query that confronts a critic of the *Rinsland-Beck Natural Test of English Usage* is the authors' very peculiar use and position of the word *natural*. No objective test of elaborate design can be a *natural* test; it is, in fact, highly artificial. But the critic soon discovers that *natural* does not in actual meaning here modify *test;* it modifies *English Usage.* That fact immediately suggests another question. What is *natural usage*? The authors give an alternative adjective—*habitual.* Here is their own explanation: "The words supplied by the student probably represent his natural or habitual language usage . . ." Could there not be a revision of the title—a revision that would accurately express the fundamental concept of the test, and at the same time carry out in the placement of adjectives one of the grammatical principles that the authors evidently wish to enforce?

The exercises which the forms provide are, for the most part, excellent. They were constructed for the purpose of correcting the types of errors that by objective experiments have been found to be most common among high-school pupils.

A few items of the test arouse specific queries. In Item 4 of Test II, Division 2, Section a, we have this interrogative sentence: "How many boys (————4————) there at your birthday party yesterday?" The key prints *were* as the correct response. When you read the completed sentence you discover that the deletion of *there* would improve the sentence.

In Test II, Division 2, Section b, we have this sentence: "I will never be able to (——2——) you geometry." When the able students fill in the proper word *teach,* may they not wonder why the authors did not use *I shall* rather than *I will*?

The items which deal with sentence structure have been carefully prepared and should in practice prove helpful in developing greater care and greater skill in placing words and phrases and clauses in positions that will make the meaning unmistakable.

The technical material in the Diagnostic Record Chart is sufficiently involved to suggest this somewhat skeptical query: How many classroom teachers will care to compute the "Cumulative Frequency" and then convert each frequency into a percentile? To "get the reciprocal of the number of cases $(1/N = 1/24 = .0417)$ and multiply by each cumulative frequency" seems a bit menacing to those who still uneasily loiter around the corridors that lead to the secret statistical chambers.

Ed Res B 19:117-8 F 14 '40. J. Wayne Wrightstone. * In techniques these tests are constructed so that the methods or items used are completion questions and controlled essay questions. The completion questions offer the usual difficulties of scoring which include, among other things, variable standards of scoring among teachers and variable interpretations of students' responses. To measure certain aspects of English usage controlled essay questions are used. If essay questions are included in the test, it would seem wise to summarize the guiding principles and findings of Stalnaker and others on how to achieve more reliable reading and grading of responses to such essay questions. The authors of this test do not provide such information or guidance in the manual for test scorers and, in the opinion of the reviewer, have weakened thereby the reliability and validity of certain parts of their test. The publishers claim that the tests are diagnostic, and the authors report that these tests can be used for diagnostic purposes because the total test score has a high coefficient of reliability. An essential condition for reliable diagnosis, however, is that the parts of the test used for diagnosis should meet reliability standards which cannot be inferred or borrowed from the reliability of a total test score. The authors of this test seem to have hold of a valuable idea which needs to be refined and improved, if the tests are to be made sufficiently practical and economical in scoring so that they will be used widely among high schools and colleges.

[1293.1]

Schonell Diagnostic English Tests. Ages 8-14; 1940; 1 form; 6d. per test; 5d. per test, 25 to 49 copies; 53(60) minutes; F. Eleanor Schonell; Edinburgh, Scotland: Oliver & Boyd, Ltd.

REFERENCES
1 SCHONELL, FRED J., AND SCHONELL, F. ELEANOR. *Diagnosis and Remedial Teaching in English.* Edinburgh, Scotland: Oliver & Boyd, Ltd. In press.

LITERATURE

[1294]

Alphabetical List of 1000 Fiction Authors Classified by Subject and Maturity Level. Grades 9-12; 1939; a revision and expansion of Jeanette Howard Foster's basic list of some 250 authors; 10¢ per copy; Irvin C. Poley and B. J. R. Stolper, assisted by Jeanette Foster and Douglas Waples; Chicago, Ill.: Evaluation in the Eight Year Study, Progressive Education Association.

REFERENCES
1 EBERHART, WILFRED. "Evaluating the Leisure Reading of High-School Pupils." *Sch R* 47:257-69 Ap '39.

[1295]

Analytical Scales of Attainment in Literature. Grades 7-8, 9-12; 1933; 1 form, 2 levels; 75¢ per 25; 15¢ per specimen set; nontimed (45) minutes; A. M. Jordan and M. J. Van Wagenen; Minneapolis, Minn.: Educational Test Bureau, Inc.
a) DIVISION 3. Grades 7-8.
b) DIVISION 4. Grades 9-12.

Carleton C. Jones, Department of English, State Teachers College, Indiana, Pa. According to the authors, *Analytical Scales of Attainment in Literature* are "designed to measure the abilities and ranges of information of the pupils." For all practical purposes, however, the scales are merely information tests; and any insinuation that other "abilities" incident to literary attainment are also measured is simply a misrepresentation of the facts. Two separate forms of the tests are available. Division 3 is designed for grades 7 and 8, and Division 4 for grades 9 to 12 inclusive; but the two forms are so nearly alike in content that there seems to be little purpose in their separate publication.

Each form of the scales is composed of four parts of forty items each. The first probes a student's "information about literature"; the second, his "information about authors"; the third, his knowledge of the "content of literature," especially in the matter of "outcomes"; and the fourth, his "general impressions" concerning particular pieces of literature, together with his knowledge of "characters." The analytical or diagnostic intent of these subtests is, of course, highly commendable. But the test items comprising each part are so little differentiated in character from the items comprising all the other parts that the diagnostic purpose of the sectioning is largely negated.

The actual content of the scales is, for the most part, exceedingly conventional; that is, the literary information which the instruments seek to explore is limited almost exclusively to the standard materials of traditional courses in school literature. The 160 items of each form are divided about equally between English and American literature, with a very few devoted to Greek and Roman mythology, to the Bible, and to three or four continental writers long popular with children. The richness of the dozen or more foreign literatures now generally included (in excellent English translations) in the curricula of progressive schools is almost entirely neglected.

Another limitation in sampling is evidenced in the scales' failure adequately to explore the various literary types. Poetry is made to assume an inordinately important place by virtue of the fact that approximately one-half of all the test items are devoted to that one literary type alone. The novel, certainly more important in present-day living than poetry, has items comprising only about one-fourth of the total. The short story, almost equally important with the novel, has items comprising only about one-eighth of the total. The rich fields of biography and the essay have been virtually disregarded, and the drama is represented by only five items, all of which pertain to Shakespeare.

Further weaknesses in sampling are evident also in the number of authors, selections, and literary periods represented. Roughly, only 50 different authors are referred to in the scales—25 English and 25 American. Of these, at least ten are mentioned five times or more; and Longfellow—to point out the most glaring violation of the principle of sampling—alone claims nearly one-eighth of the total items of each form! Moreover, a number of pieces of literature, which at best are of only minor literary significance, are given unusual prominence. For example, in one form alone four items pertain to Pyle's *Men of Iron* and three to Wiggin's *Rebecca of Sunnybrook Farm.* But probably the most damaging fault in sampling is evidenced in the tests' failure to explore modern literature. Only about one-eighth of the items pertain to the modern period (1900 on), and hardly a single item can be said to deal with truly contemporary materials. More than two-thirds of the items are devoted to authors and works dating from 1800 to 1900—which fact, of course, completely obviates the adequate sampling of other important literary periods.

Finally, the scales must be criticized on the grounds that individual test items are frequently in violation, not only of the most elementary principles of item construction, but also of the most obvious facts of literary history. For example, one item reads: "Life on the ocean was written about by (1) Irving, (2) Cooper, (3) Dana, (4) Scott, (5) Dickens"; to which the student is expected to answer "Dana", although both "Cooper" and "Scott" would be equally appropriate answers. Another item reads: "Bret Harte was (1) a short story writer, (2) an English poet, (3) an American poet, (4) an English novelist, (5) a New England novelist." For this item, Response 1 is designated as the only correct response, yet no student of American literature would be satisfied if Response 3 were not also mentioned.

Robert K. Speer, Professor of Education, New York University. These tests comprise one scale of 160 questions for grades 7-8, inclusive, and another similar scale for grades 9-12, inclusive. The scales purport to measure powers related to the following aspects of literature, each aspect being given forty questions: (*a*) information about literature; (*b*) information about authors; (*c*) outcomes; (*d*) general impressions and characters.

Despite the titles of (*c*) and (*d*) above, most of the questions are of an informational character. On the whole, these scales measure power to recall names, titles, and plot-events, with a few questions included on recall of the moods of literary classics.

There is some doubt as to the allotment of items. Thus, in the second part of the scale for grades 7-8, Information About Authors, 15 out of a total of 40 questions deal with only 4 authors: Stevenson, Scott, Poe, and Dickens. The remaining 25 questions are about 22 different authors. No mention is made of some popular classics more often found in the respective grades than certain other classics about which many questions are included.

The scales do cover a wide range of readings, however, and should prove useful for testing the memoriter aspects of learning. It is unfortunate that the authors stopped here and did not develop more questions in the field of appreciations of literary moods, effects, and interpretations.

Analytical Scales of Attainment in Literature

[1296]

Awareness Test of 20th Century Literature. Grades 9-16; 1937; 1 form; $1.50 per 25; sample copies free; 45(50) minutes; edited by Harold H. Bixler; Elmer R. Smith; Atlanta, Ga.: Turner E. Smith & Co.

H. H. Giles, Assistant Professor of Education and Research Associate in the Bureau of Educational Research, The Ohio State University. This test is valuable if only to prove that some educators are interested in contemporary writing and the use made of it by students. It is of the "Ask Me Another" type and fun to take. On the whole the authors have avoided obvious and narrow commitments to a particular line of clichés or a lofty ignorance of popular and not quite respectable literature. For example, they list Zane Grey and Harold Bell Wright as well as Mark Twain and Thomas Wolf. Section III, dealing with characters and backgrounds, exemplifies the fault of any such test made without reference to a particular situation in that it presupposes that all readers will or should, remember the same things as significant in particular books.

The test is designed to take 45 minutes and can be finished easily in 25. It takes 5 to 8 minutes to correct and record one student's work. It does not take into account sufficiently, perhaps, the immense importance of biographical and historical writing in our time. The assumptions back of the test are that the student will be compared to others in his group, and that the norm is not necessarily an acceptable standard of achievement since many factors other than class work enter in. Its chief value is to provide an objective basis for planning future reading in contemporary literature. These assumptions are valid for this test. Better still, one of a comparable nature made by students could be stimulating and useful.

Ann L. Gebhardt, Teacher of English, East High School, Madison, Wisconsin. This test is most comprehensive and approaches the subject of modern literature from several interesting angles. It is the kind of test which a teacher of English in a secondary school hesitates to criticise, because of its very nature and the nature of the ever shifting requirements of high school courses in literature. In order to check the most precocious pupils, the test would have to be revised almost annually, so that it would include current prize books and best sellers. Its apparent usefulness is limited because no three schools could agree upon what to include in their curricula, and only those few juniors and seniors who read everything because that is what they see their parents do could pass it satisfactorily. And even these students who belong definitely to a small cultured group do not often have the incentive to busy themselves with such literature.

All high schools include twentieth century literature in their courses in English, but there is a great variety in the books selected. This is partly due to the fact that tradition still clings to the "classics," which means that more recent books are on free reading lists or are projects for advanced or independent work. New books which have been made into movies would be familiar to a larger number of high school students, but even these would necessarily include only those who live in larger towns where such pictures are shown soon after their release.

There are also a few specific objections to the style of the test. In Part V several statements are misleading. For example: Item 16 states: "Bret Harte suggests that even the dissolute may be unselfish and heroic in . . ." and then lists stories by other writers as well as by Bret Harte. Item 18 states: "Sympathy for the downtrodden appears in Edwin Markham's . . ." and includes also poems of other poets. Item 37 states: "Truer happiness within her own Vermont family circle than what she might find abroad comes to the heroine of Dorothy Canfield Fisher's . . ." and includes books of other writers also.

The technique is confused. The statements are partly true-false, attributing to an author his works and those of other writers; and partly multiple choice, in that one of the quoted books is both by the specified author and characterized by the specific quality named. That might be acceptable, but it is not the technique used throughout, and the inconsistency thus created is necessarily confusing to both teacher and pupil. At least each section should conform to the same scheme if the test is to be of any real value.

In Part VI, Trends, some of the terminology would be confusing to even exceptionally "aware" students; namely, "psychographs" and "Freudian interpretation." Of course some students would understand these terms, but only a very few, and a usable test would scarcely be published for such a limited group.

It would be interesting to see a comprehensive tabulation of the results of these tests. One must not lose sight of the fact, however, that regional requirements must necessarily influence the rankings, and that the average high school English course will not quite fit any general scheme of testing, except one that is too general to be very valuable.

[1297]
Checklist of One Hundred Magazines. Grades 9-12; 1939; 5¢ per copy; Chicago, Ill.: Evaluation in the Eight Year Study, Progressive Education Association.

[1298]
Cooperative Literary Acquaintance Test. Grades 9-16; 1933-40; 40- and 45-minute editions; 25¢ per specimen set; 5¢ per test, 10 to 99 copies; Forms P and Q: Rosa Lee Walston and Edward E. Cureton with the editorial assistance of Henry W. Adams (Form P), Telfair B. Peet (Form P), Constance Churchyard, H. A. Domincovich (Form P), Constance M. McCullough (Form P), Leonard A. Rice, Arthur S. Roberts, Natalie D. Starr (Form P), Russell D. Trebilcox (Form P), Catherine L. Walston (Form P), and K. W. Wright (Form Q); New York: Cooperative Test Service.
a) FORMS 1934, 1935, AND 1936. Form 1933 is out of print; 45(50) minutes.
b) FORMS 1937, O, P, AND Q. 1937-40; 1½¢ per machine-scorable answer sheet; 40(45) minutes.

Lou LaBrant, Professor of English-Education, The Ohio State University. [Review of Form P.] The *Cooperative Literary Acquaintance Test* designed "to fill the need for a comprehensive measure of an individual's acquaintance with the field of literature" expresses all too well our present confusion in teaching literature to secondary school and college students. One hundred and fifty multiple choice questions are offered.

Just what is meant by "acquaintance" is not clear. Frequently (in over 40 of the 150 questions), correct answers could be given without the reading of a word written by the authors in question. Certainly a person may know that Moses was called "The Great Law Giver," and that Scarlett O'Hara is the heroine of *Gone With the Wind* without having read either *Old Testament* or modern novel. These and a few questions dealing with form suggest that "literary acquaintance" may mean acquisition of facts or opinions about literature.

Other questions, however, suggest that the makers of the test may have had in mind pieces chosen because they appeal to adolescent interests, or because they may be matter for close reading by students. As a means for introducing the essay, a number of anthologies have included White's article on the death of his daughter. *Ethan Frome* is a usable novel in high school. Only a few of the questions, however, appear to be offered because they sample material simple enough for independent reading by high school students. On what basis these few could be found reliable samples of the enormous amount of simple, well-written essays and novels, is not clear to this reviewer. Several questions deal with recognition of quotations from pieces presumably studied or memorized. Another considerable group calls for generalizations not warranted by the actual reading of adolescents: that Eugene O'Neill is influenced by psychoanalysis; that Chekhov expresses the tragedy among middle class people of failure to act; that Anatole France "usually" shows gentle irony. The apparent basis for selection here is that the questions deal with writers and selections frequently included in current school anthologies, and with statements made in histories of literature.

With the literature of the world from which to make selection, any sampling must be open to question. The field of this test is so extensive as to include David, Homer, Greek dramatists, Virgil, Boccaccio, Norse mythology, Shakespeare, Tolstoy, Chaucer, Cervantes, and Rousseau, along with such minor moderns as William Allen White, Hugh Walpole, and the creator of Scarlett O'Hara. When this enormous range in time, nationality, type, subject, style, and importance are to be covered by 150 questions, it is difficult to explain the inclusion of more than thirty on English poets (not including Shakespeare), with three for Browning alone. Kipling rates two! A whole precious question is used to ask the meaning of "passing fair."

Lovers of Browning might resent characterizing "Dare, never grudge the throe" as a "typical line," whatever that means, and Maxwell Anderson has himself not emphasized his writing of historical plays. These are minor matters, perhaps.

Taken as a whole the 150 questions illustrate a series of approaches: facts about the great, mere knowledge of names; recognition of popularly taught quotations from English and American verse; superficial facts about the events of certain novels or stories; generalizations about the themes or style of writers, perhaps assumed after reading one piece, perhaps read in a text on literature. That the test is a hodgepodge is no fault of its makers. It probably measures (as indeed its validation

Cooperative Literary Acquaintance Test

shows) the superficiality and almost total lack of direction in our teaching.

Edward S. Noyes, Chairman, Board of Admissions and Associate Professor of English, Yale University. [Review of Form P.] ITS APPARATUS. Materials received for review include: (*a*) a handbook describing the purpose, content, and interpretation of Cooperative achievement tests (1936); (*b*) a booklet of norms (1938); (*c*) a booklet of directions for using the Cooperative tests (1939); (*d*) a single sheet showing scaled score percentiles in each of the four college years of three types of colleges, for all forms 1932-37 of the *Cooperative Literary Acquaintance Test;* (*e*) a similar sheet (revised to May 1937) for three types of secondary schools; (*f*) a key for scoring this test (Form P, but undated); (*g*) a catalog describing Cooperative tests (Nov. 1938); and (*h*) the test itself (Form P, 1939).

There is, in all this apparatus, no indication of the student group for which the test is particularly designed, except a statement on page 14 of the catalog, that it is suitable for both school and college classes. This raises the question: What is the nature of literary acquaintance which can be measured equally well in high school freshmen and college seniors by the same test?

ITS SCOPE. The test consists of 150 items of the "controlled response" variety. Twenty-eight of these items deal with foreign literature, which might be classified as follows: Greek and Roman, 11 items; French, 4; the Bible, 4; Old English, 3 (classified here because probably read in translation); German, 2; Italian, 1; Russian, 1; Scandinavian, 1; Spanish, 1. One hundred and ten items deal with American and English literature classified as shown in Table 1.

TABLE 1

Classification of Test Items Dealing with American and English Literature in the Cooperative Literary Acquaintance Test, Form P

Period	Prose			Drama	Poetry		Total
	Fiction	Essay	Other Prose		Lyric	Other Poetry	
Before Elizabeth..	..	..	..	1	..	2	3
Shakespeare......	..	..	..	8	1	..	9
Other Elizabethans	..	1	..	2	1	1	5
17th Century.....	1	1	1	..	..	3	6
18th Century.....	2	1	1	1	2	2	9
19th Century.....	19	7	1	4	20	13	64
20th Century.....	7	..	2	2	2	1	14
Totals........	29	10	5	18	26	22	110

Twelve items defy classification by either of the two categories used above: e.g., "Albion is the poetic name for 1 Sussex," etc. The classification is based on the correct answers to items, and while probably not exactly accurate, suffices to show the scope of the test. Since 78 items deal with English and American literature since 1800, it is clearly this period with which students are supposed to be acquainted; for other periods and nationalities the items are so few and scattering as to warrant slight confidence in the breadth of literary acquaintance of even a student who scored well in all these items.

The thinness of the test, as regards any real knowledge of any single author, is revealed by an author-analysis of items dealing with English and American writers, disregarding chronology: Addison, 1 item; Maxwell Anderson, 1; Bacon, 1; Bennett, 1; Browning, 3; Bryant, 1; Bunyan, 1; Burns, 1; Byron, 2; Cather, 2; Chaucer, 2; J. F. Cooper, 1; Coleridge, 2; Dunsany, 1; G. Eliot, 1; Emerson, 1; Frost, 1; Goldsmith, 1; Hardy, 1; O. Henry, 1; Housman, 1; Howells, 1; Irving, 1; S. Johnson, 1; Jonson, 1; Keats, 2; Kipling, 2; Lamb, 1; Lanier, 1; S. Lewis, 1; Longfellow, 2; J. R. Lowell, 1; C. Morley, 1; E. Markham, 1; Marlowe, 1; Masefield, 1; Millay, 1; Milton, 3; O'Neill, 1; Poe, 1; Pope, 1; Richardson, 1; E. A. Robinson, 1; Sandburg, 1; Scott, 2; Shaw, 1; Shelley, 2; Sheridan, 1; Spenser, 1; Shakespeare, 9; Tennyson, 3; Twain, 2; H. Walpole, 1; Wells, 1; Wharton, 1; Whitman, 1; Whittier, 1; Wordsworth, 3.

Obviously, some great names, such as Swift, are absent. Equally obvious is the scanty space allotted to all but Shakespeare. The test, therefore, can scarcely give a valuable answer to the question "What does this student know about this author?" just as it cannot, in its present form, completely test the student's acquaintance with any period prior to the nineteenth century. It would probably be unfair to argue, from this analysis, that the test-makers consider it as important that a student be acquainted with Bennett as with Bacon, with Cather as with Chaucer, with O. Henry as with Johnson, or with Kipling as with Keats. They would rightly object that this test is not a measure of *knowledge*, but of "acquaintance." We return, then, to the question raised in the first paragraph. What does "acquaintance" mean?

Analysis of the content of the items would seem to show that it means strictly a "bowing acquaintance"—except, perhaps, for the dozen or so items which are of the "spot passage variety." Several items (10, 18, 25, etc.) could be answered correctly by a student who had looked through digests or tables of contents without reading the actual works. Others (2, 36, 102, 106, 148) could be answered from information obtained through the movies or movie magazines. Still others depend upon information of a fairly trivial kind. Item 88 asks the student which of five American authors listed is frequently called "The Laureate of the Common Heart." Who cares?

Another type of item, while requiring some information about the author or book mentioned, is more dangerous than those just mentioned because it implies that only one of several answers can be "correct." Consider Item 62. "Samuel Johnson's popular reputation rests largely on his 1 dictionary 2 club 3 literary dictatorship 4 eccentricities 5 kindness to young authors." The key gives 4 as the correct answer; an extremely good defense could be made for any one of the other four possibilities. A still better answer would be: 6 Boswell. Response 4 cannot be the *only* "correct" answer unless the test-makers have conducted a poll of all the people in the world who have any knowledge of Samuel Johnson. Among other items presenting roughly similar difficulties are 9, 17, 23, 59, 63, 82, 96, 100, 140.

CONCLUSIONS. If the test is taken for what it is—an index of ingenuity as much as of an acquaintance, generally superficial, with some authors and books—it should provide interesting though hardly significant information about a student or a class. If it begins to influence what literature is taught and how it is taught, the test is a potential menace. It will tend to inculcate such notions as: (*a*) that there is one and only one correct answer to any question about literature; (*b*) that the trivial and the essential are of equal importance; (*c*) that the whole work of an author can be summed up in a neat little phrase (of dubious correctness sometimes, as when Item 100 declares that "A British poet whose cynicism and pessimism are expressed in exquisite, haunting verse is A. E. Housman . . ."); (*d*) that it is much simpler and more profitable to read digests than to wade through original works of art. Since tests, once widely used, almost inevitably influence teaching, one hopes that English teachers will use this one with circumspection. Such a caution, indeed, is given by the authors of the handbook (page 7), who urge that "no test . . . can be taken as a safe guide to what specific materials should be taught in the subject tested." In spite of such warnings, the history of tests and teaching shows a constant influence of one on the other, as Louis C. Zahner clearly emphasized in his address on "The Testing and Teaching of Meaning" at the Eighth Educational Conference in New York, October 26th. The test will influence, if not the materials, at least the way in which they are presented. The able group of editorial assistants listed on the cover of Form P should consider this problem with care before a new form is issued. There are many skillfully constructed items in the present form. Item 81, for instance, requires a fairly sound knowledge of *Julius Caesar*; Item 73, again, hits at the core of the story of the "Purloined Letter"; Item 99 has four red·herrings most ingeniously but not unfairly dragged across the trail. With a scope frankly limited to a given period of literature, and with a larger number of items, answers to which can be given correctly only after a reading of the books involved, the test could be made to show something more significant about a student's acquaintance with literature than it seems to show at present.

For reviews by Carleton C. Jones and John H. Thompson, see 970.

[1299]

Cooperative Literary Comprehension Test. Grades 9-16; 1935-40; 40- and 45-minute editions; 25¢ per specimen set; 5¢ per test, 10 to 99 copies; Form Q: M. F. Carpenter and E. F. Lindquist; New York: Cooperative Test Service.
a) FORM 1936. Forms 1935 and 1937 are out of print; 45(50) minutes.
b) FORMS O, P, AND Q. 1½¢ per machine-scorable answer sheet; 40(45) minutes.

REFERENCES

1 FLANAGAN, JOHN C. "A New Type of Reading Test for Secondary-School and College Students Which Provides Separate Scores for Speed of Comprehension and Level of Comprehension," pp. 195-9. In *Practical Values of Educational Research*. National Education Association, American Educational Research Association, Official Report of 1938 Meeting, Atlantic City, N. J., February 26–March 2, 1938. Washington, D. C.: the Association, May 1938. Pp. 216. $1.50. Paper.
2 TRAXLER, ARTHUR E. "The Relation between Speed and Level of Literary Comprehension," pp. 51-56. In *1938 Achievement Testing Program in Independent Schools*. Educational Records Bureau, Educational Records Bulletin No. 24. New York: the Bureau, June 1938. Pp. xi, 59, 14. $1.50. Paper, lithotyped.
3 FLANAGAN, J. C. "A Study of the Effect on Comprehension of Varying Speeds of Reading," pp. 47-50. In *Research on the Foundations of American Education*. National Education Association, American Educational Research Association, Offi-

cial Report of the 1939 Meeting, Cleveland, Ohio, February 25–March 1, 1939. Washington, D. C.: the Association, 1939. Pp. 215. $1.50. Paper.

Lou LaBrant, Professor of English-Education, The Ohio State University. [Review of Form P.] This test is designed to go beyond the usual rate-comprehension test and examine the student's ability to recognize and understand literary devices and patterns. The writers have considerable success in presenting questions which discover whether the reader comprehends the figures of speech, tone, implied relations, and similar characteristics of the piece. There is some doubt, however, as to whether the seventy-one questions on twelve brief quotations meet the rather large ends stated in the Handbook.

The selections are brief and not especially subtle: they are simple and somewhat factual in style. No opportunity is given for testing whether the reader notes contradictions or basic assumptions. Indeed, the test itself seems to imply that literary comprehension involves merely discovering what the writer wants the reader to discover. This is undoubtedly one essential in comprehension. The test should be used, however, with full knowledge of its limitation. Limited also to excerpts of a single paragraph each, it is open to the criticism common to most reading tests, that interest in isolated bits is so slight as to weaken the performance of many students.

For the most part the test assumes that the whole is equal to the sum of the detailed parts of a paragraph, an assumption scarcely acceptable for a well-organized unit of writing. As a measure, however, of the student's ability to comprehend literary details the test is helpful for both examining and teaching.

Edward A. Tenney, Associate Professor of English, Cornell University. [Review of Form P.] This test should go far toward setting a standard of literacy for students of literature. The disrepute into which the teaching of English has fallen may be removed if tests like this one are used to judge the quality of both the teacher and the student. For if the student has not been taught to read closely and to interpret precisely, he will fare ill on this examination. The break-up of the old course of reading has often left the teacher with nothing solid to tie to and has often opened the way to vague, desultory, general classroom discussions of "social" questions wherein the mind is more likely to be titillated than trained. This test shows up both the dull student and the glib but untrained student, and it is therefore to be commended.

Its most important aspect is that it is designed to measure both "speed" of comprehension and "level" of comprehension. A study of the test reveals that there is scant relation between these two aspects of reading.[1] In other words, this means that in testing what is sometimes called "reading ability" or "power to interpret the written word" the timed test is not especially useful or especially important. Since the power to understand literature and to interpret it is what we teachers of English strive to develop and since the speed at which a student understands is of secondary or tertiary importance, this test is to be welcomed; for it enables the teacher of English to escape from the whole system of timed tests, and it also enables the slow but clear-thinking and well-trained student to meet his more agile fellow student in a situation where mere speed is of no particular advantage.

For reviews by Charles Swain Thomas and John H. Thompson, see 971.

[1300]
Davis-Roahen-Schrammel American Literature Test. High school and college; 1938; 2 forms; 50¢ per 25; 15¢ per specimen set; 60(65) minutes; V. A. Davis, R. L. Roahen, and H. E. Schrammel; Emporia, Kan.: Bureau of Educational Measurements, Kansas State Teachers College.

Paul B. Diederich, Assistant Professor of Education, The University of Chicago. The test consists of 20 titles to match with authors, 16 multiple-choice questions revealing acquaintance with 14 titles, 24 multiple-choice questions most of which reveal acquaintance with authors, 25 quotations to match with authors and titles, 20 brief statements of the central thought of literary works to match with titles, and 20 characters to match with titles. The test requires 60 minutes, is appropriate for grades nine through college, presumably after at least a year's study of American literature, and yields only a single score. Each item in the test is given one point credit. Norms are based on 641 scores reported by cooperating schools in the Every Pupil Testing Program for April, 1938. There are two comparable forms of the test.

To set such a test loose upon a state, and to set teachers to work preparing for it, would be the equivalent of a Kansas dust storm to literary appreciation. I grew up in Kansas, where this test hails from, and I still visit there occasionally. It seems to me to be as far from civilization as the North Pole. Maybe these famous Emporia tests have something to do with it, either as cause or effect. The authors are probably not to blame, for they have done a competent job with their unsavory assignment, but this test and all that it stands for does not represent, in my opinion, a promising direction of the human spirit.

Violet Hughes, Department of English, East High School, Madison, Wisconsin. As a comprehensive "achievement test for high school and college classes in the general field of American Literature," this test falls short of its purpose.

The range of selections and authors upon whom the test is based is too limited. While Captain John Smith, Governor Bradford, Jonathan Edwards, Increase Mather, Joel Barlow, Charles B. Brown, Anne Bradstreet, Michael Wigglesworth, "Boy Psalm Book," "New England Primer," Margaret Fuller, George Ripley are all included, many important authors and selections of the later nineteenth and of the twentieth century are not included. Such writers as Sinclair Lewis, Pearl Buck, Willa Cather, Ole Rolvaag, Edna Ferber, Edna St. Vincent Millay, Sara Teasdale, Helen Keller, Jane Addams are among those omitted. Missing also are questions on orators from Patrick Henry down to the present time, on many of our important patriotic songs and poems, and on drama except for *Emperor Jones* and *Clarence.*

On the other hand, undue emphasis has been placed upon the history of American literature during the Colonial and the early National periods, upon the beginnings of American literature, upon selections of junior high level, and often upon selections of relatively little importance, as *Elsie Venner* and *Blithedale Romance.* Moreover, such selections as "Barbara Frietchie," "Skipper Ireson's Ride," "Rip Van Winkle," "Legend of Sleepy Hollow," "Paul Revere's Ride," "Courtship of Miles Standish" are considered so important that two and often three or more questions are based upon them.

In some instances in Part IV, the statement of the "central thought" of a literary selection is misleading since it is the central thought of an excerpt rather than of the entire selection, as in Item 114: "Imitating the style of a good writer is a great aid to learning good English."—*Autobiography*.

The 150 questions of each form of the are of the following types: Part I, 20 questions matching a selection with its author, Part II, 40 completion questions with multiple choice; Part III, 50 questions matching quotations with source and author; Part IV, 20 questions matching central theme with selection; Part V, 20 questions matching characters with selections in which they appear.

A more helpful test for use in high schools today would include more contemporary material and questions checking the student's progress in appreciation rather than just his memory.

[1301]

English Tests for Outside Reading. Grades 9-10, 11-12; 1939; 1 form, 100 tests; $2.50 per 100; 15¢ per key for any one set; $1 per specimen set of any one set; $3.75 per complete specimen set; nontimed; Henrietta Silliman; Toulon, Ill.: the Author.
a) SET NO. 1. Grades 9-10.

Bob, Son of Battle.
Call of the Wild.
Captains Courageous.
The Casting Away of Mrs. Lechs and Mrs. Aleshine.
Daddy Long-Legs.
Florence Nightingale.
Huckleberry Finn.
Lad: A Dog.
The Lance of Kanana.
Last of the Mohicans.
The Little Shepherd of Kingdom Come.
Little Women.
Man Without a Country.
Oliver Twist.
Penrod.
Rebecca of Sunnybrook Farm.
The Secret Garden.
Seventeen.
The Three Musketeers.
Tom Brown's School Days.
Tom Sawyer.
Treasure Island.
Two Years Before the Mast.
Understood Betsy.
Wild Animals I Have Known.
b) SET NO. 2. Grades 9-10.
Adventures of Sherlock Holmes.
Aeneid.
The Amateur Gentleman.
Anne of Green Gables.
Arabian Nights.
Ben Hur.
Gulliver's Travels.
High Benton.
Hoosier School Boy.
In Brightest Africa.
Ivanhoe.
Martin Hyde, The Duke's Messenger.
Master Skylark.
Miss Lulu Bett.

The Promised Land.
Robin Hood.
Rudder Grange.
The Story of My Boyhood and Youth.
The Story of My Life—Helen Keller.
Tanglewood Tales.
Under the Big Top.
Up From Slavery.
The Virginian.
White Fang.
Wild Life in the Rockies.
c) SET NO. 3. Grades 11-12.
Abraham Lincoln.
The Alhambra.
Alice Freemen Palmer.
The Americanization of Edward W. Bok.
The Beloved Vagabond.
The Crises.
David Copperfield.
Franklin's Autobiography.
Giants of the Earth.
The Harbor.
House of Seven Gables.
Jane Eyre.
The Light That Failed.
The Little Minister.
Lorna Doone.
Man Who Married a Dumb Wife.
Maria Chapdelaine.
Mill on the Floss.
Monsieur Beaucaire.
My Antonia.
Ramona.
Representative Plays.
So Big.
The Soul of Ann Rutledge.
We—Charles Lindbergh.
d) SET NO. 4. Grades 11-12.
Adam Bede.
Adventures in Friendship.
Alice Adams.
The Bent Twig.
Covered Wagon.
David Harum.
Drums.
Gray Dawn.
The Greene Murder Case.
The Green Mirror.
Kidnapped.
Kim.
Main Street.
A Man for the Ages.
Moby Dick.
My Home in the Field of Honor.
Oregon Trail.
Pride and Prejudice.
Royal Road to Romance.
Scaramouche.
Show Boat.
Tess of D'Urbervilles.
Twelve Tests of Character.
Twenty Years at Hull House.
Woman in White.

[1302]

Literature Questionnaire: The Drama: Test 3.21. Grades 9-12; 1937; an experimental form; 5¢ per copy; 1¢ per machine-scorable answer sheet; Chicago, Ill.: Evaluation in the Eight Year Study, Progressive Education Association.

REFERENCES

1 *A Descriptive Summary of Evaluation Instruments in the Field of English*. Chicago, Ill.: Evaluation in the Eight Year Study, Progressive Education Association, March 1939. Pp. 10. Paper, mimeographed. Out of print.

[1303]
Literature Questionnaire: The Novel: Test 3.2a.
Grades 9-12; 1937; an experimental form; 5¢ per
copy; 1¢ per machine-scorable answer sheet; Chicago, Ill.: Evaluation in the Eight Year Study, Progressive Education Association.

REFERENCES

1 *A Descriptive Summary of Evaluation Instruments in the
Field of English.* Chicago, Ill.: Evaluation in the Eight Year
Study, Progressive Education Association, March 1939. Pp. 10.
Paper, mimeographed. Out of print.

[1304]
Literature Test: National Achievement Test. Grades
7-12; 1937; 2 forms; $2.00 per 25; 5¢ per specimen
set; nontimed (40-60) minutes; Robert K. Speer and
Samuel Smith; Rockville Centre, N. Y.: Acorn Publishing Co.

*H. H. Giles, Assistant Professor of Educa-
tion and Research Associate in the Bureau of
Educational Research, The Ohio State University.* The authors state that this test is relevant to the appreciation of literary effects,
qualities, moods, and the knowledge of facts.
It is extremely difficult to attempt any such
testing because in the first place there are so
many kinds of literary effects, qualities, moods,
and facts, and in the second place, a standard
test implies that the selection that must be
made is valid for all kinds of students and
teachers in all kinds of situations. To put it
bluntly, no standard test can possibly take into
account purposes and values determined by a
particular teacher and a particular group of
pupils, this with the single exception of such
tests as have no "right answers" and depend
on interpretation and further use by those who
take them rather than on scoring by any absolute method.

There is some value, which varies according to the situation, in learning how to read
and interpret the meaning and intention of an
author. Part I of the test presumes to prove
this ability. It does not raise the question of
the value of the selections given for pupil purposes. Part II deals with such qualities as
choice of words, convincingness, exaggeration,
authorship, and force. Again it is difficult to
see how any of these qualities matter except
in relationship to a purpose, more 'important
than the general purpose of getting a good
mark on a test. It is not at all sure that correct
answers in any of these cases would be a real
measure of the ability of students to analyze
effects and qualities in general. The selections
in Part III on moods, like those in the foregoing, are not chosen from literature written
in the last ten years. Part IV is certainly mis-

cellaneous and the variety is good, but it might
strike the high school student as incomplete and
irrelevant even though he might know all the
scattered facts asked for.

Such a test as this is difficult to make and
the criticisms given above are all related to one
major criticism, the omission of pupil purpose
from the assumptions back of the test. If this
omission is not important, the test is excellent
of its kind. It does require careful comparative
thinking.

*Robert C. Pooley, Associate Professor in
the Teaching of English, The University of
Wisconsin.* Any test which ventures to measure the results of literature instruction in terms
of aptitudes and appreciations rather than in
terms of facts is worthy of respectful notice.
This test consists of four parts, three of which
are nonspecific, testing the recognition of "Effects," "Qualities," and "Moods." Part IV is
called Miscellaneous Facts, and can be dis-
missed briefly. This part contains 30 items,
drawn from the whole range of English and
American literature, with side references to
French and Russian literatures. That Amy
Lowell wrote free verse, and that Jane Eyre
married Mr. Rochester are, in the eyes of the
authors, two of the 30 most important facts in
the literature of the world. Others might disagree. Had the section been labeled *Miscellaneous and Irrelevant Facts,* it would be more
accurate.

Parts I, II, and III are interesting and ingenious. They endeavor, through the comparison of short paragraphs or stanzas from
poetry, to test the pupils' sensitivity to various
aspects of mood, suggestiveness of words, degrees of humor and pathos, and consistency of
style. But while the authors must be commended for an original approach, the test is a
long cry from being a valid instrument in the
appreciation of literature. For one thing, it
touches lightly only a few of the hundred or
more recognitions and sensitivities which make
up that complex thing called appreciation. In
the second place, the exercises on the few
recognitions offered are too scanty to be really
valid. No one attempts to measure skill in
arithmetic by means of two or three problems.
Finally, the exercises are spotty in quality,
ranging from excellent to mildly absurd. For
example, the child is asked to state the effect
of the words "shall not perish from the earth"

by selecting one of these three choices; (*a*) "a dramatic tragedy," (*b*) "a defense of democratic ideals," and (*c*) "the need of a new government." The words as given suggest only one thing—*perpetuity*, which is not given in the answers. In Part II, Recognizing Qualities, the issue is confused by including some factual information worded, "paragraph IV might have been written by Daniel Defoe," etc., which is not pertinent to the test.

On the whole, this test can be given only a limited recommendation. It is definitely better than the pure fact test, and it will measure vaguely some of the elements of appreciation. But hopeful teachers will have to look further for the test of genuine, nonspecific literary appreciation.

[1305]

Questionnaire on Voluntary Reading: Test 3.31. Grades 10-12; 1939; 1 form; revision of Test 3.3; 5¢ per questionnaire; 1¢ per machine-scorable answer sheet; $1.50 per set of stencils for machine scoring; nontimed (40) minutes; Chicago, Ill.: Evaluation in the Eight Year Study, Progressive Education Association.

REFERENCES

A Descriptive Summary of Evaluation Instruments in the Field of English. Chicago, Ill.: Evaluation in the Eight Year Study, Progressive Education Association, March 1939. Pp. 10. Paper, mimeographed. Out of print.

[1306]

Stanford Test of Comprehension of Literature. Grades 7-12; 1929; 2 forms, 3 parts; 75¢ per 25 parts; 20(25) minutes per part; Mary C. Burch; Stanford University, Calif.: Stanford University Press.
a) TEST I, NARRATION AND DESCRIPTION.
b) TEST II, CHARACTER AND EMOTION.
c) TEST III, EXPOSITION.

REFERENCES

1 BURCH, M. C. *Determination of a Content of the Course in Literature of a Suitable Difficulty for Junior and Senior High School Students.* Genetic Psychology Monographs, Vol. 4, Nos. 2-3. Worcester, Mass.: Clark University Press, 1928. Pp. 163-332. $3.00. Paper.

J. Wayne Wrightstone, Assistant Director, Bureau of Reference, Research, and Statistics, Public Schools, New York, New York. The *Stanford Tests of Comprehension of Literature* are made up of ten to twelve short samples for each form. These samples are taken from books frequently recommended for use in secondary schools. According to the author, each test is designed to measure the accuracy with which certain types of literature are read. Test I contains samples from types of literature whose main interest is action and event: the adventure story, the novel of incident, the epic, and narrative and descriptive prose and poetry. Test II contains samples from types whose main interest is character

portrayal and emotional appeal such as the character sketch, the novel of emotion, lyric poetry, and the drama. Test III contains samples from types whose main appeal is to the intellect such as the essay and the oration. The functions of the tests, says the author, are to classify students of each grade into ability groups for purposes of instructions in literature, to measure growth in reading ability of an individual or group over a period of time, and to indicate what books are suitable reading materials (so far as difficulty is concerned) for a particular individual or group.

The reviewer has five criticisms of these tests as they relate to the functions claimed by the author and publisher. In the first place, the test does not measure reading comprehension of literature, but only two or three aspects of such reading comprehension. Reading comprehension is not a simple unitary process but rather a complex psychological process, involving multiple abilities of pupils. It is the opinion of the reviewer that the only kinds of reading comprehension ability measured by these tests are the ability to locate specific facts and the ability to identify general ideas in the paragraphs. Moreover, the items for such abilities are not arranged in the tests so that they can be scored and used for diagnostic purposes.

The second criticism is that the test exercises, which are paragraphs followed by questions, are not necessarily representative of the books. A primary assumption of the author is that the ability to identify the ideas in one paragraph represents the ability to comprehend the ideas and relationships of a book. This is not necessarily true and the author presents no evidence to support the assumption.

A third criticism is that the three different tests do not measure intrinsically different kinds of comprehension. The author has divided the literary selections into three arbitrary categories and has assumed that the series' three tests measure three different phases of literature comprehension. She presents no evidence to support this assumption.

The fourth criticism is that the information as to norms, validity, and reliability is entirely inadequate.

The fifth criticism is that the scores on these tests do not necessarily indicate what books children should read—a function claimed for the tests. The problem of choosing books that are suitable and interesting to boys and girls is far more complex than interpreting a score on a comprehension of literature test.

As survey tests on comprehension of paragraphs from such "classic" literature as Scott's novels, Burns' lyrics, and Emerson's essays, this series of three tests has limited values. For the modern high school curriculum and objectives of instruction in literature, this series of tests needs far-reaching reconstruction.

[1307]

Tests for the Appreciation of Literature. Grades 9-16; 1926; 1 form, 6 parts; 10¢ per set of six parts; 15¢ per specimen set; nontimed (60-100) minutes; Hannah Logasa and Martha McCoy Wright; Bloomington, Ill.: Public School Publishing Co.
a) TEST 1, DISCOVERY OF THEME.
b) TEST 2, READER PARTICIPATION.
c) TEST 3, REACTION TO SENSORY IMAGES.
d) TEST 4, COMPARISONS.
e) TEST 5, TRITE AND FRESH EXPRESSIONS.
f) TEST 6, RHYTHM.

Ann L. Gebhardt, Teacher of English, East High School, Madison, Wisconsin. One of the outstanding features of this test is its definiteness and objectivity. The average high school student has not been very enthusiastic about reading poetry, because he feels that 'here is something vague about it, so that he never knows whether he understands what it is attempting. When he takes this test he probably is not even aware of the logical, thorough way in which he is being examined, but he cannot help realizing that he is being checked on his comprehension of specific things. The test items progress from an apparently simple one, from which the teacher can at once determine whether the student can understand only an idea that is baldly stated, or whether he can grasp an idea that is imaginatively stated, through a series of increasingly difficult problems that determine where his appreciation of poetry ends.

Test 2 is perhaps a better index of the kind of teaching that preceded it than of the student's actual comprehension. Not all students can grasp the differences between the emotions the poet is attempting to arouse in the reader himself and those of the person he is writing about.

The sensory images, which are examined in Test 3, are a little harder to recognize than the simpler emotions tested in Test 2, but the transition is made logically. The references to *muscle* in Items 4 and 6 are confusing; they employ a mixed technique, demanding first recognition of personification, a figure of speech, for which there has been no adequate preparation or warning, and then discrimination between the sensory appeals of the thing personified.

Perhaps this criticism of Test 4 is a little severe, but one feels that it demands a niceness in distinction that is rather mature and sophisticated, and is often quite lost to the imaginative student who is swept away by the sensory or emotional appeal of the verse picture and forgets to be critical of it. Physical enjoyment that is so vivid, although it may never lead to keen critical perception, is nevertheless a definite achievement too seldom realized in the teaching of poetry. Too many high school students lack the capability for much more than that. Perhaps it is mere chance, but the least obvious examples of far fetched or mixed comparison are those set to the more vigorous rhythms in this group.

Although Test 5 demands those critical qualities which are not difficult to develop in a student whose standards of effectiveness are predetermined by what he hears most frequently, the problems are so definite and obvious that even the least "aware" student can pick out some examples of the things no true poet would say. Composition training and radio work should make this test easier to do than Test 4.

Test 6 is the one that unquestionably would be too difficult for the pupil who has had no training in choral reading or music. And even some of the most sensitively "aware" would have trouble in matching the patterns depicted here. In spite of this the test is a great improvement upon most tests of this nature.

Definite and objective as this set of six tests is, it would almost appear that the value of the entire group could not be defined until results from a great many student papers could be tabulated and interpreted. It is to the great credit of the compilers that its terminology and range are not confined to the classical tradition which has frightened off so many adventurers in the realm of poetry.

SPEECH

[1308]

Bryan-Wilke Scale for Rating Public Speeches. Speech audiences; 1939; 40¢ per 25; 10¢ per specimen set; nontimed (5-10) minutes; Alice I. Bryan and Walter H. Wilke; New York: Psychological Corporation.

SPELLING

[1309]

Australian Council for Educational Research Spelling Test. Ages 8-14; 1936; 6 forms; 9*d.* per booklet of tests; Victoria, Australia: Australian Council for Educational Research.

REFERENCES

1 QUANCE, F. M. *The Canadian Spellers.* Toronto, Canada: W. J. Gage and Co., 1936.

David H. Russell, Assistant Professor of Education, The University of Saskatchewan. The words of these tests are in six lists, said to be of equal difficulty for Australian children. The fifty words of increasing difficulty in each list are accompanied by illustrative sentences which contain the individual words to be written by the pupils. This is a usual form of spelling test and should be suitable for "primary school" children of from eight to fourteen years. The lists, with their accompanying sentences, are contained in a 35-page manual whose content varies from very elementary directions to teachers (such as not using the lists for teaching lists) to instructions for elaborate statistical manipulation difficult for the average teacher to perform. The manual, however, seems to accomplish its purpose of providing "reliable norms of attainment in spelling for Australian children."

The manual states clearly the methods used to obtain lists of typical useful words. It is an interesting question whether or not the system of borrowing from several United States lists and submitting these to the subjective criticism of a number of headmasters will ensure a completely valid test for Australia. It would seem that the Australian Council might undertake a word frequency count for their own country. When this was done by Quance [1] in Canada, for example, a few interesting differences were found in Canadian and American usage and such differences might also occur in Australia.

The reliability of the tests was determined by having children work two lists on successive mornings. It is expressed in terms of the probable error of a score on one list, or on the average of two lists, and not in terms of the more usual reliability coefficients.

The directions for the administration of the tests and the norms both allow the giving of "bands" or partial lists at different times of year. The norms have been worked out elaborately as age norms, percentiles, "age-in-grade" norms, and grade norms for February, May, August, and November, and are given separately for each state. All this, with norms given for "bands" at the beginning and end of the year, provides a system which seems needlessly complex for the ordinary teacher. In addition, the manual suggests corrections for the ages and also the sex of pupils for any class unusual in these respects. These may be of limited value in comparing whole classes but would seem to be of little use in understanding the difficulties of individual pupils. While the stated purpose of the manual is to "provide reliable norms of attainment in spelling" the manual seems to contain an undue emphasis on general results and an unjustified worship of norms. When this manual is placed in the hands of a teacher, it should be accompanied by one discussing the diagnosis and treatment of individual difficulties in spelling. The system of taking seven tenths of a word from a girl's score or adding seven tenths of a word to a boy's score when comparing them with the percentile tables, as suggested in the manual, or the use of norms for comparing classes, is hardly the crux of the spelling problem in elementary schools.

[1310]

Buffalo Spelling Scale. Grades 2-8; 1938; 2 forms; 15¢ per specimen set; no materials needed for pupils; (15) minutes; Allan J. Williams; Bloomington, Ill.: Public School Publishing Co.

John C. Almack, Professor of Education, Stanford University. The words in this scaled test were taken from the *Buckingham Extension of the Ayres Spelling Scale.* The grade norms are based upon results from five thousand pupils to the grade. There is no fixed time limit.

The words are presented in sentences. Since one aim is to include several test words in each sentence so as to reduce the time required for the test, a difficult problem arises. Some of the sentences do not make clear the meaning of the words, and may indeed border on the absurd, as

> *Come sit back here.*
> *Mother, send that cold child home.*
> *However, tonight father* will *change* his *store.*
> *Endeavor* to *eliminate judgment* in marking examinations.

Some half of the hundred words in each form are comprised in the interval which is expected to be covered by the second grade.

Thereafter, the word list in each grade interval is very brief: about ten words. This is a close sampling, and a longer step would give greater accuracy and refinement in the test.

The reviewer agrees that there are advantages in presenting the test words in sentences. To serve their purposes, they must be good sentences. Usually these sentences may be improved by using only one test word to each. If one does this, he then increases the amount of time the test demands for giving. It may be that some other answer can be found to this problem; it may be best to use one word to a sentence, read the whole sentence, and require the pupil to write the test word only. Or perhaps, the entire sentence may be printed, with a blank left for the test word, which is pronounced and written in the blank or in a column with other words at one side of the paper.

This test compares favorably with others of its kind. It is convenient to give and score. Its norms seem well founded.

M. E. Broom, Assistant Superintendent of Schools, El Paso, Texas. Each of the two forms includes 100 words selected from the *Buckingham Extension of the Ayres Spelling Scale.* The 100 words are included in 24 sentences in Form A and in 21 sentences in Form B. These sentences are to be read in their entirety, and then by parts thereafter, while the pupils write the sentences. The test is not timed, but the examiner is instructed to urge slow pupils to write more quickly, if they are holding back the rest of the class.

Research has shown the sentence dictation form of spelling test to be almost as valid as the dictated list of spelling words. This test has the advantage of having very few words which are not scored for correctness, with the majority of such words very easily spelled, as *on, with,* and *will.* Form B has more difficult unscored words than Form A.

Evidence is lacking in the manual as to the equivalence of the two forms, and as to the validity and reliability of the instrument. Grade placement norms are available, but the number of cases on which they were established is not stated. The test author merely says concerning these matters: "Care was taken to have the two forms of the scale balanced by an equal number of words from each column of the Buckingham-Ayres Scale. The scale was standardized by giving it to approximately five thousand pupils in each grade."

For a review by Henry D. Rinsland, see 1158.

[1311]
Davis-Schrammel Spelling Test. Grades 1-9; 1935-36; 4 forms; 15¢ per specimen set; no materials needed for pupils; (15) minutes; Vera Davis and H. E. Schrammel; Emporia, Kan.: Bureau of Educational Measurements, Kansas State Teachers College.

REFERENCES
1 Horn, Ernest. *A Basic Writing Vocabulary*: 10,000 Words Most Commonly Used in Writing. State University of Iowa, Monographs in Education, Series 1, No. 4. Iowa City, Iowa: the University, 1926. Pp. 225. Cloth, $2.25; paper, $1.75.

Walter W. Cook, Associate Professor of Education, The University of Minnesota. The words of this survey test of general spelling ability were selected from the *Buckingham Extension of the Ayres Spelling Scale.* Each of the four forms contains 96 words arranged in grade tests with enough overlapping to provide 20 words appropriate for each grade. The mean accuracy of each grade list on the original scale is 72 per cent. Percentile norms for midyear and end-of-year testing are furnished for each grade. Reliability coefficients reported for each grade list range from .84 to .93 with a mean of .87. The average probable error of measurement is reported as 1.1 words.

There is no excuse for building a spelling test in 1935 based on a pioneer scale developed in 1918. The list might at least have been checked against the most commonly used words in writing as determined by Ernest Horn in the Commonwealth Investigation.[1]

The difficulty of the words used in the test is also questionable. Although Ayres recommended that words with an average of 84 per cent correct spellings be used, and in the Springfield, and Cleveland Surveys used words of 70, and 73 per cent accuracy respectively, recent investigations are unanimous in recommending words of 50 per cent accuracy for classification purposes.

In schools using modern spelling lists and modern methods of teaching, it is difficult to conceive of any vital purpose being served by this test.

Joseph C. Dewey, Head of the Department of Education and Psychology, Westminster College. This series of spelling tests, with its four forms and its simple, easy-to-understand manual, appears to be a rather useful instrument for use in testing spelling achievement in grades one to nine. The authors state in the manual that there are four equivalent forms but submit no evidence that the four forms are actually equivalent. This leads one to the suspicion that either the forms are not actually equivalent or that the authors have been negligent in submitting evidence to support their claim.

The reliability coefficients, as given by the authors in the manual, ranging from .84 to .93 with an average of .87 seem reasonably high although the number of cases used in determining reliabilities was only 1506 with little geographical distribution, all the cases being in Kansas.

The manual is well written, easy to understand and to use. Percentile norms are provided for midyear testing as well as for end-of-year testing which is an excellent feature and enables one to use the tests at the middle of the year as well as at the end. This feature together with the four forms provided makes these tests a rather flexible and useful instrument in a variety of circumstances.

These tests provide administrators and teachers with an instrument that is easy to administer, easy to score, and to interpret. However, before choosing this test for use in any school system one must be sure that the tests are valid in terms of the word list taught by the particular school system concerned. If this is not done it may be that the tests will give a very distorted view of the effectiveness of spelling instruction in the school system.

[1312]

High School Spelling Test. Grades 7-12; 1929; 4 forms; 25¢ per specimen set; no materials needed for pupils; Harold H. Bixler; Atlanta, Ga.: Turner E. Smith & Company.

REFERENCES

1 HORN, ERNEST. *A Basic Writing Vocabulary*: 10,000 Words Most Commonly Used in Writing. State University of Iowa, Monographs in Education, Series 1, No. 4. Iowa City, Iowa: the University, 1926. Pp. 225. Cloth, $2.25; paper, $1.75.
2 SIMMONS, ERNEST P., AND BIXLER, HAROLD HENCH. *The Standard High School Spelling Scale*, Revised edition. Atlanta, Ga.: Turner E. Smith & Co., 1935. Pp. 63. $0.48. Paper.

Walter W. Cook, Associate Professor of Education, The University of Minnesota. This test is designed to measure general spelling ability at the junior and senior high school levels in order to determine which pupils may be excused from spelling classes. January norms (medians only) are furnished for grades 7, 8, 9, and 12. An exemption score of 80 is recommended.

Davis-Schrammel Spelling Test

Each of the four equivalent forms consists of 100 words selected from the *Standard High School Spelling Scale*.[2] This scale consists of the 2560 words most frequently misspelled by high school pupils selected from the 5000 most commonly used words as determined by the Commonwealth Investigation.[1]

A reliability coefficient of .93 was secured by administering Forms I and II to 132 eighth-grade pupils on successive days.

The word-used-in-sentence list dictation is employed. This technique requires that the administrator pronounce a word, read a sentence containing the word, and pronounce the word again. One test form in the hands of the administrator is required.

The test could probably be improved by selecting those words from the *Standard High School Spelling Scale*,[2] the spelling of which correlates highest with general spelling ability.

[1313]

Spelling Test: National Achievement Tests. Grades 3-4, 5-8, 7-9, 10-12; 1936-39; 2 forms; 50¢ per 25; Robert K. Speer and Samuel Smith; Rockville Centre, N. Y.: Acorn Publishing Co.
a) GRADES 3- 4. (20) minutes.
b) GRADES 5- 8. (25) minutes.
c) GRADES 7- 9. (25) minutes.
d) GRADES 10-12. (25) minutes.

For a review by W. J. Osburn, see 1161.

[1313.1]

Standard Elementary Spelling Scale. Grades 2-8; 1940; a 115-page book consisting of 3,679 words alphabetically arranged with difficulty percentages for each grade; Harold Hench Bixler; Atlanta, Ga.: Turner E. Smith & Co.

[1314]

Standard High School Spelling Scale, Revised Edition. Grades 7-12; 1925-35; a 63-page book containing 64 40-word lists to be used for either testing or teaching; 48¢ per copy; Ernest P. Simmons and Harold Hench Bixler; Atlanta, Ga.: Turner E. Smith & Co.

[1315]

Unit Scales of Attainment in Spelling. Grades 3-4, 5-6, 7-8; 1932-33; 3 forms, 3 levels; identical to the spelling tests in the battery *Unit Scales of Attainment*; 10¢ per single form; 25¢ per 25 answer blanks; 15¢ per specimen set; (15) minutes; W. A. Anderson; Minneapolis, Minn.: Educational Test Bureau, Inc.

REFERENCES

1 THORNDIKE, EDWARD L. *A Teacher's Word Book*: The Twenty Thousand Words Found Most Frequently and Widely in General Reading for Children and Young People. New York: Bureau of Publications, Teachers College, Columbia University, 1931. Pp. vii, 182. $1.60.

John C. Almack, Professor of Education, Stanford University. These spelling scales are part of an achievement battery "for measuring abilities and ranges of information." The norms for the battery were standardized on 60,000 cases in 1937.

There are three divisions, for grades 3-4, 5-6, and 7-8. A list of forty words is found in each division. The examiner is directed to "pronounce each word distinctly but not in a 'give-away' manner." A second pronunciation is allowed if it is needed, and "a short sentence or phrase may be given to convey the meaning of any word." There is no fixed time limit, but some fifteen minutes is made available. This is adequate.

Some of the words found in Division 1 for the third and fourth grades are *many, written, independent, secretary,* and *valuable.* Fifth- and sixth-grade words are *increasing, securing, height, noticeable,* and *recommendation.* Seventh- and eighth-grade words are *several, accommodate,* and *privilege.*

Key words are repeated in each division, scaled about ten steps apart, and lower in each succeeding list. The word *being* which is No. 11 in Division 1 is No. 1 in Division 2. The word *local* is No. 28 in Division 1, No. 18 in Division 2, and No. 8 in Division 3.

These scales furnish a satisfactory method for comparing spelling attainment among those pupils who have been taught these words in the grades to which they have been assigned in this test. There is such variation in the grade placement of words in different series of spelling books that the probability of identical grade placement of these words in any two spelling series or courses of study is very remote. The reviewer estimates that any two of the most used texts in spelling *for any grade* will have from twenty-five to forty per cent of their words in common; in a list of the ten most used texts, he anticipates ninety per cent will be common to all. The two or three books for consecutive grades will ordinarily have sixty per cent of their words in common.

The test also measures only a part of what is properly comprised in spelling; namely, the writing of the letters of these words in their correct order, from the pronunciation as given. Certainly, this is an important part of the results desired, but not as important as to be able to use the words in their proper meaning; to use the words in oral speech in their proper meaning, and to use them in the right form and in correct relation to each other.

To contend that any spelling test given in this fashion measures spelling attainment in general demands two big jumps between the data at hand and the generalizations: (*a*) that the sampling is adequate and significant; and (*b*) that other elements in the spelling process correlate to a significant degree with what is measured.

The statement on page 7 of the publisher's catalog (No. 24) to the effect that the profile charts are "an index of where remedial work is needed," needs considerable qualification. The diagnosis of spelling and the prescribing of remedies for deficiencies is not as simple as this suggests. Deficiencies may exist for several reasons: (*a*) because we have not made use of the forces which produce learning of spelling; (*b*) because obstacles exist to the operation of these forces; (*c*) because of lack of media or deficiencies in the media of learning; and (*d*) because of combinations of the foregoing as well as other reasons. This test is not adapted to revealing any of the major causes of spelling deficiency, though it may reveal the symptoms.

There remains also the problem of conveying to the children by some standard and uniform method the "name" of the word, the idea to be symbolized, and the meaning of the word to be spelled. Pictures may be used to do this, records on which the words have been inscribed, and by putting meaningful context which calls for the word into the hands of the subjects. This test contributes nothing new to the problem here described.

So far as statistical treatment is concerned, and so far as test mechanics are of service, this seems to be an excellent test.

G. M. Wilson, Professor of Education, Boston University. The spelling words in this scale consist of forty words in each of three divisions, namely: Division 1, grades 3-4; Division 2, grades 5-6; and Division 3, grades 7-8. It is not possible for anyone to evaluate spelling words on the basis of general impressions. It is, however, possible to apply such an instrument as Thorndike's *Teacher's Word Book* [1] and in such manner as to give at least a rough evaluation of the words.

Table 1 shows an analysis of the three divisions of words as compared with the *Teacher's Word Book.* Division 1 is designed for third and fourth grade pupils. The words in this division run up into the sixth thousand. Words in Division 2, grades 5-6, run up to the seventh, the eighth, and even the fifteenth thousand. The words in Division 3, grades 7-8, go beyond that.

TABLE 1

Frequency of Occurrence of the Words in the *Unit Scales of Attainment in Spelling*, Form B, According to Thorndike's *A Teacher's Word List*

| Thorndike's Placement | Number of Words | | |
	Division 1 Grades 3–4	Division 2 Grades 5–6	Division 3 Grades 7–8
1a	13	4	1
1b	7	5	2
2a	6	5	9
2b	7	9	4
3a	2	5	4
3b	1	2	2
4a	1	2	2
4b	0	0	0
5a	1	1	1
5b	1	2	2
6	1	0	1
7	0	1	3
8	0	3	2
9	0	0	1
10	0	0	1
11	0	0	1
12	0	0	1
13	0	0	1
14	0	0	1
15	0	1	0
16	0	0	0
17	0	0	1
18	0	0	0
19	0	0	0
20	0	0	0
Total	40	40	40

Read table thus: Of the 40 words in Division 1, 13 are listed by Thorndike as being among the first 500 words found in "the general reading for children and young people"; 7 are in the second 500; 6, in the third 500; 1, in the sixth 1,000; etc. Read likewise for Divisions 2 and 3.

The questions involved in word selection for spelling lists are primarily curriculum questions. One of these questions is: How many words should children undertake in their spelling lists? A second question is: How far up the scale of difficulty or unfamiliarity should the words run? Just a very few years ago such questions could not be answered with any degree of certainty. Today, however, we know that few eighth grade pupils have a writing vocabulary that exceeds 3,000 words. Furthermore, we know that if pupils undertake too many words, they are going to fail; that is, the primary requirement of drill is that the load shall be sizable.

The above questions indicate that the word lists in the *Unit Scales of Attainment in Spelling* are extended unreasonably. Doubtless, no words for the third and fourth grade should go above the second thousand. Many would insist that no sixth grade words should go

above the second thousand. Few who have studied the matter would extend the eighth grade list above the third thousand; certainly the fourth thousand would be the limit. In other words, this test has sadly neglected to observe the most fundamental principles relating to the curriculum and good teaching.

The test is in convenient form. It has been fully standardized. If the fundamental objections were not so weighty, the test might be looked upon with favor.

VOCABULARY

[1316]

Clinton General Vocabulary Test. High school and college; 1936; 2 forms; $1.15 per 25; 10¢ per specimen set; nontimed (30) minutes; R. J. Clinton; Corvallis, Ore.: O. S. C. Cooperative Association.

[1317]

Columbia Vocabulary Test. Grades 3-12; 1939; 1 form; $1 per 25 machine-scorable test-answer sheets; 25¢ per specimen set; nontimed (15-20) minutes; Irene Gansl and H. E. Garrett; New York: Psychological Corporation.

REFERENCES

1 GANSL, IRENE. *Vocabulary*: Its Measurement and Growth. Columbia University, Archives of Psychology, No. 236. New York: the University, March 1939. Pp. 52. $1.00. Paper.

[1318]

Cooperative Vocabulary Test. Grades 7-16; 1940; Form Q; 5¢ per test, 10 to 99 copies; 25¢ per specimen set; nontimed (10-30) minutes; Frederick B. Davis, F. S. Beers, D. G. Paterson, and Mary Willis; New York: Cooperative Test Service.

REFERENCES

Cooperative Test Service. *The Cooperative Vocabulary Test*: Information Concerning Its Construction, Interpretation, and Use. New York: Cooperative Test Service, 1940. Pp. 2. Gratis. Paper.

[1319]

English Recognition Vocabulary Test. Grades 1-16 and adults; 1937-38; 1 form; $3.50 per 100; 15¢ per specimen set; Robert H. Seashore and Lois D. Eckerson; Evanston, Ill.: Robert H. Seashore, Northwestern University.

REFERENCES

1 ECKERSON, L. E. *The Estimation of Individual Differences in the Total Size of English Recognition Vocabulary*. Unpublished master's thesis, University of Southern California, 1938.
2 SEASHORE, ROBERT H., AND ECKERSON, LOIS D. "The Measurement of Individual Differences in General English Vocabularies." *J Ed Psychol* 31:14-38 Ja '40.
3 SMITH, MARY KATHERINE. *Measurement of the Size of General English Vocabulary through the Elementary Grades and High School*. Unpublished doctor's thesis, Northwestern University, 1940. Pp. 62.

[1320]

Michigan Vocabulary Profile Test. Grades 9-16; 1937-39; a revision of the *Michigan Vocabulary Profile (see 1171c)*; 2 forms; $1.50 per 25; 3¢ per machine-scorable answer sheet; 25¢ per specimen set; nontimed (40-60+) minutes; Edward B. Greene; Yonkers, N. Y.: World Book Co.

REFERENCES

1 GREENE, EDWARD B. "Michigan Vocabulary Profile: A Sampling of Vocabularies of Superior Adults." *J Higher Ed* 9:383-9 O '38.
2 GREENE, EDWARD B. "Vocabulary Profiles of Groups in Training." *J Ed Res* 33:569-75 Ap '40.

Herbert A. Landry, Research Assistant, Bureau of Reference, Research, and Statistics, Public Schools, New York, New York. The author states in the manual that "this test is designed to give a profile of an individual's vocabulary in eight fields of information which are considered to be important and independent to a marked degree." This profile is presumed to be "more valuable than a single general vocabulary score because it shows the extent of the individual's knowledge in particular fields."

It would appear then that the chief contribution to be made by the test is in the additional information it can provide in studying the individual. One would agree that for this purpose a knowledge of the differential quality of an individual's vocabulary would be very useful in many specific situations. Value of this profile however depends upon such limiting conditions as are imposed by the extent of the validity and reliability of the instrument.

Concerning the former, it can be said that the test appears to be a valid measure of the specialized vocabulary of each of the eight different fields selected. Painstaking refinement procedures have resulted in the selection of what seems to be a graded representative sampling of the technical vocabularies involved.

Concerning the reliability of the test, the author states that the correlation between equivalent forms provides reliability coefficients for the separate subdivisions which range from .87 to .94, median .91. While they are relatively high on most of the divisions, they do not meet the minimum standard of .94 suggested by Kelley as the lowest reliability a test should have if it is to be used for individual diagnosis. The reliabilities when expressed in terms of the probable error of individual scores, which do not appear in the manual but were obtained on request from the publisher, range from .47 to .94 score points, the median is .91. There is, therefore, a one-to-one chance that an obtained score on four of the eight divisions will not vary more than approximately one score point from the true score. However, it must also be remembered that there is the same chance that the variation from the true score may be more than one score point. Now a one score point difference may seem insignificant until one inspects the table of norms. From this table, it is seen that on the lower levels, grades 9-12, the mean increase in the median scores for the eight divisions for the four year span is only 4.5 score points. Thus a one point deviation is equivalent to a one year difference in the grade norms. Within a single grade level the difference between the 31st and 69th percentile ranks seldom vary by more than two score points. Thus the possible extent of the error of measurement and its effect upon the pupil's percentile rank are apparent.

It is obvious that the scores obtained on the divisions of the test have little value unless properly interpreted. A high score on a particular division for a given grade level may be the result of several factors such as (*a*) a special interest (*b*) a formal course (*c*) the wide collateral reading common to bright pupils (*d*) certain environmental factors which result in bringing an individual into more extensive contact with a given area than is usually the case. These and other factors may operate to varying degrees in different situations. Because of this, scores become meaningful only to the extent that they have been carefully analyzed in the light of the factors that may give rise to them. This would seem to necessitate extensive use of cumulative records and interviews.

The hazards involved in an uncritical use of the test are apparent. However, since it represents the only available measure of differential vocabulary ability it can provide useful information if used with full knowledge of its limitations. Results must be carefully interpreted by persons who have both the time and the facilities to follow through each case in order to determine the real significance of an individual's scores. Further experimentation will undoubtedly lead to the overcoming of some of its present limitations for individual analysis.

The test may also be used as a general vocabulary test by combining the scores on all divisions. Percentile norms are provided for interpretation of the total scores. Used as a 240-item general vocabulary test it should provide highly reliable measures of breadth of vocabulary.

The physical aspects of the test are very satisfactory. The arrangement for machine or hand stencil scoring simplifies scoring procedure greatly. The answer sheet provides for the profile and other data and may be easily filed with a student's record for future use. The modest claims of the author together with his cautioning statements concerning its use which are included in the manual are to be commended.

Ed Res B 19:117 F 14 '40. * designed to test the vocabulary of high-school and college students in eight fields of information * The authors expect the test to provide evidence about: how growth and retention of specific information is connected with training and interest, what vocabularies are essential to certain vocations, what is the importance of vocabulary in reading, what is the importance of vocabulary in educational and vocational planning, and which terms are important tools for thinking. It would seem to the reviewer that such comprehensive and diverse purposes cannot adequately be served by this single test. The authors present little or no evidence to show that it has been used or is valid for serving any of these purposes. Further experimentation and application are needed to provide answers for these questions. The test does provide some new and challenging possibilities in vocabulary analysis, but the users of this test must finally determine for what purposes it is valuable and practical.

For reviews by Richard Ledgerwood, M. R. Trabue, John G. Darley, John M. Stalnaker, and Arthur E. Traxler of an earlier edition, see 1171.

[1321]
Schrammel-Wharton Vocabulary Test. Grades 7-12; 1938; 2 forms; 50¢ per 25; 15¢ per specimen set; 40(45) minutes; H. E. Schrammel and LaVerna P. Wharton; Emporia, Kan.: Bureau of Educational Measurements, Kansas State Teachers College.

Arthur E. Traxler, Assistant Director, Educational Records Bureau, New York, N. Y. The widespread awareness of the importance of knowledge of word meaning in school success is shown by the fact that there are now about fifty published vocabulary tests, aside from many such tests that exist as parts of other tests. These tests cover all levels from preschool through college.

The *Schrammel-Wharton Vocabulary Test*, which was used in the 1938 Nation-wide Every Pupil Testing Program, is similar in nearly every way to some of the earlier vocabulary tests. Each of the two forms contains 140 items, each consisting of a test word followed by four words from which the subject must choose

the one which defines the test word. The test is designed for use throughout the junior and senior high school and in college. It yields only a total score and has no diagnostic features. According to the manual of directions, the words were selected from the Pressey list and other supplementary lists and "all words were checked against the Thorndike word lists in order to insure an equitable distribution according to difficulty and frequency of use."

The test is long enough to be highly reliable. It is somewhat surprising, therefore, to note that a reliability coefficient of only .85 is reported in the manual of directions. This is fairly high reliability for tests in general, but it is lower than the reliability of most vocabulary tests that contain a hundred or more items. For example, the reliability of the *Inglis Test of English Vocabulary*, containing 150 items, is above .90 and that of the vocabulary part of the *Cooperative English Test*, containing 100 items, is about .95. It should be observed, however, that the reliability coefficient given for the Schrammel-Wharton test is based on the scores of only seventy-two college juniors and seniors. It is possible that further study with a more adequate sampling will show higher reliability.

The time limit for the test is forty minutes, which is long enough for most persons to complete a vocabulary test containing 140 items. This is a desirable feature. In a vocabulary test, one is interested in measuring the subject's knowledge of word meaning and not his rate of work. If the time limit is so brief that few if any pupils can cover the test in the time allowed, the scores will be determined partly by speed of reading and will not show vocabulary alone. It is noteworthy that this test avoids that pitfall.

Certain aspects of the format of the test probably involve limitations. One of these is that each test word is presented alone rather than in a sentence or phrase. A disadvantage of not presenting the words in context is that the exact meaning of each word may not be clear to the subject. For example, *draft*, word number ninety-nine in Form A, has twenty-six meanings when used as a noun, eight meanings when used as a verb, and three meanings when used as an adjective. The only clue that the person taking the test has concerning which of these thirty-seven meanings is to be applied to the word is the series of choices following it.

Another apparent limitation is that in some instances the word which the subject is expected to select as a definition of the test word is not very well suited to this purpose. For instance, in the eightieth item of Form A, the test word is *metabolism* and the expected response is *growth,* and in the second item of Form B, the test word is *possessive* and the response that is presumed to be correct is *designating.* A number of the other items could be criticized in the same way.

Fairly adequate midyear and end-of-year percentile norms for grades 7-12 are given in the manual of directions. The number of cases included in the distributions on which the midyear norms are based ranges from 327 for grade 7 to 1,311 for grade 9. The groups contributing to the end-of-year norms are smaller. As yet, the only norms for the college level are tentative norms for the beginning of the freshman year.

In all probability, the *Schrammel-Wharton Vocabulary Test* has served a useful purpose in the Nation-wide Every Pupil Testing Program, but in view of the availability of several vocabulary tests that are apparently more thoroughly validated and more adequately standardized, the recommendation of this test for use in other testing programs would hardly be warranted at its present stage of development.

[1321.1]

Vocabulary: Parr Skill-Ability Tests. Grades 9-16; 1938; 2 forms; 10¢ per test, 50 or more; 28(35) minutes; Frank W. Parr; Corvallis, Ore.: O. S. C. Cooperative Association.

[1322]

Vocabulary Power Tests. Grades 4-8, 7-9; 1938; 2 levels; 25¢ per 30; specimen set free; nontimed (15-20) minutes; Norman K. Frick; Chicago, Ill.: Scott, Foresman and Co.
a) INTRODUCTORY FORM A. Grades 4-8.
b) JUNIOR FORM A. Grades 7-9.

ENGLISH – THIRD MMY

REVIEWS BY *Harold H. Bixler, Paul S. Burnham, Ruth D. Churchill, John Cohen, Charlotte W. Croon, Edgar Dale, John S. Diekhoff, J. R. Gerberich, Harry A. Greene, Chester W. Harris, Joseph E. King, Gerald V. Lannholm, J. Paul Leonard, Robert C. Pooley, H. H. Remmers, Henry D. Rinsland, Holland Roberts, Verner M. Sims, Robert H. Thouless, Guy M. Wilson, Clifford Woody, Louis C. Zahner.*

[114]

★**Ability for English (Language): Fife Tests of Ability, Test 1.** Entrants to secondary schools (England and Scotland); 1947; 1 form; 5s. 6d. per 25; 4d. per manual; 30(35) minutes; Frank M. Earle; University of London Press Ltd.

REFERENCES

1. EARLE, FRANK M. *Tests of Ability for Secondary School Courses.* Publications of the Scottish Council for Research in Education, No. 10. London: University of London Press, 1936. Pp. xiii, 138. 5s. *

For a review by James Maxwell of the entire battery, see 8.

[115]

Iowa Placement Examinations: English Aptitude: Series EA1, Revised. Grades 12-13; 1925; Forms A, B; $4 per 100; 50¢ per specimen set including the other 10 tests in the series, postpaid; 43(50) minutes; prepared under the direction of C. E. Seashore and G. M. Ruch; M. F. Carpenter and G. D. Stoddard; Bureau of Educational Research and Service, State University of Iowa.

REFERENCES

1. STODDARD, GEORGE DINSMORE. *Iowa Placement Examinations.* University of Iowa, Studies in Education, Vol. 3, No. 2. Iowa City, Iowa: the University, 1925. Pp. 103. Paper. $1.00. *
2. LANGLIE, T. A. "The Administration of Placement Examinations." *Sch & Soc* 24:619-20 N 13 '26. * (*PA* 1:695)
3. LANGLIE, T. A. "Analysis of the Iowa Placement Tests." *J Appl Psychol* 10:303-14 Je '26. * (*PA* 1:496)
4. STODDARD, GEORGE D. "Iowa Placement Examinations." *Sch & Soc* 24:212-6 Ag 14 '26. *
5. LANGLIE, T. A. "A Comparison of 'Aptitude' and 'Training' Tests for Prognosis." *J Ed Psychol* 19:658-65 D '28. * (*PA* 3:1701)
6. STALNAKER, JOHN M. *A Statistical Study of Some Aspects of the Purdue Orientation Testing Program.* Bulletin of Purdue University, Vol. 28, No. 6; Studies in Higher Education VIII. Lafayette, Ind.: Division of Educational Reference, the University, February 1928. Pp. 68. Paper. $0.20. *
7. GERBERICH, JOSEPH RAYMOND. *A Personnel Study of 10,000 Iowa High School Seniors.* University of Iowa Studies in Education, Vol. 5, No. 3, Iowa City, Iowa: the University, 1930. Pp. 112. Paper. $1.00. * (*PA* 5:771)

8. MILLER, LAWRENCE WILLIAM. *An Experimental Study of the Iowa Placement Examinations.* University of Iowa Studies in Education, Vol. 5, No. 6. Iowa City, Iowa: the University, 1930. Pp. 116. Paper. $1.00. * (*PA* 5:799)
9. LEAF, CURTIS T. "Prediction of College Marks." *J Exp Ed* 8:303-7 Mr '40. * (*PA* 14:4739)

Robert C. Pooley, Professor of English, The University of Wisconsin, Madison, Wisconsin. A test of English aptitude for high schools and colleges consisting of four pages, to be administered in 43 minutes of actual test time. Punched keys are provided for manual scoring, and answer sheets for machine scoring. Norms are provided in the form of percentiles for the test, but these are undifferentiated for grade levels, or for the comparison of high school students with college students.

The test is in four parts. Part I tests the application of two rules of grammar; Part II is a reading comprehension test based on about thirty lines of prose; Part III is a fact-determining test from the reading of thirty-six lines of narrative poetry; Part IV is a test of the quality of construction of a prose passage, with questions on the beginning, the paragraph construction, punctuation, word choice, etc.

This test is put forward by its authors as serving the following purposes: (*a*) to afford a basis for prediction of the character of the work that each student will do in college; (*b*) to aid in selecting and admitting students; (*c*) to serve as an entrance examination in lieu of the more time-honored essay-type content examination; (*d*) to section classes for instructional purposes on the basis of mental ability; etc.

Such claims would be difficult to defend. To judge from this test the outcomes of four years of instruction in English in high schools are: (*a*) to be able to apply a grammatical rule, such as, "Avoid incongruous metaphors," to printed sentences; (*b*) to read a composition textbook and understand it; (*c*) to read a poem for such valuable experiences as, "Was the sea calm?" "How many statues were there?" "What work did the men do on the island?" (*d*) to criticize a passage in print from the point of view of an editor or an English teacher.

Nowhere, in any course of study available, can such goals be found as the principal outcomes of the teaching of English. If the test does not test what the teachers are directed by courses to study to teach, the test is invalid. It is grossly unfair to judge the results of instruction by such a test. Nor is it just to sort or segregate students for further instruction by such means. Widespread use of this test will have one positive effect; it will divert teachers from the true goals of English instruction to drill upon rules, emphasis on proofreading skills, and the reading of poetry for the cataloguing of irrelevant facts.

[116]
Basic Language Skills: Iowa Every-Pupil Tests of Basic Skills, Test C, New Edition. Grades 3-5, 5-9; 1940–45; IBM, grades 5-9; Forms L, M, N, O; 2 levels; 44¢ per specimen set of either level; H. F. Spitzer in collaboration with Ernest Horn, Maude McBroom, H. A. Greene, and E. F. Lindquist (General Editor); Houghton Mifflin Co.
a) ELEMENTARY BATTERY. Grades 3-5; $1.50 per 25; 46(60) minutes.
b) ADVANCED BATTERY. Grades 5-9; IBM; separate answer sheets need not be used; $1.60 per 25; 63¢ per 25 machine-scorable answer sheets; 30¢ per set of machine-scoring stencils; 55 or 58(70) minutes.

REFERENCES
1. EVANS, PAUL C. *A Critical Analysis of the 1936 Iowa Basic Skills Test in Language, Test C.* Unpublished master's thesis, University of Iowa, 1936.
2. VICTOR, GEORGIA C. *An Analysis of Pupil Responses to Items in Iowa Every-Pupil Test in Basic Language Skills for 1935.* Unpublished master's thesis, University of Iowa, 1936.

For reviews by Frederic L. Ayer, Gustav J. Froehlich, and Ralph C. Preston of the entire battery, see 10.

[117]
Clapp-Young English Test: Clapp-Young Self-Marking Tests. Grades 5-12; 1929; Forms A, B; 90¢ per 25; 8¢ per specimen set; 25(30) minutes; Frank L. Clapp and Robert V. Young; Houghton Mifflin Co.

Gerald V. Lannholm, Assistant Director, The Graduate Record Examination, New York, New York. This test is divided into three parts, ostensibly designed to measure the pupil's ability: (*a*) to capitalize and punctuate correctly, (*b*) to use correct word forms, (*c*) to recognize various aspects of formal grammar. The test can be scored quickly, easily, and objectively by means of the authors' patented "self-marking" technique. According to the authors, the skills selected for inclusion in the test were based on studies of error frequencies.

Published in 1929, this test was probably in advance of others in the field at that time. Although the evidence of research concerning the relative effectiveness of objective techniques for measuring a pupil's mastery of the fundamentals of correct writing is neither conclusive nor complete, the evidence is sufficiently strong to raise doubts concerning the effectiveness of the techniques employed in this comparatively old instrument. Ability to capitalize and to punctuate is measured in this test by what the reviewer has called the "locate the error" technique. The pupil need locate only the position of the error; he is not required to indicate the correct usage. In the word-form part of the test, two choices are given for each item, the pupil being directed to mark one of them as correct. The items in the third part of the test require the pupils to identify parts of speech and parts of sentences.

The sampling in the test is much too limited to have the diagnostic value implied by the authors. This may be illustrated by the fact that the test includes less than ten different punctuation usages. Interpretative material provided by the authors is limited and likely to be misleading. For example, the authors state that any pupil who is just completing the work of a given grade should make a score equal to the median score earned by all pupils finishing that grade. Similar standards are decreed for pupils of various age levels. The reviewer questions seriously the appropriateness of such an arbitrary definition of satisfactory performance for all pupils.

A coefficient of reliability of .85 is reported by the authors, who do not state whether this is based on the performance of pupils in all of the eight grades for which the test is intended or on the results for a single grade. Nor do they indicate the method used in estimating the coefficient of reliability. The authors rest their claim for validity for the test on its content, choosing to ignore the serious effect which other factors may have on its validity.

It is difficult to believe that a test in this field would retain its original form for so many years. In view of the many improved tests now available in this field, it is not anticipated that enlightened teachers or supervisors will select this edition for use in present-day classrooms.

[118]

★College Placement Test in English. College; 1941–43; Forms A, B; sold only to colleges, $1.60 per 25, postpaid; sample test free; 120(125) minutes; Hector H. Lee; Turner E. Smith & Co.

[119]

★College Preparatory Test in English. High school; 1943; 1 form; $1.25 per 25, postpaid; sample test free; (45) minutes; Hector H. Lee; Turner E. Smith & Co.

[120]

★Cooperative English Test: Lower and Higher Levels. Grades 7-12, 13-16; 1941–47; IBM; three tests available separately and in a single-booklet edition; separate answer sheets need not be used; Cooperative Test Service.

a) SINGLE BOOKLET EDITION. Grades 7-12, 13-16; 1941–43; Forms R, S, T; $3.75 per 25; 30¢ per specimen set of either level, postpaid; $1 per 25 sets of machine-scorable answer sheets; 45¢ per set of stencils; 120(130) minutes.

b) TEST A, MECHANICS OF EXPRESSION. Grades 7-16; 1941–47; Forms R, S, T, X; $1.75 per 25; 25¢ per specimen set, postpaid; 40¢ per 25 machine-scorable answer sheets; 15¢ per stencil for scoring answer sheets; 40(45) minutes; Geraldine Spaulding, W. W. Cook (Form R), and Herbert Danzer (Form X).

c) TESTS B1 AND B2, EFFECTIVENESS OF EXPRESSION: LOWER AND HIGHER LEVELS. Grades 7-12, 13-16; 1941–47; Forms R, S, T, X; 2 levels; $1.75 per 25; 25¢ per specimen set of either level, postpaid; 40¢ per 25 machine-scorable answer sheets; 15¢ per stencil for scoring answer sheets; 40(45) minutes, Geraldine Spaulding, W. W. Cook (Form R), Miriam May (Forms S and T), and Miriam M. Bryan (Form X).

d) TESTS C1 AND C2, READING COMPREHENSION: LOWER AND HIGHER LEVELS. Grades 7-12, 13-16; 1941–43; Forms R, S, T; 2 levels; $2 per 25; 25¢ per specimen set of either level, postpaid; 40¢ per 25 machine-scorable answer sheets; 15¢ per stencil for scoring answer sheets; 40(45) minutes; Frederick B. Davis, Harold V. King (Form S), and Mary Willis (Form T).

REFERENCES

1-2. See 40:1276.
3. WAGNER, MAZIE EARLE, AND STRABEL, EUNICE. "Predicting Performance in College English." J Ed Res 30:694-9 My '37. * (PA 11:3912)
4. CURETON, EDWARD E. "Evaluation or Guidance? The Report of the Eighth Annual National College Sophomore Testing Program April 17 to May 5, 1939." J Exp Ed 8:308-40 Mr '40. * (PA 14:4726)
5. SMITH, HENRY LESTER, AND EATON, MERRILL T. A Study of the English Usage, Spelling, and Vocabulary of 251 Graduate Students at Indiana University. Bulletin of the School of Education, Indiana University, Vol. 16, No. 5. Bloomington, Ind.: Indiana University Bookstore, September 1940. Pp. 68. Paper. $0.50. * (PA 15:1070)
6. TRAXLER, ARTHUR E. "The Cooperative English Test, Form Q: Correlations With School Marks and Intercorrelations," pp. 42-50. In 1940 Achievement Testing Program in Independent Schools and Supplementary Studies. Educational Records Bulletin, No. 30. New York: Educational Records Bureau, June 1940. Pp. xii, 75. Paper, lithotyped. $1.50. *

7. MASON, C. T., AND WILKINS, T. B. "Entrance Examinations and Success in College." J Negro Ed 10:54-8 Ja '41. * (PA 15:3161)
8. RYANS, DAVID G. The First Step in Guidance: Self-Appraisal: A Report of the 1940 Sophomore Testing Program. Cooperative Test Service Publications in Measurement and Guidance, Series 3, Vol. 1, No. 1. New York: Cooperative Test Service, January 1941. Pp. 35. Paper. $0.10. * (PA 15:2382)
9. CRISSY, WILLIAM J. E., AND PEDERSEN, RUTH A. The War-Time Role of the College Sophomore: A Report on the 1942 Sophomore Testing Program. Cooperative Test Service Publications in Measurement and Guidance, Series 3, Vol. 2, No. 3. New York: Cooperative Test Service, July 1942. Pp. 40. Paper. $0.10. * (PA 16:5005)
10. CRISSY, WILLIAM J. E., AND RYANS, DAVID G. The College Sophomore Appraises His Curriculum: A Report of the 1941 Sophomore Testing Program. Cooperative Test Service Publications in Measurement and Guidance, Series 3, Vol. 2, No. 2. New York: Cooperative Test Service, January 1942. Pp. 39. Paper. $0.10. *
11. DAVIS, FREDERICK B. "Fundamental Factors of Comprehension in Reading." Abstract. Psychol B 39:499-500 Jl '42. * (PA 16:5007, title only)
12. SCHNEIDLER, GWENDOLEN G., AND BERDIE, RALPH F. "Educational Hierarchies and Scholastic Survival." J Ed Psychol 33:199-208 Mr '42. * (PA 16:4181)
13. Final Sophomore Percentile Tables: The 1943 College Sophomore Testing Program. New York: Cooperative Test Service, July 1943. Pp. 6. Paper. Gratis. *
14. SIMPSON, R. G. "The Vocabulary Sections of the Cooperative English Tests at the Higher Levels of Difficulty." J Ed Psychol 34:142-51 Mr '43. * (PA 18:311)
15. Final Sophomore Percentile Tables: The 1944 College Sophomore Testing Program. New York: Cooperative Test Service, July 1944. Pp. 6. Paper. Gratis. *
16. DAVIS, FREDERICK B. "What Do Reading Tests Really Measure?" Engl J 33:180-7 Ap '44. * (PA 18:2250)
17. FOX, WILLIAM H. An Analytical Study of January-February (1943) Entering Freshmen at Indiana University. Bulletin of the School of Education, Indiana University, Vol. 20, No. 1. Bloomington, Ind.: Indiana University Bookstore, January 1944. Pp. 46. Paper. $0.50. * (PA 18:3880)
18. HENRY, LORNE J. "The Diagnostic Value of a Standardized Reading Test." Sch, Sec Ed 32:884-7 Je '44. *
19. TRAXLER, ARTHUR E. "Reliability and Intercorrelation of the Parts of the Cooperative English Test A: Mechanics of Expression," pp. 55-8. In 1944 Achievement Testing Program in Independent Schools and Supplementary Studies. Educational Records Bulletin, No. 40. New York: Educational Records Bureau, June 1944. Pp. xii, 58. Paper, lithotyped. $1.50. * (PA 18:3899)
20. TRAXLER, ARTHUR E. "The Value of the Scores on the Parts of the Cooperative Mechanics of Expression Test." Engl J 33:557-8 D '44. *
21. Final Sophomore Percentile Tables: The 1945 College Sophomore Testing Program. New York: Cooperative Test Service, August 1945. Pp. 6. Paper. Gratis. *
22. AVERILL, LAWRENCE A. "Some Uses of the ACE English Test in Worcester Teachers College." Sch & Soc 61:253-5 Ap 21 '45. * (PA 19:3147)
23. BERG, IRWIN A.; JOHNSON, GRAHAM; and LARSEN, ROBERT P. "The Use of an Objective Test in Predicting Rhetoric Grades." Ed & Psychol Meas 5:429-35 w '45. * (PA 20:2468)
24. Final Sophomore Percentile Tables: The 1946 College Sophomore Testing Program. New York: Cooperative Test Service, July 1946. Pp. 6. Paper. Gratis. *
25. DAVIS, FREDERICK B. "A Brief Comment on Thurstone's Note on the Reanalysis of Davis' Reading Test." Psychometrika 11:249-55 D '46. * (PA 21:978)
26. DAVIS, FREDERICK B. "The Factorial Composition of Two Tests of Comprehension in Reading." J Ed Psychol 37:481-6 N '46. * (PA 21:1632)
27. DAVIS, FREDERICK B. "Fundamental Factors of Reading Comprehension." Psychometrika 11:185-8 S '46. *
28. FULLER, ELIZABETH MECHEM. "The Use of Measures of Ability and General Adjustment in the Preservice Selection of Nursery School-Kindergarten-Primary Teachers." J Ed Psychol 37:321-34 S '46. * (PA 21:1640)
29. THURSTONE, L. L. "Note on a Reanalysis of Davis' Reading Tests." Psychometrika 11:185-8 S '46. * (PA 21:295)
30. Final Sophomore Percentile Tables: The 1947 College Sophomore Testing Program. New York: Cooperative Test Service, May 1947. Pp. 4. Paper. Gratis. *
31. "A Note on the Correlation Between the Iowa and Cooperative Reading Tests," p. 66. In 1947 Achievement Testing Program in Independent Schools and Supplementary Studies. Educational Records Bulletin, No. 48. New York: Educational Records Bureau, June 1947. Pp. xii, 66. Paper, lithotyped. $2.00. *

J. Paul Leonard, President, San Francisco State College, San Francisco, California. [Review of Lower Level Forms R, S, and T.] These tests represent recent achievements in the refinement of test procedures in reading and mechanical usage. Norms are provided on many cases for different types of schools. The tests are quickly scored, available for machine scoring, rather comprehensive in coverage, quickly and easily administered, and excellent to aid the average English teacher who wants to use them to supplement theme writing and observation. They are not individually diagnostic but are chiefly valuable for giving an average comparable level of achievement and for securing comparable scores on different phases of reading and expression.

The test consists of three major sections, each 40 minutes long, testing reading comprehension, mechanics of expression, and effectiveness of expression. More specifically these areas are measured through vocabulary and reading comprehension; grammatical usage, punctuation, capitalization, and spelling; sentence structure and style, active vocabulary, and organization. They are based upon careful analysis of many studies in English and in the main are designed to measure the thinking process in relation to the mechanics of reading and expression. As such, their motives are commendable, their construction unusually carefully planned and checked by sampling of items, and the scoring is designed to eliminate in so far as possible the nonessential factors frequently affecting testing. Careful precautions are given in the manual to the teacher, the claims for the test are guarded and modest, and every modern statistical device and caution have been used to make the test as accurate for its purpose as possible.

One has the feeling that superior workmanship has gone into these tests and that within the framework of statistical standards and ease of scoring they are superior. They are not meant to be individually diagnostic and thus have limited use; they are so short in length that they reduce their own reliability. In a few places one feels that a load of understanding is placed upon the pupil for quickly sensing the different ways of responding to the test items so that they may be scored easily and that in some instances, because of the time element in the test, he may be penalized for proceeding carefully. Some of the items in the grammatical section of the test can probably be "felt" by the pupil, some of the punctuation items are probably overplayed (apostrophe of possession, for instance), and the active vocabulary section

is probably more of a crossword puzzle than anything else. On the whole, however, the test is excellent for a short, quick survey of general abilities and is far superior to most tests in the statistical procedures used in building it.

Edward S. Noyes, Associate Professor of English, Yale University, New Haven, Connecticut. [Review of Higher Level Forms R, S, and T.] These three forms are nearly identical in plan and in number of items; scores on any one form should be comparable with those on any other, a fact which may be useful to teachers with several divisions.

The subtest Vocabulary (60 five-choice items, 15 minutes) is limited to synonyms. The items are said to use "words of increasing difficulty" and to demand "increasingly close discrimination among the choices." But is "piebald" (Item 60, Form R) a word more difficult than "writhe" or "cornea" (Items 1 and 4)? This reviewer sought in vain to find evidence of the need for closer discrimination among later than among earlier choices, in any one of the forms. In any item, the student who knows the meaning of the given word will find little difficulty in his choice; he who does not know must guess. The number of items seems small for exploration of vocabulary range.

The subtest Reading Comprehension (90 items, 25 minutes) is so arranged as to afford two scores: one on speed, the other on level of comprehension. Since students who finish the vocabulary section are told to go on at once to the comprehension section (some will and some will not), it would seem that speed scores would not be reliable. The selections are good in that they cover a wide range of material and are reasonably complete in themselves. The statements made about them, however, often seem dubious. Item 22, Form T, states that "the humor in this passage depends on the meaning of the word . . ." (five single words follow). Humor, in this as in most passages, is too elusive and pervading to be pinned down to any single word. Again, Item 33, Form T, states, "This passage is intended principally to be (1) humorous (2) informative (3) scientific (4) apologetic (5) critical." From the passage itself, (1), (2), and (5) are almost equally possible as answers. Similar difficulties are presented by Items 21, 22, 31, 84 in Form S and by Items 16, 48, 51 in Form T. It would be unfortunate were students to infer from such statements that writing which is informative or critical cannot at the same time be humorous.

Occasionally, students are expected to know more than the selection itself reveals. In Item 76, Form S, the passage simply does not provide the evidence necessary for a reasoned choice. Similarly, Items 33 to 36, Form S, would be difficult for anyone not familiar with the terms "romantic" and "classic" in their literary significance. In such items, the tests are not really objective despite their form. The testmaker had an attitude toward the passage; the choices he offers to the testee are based on that attitude. If the student does not adopt the same attitude, his anwers will be scored as "wrong" even though they may be entirely logical from his own premises.

The test *Mechanics of Expression* (three subtests on grammatical usage, punctuation and capitalization, and spelling; 40 minutes) consists of a series of proofreading exercises. As has long been pointed out, a student's ability to spot errors on the printed page and his ability to avoid similar errors in his own writing are two different abilities. College freshman English sections are full of students who have done reasonably well on such exercises as these but who are still lamentably prone to solecisms almost as bad. Actually, this section of the tests, in sharp contrast to the preceding one, seems hardly designed for a "higher level." Witness the emphasis on such glaring errors as "had of," double negatives, and misuse of cases and tenses.

The test *Effectiveness of Expression* (three subtests on sentence structure and style, active vocabulary, and organization; 40 minutes) provides in the first and last subtests more or less jumbled sentences to be compared with more correct ones and more or less jumbled topics to be arranged in their "best" order. Here again, the critical rather than the creative faculty is being measured; there is no necessary connection between scores on the test and the ability of the students to write accurate sentences or logically planned themes. If it is clearly understood what is being tested, I can see no objection to these exercises; but one should beware accepting their results as a true indication of "effectiveness of expression," which, after all, can only be discovered by giving the student a blank page and a pencil and setting him to write.

Cooperative English Test

The second subtest, called Active Vocabulary, is a guessing game: the student is given a brief definition of some word, the number of letters in the word, and five initial letters from which he is to select the initial letter of the word. "A man who does not belong to the army or navy is a—(8)—(1)B (2)C (3)D (4)F (5)G." This is a fearful and wonderful example of testing. (2)C, standing for "civilian," an eight-letter word, is presumably the "right" answer. But why not (4)F, standing for "farmhand," also an eight-letter word defining one who is in neither the army nor the navy? For this particular item, (4)F seems indicated, at least. This game might be fun on rainy evenings, but what it has to do with active, as opposed to passive or contemplative or retrospective, vocabulary is a bit hard to understand. Since the testee does not even have to write out the word he has in mind, the element of chance is inevitably increased: he may guess the right letter without knowing any word, or he may have a reasonable word, fitting the definition and the number of letters, which will be "wrong."

The strength of these tests lies in their sections on reading comprehension and in their comparability; the weakness, in their varying attempts to provide substitutes for writing.

Robert C. Pooley, Professor of English, The University of Wisconsin, Madison, Wisconsin. [Review of Higher Level Forms R, S, and T.] These tests are a combination of a reading skills test and two English skills tests, mechanics of expression and effectiveness of expression, brought together to permit in two hours of testing time a rather full analysis and diagnosis of English abilities at the high school and college levels. The test booklets contain answer spaces for numerical responses to be scored manually, or the booklets may be used with separate answer sheets for machine scoring. The mechanical construction of the test is excellent from the point of view of ease and objectivity in scoring and recording results. Norms are furnished at the college level for each of the parts of the test and for the total test for freshmen, sophomores, juniors, and seniors at the end of the school year and for entering freshmen. Moreover, the norms are divided into three groups according to type of college or course: I, pre-professional; II, liberal arts; III, junior and teachers' colleges.

Similar norms are provided for high schools: Group I, end-of-year norms for grades 7 through 12 in northern high schools; Group II, grades 8 through 11 for southern high schools. There is a sixteen-page manual of directions.

The test *Reading Comprehension* contains two parts: vocabulary—meaning tested by five choices, one of which is a synonym of the given word; and speed and level of comprehension—tested by responses to 17 brief reading selections drawn from widely different sources, informational, scientific, and literary. The test *Mechanics of Expression* contains 60 items of grammatical usage placed in sentences, 45 items of punctuation, and 24 items of capitalization, the latter two types presented in running prose. Spelling is presented in 60 items, each in a choice between a misspelled and a correctly spelled word. The test *Effectiveness of Expression* contains three parts. Part I measures sentence structure and style by the comparison of passages of prose placed in parallel columns and by an exercise in the choice among four versions of the same sentence. Part II is a test of active vocabulary in which the student must guess the word intended by definition and by clues to first letter and length of word. Part III measures organization by rearranging disorganized paragraphs and by completing a partial outline.

The materials of the tests are well chosen and clearly presented. The directions are simple and concise and make clear to the student the purpose of each test. Dubious and controversial usage has been avoided; so far as is possible in an objective test, the materials of English have been cast into natural settings of sentences and paragraphs. Mechanics are tested functionally rather than in isolation from English expression. It is one of the best tests available in the field of English skills.

Its principal defect is shared by all other objective tests in English: it does not test ability in English, if ability is defined as the power to use English effectively in speech and writing. It does test the power to correct errors, to proofread, to organize or reorganize material composed by others. It does not test the power to compose English and should therefore be used cautiously in the placing of students in ability groups or in the sectioning and exemption of college freshmen.

For reviews by Robert M. Bear and J. B. Stroud of Tests C1 and C2, see 497.

[121]

★Correctness and Effectiveness of Expression: Tests of General Educational Development: High School Level, Test 1. High school; 1944–45; IBM; Form B; separate answer sheets must be used; $2 per 25; 40¢ per 25 machine-scorable answer sheets; 15¢ per scoring key; 25¢ per specimen set, postpaid; worklimit (120) minutes; prepared by the Examinations Staff of the United States Armed Forces Institute; published by the American Council on Education; distributed by the Cooperative Test Service. (Also distributed by Science Research Associates: $2 per 25; 65¢ per 25 machine-scorable answer sheets; 50¢ per key; 50¢ per specimen set.)

For reviews by Herbert S. Conrad and Warren G. Findley of the entire battery, see 20.

[122]

★Correctness and Effectiveness of Expression: Tests of General Educational Development: College Level, Test 1. College; 1944–45; IBM; Form B; separate answer sheets must be used; $2 per 25; 40¢ per 25 machine-scorable answer sheets; 15¢ per scoring key; 25¢ per specimen set, postpaid; worklimit (120) minutes; prepared by the Examinations Staff of the United States Armed Forces Institute; published by the American Council on Education; distributed by the Cooperative Test Service. (Also distributed by Science Research Associates: $3 per 25; 65¢ per 25 machine-scorable answer sheets; 50¢ per key; 50¢ per specimen set.)

Charlotte W. Croon, Test Research Service, 1213 McChestney Avenue, Nashville, Tennessee. Although this test is one of a battery constructed for the special purpose of assisting in the guidance and placement of those who have been in the armed services, there is no reason why its use should be thus limited. The content is not dependent on military experience, and the norms provided are based on regular students in three types of colleges who are just completing a freshman course in English composition.

The test is not set up to be diagnostic and yields just one score. It is entirely objective and can be rapidly scored by hand or machine. The first 25 items are spelling ones of the type in which the testee selects from four words the one which is misspelled or, if he thinks all are correct, marks the fifth choice, "none misspelled." As has often been said, this technique does not require him actually to spell anything or even to recognize the correct spelling of the misspelled words. It does permit the partial testing of a large number of words in a minimum of space and time. The selection of words seemed satisfactory to this writer.

The second part consists of four themes in which errors and infelicities of the types listed below are introduced. Places where these occur (and a few where they do not) are underlined, and the testee is required to select the best of four ways to improve the underlined portion. This technique has been used many times and is always open to the criticism that areas needing rewriting are inevitably pointed out to the testee. To some degree, this objection is met by having the first choice identical with what is already in the selection and occasionally having that as the right answer.

A rough analysis of this part yielded the following distribution of items:

Punctuation (including capitalization) . 10
Grammar 15
Diction errors 16
Diction taste and style 42
Paragraph and sentence organization . . 17

In view of the intent to measure "self-education . . . as opposed to formal education," considerable emphasis on diction and especially on taste and style is desirable. Whether over half the items should fall in this category is questionable. The use of running text tends to limit both the sampling of points tested and the methods of testing (e.g., paragraph organization, an essential aspect of effective expression, is tested meagerly and indirectly by four items in which the desired answer is to leave out completely a sentence or clause). Many common errors, important enough to justify one item, are not touched on. One wonders whether the author used an outline in building the test, i.e., decided what points to cover and shaped his material accordingly, or let his material determine the items.

The first and last themes are interesting, and a good deal of ingenuity has been used in devising the items, which range from gross errors to fairly subtle distinctions. The punctuation and grammar items are clear-cut, but as soon as the author enters the subjective area of taste and style, he is on dangerous ground and should have taken every precaution to use only items that a large majority of experts will agree upon. This part could have profited from thoroughgoing criticism prior to publication, which would have eliminated most of the items that have debatable answers and ironed out rough places in the selections themselves.

The test is apparently photo-offset from Vari-Typed copy, and its appearance and legibility are marred by too much use of boldface type. There are a few misprints, one of which (in

Item 61) happens to eliminate the correct answer.

No data are given on reliability or validity. The scoring method makes no correction for chance. An examination of the percentile norms arouses some suspicion regarding the distribution of item difficulties and the efficiency and reliability of measurement. For example, only 16 raw-score points separate the 20th and the 80th percentiles in the Type I colleges. This is spreading the items pretty thin and increasing the error of measurement over the middle three-fifths of the scores. One would judge that there are too many easy and too many hard (or ambiguous) items. Probably the "correctness" items tend to be easy, and the "effectiveness" ones hard. There is no mention of the tryout of the items or the criteria used in selecting them.

For reviews by Herbert S. Conrad and Warren G. Findley of the entire battery, see 20.

[123]
★Cotswold Measurement of Ability II: English. Ages 10-11; 1947; 2 forms (Series 1, 2); 6s. per 20; 1s. per manual; 6d. per single copy; 40(50) minutes; C. M. Fleming; Robert Gibson & Sons (Glasgow), Ltd.

[124]
"Dingwall" Test in English Usage. Ages 9-10, 10-12; 1937; 1 form; 2 parts; 2 levels; 6d. per manual; 1s. 3d. per specimen set, postpaid; prepared by the Educational Institute of Scotland; University of London Press, Ltd.
a) PUPILS AGED 9-10: PUPILS' BOOKLET I. 3s. 6d. per 25.
b) PUPILS AGED 9-10: PUPILS' BOOKLET II. 4s. 6d. per 25.
c) PUPILS AGED 10-12: PUPILS' BOOKLET I. 3s. 6d. per 25.
d) PUPILS AGED 10-12: PUPILS' BOOKLET II. 4s. 6d. per 25.

Robert H. Thouless, Reader in Educational Psychology, Cambridge University, Cambridge, England. These tests are designed to give a measure of achievement in ability to write "correct" English: to use the past tense, to use the correct cases of pronouns, to use appropriate conjunctions, to punctuate, to insert capital letters, etc. Even for the older age range, there seems to be no attempt to assess skill in English usage as distinct from mere correctness. No use is made of alternative answers to be underlined or the like, so an amount of writing is required which seems undesirable in tests to be done with a time limit. The usefulness of the two forms is reduced by the fact that some of the test items are identical.

There is no indication of any measurement of the validity or reliability of the test; the small number of items in each part would probably make these low. Tentative norms are given at the end, but it is not stated from how many subjects these have been calculated, so one cannot judge how accurate they are likely to be. In any case, these norms are simply single figures indicating the average score for the chronological age for which each test was designed. There is no measure of scatter or other means of assessing how much better or worse a given score is than this average. This information is insufficient to be of any practical use for anyone who wishes to use the tests.

For review by Charles Fox, see 40:1275.

[125]

English Survey Test: Ohio Senior Survey Tests. Grade 12; 1935–41; Forms A, B; 3¢ per test; 85(90) minutes; S. L. Pressey and Maurice E. Troyer (Form B); Ohio Scholarship Tests, Ohio State Department of Education.

REFERENCES

1. MILLER, DOROTHY A. *A Comparison of Scores on the Pressey-Troyer English Survey Test With Point-Hour Ratios in Business Organization, Accounting and Business Education Courses.* Unpublished master's thesis, Ohio State University, 1944.

Charlotte W. Croon, Test Research Service, 1213 McChestney Avenue, Nashville, Tennessee. This test yields a total score and five subtest scores: grammar, spelling, capitalization, punctuation, and sentence structure. The maximum possible score on each subtest is 80. However, the sigmas (estimated from the percentiles for Form A) gives a better idea of the weighting of the five parts in the total score: grammar 15, spelling 16, capitalization 9, punctuation 20, and sentence structure 15.

The two forms were apparently constructed to cover about the same material at the same difficulty level. The percentile norms for Form A apply to pupils before they have had a remedial course, and those for Form B apply after this course. There is no information given about reliability.

Except for the sentence structure subtest, which is entirely objective, the scoring would probably have to be done by the teacher, since the pupils write in their answers. A correction for guessing in the three-choice sentence structure section would have been desirable. On Form A, a testee who knew 25 items and omitted the other 15 would score at the 50th percentile; another testee who also knew 25 items but guessed on the others would be most likely to score at the 75th percentile.

The items are crowded, and the format is poor. In the grammar section of Form A, the pupil has to decide which one of three italicized words in each line of running text is incorrect. The printing is so bad that it is hard to pick out the words.

With 80 items, one would expect good coverage of grammatical usage. Over a third of the errors are in verb number. In each form there are three items on "to" for "too." There are no items on such common errors as "hadn't ought," "of" for "have" in such a phrase as "should have gone," "can't hardly," "them" for "those," "these kind" for "this kind," double negatives, double subjects, "let's us," "use to," "like" for "as," etc. On the other hand, some of the errors included are rarely heard in real life, e.g. "all of we cheered" and "I have clumb." Also there are cases where there are two errors in one line (Item 10 in A), other cases where the error keyed is really not an error (Item 62 in B— "none" may be construed as either singular or plural), and other cases where an error can be corrected in two ways (Item 74 in B—change either the "each" to "all" or the "seem" to "seems").

The second section of the test is called Spelling Vocabulary. According to the key, it yields a score in spelling only. The items require the pupil first to think of a word from a definition used in a sentence, e.g., "His life was filled with many (disastrous circumstances, fatal happenings)," and then to write the word. If, in the example quoted, "tragedies" did not come to mind, the testee would obviously have no chance to spell it. This double-barreled technique is not in accordance with present principles of test construction.

The other parts of the test are also open to many criticisms. Six items in the punctuation section of Form A require the pupil to use a comma before the third member of a series of three. While the writer believes this is preferable, present usage permits omitting this comma. At least one of the punctuation sentences can be interpreted two ways (Item 7 in A). A number of sentences in the sentence structure section are keyed as wrong because a pronoun is used to refer to a clause; present usage allows this practice. Other items depend on technicalities; the sentence, "She received a letter from her employer that was postmarked in Washington," is perfectly clear even though "that" does not directly follow the word to which it refers.

The two forms of this test were copyrighted in 1935 and 1937. The decade since then has seen many improvements in test-construction techniques, such as preparing a careful outline of points to be covered, testing for one thing at a time, trying out the items experimentally, submitting the test to outside criticism before publication, etc. There are now several tests in this field that are more carefully planned and constructed than this one.

J. Paul Leonard, President, San Francisco State College, San Francisco, California. This is one of the senior survey tests of the Ohio State Department of Education and is designed "to help the high school senior to survey his ability in these important elements of education." The makers claim the tests were based upon research data but do not specify any definitely except the Thorndike word list for the spelling test. The test covers grammar, spelling, punctuation, capitalization, and sentence structure. The grammar test is based upon a running story with grammatical errors which the pupil is asked to identify and correct. The section on punctuation and capitalization is made up of a group of sentences without appropriate markings, and the pupil is required to correct them. The spelling section is composed of sentences, in which the word to be spelled is defined but not mentioned. The pupil is required to guess the word and spell it. The sentence structure section is made up of groups of three sentences, one of which has some incorrect form. The pupil is asked to identify the wrong structure but not to correct it.

The testmakers supply norms in terms of raw scores and percentiles. The test is rather easily scored, with the exception of the punctuation and capitalization section. Very little special statistical work has gone into the test. It is chiefly an instrument which any good teacher could make, supplied with norms for a large group of pupils. In the spelling test the pupil may guess other words than the actual one desired and will hence be marked incorrect. A good deal of time is spent trying to determine the word desired. The test is based entirely upon mechanical errors and represents nothing novel or distinctive in test building. It is a reasonably simple, comprehensive instrument to determine how well pupils can perform the operations for which it calls.

English Survey Test: Ohio Senior Survey Tests

[126]
English Test: National Achievement Tests.
Grades 3-8, 7-12; 1936-38; Forms A, B; $1.50 per 25 tests for grades 3-8; $1.75 per 25 tests for grades 7-12; 15¢ per specimen set; nontimed (40) minutes; Robert K. Speer and Samuel Smith; Acorn Publishing Co.

Harry A. Greene, Director of the Bureau of Educational Research and Service and Professor of Education, The State University of Iowa, Iowa City, Iowa. The test for grades 3–8 is a six-page survey test of 100 items. It consists of six parts: (*a*) capitalization, 10 items; (*b*) punctuation, 10 items; (*c*) language usage (sentence), 20 items; (*d*) language usage (words), 30 items; (*e*) expressing ideas, 20 items; and (*f*) letter writing, 10 items. The test for grades 7–12 is an eight-page booklet covering six phases of language skill: (*a*) word usage, 30 items; (*b*) punctuation, 20 items; (*c*) vocabulary, 20 items; (*d*) language usage—sentences, 45 items (15 points); (*e*) expressing ideas, 15 items; (*f*) expressing feeling, 10 items. A perfect score on this booklet is 110 points.

The selection of the item content of these tests seems to have been based largely on textbook analysis and personal judgment. While some objection might be registered against some of the socially improbable errors listed, the chief criticism must be of the extremely limited sampling in the several skill areas tested. Not only are capitalization, punctuation, and usage at both the word and sentence levels sampled inadequately, but many skills in these areas that receive much instructional emphasis are crowded out by a section on expressing ideas which appears to be more a reading test than a language test. In the general survey form for grades 3–8 the test of letter writing is extremely brief and unreal.

With the exception of the punctuation sections the pupil response is given by recognizing and underlining the correct form. In most exercises three choices are offered. Not only is this space-consuming in the booklet, but in some of the items the third choice adds very little to the point of the exercise. No evidence on item difficulty or item discrimination is presented. No demonstration of the validity of the testing techniques is made in the material available to this reviewer.

The tests have a number of unique features, one of which is the clever system of marking the correct choice under each item by letters found only in a specified code word. This arrangement greatly simplifies the scoring key but does make for a rather eye-tiring scoring process. The supplementary material provided with the tests is limited to a single printed sheet bearing directions to the teacher, the class record, the answer form, and the norms. While time limits are not stressed in these tests, they are clearly set forth in the directions. Grade levels corresponding to point scores earned on the tests are the only norms reported. No indication is given of the size or nature of the population on which the norms are based. No statistical evidence of the reliability of the tests is reported.

It is possible that these tests would prove very effective if treated as a part of a complete achievement test battery; but when isolated as subject-matter tests, they seem to lack the definiteness and reliability which should be expected of a useful survey or diagnostic instrument.

[127]

English Usage: Every Pupil Test. Grades 3-6, 7-9, 10-11; new form usually issued each April and December; forms April, December 1946; 2¢ per test; 1¢ per answer key; 40(45) minutes; Jessie Bechtel, Helen Kaser, and W. G. Findley under the direction of John W. Evans; Ohio Scholarship Tests, Ohio State Department of Education.

REFERENCES

1. EDMINSTON, R. W., AND GINGERICH, C. N. "The Relation of Factors of English Usage to Composition." *J Ed Res* 36:269-71 D '42. * (PA 17:2169)

J. R. Gerberich, Director, Bureau of Educational Research and Service, and Professor of Education, University of Connecticut, Storrs, Connecticut. [Review of the April and December 1946 forms.] The Every Pupil Ohio Scholarship tests of English usage are issued at three levels and in April and December forms annually. Both of the 1946 forms for grades 3 to 6 were constructed by teachers and administrators of the New Philadelphia, Ohio, public schools, while committees of Toledo junior high school teachers and of Mercer County teachers constructed the April and December forms respectively for both the junior high school and the senior high school levels. A program of test use suggested by the Ohio State Department of Education, by which the Every Pupil Tests are sponsored, consists of December testing primarily for diagnostic purposes and of April testing for measurement of progress and of achievement for three-fourths of the school year. The April and December forms for 1946 here reviewed consequently are not subject to as exact comparisons as would have been true of forms covering a school year. However, many

characteristics of the tests commented upon below are entirely independent of any expected or desirable parallelism between the two forms for one school year.

All six of the four-page tests are printed by a photo-offset or similar method from what were primarily typed originals. With the 40-minute total working time and 100 scoring points common to all, any observable uniformity or parallelism ends except in the intermediate-grade forms. Here there are five parts, allotted 20 points each, in both the April and the December forms. Tests for the junior and senior high school levels vary in number of parts from six to eight, and the tests constructed by Toledo junior high school teachers contain parts including such small numbers of items as 4, 5, and 6 and as many items as 35 and 40. Although there is no especial merit in complete parallelism and certainly there is no optimum number of items per test part, this situation nevertheless suggests to the reviewer some lack of balance among skills distinguished by numbered and named parts. The reviewer has a predisposition against 100 scoring points on any test, for the reason that interpretations based on percentages are thereby suggested to persons who still believe in percentage marking systems.

In both intermediate-grade tests, 20 scoring points each are allotted to correct usage, spelling, capital letters, punctuation, and sentence structure, with what may be an overemphasis upon capitalization and punctuation. However, the items in these tests are primarily functional rather than formal. Items are alternate response, multiple choice, and completion in nature.

The April tests at the two higher levels consist predominantly of items requiring correction of errors or at least of writing by the examinee. Formal grammar to the extent of at least 45 items of the total 200 is found in parts on subject and predicate, parts of speech, phrases and clauses, verbals, classification of sentences, and sentence sense. Other parts deal functionally with word usage, sentence structure, spelling, punctuation, and capitalization.

The December tests at the junior and senior high school levels are completion in nature to a smaller degree than are the April tests. However, formal grammar again accounts for 30 of the 200 items, in parts on punctuation and capitalization, parts of speech, and sentence patterns, whereas a more functional approach is used for parts on word usage, sentences, spelling, vocabulary, and sentence recognition.

All six tests make wide use of a completion item form which requires writing by the pupil of one or more words and in some instances also underlining of a capital letter or punctuation mark in the correction of usage errors. The scoring keys provide many instances of two, and a few cases even of three, different acceptable forms of response to items of this type. Elsewhere, such words as preposition, conjunction, etc., are to be written by the pupil, although in one part he is allowed to use Ph. and Cl. for phrase and clause. Certainly many standardized tests accomplish similar purposes with a greater degree of scorability and economy of time. For example, the *Cooperative English Test A, Mechanics of Expression* employs a rather complex but highly objective technique in measuring ability to detect and correct English usage errors.

This test series makes frequent use of items requesting the pupil to distinguish between sentences and sentence fragments or among compound sentences, simple sentences, and sentence fragments, a type of ability or aptitude often called sentence sense. Three designations appear at different levels for parts measuring this type of ability—sentence structure, sentence sense, and sentences. Although sentence structure is used in this manner at the intermediate-grade level, the same term in the April junior high school test designates items for which the pupil is asked to choose the better (or best) sentence of two (or three) for meaning exactly what it says. Furthermore, the sentence structure part of this junior high school test is almost exactly paralleled in the December senior high school test under the part heading of sentence recognition. Apparently various schools of thought are represented in the titles of parts for the different tests of this series.

Supplementary materials provided for scoring each test and for item counting the results are a mimeographed scoring key and a "Universal Class Error Sheet." The former is in ruled columns designed for strip key use, and the latter provides for recording the errors and omissions of each pupil on every item of the test. Instructions on the error check sheet conflict by recommending in one place that wrong answers be indicated by a check mark and in another place that wrong answers be indicated by a dash line. Provision is made in summary rows and columns of the sheet for obtaining individual pupil and entire class data on errors, omissions, and correct responses. Additional supplementary forms not available to the reviewer are a score distribution sheet and an item report sheet to be used by each school in forwarding results to the Ohio State Department of Education.

A supplementary tool for use in the interpretation of results is the booklet of "Percentile and Item Norms." The percentile norms for total scores of Ohio pupils are in skeleton form—deciles, quartiles, and percentiles 1, 5, 95, and 99—to the nearest one-tenth of raw score values. Interpolations from such tables are necessarily rather involved. In a section devoted to what are called item norms, percentages of Ohio pupils answering each item correctly are reported. The suggestion is made that the teacher can compare the percentage of success of her pupils on each item with the comparable percentage for Ohio pupils in general at the same grade level.

Still another supplementary tool, for use in summarizing local results, is the "Universal Class Percentile Record Blank." This blank is designed for comparing pupil and class performance with the state-wide norms and for determining pupil and class progress between tests. However, progress can be evaluated by this device only relatively and primarily within the class or grade group, by means of the direction and degree of change effected in the pupil's placement relative to state-wide norms and to local results. In the absence of some form of comparable scores, as embodied in the various types of derived scores based on the standard deviation, the amount of pupil growth is not subject to estimation. Percentile norms based on raw scores, used for both December and April tests, are valid only for relative evaluations of pupil growth.

Percentile norms for total scores show that the highest score made in eight of the ten grades covered by the test series was a perfect score and that 99th percentiles ranged from 85.0 for the third grade to 98.7, 99.3, and 99.9 of a possible 100 for the sixth, ninth, and twelfth grades respectively. Clearly some pupils were not truly measured. At the other extreme, 1st percentiles ranged from 15.0 for the third grade to 35.0, 43.7, and 45.9 for the sixth, ninth, and twelfth grades respectively. The reviewer infers that these tests lack sufficient top

English Usage: Every Pupil Test

for adequate measurement of superior pupils in the highest grade at each test level and that the tests in general are at a difficulty level considerably below that usually recommended for standardized tests. Perhaps the unfortunate tendency, if not desire, of many teachers to think and to test in percentage terms is reflected here.

These tests probably are not standardized, in the sense in which that term is ordinarily used. At least there is no evidence to indicate that the items were put through initial tryouts and that those finally included were chosen in terms of their difficulty levels and discriminative power. Comparability is obtained, moreover, only by means of percentile norms. This type of comparability is often approximated in specificity and for smaller groups by classroom teachers who determine marks by some arbitrary method based on the arithmetic mean and standard deviation or mean deviation.

The reviewer's general reaction to these tests is that they merit placement somewhere between a standardized test and a teacher-made informal objective test. He does not believe that a very high quality of workmanship went into their construction. It seems probable that many schools would be able to enlist the services of several teachers who could rather casually, with a good background of English studies but little understanding of objective testing techniques, cooperatively construct a series of tests of at least equal merit.

[128]

Essentials of English Tests. Grades 7-12; 1939-44; Forms A, B, C; $1.50 per 25; 35¢ per specimen set, postpaid; 45(50) minutes; Dora V. Smith and Constance M. McCullough; Educational Test Bureau.

Charlotte W. Croon, Test Research Service, 1213 McChestney Avenue, Nashville, Tennessee. This test is attractive, carefully constructed, and easy to take. The authors are to be commended on "confining the contents to essentials upon which there is fairly universal agreement among English authorities" and on their emphasis on validity as judged by experts in the field.

The test is divided into five parts: Spelling, 25 items; Grammatical Usage, 44 items; Word Usage, 15 items; Sentence Structure, 20 items; and Punctuation and Capitalization, 53 items (between one-fourth and one-third test capitalization). The publishers point out that persons using the test for survey purposes should notice that the parts vary in length but say that, since there is so little agreement upon the relative importance of the various phases of English usage, the authors have not attempted to apply arbitrary weightings. They apparently do not realize that, as soon as they build a test composed of several parts, they have inevitably weighted the parts in the total score. It would be better to weight the parts as they think best than to leave the weighting to uncontrolled factors.

The authors minimize the value of the test as a survey measure and stress its diagnostic aspects. They provide a Diagnostic Key to Errors, which states the point tested by each item and which appears to be a helpful teaching aid. However, norms are provided giving selected percentiles for part and total scores for grades 7 through 12 so that it is possible to determine roughly where a pupil or class stands in relation to pupils in general.

The correlation coefficient between total scores on comparable forms is given as .87 to .89. While the writer agrees that undue emphasis has sometimes been put on obtaining high coefficients, it should be pointed out that the publishers err when they imply that "introducing items so easy that all pupils would recognize them" will alter the "statistical reliability." It will merely raise all the scores equally. No coefficients are given for the parts. The writer wonders whether combining the short, and probably unreliable, Part III with Part II would not save time for both the testees and the scorers with little loss in diagnostic value.

The sampling is good. The punctuation part is particularly well constructed to cover the points to be tested in a natural and interesting way. Most of the scoring would probably have to be done by the teacher since only one part is completely objective and there are places where the scorer's judgment might enter in. It may be a little dangerous not to correct for guessing on Part IV. A tenth-grade pupil who knew eight items and omitted the rest would score at about the 20th percentile; another pupil who also knew eight items but guessed on the others would be most likely to score at the 50th percentile. The writer noticed only one item that was definitely in error, Item 42 in Part V of Form A. The key requires the capitalization of "junior" in the phrase "junior class." In Forms B and C, the authors reverse

Essentials of English Tests

themselves, and the testee is marked wrong if he capitalizes the names of school classes.

Part IV, although completely objective in scoring, is really the most subjective in content. The testee is asked to choose the one of four sentences that "most correctively and effectively states the idea." In a number of items, two or more of the choices state *different* ideas equally correctly, e.g., Item 8 in Form A, Item 4 in Form B, Item 7 in Form C. There are a few other items where the testee will find himself trying to select what the testmaker wants rather than being able to pick out one sentence as clearly superior, e.g., Items 9 and 15 in Form C, Items 9 and 20 in Form B.

The directions for administering might be improved by requiring the testees to go on to succeeding parts at appropriate intervals. In many classes, there are likely to be a few slow pupils who will spend an undue amount of time on the first parts of a test unless they are forced to move on. If the testing time were 40 minutes instead of 45, the test could be given in the average school period.

On the whole, the authors have done an excellent job in their avowed purpose of providing "teaching materials designed to orient the teacher with her instructional job in each class." The writer believes that this test will have its greatest value where the individual teacher is interested in giving it and is willing to do the scoring and interpret the results herself.

Gerald V. Lannholm, Assistant Director, The Graduate Record Examination, New York, New York. In their Manual of Directions, the authors state that this test may be used as a survey test. They also state that its chief value "probably lies in its diagnosis of individual strengths and deficiencies in the English abilities." A diagnostic key to errors helps to serve the diagnostic function of the test. Percentile norms based on total scores are presented for each of the grade levels for which the test is said to be appropriate.

The abilities which the test purports to measure are implied by the names of the five parts of the test: Spelling, Grammatical Usage, Word Usage, Sentence Structure, and Punctuation and Capitalization. The number of items in these parts varies from 15 in the word usage section to 53 in the punctuation and capitalization section. The items in the test are said to be based on skills selected according to the findings of studies of frequencies of usage and of errors. These studies are neither identified nor described. Eliminated from consideration for selection were skills upon which authorities disagree regarding the correct usage.

The authors minimize the value of a statistical evaluation of a test's effectiveness. However, they admit selecting "items which discriminate between students scoring high and those scoring low." They report that the correlation between scores on the various forms was found to be between .87 and .89.

That the authors recognized the importance of a close relationship between the purpose of a test and the nature of the task imposed upon the examinee is evident in their selection of testing techniques. In all but one of the five parts of the test, the examinee must make a written response to the items. This reviewer suggests that greater reality might have been achieved without increasing the difficulty of scoring if other techniques had been employed for measuring certain of the abilities. For example, the spelling test requires the examinee to spell only those words which he thinks are spelled incorrectly in the test copy. In the case of such words, the pupil must first examine the distorted spelling presented and determine what word it represents. Use of the list-dictation technique would eliminate this possible source of ambiguity and introduce a greater degree of reality, without increasing the scoring difficulty.

Ability in grammatical usage is measured by having the pupil evaluate the correctness of designated words or groups of words, some of which are presented correctly and some incorrectly. He is directed to correct those which he thinks are incorrect. A similar technique is employed in the word usage section. In the sentence structure section, each item presents four variations of the same thought. The pupil is to select the best of these statements. In the punctuation and capitalization section, material is presented without punctuation except for periods at the ends of some sentences. Some words are capitalized; some are not. At each of a number of underlined places, the pupil is to insert punctuation marks or capital letters if he thinks they are needed.

This reviewer considers misleading the practice of test authors generally to classify as diagnostic almost any test that covers more than one small phase of any field of learning.

Essentials of English Tests

If this practice persists, it is imperative that those who select and use tests be aware of the fact that tests vary greatly in the degree to which they may be of value in the process of diagnosis. At best, a test may assist in the identification of the specific strengths and weaknesses of individual pupils. The effectiveness of a test for accomplishing even this one step in a program of diagnosis will be limited to the extent that it fails to include a complete coverage of the specific skills involved. The effectiveness of the testing techniques employed is another limiting factor.

The *Essentials of English Tests* contain a total of 157 items. In the area of punctuation alone, authorities have identified nearly that many different usages, with several times that many variants. This test meets the criterion of complete coverage of skills more adequately than many other tests on the market. However, it still represents only a relatively small portion of the field it purports to cover. It is this reviewer's considered opinion that, despite the claim of the authors that their test has only incidental value for survey purposes, the test will be more useful for survey than for diagnostic purposes. With the substitution of improved testing techniques and the adjustment of the test's difficulty level to a smaller grade range, the test might well serve as a useful instrument for the measurement of general achievement in these aspects of correct writing.

Ed Res B 21:27–8 Ja 14 '42. William J. Jones. * no norms are reported for the college Freshmen * Each form is composed of 157 items divided into five different parts as follows: spelling, grammatical usage, word usage, sentence structure, punctuation and capitalization. More than one-third of the items are in the last part. This is probably too much emphasis on punctuation and capitalization if the test is to be used for survey purposes, as the authors suggest it may be used. Only 15 items are included on word usage, moreover. The content of the test was selected "according to the findings of studies concerning frequency of use and frequency of error." A hint concerning the way in which the authors expect their test to be used is found in the accompanying manual wherein they state that they have confined the "contents to essentials upon which there is fairly universal agreement among English authorities," believing that the presence in English tests of items upon which authorities are not agreed "has an undesirable effect upon current practice in the teaching of English." This seems to imply that the test items should be the guide for teaching practice. The tail wags the dog again! Although the authors claim that "the chief value of the examination probably lies in its diagnosis of individual strengths and deficiencies in the English abilities tested," reliabilities for part scores are not reported. The probable error of a test score for some of the parts may be high, however, for in the accompanying norms there are instances where only 1 point change in part score makes a percentile difference of 25. The reliability of the total score is reported as .89. The test is well printed and seems easy to take. The scoring stencil for Part V is ill-fitting and various answers are acceptable for certain items in the other parts.

[129]

★Examination in English: College Level. First year; 1944; 1 form (usually called Form B); 2 parts; separate answer sheets must be used; $2 per 25 of either part; 180(190) minutes; prepared by the Examinations Staff of the United States Armed Forces Institute; published by the American Council on Education; distributed by Cooperative Test Service. (Also distributed by Science Research Associates: $2 per 25 of either part; 65¢ per 25 machine-scorable answer sheets of either part; 50¢ per key for either part; 50¢ per specimen set of either part.)
a) BOOK I, READING AND LITERARY ACQUAINTANCE. Form CEn-2-B-4; 75¢ per 25 sets of machine-scorable answer sheets; 30¢ per scoring key; 35¢ per specimen set, postpaid; 120(125) minutes.
b) BOOK II, COMPOSITION. For administration only to students who have first taken Book I; Form CEn-3-B-4; 40¢ per 25 machine-scorable answer sheets; 15¢ per scoring key; 25¢ per specimen set, postpaid; 60(65) minutes.

John S. Diekhoff, Acting Chairman, Department of English, Queens College, Flushing, New York. Part I of this USAFI test has virtues which are not always found in such tests and which deserve special commendation. The four passages upon which questions are based are worth anybody's reading, for they are selected from Thoreau's *Walden,* from the *Gospel according to St. Matthew,* from Fitzgerald's *Rubáiyát,* and from Pater's *The Renaissance.* The passages themselves are well chosen. They present a variety of reading problems and are yet sufficiently alike in content to provide a basis for thought-provoking comparative questions. The passages are sufficiently difficult and the questions are sufficiently searching to tax the reading ability of very good undergraduates and to stretch their minds. The test will enhance the students' skill in reading whether or not it succeeds in measuring that skill—and I think it will measure it, too. If the selections and the questions are thought by some to demand too much of undergraduates, that is a good fault and a rare one in a time of relaxing educational standards.

The second part of the test will no doubt perform its function of measuring "literary acquaintance," but this is not so important a function. It is important to know whether a student has read Aristotle, Boswell, Corneille, and Zola. It is perhaps more important to know whether he can read them intelligently. It is certainly less important to know whether he has ever heard of them and whether he knows which is "classic," which is a biographer, which is a dramatist, and which is a "realist." This mere hearsay acquaintance, however, is what is measured by the test. Granted the limited objective, this portion of the test is good of its kind.

One may say the same of Book II, Part III, the test in composition. But I am doubtful of the ability of this kind of test to measure the really important composition skills—doubtful whether any objective-type test yet developed will do the job. It is one thing to discover whether a student recognizes correct or incorrect writing, relatively effective or ineffective writing, in what he reads for that purpose; it is another thing to discover whether he can plan and organize a composition and then write it correctly and effectively. No doubt the two skills are closely related, but they are not the same. Few teachers of composition will be willing to substitute the USAFI or any other objective test for theme reading. Many, seeking a means of supplementing and correcting their "subjective" judgment, will be glad to use the USAFI test to measure the student's ability to analyze the syntax, style, and structure of the writing of others.

[130]

★Examination in English: High School Level. Grades 10-12; 1944; IBM; 1 form (usually called Form B); 2 parts; separate answer sheets must be used; $2 per 25 of either parts; 40¢ per 25 machine-scorable answer sheets for either part; 15¢ per key for either part; 25¢ per specimen set of either part, post-paid; 180(190) minutes; prepared by the Examinations Staff of the United States Armed Forces Institute; distributed by Cooperative Test Service and Science Research Associates.
a) BOOK I, READING AND INTERPRETATION OF LITERATURE

Examination in English: College Level

AND LITERARY ACQUAINTANCE. Form SR and L-1-B-4; 120(125) minutes.
b) BOOK II, COMPOSITION. For administration only to students who have first taken Book I; Form SCp-2-B-4; 60(65) minutes.

REFERENCES

1. WHITE, VERNA, AND ENOCHS, J. B. "Testing the Reading and Interpretation of Literature." *Engl J* 33:171-7 Ap '44. *
2. WHITE, VERNA. *The Construction of a Test for High-School Students in the Reading and Interpretation of Literature.* Unpublished doctor's thesis, University of Chicago, 1945.
3. WHITE, VERNA. "Measuring Achievement in High-School English." *Sch R* 55:474-83 O '47. * (PA 21:4173)
4. WHITE, VERNA. "Measuring Competence in English of Armed Services Personnel." *Sch R* 55:345-55 Je '47. * (PA 21:4173)

Holland Roberts, Educational Director, California Labor School, Inc., San Francisco, California. These two wartime tests are modern in the sense that they not only reflect the conscious educational philosophy of the test-makers but in their construction form a unified program that anticipates the wide variation in conditions under which they may be used. A major effort has been made to insure that the tests are not mechanically applied, but that through comparative interpretations they are employed to meet the real needs of teachers and students. Adaptation to particular schools and systems has been provided for by planning the tests so that the results may be interpreted on the basis of the development of each student and be used in educational planning and individual guidance.

This provision for the great differences that exist between and within communities is an important advance in test construction and outmodes a large body of materials now used in educational measurement. Teachers who have recognized the inadequacy of the Procrustean tests that have dominated measurement can look forward to a wave of new development in the entire field of tests and measures. Testing in the past has often created a crisis in the minds of teachers and students, and at the same time a sense of fatality. If the results reached national norms, everyone relaxed and the program in operation was approved; when they were below national norms, the whip was applied and/or the program re-examined. In either case the test results were generally entombed in the files; when they have been referred to in counseling, the data have sometimes been considered in the light of a revelation from Mount Sinai.

These two tests, the one in literature and the other in composition, are designed to be administered as a unit. The literature test can be used alone but since the composition test is based upon the reading of the literature it cannot be used separately. Taken together they constitute the beginning of a core program in English.

The two-hour test, Reading and Interpretation of Literature and Literary Acquaintance, is organized in the two main divisions stated in the title. Part I on reading and interpretation is based upon four modern selections: two prose and two poetry, all centering on significant aspects of the meaning of America: "Keystones of Our National Unity" (prose); Whitman's famous poem, "Thou Mother With Thy Equal Brood"; "Western Star" (poem); and "How I Found America" (prose). These choices of core materials are distinguished for their literary quality, dramatic unity of theme, and interest and significance to the students as responsible members of our democracy. They are in sharp contrast to the miscellany of dull and unimportant scraps which are often presented to young people in reading and literature tests, for their subject matter brings the student to grips with key issues of our day in terms of his own responses to Americanism.

Here are eloquent statements of our great unfinished democratic experiment in discovering the ability of men of all nations, races, and creeds to rule themselves, presented in vivid scholarly prose, in sweeping, imaginative poetry, and in the passionate outpourings of an East Side immigrant girl caught in the tentacles of the New York sweatshop system of a generation ago.

The importance of content of this character, arranged in a pattern of fundamental meaning which is itself a vital part of the daily lives of the students, is difficult to overemphasize. When test material is chosen and organized according to such a standard, tests and the whole process of measurement reach an entirely new conception and make possible great qualitative as well as quantitative advances in educational achievement.

The multiple-choice questions that follow each of the selections make effective teaching use of the content. Many of the ninety exercises based on the selections "represent problem situations involving for their successful solution applications of knowledge and the functioning of critical reflective thinking." Ability to understand relationships and integrate them in thinking is tested rather than the older reliance upon simple recall of facts of no

relevance to the student. A part of the testing provides for comparative thinking on all four selections.

Part II tests literary acquaintance with 60 multiple-choice exercises based upon literature commonly read and studied in elementary and high schools. Some are pure memory questions of fact, but many depend upon such central understanding of the classics as:

> Macbeth deals fundamentally with the
> A. relations between husband and wife
> B. murder instigated by Lady Macbeth
> C. effect upon man of his ambition to rule over his fellows
> D. cruelty of Macbeth

The authors have also made advances in anticipating the uses of the test. They urge that teachers should "evaluate the (test) exercises in relation to the objectives of their own courses" and establish norms suitable for their own needs. A method for setting up local norms, with specific directions for translating the test scores into grades is presented, so that fair comparisons may be made with the norms given in the manual. As the authors point out, uncritical acceptance of published norms results in an exaggerated estimate of the abilities of students in schools where educational standards are high and, conversely, depreciation of student ability in schools of low scholastic status. They note that effective educational guidance and placement depend upon care in interpretation of part scores in relationship to courses "immediately in prospect."

Thorough, practical directions and materials are provided for administering, machine or hand scoring the tests, and interpreting the scores on a variety of bases. The norms are given in percentile tables so that the standing of any student, group, or class may be compared with others for the parts of the test as well as *in toto*. Such study of relative standing makes it possible to evaluate and reorient the teaching program to emphasize the objectives set up.

Part I is too rigorous for low ability groups, and the test as a whole is not suitable for retarded readers; but outside these areas it should prove of marked value for schools interested in developing higher standards of work through modern measurement.

Book II, Composition, is an hour and a half test based entirely upon three short papers written by high school students who had just taken the reading examination reviewed above. This reading furnished the subject matter for their composition. In writing their commentaries in these papers the students were guided by five key questions, such as "How are the ideas of these authors alike? How different?"; but they were instructed to prepare unified, well-organized material and to avoid making their statements a series of disjointed answers. In this they had varying success.

In taking this composition test, the student first reads each theme and then works out a series of multiple-answer exercises which involve judgments on its organization and style. After all three themes have been considered in this way, comparisons are made of their relative effectiveness in style, organization, natural use of experience, and comprehensiveness. As there are no established standards for any of these items, this section of the test is highly subjective and controversial. The foundation work for measurement in this field has not yet been done.

The second part of the work is a usage test in grammar, punctuation, and word choice constructed by a special reprinting of the three student themes. Sentences and phrases are reprinted in the left-hand column of each page, with some part underlined and numbered. In the right-hand column, two, three, or four alternative ways of writing the underlined portion are presented. The first choice is the original expression of the student. There is originality in this effort to test composition ability under conditions closely paralleling a natural life situation. It has definite advantages over the series of disconnected, isolated sentences often used for the same purpose. However, it should be clearly understood that all such exercises are concerned primarily with composition *form*. Basically they are proofreading tests and do not attempt to measure the power to compose. Composition power is concerned with conceiving and formulating ideas and action, with content—of which form is an expression. Proofreading tests have their uses, but the critical skill required to select preferred usages from someone else's writing can be at best only a minor contribution to original composition. It has not even been proved that proofing skill is an adequate test of ability to *use* accepted forms and usages in writing.

Considered, however, not as a complete composition but as a proofreading test, these exercises have definite advantages. They are based upon actual student writing and therefore present real problems of usage as they occur in daily student life rather than teacher-devised problems stated in adult language. This is an important psychological consideration generally neglected in the English classroom.

Taken as a whole, the major advantage of this test is its continuity of significant thought. To center a complete test upon the building of unity among the diverse peoples of America establishes a new high standard and a milestone in measurement. Tests constructed from such an outlook can become an integral part of creative teaching and contribute to individual and social integration.

Louis C. Zahner, Head of English Department, Groton School, Groton, Massachusetts. It is to the credit of the United States Armed Forces Institute that it disclaims any attempt to impose standards upon schools and colleges. Furthermore, it emphasizes the importance of local validation of its tests, even advising subjective analysis and judgment. This wisely moderate and all too rare view of the limitations of an objective test and of its proper function and application becomes even more striking when one considers the research and expert knowledge that have gone into the construction of the test and its percentile norms.

Book I departs from the usual technique of presenting many snippets out of context for interpretation, and instead bases its items on four long and self-sufficient passages, two of prose and two of poetry, each developing different aspects of a common theme. The authors make full use of the additional testing areas opened by this basic organization.

This part of the test is not entirely free from the faults of detail common to its type. Some of the keyed responses are too obvious, others are debatable, others can be detected by a process of elimination. Some keyed and wrong responses are ambiguously worded. To the usual assumptions of literary values which the successful test-taker must accept, moreover, are added social and political assumptions having to do with the common theme, American Democracy.

The more general problem raised by this type of test is brought no nearer to solution: the psychological processes at work in taking an objective test in reading are not those called

Examination in English: High School Level

into play in effective reading. It is one thing to select a ready-made response; it is quite another for a reader to ask himself pertinent questions and to make his own responses. Close correlation between the two, if it exists, has not been clearly established and must be accepted, if at all, on faith.

The section on literary acquaintance is likewise open to the common criticisms of this type of test. When the items move off the ground of simple and relatively insignificant fact, they must resort to oversimplified judgments and stock tags, such as the statement that "Macbeth deals fundamentally with the effect upon man of his ambition to rule over his fellows." Since some of the unkeyed responses in such items are tenable answers, each representing a part of a situation too complex to be reduced to a single phrase, such an item might better be constructed for elimination of one wholly impertinent response.

In items dealing with three or four books together, the keyed response can often be found from one book alone. For instance, in an item dealing with Jane Addams, Eve Curie, and Pasteur three of the four responses can be eliminated by anyone who knows only that Jane Addams was a social worker.

Booklet II of this test, on composition, sets up three student themes and asks questions about them ranging from organizati˜n to details of diction and punctuation. It is a thorough test of critical judgment applied to writing at the high school student's level as a writer. Whether a student who can accurately identify a possible error that has been isolated for his attention or select the best of several improvements composed for him could create, write, criticize, and revise his own composition with equal proficiency remains an open question. In spite of occasional weak spots, however, such as inclusion of responses that are highly debatable or not mutually exclusive, the formal knowledge of the principles of writing generally taught at the high school level are more ingeniously and fully tested here than in most other commercial tests.

In fact, this series of tests as a whole, if taken and interpreted as the authors advise and not as "the be-all and the end-all," should prove to be a useful adjunct to any good high school or even college freshman course in English. The authors have made a notable contribution to testing in this field.

[131]

Iowa Placement Examinations: English Training. Grades 12-13; 1925–44; IBM; 2 editions; M. F. Carpenter, G. D. Stoddard, and L. W. Miller; Bureau of Educational Research and Service, State University of Iowa.
a) SERIES ETI, REVISED. 1925–26; Forms A, B; $4 per 100; 50¢ per specimen set including the other 10 tests in the series, postpaid; 40(45) minutes; prepared under the direction of C. E. Seashore and G. M. Ruch.
b) NEW SERIES ET-2 REVISED. 1925–26; also called Quick-Scoring Edition; IBM; Form M; separate answer sheets need not be used; $1.15 per 25; 30¢ per specimen set including the other 4 tests in the series, postpaid; $1 per 100 machine-scorable answer sheets; 15¢ per stencil for scoring answer sheets; 45(50) minutes; revised by M. F. Carpenter and D. B. Stuit.

REFERENCES

1. STODDARD, GEORGE DINSMORE. *Iowa Placement Examinations.* University of Iowa, Studies in Education, Vol. 3, No. 2. Iowa City, Iowa: the University, 1925. Pp. 103. Paper. $1.00. *
2. LANGLIE, T. A. "The Administration of Placement Examinations." *Sch & Soc* 24:619-20 N 13 '26. * (PA 1:695)
3. LANGLIE, T. A. "Analysis of the Iowa Placement Tests." *J Appl Psychol* 10:303-14 Je '26. * (PA 1:496)
4. STODDARD, GEORGE D. "Iowa Placement Examinations." *Sch & Soc* 24:212-6 Ag 14 '26. *
5. LANGLIE, T. A. "A Comparison of 'Aptitude' and 'Training' Tests for Prognosis." *J Ed Psychol* 19:658-65 D '28. * (PA 3:1701)
6. STALNAKER, JOHN M. *A Statistical Study of Some Aspects of the Purdue Orientation Testing Program.* Bulletin of Purdue University, Vol. 28, No. 6; Studies in Higher Education VIII. Lafayette, Ind.: Division of Educational Reference, the University, February 1928. Pp. 68. Paper. $0.20. *
7. GERBERICH, JOSEPH RAYMOND. *A Personnel Study of 10,000 Iowa High School Seniors.* University of Iowa Studies in Education, Vol. 5, No. 3. Iowa City, Iowa: the University, 1930. Pp. 112. Paper. $1.00. * (PA 5:771)
8. MILLER, LAWRENCE WILLIAM. *An Experimental Study of the Iowa Placement Examinations.* University of Iowa Studies in Education, Vol. 5, No. 6. Iowa City, Iowa: the University, 1930. Pp. 116. Paper. $1.00. * (PA 5:799)
9. ROOT, A. R. "College Achievement." *J Higher Ed* 7:387-8 O '36. * (PA 11:477)
10. MERRILL, RUTH ATHERTON. *An Evaluation of Criteria for the Selection of Students in the School of Nursing of the University of Minnesota.* Unpublished doctor's thesis, University of Minnesota, 1937. (Summaries of Ph.D. Theses . . ., 1939, pp. 126-31.)
11. BARNETTE, W. LESLIE. "Norms of Business College Students on Standardized Tests: Intelligence, Clerical Ability, English." *J Appl Psychol* 24:237-44 Ap '40. * (PA 14:4719)
12. STUIT, DEWEY B., AND DONNELLY, MARY CARROLL. "Performance in the Iowa Qualifying Examination of Majors in Various Academic Departments With Implications for Counseling." *J Exp Ed* 8:293-9 Mr '40. * (PA 14:4754)
13. PANKASKIE, MARGARET. *Factors in Reading Achievement at the College Level.* Unpublished doctor's thesis, University of Iowa, 1941. (Doctoral Dissertations . . . 1940 and 1941, 1944, pp. 336-47.)
14. ADAMS, MICHAEL. "The Prediction of Scholastic Success in a College of Law." *Proc Iowa Acad Sci* 49:385-9 '42. * (PA 17:2871)
15. ADAMS, WILLIAM MICHAEL. "Prediction of Scholastic Success in Colleges of Law: II, An Investigation of Pre-Law Grades and Other Indices of Law School Aptitude." *Ed & Psychol Meas* 4:13-9 sp '44. * (PA 18:3271)

Robert C. Pooley, Professor of English, The University of Wisconsin, Madison, Wisconsin. This is a 4-page test of English skills in spelling, punctuation, sentence structure, and correct usage. Forms A and B are furnished with an answer key for manual scoring. Norms are presented in the form of percentiles undifferentiated for grade levels. Instructions for administration are covered by the general manual for the *Iowa Placement Examinations.*

Part I is a test of spelling. A list of 75 words is presented, of which 25 are misspelled. Space is provided for the student to rewrite correctly the misspelled words. Part II is a test of punctuation consisting of 60 sentences. The student indicates by "R" or "W" whether the sentence is correctly or incorrectly punctuated. Part III is a test of English usage consisting of 60 sentences also marked by "R" or "W." Part IV contains 45 sentences to be classified as: "good, clear, and emphatic," or "weak, confused, or ridiculous."

This test measures quite well a student's power to examine, criticize, and correct the writing of someone else. If he makes a high score in the test, he indicates that his eye can detect misspelled words and misplaced or omitted marks of punctuation. He indicates that he knows the difference between *ain't* and *isn't* and *you was* and *you were*. He can also detect a sentence which is grammatically incomplete or which presents obscure or misleading word order. In other words, as a test of the recognition of correct English it is quite satisfactory.

The use to which the test is put would have to determine its validity. If it is meant to measure the skills of proofreading and to use those as a rough index of the success the student has achieved from instruction in English, then the test is reasonably valid. If it is intended to test the power of the student to construct a good sentence, to present unified and thoughtful paragraphs and to assemble paragraphs into a successful composition, the test has no validity at all. It is the common experience of teachers of English that students who successfully pass tests of mechanical form often write with little quality, and those who write exceedingly well often fail in tests of English form. As a measure of success in the use of English, therefore, the test must be considered invalid.

Form M of the series is a test designed for machine scoring. It has been reduced to three exercises totalling 225 points. The spelling has been changed by the presentation of four different spellings of each word, the student to select the correct spelling. The punctuation exercise has been increased to 75 points and the English usage has been increased similarly. The test of sentence structure has been omitted. While the comments made above refer also to this form of the test, it is even weaker in validity than Forms A and B because the test of sentence form has been omitted. Form M is a test of proofreading in the mechanics of English

Iowa Placement Examinations: English Training

and as such is satisfactory if it is used for nothing else.

[132]

★Kentucky English Test, [Revised]. Grades 12-13; 1937–46; Form 46; 8¢ per test including scoring service; 5¢ per test without scoring service; 30(35) minutes; original test by E. J. Asher and T. E. McMullen; revision by P. L. Mellenbruch; Kentucky Cooperative Testing Service, University of Kentucky.

[133]

★Language Essentials Tests. Grades 4-8; 1941; Forms A, B; $1 per 25; 35¢ per specimen set, postpaid; 30(35) minutes; Vera Davis and H. E. Schrammel; Educational Test Bureau.

Harry A. Greene, Director of the Bureau of Educational Research and Service and Professor of Education, The State University of Iowa, Iowa City, Iowa. These tests are a revision and a slight expansion of the earlier Davis–Schrammel tests first published in 1934. The present tests are well printed in a pleasing four-page folder containing 100 items sampling four phases of language abilities: (*a*) Punctuation, 20 items; (*b*) Capitalization, 20 items; (*c*) Sentence Structure, 15 items; and (*d*) Correct Usage, 45 items.

The selection of 100 items to make a language essentials test is at best a highly difficult task. It is easy to criticize the omission or the inclusion of certain items. The items comprising these tests presumably are chosen as examples of minimal essentials as presented in the typical textbook program of language instruction. However, many items receiving heavy instructional emphasis are omitted, and some of minor importance are included. Little or no critical evidence of the validity of the individual items is presented. No analysis of item difficulty or item discrimination is reported. The language functions are all incorporated in discourse instead of in isolated exercises. The implication is that this technique results in a more lifelike reaction on the part of the pupil, although the superiority of the technique of testing language skills in meaning context has not been demonstrated.

With the possible exception of the section on usage (Part IV), the number of items is quite limited. A check of the item content with certain criterion sources indicates that in the main the items included are essential items. In Part I, a number of punctuation skills which receive considerable instructional emphasis before the end of the eighth grade are omitted. In Part II, the capitalization skills, being much less extensive in the number of variants offered, are covered much more adequately. Part III, sentence structure, is a desirable addition to a language essentials test. However, the brevity of this part of the test must seriously reduce its reliability of measurement.

The evidence on the reliability of these tests indicates that a reliability coefficient of approximately .90 may be expected when one form of the complete booklet is used, if reliabilities based on from 42 to 70 cases can be taken seriously. The reliabilities reported for the separate test parts are based on adequate populations, but unfortunately these cases are pooled from fourth- to eighth-grade sources.

The percentile norms for both midyear and end-of-year results are based upon a sampling which should be adequate to provide representative norms for most legitimate comparisons. The grade increments at the median, or at almost any of the deciles, show that the growth from one grade to the next expressed in point scores is quite limited in spite of the fact that the test comprises 100 items. An examination of the table of norms suggests that either the tests cover too wide a grade range or too many very easy items have been retained. Twenty-two points at the median level represents the typical growth from the middle of the fourth grade to the end of the eighth grade. In a number of cases the operation of chance alone would serve to wipe out the growth from one grade to the next. A variation of 1.5 points (the P.E. of a score at the sixth grade level) from the sixth grade median of 77 would bring about a misplacement in the corresponding estimated percentile equivalent of 12 percentile points because of chance alone.

These tests have secured an adequate objectivity, but as is true of most other tests of language skills, they have been forced to sacrifice something of validity in so doing. For example, the recognition of the need for a punctuation mark or a capital letter is not the valid measure of either of these skills that placing the mark or making the capital letter would be. While these tests are satisfactorily objective, the scoring technique leaves much to be desired. If considerable validity must be sacrificed for the sake of objectivity, then it would seem to be wise to go the whole distance and secure the speed and economy which results from positioned answers which may be quickly

hand scored by stencil keys or scored by one of the test scoring machines.

The provision of the diagnostic key to errors is a desirable addition to the manual for these tests. While it is true that an accurate diagnosis of language weakness could hardly be determined from one or even two responses, this key to errors should enable the classroom teacher to make a very helpful analysis of the mastery of a class on the language essentials sampled in these tests.

In the judgment of this reviewer, the Davis–Schrammel tests should be limited to survey use in grades 4–6, the grade levels in which the item content is most suitable in terms of difficulty and validity. The sampling of skills is too limited and the resulting reliability of the test parts too low to justify its use for diagnostic purposes.

[134]
★Mechanics of Written English: State High School Tests for Indiana. Grades 9-12; 1943-45; Forms A, B; 5½¢ per test; 40(45) minutes; G. S. Wykoff and J. H. McKee; Division of Educational Reference, Purdue University.

[135]
Schonell Diagnostic English Tests. Ages 9½-16; 1940; 1 form; 7d. per test, 25-49 copies, 6d. each; 1s. 9d. per manual; 53(68) minutes; F. Eleanor Schonell; Oliver & Boyd Ltd.

John Cohen, Lecturer, University of Leeds, Leeds, England. The aim of these tests is primarily to diagnose weakness, particularly in the writing of English, though they may also be employed for measuring achievement in English usage, punctuation, vocabulary and sentence structure. When the tests are employed for diagnosis, no time limit is necessary.

The five subtests include: (*a*) English usage, (*b*) capital letters and punctuation, (*c*) vocabulary, (*d*) sentence structure, and (*e*) a composition on the subject of "Home."

In constructing the test, care has been taken to embody common forms of usage, especially those with high error frequencies. Coefficients of reliability range from .82 to .94 for the first four subtests; validity coefficients for the first two subtests are .72 and .79 respectively. But since all these coefficients are based only on a sample of 119 boys, they cannot be regarded as other than tentative. Moreover, neither of the validity criteria—correction of errors for the first subtest, and punctuation of dictated prose for the second—are altogether satisfactory. The marking is highly elaborate and time-consuming and hence limits the practical utility of the test material. Nevertheless the tests, first published in 1940, have run into four editions.

Norms are given for the first four subtests in terms of averages of 1,200 pupils. The mean scores are provided for each age group 8+ to 14+, thus enabling the scores for individual pupils to be expressed in equivalent ages, which may be averaged to yield an "English" age.

Robert H. Thouless, Reader in Educational Psychology, Cambridge University, Cambridge, England. This test is intended for two purposes; for diagnosing directions of weakness in the use of English and for obtaining an estimate of ability in the use of English. For the first purpose it is recommended that the test should be given without time limit; a time limit is used, however, for the second purpose.

The parts of the test include English usage, capital letters and punctuation, vocabulary, sentence structure, and the writing of an essay. Objectivity of marking is attained in all except the last of these parts, but the assessment of ability in English can be made without the essay since norms are given separately for each part. There is an odd discrepancy between the test itself and the handbook of instructions as to what is to be the subject of the essay.

The test items are graded in difficulty so that the test can be used for a wide age range (given as 9+ to 16+). Norms are given as average performance for ages from 8+ to 14+. These norms are stated to be tentative, but since they have been derived from 1,260 pupils, they should be reasonably reliable. The validity and reliability of the test have been determined by the author and are satisfactory.

It appears to be a well-constructed test which should prove useful.

[136]

Shepherd English Test: Clapp-Young Self-Marking Tests. Grades 7-13; 1931-32; Form A; separate answer booklets must be used; $1.98 per 25 sets of test and answer booklets; 90¢ per 25 answer booklets; 12¢ per specimen set, postpaid; 45(55) minutes; J. W. Shepherd; Houghton Mifflin Co.

REFERENCES

1. MARSHALL, M. V. "Predicting Success in Freshmen English." *Col Engl* 5:219-21 Ja '44. *
2. LESLIE, LOUIS A. "Shorthand Prognosis, II." *Bus Ed World* 27:406-9 Mr '47. *

Ruth D. Churchill, Administrative Assistant, Office of Testing and Evaluation, Antioch College, Yellow Springs, Ohio. The *Shepherd*

Schonell Diagnostic English Tests

English Test, which in the course of 160 multiple-choice items divided into four subtests covers the topics of reading, words, literature, and grammar, was published in 1931. Even then, it was in all probability a mediocre test.

Detailed criticism of the items would take too long. Many of the reading-comprehension items are trivial. Part 2, called Words, containing both spelling items and items dealing with the correct choice of words, is expressed in highflown language with many of the definitions inexact. The literature items call mainly for memory of authors and story details and for the identification of quotations. The grammar items are formal and superficial, many of them calling for no more than recognition of definitions and identification of parts of speech.

The manual provided consists of one sheet, which contains a description of the test, directions for administering it, data on reliability and validity, and norms. The directions, combined with the awkward arrangement of the test booklet, are unnecessarily confusing. While the "chance-halves" reliability of the total test seems satisfactory for both forms (over .90), the validity data, consisting of correlations with first-semester grades for freshman at the University of Oklahoma, are somewhat difficult to interpret. The correlation between test scores and grades in English is .46 while the corresponding correlations with grades in modern languages and social science are .53 and .48. Perhaps the test is a better measure of verbal ability than of knowledge of "English." Norms based on 11,632 students from 19 states (but apparently all in Oklahoma or Florida colleges) are given without distinction as to the form of the test.

A review of a test as old as this one (apparently no research has been undertaken, nor any new forms published, since 1931) would scarcely seem necessary but for the fact that this test appears in the current test catalogue of a reputable company and, unfortunately, is representative of a large group of tests which continue to be listed in such catalogues even though their contents and the methods by which they were constructed have long been outmoded.

[137]

★**Tools of Written English: State High School Tests for Indiana.** Grades 7-9; 1941; 5½¢ per test; 27(35) minutes; W. R. Thompson and N. L. Gage; Division of Educational Reference, Purdue University.

[138]

★Wisconsin Language Usage Test. High school; 1939-40; Forms A, B; Form A has the title *Wisconsin Achievement Tests: Language Usage*; $1.25 per 25; 50(55) minutes; prepared by the Bureau of Guidance and Records, School of Education, and the Department of English, University of Wisconsin; manual by T. L. Torgerson and G. J. Froehlich; E. M. Hale and Co.

LITERATURE

[139]

Barrett-Ryan Literature Test. Grades 9-16; 1933; Forms A, B, C; 90¢ per 25, postpaid; 15¢ per specimen set, postpaid; 40(45) minutes; E. R. Barrett, Teresa M. Ryan, and H. E. Schrammel; Bureau of Educational Measurements, Kansas State Teachers College of Emporia.

Chester W. Harris, Assistant Professor of Education, The University of Chicago, Chicago, Illinois. Many of the obvious weaknesses of the *Barrett–Ryan Literature Test* are suggested by the copyright date of 1933; tests approximately fifteen years old are likely to be inappropriate from the standpoint of present-day teaching and evaluation. Each form includes 120 multiple-choice questions on 35 "classics." These selections are "the ones which were reported most frequently by a large number of high school English teachers as being studied in their classes." This survey must have been made in the early 1930's at the latest, if the copyright date is accurate. The "classics," as the content of these tests defines them, consist primarily of nineteenth-century American and English writings. Chaucer, Shakespeare, Milton, Bunyan, and a few eighteenth-century authors also are represented, but only one selection from the twentieth century (Frost's "Mending Wall") appears. This method of determining the content of a test usually results in creating a test whose content is inappropriate for use in any particular teaching situation.

The test is designed to measure "understanding and knowledge of literature." The test items indicate that "understanding and knowledge" means only the memory of characters' names, of quotations, of who did what, where, and when, and of hackneyed pronouncements about form or style or "theme." The test is clearly a quiz, in the sense in which present-day radio programs use that term. Use of this test as the means of evaluating student achievement in literature would assume that determining to what extent the student remembers the specified points about these particular writings gives a valid index of the effect of his experiences with literature. The "detective" approach to evaluation—i.e., the discovery of whether or not the student has read certain readings and the assumption that if he has, his achievement is satisfactory—is implicit.

Inevitably, a printed test used in a classroom carries much prestige. This test is likely to suggest to teachers that the particular selections included constitute the proper reading for students and that the reading should be directed to the end of remembering the kinds of points emphasized in the test. Further, it is likely to suggest to teachers and students certain questionable interpretations of literature. The triviality of some of the items is objectionable; the student must tell, for example, whether Evangeline traveled on the Thames, Tiber, Amazon, or Mississippi River (Item 28, Form A), and whether Bryant's water fowl is "on the water, in the air, in a tree, or on the ground" (Item 110, Form A). The key indicates that King Lear is properly regarded as "a foolish old man" (Item 55, Form A) and that the theme of "Crossing the Bar" is "death" (Item 13, Form A). Sensitive students of literature should object strenuously to such interpretations. The obvious bad writing in the test is not worthy of test authors who are members of a college English department. Item 60, Form A, when "correctly" answered, reads: "The first episode in the story is the dying of a horse"; Item 75, Form A, states: "An important element is a woman disguises as a man." Apparently, the "numerous revisions" claimed for the items were made without benefit of first-rate criticism.

The three forms are advertised as equivalent; yet the only statistical evidence given is one correlation (between Form A and Form C) of .78 for an unspecified number of college students. On the basis of this evidence, most students of measurement would reject the conclusion. Examination of the selections indicates that the three forms are far from equivalent in content. Sixty-five different selections are included in the forms; of these, thirty are common to two or more of the forms. Each form therefore includes a set of selections different from that of each of the other forms. The reported correlation of .78 supports the prediction that familiarity with one set of selections would not be highly related to familiarity with another set. High reliability (.93 to .94) is claimed for each form. Validity is indicated by

Barrett-Ryan Literature Test

correlations—again based on unspecified numbers of cases—between test scores and certain "estimates" made by teachers. The lack of pertinent information needed to evaluate these correlations—such as estimates of reliability of the teacher judgments, for example—gives one little confidence in these numbers as evidence of validity. The lack of curricular validity has already been emphasized.

[140]

Carroll Prose Appreciation Test. Grades 7-9, 10-12, 13-16; 1932-35; 1 form; 3 levels; separate answer sheets must be used; $1.50 per 25; 25¢ per 25 answer sheets; 35¢ per specimen set, postpaid; nontimed (35) minutes; Herbert A. Carroll; Educational Test Bureau, Inc.

REFERENCES
    1. CARROLL, HERBERT A. "A Standardized Test of Prose Appreciation for Junior High School Pupils." J Ed Psychol 23:603-6 N '32. * (PA 7:1573)
    2. CARROLL, HERBERT A. "A Standardized Test of Prose Appreciation for Senior High School Pupils." J Ed Psychol 23: 401-10 S '32. * (PA 7:347)
    3. CARROLL, HERBERT A. "A Method of Measuring Prose Appreciation." Engl J 22:184-9 Mr '33. * (PA 7:3561)
    4. CARROLL, HERBERT A. "Appreciation of Literature and Abstract Intelligence." J Ed Psychol 25:54-7 Ja '34. * (PA 8:2659)

Chester W. Harris, Assistant Professor of Education, The University of Chicago, Chicago, Illinois. Prospective users of a test should demand that a test manual present at the least: explicit definitions of what the test is expected to measure, descriptions of how the test was constructed, and relevant data that enable one to make judgments of the test as a measuring instrument. Carroll is to be commended for including these minimum essentials in his manuals. He singles out for measurement the "power to differentiate the good from the less good, and the less good from the very bad." His hypothesis—clearly stated—is that this power to differentiate constitutes a crucial index of the ability to appreciate prose; the term *appreciation* in the title of the test is therefore given a definite meaning. (See my review of *English: Understanding and Appreciation of Poetry* for a comment on possible meanings of *appreciation*.) The method of constructing the test and the sources of the materials used are described, and data secured from studies of the test as a measuring instrument are presented. To censure the test because it does not measure all aspects of appreciation that can be defined would be decidedly unfair. Carroll claims only to measure one index of appreciation; the score yielded by the test is designed to indicate the extent of the student's agreement, in his ranking of selections, with the criterion used.

An important assumption on which any measurement of this power to differentiate rests is that the terms "good," "less good," and "very bad" can be so defined as to secure agreement among competent judges regarding the proper category for each of the prose selections compared. Carroll's technique for securing written materials that are likely to be judged in this consistent fashion is that of drawing on three sources that presumably differ widely in literary merit for three of the four passages to be compared and of using a mutilation as the fourth. In this fashion, he has built a number of sets of exercises, each consisting of four passages and each to be responded to by ranking the four passages in order of literary merit. In each set, the first choice was drawn from a book regarded as of excellent quality, the second from books generally regarded as of poor quality, the third from the "less literary" magazines, and the fourth from mutilations. Data regarding the agreement of a group of judges (not named) among themselves and with the criterion of source are given for the college form. For some of the sets, the agreement both among judges and between judges and source is quite close; for others, the same selection has been placed in all four positions of merit by one or more of the judges. Carroll's standard for including a set is that a consensus of opinion of the judges must agree with the ranking given by the source. For one of the four passages of a set, this consensus may represent as few as 50 or as many as 100 per cent of the judges. The objectivity of the key therefore varies from set to set.

Reliability estimates for the junior and the senior high school forms are given as .70 and .71; no estimate is given for the college form. Estimates of this magnitude indicate an important limitation of the test as an instrument for the appraisal of an individual's power to differentiate. The shortness of the passages gives rise to a further limitation. The judgment of the literary merit of a novel, for example, might reasonably consider the development of character, the various principles of organization that are brought together to form a plot, and the like. A short passage of from 100 to 300 words taken from that novel is unlikely to provide a basis for such judgments. As Carroll acknowledges, the basis for judging the literary merit of these short passages is likely to be that of stylistic characteristics. In interpreting scores on this test, this restriction of the concept of literary merit should be taken into account.

Perhaps the major value of Carroll's test is that of a device to stimulate discussions of style, of literary merit, and of what constitute defensible standards by which to judge these. Presumably, many teachers are interested in helping students to arrive at defensible judgments of literary works by means of a set of principles that can be applied in many situations. For them, the final judgment and the extent to which it agrees with more "expert" opinions are important to know; but it is even more important to know the way in which this final judgment was arrived at. Carroll's work is valuable, since it leads in the direction of appraising a student's judgment in terms of expert judgment. What is needed—in addition to technically better measures of this type—is a technique for describing the principles and criteria that students use in making such judgments.

[141]

Cooperative Literary Acquaintance Test. Grades 10-16; 1940-41; IBM; Forms Q, R; separate answer sheets need not be used; $2 per 25; 25¢ per specimen set, postpaid; 40¢ per 25 machine-scorable answer sheets; 15¢ per stencil for scoring answer sheets; 40(45) minutes; Rosa Lee Walston and Edward E. Cureton; Cooperative Test Service.

REFERENCES

1. Selover, Robert B. "A Study of the Sophomore Testing Program at the University of Minnesota—Part I." *J Appl Psychol* 26:296-307 Je '42. * (PA 16:4183)

For reviews by Carleton C. Jones, Lou LaBrant, Edward S. Noyes, and John H. Thompson of earlier forms, see 38:970 and 40:1298.

[142]

★**Cooperative Literary Comprehension and Appreciation Test.** Grades 10-16; 1941-43; IBM; Provisional Forms R, T; separate answer sheets need not be used; $1.75 per 25; 25¢ per specimen set, postpaid; 40¢ per 25 machine-scorable answer sheets; 15¢ per stencil for scoring answer sheets; 40(45) minutes; Form R: Hyman Eigerman, Mary Willis, and Frederick B. Davis; Form T: Mary Willis and H. A. Domincovich; Cooperative Test Service.

REFERENCES

1. Cureton, Edward E. "Evaluation or Guidance? The Report of the Eighth Annual National College Sophomore Testing Program April 17 to May 5, 1939." *J Exp Ed* 8:308-40 Mr '40. * (PA 14:4726)
2. Johnson, A. P. *The Prediction of Scholastic Achievement for Freshman Engineering Students at Purdue University.* Purdue University, Division of Educational Research, Studies in Engineering Education II. Lafayette, Ind.: the Division, May 1942. Pp. 22. Paper. $0.35. * (PA 16:5020)
3. Johnson, A. P. *The Relationship of Test Scores to Scholastic Achievement for 244 Engineering Freshmen Entering Purdue University in September, 1939.* Unpublished doctor's thesis, Purdue University, 1942.

Holland Roberts, Educational Director, California Labor School, Inc., San Francisco, California. As the comprehension and appreciation

of literature embrace the entire scope of human life and thought, measurement in the field offers problems of corresponding difficulty. These tests are clear, well adapted to the level of secondary students, varied in form and subject, and sometimes lively and humorous. They present, however, no new basic approach and have not grappled with the underlying problems of appreciation.

Form R of the test is made up of fifteen short literary selections, half prose and half poetry. The prose selections range in length from five to fifty lines and the topics vary from the humorous autobiographical recollections of two precocious youngsters in a summer camp to James Fennimore Cooper, a summary of a novel, and a short short horror story from the Civil War. The poetry is chiefly brief excerpts of five to twenty lines taken from a wide variety of sources, from the *Bible* to "Rainbow Round My Shoulder," and spoiled versions of mediocre stanzas on miscellaneous aspects of life and love.

Form T bears a later date and gives evidence of greater experience and talent. Twelve selections were used in its construction, five prose and seven poetry. Four of the five prose selections have a rollicking humor and a marked narrative appeal for adolescents. The poetry is symbolic and philosophic, and represents sharp differences in style, content, and difficulty. The excerpts are from the *Bible* and English and American sources, and the subject matter ranges from Hebraic apostrophes to God to the pace of time in the different ages of man, the puniness and futility of human life in the struggle against the blind forces of the universe, and Napoleon's callous and hypocritical slaughter of the people in his drive for power. The prose selections range from four to seventy-five lines and the poetry from four to seventeen. From one to ten multiple-choice questions follow each selection, a total of about sixty-five for each form of the test; the majority of these questions center upon the meaning of the lines, and the others, on problems of style.

The two forms of the test are similar in structure, and superficial in content, but they are markedly different in their essential characteristic, the quality of the literature which they sample. The selections in Form R are on the whole inferior and therefore do not provide a basic measure of ability in literary appreciation or understanding. A number of them are dull and trivial. Form T offers a larger variety of lively, interesting selections, a few of them of literary power. The 40 minutes spent in taking it can be an enjoyable experience on the level of a children's game.

As a whole this test illustrates both the great difficulty of measurement in appreciation and understanding on the higher cultural levels and the inability of testmakers to conceive of measurement as an integral part of the entire process of learning and teaching. Such tests are based upon a miscellany of scraps of material, some of it with no pretensions to literary quality. They attempt to test literary understanding and appreciation without providing the student with a literary experience of intensity or significance, or integrating literature with life. There is no over-all conception or unity and no opportunity for the development of emotion or insight into the profound human relationships portrayed by a Shakespeare or a Tolstoy. Instead of helping the student grow into an author's mood, the test is limited to quickness of perception, to surface aptness rather than broad grasp and depth of penetration. The conception held by Dickens and Hugo, and by Gorky and Rolland, of literature as a great force for man's betterment is almost entirely lacking. As a whole it is difficult to see what advantage there would be in administering tests constructed according to such a pattern. The authors offer no indication of how they might be used to advance a teaching program or for individual guidance or progress.

These tests do offer some technical advances. In addition to norms in the form of percentile tables, scaled scores are given. Among other characteristics these scaled scores provide equality of scores throughout the scale so that the scores from a single school system tend to form a normal distribution. They also offer a common scale for tests, so that comparisons may readily be made of the relative standing of an individual or a class, not only on standard tests but with grades. The question is, of course, whether the test measures anything of any consequence to either students or teacher.

[143]

English: Understanding and Appreciation of Poetry: State High School Tests for Indiana. Grades 9-12; 1934–44; Forms A, B; 4½¢ per test; 40(45) minutes; G. S. Wykoff; Division of Educational Reference, Purdue University.

Chester W. Harris, Assistant Professor of Education, University of Chicago, Chicago, Illinois. A test title that contains the term *appreciation* is often interpreted somewhat differently by different persons. Some time ago, this reviewer surveyed a number of publications in order to find out how this term is defined by "experts" in the teaching of English. Two major kinds of definition were found: (a) a definition that specified certain reactions to literature on the part of students as the characteristics of appreciation and (b) a definition that specified certain abilities as the bases or indexes of appreciation. It is this second kind of definition that is pertinent in considering this test. The survey indicated that a number of different abilities were specified. Abilities that might be classified under the heading of "comprehension," such as the ability to determine word meanings, the main thought, the mood, the author's purpose, etc., were evident. Others that might be classified under the heading of "judgment," well illustrated by the early work of Abbott and Trabue, Speer, and others, also were evident. In addition, a number of other abilities, such as those Pooley has called the "basic recognitions," were specified.

This test, *Understanding and Appreciation of Poetry,* prepared by Professor Wykoff of Purdue University, attempts to measure two well-defined abilities: comprehending the mood and comprehending the main thought of selections written in verse. The term "appreciation" in the title apparently refers to the items testing the student's ability to determine the mood of the selections. The limited concept of appreciation, when compared with other concepts mentioned above, is evident.

An important consideration in selecting the content of a test, such as this one, designed to measure certain abilities of comprehension or interpretation, is that the literary materials be relatively unfamiliar to the student. If they are not, then it is always possible that the student will be able to answer items correctly on the basis of his memory of what was said about the poem in class or in a text. Such responses, of course, do not provide evidence of the ability to make such interpretations himself. The plan used in selecting the content is not specifically described; one notes, however, that several of the thirty-one selections are ones that are often interpreted for the student in texts and in class discussions. The keying of a test like this also presents problems. Particularly, one might expect students of literature to disagree about the proper term to describe the mood of a poem; that *one* term can adequately describe the mood of some of the selections is in itself doubtful. Again, information regarding the construction of the test is lacking; we are not told what judges determined the correct responses, nor how the possible responses that are listed were secured. It would have been particularly appropriate in a test of this sort to build the objective form from responses actually made by students in a free-response situation. Other limitations might be pointed out. Only a total score is recommended; yet the test is clearly designed to measure two abilities. No estimates of reliability are given. Norms based on a very small number of cases are provided; teachers using the test are urged to supply distributions of scores so that the norms may be amplified. The kind of "norm" that results from data secured in this fashion is likely to be unrepresentative of any well-defined population.

The major value of this test is that of suggesting to teachers that certain abilities in interpreting literature are important achievements. Measurement of a broader range of abilities than this test provides is needed, and the specific techniques need to be experimented with, criticized, and improved. However, a direction in which we might move—one that points away from the reliance on a measure of information about literature as *the* test of English achievement—is indicated here.

[144]

★Interpretation of Literary Materials: Tests of General Educational Development: College Level, Test 4. College; 1944–45; IBM; Form B; separate answer sheets must be used; $2 per 25; 40¢ per 25 machine-scorable answer sheets; 15¢ per scoring key; 25¢ per specimen set, postpaid; worklimit (120) minutes; prepared by the Examinations Staff of the United States Armed Forces Institute; published by the American Council on Education; distributed by the Cooperative Test Service. (Also distributed by Science Research Associates: $3 per 25; 65¢ per 25 machine-scorable answer sheets; 50¢ per key; 50¢ per specimen set.)

For reviews by Herbert S. Conrad and Warren G. Findley of the entire battery, see 20.

[145]

★Interpretation of Literary Materials: Tests of General Educational Development: High School Level, Test 4. High school; 1944–45; IBM; Form B; separate answer sheets must be used; $2 per 25; 40¢ per 25 machine-scorable answer sheets; 15¢ per scoring key; 25¢ per specimen set, postpaid; worklimit (120) minutes; prepared by the Examinations Staff of the United States Armed Forces Institute; published by the American Council on Education; distributed by the Cooperative Test Service. (Also distributed by Science Research Associates: $2 per 25; 65¢ per 25 machine-scorable answer sheets; 50¢ per key; 50¢ per specimen set.)

For reviews by Herbert S. Conrad and Warren G. Findley of the entire battery, see 20.

[146]

★Rigg Poetry Judgment Test. Grades 9-16; 1942; Forms 1, 2; 75¢ per 25; 10¢ per manual; 10¢ per set of scoring keys; 15¢ per specimen set, postpaid; nontimed (40-50) minutes; Melvin G. Rigg; Bureau of Educational Research and Service, State University of Iowa.

REFERENCES
1. YARBOROUGH, OLLIE JEAN. *An Attempt to Standardize the Rigg Poetry Test for High Schools.* Unpublished master's thesis, Oklahoma Agricultural and Mechanical College, 1938.
2. RIGG, MELVIN G. "Measuring the Ability to Judge Poetry." Abstract. *Proc Okla Acad Sci* 19:157-8 '39. * (PA 14:467)

John S. Diekhoff, Acting Chairman, Department of English, Queens College, Flushing, New York. We need not waste words on the difficulty of measuring "literary taste in the field of poetry," which (according to the Examiner's Manual) is the purpose of the Rigg test. We must regret, however, that in the manual Dr. Rigg preferred the word *taste* to the more precise word *judgment* which he uses in the title of his test.

Each form of the test presents the student with forty pairs of brief verse extracts and asks him to designate the better of each pair. One is a passage from a "recognized" poet, the other a paraphrase or parody meant to be inferior. None of the extracts is longer than six lines.

The brevity of the passages, which is said in the Examiner's Manual to be an advantage of the test, is also its weakness. It is possible on the basis of a few lines of verse to require a student to make critical judgments reflecting his knowledge of such details of composition as concreteness of diction, propriety of imagery, and correctness of prosody; but it is not possible to require judgments of the architectonic structure of a poem as a whole or of the value of the content of a poem. The stress in the Rigg test seems to be on prosody. Yet there are much more important considerations in judging a poem than minutiae of technical skill in versification, and it is whole poems that students should learn to judge. We are still waiting, I think, for a test of their skill in doing so.

If a test of student taste in or understanding of such things as prosody and minor imagery is desired, the Rigg test is probably satisfactory.

The basic assumption that the extracts from "recognized" poets are better than the parodies of them is sound, in spite of the disagreement among experts that Dr. Rigg cites. The superiority of the better passage is usually clear, but not so clear as to be obvious to the undiscriminating.

Louis C. Zahner, Head of English Department, Groton School, Groton, Massachusetts. This test "is designed to measure literary taste in the field of poetry." It is made up of forty items, each consisting of two passages of poetry from two to six lines in length. One passage is an extract from "a poet of established reputation" and the other "a parody written by a psychologist who has no standing as a poet, and who, moreover, was trying to produce something inferior." The test, in other words, uses the same general procedure as that used in the Abbott–Trabue *Exercises in Judging Poetry,* except that one parody is used instead of three.

It is fair to ask any constructor of a test exactly what he is attempting to test. What is "taste" in poetry? Since the author does not answer this question directly, the reviewer is thrown for an answer upon the implications of the test itself. "Taste" thus defined seems to be conformity to some of the more mechanical and obvious traditions of poetry as established prior to the twentieth century. (The few lines selected from later poetry are in the older, established tradition.) The test becomes little more than an exercise in detecting glaring evidence of doggerel on the one hand and lush, saccharine diction on the other. It is not designed to get at the central problem of a good interpretation of poetry, without which "taste" can hardly exist at all and with which it can safely be left to take care of itself. The "taste" tested here is the kind acquired by acceptance of stock judgments. For anything approaching a defensible test on taste a considerable context, preferably an entire poem, would be needed as a setting for the four or five lines in question. Without an adequate context their meaning, their appropriateness in mood and tone, their "taste," or anything else that concerns them cannot be properly judged. No context whatever is provided for the snippets used in this test.

One becomes even more skeptical of whether the test is examining anything worth having when one reads in the Examiner's Manual that a certain study showed "that *significant* gains in the ability to recognize good poetry were made by high school students as the result of a *three-day* training period." (Italics are the reviewer's.)

The test contains such a preponderance of quotations from well-known poems that it becomes a test in memory rather than in judgment for any person even moderately well read in poetry; and one is again led to ask how a person not even moderately well read in poetry is expected by the author to have acquired "taste."

Even were this a valid test on theoretical grounds, its percentile norms would be open to question, since for the three groups for which the norms are given, high school, college, and adult-expert, they are based on only 804, 572, and 100 papers respectively.

The Rigg test has not improved upon the Abbott–Trabue *Exercises,* its acknowledged source.

[147]

★Survey Test in American Literature. High school and college; 1940; 1 form; $1.60 per 25, postpaid; sample test free; 50(55) minutes; edited by Harold H. Bixler; Salibelle Royster; Turner E. Smith & Co.

[148]

★Survey Test in English Literature. High school and college; 1940; 1 form; $1.60 per 25, postpaid; sample test free; 50(55) minutes; edited by Harold H. Bixler; Elmer R. Smith; Turner E. Smith & Co.

MISCELLANEOUS

[149]

★P-L-S Journalism Test. High school and college; 1944; 1 form; $1.15 per 25, postpaid; 15¢ per specimen set, postpaid; 40(45) minutes; George H. Phillips, Harry Levinson, and H. E. Schrammel; Bureau of Educational Measurement, Kansas State Teachers College of Emporia.

SPEECH

[150]

★Guidance Questionnaire for Students of Speech. Grades 13-16; 1940; Form C; $2.20 per 25; specimen sets not available; 30(35) minutes; Howard Gilkinson and Franklin H. Knower; C. H. Stoelting Co.

REFERENCES

1. KNOWER, FRANKLIN H. "A Study of Speech Attitudes and Adjustments." *Speech Monogr* 5:130-203 '28. *
2. GILKINSON, HOWARD, AND KNOWER, FRANKLIN H. *Psychological Studies of Individual Differences Among Students of Speech.* Minneapolis, Minn.: Department of Speech; University of Minnesota, June 1939. Pp. ii, 196. Paper, mimeographed. Gratis. *
3. GILKINSON, HOWARD, AND KNOWER, FRANKLIN H. "Analysis of a Guidance Questionnaire for Students of Speech." *J Exp Ed* 9:175-6 D '40. * (PA 15:2359)
4. ALUSOW, FRANK TELESPORE. *A Validation of the Gilkinson-Knower Guidance Questionnaire on University of Iowa Freshman Speech Students.* Unpublished master's thesis, State University of Iowa. 1941.

[151]

★Speech Attitude Scale. Grades 9-16; 1938; Form F; $2.20 per 25; specimen sets not available; 30(35) minutes; Franklin H. Knower; C. H. Stoelting Co.

REFERENCES

1. KNOWER, FRANKLIN H. "A Study of Speech Attitudes and Adjustments." *Speech Monogr* 5:130-203 '28. *
2. GILKINSON, HOWARD, AND KNOWER, FRANKLIN H. *Psychological Studies of Individual Differences Among Students of Speech.* Minneapolis, Minn.: Department of Speech; University of Minnesota, June 1939. Pp. ii, 196. Paper, mimeographed. Gratis. *

[152]

★Speech Experience Inventory. Grades 9-16; 1937; Form C; $1.60 per 25; specimen sets not available; 15(20) minutes; Franklin H. Knower; C. H. Stoelting Co.

REFERENCES

1. KNOWER, FRANKLIN H. "A Study of Speech Attitudes and Adjustments." *Speech Monogr* 5:130-203 '28. *
2. GILKINSON, HOWARD, AND KNOWER, FRANKLIN H. *Psychological Studies of Indiv.dual Differences Among Students of Speech.* Minneapolis, Minn.: Department of Speech; University of Minnesota, June 1939. Pp. ii, 196. Paper, mimeographed. Gratis. *

SPELLING

[153]

★Kansas Spelling Test. Grades 1-3, 4-6, 7-9; 1941; Forms A, B; 3 levels; 75¢ per 25, postpaid; 15¢ per specimen set, postpaid; 15(20) minutes; H. E. Schrammel, O. M. Rasmussen, Nathan Budd, Wayne Gordon, and Fayrene Reiff; Bureau of Educational Measurements, Kansas State Teachers College of Emporia.

Henry D. Rinsland, Director, Bureau of Educational Research, The University of Oklahoma, Norman, Oklahoma. The source of words for these tests covering the elementary grades from 1 to 9 is greatly weakened by the inclusion of words from "recognized spelling texts, notably the Kansas adopted text by Ayers, Oberholtzer and Woody" in addition to words from the Buckingham extension of the *Ayers Spelling Scale,* the *Iowa Spelling Scale,* and the Thorndike *Teacher's Word List* (date not given). Even these lists are questionable, as the first two are very old and the Thorndike Word List is primarily a count of words from adult writings. There are no data given as to how the words were chosen from these lists and books or how proper grade placement was made. Since Betts, in his *Spelling Vocabulary Study* (American Book Co., 1940), has shown that seventeen authors can unanimously agree only on 6.26 per cent of a total vocabulary of 8,645 words and unanimously agree on the grade placement of one word, this reviewer cannot find any grounds for the inclusion of words from one spelling textbook or several, unless it is to test the words in that or those books only on a local basis.

The test is multiple choice, giving one correct spelling with three misspellings. Incorrect spellings used for multiple choices were obtained chiefly by an extended study of spellings, but no mention is made of the only publication of such misspellings, which is Gates' *List of Spelling Difficulties in 3876 Words* (Bureau of Publications, Teachers College, Columbia University, 1937).

The correlation between the multiple-choice form and the pronounced form varies from .55 for grade 3 to .82 for grade 2. Certainly these correlations are not high for the same words in two different settings and hardly high enough to warrant a conclusion that one test is a good test of the other. One would expect correlations well above .90 in such a situation. The coefficient of alienation is .83 for one and .56 for the other. In his *Statistics in Education and Psychology,* (Longmans, Green and Co., 1946, p. 336) Garrett says, "For *r*'s of .80 or less, the coefficients of alienation are clearly so large that predictions of individual scores based upon the regression equation are little better than 'guesses'."

The reliability coefficients between Forms A and B for all grades under grade 4 range from .72 to .86, but in grade 6 the reliability is as high as .94. Perhaps the number of words, which is only 50, has much to do with this low reliability. Fifty words can not be considered a very fair sampling for a range of three grades above grades 3 or 4; the total number of words for grades 1 to 9 is only 150! It is, therefore, seriously questioned whether the following statement in the manual is borne out by any of the published data, "Since the criterion possesses such high reliability and since the correlations between the criterion and the objective test yielded very satisfactory coefficients, the conclusion that the objective test possesses satisfactory validity seems justified."

With the more recent vocabulary research of Rinsland, *Basic Vocabulary of Elementary School Children* (Macmillan Co., 1945) now available for grades 1 to 8, in which the sampling is greater than in other studies and which is drawn from children's own writings, there seems to be little gained by the continued use of such tests as the one reviewed, which greatly lack adequate sampling in the choice of words and lack reliability coefficients high enough for any individual application. The reviewer is certain that no one spelling book or even several should be used for any test except one for local measurements.

Guy M. Wilson, Professor Emeritus of Education, Boston University, Boston, Massachusetts. In establishing validity for this test the authors used in its construction, the *Buckingham Extension of the Ayres Scale,* the *Iowa Spelling Scale,* the Thorndike *Teacher's Word Book,* and a number of recognized spelling texts, including the state-adopted text. Just how these primary and secondary sources were used, we are not told; no distribution tables are given. The purchaser and user of a test has a right to full information on validity.

The main criticisms from the standpoint of validity are that: (*a*) too much reliance is placed upon secondary sources; (*b*) words quite beyond reasonable spelling expectations are assigned for spelling in the various grades. The only primary source used in checking words is the Thorndike *Teacher's Word Book.* The authors should also have made use of the Commonwealth List at least.

The neglect of curricular considerations in the assignment of high word-value words for spelling is a serious criticism. Curricular considerations should never be subordinated to statistical considerations. Valid comparisons should be based upon familiar words for which perfect spelling is a reasonable expectation.

The multiple-choice form of the test is questionable for grade usage, or as a test of spelling. Lower-grade pupils are confused by the various forms; and merely checking is not equivalent to spelling.

When words are pronounced by the teacher, meaning can be checked. If a child does not understand a word, that word for him is not a proper spelling word and it should be omitted from the test. There should be a different word list for each grade. Right selection of words is more difficult when words are used in three grades.

Spelling for first-grade pupils is of doubtful value. If words are assigned to first-graders for spelling, they should be taken from the first five hundred words in the Thorndike *Teacher's Word Book.* Second- and third-grade pupils should not be given words above the first thousand. Words above the fourth thousand should not be assigned for spelling in any grade.

The time limit on a test is not desirable if testing is to be a part of teaching.

All told, the makers of this test appear to be more concerned with statistical results than in providing a real aid to a good teaching program.

Kansas Spelling Test

Any revisions undertaken should give more attention to curriculum and methods of teaching. In general, unless it is good teaching, it is not a good test. A good test will yield equally valid and more helpful statistical data.

[154]

★**Lincoln Diagnostic Spelling Test.** Grades 8-12; 1941–44; Forms 1, 2, 3, 4; 6¢ per test; 10¢ per specimen set; (30) minutes; A. L. Lincoln; Educational Records Bureau.

REFERENCES

1. TOWNSEND, AGATHA. "A Study of the Lincoln Diagnostic Spelling Test," pp. 49-53. In *1943 Achievement Testing Program in Independent Schools and Supplementary Studies.* Educational Records Bulletin, No. 38. New York: Educational Records Bureau, June 1943. Pp. xiii, 53. Paper, lithotyped. $1.50. * (*PA* 18:315, title only)

[155]

★**Lincoln Intermediate Spelling Test.** Grades 5-8; 1947; Forms A, B; 6¢ per test; 10¢ per specimen set; (30) minutes; A. L. Lincoln; Educational Records Bureau.

REFERENCES

1. TOWNSEND, AGATHA. "A Report on the Use of the Lincoln Intermediate Spelling Test," pp. 40-8. In *1947 Fall Testing Program in Independent Schools and Supplementary Studies.* Educational Records Bulletin, No. 49. New York: Educational Records Bureau, February 1948. Pp. xii, 69. Paper, lithotyped. $1.50. *

[156]

New Standard High School Spelling Scale. Grades 7-12; 1925–40; a 64-page book consisting of 64 40-word lists to be used for either testing or teaching and an alphabetical list of the 2560 words with difficulty values in each of grades 9, 10, 11, and 12; 48¢ per copy; Ernest P. Simmons and Harold Hench Bixler; Turner E. Smith & Co.

[157]

★**Wellesley Spelling Scale.** Grades 9-16; 1944; IBM; Forms 1, 2; 2 editions; *hand-scoring edition:* 90¢ per 25; 25¢ per specimen set, postpaid; *machine-scorable edition:* 4¢ per test; 2¢ per answer sheet; 60¢ per set of scoring stencils; nontimed (30) minutes; Thelma G. Alper and Edith B. Mallory; California Test Bureau.

REFERENCES

1. ALPER, THELMA G. "A Diagnostic Spelling Scale for the College Level: Its Construction and Use." *J Ed Psychol* 33:273-90 Ap '42. * (*PA* 17:932)

Henry D. Rinsland, Director, Bureau of Educational Research, The University of Oklahoma, Norman, Oklahoma. The purpose of the scale is to measure the student's ability to spell in high school, vocational school, and college. The authors state that they included only words which are frequently found in the written vocabulary of high school graduates and that these words genuinely represent the spelling that the student will do in the course of ordinary school or business writing. There are no data and no research studies quoted to substantiate these statements beyond the facts that the words are taken from the written themes of 363 freshmen in a required college course in English composition and that a listing of the words most frequently misspelled is given. Evidently this was done at Wellesley, but it is certainly a meager sampling for choosing the spelling words to test high schools and colleges the country over and does not warrant the attachment of the term "standardized" to a test of such limited curricular validity.

The test is published for both hand and machine scoring. The number of words tested in each scale is, in itself, a very skimpy sampling, there being only 50 words to cover the range from grade 9 to the freshman year in college. The norms, in percentiles, themselves are based on a very meager sampling; 152 college freshmen; 242, grade 12; 333, grade 11; 242, grade 10. Grade 9 percentiles were derived by extrapolation and a completion form, and therefore lack both validity and reality. Certainly test builders should begin to realize the importance of these two major sampling factors, which affect both the validity and reliability of a test. Because of the very wide range of words used by high school students and college freshmen, the selection of words studied from which some will be chosen to go in the test must be extensive. In applying the averages of *any* group to pupils the country over, as is done in the norms of a standardized and published test, test builders must not throw all principles of reliability and sampling to the wind.

Forms 1 and 2 correlate .86, which is really not high for elements as objective as multiple-choice items in spelling. The multiple-choice form was chosen because of the correlation of .75 between recognition scores from Form 1 and recall scores obtained by dictating the words in Form 2. A validity coefficient of .75 cannot be considered high and does not warrant the conclusion that the multiple-choice form is as valid as dictation, considered by most test builders as a good criterion or the best criterion. Too often ease of scoring is taken as the first criterion of a test: that is a very serious error.

No information is given as to the source of the erroneous spellings used in the multiple choices.

Guy M. Wilson, Professor Emeritus of Education, Boston University, Boston, Massachusetts. The Wellesley Spelling Scales are designed as aids in selecting the best spellers from among those who apply for secretarial jobs. The requirements are very different from those called for in a scale designed to aid a teaching-mastery program in spelling. A selection scale can properly rely more upon distribution, can use a reasonable proportion of high-value words, and can more appropriately use the multiple-choice form of test. Recognition of misspellings is a skill much needed by secretaries.

The modest claims of the authors of these scales appear to be justified by the product. The scales are conveniently arranged. Sentences are used to show the meanings of words. Comparative statistics are given. All of these features add to the usefulness of the scales.

VOCABULARY

[158]

Clinton General Vocabulary Test for High Schools and Colleges. Grades 9-16; 1936; Forms A, B; $1.15 per 25; 10¢ per specimen set, postpaid; R. J. Clinton; Cooperative Book Store, Corvallis, Oregon.

Harold H. Bixler, Director of Research and Guidance, Public Schools, Atlanta, Georgia. This test "is designed to measure the extent of a person's general reading and understanding vocabulary and not his active vocabulary."

Each form has 150 items of the multiple-choice type with four choices for each item. The author states that the words are selected from words used generally in the curriculum materials of high school and college students. They were checked by the list appearing in the Thorndike *Teacher's Word Book.* There is no time limit, but the author states that the average time required for college students is 20 minutes and for high school students 25 minutes. This would seem to be a rather short time for students in the lower high school grades in view of the number of items.

The reliability of the test, as determined by the use of the Spearman—Brown formula, is .94, based on 307 cases. This would seem to be adequate reliability for individual pupil diagnosis.

Norms provided are in the form of medians for students in grade 9 up through college grades in terms of numbers of words correct. The norm for high school freshmen, for example, is 55 words, and for high school sophomores, 61 words. This is not a very large increase from one grade to the next. The norms are not given in terms of grade equivalents.

The author also provides norms showing numbers of words in the student's vocabulary.

Thus, a score of 52 is reported as equivalent to a vocabulary of 5,540 words. The norms are based on 4,000 cases.

One of the limitations of the test is that the words are presented alone and not in sentences or phrases. This lack of context keeps the test from being a lifelike situation. In some instances, the author would do well to revise the meanings of words as given in the test. For Item 129, *sequestrate,* the correct meaning is given as *seize.* Normally one would expect *set apart* to be the correct answer, although the dictionary does give *confiscate* as a second meaning of this word.

On the whole, this test should prove to be a useful instrument for upper high school and college grades.

[159]
Columbia Vocabulary Test. Grades 3-12; 1939; IBM; 1 form; $1.10 per 25 machine-scorable test-answer sheets, with manual and hand-scoring keys; $1 per set of machine-scoring keys; 35¢ per specimen set, postpaid; nontimed (15-20) minutes; Irene Gansl and H. E. Garrett; Psychological Corporation.

REFERENCES
1. GANSL, IRENE. *Vocabulary: Its Measurement and Growth.* Archives of Psychology, No. 236. Washington, D. C.: American Psychological Association, Inc., March 1939. Pp. 52. Paper. $1.00. * (PA 13:5819)
2. BENNETT, GEORGE K., AND ROSLOW, SYDNEY. "Extension of the Norms of the Columbia Vocabulary Test." *J Appl Psychol* 25:48-51 F '41. * (PA 15: 3188)
3. REICHARD, SUZANNE. *Mental Organization and Age Level.* Archives of Psychology, No. 295. Washington, D. C.: American Psychological Association, Inc., June 1944. Pp. 30. Paper. $0.80. * (PA 19:1183)
4. SARTAIN, A. Q. "Predicting Success in a School of Nursing." *J Appl Psychol* 30:234-40 Je '46. * (PA 20:4350)

Verner M. Sims, Professor of Psychology, University of Alabama, University, Alabama. The *Columbia Vocabulary Test* is designed as a measure of the general vocabulary of pupils from grades 3 through 12. It consists of a sample of 100 words selected from a list of the "words found in 22 contemporary measures of vocabulary," arranged in order of difficulty, presented in multiple-choice test form, and printed on a single, standard, machine-scored answer sheet.

Considerable work has gone into the construction of this test, and the result is an instrument which is probably adequate as a rough measure of vocabulary. Printing it directly on an answer sheet makes for economy in use of the test and it should serve a purpose in survey studies where the concern is with group differences only.

There are, however, a number of limitations to the test which should be called to the attention of prospective users. The test items are printed in 8-point type, which is commonly assumed to be too small for use in the lower

grades. (The generally accepted minimum-size type is 14-point for the third grade, and 10- or 12-point for grades 4 to 6.) What influence this small type may have at the lower levels is not known nor was it subjected to experiment by the testmakers.

Although elaborate norms have been developed for the test, they are actually *local* norms only, being based upon a sampling of pupils from three elementary schools and one high school in New York City. No information is furnished as to how these schools were selected from the many and varied schools in New York; consequently one hesitates to conclude even that the norms are representative of this one city. Certainly they cannot be accepted for general use. Furthermore, the elaborateness of the norms (means, standard deviations, and deciles are reported for each half grade for the grades 3 through 12; grade-month means are given for grades 3 through 8; and means, standard deviations, and deciles for ages eight through thirteen) represents overrefinement of the test data. This point is well illustrated by the grade-month means. Although the standard error of a raw score on the test is reported as 3 points, the maximum increment of score found for any month was only .8 point. In other words, the chances are almost ten to one that the differences between two succeeding months do not represent actual differences in ability, and two scores would need to be more than 11 months apart before we could interpret them as almost certainly not due to chance error! Such overrefinements in standard scores are comparable to measuring weight by hefting and reporting the results to the hundredth part of an ounce. They inevitably create an illusion of accuracy which may be actually harmful in the hands of relatively unskilled users.

Finally, this test, along with most other tests purporting to measure vocabulary, actually measures ability to recognize synonyms of test words, and, at that, only one synonym (and therefore one meaning) for each test word. For example, the first word in the test, *fast,* is to be matched with *quickly;* yet Thorndike's *Century Senior Dictionary* reports a total of thirteen meanings for this word: six adjectives, four adverbs, two nouns, and one verb. Just what can we infer concerning the child's knowledge from a right or wrong response to this test situation? The fact is we have little or no information concerning the relation between the rather narrow skill measured by current vocabulary tests and the child's functioning vocabulary, either "impressive" or "expressive."

Clifford Woody, Professor of Education, University of Michigan, Ann Arbor, Michigan. The author of this test has employed more exacting criteria in selecting the words constituting the test than have been applied in choosing the words for most tests. The original lists of approximately 1,500 words from which the final selection was made consisted of the words employed in twenty-two widely used vocabulary tests designed for use from grade 1 to the college level. These words were then classified according to the level at which they appeared in Thorndike's *Teacher's Word Book*. From these classified lists, 135 words from difficulties 1 to 13 were selected. Each of these words was then incorporated into a brief sentence or phrase to make the use of the word correspond as closely as possible to the manner in which it would appear in the life process. Five response words were selected for each test item from the original list of 1,500 words. Extreme caution was employed in selecting these words: no response word should have a higher frequency rating than the test word; all response words must be of the same part of speech; all words must fit smoothly into the sentence. Only one response must be a synonym of the critical word. These precautions were taken in devising a preliminary edition of the test.

On the basis of the results obtained from administering the test to 1,041 pupils in grades 3 to 8 of a public school in Queens, New York, 100 words were selected and arranged according to percentage of pupils responding correctly. In making the final selection, attention was given not only to the percentage of correct responses but also to those words having a steady increase in successive grades in the percentage of correct responses. Furthermore, words whose individual curves of correct responses followed that for the test as a whole were selected. Thus, it should be clear that extreme care was exercised in selecting the words for the test.

The final test was standardized by administering it to 3,306 pupils in three public schools of New York City. The student populations of these three schools were considered to be typical of the total student population of the United States, but only further administration of the tests can establish the truth or falsity of this assumption. The reviewer feels that better standards can be obtained. Standards are available for boys and girls for both age and grade. The coefficient of reliability determined by the Spearman–Brown formula is .94. The standard error of measurement of a single score shows that the chances are 68 in 100 that a single score among the standardization group did not vary from the true score by more than 3 points. While the test has not been widely used and the results therefore have not been correlated with those from other standard vocabulary tests, the reviewer has no hesitation in recommending its use.

[160]

★Cooperative Vocabulary Test. Grades 7–16; 1940–41; IBM; 2 forms; 2 editions; Frederick B. Davis; Cooperative Test Service.
a) FORMS Q AND R. Separate answer sheets need not be used; $1.75 per 25; 25¢ per specimen set, postpaid; 60¢ per 25 machine-scorable answer sheets; 30¢ per stencil for scoring answer sheets; 30(35) minutes.
b) SHORT FORMS QS AND RS. $1.25 per 25 machine-scorable test-answer sheets; 25¢ per specimen set, postpaid; nontimed (10–15) minutes.

REFERENCES
1. COOPERATIVE TEST SERVICE. *The Cooperative Vocabulary Test: Information Concerning Its Construction, Interpretation and Use.* New York: Cooperative Test Service, 1940. Pp. 2. Paper. Gratis. *
2. SIMPSON, R. G. "The Vocabulary Sections of the Cooperative English Tests at the Higher Levels of Difficulty." *J Ed Psychol* 34:142-51 Mr '43. * (PA 18:311)

Edgar Dale, Professor of Education, The Ohio State University, Columbus, Ohio. The *Cooperative Vocabulary Test* contains 210 items subdivided into seven scales of 30 items each. The seven scales are equivalent, but the most discriminative items are in the first scales, the least discriminating in the last scales.

The final score does not depend upon the number of items attempted. The student who gets all the items correct on only two of the seven scales gets the same scaled score as one who gets all items right in three or more of the scales. However, the authors suggest that an unlimited time and the completion of all the scales produce the most reliable results.

All the words were selected from the Thorndike *Teacher's Word Book* and represent "a sampling from many subject-matter fields." The data show a varying number of words from each of the "thousands" levels of the Thorndike *Teacher's Word Book*, and no statement is made how the subject-matter fields were sampled.

Although the authors state that the scores "indicate the extensiveness and precision of an individual's knowledge of word meanings" and that "knowledge of word meanings is an important element in determining scholastic success," no correlations are presented between this test and indices of scholastic success.

Percentile norms for each grade level in three types of secondary schools and three types of colleges are provided and are published in the *Booklet of Norms.*

Some vocabulary tests include as correct certain items which are debatable. No such items were found here. However, a few of the choices while correct as far as the dictionary was concerned were not common uses, nor would a more suitable definition have made the test more difficult. Thus, "relic" is made synonymous with "souvenir," "churl" with "peasant."

What does the teacher have who gives this test? He will have an indication of whether an individual or a class is below, at, or above the norms. But he will not know the areas or fields of experience in which the student does well or poorly. Nor will he have any suggestions on ways of using the test to develop vocabulary. Nevertheless, the test will be one which the students will recognize as dealing with important words, one which has been constructed with real care. Further, it is a test which will give, in a few minutes, a good indication of level of general vocabulary in a college class.

Henry D. Rinsland, Director, Bureau of Educational Research, The University of Oklahoma, Norman, Oklahoma. The words in this test represent a sampling from many subject-matter fields. In the easy items only one response word is close in meaning to the word being tested, but in the difficult items the response words approach closely the meaning of the word being tested. Great care has been shown in the fine discrimination of meaning. Both the correct response and the decoys for every item are in the Thorndike list of 20,000 words and are of more frequent occurrence than the word being tested. Frequency was not taken as an index of difficulty; rather, the subjective judgment of the authors was used to supplement the frequency-level data and to exclude words from the responses which appeared to be more difficult than the word being tested.

No coefficients of reliability are given, but from experience with other Cooperative tests, they are undoubtedly between .90 and .94, sufficiently high to possess real diagnostic value.

Cooperative Vocabulary Test

The experience and reputation of the several authors warrant confidence in similar factors of the test not substantiated by published data.

[161]
English Recognition Vocabulary Test. Grades 7-16 and adults; 1938; Form 1; $3.75 per 100, postpaid; 50¢ per specimen set, postpaid; for manual see *Journal of Educational Psychology* 31:14-38 January 1940; (50) minutes; Robert H. Seashore and Lois D. Eckerson; published by Robert H. Seashore, Department of Psychology, Northwestern University.

REFERENCES
1-3. *See* 40:1319.
4. ANNEN, IDA. *The Construction, Analysis, and Evaluation of a Vocabulary Measure.* Unpublished master's thesis, University of Oregon, 1933.
5. SEASHORE, ROBERT H. "The Measurement and Analysis of Extent of Vocabulary." Abstract. *Psychol B* 30:709-10 N '33. * (*PA* 8:3720, title only)
6. LOVELL, GEORGE D. *Interrelations of Vocabulary Skills: Commonest Versus Multiple Meanings.* Unpublished master's thesis, Northwestern University. 1939.
7. SEASHORE, ROBERT H. "Further Data on the Measurement of General English Vocabularies." Abstract. *Psychol B* 36:525 Jl '39. * (*PA* 13:6500, title only)
8. SEASHORE, ROBERT H., AND ECKERSON, LOIS D. "The Measurement of Individual Differences in General English Vocabularies." *J Ed Psychol* 31:14-38 Ja '40. * (*PA* 14:3226)
9. SMITH, MARY KATHERINE. "Measurement of Size of Vocabulary of Children From 6 to 18 Years of Age (School Grades 1 to 12)." Abstract. *Psychol B* 37:581 O '40. * (*PA* 15:612, title only)
10. SMITH, MARY KATHERINE. *Measurement of the Size of General English Vocabulary Through the Elementary Grades and High School.* Unpublished doctor's thesis, Northwestern University, 1940. (*Summaries of Doctoral Dissertations . . . 1940,* pp. 298-300.)
11. LOVELL, GEORGE D. "Interrelations of Vocabulary Skills: Commonest *Versus* Multiple Meanings." *J Ed Psychol* 32:67-72 Ja '41. * (*PA* 15:3158)
12. SMITH, MARY KATHERINE. "Measurement of the Size of General English Vocabulary Through the Elementary Grades and High School." *Genetic Psychol Monogr* 24:311-45 N '41. * (*PA* 16:2082)
13. SCHULMAN, MARY JEAN, and HAVIGHURST, ROBERT J. "Relations Between Ability and Social Status in a Midwestern Community: IV, Size of Vocabulary." *J Ed Psychol* 38:437-42 N '47. * (*PA* 22:2064)
14. SEASHORE, ROBERT H. "How Many Words Do Children Know?" *Packet: Heath's Serv B El Teach* 2:3-17 N '47. *
15. SEASHORE, ROBERT H. "The Importance of Vocabulary in Learning Language Skills." *El Engl* 25:137-52+ Mr '48. *

Paul S. Burnham, Associate Director, Student Appointment Bureau, Yale University, New Haven, Connecticut. Copyrighted and published in 1938, this test is a controlled sampling of words found in the Funk and Wagnalls *New Standard Dictionary of the English Language,* 1937 edition. The test is divided into three parts. Part I consists of a general recognition test involving 173 chosen words, apparently arranged in order of difficulty. For each given word the student selects one among four choices as a synonym related to the commonest meaning of the given word. Part II is a list of 158 words taken from the dictionary's supplementary list of *proper names, geographical locations,* and *rare words.* Part III is a list of 46 *derived terms.* In both Parts II and III the problem is to give the meanings of the words or terms presented.

The sum of the correct answers can be converted into an estimate of the total English vocabulary which the student probably has at his command. Norms in terms of this total English vocabulary score are provided for grades 1 through 12, based on populations varying from 40 to 116. Norms are also available in terms of decile standing among approximately 200 state university freshmen and sophomores in educational psychology courses.

Spearman–Brown reliabilities varied from .83 (unlimited time) to .93 (20 minutes) for Part I. Decile ratings applicable to the 20-minute time limit are available but the authors recommend unlimited time. Meager evidence suggests correlations of approximately .60 with tests of reading comprehension, approximately .50 with the *Otis Advanced Intelligence Test,* and .57 with the *American Council on Education Psychological Examination.* Lack of data makes appraisal of this test difficult.

Edgar Dale, Professor of Education, The Ohio State University, Columbus, Ohio. This test aims to discover the total number of words in the vocabulary of an individual. The test is based on a sampling from Funk and Wagnall's Unabridged Dictionary. The test includes 173 general terms; 158 proper names, geographical locations, and rare words; and 46 derived terms. Provision is made for separate estimation of the total words in each of these three classes.

The 173 words in the general list are tested by a four-choice multiple-response recognition test. The proper names, geographical locations, and rare words are tested by defining, identifying, or using in illustrative sentences. Among the words in this group are *cit, frimsel, mamoul, yoghoort,* and many others like them. The 46 derived terms are tested by asking the student to think of or write, if requested, a specific instance in which each would be correctly applied, so as to describe its real meaning.

Norms are available for college groups for Parts 1 and 2. The groups on which the norms are based are not too large—237 Ohio State University students and 116 Northwestern undergraduates. "Part 3 has not yet been adequately standardized, the norms given being based upon only 120 Northwestern freshmen and sophomores who employed the self-rating criterion. . . ." (8) Preliminary work on standardization for grades 1 to 12 of school has been done but the numbers tested are still too small to be reliable.

Reliability of the test has been established only for Part 1 for college groups. Correlation between scores on the odd words with the even in Part 1 ranged from .83 to .93 for different time limits. The highest reliability was for the 20-minute time limit.

The authors state that this test was made for research purposes and has never been published commercially except in the sense that enough copies have been printed to supply people who wish to purchase them. A new pictorial form covering the easier portion of the same word list is now being standardized for children in the age range of three to ten years.

This test, of course, should be criticized on the basis of what it attempts to do—to secure a measure of the total vocabulary of an individual. If we accept the three types of test as valid and if the sampling is adequate, then we may accept a total vocabulary figure secured by this test. The writer believes that neither assumption is acceptable. While the test may prove to have great value as a correlate of other important school abilities and thus give us quick significant data about mental ability, nevertheless it does not give us the really important measures of vocabulary relating to specific areas of experience. More important than a single measure of total vocabulary are measures of specific vocabularies in science, business, geography, politics, music, and technology. Such data would be valuable for guidance and remedial work.

[162]

★**High School Vocabulary Test.** 1940; Form A; 50¢ per 20; 10¢ per manual; 15¢ per specimen set; 30(35) minutes; J. W. Chalmers; Institute of Applied Art, Ltd.

Harold H. Bixler, Director of Research and Guidance, Public Schools, Atlanta, Georgia. This test has been devised by a Canadian and published by a Canadian company. Norms are based on 1,500 intermediate and high school students in Alberta schools, grade 7–12 inclusive. However, there is no good reason why the test could not be used in schools in the United States.

The words were chosen from the Thorndike *Teacher's Word Book of Twenty Thousand Words.* The author reports that they were chosen as follows: 5 words from each 1,000 of the most common 4,000; 6 words from each 1,000 of the next most common 9,000; 5 words from each 1,000 of the next most common 4,000; and 2 words from each 1,000 of the least common 3,000.

The validity of the test may be judged from

the method of selection of the test words as listed above. Also the author reports correlation coefficients of .91 with the *Thorndike Test of Word Knowledge* and .85 with the vocabulary section of the *New Stanford Achievement Test*. As to the reliability of the test there is some question. The coefficient reported by the author is .89, based on 297 students.

One disadvantage of the test is the fact that the words are given alone and not in sentences or phrases. However, the selection of words on the whole appears to be good. There are 100 items in each form. In two instances, at least, students in the United States would be puzzled by the spelling. Item 76 is listed as *dyke* when most of our students would know it as *dike*. Item 92 is given as *silvan,* and our students would know it as *sylvan*. There are a few unusual words such as *palfrey* and *jejune*.

Norms are based on 1,939 students. The range of cases is from 119 in grade 7 to 350 in grade 10. The test would have been better if norms had been based on more students, and particularly students from a much more extensive geographical area.

[163]
Inglis Tests of English Vocabulary. Grades 9-16; 1924-27; Forms A, B, C; $1.60 per 30; nontimed (30) minutes; Alexander Inglis (Form C completed by Ralph W. Walter); Ginn & Co.

REFERENCES

1. INGLIS, ALEXANDER. "A Vocabulary Test for High-School and College Students." *Engl Leaflet* 23:1-13 O '23. *
2. NEMZEK, CLAUDE L. "Intelligence Testing at the College Level." *J Ed Res* 26:617-8 Ap '33. * (*PA* 7:4196)
3. ANDERSON, IRVING H., AND FAIRBANKS, GRANT. "Common and Differential Factors in Reading Vocabulary and Hearing Vocabulary." *J Ed Res* 30:317-24 Ja '37. * (*PA* 11:1866)
4. MILLER, CARROLL H. "Value of Certain Standard Tests for a Study of Dramatic Talent." *J Social Psychol* 9:437-9 N '38. * (*PA* 13:1753)
5. BERNARD, HAROLD W. "Some Relationships of Vocabulary to Scholarship." *Sch & Soc* 51:494-6 Ap 13 '40. * (*PA* 14:4236)
6. LANGSAM, ROSALIND STREEP. "A Factorial Analysis of Reading Ability." *J Exp Ed* 10:57-63 S '41. * (*PA* 16:1187)
7. RIKER, BRITTEN L., AND GAUDET, FREDERICK J. "The Use of Some Tests in the Prediction of Legal Aptitude." *J Appl Psychol* 25:313-22 Je '41. * (*PA* 15:4414)

Henry D. Rinsland, Director, Bureau of Educational Research, The University of Oklahoma, Norman, Oklahoma. Form A was copyrighted in 1923, 1924, and 1936; Form B, in 1924, and Form C, in 1927; therefore, the tests are fairly old. The norms are in terms of median scores for grades 9-12, college freshmen, and college graduates; the variation of percentage correct runs from 30 per cent or 45 words out of a total of 150 words for ninth-graders to 86 per cent or 129 words for college graduates.

High School Vocabulary Test

Little can be found about the steps in validation, as the reference in the description of the test gives the *English Leaflet* for October 1923 as a publication carrying the full account of the method employed in the development of the test; but this *Leaflet* cannot be obtained either from the English Society in New England, which published it, or from the printer. The coefficient of correlation for Form A with Form B is .90. The medians are within one point of each other.

Inglis reported that the words tested represented a "true sampling of the field covered by the Intelligent General Reader's vocabulary." He first made a careful analysis of the non-obsolete words other than those belonging to our everyday vocabulary of commonest words or to our special and technical vocabulary. From these he chose several lists of about 3,000 words each, and from one of these for Form A he chose words 1, 17, 33, etc.; for Form B, words 2, 18, 34, etc.; and for the other forms he evidently intended to sample in a similar fashion.

Nothing is given about the placement of these words in the Thorndike 1921 frequency count. It is evident that whatever value the present test has is based upon the superior judgment of the author in selecting words which gave fair sampling distributions from grade to grade as judged by the spacings of the median scores; to his very excellent choice of the sample sentences in which each word is given; and to the wise choice of the correct word as well as the wrong words.

It is very probable that, if the words tested in the three forms were checked against the Thorndike–Lorge *Teacher's Word Book of 30,000 Words,* a test more valid for these levels would be obtained by a thin sampling in the lower and the higher levels, say, from the fourth to the tenth thousand and from the twentieth to the thirtieth thousand; and a richer sampling from the middle levels, say, the tenth to the twentieth thousand.

[164]
★**Kansas Vocabulary Test.** Grades 4-8; 1940; 75¢ per 25, postpaid; 15¢ per specimen set, postpaid; 30 (35) minutes; H. E. Schrammel, O. M. Rasmussen, Anna Huebert, and Donald J. Tate; Bureau of Educational Measurements, Kansas State Teachers College of Emporia.

Harold H. Bixler, Director of Research and Guidance, Public Schools, Atlanta, Georgia.

This test has 85 items of the multiple-choice type. The authors state that the purpose of the test is to "measure the pupil's reading vocabulary and that it is a valuable aid for diagnosing reading weaknesses." Since the validity of any test is the most important consideration, it is well to quote the author's statement: "The words comprising the test were selected from the vocabulary in a large number of school-subject fields and other supplementary readings of interest to pupils of this school level. An attempt was made to select words from the various fields in the same proportion as the pupils will in general be confronted by them. All words were checked against the Thorndike Word Lists in order to insure an equitable distribution according to difficulty and frequency of use." Inspection of the test indicates that the author *has* included a wide variety of words.

One feature of this test is the fact that the words are presented in a sentence or phrase, e.g., "sterilize the container." This context feature makes the test more nearly a lifelike situation.

As to reliability there would seem to be some question. The authors state that the reliability coefficients range from .84 to .96, with an average of .90. Authors of other vocabulary tests have reported reliability coefficients as high as .95. The reason, of course, for low reliability is the fact that there are only 85 items in this test. The time limit is 30 minutes. It would have been better if more items had been included, and the time limit extended to a somewhat longer period.

Percentile norms are provided for midyear testing and for end-of-the-year testing for grades 4–8 inclusive. The range in number of cases is from 543 to 914. No statement is given as to the distribution of cases by states or by urban and rural areas. However, since the tests were used in the 1940 Kansas Every Pupil Test Survey, it is assumed that most of the cases are from that state. The authors do not give norms in terms of grade equivalents. Many teachers in these grades prefer grade-equivalent scores.

On the whole, the multiple-choice items listed in the test appear to be well chosen. However, some choices, intended to be the correct answers, are not so good. For instance, the expected definition of *navigable* is given as *passable*.

By way of summary, the reviewer feels that this test will serve a useful purpose.

[165]

Kennon Test of Literary Vocabulary, 1941 Edition. Prospective teachers of English in secondary schools; 1926–41; Forms I, II; $8.50 per 100; 30¢ per specimen set; nontimed (40) minutes; Laura H. V. Kennon and Irving Lorge; Bureau of Publications, Teachers College, Columbia University.

REFERENCES

1. KENNON, LAURA HALL VERE. *Tests of Literary Vocabulary for Teachers of English.* Columbia University, Teachers College, Contributions to Education, No. 223. New York: Bureau of Publications, the College, 1926. Pp. vii, 78. Out of print. *

H. H. Remmers, Director, Division of Educational Reference, Purdue University, Lafayette, Indiana. The purpose of this test in the words of the manual is "to arrive at an estimate of the control of word knowledge specifically related to the interpretation of English and American literature" and thus to be of value in "selecting for mastery of content . . . students who are preparing to teach English in the junior or senior high school, and also in counseling students toward a better orientation in their chosen field" on the assumption that "one important asset of prospective teachers of English is the possession of an extensive and special literary vocabulary."

Both curricular validation (occurrence of words in relevant types of literature and in the works of specified authors) and statistical validation (correlation of scores of teachers and prospective teachers against two older forms, item-correlation *vs.* total score and various tests as well as comprehensive English departmental examinations at Teachers College) make the statement of purposes persuasive and acceptable as having been achieved in this test at least for mine-run students and literature courses. The average item difficulty is optimal—50.6 per cent. Centile norms for the equated two forms are provided, based on 1,091 teachers and prospective teachers.

To call the correlation of .93 between each of the older Forms A and B and their new counterparts I and II a "validity coefficient," except in a narrow, statistical and rather unreal sense (validity by definition), elicits from this reviewer a demurrer re semantic liberties. But this is perhaps a very minor point. The reliability of each form was found to be .94 for the maximum range of talent (teachers and prospective teachers) investigated, and .97 for the average of both forms. It would have been desirable to include in the manual the standard error of a score on the test. Administration and scoring are simple and efficient.

[166]

Michigan Vocabulary Profile. Grades 9-16; 1937–39; IBM; Forms AM, BM; separate answer sheets need not be used; $1.90 per 25; 35¢ per specimen set, postpaid; $1.10 per 25 machine-scorable answer sheets; 40¢ per set of stencils for scoring answer sheets; nontimed (50) minutes; prepared under the direction of Edward B. Greene; World Book Co. (1939).

REFERENCES

1-2. *See* 40:1320.
3. GREENE, EDWARD B. "Vocabulary Profiles of Groups in Training." *J Ed Res* 33:569-75 Ap '40. * (PA 14:3733)
4. GREENE, EDWARD B. "Predicting the Student's Success." *J Higher Ed* 11:252-6 My '40. * (PA 14:5199)
5. JOHNSON, DONALD M. "Confidence and Achievement in Eight Branches of Knowledge." *J Ed Psychol* 32:23-36 Ja '41. * (PA 15:3156)
6. REED, HOMER B. "Why Do Some Colleges Reach A Higher Level of Achievement Than Others?" *J Ed Res* 38:161-72 N '44. * (PA 19:1348) Same: *Trans Kans Acad Sci* 47:111-21 '44. *
7. EVANS, CHESTER EUGENE. *Interrelations of Evidences of Vocational Interest.* Unpublished doctor's thesis, Ohio State University, 1946. (*Abstracts of Dissertations . . . Summer Quarter 1945–46*, 1946, pp. 51-7.)
8. THOMPSON, CLAUDE EDWARD. "Selecting Executives by Psychological Tests." *Ed & Psychol Meas* 7:773-8 w '47. *

Joseph E. King, Director, Personnel Management Consultants, Chicago, Illinois. This test measures word knowledge in eight fields of information: human relations, commerce, government, physical science, biological science, mathematics, fine arts, and sports. The basic factor tapped by the test battery appears to be verbal ability, which involves the ability to understand words and ideas, is the usual component of verbal intelligence tests, and is measured by tests of vocabulary, definitions, and same-opposites. The fact that the *Michigan Vocabulary Profile* correlates .61 with the *American Council on Education Psychological Examination* and .56 with the *Cooperative English Test* indicates its loading in factor V.

What is being measured by the *Michigan Vocabulary Profile* is probably general V plus a series of specific V's. The median correlation among the eight tests of the battery is .27 for a college sophomore group, indicating a good degree of independence between the subtests for this particular population and thus showing each score to be valuable in itself as a predictor. Since studies indicate a relationship between technical vocabulary and preference, the test may be considered to measure interest in the area. The student's score is probably also influenced by his scholastic background. In general, the profile may be said to measure the student's ability to deal with words, and to some extent his interest, in broad technical areas. In view of this, the contribution of the

test to a profile of the student's abilities and interests might be questioned. No correlation between the profile and standard tests of this type are furnished, but from the traits sampled by the *Profile* there would appear to be considerable overlap. Also, since the *Vocabulary Profile* samples word achievement more than verbal aptitude, its usefulness for predictive purposes at the high school level would probably not be as great as a measure of everyday activities related to a given area.

The test is composed of eight subtests, is administered without time limit (about 50 minutes required), and employs a separate answer sheet for both hand- and machine-scored forms. Responses are multiple choice, and two equivalent forms are available. Items were selected by the criterion of internal consistency and are arranged in order of difficulty. Equivalent-form reliabilities range from .78 to .94. Raw scores, obtained by stencil or scoring machine, are converted to percentile norms. Norms are available for 4,677 students from ninth grade to college senior. A profile sheet is contained in the test booklet to plot the student's pattern of technical vocabularies. Typical profiles for seven educational and three occupational groups are provided. The *Michigan Vocabulary Profile* thus appears to meet the desired standards of test construction and usage. The profile could be improved by allowing conversion to percentile rank to occur automatically by plotting raw scores on the profile and by adapting the profile for student use and self-interpretation. Sound interpretation of the student's vocabulary pattern requires more research as to the profiles of workers in various scholastic and occupational groups.

For a review by Herbert A. Landry, see 40:1320. For reviews by John G. Darley, Richard Ledgerwood, John M. Stalnaker, M. R. Trabue, and Arthur E. Traxler of an earlier edition, see 38:1171.

[167]

Survey Test of Vocabulary. Grades 3-13; 1931–33; Forms X, Z, X4; $1.25 per 50 copies of Form X or Y, postpaid; $1.75 per 50 copies of Form X4, postpaid; 25¢ per specimen set, postpaid; L. J. O'Rourke; Psychological Institute.

REFERENCES

1. WAR MANPOWER COMMISSION, DIVISION OF OCCUPATIONAL ANALYSIS, STAFF. "Factor Analysis of Occupational Aptitude Tests." *Ed & Psychol Meas* 5:147-55 su '45. * (PA 20:1242)

Verner M. Sims, Professor of Psychology, University of Alabama, University, Alabama. This test was developed for use in a nationwide study of vocabulary which was sponsored by the Psychological Corporation some 15 years ago and is now being offered for general use by the Psychological Institute.

The test is presented without a manual. The directions for administering and scoring are printed on the test sheet itself, and an accompanying mimeographed sheet reports the correct answers for the items and mean scores for succeeding grades from grade 3 through 12 (based upon from two to more than three thousand children at each grade).

No information is furnished concerning how the test was constructed (the original form used in the survey did report that it was based upon Thorndike's *Teacher's Word Book*); what its strengths and weaknesses are; what its reliability is; or how and when the norms were obtained (they are labeled nationwide grade norms). Nor are any suggestions offered concerning its possible uses. No attention seems even to have been given to the matter of economy of use.

The test may have served its original purpose, but the form in which it now appears makes it difficult if not impossible to arrive at a reasonable judgment concerning its worth. Unless one is willing to accept the test on the basis of the prestige of its sponsor or because of the author's reputation in the field of measurements (Dr. O'Rourke served for years as the director of research in the U. S. Civil Service Commission), there is no intelligent method by which one can decide for or against its use except to evaluate it experimentally oneself. This can only mean that from a practical standpoint the usefulness of the test is extremely limited.

Clifford Woody, Professor of Education, University of Michigan, Ann Arbor, Michigan. This vocabulary test was but one of several tests employed in a nationwide effort to determine the status of mastery of English usage in grades 3 to 13. The vocabulary test consists of 100 items of the multiple-choice type. It is based upon the Thorndike *Teacher's Word Book of Twenty Thousand Words*—a list in which the words are distributed into groups according to frequency of usage in the sources upon which the word count was based. In

building the test, five words were selected from each of the twenty levels indicated by Thorndike. Thus, the first group of five words in the test represents words in the first thousand most commonly used words; the second group of five words, those in the second thousand most commonly used words, etc. Each word chosen for the test is in a simple sentence with the word to be defined printed in capital letters. Each sentence is followed by five words from which the person taking the test must select the one which means the same as the word printed in capital letters. Care was taken in selecting the five words from which the synonym is to be chosen to select all five words from the levels of usage which are lower in frequency than that on which the word to be defined occurred. Thus, if frequency of use can be taken as a criterion of difficulty, it can be assumed that the word to be defined is always more difficult than the response words from which the synonym is to be selected. It should be pointed out that, while the above assumption tends to be true, there are many exceptions in which frequency of use is no measure of the difficulty in defining a word. While O'Rourke's initial selection of words was based upon the level upon which the words occurred in the Thorndike List, the final selection was upon frequency levels and actual difficulty determined by the percentages of correct responses made by 600 pupils in grades 3, 5, 7, 9, and 12. Only those words which were common to the Thorndike scale and the difficulty scale by actual trial were selected. Words not meeting the double requirement were eliminated.

The word lists and response words for Forms X and X4 are identical. Form X was copyrighted in 1931; Form X4, in 1940. Form X is printed on both sides of a single page; Form X4, as a four-page booklet. The time limit for Form X is 20 minutes; for Form X4, 10 minutes. The instructions for the two forms are essentially the same, although those for Form X4 are somewhat more extended and include three practice exercises not given in the instructions for Form X. Both sets of instructions call for recording the response in such fashion that scoring with a provided key is facilitated. In determining the score on each form, each correct response counts one point. Norms of achievement are provided for grades 3 to 13 based on responses from 26,008 pupils, with from two to three thousand per grade. The norms provided are for the 20-minute test, but no doubt norms for the 10-minute test are or will be available soon. Form 2 of the tests has been advertised as equivalent to Form X, and the author has indicated still other forms are being constructed and will be available in the near future. The coefficient of reliability of the test as provided by the author is .98. No coefficients of validity have been provided, but the reviewer's experience with similar tests gives assurance that one need not question the test on that basis. This test has been widely used by the United States Employment Service and in personnel work in many industries. The reviewer has no hesitation in recommending the use of this test.

[168]

★Vocabulary Test: National Achievement Tests. Grades 3-8, 7-12; 1939–43; Forms A, B; 2 levels; 85¢ per 25 tests for grades 3-8; $1.50 per 25 tests for grades 7-12; 15¢ per specimen set of either level; nontimed (15) minutes; Robert K. Speer and Samuel Smith; Acorn Publishing Co.

Clifford Woody, Professor of Education, University of Michigan, Ann Arbor, Michigan. The test for grades 3–8 consists of 50 vocabulary exercises of the multiple-choice variety printed on both sides of a single page; the test for grades 7–12 consists of two parts: Part I, Word Meanings, consisting of 60 exercises like those in the test for grades 3–8, and Part II, Word Discrimination, consisting of 20 exercises in which the pupil must complete a given sentence by selecting the appropriate word from the four given words accompanying the incomplete sentence. In the first test and in Part I of the second test, the exercises emphasize *recognition* of a synonym for a given word; in Part II of the test, the ability to select the word that completes correctly the meaning of the sentence.

The reviewer does not have available the exact method employed in selecting the words for this test, but in the catalogue describing the test occur the following statements: (a) "For each part of each test, the words used have been carefully selected and graded"; (b) in each exercise of the vocabulary test, "the base word is considered more difficult than the synonym given; therefore the pupil's choice tests his ability to compare the word with a correct word slightly less difficult." Checking the list of base or synonym words with the

levels of frequency of use on the Thorndike list of twenty thousand most commonly used words revealed little relationship in the order of the words appearing in the forms of this test and in the Thorndike levels. The catalogue indicates that each test has been used experimentally, has been analyzed by specialists, and has been checked against courses of study and content of textbooks; but no specific details have been given.

Two characteristics of the test exercises appeal to the reviewer: (a) All words of the sentence are much more simple than the word to be defined. (b) The correct response can be marked by reference to a code word, thus making an answer form unnecessary. There is no time limit for any of the tests, but approximately 15 minutes is required. Norms are given for grade and age on a month-by-month basis. A special set of norms is given for pupils with high and low IQ's. The coefficients of reliability of .94 and .95 are reported for the two tests. No coefficients of correlation with other vocabulary tests are available. The scoring by means of the code words eliminates the necessity of a scoring key, but it precludes allowing the pupils to score their own tests unless they should do so from a perfect test paper. Otherwise the pupil will have the code word and thus invalidate the use of the test for future use with other pupils.

[169]

Wide Range Vocabulary Test. Grades 3-16 and adults; 1937–45; Form B presents words in order of difficulty; Form C presents words alphabetically; $1.75 per 25, postpaid; 35¢ per specimen set, postpaid; nontimed (10) minutes; C. R. Atwell and F. L. Wells; Psychological Corporation.

REFERENCES
1. ATWELL, C. R., AND WELLS, F. L. "Wide Range Multiple Choice Vocabulary Tests." J Appl Psychol 21:550-5 O '37. (PA 12:2148)

Paul S. Burnham, Associate Director, Student Appointment Bureau, Yale University, New Haven, Connecticut. A multiple-choice form of vocabulary test, consisting of 100 words with five potential synonyms for each word. There is no time limit, and under normal circumstances approximately 10 minutes are needed. The grade range is grade 3 through adult. Two forms claimed to be equivalent are available: Form B, copyrighted in 1937, presents the words in order of difficulty; Form C, copyrighted in 1945, presents words in alphabetical order. Median scores for groups of average ages—8 through 21—are given as norms. No information is given about the size of population on which these medians were based.

The manual gives no data on reliability of either test, their intercorrelation, or correlation with other well-known measures. Subjective impression leads one to believe that this test might be useful for a preliminary screening particularly if followed by more extensive testing of the verbal factor.

[170]

★**Word Dexterity Test.** Grades 9-13; 1942; Form A; $2 per 25, postpaid; 100 or more, 6½¢ per copy, postpaid; 25¢ per specimen set, postpaid; nontimed (40-45) minutes; Shailer Peterson; the Author, 222 East Superior St., Chicago 11, Ill.

REFERENCES

1. PETERSON, SHAILER A. "Teaching the Special Vocabularies." *Engl J, Col Ed* 23:53-6 Ja '34. *
2. PETERSON, SHAILER. "The Word-Dexterity Test: A Better Measure of College Aptitude.' *Ed & Psychol Meas* 4:307-13 w '44. * (*PA* 20:326)

ENGLISH—FOURTH MMY

Reviews by *Harold H. Bixler, Charlotte Croon Davis, Frederick B. Davis, Clarence Derrick, John S. Diekhoff, Walter N. Durost, C. M. Fleming, Walter Scribner Guiler, Chester W. Harris, Walter V. Kaulfers, W. C. Kvaraceus, Gerald V. Lannholm, Margaret G. McKim, Worth J. Osburn, Robert C. Pooley, Winifred L. Post, Henry D. Rinsland, Holland Roberts, David Segal, George Spache, John M. Stalnaker, and Anton Thompson.*

[148]

★**A.C.E.R. English Usage Tests.** Ages 10–13; 1951; 2 parts; Form C ['51]; no data on reliability and validity; 3s. 6d. per manual ['51]; 6d. per scoring key; 4s. 6d. per specimen set; cash orders postpaid within Australia; 30(40) minutes; Australian Council for Educational Research. *
a) PART 1, WORD USAGE. 2s. 1d. per 10.
b) PART 2, SENTENCES. 2s. 6d. per 10.

[149]

*****Barrett-Ryan English Test.** Grades 7–13; 1929–51; IBM; Forms I ('29), II ('29), III ('29), IV ('40), V ('44), VI ('44), 1948, 1949, 1950, 1951; Forms 1944–47 out of print; manual ('43); $1.15 per 25; 35¢ per specimen set; separate answer sheets may be used; 85¢ per 25 IBM answer sheets; 25¢ per stencil for scoring answer sheets; postpaid; 50(55) minutes; E. R. Barrett, Teresa M. Ryan, E. R. Wood (I–IV), and H. E. Schrammel (1948–51); Bureau of Educational Measurements, Kansas State Teachers College of Emporia. *

[150]

*****Basic Language Skills: Iowa Every-Pupil Tests of Basic Skills, Test C, New Edition.** Grades 3–5, 5–9; 1940–47; for complete battery, see 15; 5 (Advanced Battery) or 6 (Elementary Battery) scores: punctuation, capitalization, usage, spelling, sentence sense (Elementary Battery only), total; IBM for grades 5–9; 2 levels; Forms L ('40), M ('41), N ('42), O ('43); manual ('45); battery manual ('47); 33¢ per specimen set of any one level; postage extra; H. F. Spitzer in collaboration with Ernest Horn, Maude McBroom, H. A. Greene, and E. F. Lindquist; Houghton Mifflin Co. *
a) ELEMENTARY BATTERY. Grades 3–5; $1.60 per 25; 46(60) minutes.
b) ADVANCED BATTERY. Grades 5–9; IBM; $1.75 per 25; separate answer sheets may be used; 75¢ per 25 IBM answer sheets; 40¢ per set of stencils for machine scoring of answer sheets; 55 or 58(70) minutes.

For reviews by Miriam M. Bryan and Anton Thompson of the complete battery, see 15; for reviews by Frederic L. Ayer, Gustav J. Froehlich, and Ralph C. Preston of the complete battery, see 3:10; for reviews by William A. Brownell, J. Murray Lee, and Charles W. Odell of the 1937 form of the complete battery, see 38:872.

[151]

*****California Language Test.** Grades 1–4.5, 4–6, 7–9, 9–14; 1933–50; a revision of *Progressive Language Tests* (see 40:1292); a subtest of *California Achievement Tests* (see 2); 3 scores: mechanics of English and grammar, spelling, total; IBM for grades 4–14; 4 levels; Forms AA ('50), BB ('50), CC ('50), DD ('50); manuals ('50); postage extra; 35¢ per specimen set of any one level, postpaid; Ernest W. Tiegs and Willis W. Clark; California Test Bureau. *
a) PRIMARY. Grades 1–4.5; $1 per 25; 16(25) minutes.
b) ELEMENTARY. Grades 4–6; $1.25 per 25; separate answer sheets may be used; 4¢ per IBM answer sheet; 7¢ per scoreze answer sheet; 20¢ per stencil for machine scoring of answer sheets; 20¢ per stencil for hand scoring of answer sheets; 26(35) minutes.
c) INTERMEDIATE. Grades 7–9; prices same as for Elementary; 28(35) minutes.
d) ADVANCED. Grades 9–14; $1.50 per 25; separate answer sheets may be used; 4¢ per IBM answer sheet; 7¢ per scoreze answer sheet; 60¢ per stencil for machine scoring of answer sheets; 20¢ per stencil for hand scoring of answer sheets; 31(40) minutes.

GERALD V. LANNHOLM, *Project Director, Educational Testing Service, Princeton, New Jersey.*

This series of language-correctness tests includes a test at each of four different educational levels from grades 1–14. Four forms are available at each of the first three levels, primary, elementary, and intermediate. Statements in the manual conflict with regard to the number of forms (three or four) for the advanced level. A separate manual is provided for each of the levels. Although much of the material is identical in all of the manuals, the material in certain sections is modified from one level to another. Major emphasis is given to the use of the results for identifying specific strengths and weaknesses of individual pupils. However, suggestions are also presented for the use of the results for survey or administrative purposes.

Each manual contains a fairly detailed description of the test content, a brief section on reliability and validity, instructions for preparing and using a "diagnostic profile," a discussion of the uses of the test results, directions for administering and scoring the test, and a section on norms. In comprehensiveness the manuals for this series of tests excel most of those which have come to the attention of this reviewer. A table of contents would increase its usefulness for the busy teacher.

Each of these language tests is a part of the *California Achievement Tests,* but may be used without the other tests in the battery if desired. At each of the four levels, the language test is divided into two parts. For the primary level, the two parts are designated as Mechanics of English, and Spelling. At each of the other three levels, the parts are Mechanics of English and Grammar, and Spelling. To assist the teacher in evaluating the pupil's handwriting ability, a handwriting scale is also provided at each of the four levels. A sample of each pupil's handwriting is obtained by having him write three words which are dictated at the end of the testing period.

In the primary test, the authors decided wisely to have the pupils record their answers to the exercises in the test booklet. At each of the three higher levels, the teacher may have the pupils enter their responses in the test booklet or on a specially designed "self-scoring" separate answer sheet. A single scoring key which may be used for any of the forms is provided for each of the three tests above the primary level. This is made possible by having the pupil select a coded response instead of actually writing the correct usage. This arrangement probably reduces the possibility that a teacher will use the wrong scoring key.

Despite the claims of the test authors that the primary purpose of this test series is to aid in the identification of specific strengths and weaknesses of individual pupils, it is this reviewer's opinion that the tests will serve better as measures of general achievement than they will as diagnostic-analytic instruments. This conclusion is based on the opinion that most learning of skills is specific rather than generalized and that ability to handle a given sampling of skills is not sufficient evidence to demonstrate ability to handle a different sampling of skills, even if drawn from the same family of skills. It is doubted, for example, that one can confidently assume from the fact that a pupil can handle correctly the use of a comma to set off words or phrases in apposition, that he can also use an apostrophe correctly to form the possessive case of nouns. It should be apparent, therefore, that for a test to be effective in identifying the specific skills which a pupil possesses or does not possess, each of the skills in which one is interested should be covered in the test. Further-

more, a reliable measure of a pupil's mastery of a given skill can be obtained only if the test contains an adequate sampling of situations which require the pupil to use that particular skill. None of the forms of the *California Language Test* satisfies these requirements. For example, even at the advanced level, the punctuation test contains only 10 items. This constitutes a small sampling, even for obtaining a rough indication of a pupil's general level of punctuation ability. For obtaining adequate information upon which to base a program of remedial instruction, it is entirely unsatisfactory. The advanced level test contains four items involving the use of commas. If all four items covered the same usage, some indication might be obtained regarding a pupil's ability to handle that particular use. But the test would yield no information about his ability to use the comma in other types of situations. This reviewer laments the practice of test authors to label as diagnostic nearly any test that samples more than one aspect of some field of study, whether or not the test includes an adequate sampling of each of the specific elements of learning or skill involved. He considers it equally unfortunate when teachers accept as diagnostic any test which is so designated by the author or publisher.

The authors of this test series are to be commended for their use of simpler testing techniques at the lower levels than at the higher levels and for their caution to be particularly careful about giving directions to primary pupils. In the primary level test, the nature of the exercises resembles more closely real life situations than do the exercises used in the higher level tests. In the capitalization tests at the primary level, pupils are asked to underline each letter that should be a capital letter; at higher levels, pupils are asked to indicate which of the numbered letters should be capitals. In the primary level punctuation test, pupils are asked to place needed punctuation marks in the proper places in the material printed in the test book. The higher level tests require the pupil to consider numbered places in the copy and decide which, if any, of four different punctuation marks is needed at each place. His decision is recorded as a mark under the punctuation selected. Word usage and sentence recognition exercises are included in each test above the primary level. The intermediate and advanced level tests also include a section requiring the pupil to classify each word in a sentence according to the part of speech it represents. A section covering miscellaneous elements of grammar and syntax appears in the advanced level test.

The spelling test at the primary level consists of 25 words which the authors wisely have dictated to the pupils who actually write them in the test booklet. At the other levels, the spelling test consists of 30 groups of words, the pupil being required to study each group and decide which, if any, of the words is misspelled. It is doubted that this technique provides the most dependable measure of a pupil's ability to spell words correctly in his own writing. Such a test would appear to yield more helpful information for survey purposes than for diagnostic or analytic functions.

Three estimated reliabilities are given for each of the test levels, the authors stating that the coefficients were obtained by "the Kuder-Richardson formula" (the manual does not indicate which K-R formula was used) for a single grade. Separate reliability estimates are given for Mechanics of English, Spelling, and Total Language. In view of the emphasis given in the manual on the importance and use of scores on the subsections (capitalization, punctuation, etc.), it is disappointing to find that information is not provided regarding the reliabilities of these subsections. No data are given to indicate the degree of correlation between scores on pairs of the several forms available at each of the four levels.

Several types of norms are given for each of the four levels for which the tests are available. Percentile norms are given for separate grades, for each of the three scores reported on each level of the test. For grades one through nine, two tables of percentile norms are given for each grade. One of these applies to pupils tested during the first half of the grade and the other to those tested during the second half. Grade and age norms are also presented in each of the manuals. Finally, a table is provided for use in adjusting the norms in relation to intelligence quotient medians given for each grade separately. The standardization and norms samples appear to be sufficiently large with respect to the number of pupils involved. No details are given concerning the selection of the schools in which these pupils were enrolled.

The *California Language Test* is a series of tests, available in several forms at each of four educational levels. The manuals are quite detailed and are definitely above average in the amount and value of the information presented. Provision is made at each of the three upper levels for the use of rapid scoring methods. The testing techniques employed have been used quite widely. Elaborate directions and suggestions are given for the use of the results for the diagnosis of learning difficulties. It is the opinion of this reviewer, however, that in view of the limited sampling of the many specific elements of usage in this field, more reliance should be placed on the test results for determining the general level of competence in correct writing than for diagnostic and analytic purposes.

ROBERT C. POOLEY, *Professor of English, and Chairman, Department of Integrated Liberal Studies, University of Wisconsin, Madison, Wisconsin.*

PRIMARY GRADES 1–3. There are four equivalent forms of this simple test, making possible testing and retesting of the same group with a minimum of practice effect. Three elements of English written skills are measured: capitalization, punctuation, and spelling. A brief narrative contains nine exercises in capitalization and leads into a poem of four lines. Correctly capitalizing the first word of each line is the tenth exercise. The same narrative and poem are repeated in an adjacent column for punctuation. Five exercises are furnished: two terminal periods, one comma after "said," one pair of quotation marks, and one terminal question mark. Spelling is tested by 25 dictated words from the first 500 words used in writing. For the first grade 15 of these words are used; for the second grade, 20.

Clear and easy directions for administration, and equally clear instructions for scoring, make this test easy to use. The time, 16 minutes, is appropriate to the age and attention span of the pupils, and the content of the exercises is correctly derived from the written language skills of grades 1–3 and lower 4. The title is incorrect; this is not a language test but a test of three skills in written language. Handwriting is also measured on a scale, but does not form a part of the score.

An ingenious diagnostic profile chart makes possible a quick and simple representation of the pupil's achievement in terms of grade placement and percentile rank. Diagnostic analysis is provided by a parallel chart. Because of the very few items in the test, the validity of the diagnosis may be questioned. Altogether this is a simple, specific, and convenient test of writing skills.

ELEMENTARY GRADES 4–6. Like the primary test, this test contains exercises in the mechanics of writing and spelling but adds a new section on English usage and sentences. Capitalization and punctuation are tested in sentences, 15 correct responses possible in each. Credit is given for correct responses, but no penalty is exacted for overcapitalization and overpunctuation. Thus the child loses points for failing to make a correct response but loses no points for any number of incorrect responses. This provision makes the test easier to score at the cost of accuracy in measuring the child's skill in mechanics.

The usage section employs the familiar two-choice technique: e.g. "Mary is (¹ awful ² very) pretty," in ten exercises. Some usage choices are invalid for the elementary grades, such as the distinctions between *received* and *got, may* and *can*. Sentence knowledge is measured by 10 exercises, in which the child is to distinguish between complete sentences and fragments. The spelling test at this level is not dictated, but it is a five-choice multiple response exercise in which the child selects one of four words as misspelled or indicates that none is misspelled.

Except for one or two dubious usage items, this test appears to be a convenient, easily scored, and reasonably valid test of mechanical skills in written English. Handwriting is also scaled but does not form a part of the test score.

INTERMEDIATE GRADES 7–9. The four equivalent forms of this test are similar in structure to the test for grades 4–6, with the addition of a new exercise testing knowledge of the parts of speech. A sentence of 20 numbered words is furnished. In a five-choice multiple response exercise the student must indicate the part of speech for each word in the sentence. This exercise is what used to be called "parsing," a teaching technique which properly fell into disrepute many decades ago. It is distressing to find it revived in this test. Since there is absolutely no objective evidence to support the assumption that knowledge of parts of speech contributes to a child's command of language, this section is invalid in a language test and therefore invalidates the score of the entire test as a measure of language skill.

ADVANCED GRADES 9–14. This test, prepared in three equivalent forms, consists of six sections with a total of 110 points distributed as follows: capitalization 15; punctuation 10;

words and sentences 25; parts of speech 17; syntax 13; spelling 30. The first four parts and the spelling are constructed on the patterns used in the tests for previous grades and have been described above. The new section, called syntax, consists of the identification of grammatical forms or the classification of kinds of sentences. Among the items tested are case of pronouns, degree of comparison of adjectives, principal parts of verbs, and recognition of verbals. This section, with the section on parts of speech, devotes more than one fourth of the total points of the test to formal grammar. Unless there is proof that knowledge of grammar is a factor in command of language, these 30 points are invalid in a language test, and therefore the test is invalid as a measure of language skills.

An evaluation of these tests as a series reveals the astounding fact that children are presumed to learn nothing more about language other than grammatical facts after the fourth grade. No item in the advanced tests indicates any advance over the elementary tests in English content other than in grammar. It is difficult to believe that anyone could consider the difference between a fourth grade and a twelfth grade pupil in written English to lie exclusively in the latter's ability to name a noun or select a subject, yet these tests force one to that conclusion. What factors mark growth in English skill? Surely among them are an advance in unity and the power to sustain an idea; an advance in sentence structure featuring increasing subordination; an increase in the power to organize and present materials logically; a growth in diction leading to the use of exact and colorful words in effective places. These factors are what good English teachers teach; it is upon these and similar factors that pupils should be tested. Since the *California Language Tests* ignore these basic factors, the use of the tests above the fourth grade can yield returns increasingly unrelated to the measurement of skill in language.

For reviews by Warren G. Findley, Alvin W. Schindler, and J. Harlan Shores of the complete battery, see 2; for reviews by Harry A. Greene and J. Paul Leonard of an earlier edition, see 40:1292; for reviews by C. W. Odell and Hugh B. Wood of an earlier edition of the complete battery, see 40:1193; for a review by D. Welty Lefever of an earlier edition of the complete battery, see 38:876.

[152]

*College English Test: National Achievement Tests. Grades 12–13; 1937–46; 7 scores: punctuation, capitalization, language usage, sentence structure, modifiers, miscellaneous principles, total; Forms A ('42—same as test copyrighted in 1937), B ('41); no norms for part scores; manual ('46); series manual ['44]; $2.50 per 25; 15¢ per manual; 35¢ per specimen set; postage extra; 45(50) minutes; A. C. Jordan; Acorn Publishing Co. *

For reviews by Constance M. McCullough and Robert W. Howard of Form A, see 40: 1269.1.

[153]

College Placement Test in English. College; 1941–43; 8 scores: grammar, punctuation, sentence structure, reading, syntax, vocabulary, theme, total; Forms A ('41), B ('43); no data on reliability and validity; no manual; no norms for part scores; $2.25 per 25, postpaid; specimen set not available; 120(125) minutes; Hector H. Lee; Turner E. Smith & Co. *

CHARLOTTE CROON DAVIS, *Test Research Service, 12 Normandy Road, Bronxville, New York.*

In plan and type of item the first half of this test is similar to the *College Preparatory Test in English* by the same author. In appearance it is much improved since it is spread out into twice as much space. The second half of the test, to which 60 minutes is allotted, consists of the writing of an impromptu theme on one of ten reasonably varied and stimulating topics. Although it is stated that this composition is the most important part of the examination, no directions for rating it or for combining the rating on it with the scores on the other parts are given. The condensed norms, which are based on 1,400 (Form A) or 1,500 (Form B) high school graduates, apply only to the total score on the first six parts.

As a measure of achievement in English, this test is open to some of the same criticisms as the *College Preparatory Test.* It seems odd to have 30 items on punctuation and none on capitalization. Also, reading is such an important and complex skill that it would normally be better to measure it adequately in a separate test. On the other hand, if this test is to be used only for placing college entrants in English classes, the inclusion of nine reading items may contribute to its efficiency.

Most of the items are satisfactory. More careful editing might have eliminated such slips as defining "aggregate" as "in mass" when the context reads "people in the aggregate." Replacing "aggregate" by "in mass" leads to "in the in mass." The word "capital" in "writers

make capital out of spicy gossip" probably cannot be defined in a single word. Certainly the keyed response "profit" is not close enough to be acceptable. There are a few inconsistencies in format: Part VII of Form A is called "Theme" on the cover page and "Composition" inside; the various sections are called "Parts" on the cover page and "Tests" on the key.

In summary, this test may have some value in college placement in English. However, most colleges would hesitate to include theme writing, with its attendant difficulties of scoring and unreliability of scores. Normally, a college would make much more efficient use of two hours' testing time by giving the *Cooperative English Tests* (either lower or higher level), which are completely objective, machine scorable, based on a carefully planned outline, well edited, and furnished with differentiated norms based on thousands of cases accumulated over several years of widespread use.

[154]

College Preparatory Test in English. High school; 1943; 8 scores: grammar, sentence revision, comprehension of reading, syntax, vocabulary, sentence structure, punctuation, total; 1 form; no data on reliability and validity; no manual; no norms for part scores; $1.75 per 25, postpaid; specimen set not available; nontimed (40–50) minutes; Hector H. Lee; Turner E. Smith & Co. *

CHARLOTTE CROON DAVIS, *Test Research Service, 12 Normandy Road, Bronxville, New York.*

This test is composed of seven parts, as listed above, crowded into seven 5½ by 8½ inch pages. The author has tried to cover so many areas in the time and space at his disposal that the items are spread very thin over some of them; for example, the reading comprehension score is based on four items. Perhaps the author did not intend the part scores to be interpreted separately; however, the total score is also open to question as an index of achievement in "college preparatory English." This subject, even the part of it that can be measured in tests of this type, includes so many important skills that it is not possible to cover them adequately in 40 minutes. Nevertheless, a better balanced distribution of items could have been provided. There are 15 items on punctuation and none on capitalization, 24 on grammar and none on spelling. Thirty of the 86 items are concerned with sentence structure. The writer wonders how carefully the author considered the makeup of the test.

The individual items are run-of-the-mill. In

the first item, the testee is to choose the word in parentheses that makes this sentence correct, "He left the plate (sitting, setting) under the table." Better than either would be, simply, "He left the plate under the table." An occasional item is rather silly; for example, Item 18, Part 6, reads, "And I have felt a presence that disturbs me with the joy of elevated thoughts."

Some items are badly expressed. Item B, Part 3, when completed by choice 2, reads, "Courageous impartiality is hardly to be expected in Victorian biography because their natural emotion was to praise the dead." (Whom does "their" refer to? Is praising the dead an emotion?) The sentence is not much better when completed by the keyed answer, "....because it was an era of established values accepted without question." (What does "it" refer to?) Item D, Part 3, when completed by choice 4, reads, "The author implies that courageous impartiality is a quality of truth in biography which scholarship and patient industry tried to cultivate in earlier times." (Industrious and patient *scholars* may have tried, but not scholarship and industry.) It seems to the writer that the author of a test in English expression should be especially careful to avoid loose and fuzzy sentences like those cited above. Throughout the test there is little evidence of ingenuity in devising the items or care in editing them.

The scoring is objective, though several variations from the key would surely be permissible in Part II, in which the testees write in their own revisions of defective sentences. The test is not machine scorable. Condensed norms based on 2,300 "high school graduates" are provided. No additional information about these graduates is given.

In summary, this test has little to recommend it.

[155]

*Cooperative English Test: Lower and Higher Levels. Grades 7–12, 11–16; 1940–51; IBM; 3 tests available separately and in a single booklet edition; no specific manual; descriptive folders [Mechanics and Effectiveness of Expression, '50; Reading Comprehension, '51]; general Cooperative manual ('51); norms ['40]; separate answer sheets may be used; cash orders postpaid; Cooperative Test Division, Educational Testing Service. *

a) SINGLE BOOKLET EDITION: LOWER AND HIGHER LEVELS. Grades 7–12, 11–16; 7 scores: mechanics of expression, effectiveness of expression, vocabulary, speed of comprehension, level of comprehension, total comprehension, total; 2 levels; Forms S (Lower Level, '42—some printings bear 1949 or 1950 copyright; Higher Level, '50—same as test copyrighted in 1942), T ('50 or '51—same as test copyrighted in 1943), Y

(Lower Level, '51—same as test copyrighted in 1948; Higher Level, '48), RX ('49); Forms Q, R out of print; $3.90 per 25 of any one level; 50¢ per specimen set of any one level, postpaid; $1.70 per 25 IBM answer sheets; 45¢ per set of stencils for scoring answer sheets; 120(130) minutes.

b) TEST A, MECHANICS OF EXPRESSION. Grades 7–16; Forms S ('42—some printings bear a 1951 copyright), T ('43), X ('47), Y ('50—same as test copyrighted in 1948); Forms Q, R out of print; $2.25 per 25; 50¢ per specimen set, postpaid; 80¢ per 25 IBM answer sheets; 15¢ per stencil for scoring answer sheets; 40(45) minutes; Geraldine Spaulding, Herbert Danzer (X), and W. W. Cook (Y).

c) TESTS B1 AND B2, EFFECTIVENESS OF EXPRESSION: LOWER AND HIGHER LEVELS. Grades 7–12, 11–16; 2 levels; Forms S ('42), T (Lower Level, '43; Higher Level, '51—same as test copyrighted in 1943), X ('47), Y (Lower Level, '50—same as test copyrighted in 1948); Higher Level, '48; Forms Q, R out of print; $2.25 per 25 of any one level; 50¢ per specimen set of any one level, postpaid; 80¢ per 25 IBM answer sheets; 15¢ per stencil for scoring answer sheets; 40(45) minutes; Geraldine Spaulding, Miriam May Bryan, and Janet Afflerbach (Y).

d) TESTS C1 AND C2, READING COMPREHENSION: LOWER AND HIGHER LEVELS. Grades 7–12, 11–16; 4 scores: vocabulary, speed of comprehension, level of comprehension, total; 2 levels; Forms R ('50—same as test copyrighted in 1941), S (Lower Level, '42; Higher Level, '51—same as test copyrighted in 1942), T (Lower Level, '43; Higher Level, '50—same as test copyrighted in 1943), Y ('48); Form Q out of print; $2.50 per 25 of any one level; 50¢ per specimen set of any one level, postpaid; 80¢ per 25 IBM answer sheets; 15¢ per stencil for scoring answer sheets; 40(45) minutes; Frederick B. Davis, Harold V. King (S), Mary Willis (T), Clarence Derrick (Y), Harry R. Neville (Y), Jeanne M. Bradford (Y), and Geraldine Spaulding (Y).

REFERENCES

1–2. See 40:1276.
3–31. See 3:120.
   32. CROW, CECELIA BACHRACH. *The Predictive Value of College Admissions Data.* Master's thesis, Southern Methodist University (Dallas, Tex.), 1941. (*Abstracts of theses....1941,* pp. 61–3.)
   33. ARTLEY, A. STERL. *A Study of Certain Relationships Existing Between General Reading Comprehension and Reading Comprehension in a Specific Subject-Matter Area.* Doctor's thesis, Pennsylvania State College (State College, Pa.), 1942.
   34. COOK, WALTER W. "Predicting Success of Graduate Students in a College of Education." *Sch & Soc* 56:192–5 S 5 '42. * (*PA* 17:299)
   35. MCGEHEE, WILLIAM. "The Prediction of Differential Achievement in a Technological College." *J Appl Psychol* 27:88–92 F '43. * (*PA* 17:2893)
   36. TRAXLER, ARTHUR E. "Some Comments on 'The Prediction of Differential Achievement in a Technological College.'" *J Appl Psychol* 27:176–9 Ap '43. * (*PA* 17:3603)
   37. HUMBER, WILBUR J. "The Relationship Between Reading Efficiency and Academic Success in Selected University Curricula." *J Ed Psychol* 35:17–26 Ja '44. * (*PA* 18:2581)
   38. KILBY, CLYDE S. "A Study of Freshman Tests Repeated in the Sophomore Year." *J Am Assn Col Reg* 19:217–24 Ja '44. *
   39. GLADFELTER, MILLARD E. "An Analysis of Reading and English Changes That Occur During the Freshman Year in College." *J Am Assn Col Reg* 20:527–43 Jl '45. * (*PA* 20:2073)
   40. HULT, ESTHER. "Study of Achievement in Educational Psychology." *J Exp Ed* 13:174–90 Je '45. * (*PA* 19:3494)
   41. FOX, WILLIAM H. *An Analysis of Different Methods Used in the Prediction of General University Achievement.* Doctor's thesis, Indiana University (Bloomington, Ind.), 1946. (*Studies in Education....1945–1949,* 1950, pp. 28–31.)
   42. JONES, RONALD DEVALL. "The Prediction of Teaching Efficiency From Objective Measures." *J Exp Ed* 15:85–99 S '46. * (*PA* 21:606)
   43. LINS, LEO JOSEPH. "The Prediction of Teaching Efficiency." *J Exp Ed* 15:2–60 S '46. * (*PA* 21:610)
   44. PEIXOTTO, HELEN E. "Relationship of College Board Examination Scores and Reading Scores for College Freshmen." *J Appl Psychol* 30:406–11 Ag '46. * (*PA* 21:289)

45. McGANN, MARY. "Diagnostic Testing and Remedial Teaching for Common Errors in Mechanics ot English Made by College Freshmen." *J Ed Psychol* 38:499–503 D '47. * (*PA* 22:3609)

46. *The 1948 National College Sophomore Testing Program: Final Sophomore Percentile Tables.* Princeton, N.J.: Cooperative Test Division, Educational Testing Service, May 1948. Pp. 4. Paper. *

47. ARTLEY, A. STERL. "General and Specific Factors in Reading Comprehension." *J Exp Ed* 16:181–6 Mr '48. * (*PA* 20:5122)

48. HAVENS, VIRGINIA. "A Prediction of Law School Achievement From High-School Rank, Reading Test Scores, Psychological Test Scores, and Average Grade in Pre-Law Courses." *J Ed Psychol* 39:237–42 Ap '48. * (*PA* 23:1463)

49. REMMERS, H. H., AND GAGE, N. L. *The Abilities and Interests of Pharmacy Freshmen.* The Pharmaceutical Survey, Monograph No. 1. Reprinted from *The American Journal of Pharmaceutical Education*, Vol. 12, No. 1, January 1948. Washington, D.C.: American Council on Education, [1948]. Pp. 65 plus 13 inserts. Paper. * (*PA* 22:4107)

50. RICHARDS, J. NEVIN. *The Prediction of Engineering Success From the Pre-Engineering Inventory and From the Cooperative Achievement Tests.* Master's thesis, University of Utah (Salt Lake City, Utah), 1948.

51. *College Preparatory Testing Program: A Guide to the Use of Tests and Interpretation of Results.* Princeton, N.J.: Cooperative Test Division, Educational Testing Service, [1949]. Pp. 30. Paper. *

52. *1949 National College Sophomore Testing Program: Final Report.* Princeton, N.J.: Cooperative Test Division, Educational Testing Service, [1949]. Pp. 19. Paper. *

53. *Report on the 1948 National College Freshman Testing Program.* Princeton, N.J.: Cooperative Test Division, Educational Testing Service, [1949]. Pp. 28. Paper. *

54. JACOBS, ROBERT. "Public School Testing Project: First Report," pp. 66–72. (*PA* 23:3446) In *1948 Fall Testing Program in Independent Schools and Supplementary Studies.* Educational Records Bulletin, No. 51. New York: the Bureau, January 1949. Pp. xiii, 72. Paper, lithotyped. *

55. KRATHWOHL, WILLIAM C. "An Index of Industriousness for English." *J Ed Psychol* 40:469–81 D '49. *(*PA* 24:3386)

56. REMMERS, H. H., AND GAGE, N. L. "Student Personnel Studies of the Pharmaceutical Survey." *Am J Pharm Ed* 13:6–126 Ja '49. * (*PA* 23:1004)

57. RINSLAND, HENRY D. "The Prediction of Veterans' Success From Test Scores at the University of Oklahoma," Part 1, pp. 59–72. In *The Sixth Yearbook of the National Council on Measurements Used in Education, 1948–1949.* Fairmont, W.Va.: the Council, Fairmont State College, 1949. Pp. v, 140 (variously numbered). Paper, mimeographed. *

58. STAPLETON, MARY R. *The Differential Prognostic Value of Certain Measures as Criteria for the Educational Guidance of Entering Freshman Women.* Doctor's thesis, New York University (New York, N.Y.), 1949. (*Abstracts of Theses....* [*School of Education*] *October 1948–June 1949*, 1950, pp. 137–40.)

59. TRAXLER, ARTHUR E. "Correlations Between Scores on Various Reading Tests Administered Several Months Apart," pp. 78–82. (*PA* 24:748) In *1949 Achievement Testing Program in Independent Schools and Supplementary Studies.* Educational Records Bulletin, No. 52. New York: Educational Records Bureau, July 1949. Pp. xiii, 87. Paper, lithotyped. *

60. ZWILLING, VIRGINIA T. *The Prediction of Grades in Freshman English From a Battery of Tests of Mental Ability, Interests and Aptitudes Administered to Students Entering a Liberal Arts College.* Doctor's thesis, Fordham University (New York, N.Y.), 1949. (*Dissertations. . . . ,* 1949, pp. 62–5.)

61. *College Preparatory Testing Program, 1950: A Guide to the Use of the Tests and the Interpretation of Results.* Princeton, N.J.: Cooperative Test Division, Educational Testing Service, [1950]. Pp. 30. Paper. *

62. *Report on the 1949 National College Freshman Testing Program.* Princeton, N.J.: Cooperative Test Division, Educational Testing Service, [1950]. Pp. 22. Paper. *

63. *Report on the 1950 National College Sophomore Testing Program.* Princeton, N.J.: Cooperative Test Division, Educational Testing Service, [1950]. Pp. 22. Paper. *

64. BROTHERS, WILBUR LEO. *The Relationship of Certain Factors to Effectiveness in Student Teaching in the Secondary Schools.* Doctor's thesis, Indiana University (Bloomington, Ind.), 1950. (*Thesis Abstract Series....1950*, 1951, pp. 12–8.)

65. COCHRAN, SAMUEL W., AND DAVIS, FREDERICK B. "Predicting Freshman Grades at George Peabody College for Teachers." *Peabody J Ed* 27:352–6 My '50. *

66. JACOBS, ROBERT. "A Study of the Need for Special Norms on Scholastic Aptitude and Mechanics of English Tests for College Preparatory Students in Public Schools," pp. 52–66. (*PA* 24:3895) In *1949 Fall Testing Program in Independent Schools and Supplementary Studies.* Educational Records Bulletin, No. 53. New York: Educational Records Bureau, January 1950. Pp. xiii, 70. Paper, lithotyped. *

67. JAMES, RICHARD WARREN. *Selection of Graduate Students: (1) The Adequacy of Certain Measures for Differentiating Between Two Groups of Master Candidates (2) The Value of These Measures in Prognosing Graduate Academic Achievement.* Doctor's thesis, New York University (New York,

N.Y.), 1950. Abstract: *Microfilm Abstracts* 11:53–4 no 1 '51. * (*PA* 20:2428, title only)

68. LUKER, ALBERT G. *The Validity of the Cooperative English Test in Predicting Success in English at an Engineering College.* Doctor's "Field Study No. 1," Colorado State College of Education (Greeley, Colo.), 1950. (*Abstracts of Field Studies ....1950*, 1951, pp. 97–100.)

69. MARTIN, HENRY JOHN. *A Comparison of the Composite Ability Index of College Freshmen With Grades Earned in Different Courses and Departments of Instruction at Indiana University.* Doctor's thesis, Indiana University (Bloomington, Ind.), 1950. (*Thesis Abstract Series....1950*, 1951, pp. 86–90.) (*PA* 25:7109, title only)

70. RYAN, SULER ELDON. *Some Characteristics of the 1948 Freshman Class at the University of Missouri and the Relation of These Characteristics to Academic Success.* Doctor's thesis, University of Missouri (Columbia, Mo.), 1950. Abstract: *Microfilm Abstracts* 10:84–5 no 3 '50. * (*PA* 25:4828, title only)

71. TOPETZES, NICK J., AND O'BRIEN, CYRIL C. "Mechanics of Expression at the Graduate Level." *J Higher Ed* 21:380–1+ O '50. * (*PA* 25:2660)

72. TRAVERS, ROBERT M. W., AND WALLACE, WIMBURN L. "Inconsistency in the Predictive Value of a Battery of Tests." *J Appl Psychol* 34:237–9 Ag '50. * (*PA* 25:6480)

73. TRAXLER, ARTHUR E. "Reading Growth of Secondary-School Pupils During a Five-Year Period," pp. 96–107. (*PA* 25:569) In *1950 Achievement Testing Program in Independent Schools and Supplementary Studies.* Educational Records Bulletin, No. 54. New York: Educational Records Bureau, July 1950. Pp. xiii, 119. Paper, lithotyped. *

74. VORDENBERG, WESLEY. *A Comparison of Errors Made by College Freshmen on the Cooperative English Test, Form PM, and in Themes.* Doctor's thesis, Indiana University (Bloomington, Ind.), 1950. (*Thesis Abstract Series....1950*, 1951, pp. 125–31.) (*PA* 25:7091)

75. *Final Report on the 1951 National College Sophomore Testing Program.* Princeton, N.J.: Cooperative Test Division, Educational Testing Service, [1951]. Pp. 22. Paper. *

76. *Report on the 1950 National College Freshman Testing Program.* Princeton, N.J.: Cooperative Test Division, Educational Testing Service, [1951]. Pp. 32. Paper. *

77. FARBER, ROBERT HOLTON. *Guidance Implications of the Freshman Testing Program at DePauw University.* Doctor's thesis, Indiana University (Bloomington, Ind.), 1951. (*Thesis Abstract Series....1951*, 1952, pp. 37–42.)

78. FREDERIKSEN, NORMAN. "The Influence of Timing and Instructions on Cooperative Reading Test Scores." Abstract. *Am Psychol* 6:302 Jl '51. *

79. KRATHWOHL, WILLIAM C. "Relative Contributions of Vocabulary and an Index of Industriousness for English to Achievement in English." *J Ed Psychol* 42:97–104 F '51. * (*PA* 25:8254)

80. PIERSON, GEORGE A., AND JEX, FRANK B. "Using the Cooperative General Achievement Tests to Predict Success in Engineering." *Ed & Psychol Meas* 11:397–402 au '51. *

81. SHAFFER, JOHN RICHARD. *Relationships of Certain High School Background Factors to Achievement on a Test of English Usage by Indiana University Freshmen.* Doctor's thesis, Indiana University (Bloomington, Ind.), 1951. (*Thesis Abstract Series....1951*, 1952, pp. 159–64.)

82. TRAXLER, ARTHUR E. "Intercorrelations and Validity of Scores on Three Reading Tests," pp. 79–80. (*PA* 25:6416) In *1950 Fall Testing Program in Independent Schools and Supplementary Studies.* Foreword by Ben D. Wood. Educational Records Bulletin, No. 56. New York: Educational Records Bureau, January 1951. Pp. xiii, 89. Paper, lithotyped. *

83. WALLACE, W. L. "The Prediction of Grades in Specific College Courses." *J Ed Res* 44:587–97 Ap '51. * (*PA* 26:5838)

84. WEBB, SAM C. "Predictors of Achievement in Graduate School." *J Appl Psychol* 35:265–71 Ag '51. * (*PA* 26:3054)

CHESTER W. HARRIS, *Associate Professor of Education, University of Wisconsin, Madison, Wisconsin.* [Review of Tests A, B1, and B2; Forms S, T, Y, and RX]

A common criticism of the use of objective tests in English is that they do not yield direct evidence of the ability to use English effectively in speech and writing. Instead, objective type tests, such as the Cooperative tests of mechanics of expression and effectiveness of expression, do measure directly such skills as proofreading, error location, and criticism of written materials. Two points should be made. One is that such skills may be important in their own right and as such constitute legitimate educational objectives. If so, then progress in the development of these skills should be appraised periodically in order to determine the effectiveness of those parts of the program that are designed to promote these skills. The other is that such skills may be related to the ability to use English effectively in speech and writing. If so, then measures of proficiency in these skills may provide an important index of the "real" ability. The validity of these Cooperative tests of mechanics of expression and of effectiveness of expression must be considered from both these points of view.

The description of the construction of the mechanics and effectiveness tests indicates sources that were consulted in preparing the outline of topics to be covered and the types of "errors" or infelicities to be included. The point of view of the testmakers is "modern"; they include as sources the *Experience Curriculum* of the National Council of Teachers of English, grammars by Curme and Jespersen, and studies of present-day usage. This point of view is evident in their statement: "All so-called 'errors' in written English which are considered by most linguistic scholars to be good modern usage were eliminated." A multiple choice item form is used throughout the tests. In the section on usage, the subject is asked to judge the correctness of four underlined parts of each sentence and to designate which, if any, of the four parts is an incorrect or unsuitable usage. In the punctuation section, the subject is asked to select from specified alternatives the appropriate punctuation to be inserted into a designated section of an incompletely punctuated passage. Thus the materials on punctuation—and those on capitalization as well—present incomplete rather than mutilated copy to the student. Teachers who object to presenting mutilated copy to students on the grounds that it tends to reinforce errors will prefer the presentation in the Cooperative tests to that in other tests, such as the *Tests of General Educational Development*. Those who regard the presenting of mutilated copy as necessary if the actual task of proofreading is to be approximated in a test will not.

The sentence structure and style section poses problems of comparing sentences or parts of passages and selecting the one that is best expressed. In the more recent forms, the active vocabulary type of diction item which has been criticized by several persons has been replaced by items that require a choice among given words of the most appropriate term to insert into a given sentence. The later design is preferable to the earlier one for this section; however, it is possible to quibble with the key since a single sentence often is an insufficient context to establish one response as the most suitable of those given. Also, in some of the items, clichés, such as "inhuman" treatment of prisoners, no "extra" charge for engraving, etc., are keyed as correct responses. The organization section poses problems of classification and ordering of topics and statements.

The Cooperative tests of mechanics of expression and effectiveness of expression are generally well-made tests that should be useful as measures of the kinds of skills suggested in this analysis. Whether or not these are important skills must be answered by the prospective user of the test. The question of the relationship of this type of performance to actual use of language is not answered unequivocally. The authors say:

> The *Cooperative English Expression Tests* provide objective measures of many of the various factors entering into composition ability. In developing the outline for the tests, an analysis was made of the different types of skill and knowledge which go to make up the complex ability to express oneself in English, and the tests were organized so as to measure as many of these types as possible. The tests should therefore provide reasonably accurate measures of many of the factors involved in skill in written expression.

That this is likely can readily be granted; that it is so, is not established. The one validity study referred to in the description of the tests is the 1939 study by McCullough and Flanagan[1] in which Form OM and the 1937 Form were correlated with several different criteria, one of which was the teacher's estimate of excellence in using oral and written English; the median of the product-moment coefficients of correlation between the tests and teachers' estimates was .53. As McCullough and Flanagan point out, the reliability of these estimates is probably low and the estimates were made on a five-point scale which introduces an upper limit for r that is below unity; this median value, then, is probably conservative. However, this is a study of forms of the test that are out of print, and the current forms differ in many particulars from those studied.

[1] McCullough, Constance M., and Flanagan, John C. "The Validity of the Machine-Scorable Cooperative English Test." *J Exp Ed* 7:229–34 Mr '39. * (*PA* 13:5943)

Cooperative English Test

For reviews by J. Paul Leonard, Edward S. Noyes, and Robert C. Pooley of Forms R, S, and T, see 3:120; for reviews by Robert Murray Bear and J. B. Stroud of Tests C1 and C2, see 3:497.

[156]

★**Correct English Usage Test.** Grades 9–12; 1944; 6 scores: nouns-pronouns-verbs, adjectives-adverbs-prepositions-conjunctions, capitalization and punctuation, contractions-spelling-usage, vocabulary, total; Forms I, II, III, IV; no data on reliability and validity; no norms for part scores; no description of normative population; manual ['44]; 1–4 copies, 10¢ each; 5–24, 6¢ each; 25 or more, 5¢ each; 25¢ per set of manual and keys (manual and keys free with orders of 25 or more); specimen set not available; postage extra; 40(50) minutes; Doris Taylor; Harlow Publishing Corporation. *

[157]

Correctness and Appropriateness of Expression: Iowa Tests of Educational Development, Test 3. Grades 9–13; 1942–51 (first published as a separate in 1951); for complete battery, see 17; Form Y-2 ('51—same as 1949 edition); manual ('51); general manual ('51); $3.75 per 25; separate answer pads or answer sheets must be used; $1.95 per 25 answer pads; $3 per 100 IBM answer sheets; 50¢ per scoring stencil; $2.50 per 25 first semester ('46) or second semester ('48) profiles for any one of grades 9–12; $1 per 25 self-interpreting profiles for students ('51); 25¢ per school summary report ('44); 4¢ per pupil score sheet ('48); 50¢ per specimen set; cash orders postpaid; 60(70) minutes; edited by E. F. Lindquist; John Gerber; Science Research Associates, Inc. *

For a review by Eric F. Gardner of the complete battery, see 17; for reviews by Henry Chauncey, Gustav J. Froehlich, and Lavone A. Hanna of Forms X-1 and Y-1 of the complete battery, see 3:12.

[158]

★**English IX–XII: Achievement Examinations for Secondary Schools.** Grades 9, 10, 11, 12; 1951; 4 levels; 1 form; no data on reliability and validity; no manual; Minnesota norms (median and quartile deviation) available; similar norms for other regions by special arrangement with publisher; 7¢ per test, postage extra; 60(65) minutes; edited by Walter W. Cook; prepared by a curriculum committee of high school teachers for use in the Minnesota State Board Achievement Examinations Program; Educational Test Bureau, Educational Publishers, Inc. *

[159]

★**English—9th Grade: 20th Century Test.** Grade 9; 1948–49; Form A ('48); no data on reliability and validity; no norms—author recommends the use of local norms; manual ('49); 10 or more copies, 5¢ each, postage extra; 35¢ per specimen set, postpaid; 40(45) minutes; Ardis Sanders; Benton Review Publishing Co., Inc. *

[160]

★**English—10th Grade: 20th Century Test.** Grade 10; 1950; 1 form; no data on reliability and validity; no norms—author recommends the use of local norms;

10 or more copies, 5¢ each, postage extra; 35¢ per specimen set, postpaid; 40(45) minutes; Ardis Sanders; Benton Review Publishing Co., Inc. *

[161]

★**English Test: Municipal Tests: National Achievement Tests.** Grades 3–6, 6–8; 1938–39; a subtest of *Municipal Battery* (see 20); 5 scores: language usage-sentences, language usage-words, punctuation and capitalization, expressing ideas, total; 2 levels; Forms A ('38), B ('39); no data on reliability and validity and no description of normative population in manual; no norms for part scores; Form A manual ('38), Form B manual ('39); $1.25 per 25; 35¢ per specimen set; postage extra; 30(35) minutes; Robert K. Speer and Samuel Smith; Acorn Publishing Co. *

[162]

English Test: National Achievement Tests. Grades 3–8, 7–12; 1936–44; 2 levels; Forms A ('38), B ('38); no norms for part scores; manuals ('38); series manual ['44]; 35¢ per specimen set of any one level; postage extra; nontimed (40) minutes; Robert K. Speer and Samuel Smith; Acorn Publishing Co. *
a) GRADES 3–8. 7 scores: capitalization, punctuation, language usage-sentences, language usage-words, expressing ideas, letter writing, total; $1.65 per 25.
b) GRADES 7–12. 7 scores: word usage, punctuation, vocabulary, language usage, expressing ideas, expressing feeling, total; $2.25 per 25.

WINIFRED L. POST, *Instructor in English, Dana Hall, Wellesley, Massachusetts.*

GRADES 3–8. Parts I and II test thoroughly, yet with a minimum consumption of time, a student's knowledge of important principles of capitalization and punctuation by asking him to indicate needed capitals and punctuation in ten sentences for each section.

Parts III and IV, Language Usage, offer a total of 50 multiple choice items in each of which the student is to select from three or four sentences the one sentence which is correct. These two sections would single out children from illiterate or non-English speaking homes. Their value for use in all but underprivileged communities would be lessened by the large number of options either of the conventionally illiterate sort or bearing the stamp of the testmaker manufacturing "bad" English; for example: "I did not ran away," or "I be home every day," or "It aren't my book."

Part V, Expressing Ideas, contains 20 items, each giving a sentence in capitals followed by three other sentences from which the student is to select the one which "means the same thing as the sentence in capital letters." Now these directions run into inevitable snags with language in their assumption that two different sentences can ever mean the "same" thing. It takes no semantic subtlety to question the phrase "means the same" as applied to "Ours is a government by the people and for the people" and "The people rule our country for their own good." The difficulty would be obviated by changing the directions to: "Draw a line under the one sentence which is *closest in meaning* to the sentence in capitals."

Part VI, Letter Writing, offers ten four-response, multiple choice items dealing with questions of correct form in social and business letters. Aside from misgivings about insistence on "Cordially yours" as the closing for a social letter to a friend or "Affectionately" as the proper signing off of a letter to one's best friend, the reviewer questions whether or not objective testing is a wise form for this kind of material and whether or not the material itself is vital enough to justify its place in this kind of test.

The main strengths of this test are its ease of administration and scoring, the variety of skills tested in approximately 40 minutes of working time, and the swiftness with which it would give a teacher an insight into specific strengths and weaknesses in a pupil's command of the mechanics of composition. The most conspicuous lack in the test is that it provides no measure of vocabulary—probably the most significant single criterion of a student's background, training, and native ability in English. A 25- or 30-item multiple choice vocabulary test might, in the opinion of the reviewer, take the place of a letter-writing section with a resulting increase in the worth of the test as a whole. The other general weakness of the test is the inevitable presence of a considerable number of items either too easy for an eighth-grader or beyond the reach of a third-grader. This is a weakness inherent in any test which seeks to measure people who differ so widely in age, training, and experience.

GRADES 7–12. Part I, Word Usage, consists of 30 multiple choice items ranging from a choice between literate and illiterate English to such finely drawn distinctions as exist between "frightened by" and "frightened at." Except for a few seemingly nonfunctioning items such as "She believed it to be my," the test deals discerningly with common and important usage errors. Its keyed answers enforce conservative standards of "correct" English.

In Part II, Punctuation, 20 sentences are to be punctuated. As in Part I, conservative practice is enshrined by insistence upon a comma before *and* in: "My sister's headache disap-

peared, and failed to come back." Form B, but not Form A, does recognize as optional the use of the comma before a conjunction joining two brief clauses.

In its meager 20 items, Part III, Vocabulary, secures a range of difficulty from the matching of "speak" with "talk" to recognizing "exigencies" and "requirements" as synonyms. A testing technique, however, which requires the reading of six sentences in order to sort out "start" and "begin" as synonyms seems needlessly cumbrous and time-consuming.

Part IV, Language Usage, like Part I, secures range and variety by presenting 45 skillfully devised sentences with directions to underline those which are correct.

Part V, Expressing Ideas, contains 15 items similar to those in the same part of the elementary test and suffering from the same defects. To imply that ALL MEN ARE CREATED EQUAL and "Everyone is born entitled to a fair chance in life" mean "the same thing" is linguistically naive. Otherwise, however, this part of the test does a difficult and valuable job of testing thinking power and grasp of such abstract concepts as "Freedom means an option between alternatives" or "Courage is a mean between cowardice and foolhardiness."

Part VI, Expressing Feeling, is at once the most challenging and the most questionable section of the test. The emotional intensity of words is inextricably linked with the tone in which they are uttered and with the total context out of which they come. From four sentences ripped from context, who can select with assurance or precision the one expressing the most anger, regret, confidence, courage, or despair? To do so would ignore the sometimes all-pervasive force of tone, understatement, facial expression, or temperament and circumstances of the speaker. Subtle nuances of language and emotion will perhaps always slip through the meshes of objective testing techniques.

Ease of administration, simplicity of scoring directions, variety of skills tested in a suggested time limit of about 40 minutes are the undeniable strengths of this test. The most disturbing question is the degree of finely discriminating differentiation possible in a test designed alike for seventh grade and twelfth. The inherent difficulties of measuring by the same instrument people of such widely differing ages and experience become acute in Parts III, V, and VI. The worth of sections containing only 15 to 20 items is impaired by the inevitable presence of items too easy for a twelfth grader and items beyond the reach of a seventh grader.

For a review by Harry A. Greene, see 3:126.

[163]

*English Usage: Every Pupil Test. Grades 3–6, 7–9, 10–12; 1929–51; new form usually published each April and December; 3 levels; form April 1951; no data on reliability and validity; no manual; norms ('51); 2½¢ per test; 1¢ per answer key; postpaid; 40(45) minutes; Ohio Scholarship Tests, Ohio State Department of Education. *
a) GRADES 3–6. 1930–51.
b) GRADES 7–9. 1929–51.
c) GRADES 10–12. 1929–51.

For a review by J. R. Gerberich of the April and December 1946 Forms, see 3:127.

[164]

Iowa Grammar Information Test. Grades 7–12; 1935; Forms A, B; $4.50 per 100; 30¢ per manual; postage extra; 25¢ per specimen set, postpaid; 25(30) minutes; Fred D. Cram and Harry A. Greene; Bureau of Educational Research and Service, State University of Iowa. *

ROBERT C. POOLEY, *Professor of English, and Chairman, Department of Integrated Liberal Studies, University of Wisconsin, Madison, Wisconsin.*

The purpose of this test is to measure quantitatively the product of grammar teaching in terms of the information about grammar acquired and retained by the student. The authors indicate that there is divided opinion concerning the value of grammar teaching for the improvement of English skills, but that an interest in grammar for its own sake persists. Most grammar tests, they point out, are aimed at the functional results of grammar teaching, or usage. This test deals exclusively with the materials of grammar as a body of factual information.

Each form of the test consists of 80 exercises of the 3-answer multiple response type (e.g. Grammar is a science that has to do with (1) the earth (2) plants (3) language). The categories included, with the number of exercises in each, are: kinds of sentences, 4; classes of sentences, 3; subject and predicate, 2; parts of speech, 8; antecedents, 2; phrases and clauses, 20; complements, 6; comparison, 3; classification of verbs, 8; tense, 3; mood, 3; person, 3; number, 4; case, 7; gender, 3; independent elements, 2.

The tests are completely objective and are easily scored with a simple key. The authors emphasize that each form of the test must be treated as a single part, to be taken at a single sitting and to be scored as a single measure. The test is neither diagnostic nor analytic, nor are there part scores dealing with separate phases of grammar. The single score is an objective measure of the student's retention of information about grammar. An examiner's manual explains the construction of the test forms, presents evidence for the validity and reliability of the tests, and furnishes directions for administering and scoring. Percentile norms for grades 7 through 12 are furnished for the beginning, middle, and end of the school year.

The test is honestly named as a test of grammar information, and there is every reason to believe that it measures what a student has assimilated and retained from instruction in formal grammar. The authors scrupulously avoid making any claim for the test other than a measure of retained information, and they do not attempt to evaluate in any way the place of grammar in the teaching of English skills. This restraint is highly commendable in a field where tests are frequently built on false assumptions and unsound premises.

The weaknesses of this test derive from the inherent weaknesses of English grammar rather than from any lack of skill on the part of the authors. How can a test of grammar information present crystal clear exercises to the candidate when the grammar books themselves are full of muddy definitions, confused or inexact terminology, and contradictory rules? In each form of the test, 10 or more items, or one eighth of the test, are invalid for reasons of inexact or faulty terminology, bungling definitions, or just downright bad grammar. I am sure the authors could defend each of these items by citation to a grammar book; nevertheless, erroneous information should not be listed, no matter what the source. For example, the student who takes this test must learn that "An infinitive phrase is a phrase that begins with *to,* expressed or understood, when the *to* is not used as a preposition." Note that the student, in order to identify an infinitive phrase, must look for *to;* but if it isn't there, he must know that it might be there. Furthermore, he must be skillful enough to determine whether the *to* which isn't there is or is not a preposition. When he has gone through all this, he is perhaps able to discover an infinitive phrase. Has anything more muddled and clumsy ever been perpetrated on innocent children?

Confused and confusing terminology obscures

the value of several exercises. For example, "The pronouns *I, you,* and *she* illustrate a property of pronouns known as (1) number (2) case (3) person." Are the pronouns to be considered individually or collectively? Individually they illustrate all three properties; collectively no rule can be formed, for *you* is singular and plural, nominative and objective. The three, *under special conditions,* illustrate "person," but the special conditions are not named in the exercise. Again, what clarity of grammatical distinction is served by an exercise worded like this: "A word derived from a verb and serving as a noun or as an adjective is a gerund, an infinitive, or a (1) subjunctive (2) participle (3) preposition"? The only virtue in teaching such terms as gerund and participle is to distinguish clearly between the noun and adjective functions of words otherwise similar. To lump them together this way is to create "confusion worse confounded." To do this test successfully the student must have learned specific and technical meanings for such phrases as "related group," "manner of assertion," "make complete sense," "base," and others. He must know that "A sentence that expresses emotion is exclamatory." If he claims that the sentence "The little girl sobbed as if her heart would break" is exclamatory, who would blame him? Not this reviewer, at any rate.

[165]

★**Iowa Language Abilities Test.** Grades 4–7, 7–10; 1948, c1946–48; IBM; 2 levels; 2 editions; 25¢ per interpretation manual; postage extra; 35¢ per specimen set of any one level (does not include interpretation manual), postpaid; H. A. Greene and H. L. Ballenger; World Book Co. *
a) ELEMENTARY TEST. Grades 4–7; 6 scores: spelling, word meaning, language usage, capitalization, punctuation, total; 48(55) minutes.
  1) *Hand Scoring Edition.* Forms A, B; $2.10 per 25; separate answer sheets may be used; $1.40 per 25 IBM answer sheets; 80¢ per set of stencils for scoring answer sheets.
  2) *Machine Scoring Edition.* Forms AM, BM; $2.70 per 25; separate answer sheets must be used; $1.40 per 25 IBM answer sheets; 80¢ per set of scoring stencils.
b) INTERMEDIATE TEST. Grades 7–10; 8 scores: same as Elementary Test plus grammatical form recognition, sentence sense; 46(53) minutes.
  1) *Hand Scoring Edition.* Forms A, B; $2.65 per 25; separate answer sheets may be used; $1.40 per 25 IBM answer sheets; 80¢ per set of stencils for scoring answer sheets.
  2) *Machine Scoring Edition.* Forms AM, BM; $3.10 per 25; separate answer sheets must be used; $1.40 per 25 IBM answer sheets; 80¢ per set of scoring stencils.

MARGARET G. McKIM, *Associate Professor of Education, University of Cincinnati, Cincinnati, Ohio.*

With the exception of the omission of a subtest on sentence sense at the elementary level, these tests cover the aspects of language usage typically taught in the upper elementary and high school grades. The length of the total test allows for at least 50 items in each subtest except that of grammatical form recognition at the intermediate level, and for 75 items in the language usage section. The latter has separate groups of items calling for identification of correct word, correct word form, and faulty expressions, but provides no separate scores. The authors urge teachers to secure a tally of the number of pupils missing each separate item, but give no information to show what specific points of usage are tested, or how heavily each point is emphasized. Inspection of the test suggests that certain types of items may recur more frequently than others. The most noticeable weakness is in the test of sentence sense at the intermediate level where the only skill tested is the ability to tell a sentence fragment from a complete sentence. Since each subtest is given under a short time limit, the test as a whole should be thought of primarily as a measure of general achievement, not as a diagnostic instrument.

Although the elementary test is proposed for grades 4 through 7, its use with a typical fourth grade is open to question. The difficulty of the test for children of this grade is indicated by the fact that a grade score of 5.0 can be secured on three of the five subtests with two fifths or less of the items correct. Most open to criticism are the spelling and word meaning subtests where an attempt to provide for a wide grade range has resulted in a limited number of words appropriate to the reading and spelling ability of the typical fourth grader. The short time limits for the subtests are likely to penalize the slow reader at any grade, but may work a particular hardship on younger children.

Any language test in which the child chooses one of several forms has limitations, in that it fails to indicate what the child's typical pattern of response would be were no answers suggested to him. The authors recognize this difficulty and point to the need for other types of diagnostic procedures. The attempt to set up a test which can be completely machine scored and easily hand scored has resulted in complicated directions. On each subtest a child marks his answers on a somewhat different basis. On the word meaning subtest he must work with two columns, one for indicating a synonym and the other an antonym of the key word. Where punctuation marks are to be indicated, the layout of the scoring sheet is such that the same mark is not always found in the same column. At the intermediate level, the test of capitalization calls not only for indication of words needing capitals, but also for words incorrectly capitalized. For elementary children, the wording of the directions seems unnecessarily difficult. This will not be an easy test to administer, particularly if children have had little experience with standardized tests.

The norms are based on a relatively small number of cases as yet, but the care with which the present standardization seems to have been done gives promise of a strong test from the statistical point of view. Standard scores allow for comparison of subtest with subtest and for direct comparison with the *Iowa Silent Reading Test*. Both grade norms and percentile scores are provided. Corrections have been made for the somewhat superior nature of the group on whom the tests were standardized. Split half reliability quotients for the subtests, based on approximately 155 cases at the elementary level and 100 cases at the intermediate level are for the most part in excess of .88. The lowest reliabilities, at both levels, are for the language usage subtests.

The manual of directions and a supplementary manual for interpreting the tests are written with care and should be of considerable practical use to teachers. Of particular value is a series of remedial charts in the supplementary manual for interpreting the tests. These give typical causes of low test scores and suggest ways of securing additional evidence of the deficiency and typical remedial procedures. Since teachers are urged to study class responses to specific items, a chart showing the distribution of the types of items included in the usage, punctuation, and capitalization subtests would be useful.

School systems looking for an extensive language test will find this one helpful, particularly above the fifth grade. Examiners should be carefully prepared before attempting to administer the test.

[166]

Iowa Placement Examinations: English Aptitude: Series EA1, Revised. Grades 12–13; 1925–26; Forms A ('25), B ('26); no specific manual; series manual ['26]; $5 per 100, postage extra; 60¢ per specimen set (includes the other 10 tests in the series), postpaid; 43(50) minutes; prepared under the direction of C. E. Seashore and G. M. Ruch; M. F. Carpen-

ter and G. D. Stoddard; Bureau of Educational Research and Service, State University of Iowa. *

REFERENCES

1–9. See 3:115.
10. HANSEN, G. W. *An Analytical Study of the Iowa Placement Examinations.* Master's thesis, University of Iowa (Iowa City, Iowa), 1928.
11. WITTENBORN, J. R., AND LARSEN, H. P. "A Factorial Study of Achievement in College German." *J Ed Psychol* 35:39–48 Ja '44. * (PA 18:2613)
12. EDMONSON, LAWRENCE DAVIS. *Comparative Analyses of a Test Battery Used for the Prediction of Scholastic Success at the University of Missouri.* Doctor's thesis, University of Missouri (Columbia, Mo.), 1949. Abstract: *Microfilm Abstracts* 9:64–6 no 3 '50. (PA 24:4846, title only)
13. UHRBROCK, RICHARD STEPHEN. "Construction of a Selection Test for College Graduates." *J General Psychol* 41:153–93 O '49. * (PA 24:4874)
14. TOPETZES, NICK J., AND O'BRIEN, CYRIL C. "Mechanics of Expression at the Graduate Level." *J Higher Ed* 21:380–1+ O '50. * (PA 25:2660)

CLARENCE DERRICK, *Head, English Section, Test Development Department, Educational Testing Service, Princeton, New Jersey.*

Even good achievement tests, like most baseball players, have outlived their usefulness after 20 years of service. Although the Iowa English Aptitude Test has been revised since Form A first became available in 1925, inspection of the present forms suggests that the revisions were minor. A quarter of a century ago this test may have had some virtues; today it has none. Its stated purpose is to differentiate between training in English and natural aptitude or fitness for English studies. When one analyzes the skills measured and considers that the test is only 43 minutes long, he must conclude that such a pretentious claim must have been made when true believers had implicit faith in the efficacy of the "new type" tests.

The test has four parts. In Part 1 the student indicates whether given sentences comply with a stated and illustrated rule of grammar. The authors seem to assume that the ability to recognize whether a pronoun is in agreement with its antecedent measures "aptitude," not "training." In Part 2 a reading passage is followed by 10 groups of three sentences. In each group, the task is to select the one sentence that expresses an exact idea given in the passage. A useful technique in evaluating a set of reading items is to discover how many questions can be answered without reading the passage. The reviewer obtained perfect scores on Part 2 of Forms A and B without reading the selection. The following typical item shows why such a performance was possible:

Directions: Read the passage as often as necessary. *Do not guess.* Put an X in front of the sentence in each group which expresses an idea found in the passage.
____ Direct quotations should be used only in stories and jokes.

——— Direct quotations are often quite useful in humorous stories.
——— A person cannot write a good story without using direct quotations.

Part 3, apparently designed to measure the ability to understand poetry, employs the technique familiar to users of the *Iowa Silent Reading Tests*. A poem is printed with lines and phrases bracketed and numbered. The task is to locate the bracketed portions which give the answers to unimportant factual questions. The format makes an understanding of the poem extremely difficult. A student could answer all the questions correctly and not have the slightest comprehension of the poem or the least appreciation of its value as a work of art. Part 4 is the prototype of a kind of objective exercise that has received rather extensive use since its appearance in the USAFI effectiveness of expression tests. A theme is printed in a left-hand column with questions about the theme as a whole in a right-hand column. For example, the student indicates whether commas are never used incorrectly for periods, a comma is once used incorrectly for a period, or commas are several times used incorrectly for periods. Many of the items are time consuming and inefficient. More recent uses of this item type relate the items to underlined and numbered portions of the theme.

There is no real manual for this test; the general Manual of Directions serves all 11 tests in the series. From this source, the test user can compare test scores on the English Aptitude Test with percentile norms based on a population of 12,056. He has to conjecture whether the norms represent high school or college students. When these normative data were gathered is as complete a mystery as the reason why this test continues to be offered years after it should have been respectfully interred.

W. C. KVARACEUS, *Professor of Educational Measurement, Boston University, Boston, Massachusetts.*

This test is designed to measure, in entering college students, those more specific mental abilities which constitute factors determining subsequent success in English. This instrument also presumes to be an intelligence test of a new type which might serve as a special supplement to the traditional tests of intelligence since its test items are aimed to cover only abilities in the area of English.

This specialized aptitude test is made up of four sections: Part 1 (20 items, 8 minutes) measures the ability to comprehend and apply two rules of grammar; Part 2 (10 items, 8 minutes) tests ability to read several paragraphs of a college text for accuracy of detailed information; Part 3 (15 items, 12 minutes) involves reading comprehension for accuracy in drawing inferences or general ideas; and Part 4 (20 items, 15 minutes) measures ability to evaluate various features of a written composition.

The series manual reports a reliability coefficient of .82 for the total test. Normative data include percentile equivalents on more than 12,000 cases, but the source and nature of the normative group are not disclosed. Prediction data are reported in terms of an average correlation of .50 between course grades and tests in the aptitude series, but without any mention of the types of classes or samples involved.

Sufficient data are not present in the 4-page manual to answer routine questions such as: What is the correlation between this test and the English training test? Between this test and traditional intelligence tests? What are the reliabilities of the subtests? What are the intercorrelations between subtests? Since this test, and the others in the series, have seen rather extensive use and tryout in many colleges, a substantial bibliography exists to provide some answers to these queries—if one has access to the primary sources and the inclination to use them. The series manual is inadequate as a source of information which will enable a test purchaser to evaluate the test for personal use. It is, however, a good example of the constant need for publishers to revise and to supplement accompanying test manuals with new validation, reliability, and normative data which begin to accrue in the literature after the test has been on the market for some time. Incidentally, the manual suggests 10 uses of the test results which, if followed literally, are likely to result in 10 abuses.

In view of the very restricted coverage of this instrument, the low reliability of the total test and particularly of the subtests, and the unreliability of the college instructors' marks used as criteria, it is not surprising that correlations no higher than .45 and .50 have been reported between test scores and college grades.

For a review by Robert C. Pooley, see 3:115.

[167]
Iowa Placement Examinations: English Training. Grades 12–13; 1925–44; IBM; 2 editions; no specific manual; M. F. Carpenter, G. D. Stoddard, and

L. W. Miller (New Series); Bureau of Educational Research and Service, State University of Iowa. *

a) SERIES ETI, REVISED. 1925–26; Forms A ('25), B ('26); series manual ['26]; $5 per 100, postage extra; 60¢ per specimen set (includes the other 10 tests in the series), postpaid; 40(45) minutes; prepared under the direction of C. E. Seashore and G. M. Ruch.

b) NEW SERIES ET-2, REVISED. 1925–44; also called Quick-Scoring Edition; IBM; Form M ('41); $1.75 per 25; 25¢ per series manual ('44); 50¢ per specimen set (includes the other 4 tests in the series), postpaid; separate answer sheets may be used; $3.50 per 100 IBM answer sheets; 35¢ per stencil for machine scoring of answer sheets; 25¢ per stencil for hand scoring of answer sheets; postage extra; 45(50) minutes; revised by M. F. Carpenter and D. B. Stuit.

REFERENCES

1–15. See 3:131.
16. HANSEN, G. W. *An Analytical Study of the Iowa Placement Examinations.* Master's thesis, University of Iowa (Iowa City, Iowa), 1928.
17. GIESECKE, G. E.; LARSEN, R. P.; AND WITTENBORN, J. R. "Factors Contributing to Achievement in the Study of Elementary German." *Mod Lang J* 27:254–62 Ap '43. *
18. WITTENBORN, J. R., AND LARSEN, R. P. "A Factorial Study of Achievement in College German." *J Ed Psychol* 35:39–48 Ja '44. * (*PA* 18:2613)
19. FREEMAN, KENNETH H. "Predicting Academic Success in Admissions Work." *Jun Col J* 19:33–5 S '48. *
20. UHRBROCK, RICHARD STEPHEN. "Construction of a Selection Test for College Graduates." *J General Psychol* 41:153–93 O '49. * (*PA* 24:4874)

CLARENCE DERRICK, *Head, English Section, Test Development Department, Educational Testing Service, Princeton, New Jersey.*

Tests of the mechanics of English are currently in disfavor. The modern English teacher is told that, since the function of the grammarian is to describe, not prescribe, he cannot provide firm standards of acceptable usage. The ability to recognize errors is not perfectly correlated with the ability to avoid such errors in written composition; students who obtain high scores on a mechanics test frequently write unimaginatively. While all of these things are true, to the teacher who still would like to know something about the ability of his students to spell, punctuate, and recognize common usage errors, a good mechanics test can be useful. However, the earlier edition of the Iowa English Training Test is not a good mechanics test: the later edition has limitations but can be used.

Even if the skills measured were comprehensive, which they are not, even if all the items were beyond cavil, which they are not, the earlier edition (Series ET1, Revised) could not be recommended. The fundamental reason is that there are several mechanics tests which will accomplish the modest objectives of this test without introducing its limitations—inferior format and type, almost exclusive reliance on true-false items, cumbersome scoring, an inadequate manual, and almost meaningless norms.

In the New Series (ET–2, Revised) many of the inadequacies of the earlier edition have been corrected: the type is more legible, the test is set up for quick hand scoring or for use with an IBM answer sheet, the section on recognition of effective and ineffective sentences is eliminated, the manual is greatly improved, and percentile norms based on described populations are given. Subscores measuring spelling, punctuation, and usage are obtainable. Spelling is tested in the Revised Edition by giving four spellings of a word with instructions to select the one correct spelling. A more efficient spelling item type requires the student to select the one misspelled word from five given words. With this method many more words can be tested per unit of time. The chief criticism of the punctuation and usage sections is that, since the items are true-false, there is no assurance that the student has identified the error and could correct it.

The New Series ET-2 is to be preferred to the earlier form, Series ET1. However, since the revised form tests a restricted number of skills, with equal weights given to spelling, punctuation, and usage, and since the norms are based solely on college freshmen populations, the English Training Test, New Series, falls short of being a best buy.

W. C. KVARACEUS, *Professor of Educational Measurement, Boston University, Boston, Massachusetts.*

This is the sister instrument built to accompany the English aptitude test (see 166) in the Iowa series of 11 instruments for placement of entering college students. It offers a very narrow coverage of a few skills in the language-grammar area. Forms A and B are made up of four subtests: spelling, punctuation and sentence structure, language usage, and sentence sense. The test purports to determine how well the student has mastered the fundamental content of the high school English course of study, but few teachers of English will grant it any high degree of curricular validity. Little reference seems to have been made to any study of the actual content of the high school offerings in this area. Dependence for validity in building this test was placed on the experience of college teachers whose chief contact had been with a select high school group that elected to go to college.

The manual reports a reliability coefficient of 90 for Form A. Normative data are in the form of percentiles on a substantial but anonymous sample. In view of the tremendous increase in college enrollments in recent years, together with a change in the complexion of the college population, the use of these norms, gathered in the twenties, is hardly defensible today. Under the general heading "Predictive Power of the Examinations" an average correlation of .60 is reported for the examinations in the training series against the implied criterion of college grades. However, lower correlations averaging .49 on 3,450 cases in 28 colleges are reported for the English training test in the research literature (8, 16). It is interesting to note that average correlations between tests in the training series and criteria of scholastic success are reported in the manual as higher than the correlations between tests in the aptitude series and the same criteria. In other words, the training tests are superior predictors when compared with "prognostic" tests in the same battery. However, it might be nearer the truth to say that neither predicts very effectively.

This test and the others in the series have outlived their usefulness long ago. They remain significant historically as we view the development of differential aptitude batteries.

A revised version of this test is now available in a new series (the third) in the form of a machine scored edition. This last item is in three parts: spelling, punctuation, and English usage. Normative data are available in terms of scale scores and percentiles.

For a review by Robert C. Pooley, see 3:131.

[168]
Los Angeles Diagnostic Tests: Language (A Test in Capitalization, Punctuation and Language Usage). Grades 3–9; 1927; *discontinued:* Forms 1–4; no data on reliability and validity; no description of normative population; manual ['27]; 30(35) minutes; Caroline Armstrong; California Test Bureau. *

GERALD V. LANNHOLM, *Project Director, Educational Testing Service, Princeton, New Jersey.*

The major purpose of this test appears to be the diagnosis of the individual pupil's difficulties in correct writing. To assist the teacher in classifying and tabulating the errors made on the test by each pupil, a diagnostic record sheet is provided.

The test contains 10 short sections which may be described briefly as follows. The first section presents 11 sentences and a 4-line stanza from a poem for children. Nearly all of the capitaliza-

tion is omitted, and the pupil is directed to underline each letter which should be a capital letter. In the second section, the pupil is to insert correct punctuation in six short sentences presented without any punctuation. Following these are a 9-item section on sentence recognition, another capitalization section, a word usage section of 20 two-response items, a general punctuation section, a section on the use of the apostrophe, a section requiring the pupil to form adjectives from each of nine proper nouns, an exercise involving the writing out of all parts of a friendly letter excepting the body, and a section directing the pupil to identify the part of speech of several underlined words or phrases. The various sections of the test are not timed separately.

The mechanical features of this test would discourage present-day teachers from using it. All responses are entered in the test booklet. While such a practice is desirable in the early grades, the materials can be arranged to minimize scoring difficulties without increasing appreciably the complexity of the pupil's task. As this test is designed, the scoring must be accomplished by comparing the pupil's marked booklet with a correctly marked copy or with a separate sheet which indicates the correct responses and the weight each item should receive in the total score. This scoring sheet does not have the responses arranged with the same spacing as that employed in the test booklet.

For the most part, the usage situations selected for inclusion in the test are important ones. However, the number of different skills tested within each area is rather small, especially for a test intended to be diagnostic and to be suitable for such a wide range of grade levels. The lack of any measure of spelling ability, except for the special and limited case of forming adjectives from a few proper nouns, is surprising. The inclusion of an exercise on letter writing is commendable, but the scoring of that section will certainly cause difficulties. Testing the pupil's recognition of parts of speech as such rather than measuring his ability to use them correctly is not in conformance with current practice in either teaching or testing. The relative emphasis given to some of the elements tested also appears questionable. In the first section dealing with capitalization, for example, about half of the 30 points allowed are for capitalizing the first word in a sentence. While this might be justified on the basis of frequency of usage in free writing, it is difficult to defend in terms of the percentage of errors.

This test also has some technical and editorial defects. In the first capitalization section, the personal pronoun "I" appears uncapitalized in some places and capitalized in others, enabling the uncertain but observing pupil to make correct decisions on a basis other than his mastery of capitalization. Other clues to correct capitalization may be obtained from the punctuation section on the same page, the material in that section being presented with correct capitalization. Similarly, when the pupil takes the punctuation section, he may obtain clues from the capitalization section. In a later section on capitalization which gives a list of words and terms out of context, the pupil's failure to capitalize some which carry capital letters on the scoring key may result from his interpreting the word or term differently from that intended by the test author.

Even though the primary function of the test is purportedly that of diagnosis of specific strengths and weaknesses, norms based only on total score are presented for each of grades 2–12. No description is given of the nature or size of the normative population or of the methods used in deriving these norms. The norms show exactly equal score increments from one grade level to the next for the entire range of 11 grades. Such results are so unusual that one wonders if these data were not intended to represent suggested standards rather than summary statistics based on the actual test scores received by pupils at these grade levels.

The identification of specific difficulties of individual pupils is of major importance in assisting them to master the elements of correct writing. Efficient discovery of those difficulties is facilitated by one or more good diagnostic tests. With many improved tests available in this field, it is not believed that this test, unchanged for nearly a quarter of a century, will be among those chosen for that purpose.

[169]
*Mechanics of Written English: State High School Tests for Indiana. Grades 9–12; 1940–50; 6 scores: punctuation, recognition of grammatical errors, sentence structure, vocabulary, spelling, total; Form B ['49]; Form A out of print; mimeographed; no data on reliability and validity; no manual; no norms for part scores; norms ['50]; 5½¢ per test; 15¢ per specimen set; postpaid; 50(55) minutes; Ethel Ludwig, J. H. McKee, and G. S. Wykoff; State High School Testing Service for Indiana, Purdue University. *

Los Angeles Diagnostic Tests: Language

[170]
★Morgan Test of Modern English Usage. Grades 9–16 and adults; 1949–50; title on test booklet is *Modern English Usage;* IBM; Form A ('49); manual ('50); $4 per 25 sets of test and answer sheets; separate answer sheets must be used; 3¢ per IBM answer sheet; $1 per specimen set; sample test free to qualified test users; cash orders postpaid; 40(50) minutes; Antonia Morgan and William J. Morgan; Aptitude Associates. *

WALTER N. DUROST, *Director, Test Service and Advisement Center, Dunbarton, New Hampshire.*

A competent and critical reviewer of a test looks for certain standard information in the test manual, as well as for certain characteristics in the test itself, in determining his evaluation. These things include such matters as validity, reliability, adequacy of norms, utility, etc. The manual for the present test appears to be singularly lacking in information on these points.

There is no evidence of the validity of the test except the evidence of face validity. A far more adequate statement of the purposes for which such a test would be used is needed than that given in the manual. Certainly, some usages which are colloquially acceptable are considered to be wrong, although this is said to be a test of conversational as well as written English usage. It would be interesting and helpful to know what authorities were consulted or what the author's philosophy is concerning English usage.

No data whatsoever are given concerning the reliability of the instrument. It is difficult to account for such an omission for surely some such information must be available.

The norm population is said to be national in scope and to be based upon 3,283 cases, but no statement is given as to where these cases came from or the conditions under which the tests were given. Norms are given separately by sex, and there seems to be a slight edge in favor of girls over boys in these norm tables. Providing the information separately in this way is to be considered praiseworthy, but to evaluate the differences between boys and girls by means of formulas for the standard error of the difference is a highly questionable practice. First the samples are not random, and formulas, strictly speaking, do not apply. Secondly, and more important, the question is not whether there is a statistically significant difference but rather whether there is an *instructionally* significant difference. There is no statistical test for this.

Not much can be said in favor of the mechanical arrangement of the test or of the manual. The manual is badly organized and the statements concerning the uses of the test leave much to be desired. The answer sheet is very difficult to use.

The cost of the materials is excessively high considering the nature of the test.

This test seems to represent an attempt of amateurs to play in a professional league. As such it is to be discouraged. If someone wanted a test of English usage which he would evaluate and interpret for himself, he might purchase this one to save himself the bother of duplicating the materials locally. There would seem to be little other justification.

[171]

★Objective Test in Grammar. Grades 10–12; 1950; 1 form; no data on reliability and validity; no manual; no norms; 1–4 copies, 15¢ each; 5–1000, 6¢ each; 15¢ per key (free with orders of 24 or more); 25¢ per specimen set; postage extra; nontimed (60–90) minutes; Nellie F. Falk; Perfection Form Co. *

[172]

★Objective Tests in English [Grammar]. Grades 7–9; 1950; 1 form; no data on reliability and validity; no manual; norms ('50); 1–4 copies, 15¢ each; 5–1000, 6¢ each; 15¢ per key (free with orders of 24 or more); 25¢ per specimen set; postage extra; nontimed (40–60) minutes; Gunnar Horn; Perfection Form Co. *

[173]

★The Purdue Placement Test in English: The Clapp-Young Self-Marking Tests. High school and college; 1931–41; 8 scores: punctuation, grammatical classification, recognition of grammatical errors, sentence structure, reading, vocabulary, spelling, total; IBM for Forms A, B; Forms A ('31), B ('32), C ('41); manual ['41]; $1.35 per 25 (Forms A or B only); $2.20 per 25 sets of test and answer booklet; separate answer sheets or booklets must be used; $1 per 25 answer booklets; 75¢ per 25 IBM answer sheets; 60¢ per set of stencils for machine scoring of answer sheets; 27¢ per specimen set; postage extra; Forms A, B: 40(45) minutes; Form C: 45(50) minutes; G. S. Wykoff, J. H. McKee, and H. H. Remmers; Houghton Mifflin Co. *

REFERENCES

1. QUAID, THOMAS DELL DOMA. A Study in the Prediction of College Freshman Marks. Unpublished doctor's thesis, University of Oklahoma, 1937. Pp. xii, 151. (Abstracts of Theses ....1937, 1939, pp. 20–2.)
2. LAWRENCE, WILLIAM A. An Evaluation of Achievement in the Various Colleges of the Louisiana State University with Special Reference to Certain Aspects of the Junior Division. Doctor's thesis, Louisiana State University (University, La.), 1939. (Abstracts of Theses....1939–1940, 1941, pp. 10–11.)
3. LOTT, HIRAM V. A Comparative Study of Five Criteria for Predicting Achievement in Freshman History in the Junior Division at Louisiana State University. Master's thesis, Louisiana State University (Baton Rouge, La.), 1939. (Abstracts of Theses....1939, 1940, p. 45.)
4. VARNADO, GLADYS R. A Further Study of the Predictive Value of Various Criteria on Achievement in Freshman Mathematics at Louisiana State University for the Session 1938–1939. Unpublished master's thesis, Lousiana State University, 1939. (Abstracts of Theses....1939, 1940, p. 197.)
5. BROWN, JAMES I. "A Comparison of Listening and Reading Ability." Col Engl 10:105–7 N '48. *
6. REMMERS, H. H.; ELLIOTT, D. N.; AND GAGE, N. L.

"Curricular Differences in Predicting Scholastic Achievement: Applications to Counseling." J Ed Psychol 40:385–94 N '49. * (PA 24:3407)
7. BELMAN, H. S., AND EVANS, R. N. "Selection of Students for a Trade and Industrial Education Curriculum," pp. 9–14. In Motives and Aptitudes in Education: Four Studies. Edited by H. H. Remmers. Purdue University, Division of Educational Reference, Studies in Higher Education, No. 74. Lafayette, Ind.: the Division, December 1950. Pp. iii, 63. Paper. * (PA 26:3010)
8. PRED, GORDON DAVID. "An Analysis of Orientation Test Results in the Purdue Technical Institute Courses," pp. 36–63. In Motives and Aptitudes in Education: Four Studies. Edited by H. H. Remmers. Purdue University, Division of Educational Reference, Studies in Higher Education, No. 74. Lafayette, Ind.: the Division, December 1950, Pp. iii, 63. Paper. *
9. BELMAN, H. S., AND EVANS, R. N. "Selection of Students for a Trade and Industrial Educational Curriculum." J Ed Psychol 42:52–8 Ja '51. * (PA 25:6486)

[174]

★Stanford Achievement Test [Language Arts]. Grades 4–6, 7–9; 1941–46, c1940–46; an adaptation of the reading, language usage, and spelling tests of Stanford Achievement Test (see 25); 5 scores: paragraph meaning, word meaning, language usage, spelling, total; IBM; 2 levels; Forms DM ('41), EM ('43), FM ('46); the Manual for Interpreting referred to in the directions for administering has not been published; directions for administering ('41); $2.70 per 25 of any one level; separate answer sheets must be used; 85¢ per 25 IBM answer sheets; 40¢ per set of machine scoring stencils for any one form of any one level; 55¢ per 25 profile charts ('42); postage extra; 35¢ per specimen set of any one level, postpaid; 60(65) minutes; Truman L. Kelley, Giles M. Ruch, and Lewis M. Terman; World Book Co. *
a) INTERMEDIATE LANGUAGE ARTS TESTS. Grades 4–6.
b) ADVANCED LANGUAGE ARTS TESTS. Grades 7–9.

REFERENCES
1. EATON, MERRILL T. A Survey of the Language Arts Achievement of Sixth Grade Children in 18 Counties and Six Cities in Indiana. State of Indiana, Department of Public Instruction, Research Bulletin No. 3. Indianapolis, Ind.: the Department, 1942. Pp. vii, 75. Paper. * (PA 17:3245)

For reviews by Paul R. Hanna and Claude E. Norcross and Vergil E. Herrick of the complete battery, see 25; for reviews by Walter W. Cook and Ralph C. Preston of the complete battery, see 3:18.

[175]

★Test of English Usage. High school and college; 1950; 4 scores: mechanics of writing, accurate use of words, building sentences and paragraphs, total; IBM; Forms A, B; $2.50 per 25; 35¢ per specimen set, postpaid; separate answer sheets may be used; 7¢ per Scoreze answer sheet; 3¢ per IBM answer sheet; 60¢ per set of stencils for machine scoring of answer sheets; 20¢ per set of stencils for hand scoring of answer sheets; 2¢ per 26 or more individual diagnostic records; postage extra; 100(110) minutes; Henry D. Rinsland, Raymond W. Pence, Betty S. Beck, and Roland L. Beck; California Test Bureau. *

CHARLOTTE CROON DAVIS, Test Research Service, 12 Normandy Road, Bronxville, New York.

This test consists of 150 four-choice items, distributed as follows: Test I: capitalization, 16 items; use of the apostrophe, 9 items; and punctuation, 30 items. Test II: grammar, 52 items [33 of these are selecting the correct verb form, (e.g., go, going, went, gone) to use in a given sentence]. Test III : sentence structure, 8 items ; and paragraph organization, 35 items.

It is questionable whether sections on sentence structure and paragraph organization belong in a test of *usage*. However, the skills tested in these sections are important, and it may be that the title of the test is too narrow. It might be desirable to cut the number of items on paragraph organization and to increase the number on sentence structure. Too large a portion of the test (over one fifth) is devoted to verb forms, especially since the type of item used does not seem particularly valuable. If this section were substantially cut, more items could well be included in the other grammar section, as there are many common grammatical errors not covered, and perhaps a new section could be added. The writer would like to see included a section on diction—using the proper word to express one's meaning. These items would not depend on grammatical principles but would test such distinctions as the difference in meaning between "uninterested" and "disinterested," etc.

The difficulty level seems about right, since much of the material is what might be called minimum essentials which every college freshman, and indeed every tenth grader, ought to have mastered. The test might be improved by using a few more difficult items in some of the sections.

The test is intended for diagnostic as well as survey purposes and is accompanied by an individual diagnostic record, for which the manual gives detailed instructions.

The test has been carefully prepared and analyzed. Where appropriate, the items are based on error counts in pupils' writings and Thorndike's counts of frequency of use. Kuder-Richardson reliability coefficients are supplied for the part scores and the total score at grade levels 10, 11, 12. and 13. The median coefficient for the part scores for a single grade is about .85. The coefficients for the total score are all .90 or over. The raw correlation between total score and grade in English for one sample of 125 college freshmen is .37. Percentile norms, based on 3,841 students in grades 10 through 13 in representative school districts and colleges in all parts of the country, are provided for each grade level for the three part scores and the total score.

The scores are not corrected for guessing, and the directions for administration do not touch on this point. It may be noted that a relatively ignorant or slow reading testee who guesses freely will tend to have an advantage over one who does not. For example, an eleventh grader who marks correctly the first 27 of the 43 items in Test III and omits the rest, perhaps because he does not have time to read them carefully, will have a percentile rank of 40. Another eleventh grader who also marks correctly the first 27 items in this section and rushes through the remainder guessing at random will be most likely to have a percentile rank of 65.

The writer did not notice any ambiguous or incorrect items. The punctuation section would be improved by testing occasionally for situations where no punctuation is needed. Many pupils overpunctuate. The capitalization section would be improved by placing the words that are to be considered for capitalization in the order in which they occur in the sentence. Also, in this section and others a, b, c, d are used as the choice letters for some items and e, f, g, h for others ; this peculiarity of format introduces unnecessary (and unwanted) clerical facility into the scores. In this connection, would it not be better to use numbers instead of small letters for the choices? This might speed up the testing (it quickly becomes habitual to call the choice in the third position 3, etc.) and might prevent difficulty in scoring in the situation where the testee writes his answers in the booklet. Certain small letters when hastily written are easily confused, e.g., a and d, f and h.

The appearance of the test would be improved by spreading the material out and using the two blank pages. In the writer's opinion, the green printing on pale green paper is not an improvement over the customary black on white.

In summary, this test appears to be carefully constructed and standardized and should be a useful measuring and diagnostic instrument.

[176]

★**Tests of Language Usage: Active Vocabulary and Expression: Cooperative Inter-American Tests.** Grades 8–13; 1950; 3 scores: active vocabulary, expression, total ; IBM ; 2 editions ; English edition : Forms AE, BE ; Spanish edition : Forms AS, BS ; no data on reliability and validity ; tentative norms ; $2.50 per 25 ; separate answer sheets must be used ; 80¢ per 25 IBM answer sheets ; 15¢ per scoring stencil ; 50¢ per series manual ; 50¢ per specimen set (does not include series manual), postpaid ; cash orders postpaid ; 35(45) minutes ; prepared under the auspices of the Committee on Modern Languages of the American Council on Education, Herschel T. Manual, Director of Test Construction ; Cooperative Test Division, Educational Testing Service. *

REFERENCES

1. Bou, Ismael Rodriguez. *A Study of the Parallelism of English and Spanish Vocabularies.* Doctor's thesis, University of Texas (Austin, Tex.), 1944.
2. Kelley, Frances. *A Study of the Inter-American Tests at the High School Level.* Master's thesis, University of Texas (Austin, Tex.), 1945.
3. Fife, Robert Herndon, and Manuel, Herschel T. *The 1ching of English in Puerto Rico,* pp. 171–313, 337–410. epared for the American Council on Education. San Juan, R.: Department of Education Press, 1951. Pp. xix, 410. *

Walter V. Kaulfers, *Professor of Education, University of Illinois, Urbana, Illinois.*

These tests are described as being

designed primarily for measuring ability to use, as distinguished from ability to understand, English and Spanish. * The ability to think of words and the development of a "feeling" for idiomatic expressions are especially significant in measuring progress toward the mastery of the language. A comparison of scores in the second language with scores on similar material in the native language provides a basis for interpretation which is lacking in ordinary tests of foreign languages.

In keeping with these objectives, Part I, Active Vocabulary, directs the students to "find the first letter of the [English] word that has been omitted from each sentence. The number in parentheses is the number of letters in the word." The students then record their selection of the letter on a separate answer sheet suitable for scoring either by means of a perforated stencil, or by machine.

4. He is my father; I am his —(3)— H S F R W
5. Hot is the opposite of —(4)— F A H C J

As shown by these examples, a greater degree of "active" recall is required than in the usual multiple choice type of test. In taking the examination, however, the bilingual student, like this reviewer, is likely to experience the following limitations:

a) In completing Item 4 above, a girl might, under the pressure of time, be tempted to look for the letter D (for daughter) or H (for *hija*), and then, after a little confusion, realize that she is his three-letter American *son.* This might involve a little loss of time through confusion—especially since this test is for students who are presumably not very secure in English.

b) In completing Item 5 above, the student who is more at home in Spanish than in English would be "baited into error" by the tempting choice of F for *frío*—a perfect 4-letter word—unless he realized that, after all, the English word, not the Spanish word is called for. Since these momentary but time consuming confusions beset the reviewer throughout the test, the complete avoidance of letters suggestive of possible Spanish equivalents is highly desirable in short

tests for bilinguals in which time becomes a pressing factor.

c) Since many of the vocabulary definitions contain words of rarer frequency than the key word that is to be identified, the test inevitably becomes as much a reading test as a test of active vocabulary. For example, in Item 20, Part I, Form BE, the word *implement* is not found among the first four thousand words of highest frequency in English, while the key word, *plow,* occurs among the first three thousand:

A —(4)— is a farm implement for breaking the ground. P T S F M

Apparently only the spelling *plow* (not *plough*) is acceptable here, although even abridged dictionaries usually give both. A superior student who knows both would be more confused here than the less able who know only one.

d) Item 10 of the same section does not legitimately rule out the word *jewel,* even though only the word *crown* is acceptable:

The queen wears a —(5)— on her head. J W Y C M

A more careful tryout and evaluation of the individual items would have eliminated this kind of ambiguity long before the test reached the publication stage.

e) Item 16 of the same section has a quaint foreign flavor in its use of prepositional phrase in preference to the almost universal use of the possessive construction in real life:

The son of my uncle is my —(6)— P A J S C

Similar tendencies toward classroom English are found in the upper reaches of the test of expression, as, for example, in Part II, Item 43. In this item, the student does not have much chance to make a selection in terms of a sentence "that is best from the point of view of simple speech." All choices here are rather poor by any standards of effective speech or writing.

Inasmuch as the Spanish forms of the examination are merely a translation of the English forms, limitations of a more serious nature are compounded here. Although the description of the Cooperative Inter-American Tests recognizes the fact that "a simple translation of a standardized test from one language to another was obviously not adequate because of differences in speech idiom and in culture," the language tests are nothing else. Each is a direct translation from the English without regard for the relative difficulty of the same words and expressions in the two languages. For example, in Form BS, Part I, the key word *corona* does not occur among the first thousand words of highest frequency in Spanish, but in English, it does. Although awareness of the existence of scientific frequency lists for vocabulary is evident from the descriptions of the tests, the reviewer can find little evidence of a serious use of them in Spanish as a basis for phrasing the items. Neither have the items in the Spanish forms been arranged in order of difficulty as verified by an actual tryout and item analysis of student responses. It is inconceivable that the separate tryouts of the forms on different language populations would yield exactly the same scale positions as in every single form of the present tests. Because of this bias, the reliability of the Spanish forms is probably lower than that of the English forms, though no coefficients of reliability are, as yet, available for any of the examinations.

The nature of the Spanish usage tests (Part II in each case) limits their usefulness almost exclusively to American students of Spanish or to bilingual Mexican-Americans who, through long residence in this country, have begun to live in a linguistic "no-man's-land" in which a half-breed Spanish or a half-breed English is spoken, comparable to the dialect Pennsylvania Dutch.

A native of any Spanish speaking country would, by the time he reaches grade 8 abroad, be able to score perfectly on Part II simply by eliminating usages that jar his ear as badly as an off-key note in a well known song. If the test is for bilinguals in our Southwest whose Spanish has been subject to adulteration, its usefulness is likely to be confined to those who can read Spanish. Among the majority, however, it is a spoken language only. Hence an aural comprehension test and an aural vocabulary test measuring ability to distinguish between legitimate Spanish and its adulterated forms (*e.g., patinar* vs *skatiar, frenos* vs *braques,* etc.) would serve a more useful diagnostic purpose in their case.

Although it is true that a direct comparison of scores in a second language with scores on similar material in the native language is not possible in terms of previously available tests, relative percentile ranks on substantial tests of known reliability and validity provide a safer basis for comparison than direct scores on brief tests whose rather superficial construction does not as yet meet the standards required for the purpose.

[177]
*Tools of Written English: State High School Tests for Indiana. Grades 7–8; 1941–51; Forms A ['45], B ['51]; mimeographed; no data on reliability and validity; no manual; Form A norms ['45], Form B norms ['51]; 5½¢ per test; 15¢ per specimen set; postpaid; 27(35) minutes; W. R. Thompson (A), N. L. Gage (A), and Margaret Hackett (B); State High School Testing Service for Indiana, Purdue University. *

COMPOSITION

[178]
★College Entrance Examination Board Achievement Test in English Composition. Candidates for college entrance; 1943–51; available only in College Entrance Examination Board Admissions Testing Program (see 526); 60(70) minutes; prepared by College Entrance Examination Board Committee of Examiners in English Composition in cooperation with the Staff of Educational Testing Service: 1951 membership: Edward S. Noyes (Chairman), R. Stanley Peterson, Charles M. Rice, Priscilla Tyler, and Edna R. Williams; program administered by Educational Testing Service for the College Entrance Examination Board. *

REFERENCES
1. NOYES, EDWARD S. "Recent Trends in the Comprehensive Examination in English." *Ed Rec* 21:107–19 Ja '40. *
2. WEAVER, LILLAS JEAN, AND STOKE, STUART M. "The New C.E.E.B. Examinations." *J Higher Ed* 16:37–42 Ja '45. *
3. DAVIS, SARA ELZODA. *A Study of the English Examination of the College Entrance Examination Board.* Master's thesis, Tulane University (New Orleans, La.), 1946. (*Abstracts of Theses 1946*, p. 7.)
4. PEIXOTTO, HELEN E. "Relationship of College Board Examination Scores and Reading Scores for College Freshmen." *J Appl Psychol* 30:406–11 Ag '46. * (*PA* 21:289)
5. HUDDLESTON, EDITH M. "Recent Studies of the English Composition Test." *Col Bd R* 1:45, 50–3 sp '48. *
6. FELS, WILLIAM C. "The College Board English Composition Test—Present and Future." *Ed* 71:4–10 S '50. *

CHARLOTTE CROON DAVIS, *Test Research Service, Bronxville, New York;* and FREDERICK B. DAVIS, *Professor of Education and Director of the Educational Clinic, Hunter College, New York, New York; and Director, Test Research Service, Bronxville, New York.* [Review of Forms WAC4, YAC4, ZAC1, ZAC2, and ZAC3.]

During the 1930's a number of ingenious objective techniques for measuring various aspects of the ability to write correctly were developed, and by 1940 tests employing combinations of these techniques were widely used. Validity data showed that some of them were quite promising. However, until 1947 these techniques were not made use of in the *English Composition Test* of the College Entrance Examination Board. In fact, as late as 1948, Edward S. Noyes, a member of the College Board Committee of English Examiners, wrote of some of these techniques, "one should beware accepting their results as a true indication of 'effectiveness of expression,' which, after all, can only be discovered by giving the student a blank page and a pencil and setting him to write" (3 : 120).

The attitude represented by this statement, which is composed of a straw man (no technician accepts any test result as a "true" indication of ability) and a misleading statement (setting a student to write a single composition under highly artificial conditions cannot yield a "true" indication of his effectiveness of expression), did not prevent the CEEB Committee of Examiners in English from trying out an objective section in their April 1947 examination. Their findings indicated that a full-length (60-minute) test composed of essay material would have "markedly less predictive value [of teachers' ratings of ability to write expository prose, and course grades in English] than a full-length test composed entirely of objective material" (5). Since 1947 the English Committee has developed or adapted, tried out, and used a variety of objective approaches.

Five forms of their *English Composition Test,* appearing between August 1950 and May 1951, were received for review together with analyses, descriptive statistics, and reports of research studies. No two of the forms are alike in make-up, though the same type of exercise and even a few of the same items appear in more than one form. This is unfortunate since the most compelling reason for using these tests is that they are not likely to have been seen by examinees in advance of the examination period. If items are reused, this merit is to some extent lost.

The content of the five forms reviewed was as follows:

Form WAC4: Correcting Usage and Punctuation in Sentences (35 items), Usage (65 items), and Paragraph Organization (34 items).
Form YAC4: Correcting Usage and Punctuation in Sentences (45 items), Poetry Completion (15 items), and Paragraph Organization (41 items).
Form ZAC1: Literary Comprehension (10 items), Editing for Usage and Punctuation (50 items), and Paragraph Organization (39 items).
Form ZAC2: Editing for Usage and Punctuation (47 items), and Rewriting Sentences (not objectively scorable, 42 "items").
Form ZAC3: Editing for Usage and Punctuation (45 items), and Identification of Errors in Grammar and Usage (30 items).

Some of the types of items do not seem to measure primarily aspects of English composition. One section, for example, presents several four-line stanzas of poetry from each of which one line has been omitted. For each stanza, the examinee is to select from five single lines the one that best fits into it. These items, though interesting and well-constructed, appear to measure aspects of literary appreciation and comprehension rather than composition.

Close inspection of the individual items indicates that considerable thought and ingenuity have gone into their preparation. However, some criticisms may be made of them. The items designed to test ability "to understand the organization of a piece of writing" seem distinctly below standard. Some of them appear unrelated to the *organization* of the material but test the ability to make inferences from the content; e.g., "We may infer that the writer is (1) a biologist, (2) a physicist," etc. Other items have more than one defensible answer; e.g., the stem, "If the passage were written for newspaper publication, it might well begin," is followed by five choices, any one of which might, under certain circumstances, be an answer. Other items are ambiguously phrased; e.g., "The author's own position first becomes apparent in (1) paragraph 1, (2) paragraph 2," etc. The answer hinges on whether the item means, "When is the position later identified as the author's first indicated?" or "When does it first become clear what position the author subscribes to?"

Another highly ambiguous item of a different type is the following, in which the examinee is to indicate which, if any, of the numbered words is incorrect: "Happiness is one of the intangibles which is wanted by almost everyone." Those

    1   2   3   4   5

who object to the use of "which" in a restrictive clause will argue that the answer is 1. Others will take the sentence to mean, "Happiness is one of those intangibles which are wanted by almost everyone," and will mark 2. Still others will contend that the sentence means, "Happiness is that particular one of the intangibles which is wanted by almost everyone," and will mark choice C, indicating that the sentence is correct as it stands.

The instructions about guessing are inadequate; the directions do not say whether the scoring includes a penalty for incorrect responses. Unless there is, time spent in "haphazard guessing" is far from wasted—a fact widely known among high school students and almost universally known among preparatory school students especially coached to take the College Board examinations.

The test items and the response spaces, on the answer sheets could be geared to each other in such a way that the examinee would not have to give so much attention to keeping his place. The directions for the paragraph organization sections (in which the sentences of a paragraph are scrambled and the examinee is to arrange them in proper order) are not easy for the inexperienced examinee to follow.

It is gratifying to find in recent bulletins and memoranda of the Educational Testing Service that staff members are now devoting time and energy to the preparation and assembly of English composition tests for the College Board. This task ought to be easier than that of preparing tests for general school use. The CEEB tests have an assured market and are constructed for a narrow, well-defined purpose—that of assisting in the selection of students for entrance to certain colleges. They need not be suitable for diagnostic use or for discriminating among pupils at all levels of ability. The examinees are relatively homogeneous.

When one considers that the Board has been setting examinations in English for a half century, the five forms under review are not impressive. Any one of them must be regarded as unnecessarily inadequate as a measure of ability in English composition, despite some statistical data indicating moderate correlations with previously obtained grades in English and with teachers' ratings of ability to write. If the rank and file of teachers of college-preparatory English could have the same opportunity as the reviewers to study these examinations, it is hard to believe that a chorus of disapproval would not arise.

The reliability data that the reviewers have seen were computed by means of Kuder-Richardson formula No. 20 except in two instances. Coefficients obtained for total scores on the various forms are reasonably high: .91 for YAC4, .92 for ZAC1, .93 for ZAC2, and .84 for ZAC3. All of these coefficients may be spuriously high, in varying degree, because in no instance did every examinee have time to finish, although for most parts of the various forms a large proportion of the examinees did consider every item.

[179]
Hudelson's Typical Composition Ability Scale. Grades 4–12; 1923; 1 form ['23]; no data on reliability and validity and no description of normative population in manual (for data presented elsewhere by the author, see *1*); 6¢ per scale (only 1 copy needed per class); 12¢ per manual; postage extra; 24¢ per specimen set, postpaid; 15(25) minutes; Earl Hudelson; Public School Publishing Co. *

REFERENCES
1. HUDELSON, EARL. *English Composition: Its Aims, Methods, and Measurement.* Discussion by James F. Hosic, M. H. Willing, Walter S. Monroe, and S. A. Courtis. The Twenty-Second Yearbook of the National Society for the Study of Education, Part 1. Bloomington, Ill.: Public School Publishing Co., 1923. Pp. x, 172. *
2. HUDELSON, EARL. "The Effect of Objective Standards Upon Composition Teachers' Judgments." *J Ed Res* 12:329-40 D '25. *
3. HULTEN, C. E. "The Personal Element in Teachers' Marks." *J Ed Res* 12:49-55 Je '25. *
4. HULTEN, C. E. *Experiments in Reducing the Variability of Teacher's Marks in Grading English Compositions With the Aid of a Grading Guide.* Master's thesis, University of Wisconsin (Madison, Wisconsin), 1926.
5. KNUDSEN, CHARLES W. "A Test of the Practicability of the Hudelson Typical Composition Ability Scale." *Peabody J Ed* 8:109-17 S '30. *
6. SCRUGGS, MARY. *A Study of the Hudelson Typical Composition Ability Scale.* Master's thesis, George Peabody College (Memphis, Tenn.), 1930.
7. EDMINSTON, R. W., AND GINGERICH, C. N. "The Relation of Factors of English Usage to Composition." *J Ed Res* 36:269-71 D '42. * (PA 17:2169)

WORTH J. OSBURN, *Professor of Remedial and Experimental Education, University of Washington, Seattle, Washington.*

According to the author, the aims of this scale are:

(1) to test impartially the various methods of teaching composition by measuring their results; (2) to measure those results in accurate, objective, stable, and understandable terms; (3) to furnish a common basis for comparing the writing proficiency of different pupils within the same class or school or that of pupils in different classes or schools; (4) to classify pupils fairly in compositions; (5) to grade them justly within their group; (6) to enable teachers to discover their reliability in judging the general merit of English composition; and (7) to furnish pupils an incentive to self-competition.

The paragraphs in the scale were selected from "thirty-two representative theme assignments which inspired responses most typical of the average quality of composition work done on all assignments" by nearly 800 junior and senior high school pupils in the states of West Virginia and Indiana. Each pupil wrote two compositions on related subjects and these were rated independently by eight experienced judges. In order to get the best possible composition from each pupil, motivation was provided. Stories were read to the pupils for completion. Stimulus words were given to incorporate in a composition. Thought provoking titles were suggested such as "A Trip to Heaven," "A Conversation with Mars" and the like. Practice

paragraphs were provided for use by the inexperienced teacher.

Work on this scale, which was constructed
28 years ago, was done by using the best techniques and procedures available at that time.
Hudelson must have done the best possible job
because no advance has been made upon his
work since that time. Unfortunately, however,
the scale suffers from two very serious disadvantages which seem to be inherent in all scale
making. In the first place, scales are not diagnostic. If a pupil gets a low score the teacher
has no means of knowing what is lacking or
what to do about it. The second disadvantage is
lack of reliability. The correlation of the median
judgments of the eight experienced judges on
the paired compositions ranged from .69 to .84.
Had there been only one judge (as is the case
when one teacher uses the scale) the reliability
coefficient could hardly have been more than
.40. This is not much better than sheer guessing.

The probable error of a single estimate, approximately .5, is very high. According to the
standards a 4th grade pupil is supposed to write
a composition of value 3.0; a 12th grade pupil,
one of value 6.7. The entire difference is 3.7. The
average growth per year for the eight years is
.46. But the probable error of a single rating by
an *experienced* judge is .5. This means that
even an experienced judge will misplace a child's
composition by less than a year on the scale half
of the time. During the other half he will misplace it by more than a year. Results more reliable than these can be obtained by simply ranking the pupil's composition in terms of the number of running words which he writes. This large
unreliability of experienced judges should re-
mind English teachers everywhere of what a
stupid waste of time it is for them to assign
grades to pupil's compositions. Perhaps it should
also spur some brilliant genius to devise a method of rating compositions that really is worth
while.

In spite of these serious defects the scale is
worth the 20 cents that it costs. Using it will
focus our attention on the tremendous importance of English composition and upon the urgent need for a better means of rating it. Perhaps the best thing of all to do is to buy the scale
and require each member of a class to rate the
composition of each of his classmates. An average of these ratings is the most accurate measure
that is now possible.

LITERATURE

[180]

***Ability to Interpret Literary Materials: Iowa
Tests of Educational Development, Test 7.**
Grades 9–13; 1942–51 (first published as a separate in
1951); for complete battery, see 17; Form Y-2 ('51—
same as 1949 edition); manual ('51); general manual
('51); $3.75 per 25; separate answer pads or answer
sheets must be used; $1.95 per 25 answer pads; $3 per
100 IBM answer sheets; 50¢ per scoring stencil; $2.50
per 25 first semester ('46) or second semester ('48)
profiles for any one of grades 9–12; $1 per 25 self-
interpreting profiles for students ('51); 25¢ per school
summary report ('44); 4¢ per pupil score sheet ('48);
50¢ per specimen set; cash orders postpaid; 50(55)
minutes; edited by E. F. Lindquist; Julia Peterson;
Science Research Associates, Inc. *

*For a review by Eric F. Gardner of the com-
plete battery, see 17; for reviews by Henry
Chauncey, Gustav J. Froehlich, and Lavone A.
Hanna of Forms X-1 and Y-1 of the complete
battery, see 3:12.*

[181]

*American Literature: Every Pupil Test. High
school; 1934–51; new form usually published each
April and December; form December 1951; no data on
reliability and validity; no manual; norms ('51); 2½¢
per test; 1¢ per answer key; postpaid; 40(45) minutes; Ohio Scholarship Tests, Ohio State Department
of Education. *

[182]

*An Awareness Test in 20th Century Literature.
Grades 9–16; 1937–40; Forms A ('37), B ('40); no
data on reliability and validity; no manual; norms
('37); $2.25 per 25, postpaid; specimen set not avail-
able; 45(50) minutes; edited by Harold H. Bixler;
Elmer R. Smith; Turner E. Smith & Co. *

*For reviews by H. H. Giles and Ann L. Geb-
hardt, see 40:1296.*

[183]

★Check List of Novels. High school and college;
1942–50; 15 scores: 3 scores (novels read, movies seen,
novels liked) for each of 4 categories (difficult novels,
standard novels, best-sellers, light novels) and total
group; 1 form, '50; no data on reliability and validity
in manual (for data presented elsewhere, see *1–2* below); manual ('50); norms ('42); $2.50 per 25; sep-
arate answer sheets must be used; 75¢ per 25 answer
sheets; 25¢ per specimen set; cash orders postpaid;
nontimed (50) minutes; developed by the Cooperative
Study in General Education (Ralph W. Tyler, Director); Cooperative Test Division, Educational Testing
Service. *

REFERENCES

1. COOPERATIVE STUDY IN GENERAL EDUCATION, EXECUTIVE
COMMITTEE, RALPH W. TYLER, DIRECTOR. "Second Project:
The Inventory and the Check List in Fiction," pp. 98–111. In
Cooperation in General Education. Washington, D.C.: Ameri-
can Council on Education, 1947. Pp. xvii, 240. * (*PA* 22:432)
2. DUNKEL, HAROLD BAKER. Chap. 4, "Students' Beliefs
About Fiction," pp. 121–71, 302–8, 309–11. In his *General
Education in the Humanities.* Washington, D.C.: American
Council on Education, 1947. Pp. xix, 323. * (*PA* 22:434)

JOHN S. DIEKHOFF, *Director, Center for the Study of Liberal Education for Adults, 940 East 58th St., Chicago 37, Illinois.*

With reference to 300 novels, students are asked to indicate whether they have read the novel, seen a movie based on it, read and liked it, or never read it. The list includes 30 novels classed as "difficult," 90 as "standard," 90 as "best sellers," past or present, and 90 as "light." There is not likely to be any quarrel with the classification. Such writers as Dostoevski, Meredith, and Proust are difficult; Austen, Scott, and Tarkington are standard; Hervey Allen, Margaret Mitchell, and Arthur Koestler are best sellers; Temple Bailey, Erle Stanley Gardner, and Zane Grey are light.

For its purpose, which is to inventory the reading already accomplished by high school (or college) students, the *Check List of Novels* is no doubt useful. The check list was originally designed for use with another instrument (*Inventory of Satisfactions Found in Reading Fiction*). It is described in the manual as "helpful to instructors in planning reading assignments, finding 'common denominators' for classroom discussion, and guiding individual reading programs." There is a risk (perhaps not great) that the check list will encourage students to think that to read a book—any book, Temple Bailey equally with Fielding—is somehow an action worthy of praise.

[184]

*Cooperative Literary Comprehension and Appreciation Test.** Grades 10–16; 1935–51; IBM; Provisional Forms R ('41), T ('43); no specific manual; descriptive sheet ('51); general Cooperative manual ('51); tentative high school norms ['38]; tentative college norms ['38]; $2.25 per 25; 50¢ per specimen set, postpaid; separate answer sheets may be used; 80¢ per 25 IBM answer sheets; 15¢ per stencil for scoring answer sheets; cash orders postpaid; 40(45) minutes; Mary Willis, Hyman Eigerman (R), Frederick B. Davis (R), and H. A. Domincovich (T); Cooperative Test Division, Educational Testing Service. *

REFERENCES

1–3. See 3:142.
4. HUMBER, WILBUR J. "The Relationship Between Reading Efficiency and Academic Success in Selected University Curricula." *J Ed Psychol* 35:17–26 Ja '44. * (*PA* 18:2581)

For a review by Holland Roberts, see 3:142.

[185]

*English Literature: Every Pupil Test.** High school; 1934–51; new form usually published each April and December; form April 1951; no data on reliability and validity; no manual; norms ('51); 2½¢ per test; 1¢ per answer key; postpaid; 40(45) minutes; Ohio Scholarship Tests, Ohio State Department of Education. *

[186]

★Graduate Record Examinations Advanced Literature Test.** Senior year college through graduate school and candidates for graduate school; 1939–51; available only in Graduate Record Examinations programs (see 527); 180(220) minutes; prepared by the Advanced Literature Test Committee appointed by Educational Testing Service: Don Cameron Allen (Chairman), Bradford A. Booth, E. K. Brown, John W. Spargo, and Harry R. Warfel; Educational Testing Service. *

[187]

★Interpretation of Literature Test: General Education Series.** High School; 1936–50; a revision of *An Interpretation of Literature: Test 3.1* ('36); original test published by Evaluation in Eight Year Study, Progressive Education Association; 7 scores: understanding of the story, recognizing of a person's point of view, understanding human motivation, weighing evidence supporting an ending, weighing evidence discrediting an ending, analyzing literature from a technical standpoint, total; 1 form, '50; no data on reliability and validity; no norms; manual ('50); $2.50 per 25; separate answer sheets must be used; 75¢ per 25 answer sheets; 20¢ per set of scoring stencils; cash orders postpaid; 50¢ per specimen set, postpaid; nontimed (75) minutes; Evaluation Staff (Ralph W. Tyler, Director) of the Eight-Year Study of the Progressive Education Association; published in 1950 by Cooperative Test Division, Educational Testing Service. *

JOHN S. DIEKHOFF, *Director, Center for the Study of Liberal Education for Adults, 940 East 58th St., Chicago 37, Illinois.*

This test is based upon a summary of O. Henry's story, *A Municipal Report.* Although the summary is excellent, one wishes that the student might be required to read the entire story. Since the test time is already rather long, the choice was probably made between basing it on a summary or basing it on a story assigned as outside reading. Nevertheless, the teacher, if he prefers, may assign the story in advance. Directions for scoring and interpreting the results suggest that a comparison of the summary with the whole story would be an illuminating exercise, presumably after the test has been administered.

The suggestion is characteristic of the spirit in which the test has been constructed. The manual states that "in its present form....the instrument is probably more useful as a teaching device than as a test." Its usefulness as the former is apparent, and to a reviewer not expert in techniques of testing, it seems an adequate test also.

Each section of the test approaches the story from a different point of view. The first requires the student to understand what has happened in the story (or its summary). The second requires him to understand the attitude of the narrator and to explore his own attitudes. Searching moral questions are raised as a basis for future class discussions and as an indication of the extent to which imaginative literature may be related "to the problems of living." A third section continues this exploration of the relation of literature to life by exploring the motives of the agents in the story and asking the student to judge them. Less directly (apparently not as part of the intention of the examiners) it illuminates the interplay of character and incident in a well constructed fable. Other sections test ability to weigh evidence and ability to make a literary analysis of the story in the conventional terms of setting, purpose, classification (e.g., moralistic story, love story, story of incident and plot, etc.), style, action, and author.

If new editions of the test are contemplated, two sections would benefit from revision. (*a*) The narrator in *A Municipal Report* is a fictional character. Section II of the test, "Are You Learning a Person's Point of View?," identifies the fictional narrator with O. Henry and asks the student to indicate O. Henry's point of view toward various moral problems. Unsophisticated readers are too prone to attribute the opinions of fictional characters to their authors. It should be made clear that O. Henry is the inventor of the narrator as well as of other agents in the story. (*b*) Section IV on weighing evidence is obscure. At any rate, the reviewer found close rereading necessary. There is the risk that it measures ability to understand a complex exposition rather than ability to weigh evidence.

The final section of the test, made up of somewhat leading questions, asks the student to evaluate the test itself. No assurances that "answers to this part of the test in no way affect your score on the test" will keep most students from indicating "correctly" the item which reads, "This test caused me to like the story more than I did upon first reading it"; and it seems hardly fair to entice unwary pupils into saying, "It would be interesting to take more tests in literature similar to this one." Even in this section, however, students may give the desired answers honestly as well as tactfully, for the test, attempting both to measure the student's ability to read imaginative literature and to teach while it tests, is a good one.

JOHN M. STALNAKER, *Director of Studies, Association of American Medical Colleges, Chicago, Illinois.*

In the accompanying manual of instructions, it is pointed out that this test, developed by the Eight Year Study, had long been out of print, but that interest in it continued. In response to such interest the Educational Testing Service reprinted the test.

This is not a test in the usual sense but a teaching device. It was designed to aid the secondary school teacher of literature in showing students how fiction can be analyzed and in giving students some experience in relating their reading to their own lives and problems. The test should be used in connection with class discussion; its effectiveness depends upon the skill of the teacher in using it.

As a measurement of achievement this "test" cannot be recommended. Indeed, it was not designed to be so used. The teacher of literature might well examine a specimen set of this test and determine for herself whether it is a suitable instrument to facilitate her instruction. Some teachers will find it of value while others will wish to make an entirely different approach in their teaching.

[188]

★**Inventory of Satisfactions Found in Reading Fiction: General Education Series.** High school and college; 1942–50; 11 scores: satisfactions of relaxation and pastime, escape, associational values, intimate personal relations, socio-civic, philosophy, miscellaneous informational, total informational, technical-critical, self-development, dislikes; Forms A ('50), B ('50); manual ('50); norms ['44?]; $2.25 per 25; separate answer sheets must be used; 60¢ per 25 answer sheets; cash orders postpaid; 50¢ per specimen set, postpaid; nontimed (50) minutes; developed by the Cooperative Study in General Education, (Ralph W. Tyler, Director); Cooperative Test Division, Educational Testing Service. *

REFERENCES

1. COOPERATIVE STUDY IN GENERAL EDUCATION, EXECUTIVE COMMITTEE, RALPH W. TYLER, DIRECTOR. "Second Project: The Inventory and the Check List in Fiction," pp. 98–111. In *Cooperation in General Education.* Washington, D.C.: American Council on Education, 1947. Pp. xvii, 240. * (*PA* 22:432)
2. DUNKEL, HAROLD BAKER. *General Education in the Humanities,* pp. 121–76, 297–301, 309–11. Including a section by S. H. McGuire (pp. 171–6). Foreword by Ralph W. Tyler. Washington, D.C.: American Council on Education, 1947, pp. xix, 321. * (*PA* 22:434)

HOLLAND ROBERTS, *Director, California Labor School, 321 Divisadero St., San Francisco, California.*

This revision of the inventory developed by colleges participating in the Cooperative Study in General Education is an ambitious effort "to help school and college instructors improve the pattern of student reading." It is organized in two parts. Part I consists of 90 statements of satisfactions reported by readers of fiction, with which the student is asked to agree, disagree, or to mark "uncertain." Most of the statements are individual personal responses such as "trying to guess what various characters will do" and "being reminded of places I have been," but there are a number that penetrate beneath the level of superficial generality. The authors have listed the 90 items in 6 broad categories: relaxation and pastime (10 items), escape (8), associational values (8), information (33), technical-critical (15), and self development (16). The 33 items on information are subdivided into 4 parts: intimate personal relations (9), socio-civic (10), philosophy of life and religion (8), and miscellaneous (6).

As the inventory is intended to fulfill a key function in building and guiding literature programs, the authors' approach to the field is important. They have observed "that instructors attempt to work in terms of material only rather than in terms of the satisfactions which the student derives from reading" and that students frequently confine their reading of fiction within narrow bounds, limiting themselves to adventure stories historical fiction, the works of a few favorite authors, and the like. They believe that through the use of the inventory it is "possible to determine the chief satisfactions a student now obtains from fiction" and that with this knowledge the instructor can then present his students with a program designed to improve their reading level. They believe that, if a student is told that the satisfactions he finds in his reading can be gained in greater measure in better novels, "the chances are good that he will change his reading habits for the better." Then, if the instructor points out new satisfactions to be found only in the recommended books, and the student confirms the instructor's predictions, "the change in reading habits should be permanent." To complete their program of reading guidance, the authors recommend the use of a related inventory, the *Check List of Novels*. The instructor finds out what books gave the student the satisfaction he reported and makes specific recommendations to improve the student's pattern of reading.

Clearly, this inventory is planned as part of a serious attempt to map out a major advance in teaching literature—one of the oldest established fields of creative activity. But the pub-

lisher's catalog statement makes even greater claims, stating that the inventory "provides information about....the amount and kind of material *he* (the student) *is likely to read*" (italics mine), and reveals not only the kind but the "degree" of satisfactions students believe they obtain from reading fiction. Of course there is no objective evidence that the use of the inventory will enable teachers and students to do any of these things. Some of them may be possible, but the major question is whether even then the purposes for which this instrument was devised cannot be achieved more effectively through discussion, reading records, and other ways. Until measurement of satisfactions in literature is demonstrated, we have no sure knowledge in this important field. The authors have themselves recognized certain limitations in their work, and others will be apparent to experienced teachers of literature. First, it is assumed that the data from the inventory represent reality and are reliable; yet teachers recognize that students are under grade pressure to give the kinds of responses that teachers want. Can it be assumed that students will respond spontaneously to the items in this inventory? Again, use of the inventory is entirely based upon the introspective analysis of inexperienced young people. They are asked to report whether they gain satisfaction from "feeling the beauty of the author's style" or "getting my mind off my troubles." It is possible for them to get satisfaction in these ways without being able to recognize it, or they may connect their satisfaction with an unrelated cause. Can youth who are just finding their way in the world isolate their present feelings from past experiences or from those they anticipate or desire?

A more significant weakness is the passive, static character of the majority of the questions. There is none of the enthusiasm and fire of discovering a great book, unless "getting ideas about manners and etiquette" and "feeling that I am developing my personality" can be so conceived. Not only is the use of literature as vital action lacking, but practically all sense of *doing* in the inventory is individual. The student and his book are alone in a great void. There is no suggestion of the power of group action, whose tides have made our history, nor any suggestion or conception that great literature unites men and nations and gives them security and a place in a friendly universe. Literature is treated as though it were so much baled hay, and the teaching of literature a mechanical process. The notion that human emotions should be developed according to any set of formal categories may fit a compartmentalized psychology, but teachers of literature must work in a field whose growing complexities and depth range beyond such a concept.

Part II is a series of 25 statements of "dislikes," beginning with "I dislike fiction," with which the student is asked to agree, disagree, or indicate uncertainty. The approach is negative, and the emphasis in this final section of the inventory is unrelieved by any positive suggestion.

Experience in using Part I of this inventory may disclose some positive values, particularly in stimulating discussion about specific books and thus gaining exact information from students. To the extent that it may encourage a teacher to find out more about students, it may have its uses. But other types of responses such as autobiographies of student reading, reading histories, interviews, and the students' own statements about their reading interests and satisfactions would seem to meet the needs for reading guidance more exactly and less dangerously—particularly in the hands of inexperienced or formal teachers. Certainly more experience and further careful experiment by able teachers is necessary before the inventory can be recommended for general use.

[189]

★**The Jones Book-A-Day Tests: For Checking Outside Reading of High School Pupils.** High school; 1946–52; over 3,000 tests on books commonly recommended for high school pupils; 1 form for each test; 1–99 mixed titles, 7¢ each; 100–499, 6¢ each; 25 or more of any one title, 5¢ each; postpaid; 3(4) minutes per test; Book-A-Day Series. *

[190]

*Literature Appreciation Tests.** High school; 1936–40; 13 tests; 1 form; no data on reliability and validity; no manual; tentative norms—authors recommend the use of local norms; $1.75 per 25 of any one test, postpaid; specimen set not available; nontimed (40–50) minutes per test; edited by H. H. Bixler; Turner E. Smith & Co. *

a) A MIDSUMMER NIGHT'S DREAM. 1937; Salibelle Royster.
b) AS YOU LIKE IT. 1936; Elmer R. Smith.
c) EVANGELINE. 1937; Evelyn L. Stovall.
d) HAMLET. 1938; Salibelle Royster.
e) IDYLLS OF THE KING. 1937; Luella B. Cook.
f) IVANHOE. 1938; Elmer R. Smith.
g) MACBETH. 1936; Mary J. J. Wrinn.
h) SILAS MARNER. 1936; Luella B. Cook.
i) THE ADVENTURES OF TOM SAWYER. 1940; Elmer R. Smith.
j) THE COURTSHIP OF MILES STANDISH. 1937; Evelyn L. Stovall.

k) THE HOUSE OF THE SEVEN GABLES. 1936; Holland D. Roberts.
l) THE MERCHANT OF VENICE. 1936; Elmer R. Smith.
m) TREASURE ISLAND. 1936; Luella B. Cook.

For a review by Paul B. Diederich, see 38: 976.

[191]

★**Literature Test: Municipal Tests: National Achievement Tests.** Grades 3–6, 6–8; 1938–39; a subtest of *Municipal Battery* (see 20); 3 scores: motives and moods, miscellaneous facts, total; 2 levels; Forms A ('38), B ('39); no data on reliability and validity and no description of normative population in manual; no norms for part scores; manual ['38]; $1.25 per 25 of any one level; 35¢ per specimen set of any one level; postage extra; 20(25) minutes; Robert K. Speer and Samuel Smith; Acorn Publishing Co. *

[192]

*Literature Test: National Achievement Tests.** Grades 7–12; 1937–44; 5 scores: recognizing effects, recognizing qualities, analyzing moods, miscellaneous facts, total; Forms A ('44—same as test copyrighted in 1937), B ('39); no norms for part scores; Form A manual ('38), Form B manual ('39); series manual ['44]; $2.25 per 25; 35¢ per specimen set; postage extra; nontimed (40–60) minutes; Robert K. Speer and Samuel Smith; Acorn Publishing Co. *

For reviews by H. H. Giles and Robert C. Pooley, see 40:1304.

[193]

★**Objective Tests in English [Perfection Form Co.].** High school; 1929–50; 41 tests; no data on reliability and validity; no manual; no norms; 6¢ per test; 20¢ per specimen set; cash orders postpaid; (20–40) minutes per test; Alpha Hobbs Darlington (b, g, r, t, y, cc, ee, ii), Sarah E. Dorn (jj, mm, nn), Nellie M. Falk (h, k, v, x, bb, ll, oo), Margaret Leeney (c, d, w, gg), Hannah Van Nostrand (p), Garland Miller Taylor (a, f, i, j, l, n, o, s, u, z, aa, dd, ff, hh, kk), Maye Alexander Wilson (m), and LaDuskie Wood (e, q); Perfection Form Co. *

a) AS YOU LIKE IT. 1947; 1 form.
b) DAVID COPPERFIELD. 1931–48; 1 form, '48.
c) ENOCH ARDEN. 1947–49; 1 form, '47.
d) EVANGELINE. 1929; 1 form.
e) HAMLET. 1931–48; 1 form, '48.
f) HENRY V. 1931; 1 form.
g) THE HOUSE OF THE SEVEN GABLES. 1947; 1 form.
h) HUCKLEBERRY FINN. 1950; 1 form.
i) IDYLLS OF THE KING. 1929–47; 1 form, '47.
j) IVANHOE. 1948; 1 form.
k) JOHNNY TREMAIN. 1950; 1 form.
l) JULIUS CAESAR. 1948–49; 1 form, '48.
m) KENILWORTH. 1932; 1 form.
n) KIDNAPPED. 1948; 1 form.
o) KING LEAR. 1929; 1 form.
p) THE LADY OF THE LAKE. 1929–48; 1 form, '48.
q) MACBETH. 1947–48; 1 form, '48.
r) THE MAN WITHOUT A COUNTRY. 1932; 1 form.
s) THE MERCHANT OF VENICE. 1929–49; 1 form, '49.
t) A MIDSUMMER NIGHT'S DREAM. 1931–48; 1 form, '48.
u) MOBY DICK. 1949; 1 form.
v) OLIVER TWIST. 1950; 1 form.
w) OTHELLO. 1929; 1 form.
x) THE RETURN OF THE NATIVE. 1950; 1 form.
y) THE RIME OF THE ANCIENT MARINER. 1947; 1 form.
z) ROMEO AND JULIET. 1929–49; 1 form, '49.
aa) THE SCARLET LETTER. 1932; 1 form.

bb) SHE STOOPS TO CONQUER. 1949; 1 form.
cc) SILAS MARNER. 1948; 1 form.
dd) SIR ROGER DE COVERLEY PAPERS. 1931; 1 form.
ee) THE SKETCH BOOK. 1937; 1 form.
ff) SNOW-BOUND. 1931–48; 1 form, '48.
gg) SOHRAB AND RUSTUM. 1929; 1 form.
hh) THE SPY. 1931–47; 1 form, '31.
ii) A TALE OF TWO CITIES. 1930–48; 1 form, '48.
jj) THE TEMPEST. 1948; 1 form.
kk) TREASURE ISLAND. 1947–49; 1 form, '47.
ll) TWELFTH NIGHT. 1950; 1 form.
mm) THE VICAR OF WAKEFIELD. 1947; 1 form.
nn) THE VISION OF SIR LAUNFAL. 1948; 1 form.
oo) THE YEARLING. 1950; 1 form.

[194]

*Objective Tests in English [Turner E. Smith and Co.]. High school; 1926–41; 47 tests; no description of normative population; manual ('30); $1.75 per 35 of any one test, postpaid; specimen set not available; nontimed (30–40) minutes per test; edited by George A. Rice; Mable S. Satterfield and others; Turner E. Smith & Co. *

a) A MIDSUMMER NIGHT'S DREAM. 1927–30; 1 form, '29.
b) AS YOU LIKE IT. 1926–30; 1 form, '28.
c) A TALE OF TWO CITIES. 1927–30; 1 form, '28.
d) BURKE'S SPEECH ON CONCILIATION WITH AMERICA. 1926–30; 1 form, '28.
e) THE CANTERBURY TALES. 1928–30; 1 form, '29.
f) CARLYLE'S ESSAY ON BURNS AND BURNS' POETRY. 1926–30; 1 form, '29.
g) DAVID COPPERFIELD. 1928–30; 1 form, '28.
h) DR. JEKYLL AND MR. HYDE. 1926–31; 1 form, '31.
i) ENOCH ARDEN. 1929–30; 1 form, '29.
j) FRANKLIN'S AUTOBIOGRAPHY. 1930; 1 form.
k) HAMLET. 1926–30; 1 form, '28.
l) HENRY ESMOND. 1930–34; 1 form, '34.
m) IDYLLS OF THE KING. 1927–30; 1 form, '30.
n) IVANHOE. 1926–30; 1 form, '28.
o) JULIUS CAESAR. 1926–30; 1 form, '28.
p) KING HENRY THE FIFTH. 1928; 1 form.
q) KING LEAR. 1930; *out of print.*
r) LORNA DOONE. 1929–30; 1 form, '29.
s) MACAULAY'S ESSAY ON THE LIFE OF SAMUEL JOHNSON. 1927–30; 1 form, '29.
t) MACBETH. 1926–30; 1 form, '28.
u) MILTON'S MINOR POEMS AND OTHER LYRICS. 1927–30; 1 form, '29.
v) OLIVER TWIST. 1930–34; *out of print.*
w) POE'S POEMS AND TALES. 1927–30; 1 form, '29.
x) QUENTIN DURWARD. 1927–30; *out of print.*
y) ROMEO AND JULIET. 1930–34; 1 form, '34.
z) SHE STOOPS TO CONQUER. 1929–30; 1 form, '29.
aa) SIR ROGER DE COVERLEY PAPERS. 1927–30; 1 form, '27.
bb) SILAS MARNER. 1926–40; 1 form, '40.
cc) SOHRAB AND RUSTUM. 1929–30; 1 form, '29.
dd) THE DESERTED VILLAGE. 1930; 1 form.
ee) THE HOUSE OF SEVEN GABLES. 1927–31; 1 form, '31.
ff) THE LADY OF THE LAKE. 1926–41; 1 form, '41.
gg) THE LAST OF THE MOHICANS. 1927–30; 1 form, '29.
hh) THE MERCHANT OF VENICE. 1927–30; 1 form, '30.
ii) THE ODYSSEY. 1928–30; 1 form, '29.
jj) THE OREGON TRAIL. 1930–34; 1 form, '34.
kk) THE RIME OF THE ANCIENT MARINER. 1929–30; 1 form, '29.
ll) THE RISE OF SILAS LAPHAM. 1929; 1 form.
mm) THE SKETCH BOOK. 1929–30; 1 form, '29.
nn) THE SPY. 1928–30; 1 form, '28.
oo) THE TEMPEST. 1928–30; 1 form, '28.
pp) THE VICAR OF WAKEFIELD. 1930; 1 form.
qq) THE VISION OF SIR LAUNFAL. 1930; 1 form.
rr) TRAVELS WITH A DONKEY. 1930; 1 form.
ss) TREASURE ISLAND. 1927–30; 1 form, '28.
tt) TWELFTH NIGHT. 1927–30; 1 form, '29.

uu) WEBSTER'S FIRST BUNKER HILL ORATION AND WASHINGTON'S FAREWELL ADDRESS. 1929–30; 1 form, '29.

[195]

*Stanford Achievement Test [Literature]. Grades 4–9; 1941–43, c1940–41; an adaptation of the literature tests of *Stanford Achievement Test* (see 25); IBM; Forms DM ('41), EM ('43); the *Manual for Interpreting* referred to in the directions for administering has not been published; directions for administering ('41); $1.65 per 25; separate answer sheets must be used; 70¢ per 25 IBM answer sheets; 20¢ per scoring stencil for any one form; 55¢ per 25 profile charts ('42); postage extra; 35¢ per specimen set, postpaid; 15(20) minutes; Truman L. Kelley, Giles M. Ruch, and Lewis M. Terman; World Book Co. *

WINIFRED L. POST, *Instructor in English, Dana Hall, Wellesley, Massachusetts.*

Each form contains 70 three-choice items, with a total working time of 15 minutes. The term *literature* includes material ranging from *Little Red Riding Hood* and *Rumpelstiltskin* to *Moby Dick* or *The Merchant of Venice*. The test achieves a wise balance between books of special interest to boys or to girls, with a judicious number of items drawn from classic or Norse mythology. A range of difficulty in the test items is secured not by the type of information demanded but rather by wide variations in the likelihood of a child's exposure to a given book. Each item asks for a single piece of factual information, with the emphasis predominantly on ability to spot the correct name of a character for a given book title or to attach the right book title to fit a briefly described character. For example: "The girl who lived on Sunnybrook Farm was (1) Roselle (2) Betsy (3) Rebecca."

The strong features of this test are: (*a*) the brevity and ease of administration; (*b*) the adaptability to objective test techniques of the material; (*c*) the rapidity and precision with which the resulting scores would yield information on the reading backgrounds of numbers of students too large for more individual and more subtly discriminating treatment. And this leads me to the limitations of the tests—limitations closely linked with or growing inevitably out of the strengths I have enumerated. The most significant limitation is the purely factual type of question—a type of question which precludes the possibility of getting at the quality of a child's reading or understanding. Unless used with caution, this kind of test can further the quiz-mindedness which is already tending to wipe out the distinction between an undiscriminatingly retentive memory and an inquiring or synthesizing intellect. From the standpoint of sound English teaching—a place where most of all this distinction needs to be kept alive—I should recommend these tests chiefly as time-savers. If used with a clear realization of their limitations and with critical faculties alert for the deceptive immediacy, precision, and completeness of information yielded with the apparent omniscience of an objective test score, these tests would seem to me serviceable, practical, and informative, especially when supplemented with tests of vocabulary, language skills, and comprehension.

For reviews by Paul R. Hanna and Claude E. Norcross and Vergil E. Herrick of the complete battery, see 25; for reviews by Walter W. Cook and Ralph C. Preston of the complete battery, see 3:18.

[196]
Survey Test in English Literature. High school and college; 1940; 1 form; no data on reliability and validity; no manual; no norms for part scores; no description of normative population; $2.25 per 25, postpaid; specimen set not available; 50(55) minutes; edited by Harold H. Bixler; Elmer R. Smith; Turner E. Smith & Co. *

JOHN S. DIEKHOFF, *Director, Center for the Study of Liberal Education for Adults, 940 East 58th St., Chicago 37, Illinois.*

If one wishes or is required to teach what this test tests, perhaps it will measure the students' rote learning adequately. There is a prior question, for it is one of the values and one of the dangers of externally prepared tests that they direct the teaching of those who use them. The teacher who selects this test is confirmed in a misunderstanding of the purpose of secondary school English courses; the teacher upon whom it is imposed is required to seek the wrong outcomes. For this test has little relevance to what the pupil may have read and no relevance to his understanding of what he has read. It is a test of his retention of information he might have gathered from an outline syllabus of English literature.

The pupil need have read nothing of Richardson, Fielding, Smollett, or Sterne to identify the author of *Tom Jones*. He need not have read *L'Allegro* to know that it was not by Moore, Landor, or Blake; indeed, he need never have heard of Moore, Landor, and Blake. He need not know what a heroic couplet is to know that Pope was skilled in its use. He need have read nothing but a textbook to know or to guess that

Ralph Roister Doister is an early comedy by Nicholas Udall, to have the misinformation that "in the 17th century came the first critical literary essays from the pen of John Dryden," or to know that "the Gothic novel" is "progenitor of the modern mystery tale." Since the word "progenitor" is not likely to be in his vocabulary, he must guess the answer to this question.

These illustrations suffice to show that there is no pretence that the pupil is being examined on what he has read. Surely no high school literature courses require pupils to read *Pamela, Tom Jones, L'Allegro, Ralph Roister Doister, The Rape of the Lock, The Preface to the Fables,* and *The Castle of Otranto*—the handful of titles with which we have illustrated the range of the test. If any introductory college courses do, they ought not to. The test can do nothing but harm.

[197]
★**Ullman-Clark Test on Classical References and Allusions.** Grades 8–12; 1938; 1 form; no data on reliability and validity; no description of normative population; mimeographed manual; $4 per 100, postage extra; 15¢ per specimen set, postpaid; 20(25) minutes; B. L. Ullman and Grace W. Clark; Bureau of Educational Research and Service, State University of Iowa. *

SPELLING

[198]
★**Ayer Standardized Spelling Test.** Grades 9–12; 1950; Forms 1, 2; no data on reliability and validity; $1 per 40; 10¢ per specimen set; postpaid; nontimed (30) minutes; Fred C. Ayer; Steck Co. *

REFERENCES
1. AYER, FRED C. "An Evaluation of High-School Spelling." *Sch R* 59:233-6 Ap '51. *

HAROLD H. BIXLER, *Professor of Education, Western Carolina Teachers College, Cullowhee, North Carolina.*

DESCRIPTION. This test is designed for use in high schools, norms being given for grades 9 to 12. Each pupil is to be given a test sheet, on which is printed 30 sentences. Pupils are to write the words dictated by the examiner in the blanks found in the sentences. The brevity of the test makes it possible to administer it in less than a class period.

VALIDITY. No data on validity are reported in the manual, but inspection shows that the words chosen are common words such as are found in existing spelling scales. The words are not arranged in order of difficulty.

RELIABILITY. No data are reported on the

reliability of this test. It is regrettable that the author did not include at least 50 words, as found in other standardized tests such as the *Metropolitan Achievement Tests*. The inclusion of 20 additional words would doubtless have improved the reliability of this instrument.

USABILITY. Norms are based on tests of 35,-000 high school students in 84 different cities, scattered throughout the United States. Presumably, they are also applicable to rural schools. Norms are reported in terms of averages for grades 9, 10, 11, and 12, respectively. In addition, the scores of the highest and the lowest schools are reported. A helpful feature is a table showing the percentage of pupils in grades 9, 10, 11, and 12 spelling each word correctly.

SUMMARY. This is an excellent short test, useful in situations where a quick spelling survey is desired. Teachers should compute the percentages of pupils spelling each word on the test, since norms in terms of per cents are provided. Users may find it interesting to compare results obtained on this test, where context is provided on the test sheet, with results obtained in column spelling without context.

[199]

Davis-Schrammel Spelling Test. Grades 1–9; 1935-36; Forms A ('35), B ('35), C ('35), D ('36); manual ['36]; 25¢ per set of 4 forms (only one copy needed per class); no materials needed for examinees; $1 per six sets of 4 forms; postpaid; nontimed (15) minutes; Vera Davis and H. E. Schrammel; Bureau of Educational Measurements, Kansas State Teachers College of Emporia. *

ANTON THOMPSON, *Supervisor of Research, Long Beach Public Schools, Long Beach, California.*

Although the authors have not stated the purposes for which this test was designed, the reviewer assumes that it is intended to serve as a measure of general spelling ability for pupils in grades 1–9. The tests for each grade contain 20 words. Four "equivalent" forms of the test are available. Because the words used in testing pupils of one grade overlap with those used in the next higher grade, each form includes a total of only 96 words for use in testing nine separate grades. The testing procedure is a common one: the teacher reads a sentence, states which word in the sentence is to be written, and the pupils then spell the word on locally prepared blanks. It is an inexpensive test to administer and one which requires very little class time.

As a measure of the pupil's ability to spell

the more commonly written words, this test has doubtful validity. The words were selected from the *Buckingham Extension of the Ayres Spelling Scale* and they have apparently not been checked against the more accepted frequency-counts now available. The reviewer's analysis of the words in one form of the eighth grade test shows that 9 of the 20 words are not included among the first 5,000 of the Horn list—in fact, 5 of these 9 words are not to be found in Horn's complete list of the 10,000 words most commonly written by adults.[1] A second check of this same eighth grade test shows that 11 of the 20 words are not included among the 5,000 words which Rinsland's research shows are most commonly written by eighth grade pupils.[2] Typical of words whose inclusion is questionable on the basis of frequency of child and adult usage in writing is the word "financier."

It is well known that spelling textbooks differ greatly in the words assigned to a given grade. Consequently, the validity of this test as a measure of progress in spelling achievement during a specified period must be determined by a school system through a check of the test words against those included in the local course of study.

On the basis of giving Forms A and B to 1,506 pupils in three Kansas school systems, the authors report that the reliability coefficients for the nine grades tested ranged from .84 to .93, with an average of .87. The average probable error of measurement reported is 1.1 words. Although the reported reliability meets minimal requirements, a longer test would not inconvenience the teacher and would yield a more reliable measure for the individual pupil.

Midyear and end-of-year percentile norms are supplied for each grade. According to the test catalog, these are based upon "more than 49,000 pupils in a large number of representative schools." The manual states that these scores were obtained in 1935 and 1936 from the "Nation-wide Every Pupil Scholarship Programs" which are not further described. A test purchaser working in, say, a New Jersey city school system would be interested in knowing how many of the 49,000 pupils in the norm group attended public schools in the urban centers of New Jersey and how their performance com-

---

1 Horn, Ernest. *A Basic Writing Vocabulary: 10,000 Words Most Commonly Used in Writing.* University of Iowa Monographs in Education, Series 1, No. 4. Iowa City, Iowa: College of Education, University of Iowa, 1926. Pp. 225. Paper. *
2 Rinsland, Henry D. *A Basic Vocabulary of Elementary School Children.* New York: Macmillan Co., 1945. Pp. 636.

pared with that of the total norm group. The "more than 49,000" cases include all pupils in any grade from one through nine tested at mid-year or at the year's end. The test purchaser who plans to give the test at midyear to a ninth grade class should note that the norms he will be using are based on only 342 of the pupils in the total norm group.

According to the authors' manual, the per-centile equivalent of a pupil's score means the percentage of the pupils in the norm group whose performance has been exceeded. This ex-planation may be confusing to the teacher who gives the test at midyear to first graders and concludes from the norms table that a child who spells none of the words correctly has exceeded the performance of 25 per cent of the norm population!

The manual provides the teacher with no answers to many practical questions which arise after a spelling survey. How shall the scorer mark the spelling of a word if the pupil arranges the letters in correct sequence but incorrectly capitalizes it? What procedure is advised when the average percentile equivalent for a sixth grade class tested at midyear is only 15?

This reviewer can see no important educa-tional purpose served by giving a standardized spelling test to pupils in grade one. For testing the spelling ability or spelling achievement of pupils above the first grade, this test cannot be strongly recommended. It is a short test, includ-ing a number of words infrequently written by children or adults, which has been normed on a fairly large population that has not been ade-quately defined.

For reviews by Walter W. Cook and Joseph C. Dewey, see 40:1311.

[200]

Gates-Russell Spelling Diagnosis Test. Grades 2–6; 1937; 9 scores: spelling words orally, word pro-nunciation, giving letters for letter sounds, spelling one syllable, spelling two syllables, word reversals, spelling attack, auditory discrimination, visual-auditory-kinaes-thetic and combined study methods; individual; 1 form; no description of normative population; $5.50 per 100; 75¢ per manual; 75¢ per specimen set; postpaid; Ar-thur I. Gates and David H. Russell; Bureau of Publi-cations, Teachers College, Columbia University. *

REFERENCES

1. RUSSELL, DAVID H. *Characteristics of Good and Poor Spellers.* Columbia University, Teachers College, Contribu-tions to Education, No. 727. New York: Bureau of Publica-tions, the College, 1937. Pp. 103. (PA 12:3186)

GEORGE SPACHE, *Head, Reading Laboratory and Clinic, University of Florida, Gainesville, Florida.*

This is a battery of nine tests offered for use in cases of spelling disability. Considered as a whole, the battery will contribute some under-standing of the role of certain factors in this type of academic disability. It will, for example, give some ideas concerning the student's meth-ods of spelling, of word analysis and blending, and of studying spelling. It will enable some ob-servation of his error tendencies, his knowledge of letter sounds, his auditory discrimination, the extent of reversals in his reading, and his success with various methods of learning new words. Such knowledge will be helpful to the teacher in understanding some of the reasons for the stu-dent's difficulties with spelling.

However, neither the research (1) which re-sulted in the publication of these tests in 1937 nor the research evidence available from other studies at that time or later justifies the use of some of the individual tests of the battery. The tests were chosen by a priori reasoning and re-tained in the published form without any critical examination of their validity or reliability. These criticisms may be justified in an examination of the separate tests of the battery.

Three tests are offered for observing a stu-dent's methods of spelling and his error tenden-cies: (*a*) spelling words orally (a spelling scale of 25 words), (*b*) spelling one syllable (10 non-sense monosyllables), and (*c*) spelling two syl-lables (8 nonsense 2-syllable words). Aside from the fact that the three are offered for the same purposes, it is very doubtful that they con-stitute an adequate sample of spelling perform-ance. Space does not permit the citation of the extensive research evidence which is relevant here; this has been summarized elsewhere.[1] There is ample evidence that a minimum of 100 misspelled words is necessary for a reliable sam-ple of error tendencies. Furthermore, the system of classifying spelling errors suggested in the battery is superficial and misleading in that it uses only gross categories of errors and fails to reveal the finer differences between the error tendencies of good and poor spellers.

A fourth test on giving letters for letter sounds attempts to measure the student's ability to give the name of the letter represented by a single let-ter sound. In effect, the purpose of this is identi-cal with that of the preceding tests. Certainly,

1 Spache, George. "Spelling Disability Correlates: I, Factors Probably Causal in Spelling Disability." *J Ed Res* 34:561–86 Ap '41. * (PA 15:3178)
Spache, George. "Spelling Disability Correlates: II, Factors That May Be Related to Spelling Disability." *J Ed Res* 35: 119–37 O '41. * (PA 16:771)

separate tests of the spelling of single sounds, two- or three-letter sounds, and five- or six-letter sounds as well as common words seem unnecessary duplication and may lead to rather artificial discriminations. Knowledge of how the student attempts to spell sounds can be easily obtained from an examination of his errors in an adequate size sample of misspelled common words of moderate difficulty, without this circuitous approach.

The authors felt that the inclusion of a test of word reversals is justified because of the marked frequency of this kind of reading error among poor readers. Russell (*1*) shows the same tendency among poor spellers. However, these facts are no proof of a causal role in disability. The phenomenon of reversals is universal among learners of all ages in the initial stages of their study of new materials. It is specific to the particular material being learned and not transferred to other activities. It spontaneously diminishes and disappears as orientation to the new forms increases. These facts imply that reversals are errors due to immaturity of orientation, not a cause of disability. Thus the test as used here has little or no relationship to reversals in spelling. Russell's own data (*1*) and that of others confirm the lack of relationship between reversals in reading and spelling.

The four remaining tests although some are of doubtful adequacy and reliability, are justified by the studies of poor spellers. A test of word pronunciation for evaluating sight word vocabulary, word analysis, and blending skills should aid in revealing the difficulties of poor spellers in these areas. A brief test of auditory discrimination should help to detect the extent of auditory inaccuracy in poor spellers. Two tests called "Learning to Spell Hard Words" and "Visual, Auditory, Kinaesthetic and Combined Study Methods" should give some indication of the pupil's own methods and his success with different learning procedures, even though the tests are very brief and based on the learning of words of unequal difficulty.

This battery of tests may be useful as the initial step in the observation of the difficulties of a poor speller. Some of the tests will reveal certain tendencies and skills, others will need to be supplemented by more adequate testing, as we have indicated. Several probably should not be used as they yield no additional information or because they bear little relationship to the pattern of difficulties present in spelling disability.

Gates-Russell Spelling Diagnosis Test

For reviews by John C. Almack and Thomas G. Foran, see 38:1159.

[201]

★**Graded Word Spelling Test.** Ages 5–15; 1950; Forms A, B; no data on reliability and validity; 3s. per 12; 4d. per single copy; 18s. 6d. per copy of *Diagnostic and Attainment Testing* ('50—see *1* below) which serves as the manual and includes full reproductions of both forms; postage extra; nontimed (15–40) minutes; Fred J. Schonell; Oliver & Boyd Ltd. *

REFERENCES

1. SCHONELL, FRED J., AND SCHONELL, F. ELEANOR. *Diagnostic and Attainment Testing: Including a Manual of Tests, Their Nature, Use, Recording and Interpretation.* Edinburgh, Scotland: Oliver & Boyd Ltd., 1950. Pp. viii, 168. *

[202]

*****Lincoln Diagnostic Spelling Test.** Grades 8–12; 1941–51; 11 scores: erroneous pronunciation, *ie-ei* rule, *y* to *i* rule, final *e* before suffix, double consonant before suffix, demons, English prefixes and suffixes, endings and bases derived from Latin, homonyms and words frequently confused, possessives-contractions-solids-hyphens, total; Forms 1 ['41], 2 ['42], 3 ['43], 4 ['44]; manual ['51]; norms: Forms 1 ('48–'50), 2 ('48–'50), 3 ('49–'51), 4 ('49–'51); 6¢ per test, postage extra; 25¢ per specimen set, postpaid; nontimed (30) minutes; A. L. Lincoln; Educational Records Bureau. *

REFERENCES

1. TOWNSEND, AGATHA. "A Study of the Lincoln Diagnostic Spelling Test," pp. 49–53. (*PA* 18:315, title only) In *1943 Achievement Testing Program in Independent Schools and Supplementary Studies.* Educational Records Bulletin, No. 38. New York: Educational Records Bureau, June 1943. Pp. xiii, 53. Paper, lithotyped. *

WALTER SCRIBNER GUILER, *Professor of Education, and Director of Remedial Education, Miami University, Oxford, Ohio.*

The chief purpose of this 100-word spelling test is "to attack three elements of diagnosis—pronunciation, enunciation, and the use of rules." Although the term "diagnostic" appears in the title, it seems to the reviewer that the test is analytical in nature, for it aims to identify phases of spelling which cause difficulty.

The content of the test was derived chiefly from two sources: (*a*) Lester's list of misspellings gathered from College Entrance Examination Board English examination papers and (*b*) Simmons and Bixler's *The New Standard High School Spelling Scale.* The manual states that some words were derived from Jones's "One Hundred Spelling Demons" and that others were "added in order to provide a test of fairly advanced difficulty." No mention is made of the source of the added words. Neither does the manual provide any data showing the degree of difficulty and familiarity of the added words or of the words derived from the English examination papers. In the absence of such data, the reviewer checked Form 1 of the test with Horn's *A Basic Writing Vocabulary* and found that 25 of the 100 words are beyond the 5,000 and that 11 are beyond the 10,000 words in most common use. These findings lead one to question the curricular validity of the test.

No norms based on pupil performance in public schools are available; however, percentile rank norms based on the records of private school pupils have been established both for part and total scores. No mention is made of the geographical distribution of the schools that were used in establishing the norms.

In spite of its limitations, the test possesses many good features. It represents a praiseworthy effort to discover some of the causes of spelling deficiency. Then, too, the manual provides timely suggestions for a remedial program based on the test results.

GEORGE SPACHE, *Head of the Reading Laboratory and Clinic, University of Florida, Gainesville, Florida.*

This test represents an attempt to evaluate the spelling performances of secondary school pupils. The 100 test words are divided into subgroups according to the spelling rules or conventions governing their spelling. A few in which mispronunciation, confusion of homonyms, or word elements such as prefixes appear significant are included. This use of rules is a convenient system for classifying words for testing and, perhaps, for teaching procedures. It is doubtful, however, that the method really samples error tendencies or reveals probable causes of misspelling. It ignores the real bases of spelling disability, which lie in study methods, auditory discrimination, phonic skills, handwriting, and other common factors.

Selection of the test words was made largely on the basis of frequency of misspelling. Little attention was paid to the studies of actual errors within the test words. This results in the use of test words in which the commonest and most frequent misspellings bear no relationship to their placement in subgroups in the test. For example, in Form I, Item 7, *awful,* is categorized as an example of the spelling of the suffix, *ful.* Research studies of actual misspellings of this word show that about 88 per cent of the errors occur on the *w.* Thus this item is very unlikely to function in the manner claimed for it.

Since the method of selection of test items may often result in misspellings of other types than those expected by the author, the teacher using the test should certainly be given instructions in classifying the actual errors in some meaningful and diagnostic system. Or, at least, the items should be chosen so that they will operate within the classification system suggested in the test.

This faulty method of item selection is probably responsible for the relatively poor results found in the statistical analyses cited by the author. The reliability of the entire test is apparently satisfactory for discrimination of the general spelling levels of individuals. However, the low reliabilities of the subscores indicates the tests are inadequate for the discrimination of types of errors or for comparisons among individual pupils. On some of the subscores, class averages might conceivably be used for comparative purposes. Despite the probable lack of discriminatory value in the subscores, the author offers norms for these as well as for the total scores on all four forms of the test. These norms are based on use of the test in private schools in grades 8–12. The value of these norms for public school use remains to be demonstrated.

The tests are administered by the modified list method in which each test item is inserted in an illustrative sentence. These sentences are printed on the test blank in order to standardize the administrative procedure. Research studies indicate that this is the most valid type of spelling test for assessing general performance.

It is apparent that these tests will serve certain useful purposes in evaluating spelling abilities. They will indicate with a high degree of accuracy the grade level of spelling ability of individuals. They may be used to determine class tendencies to observe certain spelling conventions. These class performances might then be used in planning group instruction in these same conventions. The tests will reveal what words from the test list the pupils misspell, and the correct spelling of these might then be taught to the group if the words are deemed essential for the spelling curriculum.

At the same time, the tests will not reveal with any great degree of accuracy why the pupils misspell, or the error tendencies of individuals. They will not indicate the knowledge or use of spelling rules by individuals or permit comparisons among the individual pupils in types of errors. Their greatest service to the teacher lies in their indications of group needs and of possible emphases in the spelling curriculum.

Lincoln Diagnostic Spelling Test

[203]

*Lincoln Intermediate Spelling Test. Grades 5–8; 1947–51; 11 scores: erroneous pronunciation-number of syllables, *ie-ei* rule, *y* to *i* rule, final *e* before suffix, double consonant before suffix, demons, English prefixes and suffixes, erroneous pronunciation-phonic quality of syllables, homonyms and words frequently confused, possessives-contractions-solids-hyphens, total; Forms A ['47], B ['48], C ['48], D ['49]; no norms for part scores of Forms B, C, D; manual ['51]; norms: Forms A ('51), B ('50), C ('50), D ('51); 6¢ per test, postage extra; 25¢ per specimen set, postpaid; nontimed (30) minutes; A. L. Lincoln; Educational Records Bureau. *

REFERENCES

1. TOWNSEND, AGATHA. "A Report on the Use of the Lincoln Intermediate Spelling Test," pp. 40–8. (*PA* 22:3648) In *1947 Fall Testing Program in Independent Schools and Supplementary Studies*. Foreword by Ben D. Wood. Educational Records Bulletin, No. 49. New York: Educational Records Bureau, February 1948. Pp. xii, 69. Paper, lithotyped. Out of print. *

WALTER SCRIBNER GUILER, *Professor of Education, and Director of Remedial Education, Miami University, Oxford, Ohio.*

This 100-word spelling test is similar in structure and in purpose to the *Lincoln Diagnostic Spelling Test.* It is designed to identify phases of spelling in which pupils encounter difficulty; it emphasizes pronunciation and the use of rules. The words are arranged in approximate order of difficulty, a feature which should enhance the validity of the test. The method employed in administering the test is the word-used-in-sentence list dictation.

The manual states that the principal sources of the selection of the words were Betts's *Spelling Vocabulary Study,* Gates's *A List of Spelling Difficulties,* and the *New York State Spelling List;* however, no mention is made of the other sources that were used. The curricular validity of the test is open to question because of the sources from which the words were selected. When there is available such a word list as Rinsland's *A Basic Vocabulary of Elementary School Children,* based on a wide sampling of children's own writings, one wonders why the author should select words for an elementary school spelling test from such sources as Betts's compilation of words from 17 spelling books and from the New York State list, the sources for which are unknown.

No data are presented showing the degree of familiarity of the test words. On checking Form I of the test with Horn's *A Basic Writing Vocabulary,* the reviewer found that 14 of the 100 words are beyond the 5,000 and that 3 words are beyond the 10,000 most commonly used words. It would be difficult to justify the inclusion of words above the 3rd thousand and certainly words above the 4th thousand in a test designed for use in the upper grades of the elementary school.

There is a serious question as to whether a test designed for use in the upper level of the elementary school should cover four school grades. Children in these grades differ widely in maturity. For this reason, a test should be designed for use in one or, at most, two school grades. Norms are available for private school pupils; however, no norms exist for public school pupils. Since the test was designed as an aid to teaching rather than as a means of selecting best spellers, the lack of norms of the latter type is not a serious limitation.

Although certain shortcomings in the test have been cited, the reviewer feels that the author has produced a very useful measuring instrument and that our profession is greatly indebted to him for constructing a type of test designed to reveal some of the major causes of spelling deficiency.

GEORGE SPACHE, *Head of the Reading Laboratory and Clinic, University of Florida, Gainesville, Florida.*

This test is an effort to evaluate the spelling performances of elementary school pupils. It consists of 100 test words commonly taught in the intermediate grades. These test words are divided into ten subgroups according to the spelling rules or conventions governing their spelling. Each of four subgroups presumably measures knowledge of a particular spelling rule, while the remaining subgroups give opportunity for the demonstration of such confusion as mispronunciation, spelling demons, homonyms, etc. This technique of grouping words according to the spelling rules they exemplify, or according to some of the elements that may contribute to misspelling is a very convenient device for classifying words for testing and, perhaps, for teaching procedures. It is doubtful, however, that the method really samples error tendencies or reveals probable causes of misspelling unless there is considerable further study of individual pupils. Furthermore, such an approach, while highly logical, would fail to reveal some of the very common bases of spelling disability. There is considerable evidence to show that the more important causes of spelling disability lie in such areas as study methods, auditory discrimination, phonic skills, handwriting, etc. Unfortunately, these primary causes of difficulty are not revealed by such a formal approach to the study of misspellings.

Another faulty assumption is present in the nature of the selection of the test words. These words were chosen largely on the basis of frequency of misspelling. Little or no attention was paid to the many research studies of the actual errors made in spelling the test words. This results in the use of some test words in which the commonest and most frequent misspellings bear no relationship to their placement in the various subgroups in the test. For example, in Form A of the Intermediate test, Item 87, *annually,* is categorized as an example of the misspelling of certain prefixes and suffixes. The research studies of actual misspellings of this word show that almost 70 per cent of the errors occur in the omission of the double *n*. Thus, this item is not likely to function in a manner claimed for it in the spelling test.

The teacher using this test will often find that misspellings are of other types than those expected by the author. Since this is the case, he should be given instruction in classifying the actual errors in some meaningful and diagnostic system. The author neither gives such instructions for the teacher nor suggests how errors are to be interpreted when they do not fall within the narrow confines of each subgroup or type. In the statistical analyses that have been made of the test, there appears to be little justification for the division into part scores. The high intercorrelations of the subscores and their low reliabilities indicate that the subgroups are probably not measuring distinctly different spelling situations. Moreover, these results indicate that the part scores are inadequate for the discrimination of types of errors or for comparisons among individual pupils. The reliability of the entire test, on the other hand, is apparently satisfactory for discrimination of the general spelling levels of individuals. Norms based on the doubtful part scores as well as on the total scores are available for grades 5–8 in private schools.

Despite these adverse criticisms, there are several practical uses for this spelling test. It may be employed with a high degree of accuracy to indicate the grade level of spelling ability of individuals. It may be used to determine group or class tendencies to observe certain spelling conventions. These group performances might then be used in planning group instruction in these same conventions. The test will reveal what words from the test list the pupils misspell, and then the correct spelling of these might be taught to the group if the words are deemed essential for the spelling curriculum. At the same time, however, the test will not reveal with any great degree of accuracy details as to why the pupils misspell, or as to the error tendencies of individuals. It will not indicate the knowledge or use of spelling rules by individuals or permit comparisons among the individual pupils in the types of errors they commit. The greatest value of the test to the teacher lies in its indications of group needs and in its desirable emphases in the spelling curriculum.

[204]

★**Morgan Spelling Test for Business and Industry.** Applicants for stenographic and secretarial positions; 1948; Forms A, B; no data on reliability and validity; manual ['48]; $2.50 per 25; 50¢ per specimen set; sample test free to qualified test users; cash orders postpaid; 20(25) minutes; Antonia Morgan and William J. Morgan; Aptitude Associates. *

HAROLD H. BIXLER, *Professor of Education, Western Carolina Teachers College, Cullowhee, North Carolina.*

DESCRIPTION. This test is designed for use in employment or guidance offices and in high school commercial classes where only a short time is available for testing. In the left-hand column will be found a list of 75 words, some correct and some misspelled. If a word is not spelled correctly, the correct spelling is to be written on the line opposite. This test, therefore, is self-administering.

VALIDITY. The authors report no data on validity, but inspection of the items reveals that they include such words as "all right," "Wednesday," and "recommend" as well as a few business terms, such as "correspondent," "receipt," and "merchandise." It is unfortunate that all words are printed with initial capital letters. This presents an unusual situation and may well affect the validity of the results.

RELIABILITY. No data are reported on reliability, but the test includes 75 items. It should, therefore, be fairly reliable.

USABILITY. Two kinds of norms are reported. A percentile table is given for a random sample of 421 office workers, including file clerks, typists, secretaries, stenographers, and administrative assistants. It would have been more helpful if stenographers and secretaries could have been reported separately. In addition, a table for interpretation is given, showing scores judged to be needed for stenographers classified as superior, average, and below average. Obviously, norms are based on a very small number of cases in comparison with other standardized tests on the market. Furthermore, no indication is given to show how the sample was selected.

SUMMARY. This test may be of some value to employers who wish to use a self-administering type of test for screening applicants. No data are available to prove that the two forms are equivalent. Hence, prospective users would be well advised to use one of the standard tests in spelling rather than this instrument.

[205]
Morrison-McCall Spelling Scale. Grades 2–8; 1923; 1 form; no data on reliability; 25¢ per scale (only one copy needed per class), postage extra; nontimed (15) minutes; J. Cayce Morrison and William A. McCall; World Book Co. *

REFERENCES
1. KENNEY, R. A. "Spelling Evaluation With Standardized Tests." *El Sch J* 46:574–8 Je '46. *
2. KYTE, GEORGE C. "When Spelling Has Been Mastered in the Elementary School." *J Ed Res* 42:47–53 S '48. * (PA 23:2892)

ANTON THOMPSON, *Supervisor of Research, Long Beach Public Schools, Long Beach, California.*

This 1923 spelling scale is still being marketed. Printed in booklet form, it consists of a manual of directions and eight word lists of equivalent average difficulty. All lists are 50 words in length. Each list contains words which range in difficulty from words judged easy enough for primary grade pupils to words considered suitable for testing capable junior high school pupils. A complete list is used in testing any grade from 2 through 8. A teacher having pupils of more than one grade classification in her classroom can test them simultaneously.

The testing procedure is familiar: the teacher pronounces a word, uses it in a sentence, repeats the word, and the pupils write the word. A pupil's score is interpreted by referring to the manual which provides data for converting the raw score to a T score, a G score (grade status), a C score (midyear classification in spelling), a B score (brightness in spelling), and a spelling age.

Words in this scale were selected from the *Buckingham Extension of the Ayres Spelling Scale.* Only words that were among the first 5,000 in Thorndike's original *Teacher's Word Book* were included. The reviewer checked one of the lists against Horn's list of 10,000 words most commonly written by adults,[1] and the Rins-

land list based upon children's writings.[2] The Horn and Rinsland studies were, of course, unavailable at the time this scale was constructed. Of the 50 words analyzed, 96 per cent were among the first 5,000 on Horn's list and 78 per cent were among the first 5,000 words which Rinsland's research shows are used by eighth grade pupils. This lends support to the conclusion that the test words are, for the most part, those commonly used in the writing of adults and upper grade children.

The manual provides explicit directions for administering, scoring, and recording the results of the test. The tables of norms are based on scores from 57,331 pupils in the rural and village schools of New York State. The norm group included about 8,000 pupils in each grade from 2 through 8, and about 1,000 ninth graders.

Balanced against the scale's desirable features are several deficiencies. Many lower grade pupils will be disturbed when given a wide range test that includes words considered difficult for junior high school students. To make matters worse, the manual sternly forbids any "unstandardized introductory remarks" through which a skilled tester might hope to build up the courage of the younger pupils. The reviewer believes the authors were somewhat naive when they wrote these lines: "If, *at the close* of the test, younger pupils should seem bewildered and confused, the examiner should smilingly encourage them by explaining that he didn't expect them to spell all the words. He should endeavor to close the test period leaving the children uniformly happy."

Although the principal reason for the examiner's reading a sentence containing a test word is to help pupils understand the word, some of the sentences offer little assistance. Illustrative of such sentences are these: "There is little *difference.*" "I am not *particular.*"

The manual provides no statistical data concerning the test's reliability. Another major fault is the lack of discussion of the possible uses of the test results.

Five pages of the manual are devoted to explaining how the teacher can convert pupils' raw scores to T scores, B scores, and other recommended units. Only those teachers who have had recent or extensive training in statistics will understand such sections as the following: "Each

---

1 Horn, Ernest. *A Basic Writing Vocabulary: 10,000 Words Most Commonly Used in Writing.* University of Iowa Mono-

graphs in Education, Series 1, No. 4. Iowa City, Iowa: College of Education, University of Iowa, 1926. Pp. 225. Paper. *
2 Rinsland, Henry D. *A Basic Vocabulary of Elementary School Children.* New York: Macmillan Co., 1945. Pp. 636.

10 units of T-score represent 1 SD (standard deviation) of distribution of 12-year-olds. Any pupil or class, for example, whose Ts is 70 has an ability that is 20 T (or 2 SD) above the mean ability of 12-year-olds."

Because the same words are used in testing pupils widely separated in grade classification, the norms reflect the sharp scaling made necessary. This places great emphasis upon the correct spelling of a single test word. Thus, a pupil correctly spelling 41 words earns a grade status of 8.0 while a pupil spelling two more words correctly earns a grade status of 8.8.

A serious weakness of the norms for most educational purposes is the fact that they are based upon rural and village pupils of one state, tested more than a quarter century ago. Comparison of the spelling ability of an urban school of the 1950's with the norm group might be interesting as a research project; however, the usual purposes for which standardized tests are given require a comparison of scores with those earned by a standardization group with similar background and preparation.

This test has undoubtedly been a valuable measuring instrument. In certain "then and now" comparisons, it may still have value although the reviewer would not recommend its use in the lower grades. For ordinary educational purposes, this scale, normed on rural and village pupils tested before 1923 in but one state, has limited usefulness.

[206]
*The New Standard High School Spelling Scale.
Grades 7–12; 1925–49; a 66–page book ('49) consisting of 2,560 words with difficulty values in each of grades 9–12; $1.32 per copy, postage extra; Ernest P. Simmons and Harold H. Bixler; Turner E. Smith & Co. *

[207]
★Rich-Engelson Spelling Test. Grades 9–13; 1947; IBM; Forms A, B; mimeographed manual; $1.05 per 25; 20¢ per specimen set; postpaid; separate answer sheets may be used; 75¢ per 25 IBM answer sheets; 25¢ per stencil for scoring answer sheets; postage extra; 30(35) minutes; Vernita Rich, Ieleen Engelson, and H. E. Schrammel; Bureau of Educational Measurements, Kansas State Teachers College of Emporia. *

HENRY D. RINSLAND, *Professor of Education, The University of Oklahoma, Norman, Oklahoma.*

The validity of this spelling test is in serious question because of (a) the age of the research on which the test is based—namely, the Buckingham Extension (1918) of the Ayres Spelling Scale (1915), the Iowa Spelling Scales (Anderson s research, 1921), and the Thorndike Word List (1921, 1931, or 1944—which one of the three Thorndike lists was used, the authors do not state) ; and (b) the simple fact that none of this research provides information concerning the specific spelling needs of high school students and college freshmen. The Ayres, Buckingham, and Iowa scales are measures of the achievement of elementary school children; all Thorndike lists are made up of words from the writing of word-talented adults. Between these two there is an unknown gap. It might as well be admitted that there are at present no facts upon which to build a valid spelling scale for the grades for which this test is intended.

The test is in the form of a list of 150 words, some correctly and some incorrectly spelled. The student is to decide for each word whether the spelling is right or wrong. Is successful accomplishment on a test of this type an indication of spelling or proofreading ability?

With validity so seriously questioned, reliabilities of from .76 to .92 are not particularly reassuring; nor do norms based on 8,477 cases provide any accurate representation of what the spelling achievement of high school students and college freshmen should be.

[208]
★Spelling and Vocabulary: Every Pupil Test. Grades 3–6; 1948–51; new form usually published each April and December; form April 1951; no data on reliability and validity; no manual; norms ('51); 2½¢ per test; 1¢ per answer key; postpaid; 40(45) minutes; Ohio Scholarship Tests, Ohio State Department of Education. *

[209]
★Spelling Errors Test. Grades 2–4, 5–6, 7–8; 1942–52; 13 scores: silent letter omission, sounded letter omission, doubled letter omission, addition by doubling, single letter addition, transposition, phonetic substitution-vowel, phonetic substitution-consonant, phonetic substitution-syllable, phonetic substitution-word, non-phonetic substitution-vowel, non-phonetic substitution-consonant, unrecognizable; 3 levels; 1 form ['42]; mimeographed; no data on reliability; [revised] manual ['52]; distribution gratis; nontimed (30–40) minutes; George D. Spache; Reading Laboratory and Clinic, University College, University of Florida. *

[210]
★Spelling: Seven Plus Assessment: Northumberland Series. Ages 7–8; 1951; for complete battery, see 24; 1 form ['51]; no data on reliability; manual ['51]; 7s. 6d. per 25; 6d. per single copy; 1s. per manual; 2s. 6d. per specimen set (includes the other 2 tests in the series); postage extra; (60) minutes; C. M. Lambert; University of London Press Ltd. *

For a review of the complete battery by Stanley D. Nisbet, see 24.

Spelling: Seven Plus Assessment

[211]

★Spelling Test for Clerical Workers. Stenographic applicants and high school; 1947; Forms A, B; manual ['47]; $2 per 25, postage extra; 50¢ per specimen set, postpaid; nontimed (15–20) minutes; Jay L. Otis, David J. Chesler, and Irene Salmi; Personnel Research Institute, Western Reserve University. *

HAROLD H. BIXLER, *Professor of Education, Western Carolina Teachers College, Cullowhee, North Carolina.*

Since this is a self-administering test, it is especially adapted for use in employment and guidance offices. The test is organized in three columns: (*a*) how word sounds, (*b*) definition, (*c*) correct spelling. The words are to be written in the third column. Each form includes 73 items.

The authors do not report the basis for the selection of the test items other than the statement that the test consists of "commonly misspelled business words." They do report correlations ranging from .64 to .82 with the spelling sections of the *Cooperative English Test* and the *Progressive Language Test*. These correlations give some indication of the validity of the test. Inspection of the items reveals that the words include both commonly used words and business terms.

Reliability of the test is satisfactory, as shown by correlations between the two forms of .96 and .90, respectively. Usability of the test may be judged by the fact that it may be taken by an individual on a self-administering basis, or it may be given to a group. Less than one class period is required.

Norms, in terms of deciles, are reported for high school graduates applying for admission to college and for employed clerical workers. These norms are based on 196 and 57 cases, respectively. Obviously, these numbers of cases are rather small for satisfactory norms. The manual gives no indication as to how these cases were chosen nor do the authors report the types of clerical jobs in which the workers were employed. The difficulty of the test may be judged by the fact that the means (norms) are 59.2 and 63.7 for the high school graduates and clerical workers, respectively, as compared with a perfect score of 73.

The authors have used a clever idea, phonetic spelling, as the basis for this test. It is to be hoped that they will assemble additional data on such groups as high school graduates applying for stenographic jobs, thus developing more usable and more dependable norms.

[212]

Traxler High School Spelling Test. Grades 9–12; 1937–40; Forms 1 ['37], 2 ['37], 3 ['39]; mimeographed manual ['37]; norms: Form 1 ('40), Form 2 ('38), Form 3 ('39); 4¢ per test; 25¢ per specimen set; postage extra; (20) minutes; Arthur E. Traxler; Educational Records Bureau. *

HENRY D. RINSLAND, *Professor of Education, The University of Oklahoma, Norman, Oklahoma.*

This spelling test is based on the old research of Ayres (1915), Buckingham (1918), and Horn (1926). Recent research has shown that spelling lists for the elementary grades based on this older research bear little relation to the vocabulary that children in those grades actually use. Accordingly, high school spelling lists based on the same research are also suspect. Until information comparable to that presented in Rinsland's *Basic Vocabulary of Elementary School Children* [1] has been secured for high school pupils, there is no way of knowing whether this test or any other spelling test adequately samples "the active vocabulary of high school pupils."

Apart from this fundamental consideration, the *Traxler High School Spelling Test* gives evidence of having been carefully planned and constructed. The test is designed to be taken on spelling sheets on which are printed illustrative sentences. The spelling word is pronounced by the examiner; and the pupil reads the illustrative sentence and then writes the word in the blank provided. This form of presentation appears to be superior to that which requires only simple recognition of right and wrong spelling. Forms 1 and 2 of the test are directly comparable in difficulty; Form 3 was purposely prepared to be more difficult than the first two forms.

Reliability coefficients for the test, secured by correlating the scores of 393 public high school pupils on Forms 1 and 2, range from .91 to .95. Percentile norms are provided for each of the three forms. These are based on scores obtained by several hundred independent school pupils in three successive programs of the Educational Records Bureau, in each of which a different form of the test was administered.

1 Rinsland, Henry D. *Basic Vocabulary of Elementary School Children.* New York: Macmillan Co., 1945. Pp. 636.

VOCABULARY

[213]

*Cooperative Vocabulary Test. Grades 7–16; 1940–51; IBM; Forms Q ('40), Z ('49); Forms R, Y, QS, RS, YS, ZS out of print; manual ('40); general Cooperative manual ('51); norms ['40]; $2.25 per 25; 50¢ per specimen set, postpaid; separate answer sheets may be used; 90¢ per 25 IBM answer sheets; 30¢ per set of stencils for machine scoring of answer sheets; cash orders postpaid; 30(35) minutes; Frederick B. Davis, F. S. Beers (Q), D. G. Paterson (Q), Mary Willis (Q), and Charlotte Croon Davis (Z); Cooperative Test Division, Educational Testing Service. *

REFERENCES

1. COOPERATIVE TEST SERVICE. *The Cooperative Vocabulary Test: Information Concerning Its Construction, Interpretation and Use.* New York: Cooperative Test Service, 1940. Pp. 2. Paper. *
2. SIMPSON, R. G. "The Vocabulary Sections of the Cooperative English Tests at the Higher Levels of Difficulty." *J Ed Psychol* 34:142–51 Mr '43. * (*PA* 18:311)
3. DAVIS, FREDERICK B. "The Interpretation of Frequency Ratings Obtained From 'The Teachers Word Book.'" *J Ed Psychol* 35:169–74 Mr '44. * (*PA* 18:2957)
4. MOCK, SANFORD J. "Cooperative Vocabulary Test, Form R, CI604A, CI605A," pp. 53–6. In *Printed Classification Tests.* Edited by J. P. Guilford with the assistance of John I. Lacey. Army Air Forces Aviation Psychology Program Research Reports, Report No. 5. Washington, D.C.: U.S. Government Printing Office, 1947. Pp. xi, 919. * (*PA* 22:4145)

For reviews by Edgar Dale and Henry D. Rinsland of Forms Q, R, QS, and RS, see 3:160.

[214]

*General Vocabulary: Iowa Tests of Educational Development, Test 8. Grades 9–13; 1942–51 (first published as a separate in 1951); for complete battery, see 17; Form Y-2 ('51—same as 1949 edition); manual ('51); general manual ('51); $3.75 per 25; separate answer pads or answer sheets must be used; $1.95 per 25 answer pads; $3 per 100 IBM answer sheets; 50¢ per scoring stencil; $2.50 per 25 first semester ('46) or second semester ('48) profiles for any one of grades 9–12; $1 per 25 self-interpreting profiles for students ('51); 25¢ per school summary report ('44); 4¢ per pupil score sheet ('48); 50¢ per specimen set; cash orders postpaid; 22(27) minutes; edited by E. F. Lindquist; K. W. Vaughn; Science Research Associates, Inc. *

For a review by Eric F. Gardner of the complete battery, see· 17; for reviews by Henry Chauncey, Gustav J. Froehlich, and Lavone A. Hanna of Forms X-1 and Y-1 of the complete battery, see 3:12.

[215]

★Holborn Vocabulary Test for Young Children. Ages 3.5–8.5; 1944–49; reprinted in 1949 from *The Language and Mental Development of Children* (see 1 below); individual; no data on reliability and validity; 1 form; 1s. per examiner's manual, postage extra; no other materials needed; (40–50) minutes; A. F. Watts; George G. Harrap & Co. Ltd. *

REFERENCES

1. WATTS, A. F. *The Language and Mental Development of Children,* pp. 48–51, 280–3. London: George G. Harrap & Co.
Ltd., 1944. Pp. 354. (Boston, Mass.: D.C. Heath & Co., [1947]. *) (*PA* 21:4427)

C. M. FLEMING, *Reader in Education, University of London, London, England.*

This test can best be evaluated if one thinks of it as an extract from the author's *The Language and Mental Development of Children* (*1*) and realises that its separate publication seems to have been intended to stimulate the interest of teachers in the study of pupils rather than to provide psychologists with a measuring instrument whose reliability has been fully established by statistical devices. On this account, it is the more to be regretted that the test is not prefaced by some discussion of the problems involved in any estimation of vocabulary and by an exposition of the importance for a teacher to understand the range of word and phrase comprehension expected from pupils ages 3–8. The facts should have been mentioned that the test was devised in the light of evidence obtained from both English and American researches and that the 100 words to be supplied as answers are fairly evenly spread through a list of the 6,000 most common English words (with specific reference to Thorndike's *Teacher's Word Book*). Information might also have been given as to the number of pupils in each age group in the sample on which the vocabulary growth curve given in the test booklet was based.

The test is, however, an interesting one. The contents are well balanced; they include simple descriptions of face and features and actions with hands and fingers, household articles, sounds, fabrics, information as to meals, quantities, occupations, the street, and children's games. While it cannot yet be recommended as a fully standardised test, it does provide enterprising teachers with a somewhat formalised means of commencing the study of their pupils.

[216]

*Michigan Vocabulary Profile Test. Grades 9–16 and adults; 1937–49; 9 scores: human relations, commerce, government, physical sciences, biological sciences, mathematics, fine arts, sports, total; IBM; Forms AM ('49—same as test copyrighted in 1939 except for norms), BM ('49—same as test copyrighted in 1939 except for norms); revised manual ('49); $2.25 per 25; 35¢ per specimen set, postpaid; separate answer sheets may be used: $1 per 25 IBM answer sheets; 40¢ per set of stencils for machine scoring of answer sheets; postage extra; nontimed (50–60) minutes; Edward B. Greene; World Book Co. *

REFERENCES

1–2. See 40:1320.
3–8. See 3:166.
9. HUMBER, WILBUR J. "The Relationship Between Read-

ing Efficiency and Academic Success in Selected University Curricula." *J Ed Psychol* 35:17–26 Ja '44. * (*PA* 18:2581)
10. HALL, WILLIAM E., AND ROBINSON, FRANCIS P. "An Analytical Approach to the Study of Reading Skills." *J Ed Psychol* 36:429–42 O '45. * (*PA* 20:1680)
11. ABT, LAWRENCE EDWIN. "A Test Battery for Selecting Technical Magazine Editors." *Personnel Psychol* 2:75–91 sp '49. * (*PA* 23:5099)
12. EDMONSON, LAWRENCE DAVIS. *Comparative Analyses of a Test Battery Used for the Prediction of Scholastic Success at the University of Missouri.* Doctor's thesis, University of Missouri (Columbia, Mo.), 1949. Abstract: *Microfilm Abstracts* 9:64–6 no 3 '50. (*PA* 24:4846, title only)
13. SUPER, DONALD E. *Appraising Vocational Fitness By Means of Psychological Tests*, pp. 474–6. New York: Harper & Brothers, 1949. Pp. xxiii, 727. $5.00. * (*PA* 24:2130)
14. GREENE, EDWARD B. "The Michigan Vocabulary Profile Test, After Ten Years." *Ed & Psychol Meas* 11:208–11 su '51. * (*PA* 26:2749)
15. LEVIN, JANICE, AND STACEY, CHALMERS L. "Awareness of Vocabulary Size: Its Relation to Class Standing and Sex Differences." *J Ed Psychol* 42:174–84 Mr '51. * (*PA* 25:7652)

DAVID SEGEL, *Specialist in Tests and Measurements, Office of Education, Federal Security Agency, Washington, D.C.*

This test is designed primarily to differentiate vocabulary ability as among eight different fields: human relations, commerce, government, physical sciences, biological sciences, mathematics, fine arts, and sports. This edition (1949) of the test is the same as the earlier edition but the manual has been revised to include additional norms and new data bearing on the validity of the test. The author sets up three problems to the solution of which he thinks the test results contribute specifically. This reviewer will consider the test in relation to these three problems.

The first problem to which the author believes the test contributes a solution is that of the growth and retention of specific information connected with specific training. As evidence for this, the author quotes a study of test scores for beginning students and for graduates of a nurses training course which shows that the vocabulary in science and especially for biological science is increased substantially by such a course. That the vocabulary in the various areas of the test is increased with training in related subject areas seems a reasonable result, and the test results may well be used in studies of the learning of individuals in various areas.

The second problem claimed to be solved by this test is the extent to which technical knowledge is related to success in a particular field. For this the manual cites norms showing that the persons in certain occupational areas have substantially higher norms in the vocabularies related to these occupations. More definite data showing the relation of certain parts of the vocabulary test to specific occupational areas or marks in certain subjects should be brought together to prove the point.

The third problem to which the author believes the test contributes is the prediction of success in a particular educational field. The normative data given in the manual do not have a bearing on the problem since the presence of a higher vocabulary score in an area related to that in which the pupil is specializing or in an occupation in which he is engaged is not a predictive situation. The higher vocabulary score in an area can be explained by the reasonable assumption that the student learned the vocabulary on the job. In fact, the author gives evidence to this effect in the manual when he shows that the biological vocabulary score increases substantially when trainees are passing through the nurses training course.

As indirect evidence on this point, the intercorrelations among the subtests may be considered. These intercorrelations are all below .55 and several are zero or practically zero. The author says in this connection, "It is evident that these figures indicate the presence of a number of fairly well isolated factors." These intercorrelations were obtained from students (sophomores in college) who were already beginning to specialize in subject areas. The point that the lack of correlation among the vocabulary score areas shows well isolated factors seems not to be well taken since the differences are those which are in large part attained through differences in learnings in the subject areas themselves.

The *Michigan Vocabulary Profile Test* is a well constructed test of vocabulary or of one type of verbal ability. It may be used, therefore, with assurance in aiding the prediction of college success in general and for educational experiments in which a vocabulary score is of value. Its use as a differential instrument—to predict success in various subject fields and occupations—should be on an experimental basis. Not enough data have been gathered and analyzed as yet to establish its validity in this particular respect.

For a review by Joseph E. King, see 3:166; for a review by Herbert A. Landry and an excerpt from a review, see 40:1320; for reviews by Richard Ledgerwood, John M. Stalnaker, M. R. Trabue, and Arthur E. Traxler of an earlier edition, see 38:1171.

[217]

★Test of Literary Essentials. Grades 10–12; 1938; 1 form; no data on reliability and validity; no manual; $1.75 per 25, postpaid; specimen set not available; nontimed (35–45) minutes; Elmer R. Smith; Turner E. Smith & Co. *

[218]

*Word Dexterity Test. Grades 7–16; 1942–50; IBM; Form A ('42); mimeographed manual ('50)—reproduced in part from 3:170(2); $2 per 25; 100 or more, 6½¢ each; 25¢ per specimen set; postpaid; separate answer sheets (IBM Form ITS 1100 A 444) may be used; IBM answer sheets must be purchased directly from the International Business Machines Corporation; nontimed (40–45) minutes; Shailer Peterson; the Author, 222 East Superior St., Chicago 11, Ill. *

REFERENCES

1–2. See 3:170.

REPRINTED FROM *The Fifth Mental Measurements Yearbook*

ENGLISH — FIFTH MMY

REVIEWS BY *Janet G. Afflerbach, M. A. Brimer, Robert S. Cathcart, John C. Daniels, Charlotte Croon Davis, Clarence Derrick, John S. Diekhoff, Jerome E. Doppelt, Reginald Edwards, Leonard S. Feldt, James A. Fitzgerald, J. Raymond Gerberich, Neil Gourlay, A. N. Hieronymus, Worth R. Jones, Gerald V. Lannholm, Constance M. McCullough, Richard A. Meade, Bernadine Meyer, John Nisbet, Stanley Nisbet, Osmond E. Palmer, Robert C. Pooley, Winifred L. Post, Roger A. Richards, J. A. Richardson, S. C. Richardson, Holland Roberts, Louise B. Scott, Geraldine Spaulding, John M. Stalnaker, Ruth Strickland, Cleveland A. Thomas, M. J. Want-man, D. K. Wheeler, and Louis C. Zahner.*

[173]

A.C.E.R. English Usage Tests. Ages 10–13.0; 1951; Form C ['46]; 2 parts: word usage, sentences; 3s. per 10 tests of either part; 1s. per scoring key; 4s. 9d. per manual ['50]; 6s. 3d. per specimen set; postpaid within Australia; 30(40) minutes; Australian Council for Educational Research. *

J. A. RICHARDSON, *Professor of Special Education, The University of British Columbia, Vancouver, British Columbia, Canada.*

Two aspects only of English usage are covered by these tests—familiarity with certain basic rules of grammar and word usage (Part 1) and recognition of correct or most effective sentence structure (Part 2). No attempt is made to assess skill in the use of vocabulary or punctuation or skill in free expression in composition. These are at least equally important aspects of English usage.

The two parts have limited value. The items of the first are classified under nine diagnostic categories. This part indicates the pupil's recognition knowledge, not the extent to which he will actually use correct word and grammar forms in practice. Correlations of .48 and .74 are given as evidence of the degree of correspondence between scores on this subtest and functional usage, the criterion being the school marks in formal grammar of two groups of sixth grade children. Quite apart from the fact that the criterion (as thus baldly stated) is inadequate, no attempt is made to interpret, for the teacher for whose use the test is intended, the significance of the correlational figures.

The same criticism is applicable to Part 2, Sentences, save that here the position is worse inasmuch as no indication at all is given of the correspondence between test success and effective written or oral expression. The item type used in this subtest—selection of the correct or most effective sentence structure from four alternative sentences—suggests that such correspondence would be low. In the writer's opinion, a much more effective test of knowledge of sentence structure is that used in the *Schonell Diagnostic English Tests* in which the testee is required himself to join given simple sentences together into a single complex sentence.

It follows from what has been written that the statistical information given on the tests is in some respects most inadequate. There are no validity figures apart from the correlations mentioned. One assumes that content validity is claimed from the manual statement (regarding the word usage test) that the items chosen "are based mostly upon errors made in children's speech and writing" and "have been shown by preliminary item analyses to discriminate between children who use words and phrases correctly and those who do not." However, no supporting figures are given. Content validity is not mentioned with respect to the sentence test. Test score stability is indicated by test-retest correlations and probable errors for one grade level only; no evidence is presented, nor is any available from the test constructors, on internal consistency. Although the subtests are both timed, there is no comment on the effects, if any, of the time limit on test performance.

On the credit side, the *English Usage Tests* were standardized, with rigorous regard for accepted sampling procedures, on 30,000 children from nearly 600 Australian schools. Maximum information is provided for the teacher with grade norms and age norms by sex for each Australian state in the form of scale scores and centile ranks. Interpretation of these statistics is adequate. Layout of tests and manuals is a model of clarity.

Despite these commendable points, the tests appear to have only limited practical value. They attempt assessment of only two aspects of English usage, ignoring others at least as important. Even within their limited coverage, they indicate only the pupil's recognition knowledge, not necessarily the extent to which he himself uses the correct English forms in his writing. The teacher, wanting to assess the "English usage ability" of his class, should use these tests, if at all, with the greatest caution and with full appreciation of their limitations.

[174]

*American School Achievement Tests, Part 3, Language and Spelling.** Grades 4–6, 7–9; 1941–58; 2 scores: language, spelling; Forms D ('55), E ('56), F ('57), G ('58); Forms D, E, F are essentially the same as Forms A, B, C copyrighted 1941–43; 2 levels; revised battery manuals ('58); $2 per 25 tests; 35¢ per specimen set of either level; postpaid; 32(45), 37(47) minutes for Intermediate, Advanced Battery; Willis E. Pratt and Robert V. Young; Public School Publishing Co. *

M. A. BRIMER, *Senior Lecturer in Educational Psychology, University College, Ibadan, Nigeria.*

At both the intermediate and advanced levels, separately timed subtests of language and spelling are presented. The language test is made up of five sections measuring usage, punctuation, capitalization, sentence recognition, and grammar; there are 65 items in all at the intermediate level and 73 at the advanced. The authors state that they have deliberately restricted content to the "tools of learning" because these are susceptible to objective testing and because their treatment is relatively constant throughout the country, and that they have drawn their material from research studies of common errors and from a large number of textbooks.

It would seem that objectivity has been a less limiting factor in the choice of content than suitability for the multiple response form. It may be that the authors have confused the two things. Language usage is probably more influenced by the prompting offered by a choice of responses than most skills; and in these tests, where the majority of the items require a choice from two alternatives, the prompting is considerable. The validity of this section as a measure of spontaneous usage is probably much lower than the representation of common errors suggests. Unprompted completion items are much more suitable for this purpose. Again, the use of the multiple choice form in the punctuation section, where the nature of the omitted punctuation has to be identified, removes the skill tested from the function involved in inserting the correct mark in a certain place. A small criticism here also is that the dots lining up the item with the answer are aligned with, and too close to, the period at the end of the sentence, possibly leading to confusion.

The capitalization and sentence recognition items arouse little comment, except that 10 items devoted to capitalization seem too much for a test of this length and that sentence recognition is more appropriately tested within continuous prose than by discrete phrases and clauses as it is here. The grammar section is very liberally interpreted and depends more heavily upon comprehension than the authors recognise. The grammar is too formal and would be better tested as usage. Some of the items involve dubious solutions. In one case, the authors have confused the logical with the grammatical object, and their use of the word "predicate" to refer to the verb alone, and not to its extension, would be authoritatively challenged.

The spelling test is composed of 50 items in which three common misspellings are used as alternatives to the right answer. There is a considerable body of feeling amongst teachers, not altogether unjustified, against the use of wrong spellings in spelling tests. Certainly, for a child who uses a common misspelling and encounters it in a test situation where it appears in print, reinforcement of the error is not unlikely to occur.

The evaluation of an attainment test intended for classroom use must take into account the adequacy of its proposed function, as well as the effectiveness of the tasks chosen to serve that function. Insofar as the concern for objectivity has undesirably restricted the content of this test, the function proposed is inadequate. Within the restricted range of tasks determined by the authors' limited interpretation of "objectivity," the representation of skills tested will suffice, though the proportionate contribution of the various skills to the total score might be challenged. Evidence in the manual of a close correspondence between results on this test and on other tests providing a more comprehensive range of English language tasks would go some way to moderate the criticism of the test's limited function.

It seems rather a pity that, after taking considerable pains to establish content validity, the authors did not think it worthwhile to correlate the tests with others which depend less upon the multiple choice form of response. There seem grounds for supposing that the test's validity measured in this way would be lower than the content validity suggests. The authors claim that the tests may be used to furnish data for remedial programmes. The limited content and length of the language sections and the absence of data or guidance on their diagnostic use suggests that teachers would be unwise to use these instruments for determining even general disabilities.

For tests of this length employing multiple choice items without correction for chance scoring, the reliabilities assessed by intercorrelating the various forms are substantial and adequate. This is probably attributable to the effectiveness of the distracting alternatives, since the authors do not report having analysed the items for internal consistency.

The norms, professedly tentative, are based on too few cases for the age and grade ranges they are supposed to cover. They are based on median scores of children in the various grades and do not appear to have been adequately smoothed, so that, for example, in the norms for the advanced level, within the score range 48 to 52 an increase of a single point of raw score is accorded between 2 and 4 months of age increase, and there is a reversal in the trend of change. While the practice of comparing a child's performance with the performance of children of different ages and grades may still be acceptable to teachers, modern tests

should attempt to provide alternative norms which are more precise in their information.

As a rough guide to the relative level of the language and spelling skills of a group of children, these tests will appeal to teachers who are not too fastidious over administration. The experienced teacher will prefer tests in which the items correspond more closely to actual classroom skills, which can more justifiably claim to provide diagnostic information, and which do not sacrifice validity for quick scoring and easy administration.

CLARENCE DERRICK, *Associate Professor of English and Humanities, University of Florida, Gainesville, Florida.*

There may be poorer tests than this one, and there certainly ought to be better ones.

The test contains six parts: Correct Usage (20 items), Punctuation (10 items), Capitalization (10 items), Sentence Recognition (10 items), Grammar (15 and 23 items), Spelling (50 items). It yields only two scores, however, one in language and one in spelling.

Correct usage is tested by asking pupils to select the correct completion for a presented sentence. Example: "I hope your mother says that you....go. a) may, b) can." The items avoid most of the disputable points although the importance of the "may-can" and the "in-into" distinctions could be argued. Most of the errors are so gross that the test is more likely to be an indicator of incompetence than proof of competence. Since all but 3 of the 80 items in the correct usage sections of the four forms examined were 2-choice items and since there is no correction for guessing, scores are inflated by chance success.

Punctuation is tested by having students indicate which punctuation mark (apostrophe, comma, period, quotation marks, question mark) is missing from the sentences presented. Since most of the items are not really 5-choice items, chance can again unduly affect scores. In the sentence "It is John's ball," for example, how many students would think a comma, an extra period, quotation marks, or a question mark were needed? Since the capitalization section has a similar format, the criticism that not all the options really function again applies. Sentence recognition is tested by deciding whether a group of words is or is not a sentence —more 2-choice items.

The grammar section requires familiarity

with grammatical terminology which may not be (should not be?) covered in a course of study for the fourth or fifth grade. Item 52 in Advanced Form E is surprising: "Which sentence is the topic sentence, that is, tells what the paragraph is about? a) one b) two c) four d) five." The examinee looks in vain for any paragraph to which the item might be referring and, not finding any, is understandably confused. Finally it dawns on him that there is an assumption (erroneous) that a topic sentence is necessarily the first sentence!

Spelling is tested with completion-type items with variant spellings. Example: "She....he would go. a) siad b) said c) saed d) sead." It would be interesting to check item analyses to discover how many of these variants are actually functioning. (According to Gates' *List of Spelling Difficulties in 3876 Words*,[1] the most common misspelling of "said" is "sed.")

The test makes use of a carbon, self-scoring technique that reduces the labor of scoring and is intriguing to pupils. It has, however, some limitations. For one, if the pupil does not mark heavily enough, the scorer may have to mark the test over so that the responses can be determined. For another, the test cannot be reused.

Like the test, the Teacher's Manual is inadequate. The manual informs the user that these tests "do not purport to be diagnostic tests," but three sentences later explains that from the results obtained on each part of the tests it is possible "to determine the general disabilities which each pupil may have." Too frequently essential data are missing. Specifically what techniques were used to compute reliability? What is meant by "checking" the original norms data against scores of 3,589 pupils in 44 school districts in 17 states and Canada? What schools? How checked?

In presenting evidence regarding the curricular validity of the test, the manual explains that the content is based on analyses of five texts, some state courses of study, and some research studies. The texts are of 1950 vintage, but the research studies are dated 1930, 1935, and 1938. Linguists have done a good deal of talking and writing since the 1930's.

From reading the manual, the reviewer gets the impression that the battery of which this test is a part was developed for a specific region (Erie County, Pennsylvania), and subse-

quently the norms were modified in some unexplained way. Because data are lacking, test users would be justified in questioning the meaning of the norms. The norms table translates uncorrected raw scores into grade and age norms. Test users who do not know the limitations of these kinds of norms should read Flanagan's discussion of grade and age equivalents in *Educational Measurement*.[2]

On all counts, the language usage test of the *American School Achievement Tests* is hardly adequate. Use it if you must; but, if you have an option, search for a test without the limitations of this one.

For reviews by J. Raymond Gerberich and Virgil E. Herrick of the complete battery, see 1; for a review by Ralph C. Preston of an earlier edition, see 4:1; for reviews by Walter W Cook and Gordon N. Mackenzie (with Glen Hass), see 3:1.

[175]

*Barrett-Ryan English Test. Grades 7–13; 1926–57; Forms 1 ('56), 2 ('56), 3 ('29), 4 ('40), 5 ('44), 6 ('44), 1946, 1948, 1954 ['55], 1955 ('56); revised manual ('56); norms: Forms 1 ['57], 2 ['57], 1946 ['46], 1948 ['48], 1954 ['56], 1955 ['57]; no data on reliability for Forms 1, 2, 1946, 1948, 1954, 1955; $1.40 per 25 tests, postage extra; 50¢ per specimen set, postpaid; 50(55) minutes; E. R. Barrett, Teresa M. Ryan, M. W. Sanders (1, 2, 1955), H. E. Schrammel (1946, 1948, 1954, manual), and E. R. Wood (manual); Bureau of Educational Measurements. *

REFERENCE

1. ANDERSON, MARY R., AND STEGMAN, ERWIN J. "Predictors of Freshman Achievement at Fort Hays Kansas State College." *Ed & Psychol Meas* 14:722–3 w '54. * (PA 29:7952)

J. RAYMOND GERBERICH, *Director, Bureau of Educational Research and Service, and Professor of Education, University of Connecticut, Storrs, Connecticut.*

Ten forms of this English test are now in print. The earliest four forms were designed for use in grades 7–12 and college, but grades 7 and 8 are not listed in the specifications for any of the six later forms and a further cutback to eliminate the college level is embodied in the 1955 and 1956 forms. "College" presumably was intended to apply only to freshmen, inasmuch as the norm tables do not provide for any higher levels.

Five purposes are listed for the tests: to classify students into sections, to discover weaknesses of individual students, to standardize work, to measure achievement, and to motivate

1 GATES, ARTHUR I. *A List of Spelling Difficulties in 3876 Words.* New York: Bureau of Publications, Teachers College, Columbia University, 1937. Pp. 166.

2 LINDQUIST, E. F., EDITOR. *Educational Measurement.* Washington, D.C.: American Council on Education, 1951. Pp. xix, 819. *

learning. Later in the manual, five uses, by implication based on the purposes previously stated, are enumerated. Uses included here but not anticipated in the purposes are: checking the efficiency of instruction, assigning school marks, and analyzing class weaknesses. It seems clear to the reviewer that uses should reflect purposes to a much greater degree than is apparent here. The lack of more coherence seems to evidence a rather traditional conception of test purposes and perhaps less than optimum care in phrasing important ideas.

Brief comments are made about content validity and some evidence is given on concurrent and predictive validity in the manual. Content validity is dealt with in one 3-line paragraph that merely lists sources of content employed and judgments sought—content of "leading textbooks and courses of study" and criticisms from "teachers and supervisors on earlier editions of the test." Correlation coefficients of .70 with an unspecified "battery of entrance tests" and of .58 and .59 with results from two specified intelligence tests furnish evidence on concurrent validity. Correlation coefficients of .66, .55, and .50 with three measures of subsequent scholastic success are presented as evidence of predictive validity. No mention is made of when these correlational data were obtained, of the age or grade groups on which they were based, or of the meaning, in either the statistical or the practical sense, of the coefficients. Only three short paragraphs of the manual are devoted to this most important characteristic of a good examination.

Split-half and alternate form reliabilities are reported. Split-half coefficients, listed as falling in the .80 to .89 range and seemingly not stepped up by use of the Spearman-Brown formula, were obtained "before the final equating of the different forms." Intercorrelations among Forms 1, 2, and 3 are reported as ranging from .76 to .85, whereas the sole reference to equivalence of other forms is found in the statement that coefficients range from .88 to .96. The latter is almost incredibly high. That these "other forms" are not very recently published seems probable, inasmuch as an earlier 4-page undated manual listing norms for Forms 1 to 3, all published originally during or before 1929, carries precisely the same statement.

It seems apparent that the 7-line statement about reliability is extremely inadequate. Pupil samples used in obtaining the data are not characterized by any indications of size, range of talent, geographical representation, testing dates, or, except for editions in p.int by 1929, forms of the test. Nor is any information given about the central tendency and variability of scores for these samples.

The 2-column format of the test booklets is uniformly poor, if one accepts as a norm the format of tests put out by the 10 or so companies publishing such instruments most widely. The type font is small, probably 9-point, and not easily read; in many instances the bold face type used to identify options is hardly distinguishable from the regular roman type. Material is frequently set without adequate leading between lines. Spacing is irregular and seemingly without pattern.

In printing the scoring keys, no attention was given to the vertical spacing of items in groups, so the scorer must vary the vertical positioning of strip keys from page to page and even from column to column instead of being able to align top edges of keys and test folders uniformly.

The various test forms seem to have similarities not much greater than chance in such matters of form and style as headings, examples, and even directions to the pupils. For example, the first part of the test is introduced in six different ways in the first six of the current forms. Examples, or sample items, also seem to be used according to whim rather than design. Forms 4 and 5 do not employ any examples, to represent one extreme. Form 3, nearest to the opposite extreme, presents examples for all parts and for all sections except one. The other forms take varying intermediate positions on this characteristic. Copyright dates also are not uniformly treated.

Circumlocutions, ambiguities, and even grammatical errors seem to be common in the directions to pupils. In the directions for Part 3, Form 1946, for example, pupils are instructed under certain circumstances to place "a '11' in the parenthesis." Almost without exception, the word "parenthesis" is used to represent the *pair* of curved lines. A further example is that directions for the second item of each pair in Part 2, Form 1955, seem to ask the pupil to indicate the *wrong* reason for a grammatical *error* he noted in the preceding item.

Two generalizations about the parts and sections of these test forms seem to be well founded. First, there is no pattern, no guiding principle, no coherence observable when the various forms are compared one with another. Second, there is no trend, no directional tendency, no transition away from or toward any type of content or testing technic observable when the forms are considered in their chronological sequence. In well standardized tests that occur in a sequence, especially when a sequence in a dynamic area has endured for a period of years, one might expect to find a pattern modified over a period of time by a trend.

Three item varieties seem to be most widely used: a plus-minus version of the basic alternate response type, a multiple choice variety with either three or four options, and a classification type of matching exercise. Form 3 uses only the plus-minus item, whereas Forms 1946 and 1948 discard it entirely in favor of multiple choice and matching varieties. Most of the other forms combine two or even all three of these types.

Although many of the test parts employ these item varieties in their simplest or basic form, some test parts present situations in which two related items appear in sequence. In one type of part dealing with a combination of functional and formal grammar, where the first of two plus-minus items is on usage and the second is on grammar controlling the usage, it seems rather strange to find that two negative answers can be expected on occasion to occur together, i.e., to find that the pupil is expected to indicate that the grammatical rule stated *does not* apply to an *error* observed. Somewhat similarly, another type of part on grammar combines by pairs a plus-minus item on correct usage and a 3-option multiple choice item on formal grammar controlling the usage. A third variation of this type of pattern combines two 3-option multiple choice items, one on usage and one on formal grammar, in a sequence or related pair. In Part 2 of Form 1946, the second item in each of three pairs contains an irrefutable, logical clue to the answer, although the clue leads to the *right* answer only if the right answer was given for the preceding usage item. Less definite clues, again misleading in some instances, appear in some other pairs of items.

Functional and formal grammar occur together in some test parts, as in several illustrations above, and separately in others. The distinctly formal grammar loading varies from around one fourth of the total scoring points in Forms 1-2 and 3-6 to more than 40 per cent in

Forms 1946 and 1948. The formal grammar items cover identification of predicate adjectives used as subjective complements, infinitive phrases, participial phrases, and present perfect passive tenses, as well as the less technical issues involving number, person, and parts of speech.

Form 1946 differs significantly from all other forms in having 160 items whereas a total of 150 items is otherwise standard. The last 20 items of Form 1946, with one exception, require two answers each. Scoring instructions specify one half point for each correct answer, ignoring the need for variation from this pattern for the one item and failing to specify what should be done with fractional scores. The front of each booklet lists the possible score of 150 on one line (160 for Form 1946), provides a space for the "number wrong and omitted" on a second line, and provides a space for "FINAL SCORE" on the third line. The implication seems to be that omissions and wrong answers should enter into the scoring. However, it appears that the "FINAL SCORE," or total number of correct answers, is to be obtained in the scoring process, so incorrect answers and omissions are incidental or else are used only by the careful scorer of his own volition in checking for accuracy.

Two tables are presented in the manual for the conversion of raw scores to percentile ranks for each grade from 7 through 13. Although the norms are reported to "be based on the scores made by 196,097 students in a large number of schools located in all parts of the country," the total number accounted for in the one table where subtotals are listed is only 195,997. The discrepancy of 100, not in itself of much consequence, was apparently carried forward from what appears to be the first, and perhaps the only other, edition of the manual, which the reviewer found in his files. The 1929 norms reported in the first manual were based on "143,633 scores made by students in the two previous years" and shown as 143,533 by subtotals, whereas the 1956 edition norms are based on these same data plus 53,464 scores of high school pupils in 1939 and 1940 and of college freshmen from 1937 to 1941.

The older edition of the manual reports end-of-year norms for 5,126 and 5,325 pupils from grades 7 and 8 respectively and shows medians of 81.3 and 86.5 for the two grades in that order. The 1956 manual bases its comparable norms for these two grades on precisely the same number of cases, but shows medians of 87 and 91 respectively. Furthermore, comparable scores for the 10th percentile are from 4 to 5 points higher in the 1956 manual than in the earlier version and approximately the same degree of discrepancy appears at the 90th percentile. Similar discrepancies in medians occur for all of the other grades, but the inclusion in the 1956 norms of the additional 53,464 scores mentioned above makes further direct comparisons impossible.

The 1956 manual reports that end-of-year norms and midyear norms are based on the 196,097 scores referred to above. The sole explanation of how this was accomplished is found in the statement that midyear norms were "statistically computed" from end-of-year data.

Some form of derived score customarily stands between raw scores and percentile ranks when scores on several parallel forms of a test are given comparability in the standardization process. A crude alternative for standardized tests would be to compute percentile ranks separately for the several forms by the use of essentially comparable normative groups. When the inconsistencies in norms noted above are viewed in the light of the attempt in these tests to give comparable meaning to raw scores, the reviewer cannot but feel that the norms are, and indeed must be, quite unreliable. The situation is not unlike that in which a teacher attempts to assign equivalent meaning to a passing mark of, say, 70, and also to every other percentage mark from 1 to 100, on several different tests.

Several interesting and rather puzzling questions may be raised in brief summary. Are norms based on pupil scores from testing done during 1927–29 and 1937–41 likely to be reliable in 1958? Are coefficients of equivalency as high as .88 to .96 more likely to be the result of a very highly consistent series of short, parallel tests than of a wide range of talent in the pupil samples on which they are based? Are test forms having wide variations in content and types of items and exercises likely to result in raw scores that are comparable? It seems to the reviewer that a negative answer to each of these questions must be given. He is forced to conclude, therefore, that these English tests do not stand up well under the careful scrutiny that modern standards of test construction demand.

[176]

*Barrett-Ryan-Schrammel English Test, New Edition. Grades 9–13; 1938–54; 6 scores: grammar, sentence, punctuation, vocabulary, pronunciation, total; IBM; Forms DM, EM ('54); manual ('54); no data on reliability for grade 9 and part scores; $3.50 per 35 tests; separate answer sheets may be used; $1.70 per 35 IBM answer sheets; postage extra; 35¢ per specimen set, postpaid; 60(70) minutes; E. R. Barrett, Teresa M. Ryan, and H. E. Schrammel; World Book Co. *

REFERENCE

1. MARTIN, RICHARD RALPH. *An Investigation of the Effectiveness of an Entrance Test Battery for Predicting Success in Law School.* Doctor's thesis, Temple University (Philadelphia, Pa.), 1954. (*DA* 16:575)

LEONARD S. FELDT, *Assistant Professor of Education, State University of Iowa, Iowa City, Iowa.*

According to the manual, this test was designed to survey student proficiency in the essential mechanics of English, to diagnose deficiencies in this area, and to facilitate grouping and placement in high school and college classes. There is little factual evidence made available to the user to demonstrate that the test performs any of these functions with greater validity than a reasonably good teacher-made examination.

In defense of test content the authors state that items are based on the "common content of leading textbooks and courses of study." How many and which ones is not specified. Criticisms by teachers and supervisors of earlier editions of the test were considered, as was a study of student errors. No bibliographic reference is made to this study, however; hence its adequacy must be accepted on faith. The authors do not indicate that they consulted published research on the nature and frequency of student errors in written language. Thus the manual contains no factual evidence which would allow the potential user to evaluate the appropriateness of content.

Usefulness as a placement instrument can be claimed for any achievement test. What is required to support this claim is evidence that the instructional program is facilitated by assignment on this basis. Even more important, the user needs evidence that placement of students on the basis of test scores is more fruitful than placement on the basis of previous grades in English or some other inexpensive alternative. No such evidence is presented in the manual.

The claims of diagnostic potential are also without proof, and careful analysis of the test itself does not support such claims. Language mechanics—correct spelling, proper punctuation, appropriate capitalization, and proper choice of word forms—is a heterogeneous body of skills, and the mastery of one will not increase the student's mastery of another. For effective diagnosis, a number of items must be included on each type of problem situation. The one item on agreement of a pronoun with its antecedent and the two items on the hyphen are obvious examples of coverage inadequate for individual diagnosis. The publisher should have specifically warned against such use rather than encouraged it.

In the reviewer's opinion, the test includes far too many items (67) on the academic aspects of language—identification of parts of speech and parts of sentences and specification of the rules governing various situations—and too few items (52) involving functional mechanics. The latter group includes no items on capitalization and spelling. Surely many teachers would have sacrificed willingly the vocabulary and pronunciation items for a greater number of items involving common problems of written expression.

A number of criticisms may be leveled at the reporting of the reliability data in the manual. Most serious, perhaps, is the absence of reliability estimates for grade 9 total score and for the various subtests at all levels. Since differential interpretations and diagnoses from subtest scores are clearly encouraged, this oversight is to be deplored. Even the estimates of total score reliability (.85 to .95 for a single grade) are of little value, since the groups on which the estimates are based are not described. The wide fluctuations in the numbers of cases (42 to 257) suggest the subjects were not randomly chosen from the standardization groups.

Midyear percentile ranks for subtest and total scores are separately tabled for each of grades 9–13. Except for these norms and beginning-of-year norms for college freshmen, percentile ranks for all other testing dates must be interpolated by the user. This might represent a considerable inconvenience for the high school principal who wished to administer the test at the beginning of the year for placement purposes or for the classroom teacher who wished to test both at the beginning and the end of the year to measure growth. Unfortunately, even the meaningfulness of the midyear norms may be seriously questioned, since only the vaguest of descriptions is given of the norms groups. While the number of cases is

impressive (32,641 high school students), test users should be wary of "national" norms that are based on samples drawn from "a large area of the country."

In summary, this reviewer does not regard this instrument as a good test of proficiency in English mechanics. The user is required to accept it more on faith than on evidence, and faith is not a trustworthy criterion for test selection.

CLEVELAND A. THOMAS, *Principal, Francis W. Parker School, Chicago, Illinois.*

Although this test seems as useful as most objective tests in the field of English, certain weaknesses must be noted. In the first place, although Test 1 is called functional grammar, many teachers would not agree that it is based on functional grammar but rather on the familiar formal grammar. It will, therefore, test knowledge of grammar in a vacuum, that is, in a way not necessarily related to speech and writing. This relationship has been constantly demonstrated by studies of the connection between the study of formal grammar and skill in speech and writing. Similarly, the subtest on the sentence is actually a test of the grammar of the sentence. There is no effort to test the student's skill in the construction of sentences. The punctuation test seems to be a reasonable selection of the conventions of punctuation. In the vocabulary items, the authors have avoided the usual trap of asking for synonyms when exact synonyms do not exist. However, there is no indication of the bases for the selection of the words included, so that just how much of a test of vocabulary this subtest actually is remains doubtful. The items on pronunciation represent an ingenious method of getting as close to pronunciation as is probably possible in an objective test. But it seems dubious, at least to this reviewer, that demonstration of knowledge of syllabication and accent placement necessarily indicates correct pronunciation.

In summary, this reviewer would urge the inclusion of work in sentence construction and items of appropriateness similar to those developed in the English achievement test of the College Entrance Examination Board in order to gain some measure not only of knowledge of the mechanics of English, but also of skill in their use. It also seems regrettable that the full contexts used in previous editions of the test (in which the items were based on several selections of paragraph length) have been deserted. A fuller context for some items in the present test would be more desirable. In general, it seems likely that this test will appeal more to those who teach formal grammar as a separate subject than to those whose interest is in whether students can speak and write creditably. Even the former type of teacher may have difficulty, however, because she will not be able to use with real reliability anything except the total score. Since only the total score is reliable, the test does not lend itself to use with the part scores. In spite of the objections noted above, the test will probably give as good an overall measure of the mechanics of English as other tests.

For reviews by G. Frederic Kuder, Robert C. Pooley, and Charles Swain Thomas of the original edition, see 40:1267.

[177]

California Language Test, 1957 Edition. Grades 1–2, 3–4.5, 4–6, 7–9, 9–14; 1933–58; previous edition (see 4:151) still available; subtest of the *California Achievement Tests;* 4 scores: mechanics of English, spelling, total, handwriting; IBM for grades 4–14; 5 levels; battery manual ('57) for each level; technical report ['58]; separate answer sheets may be used in grades 4–14; 4¢ per IBM answer sheet; 7¢ per Scoreze answer sheet; 20¢ per hand scoring stencil; 10¢ per survey data sheet ('52); postage extra; 50¢ per specimen set of any one level, postpaid; Ernest W. Tiegs and Willis W. Clark; California Test Bureau. *
a) LOWER PRIMARY. Grades 1–2; Forms W ('57), X ('57); $2.10 per 35 tests; (27–40) minutes.
b) UPPER PRIMARY. Grades 3–4.5; Forms W ('57), X ('57); $2.45 per 35 tests; 30(40) minutes.
c) ELEMENTARY. Grades 4–6; IBM; Forms W ('57), X ('57), Y ('57), Z ('57); $2.80 per 35 tests; 20¢ per machine scoring stencil; 38(50) minutes.
d) JUNIOR HIGH LEVEL. Grades 7–9; IBM; Forms W ('57), X ('57), Y ('57), Z ('57); $2.80 per 35 tests; 60¢ per machine scoring stencil; 30(40) minutes.
e) ADVANCED. Grades 9–14; IBM; Forms W ('57), X ('57), Y ('57); $2.80 per 35 tests; 40¢ per machine scoring stencil; 36(50) minutes.

REFERENCES

1. REID, T. JAMES, AND CONQUEST, GEORGE R. "A Survey of the Language Achievement of Alberta School Children." *Alberta J Ed Res* 1:39–52 Je '55. *
2. SANGSTER, C. H. "An Evaluation of the Effectiveness of a Standardized Test of Language." *Alberta J Ed Res* 2:186–202 S '56. *
3. SOPCHAK, ANDREW L. "Prediction of College Performance by Commonly Used Tests." *J Clin Psychol* 14:194–7 Ap '58. *

CONSTANCE M. McCULLOUGH, *Professor of Education, San Francisco State College, San Francisco, California.*

This is a survey test with considerable emphasis upon diagnostic uses of the pupils' responses. A "Diagnostic Profile" on the back of each pupil's booklet provides a graphic picture of his attainments and, by means of shaded areas, the location of scores typical of pupils a grade below or a grade above him. In the examiner's manual, a "Diagnostic Analysis of Learning Difficulties" classifies the errors and lists the test items which deal with particular areas.

The 56-page manual has been done with impressive care and detail. The novice is guided in the meaning of tables and scores as well as being given careful directions for administering the tests. In addition to data on reliability and norms, the concept of "anticipated achievement grade placement" is presented. This is defined as the "norm performance of a nation-wide sample of students in the same school grade and having comparable chronological age and mental ability characteristics." Graphs present separately the curves for mechanics of English and spelling scores for children in different grades whose IQ's vary from 80 to 135. While this seems very significant for use in subjects which are largely developed in school, it seems rather misleading to present such a means of interpretation for the mechanics of English score when word usage is included in the score. Considering the wide variations of knowledge of good usage with which children come to school, the little that intelligence has to do with it, the little that teachers have to do for some children and the much they have to do for others, and the importance of ear training (indeed, parroting), the presence of word usage in the score makes such a chart an interesting statistical feat rather than anything of value to the teacher of usage. (My parakeet uses good English and learns fast—and has only a bird brain.)

The 1957 Technical Report on the *California Achievement Tests* is as good as an elementary course in test construction and standardization. It describes in detail the way in which the tests were standardized, how the results were treated, and why certain methods were used.

The batteries for the first four grades are introduced as "games," giving a cheerful slant to an old form of torture. The authors wisely have the teacher read aloud the sentences in the lower primary tests, so that the reading difficulty is minimized or removed. The vocabulary of the tests is well controlled, but, as every teacher knows, there are always some children who cannot read the test of their grade level even though it is relatively easy. For such children, the teacher might well read or have another pupil read aloud the passages of the higher test batteries, or administer a test for a lower grade. Otherwise, the test will be a reading test instead of a language test.

The mechanics tests present successive sentences, sometimes in a running text, with numbers over certain words or at crucial points. One response (right or wrong or multiple choice) is required for a line; thus, each answer space at the right of the page is in perfect alignment with a crucial point. Narrative form, letter form, and unrelated sentences are used. Unfortunately, clues to correct responses may be deduced in certain instances by the surrounding material. If, for example, all sentences begin with a capital except one and the first word of this sentence is numbered as crucial, it is pretty clear that this should have a capital, too.

The spelling test for the first four grades is a dictated test, the first five words of which provide handwriting samples for the grading of the child's handwriting by a scale in the answer key. The words are well chosen and are representative of useful words at the levels tested. Unfortunately, the authors do not provide suggestions for the possible diagnostic value of such a test or show the types of spelling errors that indicate kinds of spelling difficulties and needs.

Beginning with the elementary level, the tests are called tests (not games) and are machine scorable as well as hand scorable. The spelling test at this level presents rows of four words, any one of which may be misspelled. Thus 120 words are reviewed by the pupil. The words include samplings of different vocabulary levels: the words "most" and "dispatch" are in the same test. Thus the teacher can see the height as well as the depth of a student's spelling ability and need.

The handwriting test in the upper level tests is a 2-minute test in which the pupil writes a sentence containing all the letters of the alphabet.

On the backing sheet of the Scoreze answer sheet, the point being tested in each item is indicated. Thus the teacher who wishes to chart a student's strengths and weaknesses can do so as he marks the paper.

The repetition of certain basic items at successive levels of the test means that the high school teacher will not be alerted to such things as misuse of the possessive with gerund while the student is still writing and saying, "I wish I had of knowed." This is a well constructed battery for survey purposes, and its many suggestions for diagnosis give the teacher some ideas for teaching on the basis of the results.

WINIFRED L. POST, *Instructor in English, Dana Hall, Wellesley, Massachusetts.*

Each test consists of two main sections: the first includes three subtests on capitalization, punctuation, and word usage; the second tests spelling. Each of the five tests also offers an optional measure of penmanship.

Because capitalization and spelling are almost completely subject to arbitrary rules, the tests in these areas will be more uniformly satisfying to English teachers than the tests of either punctuation or usage. Some English teachers may question the heavy stress on capitalization, at least at the advanced level, but all will agree that the capitalization sections measure skillfully, efficiently, and thoroughly—through the use of increasingly complex sentences—the student's ability to apply all important rules for capitalization.

In the punctuation sections, almost all the items are confined to those areas of punctuation which are governed by rules. Many teachers may feel that any full-scale testing of skill in punctuation, at least for the high school grades, ought to pose some problems which a student can solve only by awareness of just what punctuation the intended meaning of the sentence requires. And certainly any high school test ought to include some testing of ability to use the semicolon and possibly the dash.

The third section, word usage, has the drawback throughout the series of the 2-choice item which is wide open to guessing. Items on each test range from a choice between literate and illiterate English to choices involving fairly subtle distinctions in idiom. Even the most difficult items, however, demand only a knowledge of rules and, increasingly for grades 7 and over, a familiarity with grammar terminology.

For measuring students in grades 1–8, these tests are skillfully constructed with ingeniously contrived equivalence among their many forms. They are easy to administer and score as well as highly practical for any school which wants separate scores in capitalization, punctuation,

California Language Test

word usage, and spelling. For some English teachers, the title *California Language Test* may be misleading. The manual calls the capitalization, punctuation, and word usage sections tests of "Mechanics of English," a phrase which accurately and modestly defines their scope and purpose. They measure with precision and efficiency only those areas of language in which rules of right and wrong are final arbiters. They leave untested judgment, sensitivity, and ability to solve problems by grasp of meaning rather than by remembered rules. According to the manual, each of these tests is "designed for adequate measurement throughout the full range of ability found in almost any school group." Yet, in the test for grades 9–14, there is little attempt to test such important problems in language as the dangling element, the misplaced word, phrase, or clause, the squinting modifier, the lack of parallel structure, faulty comparisons, missing or illogical transitions, and illogical metaphor. The *College Entrance Examination Board Achievement Test in English Composition* has already shown that these areas in language can be tested validly and reliably by objective test techniques. Therefore, in the judgment of this reviewer, no test which fails to reckon significantly with these elements of language can rightly claim that it is testing "the full range of ability" of students in grades 9–14.

For reviews by Gerald V. Lannholm and Robert C. Pooley of the 1950 edition, see 4:151; for reviews by Harry A. Greene and J. Paul Leonard of an earlier edition, see 40:1292. For a review by Charles O. Neidt of the complete battery, see 2; for reviews by Warren G. Findley, Alvin W. Schindler, and J. Harlan Shores of the 1950 edition, see 4:2; for a review by Paul A. Witty of the 1943 edition, see 3:15; for reviews by C. W. Odell and Hugh B. Wood of an earlier edition, see 40:1193; for a review by D. Welty Lefever, see 38:876.

[178]
College English Test: National Achievement Tests. Grades 12–13; 1937–43; 7 scores: punctuation, capitalization, language usage, sentence structure, modifiers, miscellaneous principles, total; Forms A ('42, identical with test copyrighted in 1937 except for minor changes), B ('41); directions sheet for Form A ('43), directions sheet for Form B ('42, identical with sheet copyrighted in 1937 except for minor changes); teachers' guide ['44]; no norms for part scores; $3.75 per 25 tests; 50¢ per specimen set; postage extra; 45(50) minutes; A. C. Jordan; Acorn Publishing Co. *

California Language Test

OSMOND E. PALMER, *Associate Professor, Office of Evaluation Services, Michigan State University, East Lansing, Michigan.*

The two forms are parallel in form and quite close in content, except as noted in the subsequent discussion. The test must be hand scored. In the punctuation section, the student is to insert the proper marks and enclose them in parentheses (for easier identification by the rater?). In the capitalization section, the words which need to be capitalized are to be underlined. The next three sections require the student to draw a line under the best of four sentences. (It would be much simpler merely to circle the letter of the right response.) The last section requires matching; the letter of the right response is written before the item.

The 4-page teachers' guide covers a whole series of English tests, but only one brief descriptive paragraph (and the corrected odd-even reliability figure .88) can be taken as referring specifically to the *College English Test*. The directions, space for recording class scores, the answer keys, and the norms are all contained on a single sheet. The norms are not convincing. They are given in median scores by month for grades 11–13. Each month at the high school level shows exactly a one-point increase over the month before. The college norms begin one point above the highest high school figure and increase by one or two points a month for nine months. Even if the test had been more carefully constructed and had a higher reliability, it could not measure progress as minutely as this.

The test, in parts at least, is unrealistic and arbitrary, occasionally careless, and not completely consistent from one form to the other. One item in each form tests for punctuation of a Biblical reference. Form A requires "1 Sam. IX. 13" and Form B, "Deut. 5:11–21." In one answer, the items in a bibliography entry are ·separated by commas; in the other, by periods. In Form B, the key calls for three commas in "The French king Henry IV of Navarre ruled from 1589–1610." With respect to capitalization, the student is expected to know that a Latin sentence, when it appears on the Great Seal of a state, would have every word capitalized and how to treat the "whereases" in a formal declaration. At the other extreme, he is tested for the capitalization of "I" and "United States," both of which appear properly capitalized in other parts of the same section. One form calls for the capitalization of "western" in the phrase "the western part of the state"; both forms insist that "spring" in "South American Spring" is capitalized.

Part 3, Language Usage, is quite different in the two forms. This is probably due to the fact that in the earlier Form A so many of the right answers are unnatural—"Them who failed, we also praised"; "Let us fellows go, for we are better than they"; and "Can you tell me if I may go, or will I have to see to [sic] the principal." Occasionally, there would seem to be two acceptable answers. For examples: "Lincoln's assassination caused much trouble" or "An act that caused much trouble was the assassination of Lincoln"; "Can you tell me if it is raining," "Can you tell me whether it is raining," or "Can you tell me whether or not it is raining?" In one case the attempt to test for who-whom led to a confusion in the keying. This is supposed to be right: "Tell him that whomever we see coming will be the man whom we are instructed to arrest." Both forms reject a one-he sequence in favor of one-one. Form B does not test for so many out of the way points and its sentences are a little less awkward, but some responses are still dubious.

The sections on sentence structure and modifiers illustrate some of the same difficulties and introduce a new one. In order to get the four choices of response, the authors frequently test for two different things simultaneously—a matter of emphasis plus the one-one sequence; tense plus order; shall-will plus can-may.

Some of the "Principles" which form the key list in the last section are not mutually exclusive, so that a student could well mark one of several responses. For instance, an "incorrect use of the expletive there" might also be an example of an "unnecessary change of subject." An "unnecessary change of subject" might also involve a "lack of parallel structure." An "incomplete comparison" could also be an "illogical comparison." It is a little hard to make a distinction between "lack of parallel correlative elements" and "lack of parallel structure for parallel ideas," or between "incorrect co-ordination" and "unnecessary double-barreled co-ordinating construction."

Because this test does not reflect current language practices and because it is not carefully made, it could well be allowed to go out of print.

For reviews by Constance M. McCullough and Robert W. Howard of Form A, see 40: 1269.1.

[179]

*Cooperative English Test: Lower and Higher Levels.** Grades 7-12, 11-16; 1940-56; IBM; 3 tests available as separates and in a single booklet edition; no specific manual; general Cooperative manual ('51); descriptive folders [Mechanics and Effectiveness of Expression, '56; Reading Comprehension, '51]; norms ['40]; separate answer sheets must be used with Form Z, optional with other forms; postage extra; Cooperative Test Division, Educational Testing Service. *

a) SINGLE BOOKLET EDITION: LOWER AND HIGHER LEVELS. Grades 7-12, 11-16; 7 scores: mechanics of expression, effectiveness of expression, vocabulary, speed of comprehension, level of comprehension, total comprehension, total; IBM; Forms T ('50 or '51, same as test copyrighted in 1943), Y (Lower Level, '51—same as test copyrighted in 1948; Higher Level, '48); RX ('49), Z ('53, same as test copyrighted in 1951); 2 levels; directions for hand scoring answer sheets ['49]; $4.95 per 25 tests; $1.95 per 25 IBM answer sheets; 60¢ per set of scoring stencils; 120(130) minutes.

b) TEST A, MECHANICS OF EXPRESSION. Grades 7-16; IBM; Forms T ('43), X ('47), Y ('50, revision of Forms Q and R; same as test copyrighted in 1948), Z ('53); $2.50 per 25 tests; $1 per 25 IBM answer sheets; 25¢ per scoring stencil; 40(45) minutes; Geraldine Spaulding (T, X, Y), Herbert Danzer (X), W. W. Cook (Y), Janet Afflerbach (Z), Miriam M. Bryan (Z), and Paula Thibault (Z).

c) TESTS B1 AND B2, EFFECTIVENESS OF EXPRESSION: LOWER AND HIGHER LEVELS. Grades 7-12, 11-16; IBM; Forms T (Lower Level, '43; Higher Level, '51—same as test copyrighted in 1943), X ('47), Y (revision of Forms Q and R; Lower Level, '50—same as test copyrighted in 1948; Higher Level, '48), Z ('53); $2.75 per 25 tests; $1 per 25 IBM answer sheets; 25¢ per scoring stencil; 40(45) minutes; Geraldine Spaulding (T, X, Y), Miriam M. Bryan, Janet Afflerbach (Y, Z), Catherine Dodd (Z), and Paula Thibault (Z).

d) TESTS C1 AND C2, READING COMPREHENSION: LOWER AND HIGHER LEVELS. Grades 7-12, 11-16; 4 scores: vocabulary, speed of comprehension, level of comprehension, total; IBM; Forms R ('50, same as test copyrighted in 1941), T (Lower Level, '43; Higher Level, '50—same as test copyrighted in 1943), Y ('48), Z ('53); 2 levels; directions for hand scoring ['49]; $3.25 per 25 tests; $1 per 25 IBM answer sheets; 25¢ per scoring stencil; 40(45) minutes; Frederick B. Davis, Mary Willis (T), Clarence Derrick (Y), Harry R. Neville (Y), Jeanne M. Bradford (Y), Geraldine Spaulding (Y), and Charlotte Croon Davis (Z).

REFERENCES

1-2. See 40:1276.
3-31. See 3:120.
32-84. See 4:155.
85. HESTON, JOSEPH C. "The Graduate Record Examination vs. Other Measures of Aptitude and Achievement." Ed & Psychol Meas 7:618-30 au '47. * (PA 22:3210)
86. LINDSAY, REX B. Predicting Success in the Lower Division at the University of Utah. Master's thesis, University of Utah (Salt Lake City, Utah), 1947.
87. MURPHY, HAROLD D., AND DAVIS, FREDERICK B. "College Grades and Ability to Reason in Reading." Peabody J Ed 27: 34-7 Jl '49. *
88. BERNER, WILLIAM. An Evaluation of the Freshman Testing Program at Southern Methodist University. Master's thesis, Southern Methodist University (Dallas, Tex.), 1951.
89. KNICKERBOCKER, K. L. "Placement of Freshmen in First-Quarter English." J Higher Ed 22:211-5+ Ap '51. * (PA 26: 520)
90. WELSH, MARY L. A Comparison of Two Psychological Examinations in Predicting Academic Success of Ohio Univer-

sity Students. Master's thesis, Ohio University (Athens, Ohio), 1951.

91. *Final Report on the 1951 National College Freshman Testing Program.* Princeton, N.J.: Cooperative Test Division, Educational Testing Service, [1952]. Pp. i, 27. *

92. ANDREW, DEAN C. "Predicting College Success of Non-High-School Graduates." *Sch R* 60:151–6 Mr '52. *

93. FREDERIKSEN, NORMAN. "The Influence of Timing and Instructions on Cooperative Reading Test Scores." *Ed & Psychol Meas* 12:598–607 w '52. * (*PA* 27:6741)

94. FREEHILL, MAURICE F. "Student Self-Estimates as Guidance in Selecting Courses." *Col & Univ* 27:233–42 Ja '52. *

95. LIEN, ARNOLD JUEL. "A Comparative-Predictive Study of Students in the Four Curricula of a Teacher Education Institution." *J Exp Ed* 21:81–219 D '52. *

96. VORDENBERG, WESLEY. "How Valid Are Objective English Tests?" *Engl J* 41:428–9 O '52. *

97. WELCH, W. BRUCE. *An Examination of the Usability of Selected Standardized Tests of Mental Ability and Achievement for College Groups With Atypical Socio-Economic Status.* Doctor's thesis, Indiana University (Bloomington, Ind.), 1952.

98. ANDERSON, SCARVIA B. "Prediction and Practice Tests at the College Level." *J Appl Psychol* 37:256–9 Ag '53. * (*PA* 28:6583)

99. BARRETT, DOROTHY M. "Correlation of Survey Section of Diagnostic Reading Tests and of Test C2: Reading Comprehension With College History Grades." *J Ed Res* 46:465–9 F '53. * (*PA* 28:1461)

100. CARLIN, LESLIE C. "A Longitudinal Comparison of Freshman-Senior Standing." *J Ed Res* 47:285–90 D '53. * (*PA* 28:6586)

101. COLEMAN, WILLIAM. "An Economical Test Battery for Predicting Freshman Engineering Course Grades." *J Appl Psychol* 37:465–7 D '53. * (*PA* 29:1562)

102. JENSON, RALPH E. "Predicting Scholastic Achievement of First-Year Graduate Students." *Ed & Psychol Meas* 13:322–9 su '53. * (*PA* 28:4833)

103. KERN, DONALD WARREN. *The Prediction of Academic Success of Freshmen in a Community College.* Doctor's thesis, New York University (New York, N.Y.), 1953. (*DA* 15:85)

104. MORTVEDT, AUDREY R. *Relative Effectiveness of a Local English Test, the ACE L-Score, Cumulative Grade Average, and the Cooperative General Culture Test in the Selection of Upper-Class Regent's Scholarship Winners.* Master's thesis, University of Nebraska (Lincoln, Neb.), 1953.

105. RUSSON, ALLIEN R. *The Prediction of Scholastic Achievement of Business Education Majors at the College Level.* Doctor's thesis, University of California (Los Angeles, Calif.), 1953.

106. SATZ, MARTIN ALLEN. *The Relationship Between Eleven Independent Variables and Academic Performance in Nine Social Science Areas at the University of Washington.* Doctor's thesis, University of Washington (Seattle, Wash.), 1953. (*DA* 14:635)

107. SPAULDING, GERALDINE. "A Note on the Interpretation of Scaled Scores for Form Z of the Cooperative English Test." *Ed Rec B* 61:72–4 Jl '53. * (*PA* 28:4863)

108. VOTAW, DAVID F., AND LAFORGE, PAULA K. "Rapid Hand Scoring of Cooperative English Tests." *Jun Col J* 24:214–8 D '53. *

109. WEBB, SAM C., AND McCALL, JOHN N. "Predictors of Freshman Grades in a Southern University." *Ed & Psychol Meas* 13:660–3 w '53. * (*PA* 28:6598)

110. BOLTON, EURI BELLE. "The Predictive Value of the Columbia and the Michigan Vocabulary Tests for Academic Achievement." *Peabody J Ed* 32:9–21 Jl '54. * (*PA* 29:7954)

111. CHAPPELL, TOLAN L.; CALLIS, ROBERT; RENZAGLIA, GUY A.; AND SPOHRER, MYRON A. "The Differential Prediction of Achievement at the University of Missouri." *Ed & Psychol Meas* 14:724–5 w '54. * (*PA* 29:7955)

112. FREEHILL, MAURICE F. "The Co-operative English Test in Academic Counseling." *Col & Univ* 29:244–52 Ja '54. *

113. GUAZZO, EUGENE J., JR. *Predicting Academic Success of Architecture Students.* Master's thesis, Alabama Polytechnic Institute (Auburn, Ala.), 1954.

114. LAYTON, WILBUR L. "The Relation of Ninth Grade Test Scores to Twelfth Grade Test Scores and High School Rank." *J Appl Psychol* 38:10–1 F '54. * (*PA* 29:1570)

115. MARTIN, RICHARD RALPH. *An Investigation of the Effectiveness of an Entrance Test Battery for Predicting Success in Law School.* Doctor's thesis, Temple University (Philadelphia, Pa.), 1954. (*DA* 16:575)

116. SEIGLE, WILLIAM F. "Prediction of Success in College Mathematics at Washburn University." *J Ed Res* 47:577–88 Ap '54. * (*PA* 29:2982)

117. BOYD, JOSEPH DON. *The Relative Prognostic Value of Selected Criteria in Predicting Beginning Academic Success at Northwestern University.* Doctor's thesis, Northwestern University (Evanston, Ill.), 1955. (*DA* 15:1780)

118. BUCKTON, LAVERNE, AND DOPPELT, JEROME E. "Freshman Tests as Predictors of Scores on Graduate and Professional School Examinations." *J Counsel Psychol* 2:146–9 su '55. * (*PA* 30:3453)

119. CHAHBAZI, PARVIZ. "The Prediction of Achievement in a College of Agriculture." *Ed & Psychol Meas* 15:484–6 w '55. * (*PA* 30:7754)

120. CHAPMAN, HAROLD MARTIN. *The Prediction of Freshman Scholarship From a Combination of Standardized Test Scores*

and High School Grades. Doctor's thesis, University of Houston (Houston, Tex.), 1955. (*DA* 15:1201)

121. GUSTAD, JOHN W., AND FISH, JANICE P. "The Use of the Cooperative Mechanics of Expression Test in Classification at the College Freshman Level." *Ed & Psychol Meas* 15:436–40 w '55. * (*PA* 30:7761)

122. HAYNES, JERRY O. *Some Predictive Factors of Academic Success in Two Curricula of a Land-Grant College.* Master's thesis, Alabama Polytechnic Institute (Auburn, Ala.), 1955.

123. MELTON, RICHARD S. "Differentiation of Successful and Unsuccessful Premedical Students." *J Appl Psychol* 39:397–400 D '55. * (*PA* 30:7769)

124. MULLINS, CECIL J. "The Effect of Reading Ability on Two Standardized Classification Tests." *J Ed Psychol* 46:189–92 Mr '55. * (*PA* 30:1627)

125. POUNDS, RALPH L. "Prediction of Academic Success at the University of Cincinnati, Teachers College: Progress Report II." *Yearb Nat Council Meas Used Ed* 12(pt 2):12–31 '55. *

126. ROYER, J. EVERETT. *Selection and Use of Certain Factors Significant in Predicting Achievement of Students in First-Semester Accounting at the University of Miami, 1950–1953.* Doctor's thesis, Indiana University (Bloomington, Ind.), 1955.

127. SKUBA, MICHAEL. "An Analysis of English Errors and Difficulties Among Grade Ten Students in the Smoky Lake School Division." *Alberta J Ed Res* 1:15–23 D '55. *

128. ANDERSON, RODNEY EBON. *The Use of Entrance Tests in the Differential Prediction of Freshman College Achievement, and the Effect of an Item Analysis on the Efficiency of the Predictive Batteries.* Doctor's thesis, Indiana University (Bloomington, Ind.), 1956. (*DA* 16:2344)

129. HOUK, CLIFFORD C. *An Investigation of the Relationship Between General Chemistry 3 at Ohio University and Various Measures of Achievement.* Master's thesis, Ohio University (Athens, Ohio), 1956.

130. SMITH, GEORGE B. *Who Should Be Eliminated? A Study of Selective Admission to College.* University of Kansas Publications, Kansas Studies in Education, Vol. 7, No. 1. Lawrence, Kan.: School of Education, the University, December 1956. Pp. 28. *

131. TRAXLER, ARTHUR E. "Reliability of Cooperative Achievement Tests for Independent Secondary School Pupils." *Ed Rec B* 68:64–8 Jl '56. * (*PA* 31:8853)

132. WEBB, SAM C. "Differential Prediction of Success in Graduate School." *J Ed Res* 50:45–54 S '56. * (*PA* 31:6685)

133. FRICKE, BENNO G. "Speed and Level Versus Rate and Accuracy of Reading." *Yearb Nat Council Meas Used Ed* 14:73–7 '57. *

134. HENDERSON, HAROLD L. "Predictors of Freshmen Grades in a Long Island College." *Ed & Psychol Meas* 17:623–7 w '57. *

135. HEWER, VIVIAN H. "Vocational Interest-Achievement-Ability Interrelationships at the College Level." *J Counsel Psychol* 4:234–8 fall '57. *

136. MANUEL, HERSCHEL T. "Aptitude Tests for College Admission." *Yearb Nat Council Meas Used Ed* 14:20–7 '57. *

137. RICHARDS, JAMES M., JR. "The Prediction of Academic Achievement in a Protestant Theological Seminary." *Ed & Psychol Meas* 17:628–30 w '57. *

138. BARRETT, RICHARD S. "The Process of Predicting Job Performance." *Personnel Psychol* 11:39–57 sp '58. *

139. BERRY, CHARLES A., AND JONES, ARLYNNE L. "The Predictive Value of the Tests of the National Testing Program for Grambling College Freshmen." *Negro Ed R* 9:23–33 Ja '58. *

140. GOWAN, J. C. "Intercorrelations and Factor Analysis of Tests Given to Teaching Candidates." *J Exp Ed* 27:1–22 S '58. *

141. JENSEN, VERN H., AND CLARK, MONROE H. "A Prediction Study of Cooperative English Test Scores." *Personnel & Guid J* 36:635–6 My '58. *

142. MOORE, CHARLES W. *Some Relationships Between Standardized Test Scores and Academic Performance in the College of Business Administration of the University of Houston.* Doctor's thesis, University of Houston (Houston, Tex.), 1958. (*DA* 19:356–7)

For a review by Chester W. Harris of Forms S, T, Y, and RX, see 4:155; for reviews by J. Paul Leonard, Edward S. Noyes, and Robert C. Pooley of Forms R, S, and T, see 3:120. For reviews by Robert Murray Bear and J. B. Stroud of the reading test, see 3:497.

[180]

*Coordinated Scales of Attainment: English.** Grades 4, 5, 6, 7, 8; 1946–54; subtest of *Coordinated Scales of Attainment;* 3 scores: punctuation, usage, capitalization; IBM; Forms A ('46), B ('49) ; 5 levels; directions for administering ['52] ; battery manuals (A, '54; B, '49) ; separate answer sheets must be used;

$1.70 per 25 tests; $1 per 25 IBM scorable answer sheets; 25¢ per scoring stencil; $1 per specimen set; postage extra; (45) minutes; Dora V. Smith; Educational Test Bureau. *

For a review by Alvin W. Schindler of the complete battery, see 4:8; for reviews by Roland L. Beck, Lavone A. Hanna, Gordon N. Mackenzie (with Glen Hass), and C. C. Ross of batteries 4–8, see 3:6.

[181]

*Correctness and Effectiveness of Expression. High school, college; 1944–57; subtest of *Tests of General Educational Development;* IBM; 2 levels, 2 forms: high school, Form B ('44), college, Form B ('43); revised manuals: high school level ('56), college level ('54); $2.50 per 25 tests of either level; separate answer sheets must be used; $1 per 25 IBM answer sheets; 50¢ per specimen set; postage extra; (120) minutes; prepared by Examination Staff of United States Armed Forces Institute; Veterans' Testing Service, American Council on Education. *

For a review by Charlotte W. Croon of the college level, see 3:122. For a review by Robert J. Solomon of the complete battery, see 27; for a review by Gustav J. Froehlich of Form B, see 4:26; for reviews by Herbert S. Conrad and Warren G. Findley, see 3:20.

[182]

★Cotswold Junior English Ability Test. Ages 8–9; 1949–52; forms A ['49], B ['52]; 9s. per 20 tests; 5½d. per single copy; 1s. per manual; postage extra; C. M. Fleming; Robert Gibson & Sons (Glasgow), Ltd. *
a) JUNIOR ENGLISH A. Form A ['49]; manual ['49]; 28(35) minutes.
b) JUNIOR ENGLISH B. Form B ['52]; manual ['52]; 35(45) minutes.

M. A. BRIMER, *Senior Lecturer in Educational Psychology, University College, Ibadan, Nigeria.*

Though the norms for both forms of this test extend from 8-0 to 9-11 years and the tests are similar, they differ in difficulty and in some of the processes tested. Form A has 51 scored items and Form B, 70. The mean raw score on Form A at age 8-11 is 30, while on Form B it is 22. Thus the author is quite right to recommend Form A for 8-year-old and Form B for 9-year-old children. Both forms of the test and the tasks included are part of the outcome of the author's own researches into the basic primary school subjects, which she reports separately.[1] The items were selected after having been tried out and analysed for difficulty and internal consistency. Items found to

1 FLEMING, C. M. *Research and the Basic Curriculum.* London: University of London Press Ltd., 1946. Pp. vii, 120. *

be ambiguous after scrutiny of children's responses were discarded.

In each form there are six separately timed subtests covering reading comprehension, language usage, written composition, short term recall of material read, and accuracy in transcription. There is a progressive increase in difficulty throughout the tests and a well developed unity of the parts. The reading comprehension links the content by making each paragraph part of a single story. This has the merit of reducing the artificiality of the testing situation and of aiding the orientation of young children when they are required to adjust rapidly from one task to another. Teachers of English in primary schools will recognise that, both in this respect and in the skills emphasised, the test is adjusted to the standpoint of the classroom.

On the back cover of the booklet there is a short practice test which adequately familiarises the children with the type of material they will encounter in the test proper, and with the kind of responses they will be required to make. The practice is necessary since the children are required to read the instructions for themselves in the test proper. An example preceding each subtest would undoubtedly have helped a great deal to extend discrimination to the lower ability ranges where the test is at present most weak.

There are rather more selective response items than necessary and more direct questions with single word answers than are desirable. Children grasp completion items rather more readily than those involving selective underlining, and the response made has the advantage of completing a unit of sense, which is a desirable exercise in itself. As a general rule, tests for classroom use should avoid testing techniques which are not a function of the skill being tested.

Instructions for administration are clear and leave little to chance, and despite their similarity to the usual classroom exercises, the scoring of the items remains objective. Marking takes a little longer than with many objective tests and a certain amount of judgment is required of the marker.

The reliability of Form A has been estimated at .97 by the split-half technique and at .94 by the test-retest technique. The figure of .97 confirms the success of the system of item selection used in producing high internal consistency.

Cotswold Junior English Ability Test

The figure of .94 indicates that the whole procedure of administering, working, and scoring the test produces highly consistent results on two occasions. The reliability of Form B is not reported, but the similarity of the two forms and the fact that Form B is longer suggests that it will prove to be at least as reliable as Form A. No evidence of validity is reported in the manual, but reference is made to *Research and the Basic Curriculum* as the basis of the form and content of the test.

The norms for both forms are presented as standardised scores with a mean of 100, a standard deviation of 15, and a normalised distribution. These have the effect of comparing each child's performance with that of a representative group of English children of the same age. Neither form is at its best at the lower extreme of its range. The lower 10 per cent of 8-year-old children make scarcely any score. Norms are provided from 8-0 to 10-0 years, but Form A at least is restricted at the top of its range. It would be better to employ the test well within the limits of its range.

In summary, this is a test to be recommended for classroom use, particularly to those teachers who wish to have tests closely related to classroom exercises. It is rare to find a test of this nature standardised on such a large population.

JOHN C. DANIELS, *Lecturer in Education, University of Nottingham, Nottingham, England.*

It is claimed by the author that these tests have been "devised to measure....the mastery of vocabulary....and the comprehension and use of what is commonly called English" of 8-year-olds. The two tests consist of six subtests, all timed separately. For example, in Form B, subtests 1 and 2 are reading comprehension tests of the type in which the child reads a story silently and then answers five questions on the text. In this case the passages for subtests 1 and 2 are two halves of one longer story. Subtest 3 consists of a story with missing words to be found and underlined in a column to the right of the text. After this, the child is to compose and write out in full two sentences about the story. Subtest 4 consists of direct questions, with answers to be recalled, on the story of subtest 3, plus a test in which the child has to find and underline certain synonyms for words underlined in the text of another story. Subtest 5 is a spelling test, the words to be spelt being read out aloud and their use illus-

trated in sentences. Subtest 6 consists of deciding which of 10 sentences are "commands" and copying these in full, marks being subtracted for errors of copying.

The author explains the rationale of the test in her work *Research and the Basic Curriculum*. It is, she claims, based upon "careful analysis of the difficulties in reading and the processes used in written composition." Certainly the validity of the tests must rest upon the validity of Fleming's analysis, for it is otherwise difficult to see how this empiricist mish-mash of tests could give valid estimates of any recognisable factor other than a rather rough and ready estimation of *g*. Norms are given as standardised scores, with age allowances, having a mean of 100 and, apparently, a standard deviation of 15.

So much depends upon 8- and 9-year-olds being sufficiently "test-trained" to be able to follow the detailed plan of work which has to be carefully controlled by the teacher that, since no reliability coefficients are quoted, your reviewer must be allowed to venture the opinion that retest reliability would be found to be low. The complexity of the testers' and markers' tasks will also militate against high reliability. However, since there is a grave shortage of good tests of general "scholastic" ability at this age level, these tests will no doubt find many satisfied users.

[183]

Cotswold Measurement of Ability: English. Ages 10–12.5; 1947–54; 6 forms: labeled Series 2 ['47], 3 ['49], 4 ['51], 5 ['52], 6 ['53], 7 ['54]; incomplete norms for Series 2–5; 9*s.* per 20 tests; 5½*d.* per single copy; 1*s.* per manual (dates as for tests) for any one series; postage extra; 35(50) minutes; C. M. Fleming and J. W. Jenkins (manual for Series 2); Robert Gibson & Sons (Glasgow), Ltd. *

M. A. BRIMER, *Senior Lecturer in Educational Psychology, University College, Ibadan, Nigeria.*

These tests are designed as measures of attainment in English at the stage of transfer from primary to secondary schools in England and Wales. They are produced annually for use by education authorities in their selection procedures, and distribution is restricted during this critical, initial use. They are eventually released and published with norms based on quite large numbers of English children. While the original function remains in evidence to the extent that the greater discrimination occurs above the mean, the tests have nevertheless sufficient range for general classroom measurement.

The tests have been constructed on the evidence derived from the author's own researches into the difficulties children encounter in reading and the processes by which written composition takes place. Each test is made up of about 112 scored items arranged in four separately timed subtests. The tasks presented are essentially of functional English, concentrating upon reading comprehension and composition. The reading comprehension relies a great deal, perhaps too much, on inference from context. The complexity of the inference gradually increases since, although questions follow each paragraph, the paragraphs continue the theme and the questions integrate material from the preceding paragraphs. Composition is tested analytically by selective response, completion type items within a continuous prose passage, and by the arrangement of sentences into a sensible order after first selecting them from among others to be relevant to a given theme. These two tasks probably approach as close to an objective assessment of written composition as it is possible to get. Vocabulary is tested within the context of a sentence and spelling is tested with a completion item which avoids the pitfalls of employing misspellings as distractors or phonetic spellings as clues. An interesting exercise in precise expression is also included, in which the children are required to select two sentences which mean most nearly the same as a given model.

The tests are intended to be used with the arithmetic and mental ability tests of their batteries, which justifies the placing of the practice test for the English test on the back cover of the arithmetic booklet. Nevertheless, it does inconvenience those users who wish to employ the tests separately, since it is necessary to give the practice test if the norms are to be strictly applicable. On the back covers of the English booklets, short tests of visual acuity are presented. No great precision of measurement is attempted, since they are intended as indications of the children's effectiveness with the size of type used in the tests rather than as measures in their own right. No norms or other form of guidance is given for the interpretation of performance.

The administration is strictly controlled and presents no difficulties apart from the placing of the practice test referred to above. Marking is objective but rather laborious since no mark column is provided and composite marks are sometimes accorded to the same response.

The norms are presented in the form of standardised scores with a mean of 100 and a standard deviation of 15. In effect, they compare the child's performance with that of a representative group of English children of the same age. The scores are grouped into decile ranks for ready interpretation.

The tests are well constructed and cover processes which teachers consider important and which are often missing from other tests of English. The continuity of a single theme throughout each test reduces the artificiality of the testing situation. The tests have well established norms and adequate reliability. More information on the construction of the tests and more extensive guidance to teachers on the interpretation of the scores would improve the manuals.

S. C. RICHARDSON, *Lecturer in Psychology, Hillcroft College, Surbiton, Surrey, England.*

This test is in six forms which are roughly similar. Each is developed around comprehension passages and groups of sentences. Questions follow each section. Items other than comprehension items (spelling and vocabulary questions, for instance) are related to the themes of the passages. The great advantage of this design, in the reviewer's opinion, is that it avoids the use of short, disconnected items which make up most objective tests and which must, to some extent, favour the nonperseverative candidate. Some questions demand sustained thought and the capacity to build up and use mental content. Writing capacity is tested to some extent by a question requiring an answer six sentences long, though the material is not original.

The material of the tests seems likely to be independent of any particular teaching method and should be suitable for children from any school. The grammatical and syntactical questions have been chosen to test some of the points of difficulty revealed by research into the nature of children's errors in writing English. The tests have good reliabilities and have been standardised on large groups of children. Practice material and "warming-up" questions are supplied.

One type of item, occurring in only one form of the test, might perhaps be criticised. This is

Cotswold Measurement of Ability: English

one where the child is asked to write four lines of verse from memory. The product is scored for spelling and punctuation. This question must surely yield material varying widely in difficulty, with a tendency for the abler children to produce more difficult material.

It would be useful to know more about the criteria of external validity mentioned in the manual. In the absence of exact information, the test seems a good measure of the ability to understand English and, to a lesser extent, of the ability to use it. It is notoriously difficult to construct a good, objectively scored English test. The criticisms which apply to many tests of this kind are (*a*) that they instigate undesirable teaching methods and (*b*) that they test only the more mechanical aspects of English ability. The Cotswold test, in the reviewer's opinion, avoids the first of these difficulties and goes some way towards overcoming the second.

[184]

*English: Every Pupil Scholarship Test. Grades 2–4, 5–6, 7–8, 9–12; 1926–58; new form usually issued each January and April; 4 levels; norms available following testing program; no data on reliability; 4¢ per test; 4¢ per scoring key; postage extra; 40(45), 50(55) minutes for grades 2–8, 9–12; Bureau of Educational Measurements. *

[185]

*English IX-XII: Achievement Examinations for Secondary Schools. High school; 1951–53; Forms 1 ('51), 2 ('52), 3 ('53); no specific manual; series manual ('57); no data on reliability and validity; norms: Forms 1 ['52], 2 ['53], 3 ('53); 10¢ per specimen set; postage extra; [60–90] minutes; Educational Test Bureau. *
a) FORMS 1 AND 3. Grades 9, 10, 11, 12; 10¢ per test.
b) FORM 2. Grades 9–10, 11–12; $2.75 per 25 tests.

[186]

★English IX-XII: Midwest High School Achievement Examinations. Grades 9, 10, 11, 12; 1955–57; Forms A ('55), B ('57); 4 levels; no specific manual; no data on reliability; norms: [A, '55; B, '57]; 10¢ per test, postage extra; Form A: 60(65) minutes; Form B: 90[95] minutes; Educational Test Bureau. *

ROGER A. RICHARDS, *Assistant in Secondary Curriculum, New Jersey State Department of Education, Trenton, New Jersey.*

The most serious shortcoming of these tests is the total lack of information about them. The prospective user is not even told how much time is required to administer the tests. A single sheet of paper folded to make a 4-page brochure is entitled "Manual," but the data generally contained in such a publication are not provided. The so-called "Rationale" might better be referred to as a thumbnail sketch of the history of American education (and not a very good sketch). The statement labeled "Purpose" is as follows:

> The purpose of these High School Achievement Examinations is to motivate efforts of accomplishments by the students. A less easily arrived at purpose is that of motivating thinking ability. However, these Examinations make a real effort to stimulate thinking ability based on mastery of contents resulting from efforts of work.

How they make that effort is a mystery to this reviewer, and the publishers are apparently content to let it remain that way to all readers. The manual—which apparently serves science, mathematics, history, and language tests as well as those under review here—states that the "norms are established at the end of each school year." But how they are established is not divulged. The terms "validity" and "reliability" are not mentioned in the manual.

The reviewer infers that the tests are intended to provide a basis for grading students at the end of a year's work in English. That they are worthless for such a purpose would be quite obvious to almost any teacher who looked at a copy of any one of them. In order to construct any test to measure achievement in a course, one must start with a knowledge of the course. If he is to include some spelling words, he must select them from those which the students have supposedly learned during the term. If he is to ask questions about literature, he must base them on the literary works which the students have read. Unfortunately, we are not told anything about the type of English course upon which these tests are based. The reviewer hopes that no such course exists, and he is reasonably confident that it does not.

The provision of two forms for each grade leads one to hope that the forms might be equivalent. But an examination of the contents leads the reviewer to suspect that the two forms for any grade are quite different. Again, the publishers have chosen not to clarify this point.

With so many basic deficiencies, these tests do not warrant the space that would be required to consider some of the more detailed matters such as item writing, format, and scoring. In the opinion of the reviewer the tests do not warrant serious consideration for use as evaluation instruments. English teachers who are looking for good standardized tests would do well to continue their search.

[187]

★English Progress Tests A–F. Ages 8, 9, 10, 11, 12, 13; 1952–57; 1 form; 6 levels; 7s. per 12 tests; 8d. per

single copy; 1s. per manual of any one test; postage extra; A. F. Watts (*a, c, f*) and M. A. Brimer (*b, d, e*); published for the National Foundation for Educational Research in England and Wales; Newnes Educational Publishing Co. Ltd. *
a) ENGLISH PROGRESS TEST A. Age 8; 1952; 1 form ['52]; manual ['52]; no data on reliability; 39(45) minutes.
b) ENGLISH PROGRESS TEST B. Age 9; 1956–57; 1 form ['56]; manual ['57]; (45) minutes.
c) ENGLISH PROGRESS TEST C. Age 10; 1952; formerly called *English Grading Test 3*; 1 form ['52]; manual ['52]; no data on reliability; (55) minutes.
d) ENGLISH PROGRESS TEST D. Age 11; 1956; 1 form ['56]; manual ['56]; provisional norms; (45) minutes.
e) ENGLISH PROGRESS TEST E. Age 12; 1956; 1 form ['56]; manual ['56]; provisional norms; (45) minutes.
f) ENGLISH PROGRESS TEST F. Age 13; 1953; 1 form ['53]; manual ['53]; no data on reliability; (55) minutes.

NEIL GOURLAY, *Professor of Education, University of the Witwatersrand, Johannesburg, Union of South Africa.*

The series is "designed to provide a continuous assessment of English skill from 8–14." There is a test and manual for each age level. Various skills are involved: vocabulary, spelling, reading comprehension, rewording of sentences, direct and reported speech, punctuation, and several others. Vocabulary and spelling enter into all the tests, but only a limited sample of the other skills is tested at each level, the sample varying appropriately from age to age.

Most of the tests would appear to have been well standardised and, where the standardisation might be inadequate, this has been stated. The standardisation procedure adopted enables the user to convert raw scores to transmuted scores, which, for the age group concerned, are distributed with mean 100 and SD 15. Age corrections can then be applied to obtain standardised scores for all ages *within* the age group. A difficulty arises for the teacher using the tests with pupils whose ages range over two or more of the age groups. If an allowance is to be made for age, the teacher has little option but to use standardised scores; and, since the standardisation of each form is limited to an age group, two or more forms of the test will therefore be required. This has certain obvious disadvantages. It is in fact doubtful whether much is gained by the method of standardisation adopted. A set of age norms for each form of the test would probably have increased the tests' usefulness.

A certain amount of the scoring is subjective. This is a disadvantage, but it is compensated for by the increased scope of the items which must improve validity.

There is no doubt that the series is well constructed and can be recommended to teachers and other test users. But, as stated above, a simpler form of standardisation would probably have increased its usefulness.

STANLEY NISBET, *Professor of Education, University of Glasgow, Glasgow, Scotland.*

These tests are designed to "give teachers an idea of the progress a pupil has so far made in mastering the English language." They cover reading comprehension, vocabulary, sentence construction, written expression, punctuation, spelling, and simple grammatical usage.

A special feature is their preference for "free" responses, which require the pupil to write a word or a sentence, and the consequent avoidance of strictly "objective" items (e.g., multiple choice). The manuals give guidance to markers, with examples of acceptable and unacceptable answers. This characteristic helps the tests to give adequate credit to pupils whose teachers have followed "more liberally conceived programmes," as opposed to those who teach English too mechanically. On the other hand, much is left to the subjective judgment of the marker; the reviewer quite often found it difficult to decide whether certain answers on scripts were acceptable or not.

Kuder-Richardson (formula 20) reliability coefficients are quoted for Tests B, D, and E only. They are high (around .95) and indicate that, provided the same person marks all the scripts in a group, a satisfactorily stable assessment is obtained. We do not know, however, to what extent different markers would agree in assessing the same scripts. The reliability quoted merely assures us that the self-consistency of the single marker on a single occasion is high enough not to impair the inherent stability of the test, which is itself high.

Test B was standardized on a representative sample of about 4,500 children. Figures are not provided for the other tests. In the case of Tests D and E, users are warned that the standardizing sample was too small to make the norms trustworthy. The layout of the norms in the manuals is clear, but there is a lack of uniformity in the way in which they are presented in the different manuals. This is probably due to the fact that the tests were produced at different times and by two different authors. If a new edition is contemplated, it would be helpful if a uniform presentation were adopted. It is

English Progress Tests A–F

only fair to say, however, that no great importance is claimed for these norms.

The reviewer has doubts about several small details in some of the marking keys, but on the whole they are clear enough.

It may be concluded that the tests can be recommended for internal classroom use as being preferable to most English tests of a more mechanical type. They have been constructed, often ingeniously, to discover whether pupils can in fact *use* English. The norms, however, should be treated with great caution or not used at all, and, in the absence of strict precautions to ensure consistency among markers, the tests should not be used for any external purpose (e.g., grading pupils or comparing schools or classes).

[188]

*English Survey Test: Ohio Scholarship Tests: Ohio Senior Survey Tests. Grade 12; 1935–54; 6 scores; grammar, spelling, capitalization, punctuation, sentence structure, total; Forms A ('53), B ('54); mimeographed battery manual ['53]; no data on reliability; 4¢ per test; 50¢ per battery teacher's manual ('35); cash orders postpaid; 150(160) minutes; Mary H. Hutchison; Ohio Scholarship Tests. *

For reviews by Charlotte W. Croon Davis and J. Paul Leonard of the original edition, see 3:125.

[189]

★English Test (Adv.). Ages 12–13; 1954–58; forms 1 ['54], 2 ['57], 3 ['58]; distribution restricted to directors of education; 8s. 3d. per 12 tests; 9d. per single copy; 1s. 7d. per manual; postage extra; 50(55) minutes; published for National Foundation for Educational Research in England and Wales; Newnes Educational Publishing Co. Ltd. *
a) ENGLISH TEST (ADV.) 1. 1954–55; manual ['55]; G. A. V. Morgan.
b) ENGLISH TEST (ADV.) 2. 1957; manual ('57).
c) ENGLISH TEST (ADV.) 3. 1958; manual ('58).

[190]

*English Test: Municipal Tests: National Achievement Tests. Grades 3–6, 6–8; 1938–56; subtest of *Municipal Battery;* 5 scores: language usage-words, language usage-sentences, punctuation and capitalization, expressing ideas, total; 2 forms; 2 levels; no data on reliability; no norms for part scores; $1.75 per 25 tests; 50¢ per specimen set of either level; postage extra; 30(35) minutes; Robert K. Speer and Samuel Smith; Acorn Publishing Co. *
a) GRADES 3–6. 1938–55; Forms A ('55, identical with test copyrighted in 1938), B ('39); directions sheet ('38).
b) GRADES 6–8. 1938–56; Forms A ('52, identical with test copyrighted in 1938), B ('56, identical with test copyrighted in 1939); directions sheets (A, '38; B, '39).

For a review by J. Murray Lee of the complete battery, see 18; for a review by Ralph C. Preston, see 4:20; for reviews by A. M. Jordan

of the complete battery for grades 6–8 and Hugh B. Wood of the batteries for grades 6–8, see 40:1191.

[191]

*English Test: National Achievement Tests. Grades 3–8, 7–12; 1936–57; 2 forms; 2 levels; no norms for part scores; 50¢ per specimen set of either level; postage extra; (40) minutes; Robert K. Speer and Samuel Smith; Acorn Publishing Co. *
a) GRADES 3–8. 1936–38; 7 scores: capitalization, punctuation, language usage (sentences), language usage (words), expressing ideas, letter writing, total; Forms A ('38), B ('38); directions sheet ('38); no data on reliability; $2.50 per 25 tests.
b) GRADES 7–12. 1936–57; 7 scores: word usage, punctuation, vocabulary, language usage (sentences), expressing ideas, expressing feeling, total; Forms A, B ('52, identical with tests copyrighted in 1938); directions sheets (A, '57; B, '52); teachers' guide ['44]; no data on reliability for Form B; $3 per 25 tests.

For a review by Winifred L. Post, see 4:162; for a review by Harry A. Greene, see 3:126.

[192]

★English Test 2. Ages 12–13; 1952; 1 form ['52]; 8s. 6d. per 12 tests; 9d. per single copy; 1s. per manual ['52]; postage extra; 60(65) minutes; G. A. V. Morgan; published for the National Foundation for Educational Research in England and Wales; Newnes Educational Publishing Co. Ltd. *

REGINALD EDWARDS, *Lecturer in Educational Psychology, University of Sheffield, Sheffield, England.*

This test was produced in response to a demand from teachers of children between 12 and 14 who attend secondary modern schools—that is, those who academically fall below the 80th percentile. A panel of teachers cooperated in its production. A reasonable attempt has been made to sample what is usually taught to children of this age, bearing in mind that each school is autonomous in this respect. The test covers: selective and inventive vocabulary, reported speech, grammatical usage, knowledge of idiom and conventional patterns of language, sentence joining, punctuation, reading comprehension, poetry completion, spelling, and the use of the dictionary. The test contains 120 items in two separately timed sections. The time limits are said to be generous in order that slow readers will not be unduly penalised. In fact, the second half of the test is found by children to be much harder than the first, so that the limits for the second half are none too generous for children of average ability.

The first section consists of 15 questions dealing with idiomatic expression, 15 on vocabulary and meaning, and 30 on grammatical rules, usages, punctuation, etc. For its kind, this is a most useful section, though it could be argued that each individual usage might be tested separately, and tested in a better way. The second half of the test is heavily concentrated on exercises based upon a dictionary extract (20 items) and passage comprehension and sentence completion items. This section might well be a test of verbal intelligence.

Although intended for secondary modern school children, the test was standardized upon "two complete age groups of pupils attending all types of secondary school" in two areas, one rural and one urban. Thus, the standardization population included the academically brightest 20 per cent. This procedure is still useful with a single age group, but some care is necessary in its extension. After two years, the academically gifted will pursue a much different course than the less gifted, and, as is known, measured verbal intelligence among the less gifted will tend to decline in comparison with that of those pursuing a more academic course. The standardization showed the expected sex difference in favour of girls which exists between ages 10 and 13. In this case, a significant difference of 7.5 points of raw score was found, but separate norms for boys and girls are not available. Although more boys than girls (1,920 against 1,841) were included in the standardization group, the table of norms gives the mean raw score at the middle of the age range as 69. The reported mean scores are boys, 62.47 and girls, 69.97. These facts detract from the value of the norms provided.

It still remains to be asked, what does the test measure? One of the declared aims of the National Foundation for Educational Research is to produce verbal intelligence tests, English attainment tests, linked ability and attainment tests, and diagnostic tests in basic subjects. Certainly this test cannot be used diagnostically, save in a rough and ready way, as it contains too few items of most kinds to be sufficiently diagnostic. Equally, it can scarcely be a verbal intelligence test, though, on the basis of factor analysis of material analogous to that in the test, its items are said to have "high loadings in a factor representing verbal ability." Indeed, from these facts the test's validity is argued. But a knowledge of the wide range of item difficulty and of the test's sampling of vocabulary and comprehension would enable anyone to guess at this high loading on verbal ability. It would seem, therefore, that this is a test

which measures a composite of ability and attainment. As such, its usefulness outside its country of origin must be limited. However, in England, it satisfies teachers who feel that it measures the kind of teaching that goes on in school, where spelling, punctuation, and sentence structure are still important in a subject commonly called "English."

S. C. RICHARDSON, *Lecturer in Psychology, Hillcroft College, Surbiton, Surrey, England.*

This test is intended for secondary modern school children. The questions were suggested by a panel of teachers and appear to be fairly closely related to the teaching methods most commonly used in these schools. Children taught in a different way may be at some disadvantage in the test.

The test includes questions on spelling, vocabulary, sentence construction, and comprehension. There is also a section testing the ability to use a dictionary. Many of the items are nicely designed to give objective scoring without appearing too artificial. In some, the candidate is required to construct a fairly long sentence out of given material.

It seems to the writer a pity that one or two of the questions have a social class bias. No middle class child, however backward in English, is likely to give as a correct answer, "Someone has taken Mary's pencil off of her," or "the man....is the one who learnt me to swim," though, with a predominantly working class group, such items may have validity. Since, in some circumstances, tests influence teaching methods and content, it also seems regrettable that so many of the questions favour the depressing form of English teaching which consists in training children in the use of clichés ("fall between two stools" and "show the white feather," for examples). The poetry completion section is perhaps open to criticism on the ground that the poem is a fairly hackneyed one and some children may already know it by heart.

Apart from some very indirect factorial evidence, there is nothing to show, objectively, exactly what the test measures. The authors suggest that it measures "mechanical English" (spelling and punctuation) and "comprehension and creativity" (reading comprehension and writing). This last claim seems to the writer a trifle optimistic. It seems to rest chiefly on the poetry completion items. The difficulty of test-

English Test 2

ing this ability objectively does not seem to have been solved in the test and it should probably be used in conjunction with an essay paper if a full measure of English ability is required.

The test has reasonably generous time limits and high scores should not depend to a great extent on speed. It has a high (Kuder-Richardson) reliability, and gives a good spread of raw scores. Since British tests of English for the 12–14 age group are relatively scarce, it will be a useful addition.

CLEVELAND A. THOMAS, *Principal, Francis W. Parker School, Chicago, Illinois.*

The content of this test is sufficiently different from American tests that extensive attention must be paid to it. Section 1 of the test is made up of 60 consecutive items with no time breaks but only simple directions for the various parts of the section. Vocabulary is tested by asking students to select the proper item from among six to match a definition. Students are also asked to select one idiomatic use from among six to fit the context of a given sentence. Ability to handle indirect quotations is tested by asking the student to fill in blanks in an indirect quotation on the basis of a previously stated direct quotation. Ability to combine ideas is tested by asking the student to join two or three short sentences into one. In the spelling sections, one form of a word is given and the student is asked to write the proper form of the given word in a sentence. Punctuation is tested by asking the student to supply the proper mark at designated spots in given sentences.

Section 2 includes an extract from a dictionary for use in answering a series of questions. Spelling is tested by giving some letters of a word in a sentence and asking the student to write the whole word, for example, st_p_d for "stopped." The section also includes short passages followed by comprehension questions such as "Find the *four* words, occurring *together* in the passage, which mean nearly the same as 'still to come.' "

This is an interesting test which attempts to put the emphasis squarely on the use of the language rather than on knowledge about it. American teachers and testers may feel that some parts of the test will not test what they are supposed to test. For instance, the example of the reading comprehension item above raises the question of whether reading comprehension

of the passage or only of the specific items within the passage is actually being tested. The test will not render specific diagnosis of the various aspects tested, but only a total score. It should be of interest to any teacher of English as evidence of British emphases. It would also be useful to the experimentally minded or to those who would like to measure their students against British students.

[193]
★English Tests 1, 3–8. Ages 10–11; 1951–58; 7 forms; distribution restricted to directors of education; 7s. 6d. per 12 tests; 8d. per single copy; 1s. 7d. per manual; postage extra; G. A. V. Morgan (a–d) and M. A. Brimer (e); published for National Foundation for Educational Research in England and Wales; Newnes Educational Publishing Co. Ltd. *
a) ENGLISH TEST 1. 1951–58; form 1 ['51]; manual ['58]; 45(50) minutes.
b) ENGLISH TEST 3. 1952–53; form 3 ['52]; manual ['53]; 50(55) minutes.
c) ENGLISH TEST 4. 1953–57; form 4 ['53]; manual ('57); 40(45) minutes.
d) ENGLISH TEST 5. 1954–55; form 5 ['54]; manual ('55); no norms for ages 11-6 to 11-11; 50(55) minutes.
e) ENGLISH TEST 6. 1955–56; form 6 ['55]; manual ('56); no norms for ages 11-10 to 11-11; 50(55) minutes.
f) ENGLISH TEST 7. 1956–57; form 7 ['56]; manual ('57); 50(55) minutes.
g) ENGLISH TEST 8. 1957–58; form 8 ['57]; manual ('58); 50(55) minutes.

[194]
*English Usage: Every Pupil Test. Grades 3–4, 5–6, 7–9, 10–12; 1929–58; new form usually issued each December and April; 4 levels; norms available following testing program; no data on reliability; 3¢ per test; 1¢ per scoring key; cash orders postpaid; 40(45) minutes; Ohio Scholarship Tests. *

For a review by J. R. Gerberich of the 1946 forms, see 3:127.

[195]
★Greene-Stapp Language Abilities Test: Evaluation and Adjustment Series. Grades 9–13; 1952–54; 5 scores: capitalization, spelling, sentence structure, punctuation, usage; IBM; Forms AM ('52), BM ('53); manual ('54); no norms for grade 13; separate answer sheets must be used; $6.40 per 35 tests; $1.70 per 35 IBM answer sheets; postage extra; 35¢ per specimen set, postpaid; 80(95) minutes in 2 sessions; Harry A. Greene and Helen I. Stapp; World Book Co. *

REFERENCE
1. CROOK, FRANCES E. "Interrelationships Among a Group of Language Arts Tests." *J Ed Res* 51:305–11 D '57. *

RICHARD A. MEADE, *Professor of Education, University of Virginia, Charlottesville, Virginia.*

This test is designed to measure proficiency in five areas of language study. It is administered in two periods of 50 and 45 minutes, respectively. The directions seem clear, and it should not be difficult for any teacher who has read them with care to give the test. The test may be machine scored; however, a convenient stencil is furnished for hand scoring.

The manual is an adequate one. It gives understandable directions for scoring and treats well the kinds of interpretation of results which are possible. Raw scores obtained may be easily converted by the use of tables into percentile ranks and standard scores. There is also a clear section on the use of the results and suggestions for conducting remedial work. In general, these suggestions are clear, but, in a few instances, they are vague. Also, the contents of the test should never determine the objectives of a classroom. Test items may be based on content which a given class or pupil should not attempt. Hence, remedial work should relate only to those items that are in accord with goals already set without regard to the content of this test.

Characteristics of the group upon which the test was standardized are given in the manual, and users are warned to interpret results in the light of this information. This point is an excellent one for a manual to make, and teachers should consider it with care.

The capitalization, spelling, and punctuation subtests are adequate and are geared to actual performance at this level. However, the subtests on sentence structure and so-called applied grammar and on usage and so-called applied grammar are open to some question. In both these subtests, there is more stress on grammatical understanding than on ability to identify correct or incorrect structure and usage. The only way the subject can indicate that a sentence is incorrect is to assign a grammatical reason for the error; he receives no credit unless he evidences this knowledge. Hence, the user must decide whether or not it is his purpose to test thorough grammatical knowledge that includes the full understanding of standard terminology.

In addition, the subtest on usage takes no note of colloquial (informal) usage. About one third of the items involve usages that many authorities would consider correct for informal language purposes. There is no direction to the subject to tell him that the test is based on very formal usage. English teachers themselves differ in their points of view about correct usage. So, here again, the user must decide whether this test is in keeping with his own philosophy.

All in all, the *Greene-Stapp Language Abili-*

ties Test is a well constructed test that adequately covers the areas it includes. If the user takes into account the two points made above about grammar and usage, he should find this test convenient and usable in terms of his purposes.

OSMOND E. PALMER, *Associate Professor, Office of Evaluation Services, Michigan State University, East Lansing, Michigan.*

A lot of work has gone into these tests but the results are dubious.

The manual is unusually complete and even has suggestions for analyzing the errors a student makes and for correcting them. The tests seem to have been constructed after good tryouts. They were standardized on an adequate population; reliabilities (fair) were found; and standard scores were established which allow direct comparison with Terman-McNemar IQ's and with other tests in the series.

Each of the five parts of the test is long enough to give a fairly detailed picture of the student's mastery. But all sections do not seem to do an equally good job. The section on capitalization covers its area pretty thoroughly. That on punctuation is likewise quite thorough, but it is not quite as meaningful. A word in a sentence is underlined and the student is given a choice of four marks of punctuation which might be used before, after, or within the word. A fifth choice is that no punctuation is necessary. In half the cases, the choice probably reduces itself to comma (or period) or nothing. In addition, where two spots in a sentence are marked, the same punctuation is required at both spots. The correct decision at one point automatically ensures a correct answer at the other; but it is here, in the omission of one of two necessary commas, that students frequently err.

The spelling section is not so carefully worked out as these two. The setup itself is a little disturbing. Each item consists of four words printed horizontally across the whole width of the page. One or none of these words may be correctly spelled. Since it is easier to glance down a column than to span a page, the good speller may be tempted to see how often the correctly spelled word is the first response in an item. In this manner he could get 10 of the 45 items without looking at three of the four words tested. The misspellings are supposed to have been taken from student papers, but a number of them look so strange that it is doubtful if many students will even recognize them. There is a fair representation of words testing for final *e,* final *y, al* plus *ly,* and doubling. For some reason there are no examples of *ie-ei* words. Also, some of the more commonly misspelled words are missing: grammar, separate, athletics, arctic. There would have been room for these, for about 10 words are needlessly (?) repeated with different spellings in different items, and a few that appear are expendable: voucher, statistics, millinery, embroidery.

What one learns about a student from the two remaining sections, Sentence Structure and Applied Grammar, and Usage and Applied Grammar, is ambiguous. Each item in the sentence structure test has as its stem a sentence. The first response is always, "The sentence is correct." The other three, which suggest ways in which the sentence may be corrected, are an assortment of about 25 statements used, in set patterns or randomly, throughout the 38 items. In fewer than half the cases are these three foils homogeneous or do they all have relevance to the point being tested for in the sentence. For instance, in Item 3, Form AM, the sentence "He wants us to appreciate fully what he has done for this community" is correct. Two of the responses, suggesting corrections of a dangling participle or a dangling gerund, do not seem to have much relevance to this sentence. Nor does the third seem much more apropos: "Leave out a word or phrase that repeats an idea." In 9 cases out of 11 (both forms) when the response "Leave out an unnecessary conjunction before a relative pronoun" is used, there is no such combination in the sentence. This means that a student can eliminate one or two responses simply because they cannot apply to the situation. It also means that if he does pick one of these nonrelevant responses, he is confused by something other than what the item seems to be testing. For diagnosis it also suggests an analysis of the wrong responses for each student individually to find out exactly what is bothering him. Does he mistake an infinitive for a gerund? Does he know what a verbal is?

Test 5, Usage, has the same arrangement as the sentence structure test, but the student has to consider only the one word underlined in the sentence. There is a greater variety in the responses, but some 25 are used frequently. Here,

too, the foils are frequently not to the point. For example, the sentence "Everyone should prepare *his* lessons on time" obviously tests for agreement in number between pronoun and antecedent. The first response, which calls for agreement in gender, is either irrelevant or misleading—how is a student to know whether only girls are involved? The second introduces the problem of the antecedents of reflexive pronouns. And the third response jumps to: "A pronoun used with a gerund to show ownership should be in the possessive case."

Aside from the need here, too, to analyze wrong answers to find a student's specific weaknesses, there is another difficulty. Most of the responses are statements of principle, such as, "The present tense should be used for facts permanently true," and, "The nominative case should be used after a copulative or linking verb." The student undoubtedly assumes that these statements are true and needs to decide only if they are relevant. But of the specific statements introduced as responses, only 9 (5 of these being right answers) of 41 in both forms of the test are correct statements. Eleven might be true of some sentences in some contexts, but 21 are not true for the sentence tested for or for any sentence. Since, throughout the sentence structure test and in most cases here, the student did not have to question the accuracy of the responses, he may fail to do so in the case of these 30-odd responses. Does this help to make the usage test the hardest part of the tests?

If these are speeded tests, and the reviewer's guess is they are (he would estimate that it would take at least 120 minutes instead of 80 to finish them), several other problems are introduced. They may be easier than the 50th percentile difficulties (about 44 per cent correct for 9th graders and about 60 per cent for 12th) reflected in the total score norms would indicate. The reliability, too, figured as it was on the split-half formula, may be spuriously high. The main problem, however, is the significance of the scores. The difference between two scores may be due to a greater knowledge of the matters tested, or it may be due merely to speed. Does the 12th grader get a higher percentage of items attempted right than the 9th grader, or did he simply get more right because he answered more items?

These tests, if carefully used, can tell us

something about our students, but others should prove more fruitful.

[196]

★Hoyum-Schrammel English Essentials Tests. Grades 3–4, 5–6, 7–8; 1955–56; Forms A ('55), B ('55), C ('56), D ('56); 3 levels: primary, intermediate, advanced; manual ['56]; no data on reliability for Forms C and D; $1.25 per 25 tests, postage extra; 25¢ per specimen set of any one level, postpaid; 40(50) minutes; Vera Davis Hoyum and H. E. Schrammel; Bureau of Educational Measurements. *

WORTH R. JONES, *Assistant Professor of Education, University of Cincinnati, Cincinnati, Ohio.*

Forms for the primary grades consist of parts covering sentence recognition, capitalization, punctuation, correct usage, and alphabetization. Forms for grades 5–8 consist of parts covering sentence recognition, capitalization, punctuation, correct usage, and reference materials, such as guide words and an index.

No publication date is indicated in the manual, which contains reliability data and limited information for Forms A and B of the tests. Data for Forms C and D are not given. The manual is extremely brief in its explanation of the development of the tests. Although the statement is made that the tests may be used for both survey and diagnostic purposes, the norms are based only on total scores. These norms were computed from the scores made by 22,485 pupils located in "many representative" schools in "twenty-three different states." No further information on this point is included.

Reliability coefficients for Forms A and B are reported as ranging from .87 to .96, and the standard error of scores, from 2.8 to 6.3. Reliability data are based on results obtained from pupils in "a number" of schools, located in Arkansas, Colorado, Kansas, and Nebraska. An adequate description of the reliability studies is lacking.

The authors' description of attempts to establish the validity of the tests also leaves much to be desired. The content of the tests is reportedly based on the common content of 11 sets of leading textbooks, with items "somewhat in proportion as they were stressed in these sources." The authors assert that criticisms from teachers, supervisors, and test construction specialists were carefully considered in the making of revisions and improvements, although such individuals are not otherwise identified.

An examination of the tests reveals the following technical and editorial errors:

a) Form C, grades 3–4, Part 2, Item 16: The word "be" has been omitted from the sentence.

b) Form A, grades 7–8, Part 3, Item 37: The word "though" evidently should be "thought."

c) Form A, grades 7–8, Part 4, Item 58: "The students [1. choose 2. chose 3. choosed] Carl as team captain." Although "chose" is the desired answer, is it not true that "choose" might be equally correct, depending upon the context?

d) Form D, grades 7–8, Part 6: The example is incorrectly marked. The correct answers should be 12 and 20 rather than 12 and 22.

e) Sections pertaining to capitalization require the pupils to identify letters in heavy type. It is questionable as to whether there is enough distinction between the heavy type and the light type in some of the items.

f) It is the opinion of the reviewer that the directions for marking the punctuation sections on the forms for the primary grades probably will confuse the students. For example, Form C, grades 3–4, uses the term "parentheses" to refer to both brackets and parentheses. At all levels these sections require the pupil to refer to a single list of answers before marking each item. Much time might be wasted through this procedure. It appears highly possible that ease of marking has been sacrificed for ease of scoring.

Because of the inadequacies of the manual, the lack of data on reliability for Forms C and D, the poor format, and the errors within the tests, the reviewer is unwilling to recommend these tests to prospective users.

RUTH STRICKLAND, *Professor of Education, Indiana University, Bloomington, Indiana.*

Each of the tests covers sentence recognition, capitalization, punctuation, and certain aspects of usage. The remainder of each test deals with the use of reference and resource materials. No attention is given to word meanings, writing style, or spelling.

The tests of sentence recognition follow an identical pattern from grade 3 through grade 8. They test recognition of fragments, run-on sentences, and simple sentences—mainly declarative. There is relatively little difference in maturity and complexity between the sentences for the primary grades and those for the advanced grades. The content dealt with at the three test levels differs little.

Part 2 of each test deals with capitalization. In each case the letter to which the child is to respond is indicated in darker type. The child is not asked to find an error in a sentence or to look at the sentence as a whole—the way he would experience it in his own writing. He is told to respond only to the one letter in heavy type in the context of the sentence. Because the dark type differs in size from the rest of the type, it is, in a few instances, difficult to locate the letter to which attention is called.

Knowledge of punctuation is tested in Part 3 of each test. The answer choices for the section are listed at the beginning of the section. Parentheses or brackets appear at the point which is to be tested. It appears likely that many children will receive considerably higher scores on this subtest because attention is directed to a specific spot, whether it calls for punctuation or not. The child might not have recognized the need for attention at that point had he not been called upon to consider it.

Part 4 of each test deals with usage. In the test for grades 3 and 4 common verb errors, double subjects, and a few other common errors are included. The two final items of Forms A and B which link a pronoun with a noun as a double subject seem very difficult for this level. Forms C and D for grades 3 and 4 have an added part dealing with contractions and possessives. These do not appear in Forms A and B.

The usage section of each of the intermediate forms contains 50 items, some of which test the same elements which appear in the easier tests. Again at this level a new Part 4 dealing with contractions, possessives, and plurals appears in Forms C and D but not in Forms A and B.

The final section of the tests for grades 3 and 4 and Forms C and D for grades 5 and 6 deals with alphabetization. Directions are clearly stated so that children ought to have little difficulty with these items.

Forms A and B of the intermediate test have two sections which do not appear in Forms C and D. Part 5 of Forms A and B deals with reference materials. Section A is concerned with the use of guide words as one finds them in a dictionary and Section B with the use of an index. The questions dealing with the index would be difficult for many pupils of grades 5 and 6.

The four forms of the intermediate test differ considerably in difficulty and in content. Forms C and D appear distinctly easier and more within the scope of the majority of pupils of this age than do Forms A and B.

Part 5 of Forms A and B of the tests for grades 7 and 8 deals with reference materials. It is essential that children learn to use reference resources easily and effectively but there is some question as to whether these skills fall

within the scope of an English test. Also the items dealing with reference materials in Forms C and D of this test seem distinctly easier than those of Forms A and B. Part 6 of Forms C and D is concerned with the location of authors and topics in card index drawers.

At all grade levels, the directions for the test are to be read by the pupils. This adds considerably to the difficulty for many pupils at grades 3 and 4. At each grade level there is a great deal to cover in a 40-minute period.

What really constitutes skill and power in the use of language is not touched upon here. The ability to express an idea or a series of ideas in organized, clear cut sentences and well-knit paragraphs and to set them down in a form which will carry meaning to a reader is in no way measured in these tests.

[197]
*The Iowa Tests of Educational Development: Test 3, Correctness and Effectiveness of Expression. Grades 9–13; 1942–58; IBM; Forms X-3S, Y-3S ('52); examiner's manual ('58); battery manual ('54); pupil profile leaflet, fourth edition ('58); profile card (no date); separate answer sheets must be used; $3 per 20 tests; $5 per 100 IBM answer sheets; 50¢ per hand and machine scoring stencil; 50¢ per specimen set; 50¢ per battery manual; postage extra; 60(70) or 40(50) minutes (class period version); prepared under the direction of E. F. Lindquist; Science Research Associates. *

For reviews by J. Murray Lee and Stephen Wiseman of the complete battery, see 17; for a review by Eric F. Gardner of Forms X-2 and Y-2, see 4:17; for reviews by Henry Chauncey, Gustav J. Froehlich, and Lavone A. Hanna of Forms X-1 and Y-1, see 3:12.

[198]
Modern English Usage Test. Grades 9–16 and adults; 1949–50; IBM; Form A ('49); manual ('50); no data on reliability and validity; separate answer sheets must be used; $4 per 25 tests; 50¢ per specimen set; cash orders postpaid; 40(50) minutes; Antonia Bell Morgan; Aptitude Associates. *

HOLLAND ROBERTS, *Director, Academic Freedom Committee, San Francisco, California.*

The author has designed this test to cover a very wide field: conversation and written English in secondary schools, colleges and universities, business schools, and business and industry. The manual states that it has been standardized nationwide on 3,283 high school students and 171 male high school graduates, 63 holding the bachelor's degree, and 67 with unspecified advanced degrees.

The test consists of 130 sentences, with one

or more words underlined to indicate some point of usage. The student is asked to mark each sentence T for "correct" or F for "incorrect."

Interested teachers will find a number of problems in considering what the test offers, as little or no information is provided on a number of key questions: how the test was constructed, how the standardization was done, and how the test is to be used in improving usage in teaching programs. In particular, there is no reference to authority for the choice of the 130 usage items which make up the body of the test nor any indication that the author recognized or made use of the important studies in the field of English usage issued by the National Council of Teachers of English and other authoritative and scholarly organizations. There is no reference to any authority anywhere in the manual, scoring key, or test. The result is general confusion. Colloquialisms and idiomatic English are accepted at times and rejected at others for undisclosed reasons. Positive positions are taken on cases of divided usage, and even against generally accepted usage: "It's up to you and *I* to set a good example" is considered acceptable usage, but not "Bill has worked here longer than *I*."

The use of the nominative in "Who do you have in mind?" is rejected, although it is in almost universal use and is given as established by Leonard in *Current English Usage* and Marckwardt and Walcott in *Facts About Current English Use,* and approved by Kennedy in *English Usage* as "natural" and "almost inevitable." In the *Oxford English Dictionary* it is called "common in colloquial use" and Shakespeare, Southey, and Hardy are cited in support. At times it is not clear what usage is in question, as in the sentence: "He will *succeed* if he continues to work hard." The author does not accept this usage but gives no reason. A number of cases of divided usage are included such as: "Ben talks *like* he knew everything." The author of the test accepts this usage, although Leonard and Kennedy report it as "disputable" and the Oxford dictionary notes that it is "generally condemned as vulgar or slovenly."

Finding ways to rationalize such diverse unilateral decisions would tax the ingenuity of the nimblest. Most teachers and supervisors will prefer to use the *Cooperative English Test* or make their own teaching tests which place major emphasis upon learning the large body of accepted usage and subordinate the debatable usages which illustrate the ebb and flow of change and the presence all about us of different levels of language.

For a review by Walter N. Durost, see 4:170.

[199]

★The New Purdue Placement Test in English. Grades 11–16; 1931–55; 8 scores: punctuation, grammar, sentence structure, reading (study), reading (pleasure), vocabulary, spelling, total; IBM; Forms D, E ('55); preliminary manual ('55); only norms are tentative grade 13 norms for total score; separate answer sheets or booklets must be used; $2.70 per 35 tests; $1.35 per 35 IBM answer sheets; $2.10 per 35 answer booklets; 42¢ per machine scoring stencil; 60¢ per specimen set; postage extra; 65(75) minutes; G. S. Wykoff, J. H. McKee, and H. H. Remmers; Houghton Mifflin Co. *

REFERENCES

1–9. See 4:173.
10. JOHNSON, A. PEMBERTON. "Counseling Engineering Freshmen." *Ed & Psychol Meas* 13:133–44 sp '53. * (PA 28: 1566)
11. SEVERANCE, KATHERINE M. *The ACE and the Purdue English Placement Tests as Predictors of Academic Success at Baylor University.* Master's thesis, Baylor University (Waco, Tex.), 1953.
12. BAKER, PAUL CLEO. *Experiments in Variable Selection for Prediction of Academic Achievement.* Doctor's thesis, Purdue University (Lafayette, Ind.), 1955. (DA 15:2565)
13. DUNGAN, EARL WILLIAM. *An Evaluation of the Orientation Test Battery at Dickinson State Teachers College for Purposes of Prediction and Counseling.* Doctor's field study, Colorado State College of Education (Greeley, Colo.), 1955.
14. BONNER, LEON WILLIAM. *Factors Associated With the Academic Achievement of Freshmen Students at a Southern Agricultural College.* Doctor's thesis, Pennsylvania State University (State College, Pa.), 1956. (DA 17:266)

GERALD V. LANNHOLM, *Program Director, Educational Testing Service, Princeton, New Jersey.*

The authors of the *New Purdue Placement Test in English* state that its primary purpose is "to sample the knowledge possessed by high school seniors or college freshmen of what is called 'good English.'" An examination of the content of the test reveals that the authors were either unnecessarily modest in this claim or had in mind a much broader concept of "knowledge" than that used by this reviewer. While it is clear that knowledge is required to respond correctly to the test exercises, the successful examinee must also be able to apply such knowledge.

The names of the various parts of the test indicate the general areas covered: recognition of grammatical errors, punctuation, sentence clearness and effectiveness, reading, vocabulary, and spelling. In each of the first three of these parts, the authors employ a 2-response (right or wrong) type of exercise. In the first part, the examinee is to study each of the 30 sentences and indicate whether or not it contains an error in grammar. In the second, he is to decide, for

each of 45 sentences, whether or not it is punctuated correctly. In the third, he is to indicate,
for each of 30 sentences, whether or not it is
clear and effective. In none of these parts is he
asked to identify the error or to supply a correction. To measure reading ability, two reading selections (constituting the fourth and fifth
parts, respectively) with 14 four-choice questions based on each are presented. In the vocabulary part, the examinee is required to indicate
which of the five words given for each of 45
key words means most nearly the same as the
key word. The spelling part includes 45 items,
each of which is made up of three different
words plus the word "none"; the examinee is
to select the misspelled word, if any, in each
item. Each of the seven parts has its own time
limit, with 65 minutes being allotted for the 225
items in the total test. The answer sheet provides space for recording the score on each part.

Labeled a "preliminary edition," the manual
nevertheless represents a fairly complete job.
It contains considerable information to assist
the prospective user in evaluating the usefulness of the test for his particular purpose, directions for administering and scoring the test,
and interpretative data, the source of which is
described in some detail. The data, all based on
the use of the test at Purdue University, include percentile and T score norms for total
score, estimated reliability coefficients and
standard errors of measurement for part scores
and total score, intercorrelations among the
part scores and total score, and correlations of
the test scores with scores on a number of other
tests.

The authors report that the principal use of
the test scores has been for placement in English courses. While they do not present direct
evidence on the effectiveness of the test scores
alone for that purpose, they cite correlations
between the test scores and grades in English
courses for freshmen at Purdue University assigned to English courses at three different
levels on the basis of their scores on this test
and other data. Raw correlation coefficients
ranging from .08 to .34 were obtained for the
separate courses. Corrected for restriction of
range in test scores, the estimated correlations
ranged from .84 to .86. The authors' statement
that "the validity of this test is near .85" may
be misleading to readers who do not realize that
validity is a specific rather than a generalized
concept.

Without the information given in the manual,
some might be inclined to underestimate the
quality of this test on the basis of the overemphasis on error recognition, the use of the
right-wrong item type, the relatively small
sampling of specific skills within ability areas,
and the lack of exercises requiring the student
to produce good writing. Although this reviewer believes that the prospective user should
always examine any test before making a decision on its quality, this test demonstrates the
soundness of the adage which says that "the
proof of the pudding is in the eating." The evidence presented indicates that the test has a
high degree of effectiveness for the placement
of college freshmen in English courses.

M. J. WANTMAN, *Visting Director of Educational Measurement and Research, University
of Malaya, Singapore.*

The primary purpose of this test is stated as
being "to sample the knowledge possessed by
high school seniors or college freshmen of what
is called 'good English.' " The test is specifically
designed for use in the placement of freshmen
students at Purdue in advanced English, standard English, and remedial English classes. The
test seems to be adequate for placement purposes.

The typography of the test and its format
are not impressive. The type in Parts 2, 4, and
6, covering punctuation, reading, and vocabulary, is small. The booklet is stapled at the top
of the long side of the pages rather than at the
side.

Either IBM answer sheets or the "self-
marking answer booklets" must be used. There
is no provision for recording answers in the
test booklet. The layout of the IBM answer
sheet is good, but that of the self-marking answer sheet is crowded, particularly for the vocabulary part. The printing of the names of the
parts on both the IBM answer sheets and the
self-marking answer booklets would have minimized the possibility of a student's marking his
answers in the wrong place.

The directions for administering the test are
clear and straightforward. A student is allowed
to work on a particular part only during the
time announced for that part. It may be difficult
to proctor students to be sure they are conform-
ing to this instruction since neither the pages of
the test booklet nor the parts of the answer

sheets are labeled with large distinguishing marks.

The norms reported are marked "tentative" —which indeed they should be. They are based on 1,310 and 1,306 first year students at Purdue for Forms D and E, respectively. The cases for Form D include 1,037 men and 273 women; the Form E norms are based on 1,029 men and 277 women. Separate norms are provided for men and women because "it has been found that, on the average, women in the first year of college score higher on this test than do men."

The table of norms presents raw scores, percentile ranks, and T scores. The T scores have been normalized so that they should not be interpreted in terms of standard deviation units. For example, a raw score of 195 for a man on Form E is reported as a T score of 64. A T score of 64 implies the student is 1.4 standard deviations above the mean for men on this test. A raw score of 195 for a man on Form E is, in fact, almost 2.7 standard deviations above the mean for men. Another apparent weakness in the norms is the lack of comparability of results for the two forms. A raw score of 195 for a man on Form D, for example, is converted into a T score of 77. The authors enumerate other important reasons why "caution in the use of these norms is strongly recommended," and indicate that new norms will be published.

The reliabilities reported were computed by the Kuder-Richardson formula 20. The directions for administering the test suggest that speed is a factor ("An error of a few seconds in the time allowed may mean a difference of several points in a score.") in spite of the claim that "the test has more the nature of a power test than of a rate or speed test." While the latter statement is no doubt true, speed is enough of a factor to make the Kuder-Richardson reliabilities overestimates. If Forms D and E are really equivalent, parallel forms reliabilities would be a better indication of reliability.

Since the time limits for the various parts range from 7 minutes to 11 minutes, the reliabilities of the scores, as might be expected, are not high enough to warrant the use of the part scores. The reliabilities reported for Part 3, Sentence Clearness and Effectiveness, and Parts 4 and 5, Reading, are the lowest, being .68, .80, and .77, respectively, for Form E. The standard errors are relatively large. In Part 4, for example, where the maximum possible score is 15, the standard error is 1.83. The reliabilities reported for total scores are adequate. They are .94 and .96 for Forms D and E, respectively.

In spite of a suggestion made early in the manual that the test was not designed as a predictive device, the authors later present as evidence of validity correlations between test scores and grades in English courses and between test scores and first semester grade point index. The correlations reported have a modal value in the neighborhood of .30, which, when the correlations are corrected for restricted range, rises to the neighborhood of .80. The data presented suggest that .80 highly overestimates the correlational value. It is probably somewhere between .30 and .80.

The correlations between total scores on the test and a "Verbal Factor Score" (no indication of the source of this score is given) for various groups of students suggest that these two values are measures of the same thing. For the groups in which the number of cases is over 200, the correlations range from .8676 to .9035. The reporting of coefficients of correlations to four decimal places is amazing when it is noted that one such 4-decimal place value is based on 14 cases and when cognizance is taken of the known competence in statistics of at least one of the authors.

The *New Purdue Placement Test in English* is a good test for measuring the "fundamentals of English." Even though there are still a few items for which the answers are probably controversial, the authors seem to have succeeded in not being "too doctrinaire in attitude, neither too liberal nor too conservative." The evidence of validity for English placement and for predicting success in first year performance at Purdue is strong enough to warrant universities' using this test for these purposes at their institutions provided they establish their own norms and determine evidence of validity based on their own students.

[200]

★**SRA Achievement Series: Language Arts.** Grades 2–4, 4–6, 6–9; 1954–57; title on some tests for grades 2–6 is *How Should We Say This?*; 2–3 scores: capitalization-punctuation, grammatical usage, spelling (grades 4–9 only); IBM for grades 4–9; Forms A, B; 3 levels; technical supplement, second edition ('57); separate answer sheets must be used in grades 4–9; 50¢ per teacher's handbook ('55); 50¢ per administrator's manual ('56); $1 per technical supplement; postage extra; Louis P. Thorpe, D. Welty Lefever, and Robert A. Naslund; Science Research Associates. *
a) GRADES 2–4. Forms A ('55), B ('57); examiner's

manual, second edition ('57) ; $1.70 per 20 tests ; $1 per scoring stencil ; (105) minutes in 2 sessions.

b) GRADES 4–6. IBM ; Forms A ('54), B ('56) ; examiner's manual ('56) ; $2 per 20 tests ; $5 per 100 IBM scorable answer sheets ; $1 per set of machine scoring stencils ; 50¢ per hand scoring stencil ; 75(90) minutes.

c) GRADES 6–9. IBM ; Forms A ['55], B ('56) ; examiner's manual ('56) ; prices same as for grades 4–6 ; 60(75) minutes.

CONSTANCE M. MCCULLOUGH, *Professor of Education, San Francisco State College, San Francisco, California.*

These tests constitute a basic literacy measure for the grades concerned, in the form of a proofreading test of capitalization, punctuation, usage, and (for grades 4–6 and 6–9 only) spelling. The punctuation, capitalization, and usage items are strewn throughout a series of stories so that the examinee is required to be aware of all three types of error. The points of error are numbered, and correspondingly numbered items on the right hand side of the pages present two or more possibly correct answers from which to choose. Narrative materials are used in the spelling tests for grades 4–6 and 6–9, crucial words underlined, and multiple choice spelling versions given in the right hand margin.

These tests have much in their favor. The Examiner Manual offers clear directions for administering the tests and classifying the items for scoring.

The Teacher's Handbook provides some interpretation of scores and suggestions for follow-up of deficiencies. The Manual for the School Administrator explains that item selections were based on analysis of textbooks, courses of study, expert opinion, and research studies. Tables in the manual show a breakdown of the actual intent of each item. The Technical Supplement is a veritable textbook on the construction and standardization of the tests, the manner in which the batteries were equated, and the procedure followed for establishing norms. It is important to note that the norms are based upon May testing, and require a different interpretation if the tests are to be given at another time of year. Reliability coefficients on total usage items and combined capitalization and punctuation items range from .78 to .91, and seem to be slightly lower for the higher levels within each battery.

Needless confusion is avoided by the fact that the examinee makes only one kind of response throughout the entire test. The narra-

tive material includes personal letters, business letters, and even poetic form, as well as conversation. The subject matter reflects natural child life at the levels tested. The most basic errors are tested more than once, so that a more dependable diagnosis is possible. Forms A and B, slightly different in subject matter, are utterly identical in the types of item tested and the order of their occurrence.

On the negative side it might be mentioned that the narrative form and the mixture of types of item mean a more complicated kind of answer key and pupil inconvenience in finding the space intended for answers. Although the vocabulary of the tests is relatively easy for the grade levels concerned, there will doubtless be some children for whom the test is one of reading ability rather than language. Such children should have the items read to them or be given the next easier test.

Test users should know that the tests at each level are more discriminating at lower score levels than at higher score levels. As a basic literacy test, the test contains few niceties which would characterize the high scorers. On the other hand, some of the niceties are actually no longer disputed usages and probably reflect educational lag rather than linguistic truth. Examples are : *can* for *may,* come *and* see, every*one* —*they,* and off *of.* For the teacher who wishes to identify a child's specific needs, the omission of some errors, like "ain't," seems unfortunate.

The spelling test reflects spelling ability at a difficulty level rather than a child's ability to spell demons common to all educational levels. The test does not provide a way of diagnosing the kinds of spelling error the pupil makes. The presence of "to, two, too" and "they're, their, there" under usage instead of under spelling seems odd.

In general, the tests have been constructed with admirable care and concern for the purposes of possible users.

WINIFRED L. POST, *Instructor in English, Dana Hall, Wellesley, Massachusetts.*

All three tests in this series measure skills in capitalization, punctuation, grammar, and usage. One form of the test for grades 4–6 and both forms of the test for grades 6–9 measure skill in spelling in a separate section.

The test for grades 2–4 consists of four passages, mainly narrative, on such subjects as pet dogs, pet birds, or birthday parties. The print is large, the instructions are simple, and the opening page is inviting. Throughout the test portions of the text are underlined, and either one or two alternatives are offered for each underlined portion. The student indicates his choice by a mark in his test booklet. The items range in difficulty from a choice between "had brang" and "had brought" to a choice between "they" and "he" to refer to the pronoun "everyone."

The test for grades 4–6 is in form like that for grades 2–4, except that it offers the option of a separate answer sheet for machine scoring, and, in Form B, provides a section which tests ability to spot spelling errors in a continuous passage. The other sections of the test also consist of continuous passages, still mainly narrative, but with heavy use of dialogue and letters for testing skills in punctuation. The variety of problems offered in punctuation is an evident strength of the test, though thoughtful English teachers may question the assumption that even the allegedly quoted informal conversation of children must adhere to ultra-conservative standards of formal "good English." The grammar-usage items range in difficulty from a choice between illiterate and literate English to rather subtle distinctions between restrictive and nonrestrictive elements. Those items which require a student to read fairly long, fairly complex groups of words and then indicate whether or not these groups of words form a complete sentence will be warmly received by all English teachers. This test, unlike the test for grades 2–4, assumes that the student has some knowledge of common technical terms and that he will be able to select the correct term to describe underlined groups of words.

The test for grades 6–9 differs from that for grades 4–6 mainly in the increased complexity of the reading material and the inclusion of descriptions and evaluations as well as narratives. Like the lower level test, this one includes a separate spelling section requiring the student to find spelling errors in context. All four sections preceding the spelling section present a rich variety of items on punctuation, grammar, usage, and capitalization. Here, too, the items range in difficulty from a choice between "We *seen* him" and "We *saw* him" to a choice between "try *and*" and "try *to*."

The title for these tests is misleading. "Mechanics of English" would be a less pretentious and a more precisely descriptive title for tests which, within the sharply defined areas of capitalization, punctuation, grammar, usage, and spelling, measure admirably what they set out to measure. Ease of administration, ease of scoring—either by schools themselves or by the scoring service offered by SRA—the provision of complete data for interpreting scores for individual students and evaluating them in the light of norms based on carefully selected groups of public school students, the carefully and ingeniously contrived equivalence of forms, the attractive format, and the use of intrinsically interesting materials are the outstanding strengths of these tests. Teachers who are alive to recent developments in the teaching of language will especially welcome the use of connected material which forces the student throughout the test to reckon with a total context rather than to deal with isolated sentences. English teachers whose concept of language teaching includes more than those situations governed by a hard and fast rule of right and wrong will find these tests excellent as far as they go, but may wish to supplement them with other items which seek to test judgment, awareness of meaning as sometimes the sole determiner of what punctuation needs to be used, where a word or phrase or clause should be put in its sentence, when words or phrases can be deleted without loss of meaning, or when the relationship of ideas in a sentence requires the subordination of one of two clauses within the sentence. English teachers trained in testing may cavil over the considerable number of items in this test which offer the student only two choices; and the teachers who want the separate skills in mechanics of English measured in separate sections will prefer the *California Language Test*. In the opinion of this reviewer, however, one of the outstanding advantages of these tests is the very fact that the student is not told to look for only one kind of problem in each section. He must have the flexibility to deal with many kinds of language problems within each section of the test; this is closely in line with the realities of meaning, language, and the written word.

For reviews by Warren G. Findley and Worth R. Jones of the complete battery, see 21.

[201]

★**Scholastic Achievement Series: English-Spelling.** Grades 2.5–3, 4–6, 7–9; 1954–55; various titles used by publisher; for Catholic schools; subtest of *Scholastic Achievement Series;* 4 scores: punctuation and capitalization, correct usage, English total, spelling;

IBM for grades 4–9; 2 forms; 3 levels; separate answer sheets may be used in grades 4–9; $1.75 per 35 IBM scorable answer sheets; 24¢ per scoring stencil; 50¢ per specimen set of any one level; postage extra; (40–50) minutes; Oliver F. Anderhalter, R. Stephen Gawkoski, and John O'Brien; Scholastic Testing Service, Inc. *

a) PRIMARY TEST. Grades 2.5–3; Forms A ('54, identical with English-spelling tests of complete battery copyrighted in 1953), B ('55); battery manual ('55); $2.70 per 35 tests.

b) ELEMENTARY TEST. Grades 4–6; IBM; Forms A ('54), B ('55); battery manual ('55); $3.75 per 35 tests.

c) ADVANCED TEST. Grades 7–9; IBM; Forms A ('54), B ('55); battery manual ('55); $3.75 per 35 tests.

GERALDINE SPAULDING, *Consultant, Educational Records Bureau, New York, New York.*

The manuals provided with these tests are those prepared for the complete battery, with a separate manual for each level. The text of the three manuals is the same except for the descriptions of test content and directions for administering. The figures in tables giving reliability and related data are the same in the primary and elementary manuals, but, without explanation, the corresponding table in the advanced manual gives different figures. Several varieties of reliability index are shown, but each represents the median of a number of single-grade indices. There is no indication of how much variation in reliability there was from grade to grade. The median split-half reliabilities given in the primary and elementary manuals are .90 for total English score and .91 for spelling score; those in the advanced manual are .91 for total English and .95 for spelling. More detailed information on reliability, grade by grade, would be more useful than the variety of indices given.

The manuals do give relatively complete information on the procedures of construction and standardization. Detailed directions for administering, scoring, and tabulating are given. The instructions to the examiner for some of the spelling tests are rather muddled, but examiners will doubtless know how to proceed. There is an error in the directions (for use when answers are marked in the booklets) for Test 1A, elementary level: "select its number as the answer" should read "select its *letter* as the answer."

The choice of content is based on the analysis of the courses of study in a large number of Catholic schools. The content of the English tests, reflecting that analysis, would appear to confirm the need for a special test for Catholic schools, since the emphasis differs from that found in most achievement batteries. A rather superficial difference (as far as measurement is concerned) is that some of the sentences used to provide testing situations are on religious subjects. A more fundamental difference is in the weight given to formal matters of language in the elementary and advanced tests. The primary English test consists only of subtests on punctuation, capitalization, and correct usage; but at the two higher levels, three more subtests are added to these parts, all dealing with information *about* language—knowledge of rules, statements of principles, identification and classification of conventional linguistic elements, and information about specific techniques of writing and speaking. Non-Catholic schools would probably consider this kind of material greatly overemphasized in the tests.

The usage tests employ the conventional technique of requiring the examinee to choose between a right and a wrong word or form of word given in a sentence. The chief problem in such items is that of devising sentences in which the wrong choice is not too farfetched. Even when the grammatical distinction involved is a suitable one, the specific sentence, using the wrong choice, sometimes looks very artificial. A number of items in Test 3 exhibit this defect. In usage items, the wrong choices ought to conform to *real* uneducated or childish patterns of speech, and should not have a "manufactured" look. One might expect that item analysis would reveal defects of this kind, but even if it did not, it is doubtful that such items are really testing what the test is designed to measure.

In general design and printing, the test booklets are clear and reasonably attractive, though conservative. The grade-equivalent conversion tables are printed in very small type, but this, unfortunately, is a defect common to many achievement batteries. The machine scorable answer sheets fall far short of the standard of the booklets. The small letters identifying choices are blurred and barely legible. The conversion tables on the Form A answer sheet are in microscopic type and are almost completely illegible. The tables on the Form B answer sheet are in larger and clearer type, but on neither form are the tables conveniently placed for machine scoring. These deficiencies should be corrected in later printings.

In general, the content of the capitalization, punctuation, and usage sections is conventional, and the kind of item used presents no innovations. The tests, presumably, correspond more closely in emphasis, and probably in grade placement of topics, to the curriculum of Catholic schools than do tests designed primarily for use in public schools.

RUTH STRICKLAND, *Professor of Education, Indiana University, Bloomington, Indiana.*

Each of the tests contains a section dealing with punctuation. These sections are satisfactorily graduated in difficulty, but all of them call upon children to take note of certain designated points. There is no means of ascertaining whether children would recognize these as points needing attention if they were proofreading their own writing. The subtests on capitalization, on the other hand, do require children to locate and mark the points at which capital letters are needed.

The test for grades 2 and 3 also contains a correct usage section that deals mainly with common verb errors and homonyms.

The test for grades 4–6 includes a two-part section dealing with various aspects of grammar: sentences, phrases, clauses, parts of speech, and syntax. A great deal more knowledge of abstract grammar—parts of speech, definitions, and syntax—is called for here than is now thought desirable for these grades by many authorities in the field of English. Test 3 is concerned with correct usage. Parts of it deal with common errors and parts of speech with refinements which, in teaching practice, are often left for a slightly later age. Test 4 is concerned with oral and written English. The attention here is centered on structure, definition, and the mechanics of writing.

The test for grades 7–9 starts with punctuation and capitalization, as do the others. Test 2A deals with sentences, phrases, and clauses. Test 2B is concerned with parts of speech and syntax. Again, in both of these sections, an unusually extensive knowledge of abstract, structural grammar is called for—far more than many authorities advocate for this level. Test 3 deals with correct usage and reflects more closely what most teachers of English would expect children of these ages to know. In fact, it would be quite an easy test for children of this level who have experienced the emphasis on correct usage that is commonly thought good for elementary and junior high school age young people. In Test 4, on oral and written English, the 22 multiple choice questions deal mainly with form and definition.

Each test in the series ends with a section on spelling consisting of 35 dictated words.

At all grade levels, the directions for the tests are given orally to the pupils. Scoring keys are provided with all testing materials. Grade equivalents are provided for each test in convenient conversion scale form following each test in the booklet. All grade placements are in terms of tenths of a year. Corresponding percentile ranks are also given. Scores on the various subsections are not convertible into grade equivalents but do have diagnostic value. Diagnostic profiles can be plotted from them.

These tests raise some fundamental and truly amazing questions. Is a child in the middle grades who knows how many parts there are in "every" paragraph or friendly letter, who can fit together a definition of a homonym or synonym, and who knows *exactly* how many inches of margin to leave at the right side of a page, through that knowledge a writer? Can one learn to speak or write through definitions and mechanics alone? Of what does growth in the use of English consist?

Growth in expressing ideas through clear, well organized writing is in no way touched upon in any part of any of the tests. English is treated throughout the tests as a machine or a jigsaw puzzle, not a living, organic language. One could designate and name every bone and muscle that makes up the human frame and still know nothing about a human being as a living, breathing entity. In these tests English is treated as an unrelated mass of discrete parts without color or motion or life. In no way is it approached as a means of communication. It would appear that a child could pass these tests with perfect scores and still be unable to put on paper, between an initial capital and a final period, anything that would be worth writing or reading.

Research on the teaching of grammar makes it fairly clear that grammar, as it is handled in the tests for grades 4 to 9, is little if at all used by children. Much that is covered here would be of value only to superior 10th to 12th grade students who are headed for college. It would have no significance for the majority of high school students at any level. Use of these tests can only yield results which are unrelated to the measurement of skill and power in the use of language.

Scholastic Achievement Series: English-Spelling

For reviews by William E. Coffman and James R. Hayden of the complete battery, see 23.

[202]

★**Survey Tests of English Usage.** Grades 9–13; 1947–49; Forms E ('47), H ('48), S ('49) for use at the beginning of either semester; Forms G ('47), N ('48), T ('49) for use during the second semester; Forms J, K ('49) based on the book *Self-Aids in English Usage;* title on Forms T, N, and G is *Achievement Test of English Usage;* no manual; directions sheet (no date); teacher's remedial sheet ('47); tentative norms for Form J; no data on reliability and validity; 90¢ per 30 tests of any one form; postage extra; 25¢ per specimen set, postpaid; (35–40) minutes; L. J. O'Rourke; Psychological Institute. *

[203]

***Tressler English Minimum Essentials Tests, Revised Edition.** Grades 8–12; 1932–56; IBM; Forms A ('54, identical with test copyrighted in 1941 except for changes in 4 items), AM ('56, machine scoring edition of Form A), B ('41), C ('41); manual ['55, identical with sheet copyrighted in 1941 except for minor changes]; separate answer sheets must be used with Form AM; $1.75 per 25 tests; 5¢ per IBM answer sheet; 25¢ per machine scoring stencil; 30¢ per specimen set; postpaid; (40–50) minutes; J. C. Tressler; Public School Publishing Co. *

COMPOSITION

[204]

***College Entrance Examination Board Achievement Test in English Composition.** Candidates for college entrance; 1943–58; for more complete information, see 599; IBM 60(80) minutes; program administered by Educational Testing Service for the College Entrance Examination Board. *

REFERENCES

1–6. See 4:178.
7. NEWMAN, SIDNEY H.; FRENCH, JOHN W.; AND BOBBITT, JOSEPH M. "Analysis of Criteria for the Validation of Selection Measures at the United States Coast Guard Academy." *Ed & Psychol Meas* 12:394–407 au '52. * (*PA* 27:6159)
8. DYER, HENRY S. *College Board Scores.* New York: College Entrance Examination Board [1953]. Pp. xxiii, 70. * (*PA* 28:4936)
9. OLSEN, MARJORIE A. "The Predictive Effectiveness of the College Entrance Examination Board English Composition Test." Abstract. *Am Psychol* 8:411 Ag '53. *
10. WEBB, SAM C., AND McCALL, JOHN N. "Predictors of Freshman Grades in a Southern University." *Ed & Psychol Meas* 13:660–3 w '53. * (*PA* 28:6598)
11. College Entrance Examination Board. *English Composition: A Description of the English Composition Test of the College Entrance Examination Board.* Princeton, N.J.: the Board, June 1954. Pp. 35. * (*PA* 29:1443)
12. MILLER, PETER M. "An Analysis of Error-Types Used in the Interlinear Exercise of the College Entrance Examination Board's English Composition Test." *Yearb Nat Council Meas Used Ed* 11:19–22+ '54. *
13. DYER, HENRY S., AND KING, RICHARD G. *College Board Scores: Their Use and Interpretation, No. 2.* New York: College Entrance Examination Board, 1955. Pp. viii, 192. * (*PA* 30:1616)
14. ELEY, EARLE G. "Should the General Composition Test be Continued? The Test Satisfies an Educational Need." *Col Board R* (25):9–13 w '55. *
15. PEARSON, RICHARD. "Should the General Composition Test be Continued? The Test Fails as an Entrance Examination." *Col Board R* (25):2–9 w '55. *
16. SWINEFORD, FRANCES. "Reliability of an Interlinear Test of Writing Ability." *Sch & Soc* 81:25–7 Ja 22 '55. *
17. College Entrance Examination Board. *A Description of the College Board Achievement Tests.* Princeton, N.J.: Educational Testing Service, 1956. Pp. 133. * (*PA* 31:1745)
18. FISHMAN, JOSHUA A. *1957 Supplement to College Board Scores No. 2.* New York: College Entrance Examination Board, 1957. Pp. vi, 206. Paper. *
19. EVENSON, A. B., AND SMITH, D. E. "A Study of Matriculation in Alberta." *Alberta J Ed Res* 4:67–83 Je '56. *
20. FRENCH, JOHN W. "Validation of New Item Types Against Four-Year Academic Criteria." *J Ed Psychol* 49:67–76 Ap '58. *

For a review by Charlotte Croon Davis of earlier forms, see 4:178.

[205]

★**College Entrance Examination Board Advanced Placement Examination: English Composition.** High school seniors desiring credit for college level courses; 1954–58; for more complete information, see 600; 180(200) minutes; program administered by Educational Testing Service for the College Entrance Examination Board. *

ROBERT C. POOLEY, *Professor of English and Chairman, Department of Integrated Liberal Studies, University of Wisconsin, Madison, Wisconsin.* [Review of Form FBP.]

This test is designed for the use of colleges to evaluate students who have taken advanced courses in English composition in schools, and are seeking recognition of this work at the college level in the form of advanced standing or credit upon admission. It is therefore set at a level above ordinary college entrance tests. Unlike tests which deal with subject content areas, this test is not objective in character, and relies upon the skill of readers within the procedure set up to insure a reasonable degree of objectivity.

In a period of three hours the candidate is required to write three essays of one hour each. One of these calls for the ability to read, understand, and evaluate a critical passage of an advanced nature, pointing out and evaluating the effectiveness of the rhetorical aspects of the passage. Another calls for the thoughtful response to the implications of a quotation, in which a student may display his own resources from reading and experience. The third is a constructive development of one of several topic statements or ideas.

Inasmuch as the power to write effectively is the end result of instruction in composition, this test is aimed at the very heart of the skills and abilities to be tested. It is centered upon the power to think, organize, and compose English expository prose, and upon this power alone. To the extent that the quotations and topics arouse the optimum response from the candidates and permit the fullest display of their competence, the test is as nearly perfect for its purpose as any test can be. However, since it is not objective in nature, its true validity rests upon the impartiality of judgment of the readers.

Having been devised by independent committees of school and college teachers, the test was administered in 1957 to properly qualified high school students and a cross section of college freshman students from colleges representative of those the high school students might enter. The papers were mixed without identification before going to the readers. The chief reader read a sample of examination booklets and prepared tentative standards for each section. These standards were discussed in a training session with the corps of readers to establish a uniform interpretation of the standards. Each essay was read only once, but different readers were assigned to the separate essays, so that each book was read by three readers. Essays were rated on a 15-point scale, the raw scores were distributed, and by analysis of the chief reader were converted to grades on a 5-point scale: 5 (high honors), 4 (honors), 3 (creditable), 2 (pass), 1 (fail). In the 1957 examination 61 high school students, or 9 per cent of the high school group achieved grade 5, high honors; not one of the college sample achieved this grade. Although the college sample was only a little over 10 per cent of the size of the high school group, the failure of anyone of this group to achieve grade 5 is indicative of the high level set for the evaluation of advanced standing in composition.

Provided the same procedures are followed in subsequent years in reading and evaluation, this test can be highly commended for testing precisely what it intends to test, for setting a high level of performance and challenge to the candidate, and for establishing a basis of evaluation which is confirmed by cross reference to a college level sample of students. The growing concern for the advancement of superior students, and the difficulty of establishing fair and equitable procedures for the granting of advanced standing or credit on the campuses of many different institutions make this test particularly desirable as one yielding a nationally established set of grades which are reported to the college of the candidate's choice and are there interpreted and utilized as the proper authorities decide.

[206]

★Sequential Tests of Educational Progress: Essay Test. Grades 4-6, 7-9, 10-12, 13-14; 1957; Forms A, B, C, D; 4 levels; $1 per 20 tests; $4.25 per manual of any one level; $5 per specimen set; postage extra; 35(40) minutes; Cooperative Test Division, Educational Testing Service. *

a) LEVEL 4. Grades 4-6; Forms 4A, 4B, 4C, 4D.
b) LEVEL 3. Grades 7-9; Forms 3A, 3B, 3C, 3D.
c) LEVEL 2. Grades 10-12; Forms 2A, 2B, 2C, 2D.
d) LEVEL 1. Grades 13-14; Forms 1A, 1B, 1C, 1D.

REFERENCE

1. BLACK, DONALD B. "A Note on the Use in Alberta of the Sequential Tests of Educational Progress: Essay Test." *Alberta J Ed Res* 4:172-80 S '58. *

JOHN S. DIEKHOFF, *Dean, Cleveland College, Western Reserve University, Cleveland, Ohio.*

Teachers of English composition at any school level will agree that the best way to judge a student's ability to write is to read something he has written. They will also agree that any teacher's judgment of a single brief composition is not very reliable. The simple experiment of having every English teacher in a school or department grade the same set of student papers always has disturbing results and makes the point for most of us.

The formulators of the STEP essay tests recognize that writing is the test of writing. They provide essay topics at four levels: grades 4-6, grades 7-9, grades 10-12, and the freshman and sophomore years of college. For each level there are four forms of the test, i.e., four sets of essay topics, so that students may be tested more than once. There are careful instructions for the administration of the tests, sample essays on each topic ranked in terms of their quality, and instructions for scoring the essays and translating numerical scores into percentile ranks, and the like.

"The problem," say the directions for scoring, "is to score papers in such fashion that an independent scorer will come up with the same results." Indeed this is the problem. The sample essays with their assigned scores, to which essays on the same topics may be compared, and the eminently sensible instructions for the test reader constitute the attempt to solve this problem.

Accepting as he does the assumption that the best test of writing is writing, this reviewer does not see how it could be done much better. The essay topics are appropriate to the several school levels. The sample essays present clear differences in quality—one wishes student themes were always so clearly "high," "low," or "middle." The test reader is warned against his preconceptions of identifiable students, against letting "neatness" become a criterion in judging papers written under test conditions, against his "pet peeves," and happily against fruitless interminable rereading of papers difficult to score.

At bottom, however, these tests are essay tests. Assigning numerical scores, converting those scores into percentile ranks, recording them on the student's "profile," and comparing them with national and local norms will not make the test reader's critical judgment more exact. The sample essays, the *caveats* for the test reader, and the awareness that he is working with nationally used tests ought to make him more careful, however.

JOHN M. STALNAKER, *President, National Merit Scholarship Corporation, Evanston, Illinois.*

The STEP essay test requires a student to spend 35 minutes writing on a single topic which is specified. There are 16 tests, four forms at each of the four grade levels. Each test booklet consists of eight pages. The first page gives general directions which are identical for all levels whether it be the fourth grade or the sophomore in college. The second page gives six or eight lines of explicit directions for the writing and of course is different in each of the 16 forms. The student is not told the length that his essay should be but he is told after he has spent five minutes planning that he will have 30 minutes to complete the writing. The remainder of the test booklet consists of five ruled blank pages for the actual writing.

In addition to the test booklets there are four handbooks—one for each of the four grade levels but these are identical except for the sample comparison essays which are given on pages 9-17. One handbook contains the comparison essays for all four forms of one grade level.

The essays are to be evaluated by the classroom teachers who are given instructions to read them on a 7-point scale. The planning committee felt that it was concerned only with recommending broad criteria for judgment in reading. The committee suggested three factors to be evaluated in the reading: originality of thought, 50 per cent; style, 30 per cent; and convention, 20 per cent. Five comparison essays are given for each form: one graded 6 (high), one graded 2 (low), and three graded 4 (middle). The teacher is instructed to match the essay she is grading against the most com-

parable comparison essay and assign the appropriate grade.

Tables are given to translate the raw score into a converted score for which percentile ranks are given. These are based on the publisher's norming program of 5,000 students in grades 4 to 14, each of whom took two forms of the preliminary essay test.

The tests were developed from questions written by teachers, but it is stated that the final responsibility for the design and development rests with the ETS staff. The topics require personal narrative, exposition, argument or persuasion, and analysis of a problem or a situation.

Some statistics are given. Reading reliabilities for the selected experts who did the reading for the norms are low, ranging from .50 to .73, and score reliabilities are reported ranging from .50 to .62. The relationship between the essay test and the objective STEP test on writing ability is reported as ranging from .61 to .70, or about the same as the relationship between one essay test and another.

Some additional information on reader reliability might be helpful. A simple distribution of the scores assigned is itself frequently revealing. What is the reading reliability for the average classroom teacher who has no instruction other than that given in the handbook?

It is obvious that this is not a test of the usual type. Its use is limited. The scores must be cautiously interpreted in the light of the quality of the reading, and the general lack of reliability.

In the promotional literature about this test it is said that "means should be found to encourage English teachers....by making available some standardized essay materials. The STEP essay tests are planned to satisfy a part of this need." There is much to be done in improving the teaching of English and, if this effort helps, we should favor it. There are, of course, other approaches which may be fruitful.

LOUIS C. ZAHNER, *Head, English Department, Groton School, Groton, Massachusetts.*

Few teachers, administrators, or businessmen who employ the product of schools and colleges would deny that written composition is deteriorating. The wholesale substitution of objective tests for essay examinations in all subjects may well be a major cause of the deterioration; for testing influences teaching to a degree little short of control. For this reason, if for no other, the test here reviewed deserves use wide enough to establish it as a permanent part of testing programs, and thoughtful enough to provide its sponsors with data for its continuing improvement—improvement that does not convert it into a straddle between essay and objective tests, but strengthens it as the straightforward "free response" essay test it now is. If this latest attempt to establish an essay examination goes the way of its predecessors and becomes the last, a decisive battle may well have been lost.

This test is exactly what it claims to be—an examination in composition. It examines the testee's ability to write by setting him an assignment in writing. The subjects set, moreover, are on the whole realistic and well selected at each level to provide pupils with natural subjects about which they can be expected to have something of their own to say. The test has the same sort of solid validity as that of a swimming test that requires the testee to swim in the water; it is not concerned about how the details of his anatomy as measured on land correlate with those of other swimmers of known ability.

But similar tests have been killed by two disorders that have come to be considered congenital: the difficulty and expense of administration and reading; and the "unreliability," or lack of uniformity, in the reading.

This test meets the first difficulty quite simply: it is locally administered and read. The only expense is that of the teacher's time. Once the reader has examined the handbook, this should not be excessive. The scoring is on a 7-point scale; the essay topics are not structured, and hence do not require meticulous point-by-point checking of details of content. The handbook provides full conversion tables, norms, and instructions for conversion of scores into percentiles.

The second difficulty—reliability of reading —is more menacing. The method used is to give the reader sample answers with which to match the answers of his students. These samples have been selected and scored by a representative group of experienced teachers, who arrived at their conclusions in meetings at which they had ample opportunity for full discussion of criteria and standards of reading in general and for reconciling differences of opin-

ion in the scoring of individual essays. The handbook gives also the figures for the reliability of the reading achieved by this group of experienced teachers. They are impressive. But it must be remembered that the reading of even this select group had to be carefully standardized and controlled, and that uniformity of reading was achieved through a somewhat intricate process carried on under unusually favorable circumstances.

It is doubtful whether local readers of the test can be expected to achieve uniformity among themselves or with the group that scored and selected the sample answers. The user of the test is guided by only a very few samples and an analysis of them so meager as to be negligible. The only scores illustrated by samples are 6, 4, and 2. The highest score, 7, is not illustrated, nor are 5, 3, and the lowest, 1.

From one to three samples are given for each score. The analytical comments are of little help. None are given on samples scored 6 or 2. The most voluminous, all on samples scored 4, run: "Thought O.K.; mechanics weak," or "An average in thought, style, and mechanics." There is nothing on such matters as organization or, in fact, on any other elements of composition.

What a reader needs to know as he attempts to "match" his papers with the samples is not *how* a committee of experts agreed to score an essay, but *why* they agreed to score it as they did. Here the committee could well follow the example set by Noyes, Sale, and Stalnaker in a monograph [1] published in 1945.

Provision of more divergent samples and fuller, more searching analysis of samples would serve two essential purposes: it would make for reading that would tie in with greater reliability to the published norms and percentiles; and it would give a teacher a clearer idea about what qualities the experienced and highly qualified teachers who made up the reading committee consider to be desirable in composition and its teaching.

Even without such a full support of analysis of sample answers to establish more uniform reading, the test is likely to prove stimulating to a class and useful to a teacher.

1 NOYES, EDWARD SIMPSON; SALE, WILLIAM MERRITT, JR.; AND STALNAKER, JOHN MARSHALL. *Report on the First Six Tests in English Composition: With Sample Answers From the Tests of April and June 1944.* Princeton, N.J.: College Entrance Examination Board, 1945. Pp. 72. *

For reviews by Robert W. B. Jackson and Wilbur L. Layton of the complete battery, see 24.

[207]
★Sequential Tests of Educational Progress: Writing. Grades 4–6, 7–9, 10–12, 13–14; 1956–57; IBM; Forms A, B ('57); 4 levels; manual ('57); battery directions ('57); no data on reliability of Form B; separate answer sheets must be used; $3.95 per 20 tests; $1 per 20 IBM scorable answer sheets; 45¢ per scoring stencil; $1 per manual; $1 per battery technical report ('57); $1.25 per specimen set; postage extra; 70(90–100) minutes; Cooperative Test Division, Educational Testing Service. *
a) LEVEL 4. Grades 4–6; Forms 4A, 4B.
b) LEVEL 3. Grades 7–9; Forms 3A, 3B.
c) LEVEL 2. Grades 10–12; Forms 2A, 2B.
d) LEVEL 1. Grades 13–14; Forms 1A, 1B.

CHARLOTTE CROON DAVIS, *Test Research Service, Bronxville, New York.*

Approximately 50 educators participated directly in the construction of the STEP writing tests: a steering committee of 5, a planning committee of 5, 14 test authors, including members of the planning committee, and 32 critical reviewers. The test materials were prepared at workshop sessions lasting several weeks. Committees of teachers designed the tests; items were written by subcommittees of teachers; other teachers served as critics; test experts gave technical assistance. These cooperative procedures have advantages and drawbacks. They are excellent for educating test users, fostering good public relations, and gaining acceptance and effective advertising for the tests. On the other hand, they are expensive and time-consuming. More serious is the fact that creative work of this kind done by committees tends to be neither very poor nor conspicuously good; it reflects the compromises inevitable in committee functioning. Usually a better test is produced if committees serve in advisory capacities, where they are invaluable, and some one competent, experienced individual has responsibility and authority. In the reviewer's opinion, these general observations are borne out by a careful examination of these tests.

In addition to the objective tests under review here, the STEP battery contains essay tests of writing, in which the examinees write compositions on assigned topics and which, scored by a semiobjective method, are said to produce reliable results. With this provision for tests of writing in which the examinees actually write, it might have been advisable to limit the objective tests to those aspects of expression that can be directly measured by objective methods. Techniques of measuring the abilities to "think critically in writing," "write material appropriate for a given purpose," and "write effectively" used in tests in which the examinees do *no* writing are necessarily indirect. They measure primarily other skills, more or less closely related to these abilities.

Whether or not these tests measure writing ability, they definitely appear to measure reading ability. Each form consists of 8 to 10 selections written by pupils, each followed by several items based on the selection. The amount of reading per item is large. For example, one selection in Form 1A with its 8 items has about 1,000 words, or 125 words per item. Many items depend on such recognized reading skills as getting the main idea of a selection, following its structure, or deciding which statements need supporting evidence. It seems to the reviewer that these tests must substantially overlap the reading tests in the battery.

The selections are well chosen to provide variety, face validity, and difficulty suitable to the four levels. Whether the authors were wise to use largely pupil assignments that had been graded *poor or failing* is dubious. The explanations preceding some selections of how they came to be written are helpful and could have been given more often; e.g., a setting for "Black Blaze" in Form 1A might have clarified Items 13 and 14. With only 60 items per test, coverage of the wide field of English expression is necessarily thin in spots; e.g., spelling, an important skill in the intermediate grades, is touched on by just two or three items in Form 4A, none in 4B.

On the whole, the items are clear and direct and require the application of information or skills to new material. They can be classified into two general types: (*a*) those that test only *correctness* of expression, in which three of the four choices are clearly incorrect, (an exception is 4A, Part I, Item 1, which has two correct choices, only one of which is keyed) and (*b*) those that require selecting the most appropriate or effective choice. Ideally, in the second type the examinee should not be able to rule out distractors as "mechanically" incorrect. However, many items of this type are really mixtures of effectiveness and correctness. This double-barreledness may be almost inevitable if the number of choices cannot be varied to fit the point tested and if the items are not to have more than one defensible answer. Nevertheless, some items, especially at the higher levels, seem to the reviewer to include two defensible choices or to have *no* choice that seems just right or particularly good; e.g., 4B-I-9, -II-8; 3A-I-21; 3B-I-19, -II-15; 2A-II-1; 2B-I-19, -II-2, -3, -5, -8; 1A-I-9, -II-8; 1B-I-3, -II-7, -10. Some items overlap or give clues to the answers to other items: e.g., 4B-I-9, -13; 3A-I-7, -10, -12; 3B-I-8, -10; 3B-II-20, -21; 2B-I-16, -17; 2B-I-25, -28. Systematic review of the test materials by one or two experienced critics during the construction process should have called attention to most of these items at a time when they could conveniently have been revised or abandoned.

The statistical framework for the tests received expert attention. The items were pretested and analyzed; the eight forms were equated both horizontally (Form A with Form B at each level) and vertically (Level 4 with Level 3, Level 3 with Level 2, etc.), and all raw scores converted to a single scale. The norms are based on a national sample scrupulously chosen to be representative. They are presented by grades and are in the form of percentile bands which automatically indicate the accuracy of the scores. For example, the chances are about two out of three that a fifth grader who obtains a score of 250 will have a true percentile rank somewhere between 35 and 60. Parallel form coefficients are not provided.

The directions for administration and scoring, which are the same for most of the tests in the battery, are well presented but are questionable in certain respects. Parts I and II may be given at different sessions. As the examinees are free to use extra time at the end of the second session to return to Part I, they are also free to improve their Part I scores by changing their answers as a result of consultation or study about particular items during the time between sessions. The instruction to guess on "too difficult" items is necessary, since the score is the number right, and it is regarded as effective since the *average* number of omissions in the 100-case samples used for estimating reliability was very low. However, this does not insure that an *individual* pupil, unwilling to guess even when told to do so, may not fail to mark a sizable number of items. A scoring method that corrected for *failure* to guess might minimize the effect of this personality factor or lack of testwiseness.

Some examinees might benefit from directions specific to these tests. They could be told to read each selection before attempting the accompanying items and could be made aware, through samples, that there may be items in which the keyed response is to leave the point under consideration just as it is expressed in the selection (some naive pupils feel that some change must be needed or the point would not be brought up), and items like 1B-I-8, in which *all* the choices are at least partially correct and the last choice, which includes the other three, is keyed.

Although, on the whole, the format of the tests is satisfactory, the arrangement would be more convenient for the examinee if all choices, no matter how short, were placed in a single column, B directly under A, etc., and if the items based on a selection always appeared on the same page as the selection or on the facing page.

Probably the most notable feature of these tests is that they are available at four levels, with a single, continuous score scale. Regarded as a whole, they should provide, within the limitations of the individual forms, a valuable standardized instrument for measuring a pupil's growth over many years in the abilities tested. The tests should also be useful for evaluating classes, grades, and larger groups on the basis of the norms supplied. Although the tests might be improved both in general design and in specific content, the authors are to be commended for making progress in testing some of the important but hard-to-measure skills related to good writing.

JOHN M. STALNAKER, *President, National Merit Scholarship Corporation, Evanston, Illinois.*

The STEP test in writing is designed "to measure comprehensively the full range of skills involved in the process of good writing," a rather heavy assignment for a 70-minute objective test. There are two forms of the test at each of four grade levels (4-6, 7-9, 10-12, 13-14), or eight tests in all. There is a 12-page set of directions for administering and scoring, a 36-page manual for interpreting scores, and a 60-page technical report which covers all STEP tests except the essay test.

Each 12-page test booklet contains 60 questions for which the student selects the best an-

Sequential Tests of Educational Progress: Writing

swer from among four choices. An IBM type answer sheet is used. The questions concern a passage, the sentences of which are numbered. In general, 8 to 10 brief passages are included in each of the tests. The test is divided into two parts, each requiring 35 minutes of testing time. The time is said to be ample for most pupils. The single score is the number of items answered correctly.

Most of the items propose several revisions of a sentence in the passage, but some of the items concern spelling and mechanics. The test is said to cover organization, conventions, critical thinking, effectiveness, and appropriateness. Most of the passages are intentionally quite poorly written. One must sympathize with the student who is sensitive to the written word and to style, for the reading of such passages and the options given for change can constitute an ordeal.

In the manual for interpreting scores, a good deal of space is given to converting scores and interpreting the results. The statement is made that *"there is no such thing as an absolute score on a test"* by which apparently is meant that a score on a specific test does not necessarily reflect precisely the true ability of the person tested. Users are encouraged to interpret the converted test scores by percentile bands (confidence intervals) in which one score is said to lie between say the 51st and the 72nd percentiles.

Individual score norms are given for the various grades. They are based in some instances on relatively small numbers of students (under 200). Validity is said to be insured because qualified persons have constructed the tests—a highly questionable statement, especially in this type of test.

Form A is, in general, slightly less reliable than the other tests in the series. No reliability data are given for Form B. Test scores correlate with the verbal factor scores of an aptitude test between .68 and .83.

Some of the claims made for the test would appear to have been written with an eye on sales promotion rather than on any evidence reported. On the other hand, the test, while offering nothing new or distinctive in test construction, appears to have been prepared with care, by competent people using approved procedures. It will doubtless yield results of value in many classrooms.

LOUIS C. ZAHNER, *Head, English Department, Groton School, Groton, Massachusetts.*

This is not a test *in* writing. Whether it can legitimately be called a test *of* writing is debatable. A more accurately descriptive, though somewhat unwieldy, title would be "A Test in the Recognition of Appropriate Usage, and of Logical and Effective Written Expression." It falls somewhere between a test of proofreading and one of editing. It requires more than a proofreader's correction of errors in mere mechanics, and less than an editor's or author's revision; for the editor or author has to produce his own rewording for what he himself considers to be weak spots, while this test demands only the selection of the most effective of several ready-made versions for spots already pinpointed.

Put another way, this is an objective test of what is essentially a subjective process; for all writing of whatever sort is "creative," a melding of content and forms according to some design—"design" in the sense not only of artistic and effective shaping, but of purpose.

In the piecemeal dealing with details to which an objective test of expression must resort, the quality of the thought and design of the composition as a whole is lost sight of. This is perhaps unavoidable: appraisal of the qualities of a complete composition would convert the test into one of reading. But the omission poses a stubborn question. If writing is the union of whole thought and design, can proficiency in the art be appraised by a test that touches on neither? The question is particularly embarrassing for a test of writing that requires no writing at all on the part of the testee.

In spite of this, it may still prove to be true, when validity studies have been completed, that most proficient writers will do well on this test and most poor writers badly. But this is not to say that all who score high are proficient writers, or that all who score low are defective writers. All racehorses are quadrupeds, but not all quadrupeds are racehorses.

Within the limits set any test in composition by the requirements of objective testing, this is a strong test, well conceived and well executed. Its use of student writing as a base is realistic. Its coverage of the details of structure, usage, rhetoric, and logic is wide and nicely attuned to the grade levels tested.

This test and its companion piece, the STEP

essay test, may well complement each other. The writing test has coverage of details of composition, and built-in reliability of scoring. But it loses sight of a work as a whole, and is questionable in its validity. The essay test, on the other hand, is questionable in the reliability of its scoring, and it pays little attention to the many details of the "skills" of written composition. It does, however, have built-in validity, and it emphasizes the appraisal of the testee's work as a whole. As complementary parts of a program in testing written composition, a program in which each would tend to correct the mistakes of the other, they would be a strong combination. Such a program would have to be local: while the writing test, which is machine scorable, can be used in a program of any geographical extent, the essay test, which is locally read, might be impracticable for use in any unit larger than a city school system.

Taken singly, this test at least indicates how much a student knows about the skills of written composition, even though it leaves open the question of whether or not he can apply them in practice; and it directs the attention of student and teacher alike to the importance of details.

For reviews by Robert W. B. Jackson and Wilbur L. Layton of the complete battery, see 24.

LITERATURE

[208]

★**American Literature: Every Pupil Scholarship Test.** High school; 1958; new form usually issued each April; norms available following testing program; no data on reliability; 4¢ per test; 4¢ per scoring key; postage extra; 60(65) minutes; Bureau of Educational Measurements. *

[209]

*****American Literature: Every Pupil Test.** High school; 1934–58; new form usually issued each April; norms available following testing program; no data on reliability; 3¢ per test; 1¢ per scoring key; cash orders postpaid; 40(45) minutes; Ohio Scholarship Tests. *

[210]

★**Center-Durost Literature Acquaintance Test: Evaluation and Adjustment Series.** Grades 11–13; 1953, c1952–53; IBM; Form AM ('53); manual ('53); no college norms; separate answer sheets must be used; $3.60 per 35 tests; $1.40 per 35 IBM answer sheets; postage extra; 35¢ per specimen set, postpaid; 40(50) minutes; Stella S. Center and Walter N. Durost; World Book Co. *

REFERENCE

1. DUROST, WALTER N. "Issues in the Measurement of Literature Acquaintance at the Secondary-School Level." *J Ed Psychol* 43:31–44 Ja '52. * (PA 26:7210)

HOLLAND ROBERTS, *Director, Academic Freedom Committee, San Francisco, California.*

This test illustrates some complex problems which educators face in attempting to measure cultural values. The authors state in the manual that "the test is designed to measure one's acquaintance with worth-while literature" focusing "attention on the fact that there are thoughts, feelings and convictions that are an essential part of Anglo Saxon culture"; further, that "to be without at least an acquaintance with literature embodying these traditions is to lack an essential element of literacy."

They consider that the test serves "as a survey instrument" and "as an instructional device," and specify four specific uses: (*a*) "to survey the literature acquaintance of high school students and college freshmen" and to establish the 85 books sampled in the test as "a basic reading list for both high school and college freshmen classes"; (*b*) to guide the teacher of literature in placing emphasis in the class work; (*c*) to stimulate and measure breadth of reading in club work; and (*d*) to stir adults in extension classes to fill in gaps in their reading.

To achieve these important objectives, students are asked to identify 65 short quotations of a few sentences or lines by matching each with one of three titles printed below. American and English literature are about equally represented in the 53 prose and 12 poetry samples chosen for the test and strike a balance between the classics and modern writing.

In deciding whether this test is a valuable tool, teachers and supervisors will be interested in examining some of its basic assumptions: (*a*) that our high schools should concentrate on a small specific body of writing which our students ought to know, or they will lack "an essential element of literacy"; (*b*) that American secondary schools should concern themselves primarily with the development of "Anglo Saxon culture" and "traditions" to the virtual exclusion of most of world literature; (*c*) that a rigid, limited test of ability to identify small pieces dissected from literature should be used to evaluate and so set the basic pattern for teaching literature; (*d*) that the test measures something significant—something more than casual acquaintance with the literature from which the samples are taken; (*e*) that the books from which the selections were taken represent "worthwhile" reading for our high

school juniors and seniors and college freshmen living in our modern world.

The testmakers supply little evidence other
than traditional authority to support these basic
assumptions. Today as the world grows daily
more unified and the peoples of every nation
are reaching out to each other to make man-
kind one family, both the general public and
educational leaders are advocating that our
schools recognize in their teaching that our nations has its origins in many peoples and cul-
tures. They see Anglo Saxon culture and its
rich literature as one of many notable contributions to our worldwide heritage. Teachers and
the public are moving away from preoccupation with traditional English and American literature to concern themselves with some of the
contributions of world literature. The great
books of French, Spanish, Scandinavian, German, Jewish, Italian, Slavic, African, Indian,
Arabian, and Chinese literature are vital reading for our youth if they are to take their places
among the cultured peoples of Latin America,
Europe, Africa and Asia.

The authors have given two places in their
test to Louisa May Alcott, with quotations
from *Little Women* and *An Old Fashioned
Girl,* but they have found no room for
Cervantes' *Don Quixote* or any other representative of Spanish letters. There are two titles
by Edna Ferber and two by Booth Tarkington,
but none by Dumas, Hugo, Heine, Mann, Lager-
lov, Nexo, Gogol, Chekhov or Tolstoi. Inter-
cultural relations are increasing in importance
today for all people and especially for those
nations who hold a major position in world
affairs. Curriculum makers, parents, and our
youth are proposing that secondary English
classes explore the possibilities of world literature for contributing to one world at peace,
with liberty and justice for all. From the view-
point of the United Nations, a literature acquaintance test which gives no hint that notable books by Tagore, Sophocles, Pushkin,
Turgenev, Voltaire, Rousseau, Anderson, Omar
Khayyam, Confucius, and Lao-tse exist might,
to paraphrase the manual, be said to lack some
"essential elements of literacy."

However, even if the test were more exactly
entitled "An *Anglo American* Literature Acquaintance Test," it would still be subject to
sharp criticism. Some of the literature included
is too juvenile for high school juniors and seniors. *Treasure Island, Ivanhoe, Rip Van Win-*

kle, Kidnapped, Call of the Wild, Little Women
and *The Deacon's Master Piece* are commonly
read anywhere from the fifth grade through
junior high school. Others, like *The Little Minister* and *Gone with the Wind,* are of doubtful
literary value. A few notable pieces such as
Milton's *L'Allegro* have been found by several
generations of English teachers to be beyond
the experience and outside the interests of
many 17-year-olds.

On the whole, curriculum makers and the
College Entrance Examination Board have
been moving rapidly away from the narrow confines of a rigid test based on the identification
of minute pieces of writing toward the broader
and deeper perspective of understanding and
assimilating the central meanings of literature
for our generation. In this respect the test presents other unresolved problems. Is there any
certainty that recognition of the source of a
quotation means that the student has either
read the book or poem or assimilated its significant meanings? He may have skimmed over
it, seen a movie or read a comic book version,
read a review or summary, or picked up enough
names and factual information about it from
casual discussion to pass the test. As the authors note in the manual, "Many of the [po-
etry] quotations are as familiar as proverbs."
On the other hand, what reason do we have to
say that failing to identify one short, often unimportant quotation from a book or poem is
proof that the student has not read and understood it? How can we know that the episodes
selected by the testmakers are, as they have
stated, "unforgettable if one has read the
books"? No studies are cited or evidence given
to support this view. On both these counts the
test is subject to question.

A standardized measuring instrument should
serve the purposes of a changing, growing educational program if it is itself to pass the basic
test of utility; it should not attempt to dominate
it, and it should not stereotype the educational
process. This test restricts and cramps the
teaching of literature. It has neither the depth
nor the scope to meet the crisis in American
education and culture.

For the present we must continue to rely
on such unstandardized tests of acquaintance
with literature as listing by students of reading done, accompanied by informal annotations,
informal and formal dramatizations of novels
and stories and plays, interviews with students

Center-Durost Literature Acquaintance Test

on their reading, biographical histories of student reading experiences, and class, club, and small group discussions that apply to the issues of our day the significant meaning of the wide scope of our heritage of English, American, and world literature.

A precise instrument would be valuable, but the important thing is to keep clearly before us the objective of the teaching of literature—the firing of young minds for the never ending search for the best that has been felt and said and thought, and its use in improving the world in which we live and the world we are building.

[211]

★College Entrance Examination Board Advanced Placement Examination: Literature. High school seniors desiring credit for college level courses; 1954–58; for more complete information, see 600; 180(200) minutes; program administered by Educational Testing Service for the College Entrance Examination Board. *

John S. Diekhoff, *Dean, Cleveland College, Western Reserve University, Cleveland, Ohio.* [Review of Form FBP.]

This test depends for its value on the critical judgment and consistency of its readers. It is made up of three essay questions of kinds familiar to college students in literature and therefore appropriate for the purposes of the test. Each essay is graded, on a 15-point scale, on different categories to which the student's attention has been specifically directed. All three essays are weighted equally in obtaining the total score. As with other tests among the Advanced Placement Examinations, final test grades of 5, representing highest honors, to 1, fail, are reported.

One question asks for critical comment on a contemporary lyric that the reviewer is unable to identify. The question gives some guidance by suggesting points to be discussed; perhaps it suggests too many points. The poem is not one that the reviewer would choose for the purpose, but there is plenty for the student to understand and to discuss, and it will serve.

A second question asks for comment on a brief narrative passage, so familiar to the reviewer that there is risk that it will also be familiar to some students. Some may have studied it. Indeed, it is included with detailed analytical questions in a widely used college freshman anthology. Here again, specific questions are asked to focus the student's comment on particular aspects of the writer's technique; but the student is also asked to call upon his

knowledge of other literature for the discussion of the advantages and limitations of a specified literary device.

The final question requires the student to draw entirely upon what he has read in the past. A genre is specified and an approach to its discussion, but the books to be drawn upon for illustration are not specified. The reviewer is pleased at the assumption that the student has done some private reading and that he should be encouraged to comment on it.

All in all, the examination gives the student an opportunity to show that he knows how to read literature of different types and to demonstrate the extent of his reading. Knowledgeable test scorers should be able to judge whether or not he has achieved college competence in literature and colleges should be willing to trust their judgment.

[212]

★English Language and Literature: National Teacher Examinations. College seniors and teachers; 1940–58; for more complete information, see 538; IBM; 80(90) minutes; Educational Testing Service. *

For reviews by William A. Brownell, Walter W. Cook, and Lawrence G. Derthick of the entire series, see 538; for a review by Harry N. Rivlin of an earlier edition, see 4:802.

[213]

★English Language and Literature: Teacher Education Examination Program. College seniors preparing to teach secondary school; 1957; for more complete information, see 543; IBM; 80(95) minutes; Educational Testing Service. *

For a review by Walter W. Cook of the entire series, see 543.

[214]

*English Literature: Every Pupil Test. High school; 1934–58; new form usually issued each April; norms available following testing program; no data on reliability; 3¢ per test; 1¢ per scoring key; cash orders postpaid; 40(45) minutes; Ohio Scholarship Tests. *

[215]

*The Graduate Record Examinations Advanced Tests: Literature. College seniors and graduate students; 1939–56; for more complete information, see 601; IBM; 180(200) minutes; Educational Testing Service. *

Robert C. Pooley, *Professor of English and Chairman, Department of Integrated Liberal Studies, University of Wisconsin, Madison, Wisconsin.* [Review of Form EGR.]

Designed for the evaluation of students having completed a four-year undergraduate program of liberal studies, with a major or minor in English literature and with some correlative work in modern European literatures, this test was prepared under the auspices of a committee of six members appointed from a panel nominated by the Modern Language Association of America. The test consists of 229 individual exercises in sequence to be performed in three hours' time. All questions are of the multiple choice type, providing in a few instances three choices, in many, four choices, and in the majority, five choices. Answers are recorded by special pencil on a numbered answer sheet for machine scoring.

Although the parts are not marked off by separating enumeration, this examination consists of six recognizable divisions: (a) knowledge of specific works of literature and their authors, approximately 35 per cent of the total; (b) interpretation of meaning from passages of verse, requiring no previous knowledge although recognition of the passage and its context undoubtedly assists the interpretation, about 11 per cent; (c) identification of the author or title of a work from a specific passage, in which pure memory or recall is subordinated to selection on the basis of content and qualities of style exhibited in the passages, which are about equally divided between prose and verse, about 9 per cent; (d) ability to read, understand, interpret, and give judgments of value concerning content and structure of verse, about 14 per cent; (e) understanding and evaluation of prose passages of literary criticism, including the ability to relate critical judgments to a wide variety of specific authors and works, about 13 per cent; (f) evaluation of poetry on the basis of poetic qualities, including value judgments of diction, metrics, consistency, and emotional tone, about 18 per cent.

The content as a whole is of a very high order, apparently most thoroughly sifted and weighed prior to selection to offer a fair and reasonable measure of attainment in knowledge, skills, judgments, and appreciations in literature truly representative of English, American, and continental traditions. The specific exercises are carefully worded to avoid ambiguity, yet are sufficiently mature and technical to test the well trained, widely read student. Most successful is the balance between factual knowledge of literature and literary persons, and ability to recognize and deal critically with literary values. For the purposes of such a test as this the balance between knowledge and

power is extremely important, and has been very well achieved. In matters of detail it is difficult to satisfy everyone. Some of the facts selected to test knowledge seem overspecific, yet they may be defended as specific to very widely read selections. In the selection of particular authors and works for fact and judgment the test represents a very conservative tradition of courses in literature; the student who has followed such a conservative pattern of courses will have an advantage over others.

The chief adverse criticism is addressed to the imbalance between verse and prose in the content of the examination. It is heavily weighted to verse, and correspondingly weak in literary judgments of fiction, both novel and short story, the informal essay, and drama as a literary type. The student who by personal taste or fortunate pressure has applied himself to the poetic tradition in literature will reap his reward in this test.

In total, however, the test is excellent, and is well designed for the purpose of evaluating the attainment in literature of an applicant to a graduate school. Within the limits imposed by objective techniques in testing, this test comes as close as is reasonable and presently possible to a fair evaluation of knowledge of literature in the Anglo-American tradition, and of power to deal independently with literature and to arrive at sound value judgments in literature.

For a review by Harold Seashore of the entire series, see 601.

[216]
*Interpretation of Literary Materials. High school, college; 1944–57; subtest of *Tests of General Educational Development;* IBM; 2 levels, 2 forms: high school, Form B ('44), college, Form B ('43); revised manuals: high school level ('56), college level ('54); $2.50 per 25 tests of either level; separate answer sheets must be used; $1 per 25 IBM answer sheets; 50¢ per specimen set; postage extra; (120) minutes; prepared by Examination Staff of United States Armed Forces Institute; Veterans' Testing Service, American Council on Education. *

For a review by Robert J. Solomon of the complete battery, see 27; for a review by Gustav J. Froehlich of Form B, see 4:26; for reviews by Herbert S. Conrad and Warren G. Findley, see 3:20.

[217]
*The Iowa Tests of Educational Development: Test 7, Ability to Interpret Literary Materials. Grades 9–13; 1942–58; title on Form Y-3S is *Interpretation of Literary Materials;* IBM; Forms X-3S, Y-3S ('52); examiner's manual ('58); battery manual ('54);

pupil profile leaflet, fourth edition ('58); profile card (no date); separate answer sheets must be used; $3 per 20 tests; $5 per 100 IBM answer sheets; 50¢ per hand and machine scoring stencil; 50¢ per specimen set; 50¢ per battery manual; postage extra; 50(60) or 40(50) minutes; prepared under the direction of E. F. Lindquist; Science Research Associates. *

For reviews by J. Murray Lee and Stephen Wiseman of the complete battery, see 17; for a review by Eric F. Gardner of Forms X-2 and Y-2, see 4:17; for reviews by Henry Chauncey, Gustav J. Froehlich, and Lavone A. Hanna of Forms X-1 and Y-1, see 3:12.

[218]

*Literature: Every Pupil Scholarship Test. Grades 7–8, 9–12; 1928–58; new form usually issued each January and April; 2 levels; norms available following testing program; no data on reliability; 4¢ per test; 4¢ per scoring key; postage extra; 40(45) minutes; Bureau of Educational Measurements. *

[219]

*Literature Test: National Achievement Tests. Grades 7–12; 1937–57; 5 scores: recognizing effects, recognizing qualities, analyzing moods, miscellaneous facts, total; Forms A ('44, identical with test copyrighted in 1937), B ('54, identical with test copyrighted in 1939); directions sheet for Form A ('44), directions sheet for Form B ('57, identical with sheet copyrighted in 1939 except for minor changes); teachers' guide ['44]; no data on reliability for Form B; no norms for part scores; $3 per 25 tests; 50¢ per specimen set; postage extra; 40(50) minutes; Robert K. Speer and Samuel Smith; Acorn Publishing Co. *

For reviews by H. H. Giles and Robert C. Pooley, see 40:1304.

SPEECH

[220]

★The Graduate Record Examinations Advanced Tests: Speech. College seniors and graduate students; 1953; available only in the Institutional Testing Program of *The Graduate Record Examinations* (see 601); IBM; 180(200) minutes; Educational Testing Service. *

For a review by Harold Seashore of the entire series, see 601.

[221]

★Weidner-Fensch Speech Screening Test. Grades 1–3; 1955; individual; Forms A, B; hectographed manual; no data on reliability; $3.50 per examiner's kit including 50 record blanks; $1 per 20 record blanks; postage extra; [20] minutes; William E. Weidner and Edwin A. Fensch; Psychometric Affiliates. *

ROBERT S. CATHCART, *Associate Professor of Speech*, and LOUISE B. SCOTT, *Assistant Professor of Speech, Los Angeles State College, Los Angeles, California.*

This test purports to "screen out children with speech difficulties from those who have normally developed speech." It uses 33 simple pictures in a 4-page booklet to which "children suspected of defective speech" are asked to respond. The pictures are so designed and arranged that "the eleven consonant sounds which are most often defective in children" will be tested in their initial, medial, and final position in word forms. A record sheet for each form includes the question to go with each picture, the word response desired, the sound being tested, and space in which to score the response.

This test is easy to understand and simple to administer, requiring no previous testing experience or special equipment. It can be completed in less than 10 minutes. A single booklet can be used a number of times with only a record sheet needed for each new subject. Unfortunately, the test's simplicity and economy are not matched in validity and reliability. The data furnished in the test manual do not establish its validity and reliability, and a careful examination of the test itself reveals weaknesses which create doubts about the test's ability to screen out consistently articulatory problems.

One weakness of this test has to do with the pictures which are used to get word responses. To work properly, the pictures must always elicit the *same* desired response, that is, a picture of a dog for the final "g" sound and a goat for the initial "g" sound. Ideally, the "name" of the picture should be obvious to all children and the word response elicited should be so simple that the desired sound can be clearly distinguished. In the Weidner-Fensch test there are a number of pictures which do not get the desired response. For example, there is a picture of a baby in a baby carriage to which most children would respond "baby carriage"; however, the response desired is "buggy," to the test for the medial "g" sound. Another picture is of a horse-drawn coach of Louis XIV vintage to which TV era children would respond "stage coach," but the sound to be assessed is the final "dz" sound as in "carriage." Random applications of the test to first and third grade children revealed four pictures in each form to which *no child ever gave the desired response*. Add to this further problems which would obviously be created by regionalism (a "violin" is a "fiddle" in some regions and there is no "r" sound in a Boston "car") and socioeconomic differences (some upper-middle class children did not recognize the wringer-type "washing machine" used for the medial "sh" sound), and one has reason to doubt the validity of the test.

There are some data in the manual about the construction and validating procedures used by the authors but it is not specific or detailed. They state that the pictures selected were originally presented to 474 children in the first, second, and third grades, after which nine picture changes were made and tried out with 87 other children. Then the revised test was given to 321 similar children. The authors then concluded that "all object items now have high specific word recall recognition value," a statement which is hardly warranted by the data presented. Other vague and unsupported statements like "recognition is a bit higher in the third than in lower grade levels" do little to establish confidence in their validating procedures. Reliability is not mentioned in the manual.

One can infer from the manual that the test is to be given by a "therapist" because this word is used when information about scoring the test is presented; however, the word "examiner" is used in four other places with no explanation or clarification. One can hardly conceive of a trained speech therapist who would need a test like this to locate sound difficulties; and if it is to be applied by the "untrained" classroom teacher, then there is the problem of his ability to recognize misarticulated sounds when he hears them. This latter point presents an even greater problem when one notes that a number of words in the test call for difficult sound blends and syllabics (e.g., shirt, star, flag, and bottle). In words like these it would be very hard for the untrained ear to detect just what sound was causing the difficulty.

Finally, one could question the selection of "the eleven consonant sounds which are most often defective" because such common sound problems as "n" and "ng" are omitted; whereas sounds like "s" and "r," which are common problems in the first grade but become less so in the third grade, are included.

All in all, the Weidner-Fensch test seems to have been constructed without rigorous experimental procedures and without a basic understanding of the problems involved in standardizing a general speech test. Its use and value appear severely limited by these shortcomings.

Weidner-Fensch Speech Screening Test

SPELLING

[222]

★A.C.E.R. Spelling Test (Form C). Grades 3-4, 4-5, 5-6, 6-7, 7; 1946-51; 1 form; 5 levels; 3s. 6d. per manual ['51]; postpaid within Australia; (30) minutes; Australian Council for Educational Research. *

J. A. RICHARDSON, *Professor of Special Education, The University of British Columbia, Vancouver, British Columbia, Canada.*

The form of these tests is rather an unusual one. Complete sentences are dictated to the pupils, but only some of the words are marked. The children are aware from the instructions that spelling is being tested but do not know which of the words they write will actually be scored. This seems to the reviewer to be, on the whole, a better method of testing spelling than the more usual one employed in the very widely used 1935 A.C.E.R. spelling tests where the examiner dictates each successive word in the list, uses it in a given illustrative sentence, and then repeats the word. The first method—writing the words in context—approximates more closely the practical situation of composition or letter writing.

The 1946 tests are intended for use in all six Australian states on the apparent assumption that the words chosen are equally appropriate throughout the continent. An even more dubious procedure in construction was the selection of words for preliminary trial from two American lists. Even though these lists were supplemented by "some typically Australian words" (no further information being provided) and by "a group of difficult words from a commercially published spelling book," there must still be a major doubt concerning the content validity of the tests. This, incidentally, is the only validity referred to in the manual. Though the tests were constructed and used for the A.C.E.R. curriculum survey of 1946, no further information concerning them has subsequently appeared. There is a similar lack of information on the internal consistency of the tests.

As with all of the attainment tests used in the 1946 survey, the sample of 30,000 children from nearly 600 schools throughout Australia is more than adequate. Grade norms only, in the form of 15-point scale scores and centile rank equivalents, are provided. It is a pity that steps have not been taken, subsequent to the original standardisation, to provide age and age-in-grade norms to give these spelling tests the comprehensive coverage in respect to norms which is such a useful feature of other A.C.E.R. tests.

The manual presenting the spelling lists falls short of the usual high standard of A.C.E.R. publications. Although it contains useful general information on the significance of test scores, on the devising of the 15-point scale, and, in an appendix, on basic statistical concepts, unfortunately it does not give by any means sufficient details about the tests with which it is concerned—their validity, the interpretation of scores, and their usefulness to teachers. Moreover, the manual is marred by inferior technical production—crowded pages and poor print.

In short, although the tests appeal to the reviewer as a well devised and effective means of testing proficiency in spelling, they are recommended only with some reservations. More information is needed about validity and the significance and usefulness of the scores; further work to provide more comprehensive norms for the tests is also desirable. At present, with only meagre manual information as the basis for judgment, the teacher is probably justified in his preference for the 1935 A.C.E.R. spelling tests (see 40:1309).

D. K. WHEELER, *Senior Lecturer in Education, University of Western Australia, Nedlands, Australia.*

These tests consist of five sentence lists, of which lists A, B, and C are intended for grades 4, 5, and 6 in four Australian states and grades 3, 4, 5 in Queensland and Western Australia; list D is for grade 7 in South Australia and grade 6 in Western Australia and Queensland; and list E is for grade 7 in Queensland. In all, there are 33 sentences containing 102 different words to be marked (55–60 words in any one sentence list). Over 75 per cent of the words are common to any two consecutive lists.

The scored words were derived from four sources: Coleman's[1] list of 3,017 words; Horn's[2] basic writing vocabulary of 10,000 words, "typically Australian words" (*wallaby, boomerang, eucalypts, corroboree,* and *black-*

fellows); and difficult words from a commercially published spelling book. No good reasons are given for the insertion of any "typically Australian" words, or for these words in particular. Why *wallaby* rather than *kangaroo? Eucalypts* is probably used more often in California than in Australia. *Blackfellows* (equivalent of "niggers") is suspect in terms of human relations programs.

Of the 97 general words, 67 are found in Coleman's list, though doubt is likely to arise about their random selection when *pour* and *powder* (listed together in Coleman) appear in the same sentence in the test. These 67 words are also found in Horn's list. Of the remaining 30 words, 20 are in or above Horn's first 5,000, and 9 are not listed. Presumably these 9 are derived from the commercial speller. It is difficult to see why words should be chosen at random from Horn's list. Surely a standardized test at the elementary level would have considerably more curricular validity if it sampled only the first three or four thousand most frequently used words. Coleman's list gives neither frequency nor difficulty, but the average grade placement of 34 of the 38 words common to lists A, B, C is, according to Gates,[3] 6.3.

If the three lists are considered separately, there is the same high proportion of less frequently used words. Only 50 per cent are in Horn's first 3,000. From 30 to 40 per cent are in or above the fourth thousand for the grade indicated by Rinsland,[4] or else are not listed as used in the grade for which the list is intended. List D has 25 words (of 60) in or above Horn's fifth thousand, and 6 not listed; list E has 28 words in or above the fifth thousand, and 9 not listed. List D has 16, and list E, 23 words not listed in Rinsland's basic vocabulary of 25,000 words. No reasons are given why these words should be included.

The manual suggests that the random selection of words from comprehensive spelling lists should serve to make the lists for each grade fairly representative of the children's spelling vocabulary. The above data cast some doubt on this statement and hence on the validity of the words in these lists of sentences.

All standardized spelling tests suffer from limited usefulness in the direction and appraisal of instruction, but these have two particular

1 COLEMAN, WILLIAM H. *A Critique of Spelling Vocabulary Investigation.* Colorado State Teachers College, Education Series No. 12. Greeley, Colo.: the College, 1931. Pp. 119.
2 HORN, ERNEST. *A Basic Writing Vocabulary: 10,000 Words Most Commonly Used in Writing.* University of Iowa Monographs in Education, Series 1, No. 4. Iowa City, Iowa: the University, 1926. Pp. 225.

3 GATES, ARTHUR I. *A List of Spelling Difficulties in 3876 Words.* New York: Bureau of Publications, Teachers College, Columbia University, 1937. Pp. 166.
4 RINSLAND, HENRY D. *A Basic Vocabulary of Elementary School Children.* New York: Macmillan Co., 1945. Pp. 636.

drawbacks: (*a*) the fact that the words represent only a small sampling of those on the lists which children tested are required to learn; and (*b*) the low social usefulness of many of the words tested. To what extent they test general spelling ability, as distinct from ability to spell these particular words, is a moot point. Lists A, B, and C are probably useful as a rough indication of how children stand compared with other children in the same state (since most states use one list throughout). The usefulness of lists D and E is more doubtful.

[223]

Coordinated Scales of Attainment: Spelling. Grades 4, 5, 6, 7, 8; 1946–54; subtest of *Coordinated Scales of Attainment;* IBM; grade 4: Forms A ('46), B ('49); grades 5–8: Forms A, B ('49); 5 levels; directions for administering ['52] for each level; battery manuals (A, '54; B, '49); separate answer sheets must be used; $1.90 per 25 tests; $1 per 25 IBM scorable answer sheets; 10¢ per scoring stencil; 50¢ per specimen set; postage extra; (45) minutes; James A. Fitzgerald; Educational Test Bureau. *

For a review by Alvin W. Schindler of the complete battery, see 4:8; for reviews by Roland L. Beck, Lavone A. Hanna, Gordon N. Mackenzie (with Glen Hass), and C. C. Ross of batteries 4–8, see 3:6.

[224]

Graded Word Spelling Test. Ages 5–15; 1950–55; Forms A, B ['50]; no data on reliability; no norms; 3s. per 12 tests; 4d. per single copy; 1s. 6d. per manual ['55]; postage extra; [15–40] minutes; Fred J. Schonell; Oliver & Boyd Ltd. *

JOHN NISBET, *Lecturer in Education, University of Aberdeen, Aberdeen, Scotland.*

The 100 words in each of the two forms of the test are arranged in groups of 10, the first group covering attainment at age 5–6, the next group at age 6–7, and so on up to age 14–15. Administration is oral, subjects writing the words on a blank sheet of paper as the tester first reads out the word, then the word "embedded in an explanatory sentence," and finally the word repeated. It is left to the tester to invent explanatory sentences; skill in inventing these sentences may affect scores.

The manual includes no data on construction or reliability, but a personal communication from the author gave the following information. A pool of words drawn mainly from the author's Essential Spelling List was given to approximately 2,000 English children, about 200 in each age group from 5–15 years. After elimination of words which were unsuitable in terms of statistical criteria, 10 words were

chosen for each age group, each word having been spelled correctly by 45 to 55 per cent of the age group. The last 20 words include more difficult words to allow headroom for the ablest (e.g., miscellaneous, hydraulic). Reliability (test-retest on 195 children, age unspecified) was .96. Since girls scored higher than boys on the average, the author considered giving separate norms for boys and girls; but having checked scores from some 10,000 children, he suggests that separate norms would merely add 1 or 2 months of score to boys' scores and subtract 3 or 4 months from girls' scores between the ages of 7 and 13 years.

It is unfortunate that these data were not included in the manual, for their absence suggests a less systematic construction. The merit of the test is that it can be administered without expense to an entire class at one time, and that the "spelling quotient" is simple to calculate and easy to understand. Spelling standards, however, vary considerably between areas and over quite short periods of time; and as the representativeness of the standardisation group is uncertain, the norms may not be generally valid. The nature of the construction of the test complicates any revision of test norms with changing standards. Nevertheless, the lists provide a convenient rough check on spelling attainment between ages 8 and 12, and are widely used for this purpose in Britain.

[225]

Lincoln Diagnostic Spelling Tests. Grades 5–8, 8–12 or 9–12; 1941–57; 2 editions; (30–40) minutes; A. L. Lincoln.
a) [EDUCATIONAL RECORDS BUREAU EDITION.] Grades 5–8, 8–12; 4 forms; 2 levels; manual ('51); 6¢ per test; postage extra; Educational Records Bureau. *
　1) *Lincoln Intermediate Spelling Test.* Grades 5–8; Forms A, B, C ('49, identical with tests published in 1947 and 1948), D ('49).
　2) *Lincoln Diagnostic Spelling Test* [*Advanced*]. Grades 8–12; Forms 1 ('49, identical with test copyrighted in 1941), 2 ['42], 3 ['43], 4 ['44].
b) LINCOLN DIAGNOSTIC SPELLING TESTS [PUBLIC SCHOOL PUBLISHING COMPANY EDITION]. Grades 5–8, 9–12; 2 forms; 2 levels; manual ('56); tentative norms; $2.25 per 25 tests; 50¢ per specimen set; postpaid; Public School Publishing Co. *
　1) *Intermediate.* Grades 5–8; Forms A, B ('56, same as Forms A, B of the *Lincoln Intermediate Spelling Test* published in 1947 and 1948).
　2) *Advanced.* Grades 9–12; Forms A, B ('56, same as Forms 1, 2 of *Lincoln Diagnostic Spelling Test* published in 1941 and 1942).

REFERENCES

1. TOWNSEND, AGATHA. "A Study of the Lincoln Diagnostic Spelling Test." *Ed Rec B* 38:49–53 Je '43. *
2. LUNTZ, LESTER. "A Comparison of Results Obtained With Dictation and Multiple-Choice Spelling Tests." *Ed Rec B* 65: 76–84 F '55. * (PA 29:7866)

For reviews by Walter Scribner Guiler and George Spache, see 4:202–3.

[226]

★**Phonovisual Diagnostic Spelling Test: A Test for All Consonant Sounds and the 17 Fundamental Vowel Sounds.** Grades 3 and over; 1949; 1 form; no data on reliability; no norms; 75¢ per 50 tests; 10¢ per single copy; cash orders postpaid; administration time not reported; Lucille D. Schoolfield and Josephine B. Timberlake; Phonovisual Products, Inc. *

[227]

Spelling and Vocabulary: Every Pupil Test. Grades 3–4, 5–6, 7–9, 10–12; 1948–58; new form usually issued each December and April; 4 levels; norms available following testing program; no data on reliability; 3¢ per test; 1¢ per scoring key; cash orders postpaid; 40(45) minutes; Ohio Scholarship Tests. *

[228]

★*Spelling Errors Test.* Grades 2–4, 5–6, 7–8; 1948–55; 1 form ['55]; 3 levels; 25¢ per set of record blank ['55] and manual ['55]; postage extra; [15] minutes; George Spache; the Author, University of Florida, Gainesville, Fla. *

REFERENCE

1. LAMPARD, DOROTHY M. "A Study of Spelling Disabilities in Grades Four, Five, and Six." *Alberta J Ed Res* 1:48–59 D '55. *

[229]

Spelling: Every Pupil Scholarship Test. Grades 3, 4–6, 7–8, 9–12; 1928–58; new form usually issued each January and April; 4 levels; norms available following testing program; no data on reliability; 4¢ per test; 4¢ per scoring key; postage extra; 15(20), 30(35) minutes for grades 3–8, 9–12; Bureau of Educational Measurements. *

[230]

Spelling Test: National Achievement Tests. Grades 3–4, 5–8, 7–9, 10–12; 1936–57; 2 forms; 4 levels; no data on reliability; $1.25 per 25 tests; 50¢ per specimen set of any one level; postage extra; (25) minutes; Robert K. Speer and Samuel Smith; Acorn Publishing Co. *
a) GRADES 3–4. 1936–57; Forms A ('57, identical with test copyrighted in 1939), B ('39); directions sheet ('39).
b) GRADES 5–8. Same as for *a*.
c) GRADES 7–9. Same as for *a*.
d) GRADES 10–12. 1936–56; Forms A ('56, identical with test copyrighted in 1939), B ('39); directions sheet for Form A ('42, identical with sheet copyrighted in 1939), directions sheet for Form B ('39).

JAMES A. FITZGERALD, *Professor of Education, University of Scranton, Scranton, Pennsylvania.*

The sources and the objectives of the vocabulary of these spelling tests are not stated by the authors, nor is the validity of the tests indicated. However, an analysis of one of the two forms for each level indicates that they have a degree of curricular validity. Forty-seven of the 50 words in Form B, grades 3–4, are included among the 2,650 words most commonly written by children and adults in Fitzgerald's *A Basic*

Life Spelling Vocabulary.[1] All 50 are in Horn's adult list [2] of 10,000 words. All are included in Rinsland's *A Basic Vocabulary of Elementary School Children.*[3]

Twenty-six of the 60 words in Form A, grades 5–8, are in Fitzgerald's vocabulary; 57 are in Horn's (53 among his most common 5,000 words); and 56 are in Rinsland's.

Forty-nine of the 60 words in Form B, grades 7–9, are among Horn's 10,000, but only 36 are within the 5,000 most useful words of adult writing. On this level, a list of 60 words of which 24 are beyond the most common 5,000 and 11 beyond the most common 10,000 words of adult writing may be criticized on the basis of curricular validity. In addition, some prospective test users may be concerned because 15 of these 60 words are not found in Rinsland's vocabulary.

Many of the 60 words presented in Form A, grades 10–12, may be questioned on the basis of utility. Only 26 of these words are in Horn's list of 10,000. In other words, 34 are not within the 10,000 most common words in adult writing. Only 11 are among Horn's most common 5,000; 49 of the 60 are beyond the 5,000 most useful words in adult writing. Thirteen are not included in the Thorndike-Lorge *Teacher's Word Book of 30,000 Words.*[4] If the purpose of the test is to test pupils upon words generally useful in writing, the value of the test is questionable because some of these words will seldom, if ever, be used in writing by ordinary individuals. Therefore, although the tests have curricular validity on the two lower levels, their validity is low at the two higher levels.

No manual is presented, but norms are provided for each test at each level. The purpose of the tests is not stated, but it may be inferred from the accompanying norms that the objective is to rate the spelling ability of individuals.

The manner of administering the tests is clearly described. Each word to be spelled is to be pronounced, read in a prepared sentence, and pronounced a second time. Some sentences, however, do not clearly indicate the meaning of words. Examples of such sentences are: "Call

1 FITZGERALD, JAMES A. *A Basic Life Spelling Vocabulary.* Milwaukee, Wis.: Bruce Publishing Co., 1951. Pp. 161.
2 HORN, ERNEST. *A Basic Writing Vocabulary: 10,000 Words Most Commonly Used in Writing.* University of Iowa Monographs in Education, First Series No. 4. Iowa City, Iowa: the University, 1926. Pp. 225.
3 RINSLAND, HENRY D. *A Basic Vocabulary of Elementary School Children.* New York: Macmillan Co., 1945. Pp. 636.
4 THORNDIKE, EDWARD L., AND LORGE, IRVING. *The Teacher's Word Book of 30,000 Words.* New York: Bureau of Publications, Teachers College, Columbia University, 1944. Pp. xiii, 274.

a *physician* at once," "The new *tariff* is too high," "He is *altogether* too bold," and "Be less *equivocal* in your answers." From these sentences, it would be difficult, if not impossible, for pupils who were unacquainted with the words to infer the meanings of *physician, tariff, altogether,* or *equivocal.*

Unfortunately, many pupils on all levels will find that insufficient room is allowed for writing the words in the blanks. This defect can be very easily corrected by the publisher.

Despite their limitations, these tests have value for determining the comparative spelling abilities of pupils in a class or in different schools in a district. The two comparable forms at each level should have some value for determining the spelling progress of individuals, particularly on the two lower levels where the validity of the word lists is highest.

For a review by W. J. Osburn, see 38:1161.

[231]

*Traxler High School Spelling Test. Grades 9–12; 1937–55; Forms 1 ('55, same as 1937 test), 2 ('55, same as 1937 test), 3 ('55, same as 1940 test) ; manual ('55) ; norms based upon testing in private schools in 1937–40; $1.75 per 25 tests; 50¢ per specimen set; postpaid; administration time not reported; Arthur E. Traxler; C. A. Gregory Co. *

For a review by Henry D. Rinsland, see 4:212.

[232]

*Wellesley Spelling Scale. Grades 9–16; 1944–57; IBM; Forms 1 ('57, identical with test copyrighted in 1944 except for one item), 2 ('57, identical with test copyrighted in 1944) ; manual ('57) ; $1.75 per 35 tests; separate answer sheets may be used; 3¢ per IBM answer sheet ; 20¢ per scoring stencil ; postage extra; 25¢ per specimen set, postpaid; (15–20) minutes; Thelma G. Alper and Edith B. Mallory; California Test Bureau. *

REFERENCE

1. ALPER, THELMA G. "A Diagnostic Spelling Scale for the College Level: Its Construction and Use." *J Ed Psychol* 33: 273–90 Ap '42. * (PA 17:932)

JANET G. AFFLERBACH, *Editor, Professional Examination Service, American Public Health Association, New York, New York.*

The *Wellesley Spelling Scale* is a compact and practical test of 50 items of the multiple choice type. The examinee chooses among one correct spelling and three incorrect spellings of a word for which a context setting is supplied. The answer sheet is well designed, with more than usual precaution taken to insure the use of proper norms in interpreting the score. A simple scoring key is provided, the same for both forms. An unusually com-

plete manual contains a detailed description of the construction and purposes of the test, precise directions for administering and scoring it, and sensible suggestions for interpreting the test results.

The choice of key words is excellent. Among them are examples of generally accepted "pitfalls" to avoid in spelling, including the formation of the past tense from the present (occur-red), of adverbs from adjectives (definite-ly), and of "agent-devoting" nouns from verbs (descend-ants). The very "everydayness" of the key words enhances the practicality of the tests for the classroom teacher. Here the student meets the kind of words he is likely to need in ordinary personal or business writing. No attempt has been made to include bizarre, "spelldown" favorites, highly technical terms, or new words of uncertain status.

However, to judge the scale on the merits of words included rather than of words omitted is the chief concern. These scales are obviously a good tool with which to discover poor spellers and to determine the type of remedial instruction that is needed. The scales are also valuable in determining the amount of progress made after a specific course of spelling instruction. The availability of two forms makes such measurement a practical possibility. With the two forms very well balanced in choice of key words, the test user can be confident of coverage of similar rules and exceptions regardless of which form he selects.

The reviewer found only three items to which exception could be taken. In Item 44, Form 1, the exclusion of *criticising* as a correct spelling is debatable. Certainly a spelling allowed by Webster's unabridged dictionary should be accounted for in the scoring key. The appearance of *affect* (Item 14, Form 1) and *effect* (Item 6, Form 2) with identical choices places undue emphasis upon what is basically a problem in vocabulary rather than in spelling since the speller must be able *first* to discriminate from contextual clues between the two and *secondly* to spell the words correctly. This is not true of other words in the scale.

The value of the *Wellesley Spelling Scale* for the purposes indicated is not diminished to any significant extent by the specific criticisms noted. The instrument, with its thorough and attractive accessory materials, represents a sensible answer to the need for a practical ready-made measuring device in spelling for grades 9 through 13.

For reviews by Henry D. Rinsland and Guy M. Wilson, see 3:157.

VOCABULARY

[233]

★**Durost-Center Word Mastery Test: Evaluation and Adjustment Series.** Grades 9–12; 1951–52, c1950–52; 3 scores: vocabulary, vocabulary in context, use of context; IBM; Form AM ('51); manual ('52); separate answer sheets must be used; $4.15 per 35 tests; $1.70 per 35 IBM answer sheets; postage extra; 35¢ per specimen set, postpaid; 60(80) minutes in 2 sessions 2 to 7 days apart; Walter N. Durost and Stella S. Center; World Book Co. *

A. N. HIERONYMUS, *Associate Professor of Education, State University of Iowa, Iowa City, Iowa.*

ORGANIZATION AND CONTENT. This test consists of two parts. Part 1 is a 100-item multiple response vocabulary test. Part 2—to be administered "several days, preferably a week" later—is an exact duplicate of Part 1, with the notable exception that each item is preceded by a sentence in which the word to be defined is employed in context. Part 1 provides a measure of general vocabulary; Part 2, a measure of the knowledge of words when they are used in contextual material. A third score is obtained as the difference between the two part scores. This difference score, labeled Use of Context, is intended to yield evidence on "the extent to which the student is able to learn the meanings of unknown words by seeing them in typical context situations."

As a general vocabulary test, Part 1 is highly satisfactory. Words were selected so as to be representative with respect to source, parts of speech, and social utility, and they were submitted to an adequate tryout. Distributions of tryout item difficulty indexes are presented and appear to be close to ideal.

While norms and evaluational evidence are presented for Part 2, the authors recommend basing instructional follow-up primarily on the results from Part 1 and Use of Context scores.

RELIABILITY. Both alternate form and split-half within-grade reliability coefficients are reported for one community. In view of the generally recognized superiority of alternate forms reliability data, one wonders why the split-half coefficients were even reported, and, more par-

ticularly, why the standard errors of measurement were based on split-half coefficients rather than on alternate forms data.

Reliability data are conspicuously absent for the Use of Context score which the authors term "perhaps the most significant measure to be derived" from the test. The logic of assessing the extent to which an individual is able to learn the meaning of unknown words from context is very appealing. Obtaining scores on this ability would appear to be the main reason for giving this particular test. Important scores for which norms are provided should be accompanied by reliability coefficients. Also missing are correlations between part scores; such correlations would shed light on the reliability or lack of reliability of the Use of Context scores. The only empirical evidence bearing on the behavior of these scores is in the form of correlations with IQ, which are .24, .02, −.11, and −.24 for grades 9, 10, 11, and 12, respectively.

INTERPRETATION OF RESULTS. The standardization was conducted in 1950 as a part of the standardization of the Evaluation and Adjustment Series. No information is given about methods of selecting the norms sample. The numbers of pupils (2,405 to 3,880 per grade), schools (54), and states (24) involved are given. The median CA's and IQ's supplied are of dubious value.

Standard scores and percentile ranks are supplied for Parts 1 and 2 for fourth- and ninth-month testing in each of the four grades. Percentile norms for Use of Context difference scores are given for all grades combined.

No provision is made for measuring growth. Since identical standard score distributions are used for each grade level, growth must be inferred from change in status. All the user can conclude from such data is that a given student gained more than or less than others with the same initial score.

A case is made for comparing scores made on the Durost-Center test with those on an intelligence test "with the idea of making further use of the two measures in a diagnostic and remedial sense." This would seem to be carrying the notion of expectancy too far, especially since obtained correlations between the vocabulary scores and IQ's run about as high as the correlations between equivalent forms of so-called tests of intelligence.

OVERALL EVALUATION. As a vocabulary test, either Part 1 or Part 2 is eminently satisfactory.

A second score probably adds little important knowledge about the student. The difference between the part scores (Use of Context) is probably too unreliable to be of much significance.

[234]

*The Inglis Tests of English Vocabulary. Grades 9–16; 1923–51; Forms A, B ('51, identical with forms copyrighted in 1923, 1924, except for change in format), C ('27); directions sheets (A, '23; B, '24; C, '27); no norms for grades 14–16; $3 per 30 tests, postpaid; specimen set not available; (40) minutes; Alexander Inglis; Form C completed by Ralph W. Walter; Ginn & Co. *

REFERENCES

1–7. See 3:163.
8. DOWNING, C. M. "A Lower Extension of the Inglis Tests of English Vocabulary." *Engl Leaflet* 32:21–30 F '33. *
9. LANGSAM, ROSALIND S. *A Factorial Analysis of Reading Ability.* Doctor's thesis, New York University (New York, N.Y.), 1941.
10. UHRBROCK, RICHARD STEPHEN. "Construction of a Selection Test for College Graduates." *J General Psychol* 41:153–93 O '49. * (PA 24:4874)

For a review by Henry D. Rinsland, see 3:163.

[235]

*The Iowa Tests of Educational Development: Test 8, General Vocabulary. Grades 9–13; 1942–58; IBM; Forms X-3S, Y-3S ('52); examiner's manual ('58); battery manual ('54); pupil profile leaflet, fourth edition ('58); profile card (no date); separate answer sheets must be used; $3 per 20 tests; $5 per 100 IBM answer sheets; 50¢ per hand and machine scoring stencil; 50¢ per specimen set; 50¢ per battery manual; postage extra; 22(30) minutes; prepared under the direction of E. F. Lindquist; Science Research Associates. *

For reviews by J. Murray Lee and Stephen Wiseman of the complete battery, see 17; for a review by Eric F. Gardner of Forms X-2 and Y-2, see 4:17; for reviews by Henry Chauncey, Gustav J. Froehlich, and Lavone A. Hanna of Forms X-1 and Y-1, see 3:12.

[236]

★New Standard Vocabulary Test. Grades 7–12; 1955–58; reprinted from the Educational Edition of the *Reader's Digest;* IBM; Forms A ('55), B ('56), C ('56), D ('57), E ('57), F ('58); manual ('58); $2.50 per 35 tests; $3 per 100 IBM answer sheets; 30(35) minutes; Miriam M. Bryan, Janet G. Afflerbach, and Herbert A. Landry; Educational Department, Reader's Digest. *

RICHARD A. MEADE, *Professor of Education, University of Virginia, Charlottesville, Virginia.*

This vocabulary test consists of 125 four-response multiple choice items. The words represent a sampling from the Thorndike-Lorge word list [1] and also from words that have come

1 THORNDIKE, EDWARD L., AND LORGE, IRVING. *The Teacher's Word Book of 30,000 Words.* New York: Bureau of Publications, Teachers College, Columbia University, 1944. Pp. xiii, 274.

into general use since the creation of that list.

Of the four forms reviewed, two are designed for administering in the fall and the other two in the spring. It is the purpose of the test to provide a means for discovering the extent of vocabulary growth of pupils during the school year. In addition, pupil achievement may be compared with that of the large group of pupils upon whom the test was standardized.

The test is quite simple in both administration and scoring. An adequate manual provides clear directions and suggestions for using, scoring, and interpreting results. The test provides teachers of grades 7–12 with a simple, reliable, and usable test.

OSMOND E. PALMER, *Associate Professor, Office of Evaluation Services, Michigan State University, East Lansing, Michigan.*

These tests originated in vocabulary quizzes of the Student Guide section of the *Reader's Digest Educational Edition,* but they were prepared by test experts on the basis of the Thorndike-Lorge 30,000 word list and more recent words, and extensively tried out. From the tryouts the better items were chosen and comparable forms developed on the basis of 5,000–8,000 students per form. Large and small school systems in all parts of the country were used. The reliability of the tests is satisfactory and the norms seem reasonable, showing an improvement at the median of from 5 to 7 points between testings with fall and spring forms and from 6 to 10 points between one grade and the next.

There are 125 words in each form, presented in short phrases. The student is to choose from among four responses the response which most nearly corresponds to the meaning of the underlined word in the phrase. The time allowed for each test, 30 minutes, seems too short, for even college students often fail to finish 50-word vocabulary tests in 15 minutes.

These tests may be used to assess a student's individual progress, his standing in his class, and his wealth of vocabulary as compared to national averages. The words chosen seem fair enough, considering the grade range involved. The words range from easy to difficult and there do not seem to be too many at either extreme.

The authors' claim of careful tryout and careful selection of items seems borne out by inspection. In many cases the choice of foils for a word is ingenious. In general, the authors have avoided the trap of making the responses harder than the word being tested. In only a few cases can one quarrel with the right answer or the value of the foils. These are minor objections and there are few of them to raise. The tests should serve as a convenient and reliable measure of vocabulary growth.

[237]

★Purdue Industrial Supervisors Word-Meaning Test: Purdue Personnel Tests. Supervisors; 1952; 1 form; preliminary manual; $2.50 per 25 tests, postage extra; 50¢ per specimen set, postpaid; 15(20) minutes; Joseph Tiffin and Donald A. Long; distributed by University Book Store. *

REFERENCES

1. LONG, DONALD A. *Construction of an Industrial Vocabulary Test.* Master's thesis, Purdue University (Lafayette, Ind.), 1952.
2. SAWYER, JACK. *Self-Insight and Supervisory Performance.* Doctor's thesis, Purdue University (Lafayette, Ind.), 1955. (*DA* 15:1892)

JEROME E. DOPPELT, *Assistant Director, Test Division, The Psychological Corporation, New York, New York.*

This instrument is designed to determine the relative ability of supervisors to understand words which may appear in material directed to them. The test includes 60 four-choice vocabulary items of the synonym type, administered in 15 minutes. The preliminary manual gives a table of percentiles based on "180 industrial supervisors in a variety of plants." The odd-even reliability of the test, apparently determined for the same industrial supervisors, was found to be .92. Means and standard deviations are not given.

It is noted on the test booklet that "this test consists of words found in printed material that had been distributed to industrial supervisors." The attempt to achieve a certain amount of face validity by this method of selection is, of course, commendable. There is, however, no reason to believe that such words, in themselves, guarantee a suitable measuring instrument. More important for the test user is evidence that the test is effective in discriminating among supervisors. Unfortunately, such evidence is not given in the current (1952) manual, which states that "validity studies are now in process and will be published as soon as available."

There is a need for additional information on this test. The lack of validity data is a crucial weakness. Further normative and reliability data for groups that are not as broadly defined as "supervisors in a variety of plants" would

also be helpful. Until such information is available and can be evaluated, the reviewer feels the test cannot be recommended for use.

BERNADINE MEYER, *Assistant Professor, School of Business Administration, Duquesne University, Pittsburgh, Pennsylvania.*

This test is designed "to determine the relative ability of supervisors (or prospective supervisors) to understand those words which may appear in material directed to them." The test consists of 60 words, for each of which the testee is to select one of four possible definitions.

Directions for taking the test are readily understandable and easy to follow, as are also the directions for administering. The test user is entitled to more information about the construction of the test than is given in the manual. The manual states that the test was constructed from an original list of 500 words taken from the *Supervisors' Memory Jogger.* However, it does not tell how the 500 words were selected or why the Jogger was used. There is an implication that the Jogger contains the same vocabulary found in other written materials directed to industrial supervisors, but there is no evidence offered to support this implication.

The manual further states that the list of 500 words was reduced to 60 words by "a series of pooled judgment and internal consistency item analysis steps" described by one of the test authors in a Master's thesis. Since the probability that test users will read this thesis is extremely remote, the manual should describe the steps and indicate whose judgment was involved.

No information is given concerning the method used to select the words given as possible definitions. In some cases the test tests knowledge of the meaning of one or more of the words given as possible definitions. For instance, the word to be defined in Item 13 is "impracticable." Given as possible definitions are: "implacable," "plausible," "infeasible," and "imaginable." One might know the meaning of the word "impracticable" but be unable to answer correctly because he does not know the meaning of "implacable," "plausible," and "infeasible."

Percentile rank equivalents for raw scores are provided. The manual states that "these norms are based on 180 industrial supervisors in a variety of plants." Again, there is need for additional information : Were these experienced or beginning supervisors? How were they selected? Were they readers of the *Supervisors' Memory Jogger?* How much variety was there in the plants involved?

Reliability of the test, estimated on odd-even items, is reported as .92 for a group of 180 industrial supervisors, presumably the supervisors in the normative group. Validity studies for the test are reported only as being in process.

All in all, this is a simple, easily administered, easily scored test. However, with only sketchy information concerning test construction and with validity undetermined, one cannot enthusiastically endorse it.

[238]

★Quick-Scoring Vocabulary Test: Dominion Tests. Grades 9–13; 1958; preliminary manual; Forms A, B; $1 per 25 test-answer sheets; 10¢ per scoring key; 75¢ per complete specimen set; postage extra; 20(30) minutes; Department of Educational Research, Ontario College of Education, University of Toronto; distributed by Guidance Centre. *

[239]

*Survey Test of Vocabulary. Grades 3–12; 1931–48; Forms X4 ('40), Z4 ('48); no manual; key-norms sheets (no dates) ; no data on reliability; $1.95 per 50 tests, postage extra; 25¢ per specimen set, postpaid; 20(25) minutes; L. J. O'Rourke; Psychological Institute. *

REFERENCES

1. See 3:167.
2. STEAD, WILLIAM H., AND OTHERS. *Occupational Counseling Techniques: Their Development and Application.* New York: American Book Co., 1940. Pp. ix, 273. *
3. JANUS, SIDNEY. *The Prediction of Learning Ability for Certain Types of Mechanical Skill.* Doctor's thesis, George Washington University (Washington, D.C.), 1944.
4. LITTLETON, ISAAC T. "Prediction in Auto Trade Courses." *J Appl Psychol* 36:15–9 F '52. * *(PA 26:7256)*

For reviews by Verner M. Sims and Clifford Woody, see 3:167.

[240]

*Vocabulary: Every Pupil Scholarship Test. High school; 1935-58; new form usually issued each January and April; norms available following testing program; no data on reliability; 4¢ per test; 4¢ per scoring key; postage extra; 40(45) minutes; Bureau of Educational Measurements. *

[241]

*Vocabulary Test: National Achievement Tests. Grades 3–8, 7–12; 1939–57; 2 forms; 2 levels; 50¢ per specimen set of either level; postage extra; (15) minutes; Robert K. Speer and Samuel Smith; Acorn Publishing Co. *

a) GRADES 3–8. Forms A ('57, identical with test copyrighted in 1939), B ('40) ; directions sheets (A, '43; B, '40) ; no data on reliability; $2 per 25 tests.

b) GRADES 7–12. 2 scores: vocabulary, word discrimination; Forms A ('51, identical with test copyrighted in 1939), B ('54, identical with test copyrighted in 1939) ; directions sheet for Form A ('51, identical with sheet copyrighted in 1939), directions sheet for Form B ('40) ; teachers' guide ['44] ; no data on reliability for Form B ; $2 per 25 tests.

For a review by Clifford Woody, see 3:168.

ENGLISH – SIXTH MMY

REVIEWS BY *J. Douglas Ayers, Hillel Black, M. Alan Brimer, Miriam M. Bryan, Henry Chauncey, William E. Coffman, Charlotte Croon Davis, Clarence Derrick, Leonard S. Feldt, J. Raymond Gerberich, Marvin D. Glock, Albert N. Hieronymus, Stephen Hunka, Margaret F. Lorimer, William H. Lucio, T. R. Miles, Stanley Nisbet, Victor H. Noll, Osmond E. Palmer, A. E. G. Pilliner, Gus P. Plessas, Robert C. Pooley, Roger A. Richards, Holland Roberts, Benjamin Rosner, H. J. Sants, Richard E. Schutz, John C. Sherwood, George D. Spache, Bernard Spolsky, Robert E. Stake, John M. Stalnaker, and George P. Winship, Jr.*

[248]

*American School Achievement Tests: Part 3, Language and Spelling. Grades 4-6, 7-9; 1941-63; subtest of *American School Achievement Tests*; 2 scores: language, spelling; 4 forms (2 sheets); Forms D, E, and F are identical with Forms A, B, and C copyrighted 14 years earlier except for format; 2 levels; $3 per 35 self-marking tests; 50¢ per specimen set of either level; postage extra; Willis E. Pratt, Robert V. Young, and Clara E. Cockerille (manuals); Bobbs-Merrill Co., Inc. *
a) INTERMEDIATE BATTERY. Grades 4-6; Forms D ('55), E ('56), F ('57), G ('58); battery manual ('61, 17 pages); 32(45) minutes.
b) ADVANCED BATTERY. Grades 7-9; Forms D ('56), E ('56), F ('57), G ('58); battery manual ('63, 17 pages); 37(50) minutes.

REFERENCES

1. GROFF, PATRICK J. "Parts of Speech in Standardized English Tests." *Sch R* 69:457-60 w '61. *

For reviews by M. A. Brimer and Clarence Derrick, see 5:174. For reviews of the complete battery, see 2, 5:1, 4:1, and 3:1.

[249]
*Analytical Survey Test in English Fundamentals. Grades 9–13; 1932–57; formerly called *Diagnostic Survey Test in English Fundamentals;* 8 scores: spelling, capitalization, punctuation, sentence organization, sentence structure, grammatical usage, grammatical terminology, total; Forms 3 ['57], 4 ('57), (8 pages); mimeographed manual ('57, 10 pages); no data on reliability of current forms; tentative norms; $3.50 per 35 tests; 50¢ per specimen set; postage extra; 33(45) minutes; J. Helen Campbell and Walter Scribner Guiler; Bobbs-Merrill Co., Inc. *

REFERENCES

1. GUILER, WALTER SCRIBNER. "Capitalization Disabilities of College Freshmen." *J Am Assn Col Reg* 22:317–27 Ap '47. *
2. GUILER, WALTER SCRIBNER. "Punctuation Disabilities of College Freshmen." *J Am Assn Col Reg* 22:183–91 Ja '47. *

LEONARD S. FELDT, *Professor of Education, State University of Iowa, Iowa City, Iowa.*

The main purpose of this test, as stated in the mimeographed manual, is "to discover the particular phases of the mechanics of English usage in which individual students (or the class as a whole) need further training." To perform this diagnostic function the authors have included 20 items on spelling, 16 on capitalization, 16 on punctuation, 8 on sentence organization, 16 on sentence structure, 16 on grammatical usage, and 8 on grammatical terminology. The reader who doubts that such short subtests could yield scores which are sufficiently reliable for diagnostic purposes will find no data in the manual to allay these fears. He will find other inadequacies as well.

Content validity is obviously a crucial characteristic of an instrument of this kind, but the manual presents practically no evidence on which to base judgment. The authors state that curriculum validity was insured by including "only those usages that have high functional value and that thereby constitute legitimate educational objectives. The criterion used in judging functional value was whether or not violation of the usage constitutes a flagrant language error." There is no indication, however, that the authors have referred to the research on the incidence of various errors, to the curriculum publications of the National Council of Teachers of English, or to studies bearing on the acceptability of many usages encountered in formal and informal writing. Thus the case must rest on the potential user's personal evaluation of the test content.

Throughout the manual the authors state that they are concerned with skills of functional value. Yet in Part 2, Sentence Structure, the student may lose eight points if he cannot identify the principles which have been violated in a series of poorly constructed sentences. It is not enough that he recognize a sentence is faulty, but he must know which of seven principles account for the fault. In Part 7, Grammatical Terminology, the examinee may lose eight points if he cannot identify the technical names of parts of sentences. These may be functional skills in learning about the structure of the English language, but they hardly seem functional skills in the use of language. One might also argue that a number of the items fail to represent examples of flagrant errors. For example, the Sentence Structure subtest includes the following item: "One reason that camels are used on the desert is because their ....feet do not sink in the sand." According to the key, this sentence is unacceptable, since a clause beginning with *because* cannot be used as a predicate noun. Many teachers of English may agree. Leonard and others,[1] however, in their survey of linguists and teachers, conclude, "The opinions of the judges in this instance leave little doubt that the expression is acceptable colloquially." Other usages scattered through the test fall into the category which Marckwardt and Walcott [2] call "disputable"—constructions upon which linguists and teachers evidence substantial difference of opinion. Clearly, the reaction of a potential user to this test will be conditioned by the degree to which his definition of flagrant error is consistent with that of the authors.

One final bit of evidence bearing on validity concerns the correlation of scores on an earlier edition with first semester English grades. A coefficient of .65 is reported in the manual, but no details are offered as to the institution involved, the nature of the examinee population, or the skills represented in this grade criterion. The obtained coefficient is therefore relatively meaningless.

Despite the absence of concrete evidence of validity in the manual, individual teachers might react favorably to the test content. Other aspects of the test more surely deserve criticism. Though separate scores are to be obtained on individual parts and the presence of specific

1 LEONARD, STERLING ANDRUS. *Current English Usage,* p. 145. National Council of Teachers of English, English Monographs, No. 1. Chicago, Ill.: the Council, 1932. Pp. xxii, 232. *
2 MARCKWARDT, ALBERT H., AND WALCOTT, FRED C. *Facts About Current English Usage,* p. 112. National Council of Teachers of English, English Monographs, No. 7. New York: D. Appleton-Century Co., Inc., 1938. Pp. 144.

weaknesses is to be inferred from these scores, no reliability data are reported for the subtests. Only one reliability coefficient is presented in the manual; it pertains to the total score for an undescribed group of college freshmen. No reliability information at all is available for grades 9 through 12. Minimum standards of excellence in test development have advanced quite far beyond the point where such meager evidence can be regarded as sufficient.

Were the aforementioned weaknesses not enough to cause potential users to look elsewhere for a test of language skills, the faulty standardization of this test would surely constitute sufficient grounds for its rejection. The norms consist solely of median scores on each part and total for groups that are not described in any respect. Test users have rightfully come to expect more complete tables of norms and relatively comprehensive descriptions of the samples on which the norms are based. Since the present manual contains no information whatever about the norms groups, even the scant data that are provided are practically useless.

In summary, the faults of this test appear to outweigh its virtues by a wide margin. If a potential user is attracted to the particular sets of items in each subtest, he should realize that he is getting little more for his money than a collection of pre-tried exercises. He should be prepared to investigate reliability extensively before using the test for diagnostic purposes and to develop his own norms. While most standardized tests of language facility have not been favorably reviewed in the past, other tests, such as the *Cooperative English Tests [1960 Revision]*, will probably have greater appeal for the majority of English teachers.

ROGER A. RICHARDS, *Assistant Professor of English, Jersey City State College, Jersey City, New Jersey.*

The manual accompanying this test states, in a sentence of curious structure, that "The revised edition has the further advantage over the earlier edition in that [*sic*] it can be administered in less time, 33 minutes instead of 38." This statement illustrates one of the many ways in which the attempt to make a test administratively attractive can rob it of its validity. The stated purpose of the test is sufficiently ambitious in itself to give rise to mild suspicion: "The main purpose....is to discover the particular phases of the mechanics of English usage in which individual students (or the class as a whole) need further training. It is also designed to measure general achievement in the mechanics of English usage." To claim that such a noble purpose can be served by only 33 minutes of testing time seems incredible.

The seven parts of the test reflect varying degrees of inadequacy. Time limits for individual subtests range from three to six minutes. None of the parts contains more than 20 items, and two, covering the broad fields of "Sentence Organization" and "Grammatical Terminology," consist of only eight. The rest are tests of 16 questions. It is especially inconceivable that the 20-word subtest can adequately appraise overall spelling ability of students in the range from ninth grade through first year of college.

Statistical data concerning the test are grossly inadequate. No information concerning validity or reliability of the various parts is given. We are told only (*a*) that for 350 college freshmen, scores on the earlier forms of this test correlated .65 and .62 with first semester English grades and total first semester average, respectively, and (*b*) that the reliability of scores "made by more than 300 college freshmen on the two test forms [the earlier Forms 1 and 2]" was .90. A single set of norms for both of the current forms is presented solely in terms of median part scores and total scores for students at each grade level from 9 through 13. No information is given concerning the origin of the norms. For all the test user knows, they might be based on nothing more than speculation. What relevance they could possibly have to the present-day performance of students is not clear. If they are based on some sort of evidence, we are in grave trouble. Consider, for example, the spelling section. Each item presents three alternative spellings of some commonly used word. Many of the distractors seem invented just to furnish multiple responses. We have, among others, these: "decidedly, decidedaly, decidedly," "satisfactorily, satisfactorely, satisfactorally," "curosity, curiosity, curiosety," "courtesies, curtesies, curtisies." Confronted with such choices, the median college freshman, according to the norms, makes a score of only 14 out of 20!

Some of the scoring procedures seem inappropriate. In Parts 2 (Capitalization) and

3 (Punctuation), the score is determined by the number of sentences right; the result is that on the Form 4 capitalization subtest, item 1, containing a single capital letter, and items 8 and 12, requiring no capitals, are weighted the same as item 2, which requires 10 capitals! It is doubtful that Part 4 measures skill in "Sentence Organization," though this reviewer must confess that he has no idea of what language skill is referred to by the term or how, if it exists, the skill differs from "Sentence Structure" covered by Part 5. Whatever is involved, the key is inadequate. It makes no provision for giving credit to a student who rearranges "disconnected groups of words" to form interrogative sentences. And a student with keen insight into language would have difficulty accepting the "right" reconstruction of item 2 of Form 3: "(1) made to carry (2) with folding blades (3) in the pocket (4) is a knife (5) a pocket knife." According to the key this sentence should read "A pocket knife is a knife with folding blades made to carry in the pocket." The misplaced modifying phrase "made to carry" is not likely to cause any breakdown in communication, but its appearance seems unforgivable in a test designed to measure a student's ability in "Sentence Organization."

In addition to the multitude of similar measurement crudities, the approach to language reflected by the test will be objectionable to the more enlightened English teachers in today's schools. Many parts of the test confront the student with tasks that he will never meet except on such exercises as these. Moreover, no awareness of such vital linguistic considerations as levels of usage, the importance of appropriateness, or the constant change in language shows through.

These tests ought to be withdrawn from the market. If they are permitted to continue in circulation, however, they should not be used except as the basis of class discussions. Even then, they will probably appeal only to teachers of an extremely traditional orientation.

[250]

*Barrett-Ryan English Test. Grades 7–13; 1926–61; IBM; Forms 1 ('56), 2 ('56), 3 ('58), (4 pages, revisions of tests copyrighted in 1929), 6 ('44), 1948, 1954 ['55], (4 pages); revised manual ('58, 6 pages); supplementary norms: Forms 1 and 2 ['57], Form 3 ('61), Forms 1948 and 1954 ['48, same as norms originally issued for Form 1948 alone]; $1.40 per 25 tests; separate answer sheets may be used; 85¢ per 25 IBM

answer sheets; 30¢ per scoring stencil; postage extra; 50¢ per specimen set, postpaid; 50(55) minutes; E. R. Barrett, Teresa M. Ryan, M. W. Sanders (1, 2, 3), H. E. Schrammel (1948, 1954, manual), and E. R. Wood (manual); Bureau of Educational Measurements. *

REFERENCES

1. ANDERSON, MARY R., AND STEGMAN, ERWIN J. "Predictors of Freshman Achievement at Fort Hays Kansas State College." Ed & Psychol Meas 14:722–3 w '54. * (PA 29:7952)
2. GROFF, PATRICK J. "Parts of Speech in Standardized English Tests." Sch R 69:457–60 w '61. *

CLARENCE DERRICK, *Professor of English, and Chairman, Humanities Department, University of Florida, Gainesville, Florida.*

Wines and cheeses improve with age; objective English tests do not. The *Barrett-Ryan English Test* was first published in 1926, and the revised forms suffer from the influence of the earlier editions. Even more important, in the confusion of form designations, the unwary purchaser may fail to recognize that Form 6 (1944), Form 1948, and Form 1954 differ significantly from revised Form 3 (1958). If one has to use the Barrett-Ryan test, he will be better off using the 1956–1958 revisions. This review will concentrate on these later forms with only passing reference to the earlier editions.

In Part 1, Punctuation, 30 items test the use of the colon, comma, question mark, semicolon, apostrophe, hyphen, double quotation marks, simple quotation marks. The principal difficulty is that the item type used reduces most of the items to two, or at best, three-choice items although they are apparently five-choice items. For example, the student is asked to select for an indicated spot in a sentence the appropriate mark from a key list containing these possibilities—colon, comma, question mark, semicolon, no punctuation. The first sentence in Form 1 is, "Omaha, Nebraska ( ) is known as a cattle market." It doesn't take much knowledge to eliminate the question mark, the colon, and the semicolon as possibilities. The 10 capitalization items in Part 2 are presented in the same manner as true-false items. The student has a fifty-fifty chance of getting these items correct by guessing. Part 3, The Sentence, tests sentence structure, diction, and recognition of the complete sentence. This 45-item section also calls for a true-false type of response. The subtest on recognition of the complete sentence uses an informal letter as the text, a poor choice since there is a freedom in the informal letter which is not present in more formal writing. Part 4, Verb Usage, contains 15 more true-false type items of verb forms frequently confused. Part 5, Grammar, has 50 paired true-false items. In the first item of a pair, the student indicates whether or not an error is present; and in the second item of the pair, he indicates whether or not a stated reason is applicable to that error. The aroma of the traditional textbook hangs heavy over this part of the test. Considerable emphasis is given to who-whom, whoever-whomever problems. One correct sentence is this rhetorical gem: "The class elected me, who am the youngest, as president." (Whoever-whomever) permitted this sentence to stand as "correct" has a tin ear.

Only the barest minimum of information on reliability and validity is reported in the manual. Similarly, the norms for the test are based on populations described as midyear high school students and beginning-of-the-year college freshmen. What high school students? What college freshmen?

Other inadequacies of the *Barrett-Ryan English Test* could be discussed; but enough limitations have been suggested to lead to the conclusion that there are other tests which are much more useful in providing the teacher with information about a student's proficiency in punctuation, capitalization, the sentence, verb usage, and grammar.

For a review by J. Raymond Gerberich, see 5:175.

[251]

*California Language Test, 1957 Edition With 1963 Norms.** Grades 1-2, 2.5-4.5, 4-6, 7-9, 9-14; 1933-63; subtest of *California Achievement Tests;* 4 scores: mechanics of English, spelling, total, handwriting; IBM and Grade-O-Mat for grades 4-14; 2-4 forms ('63 printings, c1957-63, are identical with tests copyrighted in 1957 except for profile); 5 levels; battery manual ('63, c1957-63, 53-70 pages) for each level; battery technical report ('57, 48 pages) on 1957 edition with 1957 norms; battery individual profile ('63, 2 pages) for each level; no norms for grades 13-14; separate answer sheets or cards may be used in grades 4-14; 5¢ per IBM answer sheet; 9¢ per Scoreze answer sheet; 3¢ per set of Cal-Cards; 4¢ per set of Grade-O-Mat scorable punch-out cards; 20¢ per either IBM answer sheet or Cal-Card hand scoring stencil; 20¢ per either IBM answer sheet or Grade-O-Mat machine scoring stencil; 2¢ per profile; postage extra; technical report free; 75¢ per specimen set of *a* or *b,* $1 per specimen set of *c, d,* or *e;* postpaid; Ernest W. Tiegs and Willis W. Clark; California Test Bureau. *
a) LOWER PRIMARY. Grades 1-2; Forms W ('63), X ('57), (8 pages) ; $2.45 per 35 tests; 27(40) minutes.
b) UPPER PRIMARY. Grades 2.5-4.5; Forms W ('63), X ('57), (6 pages) ; $2.80 per 35 tests; 30(40) minutes.

c) ELEMENTARY. Grades 4-6; IBM and Grade-O-Mat; Forms W ('63), X ('57), Y ('63), Z ('57), (10 pages) ; $3.15 per 35 tests; 40(50) minutes.
d) JUNIOR HIGH LEVEL. Grades 7-9; IBM and Grade-O-Mat; Forms W ('63), X ('57), Y ('57), Z ('57), (10 pages) ; $3.15 per 35 tests; 32(40) minutes.
e) ADVANCED. Grades 9-14; IBM and Grade-O-Mat; Forms W ('63), X ('57), Y ('57), (14 pages) ; $3.15 per 35 tests; 38(48) minutes.

REFERENCES

1-3. See 5:177.
4. GROFF, PATRICK J. "Parts of Speech in Standardized English Tests." *Sch R* 69:457-60 w '61. *

RICHARD E. SCHUTZ, *Professor of Education, and Director, Testing Service, Arizona State University, Tempe, Arizona.*

Although no changes have been made in item content, the 1957 edition of the *California Language Test* has been restandardized and now appears with 1963 norms. The manual gives three reasons for renorming the test: (*a*) to maintain the proper relationship with the 1963 revision of the *California Test of Mental Maturity,* which was normed at the same time, (*b*) to utilize newly determined age-grade relationships, (*c*) to update the norms in line with curriculum changes since 1957.

The dominant reason for the renorming appears to be the 1963 revision of the CTMM series. The age-grade relationships were derived directly from the CTMM standardization program. And if curriculum change was indeed an important consideration, this should have required a complete revision of the test content in line with the modified curriculum rather than simply an updating of norms for outmoded test content.

How do the new norms compare with the old? A comparison of the 1963 and 1957 age-grade relationships shows students in 1963 consistently 2-3 months older at each grade level. This appears to indicate a reversal of the declining age-in-grade trend observed between the early 1920's and the mid-1950's. It is difficult to account for such a consistent reversal throughout the grades from elementary school through college in the brief period between 1957 and 1963. The manual makes no attempt to explain the changes or their determinants.

The changes in the test norms are less regular. At the primary level the 1963 derived normative scores run consistently lower than the 1957 norms in both mechanics of English and spelling. For example, a raw score of 35 yields a grade placement of 1.9 on the 1963 norms and 2.3 on the 1957 norms. A raw score of 10 on the spelling test yields a 1963 grade

placement of 2.7 versus 3.9 in 1957, a difference greater than one full grade. Disregarding
sampling errors, this difference indicates that
language instruction has improved considerably
in the lower grades. With differences of this
magnitude, the new norms may come as a shock
to primary teachers when they compare their
class results with those obtained in previous
years with 1957 norms. "Falling back" six
months to a year in terms of grade placement
may be regarded by the individual teacher as a
slap in the face for present efforts rather than
as a pat on the back for past efforts in upgrad-
ing language instruction generally. It is hoped
that a knowledgeable person will be on hand
to help interpret the comparison, since the
manual does not anticipate the need for this
kind of help.

At the elementary level, the mechanics of
English norms are uniformly 3 to 5 grade
placement scores lower at the fourth through
sixth grade range for which the test is designed. Differences in the spelling norms at
the elementary level are complicated. At grade
placement 4.0 there is a 2 point difference with
the 1963 norms lower. At 6.0 there is a 6 point
difference with the 1963 norm again lower.
These differences are difficult to account for
other than in terms of sampling error.

At the junior high school and advanced
levels, differences between the 1957 and 1963
mechanics of English norms are slight and not
in any consistent direction. The 1963 spelling
norms, on the other hand, are uniformly higher
than the 1957, with differences of 1–4 points
from the ninth through twelfth grade range.
This difference suggests that the terminal spelling achievement of current high school graduates may be somewhat below the accomplishment of their 1957 counterparts, which leaves
a rather unpleasant taste following the pleasant
swallow of improvement in the early grades.

Unfortunately, it is impossible to separate
sampling error from true variability in assessing any of the normative differences. In fact,
the entire 1963 standardization program is so
ill-defined in the manuals that the sample's
representativeness of any population rests on
little more than faith. It is clear, however, that
the 1963 standardization strategy represents a
radical departure from that utilized in 1957.
In 1957 about 70,000 students from 341
schools in 48 states were involved in the standardization. In 1963, only 15,351 students were

involved, with the number of schools and states
not reported. The 1957 manuals describe in
considerable detail the sampling criteria used in
selecting the standardization participants. The
1963 revised manuals state only that the sample
was obtained from two phases: "(1) independent class units from seven geographic
regions representing forty-nine states, and (2)
complete school systems, including all students
in Grades 1 through 12 from five school systems located in the northeastern, eastern, central, and western areas of the United States."
Test data from the two phases were combined
in generating the norms.

The 1963 tables of norms are much more
conveniently presented in the manuals than
were the 1957 tables. All of the grade placement norms for the reading, arithmetic, and
language tests are grouped on single pages
rather than separated by test. Percentile ranks
are presented for separate grades and in terms
of raw scores, rather than across grades and
in terms of grade placement scores as in 1957.
In addition, stanine intervals and T scores are
included with the percentile ranks. Anticipated
grade achievement norms are tabled rather
than graphed. These layout modifications will
save users much time and reduce clerical errors
in manually performed conversions.

There may be some administrative confusion
in transferring from the 1957 to the 1963
norms. The 1957 answer sheet with its diagnostic profile in terms of grade placement is
still usable for responses. The 1963 answer
sheet includes a profile based on the revised
norms. The diagnostic profile included on the
answer sheet is of importance, since it contains
grade placements for the subscores of capitalization, punctuation, and word usage available
from no other source. Since no reliability data
are reported for these subscores, however, extreme caution should be exercised in their use.

The only other innovation in the 1963 revision is the availability of specially devised
mark-sense and porta-punch cards as response
recording modes at the elementary levels and
above. Although no evidence is given concerning the comparability of results obtained via
these various response modes, they may prove
of interest to school systems which have data
processing equipment readily available.

The basic content and organization of the
California Language Test have changed little
from the days of the *Progressive Achievement*

Tests. This stability can be defended without great difficulty in the areas of capitalization, punctuation, and spelling. A defense of the word usage subsection is more difficult in light of present knowledge in descriptive and structural linguistics. However, the lag between scientific advances and classroom instruction is probably sufficient to maintain the curricular validity of "usage" items for the majority of classrooms for some time to come. Even so, many would regard the generality of the title "Language Test" to be inappropriate without consideration of such topics as dialect differences, structural patterns, and verbal expression.

For reviews by Constance M. McCullough and Winifred L. Post, see 5:177; for reviews by Gerald V. Lannholm and Robert C. Pooley of the 1950 edition, see 4:151; for reviews by Harry A. Greene and J. Paul Leonard of an earlier edition, see 40:1292. For reviews of the complete battery, see 3, 5:2, 4:2, 3:15, 40:1193, and 38:876.

[252]

★**Canadian Achievement Test in English (CATE).** Grade 10; 1961–63; this test and tests 5, 365, 565, and 566 make up the *Canadian Test Battery,* grade 10. 1 form ('61, 11 pages) ; 2 editions of manual (for use also with test 365) : hand scoring ('63, 7 pages), machine scoring ('63, 8 pages) ; supplementary data ('63, 6 pages) for the battery ; separate answer sheets or cards must be used; $1.25 per 25 tests; $1 per set of 50 hand scoring answer sheets and hand scoring manual; 20¢ per hand scoring stencil; 20¢ per 15 battery profiles; 50¢ per set of 25 IBM answer cards (machine scoring through the Department of Educational Research only) ; 10¢ per machine scoring manual; 50¢ per specimen set; $2.15 per battery specimen set; postage extra; 60(70–75) minutes; Department of Educational Research, Ontario College of Education, University of Toronto; distributed by Guidance Centre (machine scoring manual and answer cards must be purchased from the Department of Educational Research). *

REFERENCES

1. D'OYLEY, VINCENT R. *Technical Manual for the Canadian Tests: Statistical Data on the Carnegie Study Tests of Academic Aptitude and Achievement in Grades 8, 9, and 10 in Ontario Schools and Grades 7 and 8 in Toronto Schools.* Carnegie Study of Identification and Utilization of Talent in High School and College, Bulletin No. 4. Toronto, Canada: Department of Educational Research, Ontario College of Education, University of Toronto, 1964. Pp. viii, 50. *
2. D'OYLEY, VINCENT R. *Testing: The First Two Years of the Carnegie Study 1959 to 1961: Analysis of Scores by Course, Sex, and Size of Municipality.* Carnegie Study of Identification and Utilization of Talent in High School and College, Bulletin No. 6. Toronto, Canada: Department of Educational Research, Ontario College of Education, University of Toronto, 1964. Pp. ix, 53. *

BERNARD SPOLSKY, *Assistant Professor of Education, McGill University, Montreal, Quebec, Canada.*

This test was "developed for use in the Carnegie Study of Identification and Utilization of Talent in High School and College, a longitudinal study of approximately 90,000 Grade 9 students enrolled in Ontario schools in September, 1959"; the norms supplied are based on a total population of approximately 60,600 students in grade 10 in Ontario schools in 1960–61. The test is available in 1963 in both machine and hand scoring editions, each edition being accompanied by full and clear directions for administration.

Lacking a statement on the part of the authors as to what specific abilities the test is aimed to measure or as to what achievement in English is held to mean, one is forced to draw inferences from the test itself. Work in grade 10 in English includes the development of abilities in reading and expression; the former includes comprehension and appreciation, and the latter both the mechanics (spelling, punctuation, acceptable usage) and the effectiveness of expression. One would expect then that a test of achievement in English would give some sort of attention to each of these areas. But this test falls far short of the ideal: it omits effectiveness of expression entirely, pays only lip service to comprehension and appreciation, and concentrates on those aspects of mechanics which are most susceptible of objective testing. This becomes evident when one considers the type of item used: of 110 items, 43 test what might be called elementary editorial ability by calling on the student to mark incorrect forms and another 21 call for the application of traditional grammatical terminology.

This failure of the test to reflect the aims of English teaching is also made clear when one looks at the content of the various sections. The section headed "Comprehension and Appreciation," for instance, seems to be concerned not with these abilities but with the student's ability to apply critical labels. The three questions on a prose passage do not test understanding of the passage but call for the selection of responses dealing with intention and means: the student has to decide the application of such vague expressions as "building to a climax," "creating atmosphere," and "producing contrast," and to decide whether atmosphere was created by "vivid verbal constructions" or "vague adverbs." Questions asked about a ten-line extract from a poem are similarly unsuitable: in one item, the question refers to "the poem," with the result that a student who knew the whole poem would be led to an incorrect response to two items; three items are concerned with terminology; one asks for identification of the line in which the poet makes "most effective use of repetition of words and sounds to make the picture more forceful" (the response given as correct ignores the frequent use of alliteration throughout the extract and chooses the line with the greatest number of repeated words, the least effective line in the whole extract); and two ask for identification of metaphors. The last three items of this section call for selection of expressions that will "contribute *most* towards the effectiveness" of given sentences; the answers required involve rather the selection of the most usual word or expression for the context; in other words, this is a test of vocabulary, or, more precisely, of ability to use clichés. The section as a whole does not test comprehension and even reflects a considerable lack of appreciation of language.

The test must be considered, therefore, as measuring certain areas of the mechanics of English. Even these items are not well chosen. The punctuation section includes two items where decisions are not covered by hard-and-fast rules but are matters of stylistic variation, and one where something that is clearly direct speech is to have two punctuation marks added but is to be left without quotation marks. The vocabulary section consists of five items requiring completion of sentences with the best of five words and nine requiring choice of a synonym. Unfortunately, the sentences do not fully control the choice of words (for instance, one is as likely to have second helpings of food because of its succulence, pleasantness, or refreshing nature as because of its palatability). And the various synonyms offered are at times equally satisfactory (the *Shorter Oxford Dictionary,* for instance, gives for the word *contraction:* "shrinking, narrowing;....the action of contracting or establishing by contract," but the test demands that the student choose between "an agreement," "a shrinking," and "a narrowing"). The major part of the grammar and usage section calls for the student to mark incorrect forms. I referred to this above as elementary editorial ability; actually, it is less than this. The errors are embedded in sentences that have been constructed to contain at least three crucial usages, each of which is underlined; it is thus not a measure of the student's ability to select errors himself. The sentences produced read very strangely. Many of them are most unlikely to have any existence outside a grammar book, e.g., "Your friends may approve of *your* going, but I, who *am* your mother, *forbids* it." What seems to be called for in many of the items is ability to recognise that certain words are out of place in the extremely formal style set up by the other usages, or, alternatively, ability to recognise the items that might be marked wrong by cautious teachers. Generally, the test does not call for any normally accepted forms to be marked incorrect, but many of the correct forms represent a preciousness of usage that is old fashioned.

Satisfactory split-half reliability coefficients are provided. On the other hand, validity data showing intercorrelations of the test with two other tests in the battery (*Canadian Achievement Test in Mathematics and Canadian Achievement Test in French*) and with school marks (based on a random sample population of 1,000) indicate that the test is not so much a measure of English achievement as a reflection of some more general ability in school work: one notes that it is about as good as a predictor of the grade 10 French mark (correlation of .56) and of marks for the other two tests (.53, .54) as it is in predicting the grade 10 English mark (.58).

Taking all these factors into consideration, one feels that, whatever its use may have been in the study for which it was prepared, the CATE has little to recommend it as a test of achievement in grade 10 English.

[253]

★Canadian English Achievement Test (CEAT). Grades 8.5–9.0; 1959–63; this test and tests 445 and 567 make up the *Canadian Test Battery,* grades 8–9; 3 or 4 scores: reading comprehension, effectiveness of expression, and (grade 9 only) mechanics of expression, or (grade 8 only) punctuation-capitalization, grammatical usage; 1 form; separate parts 1 ('59, reading comprehension), 2 ('59, mechanics of expression), 3 ('59, effectiveness of expression; items selected from earlier forms of *Cooperative English Test: Lower and Higher Levels*), (6 pages); 2 editions of battery manual: hand scoring ('63, 11 pages), machine scoring ('63, 13 pages); supplementary data ('63, 6 pages) for the battery; battery profile ('63, 2 pages); no data on reliability of part 1; separate answer sheets or cards must be used; $1.25 per 25 tests; $1 per set of 50 hand scoring answer sheets and hand scoring manual; 20¢ per hand scoring stencil; 20¢ per 15 battery profiles; 50¢ per 25 IBM answer cards (machine scoring through the Department of Educational Research only); 10¢ per machine scoring manual; 50¢ per specimen set; $2.75 per battery specimen set;

postage extra; 30(40–45) minutes per part; Department of Educational Research, Ontario College of Education, University of Toronto; distributed by Guidance Centre (machine scoring manual and answer cards must be purchased from the Department of Educational Research). *

REFERENCES

1. D'OYLEY, VINCENT R. *Technical Manual for the Canadian Tests: Statistical Data on the Carnegie Study Tests of Academic Aptitude and Achievement in Grades 8, 9, and 10 in Ontario Schools and Grades 7 and 8 in Toronto Schools.* Carnegie Study of Identification and Utilization of Talent in High School and College, Bulletin No. 4. Toronto, Canada: Department of Educational Research, Ontario College of Education, University of Toronto, 1964. Pp. viii, 50. *

2. D'OYLEY, VINCENT R. *Testing: The First Two Years of the Carnegie Study 1959 to 1961: Analysis of Scores by Course, Sex, and Size of Municipality.* Carnegie Study of Identification and Utilization of Talent in High School and College, Bulletin No. 6. Toronto, Canada: Department of Educational Research, Ontario College of Education, University of Toronto, 1964. Pp. ix, 53. *

J. DOUGLAS AYERS, *Associate Professor of Educational Psychology, University of Alberta, Edmonton, Alberta, Canada.*

The *Canadian English Achievement Test* is one of several tests "developed for use in the Carnegie Study of Identification and Utilization of Talent in High School and College, a longitudinal study of approximately 90,000 Grade 9 students enrolled in Ontario schools in September, 1959." The test has three subtests: Reading Comprehension, Mechanics of Expression, and Effectiveness of Expression.

The directions for administration have certain flaws, one of which is crucial. Both the directions for administration and the test booklets for Reading Comprehension and Effectiveness of Expression fail to inform the students whether they should "guess" or not. This is a very serious oversight as testwiseness and willingness to guess are affected by previous experience with both standardized and teacher made tests. Consequently variation in testing conditions is introduced by lack of standard directions on guessing and the effect on the reported norms is unknown. Certainly, the individual teacher can make no interpretation about the relative standing of the students in her class. The directions for Mechanics of Expression, on the other hand, caution against wild guessing. Then in scoring for grade 9 the wrongs are subtracted from the rights whether there are two or three alternatives, but there is no correction for guessing for grade 8. There is also a minor flaw. The manual states that the Mechanics of Expression subtest "is considered as having two parts for Grade 8." Some teachers, therefore, may allow 30 minutes for each part. Such confusion could be avoided

easily by saying that the test has two subscores within one time limit.

Reading Comprehension is undoubtedly the poorest of the subtests. It involves only three aspects of comprehension (main idea, suitable title, and simple deduction) and does not involve such important aspects as inference, implication, purpose of passage, and relevant versus irrelevant detail. The 10 short simple paragraphs are all of approximately the same length. Such selections do not allow for development of ideas within a passage and for selecting and synthesizing several ideas to obtain the main idea. In fact, the main idea in short paragraphs becomes the topic sentence. In several instances the conclusion is not from the paragraph as a whole but from an isolated statement within it. Flexibility of approach is limited because the passages are nearly all description and precluded because the questions for each paragraph are posed in identical form.

The punctuation section of Mechanics of Expression has a uniform three-alternative format which prevents the use of some seductive misleads, for example, a comma in item 14. Item 13 has no correct answer due either to a misprint or lack of item analysis. The capitalization section has 35 questions in 98 words, and 75 per cent of the text is geographical. Five of the capitals occur at the beginning of sentences. In each of the items in the grammatical usage section the testee has only to choose from two options. This type of item has almost disappeared from modern tests as it should.

While the individual items in Effectiveness of Expression were borrowed from earlier editions of the *Cooperative English Test,* the format, time limit, and proportion of items of various types has been changed. In addition, the directions for Sections D, E, and F have been made unnecessarily complicated and repetitive and the items space consuming.

The norms for grade 9 are based on virtually all students in Ontario in November 1959, but as was pointed out above, the lack of standard directions has an unknown effect on the reported percentile norms. The grade 8 norms are based on a representative sample of approximately 6,500 Ontario students tested in May 1962. On the subtests that can be compared, means for grade 8 are one point higher than for grade 9. The reasons for such a difference are not indicated. In any case, if this test is to be used over several grades it should have progressively higher means over successive grades.

The manual contains no data on item analysis, reliability, or validity, but recently some data have become available on reliability and validity. The split-half reliability of Mechanics of Expression for 200 cases in grade 8 is quoted as .93, and at grade 9 it is .92; for Effectiveness of Expression, the reliabilities are .80 and .86. For Reading Comprehension, K-R reliabilities of .63 and .61 are reported.

It should be noted that the *Canadian English Achievement Test* is not "Canadian" nor has it been standardized on a Canadian population. Also, because of variations in grade structure between provinces, Ontario norms are unlikely to be appropriate outside that province. It would seem that this test was hurriedly thrown together before its original use in 1959 and that it has now been published without any further study or analysis.

BERNARD SPOLSKY, *Assistant Professor of Education, McGill University, Montreal, Quebec, Canada.*

Norms are provided for grades 8 and 9, the former being based on what is called in the manual "a representative sample" of approximately 6,500, the latter on a total population of 85,000. The grade 8 norms for Parts 1 and 3 (the only parts comparable, for there is a different system for marking Part 2 for each grade) are higher than those of grade 9. This may be explained by the different time of year at which the test was administered to each grade, but it does suggest that the norms must be used with very considerable care, and serves to cast doubt on the validity of the test as a whole.

Part 1, Reading Comprehension, presents 10 passages that range in difficulty from a school textbook to J. S. Mill and asks each time for the choice of best title, main idea, and a conclusion. Generally, this is well done, although the rigidity of the structure leads to some questions that are not as good as they might be: some items are ambiguous (in one, for example, the student is expected to conclude that the main idea of a passage mentioning air mileage and air freight has to do with air travel) and some of the selections of titles involve an ability apart from comprehension.

Part 2, Mechanics of Expression, is less sat-

isfactory. In the punctuation section the student is asked to choose which of three possibilities (two alternatives and a "no punctuation") should be placed at a numbered point. Ability to do this is not necessarily the same as ability to punctuate an unpunctuated selection or to use punctuation in one's own writing. One item offers as the correct answer the wrong pair of quotation marks (" instead of " to open a quotation). The section on capitalization follows the same system, except that only two alternatives are used. The remainder of the test is on usage, the student being required to choose which of two forms is "correct" in the sentence given. In grade 9 Mechanics of Expression is treated as one test, with incorrect responses being deducted from the total correct; in grade 8, the test is considered as having two parts, the score being the total correct. No explanation is given for the change in system. As so often seems to happen in an objective test of usage, the items call for standard schoolroom usage, completely ignoring all questions of levels and functional varieties. In other words, while the test may show how much the student has learned about "correct" forms, or, more likely, something about his social and economic background, it will not show whether or not he appreciates what is implied by appropriateness of usage. This is clear from the instruction ("decide which of the two forms given is correct"). The student with understanding of usage is not the one who will say that *it is I* is correct (and one is surprised to find this form called for when *it is me* has been shown to be sanctified not merely by the usage of the majority of educated speakers but also by the historical development of the language) but the one who realises that while *busted* is normal and acceptable in many levels of conversation, *burst* is preferred in formal situations. Its blurred conception of usage will vitiate the test for anyone who is aware of current scholarship and attitudes in this field.

Part 3, Effectiveness of Expression, contains items from earlier forms of the *Cooperative English Test*. It is an interesting attempt to measure objectively a subjective ability. Eleven items involve choosing the best way of expressing an idea, ten are concerned with choice of the best word to complete a sentence, two sections call for the ordering of sentences and paragraph headings, and the last asks that certain pieces of information be classified according to which of several parts of a composition they would fit. Clearly, this section does measure some of the abilities involved in effective expression, but just as clearly it will provide only a very limited picture of the student's ability to write.

Taking all this into consideration, one feels that the test requires considerable revision before it will be ready for more than experimental use.

[254]

*College Entrance Examination Board Advanced Placement Examination: English. High school students desiring credit for college level courses or admission to advanced courses; 1954–63; replaces the separate tests in literature and English composition which were formerly part of the program; for more complete information, see 761; 180(200) minutes; program administered for the College Entrance Examination Board by Educational Testing Service. *

For a review by Robert C. Pooley of an earlier form of the English composition test, see 5:205; for a review by John S. Diekhoff of an earlier form of the literature test, see 5:211.

[255]

*Cooperative English Test: Usage, Spelling, and Vocabulary. Grades 7–16; 1932–51; 4 scores: usage, spelling, vocabulary, total; IBM; Forms OM ('38, 14 pages), PM ('39, 15 pages); manual ('51, 4 pages); norms booklet ['38, 8 pages]; separate answer sheets must be used; $4 per 25 tests; $1 per 25 IBM answer sheets; 50¢ per set of scoring stencils; postage extra; $1 per specimen set of this test and three other English tests, cash orders postpaid; 70(80) minutes; M. F. Carpenter, E. F. Lindquist, W. W. Cook, D. G. Paterson, F. S. Beers, and Geraldine Spaulding; Cooperative Test Division. *

REFERENCES

1–11. See 40:1271.
12. STUCKY, MILO O., AND ANDERSON, KENNETH E. *A Study of Persistence in College Attendance in Relation to Placement-Test Scores and Grade-Point Averages.* University of Kansas, School of Education, Kansas Studies in Education, Vol. 9, No. 2. Lawrence, Kan.: the School, April 1959. Pp. 58. *
13. STUCKY, MILO O., AND ANDERSON, KENNETH E. "A Study of the Relationship Between Entrance-Test Scores and Grade-Point Averages and Length of Stay in College." *Yearb Nat Council Meas Used Ed* 16:164–70 '59. *
14. McKEY, ELEANOR F. "The Standardized Test—Are Improvements Needed?" *Engl J* 49:35–7 Ja '60. *
15. BARNHART, E. L., AND ANDERSON, KENNETH E. *A Study of the Relationships Between Grade-Point Averages, Placement-Test Scores, Semester Hours Earned, and Area of Major Interest for the Group Who Entered the University of Kansas in the Fall of 1954.* University of Kansas, School of Education, Kansas Studies in Education, Vol. 11, No. 1. Lawrence, Kan.: the School, January 1961. Pp. 36. *
16. TAULBEE, GEORGE C., SR. *Construction and Validation of a Scale for Predicting Graduation From a College of Optometry.* Doctor's thesis, University of Houston (Houston, Tex.), 1963. (DA 24:387)

MARGARET F. LORIMER, *Associate Professor, Office of Institutional Research, Michigan State University, East Lansing, Michigan.*

The *Cooperative English Test,* widely used for many years in high schools and colleges, is designed to measure achievement in three areas: usage, spelling, and vocabulary. Scores for each of the three areas and the total score have been translated into percentile ranks for secondary students in public schools in the South, in public schools in the East, West, and North, and in private schools, and for entering freshmen in preprofessional colleges, in liberal arts colleges, and in junior colleges and teachers colleges. Since the norms were established many years ago (1938), they are possibly outdated by now.

The usage test is divided into four parts, each separately timed: a 75-item (60 items in Form PM) grammar and diction test, a 60-item punctuation test, a 30-item capitalization test, and a 15-item sentence structure test. The first three of these ask the student to choose the best from two to five choices for insertion at a given point. The fourth part offers four versions of the same sentence and asks the student to choose the best of the four.

The spelling test of 45 items lists five words for each item, any or none of which may be wrong. The most seasoned writer and reader soon finds any confidence in his spelling ability shaken as he works through the lists of words, many of which are taken from collections of words most often misspelled.

The vocabulary test of 100 items offers five synonyms for each word. Many of the words might be expected to be in the reading vocabularies of advanced high school and college students, but few of them would be in their speaking vocabularies.

The division of the battery into six distinct tests helps the teacher in diagnosing the student's errors, but it removes from the student the responsibility of spotting errors and leaves him only the responsibility of choosing the best of several alternatives.

The test may be useful in measuring the degree to which a student has mastered the basic rules of grammar and punctuation, and to some extent useful in measuring the extent of his reading vocabulary and his ability to proofread for spelling errors. It does not test ability to write or to speak effectively. It resembles tests which might be found at the end of a workbook of English exercises.

John M. Stalnaker, *President, National Merit Scholarship Corporation, Evanston, Illinois.*

That this test enjoys enough annual usage to justify the publisher's continuing to reprint it suggests that some users find it of value in comparison with the newer tests now available in this area. The test covers usage, spelling, and vocabulary. The usage section is divided into four parts: grammar and diction, punctuation, capitalization, and sentence structure, each separately timed for a total of 40 minutes. Spelling is allowed 10 minutes, and vocabulary 20 minutes.

In the usage test, one of two or more alternate words or phrases is to be checked as the most appropriate for the sentence. In the punctuation section, some 60 places are numbered in an essay and the student is asked to choose for each the appropriate punctuation mark from several given on an answer sheet. In the capitalization exercise, the student indicates whether or not each of 30 marked words should start with a capital letter. Not all errors, however, are marked. Thus, even the corrected sentence may be a poor one containing errors. In the sentence structure section, a sentence is presented in four ways; in each group the sentence which is better than any of the others is to be checked.

In the spelling test, groups of four different words are presented, with the student marking which, if any, is incorrectly spelled. Finally, the vocabulary test asks for the selection of one of five words which most nearly corresponds in meaning to a stimulus word.

The answer sheet gives a table for changing raw scores into scale scores. The norm booklet, undated, gives percentile ranks for several groups and grades within groups, e.g., end of tenth grade, public secondary schools of the South. A manual of directions describes the administrative regulations and the scoring, which is based on corrections for guessing. The booklet "Introduction to the Norms," dated 1938 and referred to in the norms booklet, is out of print.

The chief limitation of this test is the one common to all objective tests in English. It does not measure directly what the teacher means by the ability to write clearly and accurately. However, the scores relate to writing ability measured in other ways, although no evidence of this type is presented.

As long as there is a demand, one might wish that such tests and norms were revised periodically, and a discussion of the validity and significance of the test given. However, the limited number of users, one assumes, have developed their own norms. The publisher has covered the same major content in the 1960 revision of the *Cooperative English Tests* (see 256), for which 1960 norms are given. For most users, the 1960 revision will be preferable to this test.

For reviews by Carleton C. Jones, Jeanette McPherrin, Louis C. Zahner, Henry D. Rinsland, and L. K. Shumaker of Form PM and earlier forms, see 40:1271; for reviews by John M. Stalnaker, Charles S. Thomas, and John H. Thompson, see 38:961.

[256]
Cooperative English Tests, [1960 Revision]. Grades 9-12, 13-14; 1940-60; revision of *Cooperative English Test: Lower and Higher Levels;* 6 scores: vocabulary, reading comprehension (level, speed, total), English expression, total; IBM; Forms A, B, C, ('60); 2 levels (tests labeled, say, for grades 13-14, Form 1A; for grades 9-12, Form 2A); 2 tests (reading comprehension, English expression) available in separate booklets (7-11 pages) or a single booklet (16-18 pages); directions for administering ('60, 16 pages); manual for interpreting ('60, 42 pages); technical report ('60, 35 pages); distribution of Form 1C restricted to colleges; separate answer sheets must be used; $4 per 20 copies of either test; $6 per 20 tests (single booklet); $1 per 20 IBM scorable answer sheets for both tests; 25¢ per scoring stencil for either test; $1 per 20 Scribe answer sheets for both tests (scored by the publisher only); $1 per manual for interpreting; $1 per technical report; postage extra; $2 per specimen set, cash orders postpaid; 40(45) minutes per test; revision by Clarence Derrick, David P. Harris, and Biron Walker; Cooperative Test Division. *

REFERENCES
1-2. See 40:1276.
3-31. See 3:120.
32-84. See 4:155.
85-142. See 5:179.
143. MOFFETT, CHARLES R. *Operational Characteristics of Beginning Master's Students in Educational Administration and Supervision.* Doctor's thesis, University of Tennessee (Knoxville, Tenn.), 1954.
144. JONES, WILLIAM ALTEN. *The Adequacy of Certain Measures Used in the Selection of Freshman State and Merit Scholarship Recipients at Indiana University.* Doctor's thesis, Indiana University (Bloomington, Ind.), 1955. (DA 15:1553)
145. LUTON, JAMES N. *A Study of the Use of Standardized Tests in the Selection of Potential Educational Administrators.* Doctor's thesis, University of Tennessee (Knoxville, Tenn.), 1955.
146. JEX, FRANK B. *University of Utah Studies in the Prediction of Academic Success.* University of Utah Research Monographs in Education, Vol. 1, No. 1. Salt Lake City, Utah: the University, July 1957. Pp. ix, 51. *
147. PETRO, PETER K. *Student Aptitudes and Abilities Correlated With Achievement in First Semester High School Bookkeeping.* Master's thesis, Iowa State Teachers College (Cedar Falls, Iowa), 1957.
148. BELAI, LOUISA. "A Comparative Study of the Results of Standardized Tests and Achievement at a Liberal Arts College for Women." *J Ed Res* 52:94-100 N '58. * (PA 33:11014)
149. METZGER, STANLEY MILES. *A Study of Selected Characteristics of the Male Graduates and Scholastic Drop-Outs of*

the *1951 Freshman Class Entering State University of New York Teachers College at Cortland.* Doctor's thesis, Syracuse University (Syracuse, N.Y.), 1958. (*DA* 19:2020)

150. NUNNERY, MICHAEL Y. *A Study in the Use of Psychological Tests in Determining Effectiveness and Ineffectiveness Among Practicing School Administrators.* Doctor's thesis, University of Tennessee (Knoxville, Tenn.), 1958. (*DA* 19:1276)

151. SAVAGE, H. W. *An Evaluation of the Cooperative English Test of Effectiveness of Expression for Use in Ontario.* Atkinson Study of Utilization of Student Resources, Supplementary Report No. 1. Toronto, Canada: Department of Educational Research, Ontario College of Education, University of Toronto, 1958. Pp. vi, 39. *

152. WEBB, SAM C., AND GOODLING, RICHARD A. "Test Validity in a Methodist Theology School." *Ed & Psychol Meas* 18:859–66 w '58. * (*PA* 34:2123)

153. WIGGINS, NEWTON W. *The Predictive Ability of the Total and Partial Raw Scores of the A.C.E. Psychological Examination, the Cooperative English Tests, and High School Marks in Determining the Scholastic Success of Prospective Freshmen at Western Illinois University.* Master's thesis, Western Illinois University (Macomb, Ill.), 1958.

154. AKAMINE, TOSHIO. *A Study of High School Students' Records and Certain Test Scores as Predictors of Academic Achievement at the State College of Washington.* Doctor's thesis, State College of Washington (Pullman, Wash.), 1959. (*DA* 20:955)

155. BLACK, D. B. "A Comparison of the Performance on Selected Standardized Tests to That on the Alberta Grade XII Departmental Examination of a Select Group of University of Alberta Freshmen." *Alberta J Ed Res* 5:180–90 S '59. * (*PA* 34:6559)

156. EINSPAHR, MARTIN HARLEY. *The Construction and Validation of Scales for Predicting Academic Success in College.* Doctor's thesis, University of Houston (Houston, Tex.), 1959. (*DA* 20:3366)

157. GUTEKUNST, JOSEF GRANT. *The Prediction of Art Achievement of Art Education Students by Means of Standardized Tests.* Doctor's thesis, Temple University (Philadelphia, Pa.), 1959. (*DA* 20:3202)

158. HENDERSON, HAROLD L., AND MASTEN, SHERMAN H. "Six Predictors of College Achievement." *J Genetic Psychol* 94:143–6 Mr '59. * (*PA* 36:4KL43H)

159. LEAHY, DOROTHY M. "Reading Ability of College Home Economics Students." *Calif J Ed Res* 10:42–8 Ja '59. * (*PA* 34:2106)

160. NUNNERY, MICHAEL Y. "How Useful Are Standardized Psychological Tests in the Selection of School Administrators." *Ed Adm & Sup* 45:349–56 N '59. * (*PA* 35:7092)

161. STACK, SHIRLEY ELLEN. *A Study of the Relationships Between Prospective Teachers' Scores on the Chicago Certification Examination and on Standardized Ability and Achievement Tests.* Doctor's thesis, Northwestern University (Evanston, Ill.), 1959. (*DA* 20:2160)

162. STINSON, PAIRLEE J., AND MORRISON, MILDRED M. "Sex Differences Among High School Seniors." *J Ed Res* 53:103–8 N '59. *

163. ALOIA, ALEX D., AND SALINDA, JUAN F. "A Correlation Study Between Grades in English and Cooperative English Test Scores of College Freshmen." *Calif J Ed Res* 11:7–13 Ja '60. * (*PA* 34:8393)

164. BLACK, DONALD B. "The Prediction of Freshman Success in the University of Alberta From Grade XII Departmental Results." *Alberta J Ed Res* 6:38–53 Mr '60. *

165. KIMBELL, FONTELLA THOMPSON. *The Use of Selected Standardized Tests as Predictors of Academic Success at Oklahoma College for Women.* Doctor's thesis, University of Oklahoma (Norman, Okla.), 1960. (*DA* 20:4335)

166. VINEYARD, EDWIN E., AND BAILEY, ROBERT B. "Interrelationships of Reading Ability, Listening Skill, Intelligence, and Scholastic Achievement." *J Develop Read* 3:174–8 sp '60. * (*PA* 35:1274)

167. ZABEL, RONALD L. *The Determination of the Ability of the Total Score of the Cooperative School and College Ability Test, the Total Reading Comprehension Score of the Cooperative English Test, and High School Rank to Predict Scholastic Success of Freshmen at Western Illinois University.* Master's thesis, Western Illinois University (Macomb, Ill.), 1960.

168. BESSENT, EDGAR WAILAND. *The Predictability of Selected Elementary School Principals' Administrative Behavior.* Doctor's thesis, University of Texas (Austin, Tex.), 1961. (*DA* 22:3479)

169. CENTI, PAUL. "Intellective and Language Factors Related to College Success." *Cath Ed R* 59:319–22 My '61. *

170. COPEMAN, JAMES; PASCOE, ROBERT; AND WARD, GEORGE, II. "The Edwards Personal Preference Schedule and Revised Cooperative English Test as Predictors of Academic Achievement." *Proc W Va Acad Sci* 33:124–6 '61. * (*PA* 36:5KL24C)

171. EELLS, KENNETH. "How Effective Is Differential Prediction in Three Types of College Curricula?" *Ed & Psychol Meas* 21:459–71 su '61. * (*PA* 36:2KJ59E)

172. GREENBERG, BRADLEY S. "Predicting Journalism Student Ability." *Journalism Ed* 16:60–5 su '61. *

173. GROFF, PATRICK J. "Parts of Speech in Standardized English Tests." *Sch R* 69:457–60 w '61. *

174. SWANSON, EDWARD O., AND BERDIE, RALPH F. "Pre-

dictive Validities in an Institute of Technology." *Ed & Psychol Meas* 21:1001–8 w '61. Errata: 22:258 su '62. *

175. SWEENEY, MARY ROSE. *A Study of the Relationship of the Quantity of High School English to College Performance in English.* Doctor's thesis, University of Kansas (Lawrence, Kan.), 1961. (*DA* 22:2640)

176. WOLINS, LEROY; MACKINNEY, A. C.; AND STEPHANS, PAUL. "Factor Analyses of High School Science Achievement Measures." *J Ed Res* 54:173–7 Ja '61. * (*PA* 35:7129)

177. BERDIE, RALPH F.; LAYTON, WILBUR L.; HAGENAH, THEDA; AND SWANSON, EDWARD O. *Who Goes to College? Comparison of Minnesota College Freshman, 1930–1960.* Minneapolis, Minn.: University of Minnesota Press, 1962. Pp. vii, 56. *

178. CASH, W. L., JR. "Predictive Efficiency of Freshman Entrance Tests." *J Psychol Studies* 13:111–6 Je '62 [issued F '64]. *

179. GILLESPIE, HORACE FORD. *The Construction and Validation of Scales for Predicting Academic Success in College in Specified Subject Matter Areas.* Doctor's thesis, University of Houston (Houston, Tex.), 1962. (*DA* 23:1576)

180. JONES, REGINALD L., AND SIEGEL, LAURENCE. "The Individual High School as a Predictor of College Academic Performance." *Ed & Psychol Meas* 22:785–9 w '62. * (*PA* 37:7189)

181. JUNGEBLUT, ANN. "Some Results of the 1960 Revision of the Cooperative English Tests in a Small Group of Independent Schools." *Ed Rec B* 80:49–55 F '62. *

182. LEWIS, JOHN W. "Utilizing the Stepwise Multiple Regression Procedure in Selecting Predictor Variables by Sex Group." *Ed & Psychol Meas* 22:401–4 su '62. * (*PA* 37:3871)

183. REID, JOHN W.; JOHNSON, A. PEMBERTON; ENTWISLE, FRANK N.; AND ANGERS, WILLIAM P. "A Four-Year Study of the Characteristics of Engineering Students." *Personnel & Guid J* 41:38–43 S '62. * (*PA* 37:5655)

184. RUDD, JOHN PAUL. *A Study of the Validity of Selected Predictors for Placement in Three-Rail Curricula.* Doctor's research study No. 1, Colorado State College (Greeley, Colo.), 1962. (*DA* 24:184)

185. VICK, MARY CATHARINE, AND HORNADAY, JOHN A. "Predicting Grade Point Average at a Small Southern College." *Ed & Psychol Meas* 22:795–9 w '62. * (*PA* 37:7205)

186. BOWMAN, ALDEN E.; COBERLY, R. L.; LUCAS, DONALD; AND WHALEY, EARL R. "Selection and Performance of Scholarship Hall Award Winners." *J Col Student Personnel* 4:220–6+ Je '63. *

187. HUGHES, BILLIE EDWARD. *Predicting Achievement in a Graduate School of Education.* Doctor's thesis, North Texas State University (Denton, Tex.), 1963. (*DA* 24:1448)

188. KING, DONALD THOMAS. *A Comparison of a College Generation of Rural and Nonrural Students in Selected Colleges of Arkansas With Respect to Academic Success and Number of Semesters of Undergraduate Study Completed.* Doctor's thesis, University of Arkansas (Fayetteville, Ark.), 1963. (*DA* 24:626)

189. MACK, LAURENCE L. "Examining the Efficiency of Predictors Presently Being Used at the University of Alberta." *Alberta J Ed Res* 9:100–10 Je '63. *

190. MORICE, HERBERT OSCAR. *The Predictive Value of the High School Grade Point Average and a Select Group of Standardized Tests for Junior College Achievement.* Doctor's thesis, University of Houston (Houston, Tex.), 1963. (*DA* 24:1482)

191. NORTH, ROBERT D. "Results of the ERB Public School Norms Project, 1962–63." *Ed Rec B* 84:72–4 Jl '63. *

192. SASSENRATH, JULIUS M., AND FATTU, NICHOLAS A. *Relationships Among Factors Obtained for Elementary and Secondary Student Teachers.* Bulletin of the School of Education, Indiana University, Vol. 39, No. 5. Bloomington, Ind.: Bureau of Educational Studies and Testing, the School, September 1963. Pp. vii, 34. * (*PA* 38:6666)

193. WILLIAMS, JOHN E., AND JOHNSTON, ROBERT A. "The Area Tests of the Graduate Record Examination as a Partial Criterion of Academic Success." *J Exp Ed* 32:95–100 f '63. *

194. ZIMMERER, ANN MORGAN. *A Study of Selected Variables for Predicting Success in a College of Engineering.* Doctor's thesis, University of Houston (Houston, Tex.), 1963. (*DA* 24:842)

LEONARD S. FELDT, *Professor of Education, State University of Iowa, Iowa City, Iowa.*

The *Cooperative English Tests* measure achievement in two general areas: written expression and reading. It seems appropriate to consider each area separately and then to return to issues relevant to the entire battery.

ENGLISH EXPRESSION TEST. The validity of multiple choice English tests as a substitute for more tedious evaluation procedures based on student themes has long been challenged by teachers of composition. In the test manual the authors seek to reassure the user on this point, claiming that "evidence suggests that ability to do well on this kind of test is related to ability to write well in an 'essay' situation." Those who can accept this proposition will find many virtues in the English effectiveness portion of this test. The content is based on at least one authoritative study of student errors and was checked by a competent panel of composition teachers. The specific error situations covered by the exercises are itemized in detail, permitting the potential user to make an informed judgment concerning the adequacy of test coverage. Counterbalancing this generally favorable impression of content validity is the absence of items bearing on the broader aspects of writing quality. The test does not assess the student's ability to select a phraseology more appropriate to one kind of writing than another, to organize ideas effectively, or to break a composition into meaningful paragraphs. None of the items force the student to consider appropriateness of content, the logical ordering of ideas, or the adequacy of an introduction or conclusion. Teachers who are primarily concerned with measuring these abilities might well follow the publisher's advice and consider the use of the STEP essay and writing tests.

READING COMPREHENSION TEST. The reading subtest is less likely to evoke the misgivings which many teachers harbor about multiple choice tests of writing ability. The selections are varied in content and in length, and pose a variety of comprehension problems. Some of the reading material is humorously anecdotal, some is predominantly factual, and some emphasizes subtleties of mood or feeling. The questions based on literary excerpts frequently call for judgment of those elements which contribute to the effectiveness of the selection. The questions over natural science or social studies materials, on the other hand, often tend to dwell on factual details. There are no questions, for example, that call for the recognition of implicit assumptions by the writer, the deduction of conclusions or generalizations from presented data, or the differentiation of fact from opinion. Thus the skills emphasized in the test are probably more representative of the reading skills of concern to teachers of English than to teachers of the sciences or social studies.

The test yields one comprehension score which is largely unaffected by rate and a second comprehension score that is very much affected by rate. No pure rate measure, in terms of words per minute, is obtained. At the high school and college levels remedial reading efforts are largely concerned with the improvement of rate. If this test were to be used to identify potential candidates for a rate improvement class, selection would have to be made by comparing the power score with the score which reflects both power and speed. One might wonder whether a scoring scheme which yields operationally independent measures of these two aspects of reading might not be more useful, diagnostically, in this classification problem.

TECHNICAL DATA. The two manuals which accompany these tests provide a wealth of technical data on validity, reliability, scaling, and norming. In addition to information bearing on content validity, the manual includes a summary of the results of about twenty predictive validity studies primarily against grade criteria. All but one of these involve earlier forms of the reading comprehension test. The median coefficient is in the .40–.45 range, a value quite consistent with other research in this field. Reliability data are reported for grades 10 and 12 only, a deficiency to be lamented. Since the standard error of measurement plays an important role in the interpretive techniques suggested by the publisher, one might wonder how the standard error values were arrived at for grades 9, 11, and 13.

The national norming studies for this edition were carefully planned and executed, though that ever-present difficulty—the non-cooperating school—was encountered to a significant degree. The publisher provides spring percentile rank norms for grades 9–12 and college sophomores, fall norms for college freshmen. For groups tested at other times of the year, the publisher recommends the most nearly appropriate norms table and warns that standings will be slightly under or overestimated. Since this warning appears to constitute an invitation to the user to adjust or interpolate within the tabled ranks, it probably would have been wiser for the publication agency itself to have provided a more complete set of norms, even if these could be derived only by interpolation.

INTERPRETIVE TECHNIQUES. In this test, as in other recent CTD publications, a strong emphasis is placed on percentile rank bands, rather than on single-valued estimates of a student's rank. While cautious interpretation of test results is certainly desirable, this reviewer feels that the mandatory use of a confidence interval is not the best means to insure caution. In practice, the use of an interval appears to lead to the same types of "inappropriate" statements about a student's performance that were formerly made from a single-valued estimate of his rank. For example, one manual example involves a boy whose percentile rank band extends from 75 to 90. The user is told that this means "about 10% of freshmen in the norms group score higher and about 75% score lower." This is a regrettable corruption of the notion of a 68 per cent confidence interval.

On a quite different point, the publishers surely deserve criticism. In the interpretation of class performance, they suggest that teachers conduct an informal item analysis via a show of hands to determine per cent of error for each item. These data are then to be referred to the classifications of item content to determine where additional teaching emphasis should be laid. Such interpretations, based as they are on clusters of two or three items, are extremely untrustworthy, and measurement authorities have consistently warned against this practice. It seems incongruous that the publisher be so concerned about unreliability of the total scores of individual students and so unconcerned about the unreliability of class performance on individual items. Does a high percentage of error on *one* specific exercise necessarily suggest a class weakness on *all* such situations?

SUMMARY. Despite the reservations noted above, this reviewer has no hesitancy in strongly recommending these tests. They are well constructed, efficient instruments and should prove extremely useful to every teacher who recognizes and accepts their basic limitations.

MARGARET F. LORIMER, *Associate Professor, Office of Institutional Research, Michigan State University, East Lansing, Michigan.*

The *Cooperative English Tests* are intended to measure the achievement of high school and college students in two areas: reading and written expression. The two tests are available in separate booklets or in a single booklet and can be administered separately if desired. Since the general directions and time limits are the same for both tests and for all forms at each level, more than one test or more than one form can be administered simultaneously.

Scores may be used for academic advisement, placement, and evaluation. Adequate directions for their use and a helpful student profile are provided.

College norms seem to be based on a very limited sample of students; high school norms, though based on greater numbers of students, are hardly representative of the various regions or of the general population. High schools in the sample are located for the most part in small towns in rural areas. Interpretation of scores on the basis of these norms should take these facts into consideration.

The 1960 edition incorporates a number of revisions, all apparently based on sound reasons: choices for each item have been reduced to four; the number of reading items has been reduced from 90 to 60; the mechanics and effectiveness items have been combined into one test; and a new type of mechanics item has been introduced which places on the student responsibility not only of correcting the error but of finding it.

The reading comprehension test has two parts: a vocabulary test and a reading test of 60 items each. Each vocabulary item consists of a word out of context and four choices of synonym. Most words included are in fairly common use. For the student who is at all familiar with the word, the choice is simple. One wonders, however, whether such words as "divagation," "concatenation," and "encomium" are valid choices for any vocabulary test.

The reading test consists of passages varying from 60 to 300 words and covering a wide range of subjects and types of materials. Most are sufficiently relevant and interesting to engage students of the age for which the test is intended. Most are appropriate; those which fall short are those which demand some specific previous knowledge or experience, as for example knowledge of the meaning of "aperture" in the selection and use of a camera or of "quadrant" in the passage dealing with the area around the South Pole. Also of questionable appropriateness are those fragments the meaning of which depends heavily on what has come before. Some, as in Form 2C, 55–57 and Form 1B, 39–42, leave the reader without sufficient orientation; others, as in Form 1B, 21–25, could easily have been clarified if the editors had inserted a few words. It is doubtful if the skill of figuring out what went before, who is who, or who is on whose side is a reading skill or even worth one's time.

The items imply that "reading" encompasses many skills ranging from those which demand no more than spotting information without regard for its importance, to those which demand considerable depth of understanding. How much validity one is willing to concede to the test depends on his acceptance of the range of the skills included. To the teacher who holds high the value of getting students to read for main ideas, to think critically about the ideas involved, and to draw inferences, it is irksome for a test to require and therefore place value on the ability to go back and count the number of kinds of thrushes mentioned in a long passage about thrushes found in the United States. On the other hand it is gratifying to see the many passages which do ask the student to interpret and make judgments.

The way any set of test items is keyed is sure to raise some controversy. Most indefensible to students (and the manual suggests that the tests be followed up by class review of the test) are the keys to the items which ask what a good title for the selection would be. The "correct" answer is often puzzling, and it is doubtful if these items add much to the test since a really valid judgment must rest on much more of a passage than the fragment presented. Also indefensible are the keys to items involving a judgment based on one's point of view or attitude. One's understanding or interpretation of what he reads is necessarily filtered through his values; hence the passage about the student who believed it important to "work for his college" by playing football is comprehended differently by the one who shares the student's view and the one who shares the views of the English teacher who keyed the item. In such a case the "good" reader is one who is perceptive enough to anticipate the view of English teachers who make and key such items.

Students also point out—with justification—that the keys do not take into consideration that people differ in what they find amusing.

When a man is so unimaginative as to be amusing, it is hardly fair to ask the student to choose between "amusing" and "unimaginative" to describe the man.

The expression test is divided into two parts: an effectiveness test of 30 items which supplies four words or phrases to be inserted into or used to complete a sentence, and a mechanics test of 60 items, each a sentence printed on three lines, one of which or none of which may contain an error.

The effectiveness items appear to be an improvement over the jumbled sentences used in the earlier edition. They probably come as close as possible to measuring the precision with which a student chooses his words; however the ability to choose the best word from a list of four is a different task indeed from thinking of the right word or recognizing the word one chooses as a solecism as one composes a theme. The test undoubtedly serves some use in measuring a student's ability to criticize writing, but the only adequate test of effectiveness is to give the student a subject, a blank sheet of paper, and a pen, and ask him to write.

The mechanics test is basically an exercise in proofreading. Controversial usage and rules for punctuation have for the most part been avoided. It is unfortunate that errors in spelling are included with those in usage and punctuation. Such a combination lessens the diagnostic value of the test and consumes time which might better be devoted to other tasks. In essence, the test asks the student to check the spelling of hundreds of words. Some of the usage errors seem far too obvious, especially on the college forms. To be sure, "he don't," "you was," and "his mother learned him" are errors found in the speech patterns of students, and on that basis can be justifiably included; but one wonders just what such items measure—perhaps nothing more than a student's ability to recognize those expressions which displease English teachers. Again the real test of a student's mechanics is his speech and writing, his creative faculty, not his critical faculty.

One final criticism stems from the experience of the writer in administering this battery to hundreds of students in successive sessions. When the single booklet was used, but only the reading test administered, we could never be sure that the students previously using the books had closed them with the reading test on top since both covers are the same color and have the same general appearance. It would be an invaluable aid if the cover of the expression test could be a different color from that of the reading test.

This battery of tests has undoubted merit and is probably among the best on the market. It is not without its shortcomings which have been pointed out here chiefly to emphasize what all of us know but wish we did not have to admit—that the measurement, if not the formal teaching, of language skills is so complex and so evasive as to be almost impossible.

J Counsel Psychol 7:225–6 f '60. *Laurence Siegel.* Every once in a while a reviewer is privileged to consider a test that is truly outstanding. The new battery of *Cooperative English Tests* afforded such an opportunity. The techniques utilized for test development and standardization set a high standard for test constructors; the Technical Report is written with unusual care and lucidity; the testing materials themselves are highly attractive; and the ancillary materials provided for teachers, counselor and pupils are well designed. * It is impossible, in a review of this type, to do justice to the ingenious sampling procedures employed for various aspects of the standardization process. * The student of test construction procedures will find that a careful reading of the Technical Report proves to be enlightening and, at times, almost inspiring. The presentation made in the Report is so carefully done that this reviewer found that it anticipated every one of his procedural objections or questions. * The only weakness evident in the manual is in the reported predictive validity. Although a sizable number of prediction studies with earlier forms of the Reading Comprehension subtest are summarized in tabular form, no such studies are reported for the 1960 revision. * There is little doubt that the revision of the battery will prove to have reasonably high predictive validity against the usual criteria of scholastic success. *

For reviews by John C. Sherwood and John M. Stalnaker of the expression test, see 258; for a review by Chester W. Harris of the mechanics and expression tests of the earlier edition, see 4:155; for reviews by J. Paul Leonard, Edward S. Noyes, and Robert C. Pooley, see 3:120. For reviews by W. V.

Clemans and W. G. Fleming of the reading test, see 806; for reviews by Robert Murray Bear and J. B. Stroud of the earlier edition, see 3:497.

[257]

*English: Every Pupil Scholarship Test. Grades 2–4, 5–6, 7–8, 9–12; 1926–64; new form (4 pages) usually issued each January and April; forms from previous testing programs also available; 4 levels; general directions sheet ['63, 2 pages]; no data on reliability; norms for new forms available following testing program; 4¢ per test; 4¢ per key; postage extra; 40(45) minutes for grades 2–8, 50(55) minutes for grades 9–12; Bureau of Educational Measurements. *

REFERENCES
1. GROFF, PATRICK J. "Parts of Speech in Standardized English Tests." *Sch R* 69:457–60 w '61. *

[258]

*English Expression: Cooperative English Tests [1960 Revision]. Grades 9–12, 13–14; 1940–60; separate booklet edition of expression subtest of *Cooperative English Tests [1960 Revision]*; revision of *Mechanics of Expression: Cooperative English Test: Lower and Higher Levels, Test A* and *Effectiveness of Expression: Cooperative English Test: Lower and Higher Levels, Tests B1 and B2;* IBM; Forms A, B, C, ('60, 7 pages); 2 levels (tests labeled, say, for grades 13–14, Form 1A; for grades 9–12, Form 2A); battery directions for administering ('60, 16 pages); battery manual for interpreting ('60, 42 pages); battery technical report ('60, 35 pages); distribution of Form 1C restricted to colleges; separate answer sheets must be used; $4 per 20 tests; $1 per 20 IBM scorable answer sheets for the battery; 25¢ per scoring stencil; $1 per 20 Scribe answer sheets for the battery (scored by the publisher only); $1 per manual for interpreting; $1 per technical report; postage extra; $2 per specimen set of the battery, cash orders postpaid; 40(45) minutes; revision by Clarence Derrick, David P. Harris, and Biron Walker; Cooperative Test Division. *

JOHN C. SHERWOOD, *Professor of English, University of Oregon, Eugene, Oregon.*

If testmaking in composition had never become "scientific," if statisticians and psychologists had never concerned themselves with the process, a reviewer of the *Cooperative English Tests* would have a comparatively easy task. If he considered merely the tests as they stand, without any reference to the process by which they were prepared or the results which they produce in practice, he could simply enumerate certain seeming advantages and mention a few not very urgent objections. Unhappily, we know that test evaluation is no such simple process. But let us begin with the test.

The most obvious merit of the test is its efficiency—a combination of relative brevity (testing time is 40 minutes) and relatively good coverage of the different aspects of "expression," of the details of composition—sentence

English Expression: Cooperative English Tests

structure, diction, and the like—as distinguished from such broader aspects as unity and organization. (A distinction is made between "mechanics" and "effectiveness" in the arrangement of the test.) One is impressed with the generally high quality of the items. The accusation is sometimes made that the student taking an objective test is compelled not so much to *produce* a correct answer as to try to *guess* what answer will suit the testmaker, and the problem could well be troublesome in the area of style, where personal prejudice and current taste inevitably enter in. But assuming the values generally held by college teachers today, it is usually easy to spot the answer expected by the testers—though one form falls down somewhat in this respect, as will be noted later.

No "objective" test measures the ability to write; it tests certain critical powers which are related to the ability to write. In one way the mechanics section of this test comes nearer to the actual writing of themes than some tests, including its own ancestors. It does simulate one part of the writing process, the period of proofreading and revision. Any teacher of remedial English knows that some students can become quite proficient in spotting errors in workbook exercises, where they know what they are looking for, without being able to detect the same errors in their own themes. The mechanics section differs from a workbook exercise and resembles a set of sentences in a theme at least to the extent that a given item may contain any one of the standard errors or none at all. If the Cooperative test cannot test the actual ability to write, it does at least test the ability to evaluate what has been written.

In this connection we should note that on this test the student is required to do no more than spot errors or choose between more and less effective constructions; some other tests would require him to cite specific rules and know a specific terminology. The approach used by the Cooperative test would seem preferable in an age of competing grammars and terminologies. In most other respects the test is rather conservative. The gerund still takes the possessive, and even the innocently colloquial use of *most* for *almost* could cost the student a point. The liberal grammarian would doubtless find the test usable, but not exactly to his taste.

Against these virtues—assuming that conservatism is a virtue—we may set a few apparent objections. Although the coverage of "expression" is relatively thorough, one form (1A) shows a lack of balance in the "effectiveness" section, where 20 out of 30 items are concerned with exact word choice, leaving only 10 for all other stylistic problems put together. In this same form are several diction items where more than one answer could be considered correct—or to be more exact, in which several of the four choices would yield perfectly plausible English sentences; the sentences would indeed differ slightly in meaning, but there is no clear basis in the context for preferring one to the other. Did "we" (in item 23) eat the food because it was "nutritive" or "palatable" or "refreshing"? It might well have been all three, and our motive for eating it would have depended on the state of our appetites at the time. To make a rational choice between two words the student must have a clear picture of the situation to which the sentence refers; otherwise he might distinguish the words precisely and yet not know which to use.

To stop with a simple examination of the test would be most unjust to both testers and users; we cannot ignore the formidable effort that went into preparing both the test and the technical apparatus that goes with it. One hesitates to cast doubts on a particular item, for instance, when it might very well be that this item has proved in practice to be one which the better students answer in accord with expectation. A test heavily weighted toward diction may be objectionable or it may not; possibly discrimination in this area is symptomatic of general verbal competence, so that such a test might in fact be as sound as one seemingly better balanced. At the same time we must understand what soundness means in this context. It means well-established norms, consistency from form to form and in repeated testings, and other things susceptible of precise statistical measurement. It even means that a careful user of the test will know when *not* to expect absolute precision—he will know that "converted scores" which look significantly different may lose that significance when translated into "percentile bands." What soundness in a test of this kind does not mean, unfortunately, is more than a rough prediction as to how well a student will actually write.

English Expression: Cooperative English Tests

"It is not a direct measure of writing ability, but evidence suggests that ability to do well on this kind of test is related to ability to write well in an 'essay' situation." An experiment at the University of Florida produced a correlation of .54 between one form and essay examinations. Precisely what this means is hard to say, however, since essay grading is itself such a variable and subjective process.

These final doubts apply to objective tests in general, and not merely to the Cooperative; in fact, as already indicated, the Cooperative test more closely approximates the ordinary writing process than some. The test is compact and efficient; it has been carefully done and is provided with all the technical apparatus one could expect. At a time when grammarians are in conflict, it will probably suit all but the very liberal. As long as objective tests remain a necessity in the administration of composition courses, the *Cooperative English Tests* should remain in favor.

JOHN M. STALNAKER, *President, National Merit Scholarship Corporation, Evanston, Illinois.*

A promotional brochure issued by the publisher states: "The 1960 revision of the Cooperative English Tests is a distinctive contribution to the testing world, representing, as it does, a combination of measurement characteristics which have worked in thousands of practical situations over many years and the latest developments in the tests-and-measurements art."

In each of three forms at each level, the first 15 minutes are used for measuring effectiveness, which "refers to the choice of the written expression which precisely conveys the meaning intended." Mechanics (25 minutes) "refers to usage, spelling, punctuation, and capitalization." The student is given a series of three-line sentences, and asked to identify in each sentence the line in which any mechanics error occurs, or to indicate that the sentence contains no such error. The kinds of errors used have been taken from a list of errors compiled from a group of about 20,000 actual themes gathered from various sections of the country.

No grade designations appear on the test booklets, but two levels of the test are available. Form 1 is for college freshmen and sophomores. Form 2 is for students in grades 9–12.

Each level has three forms of the test. Some advanced tenth grade students, for example, could take Form 1A (for college freshmen or sophomores) though most would take Form 2A (for grades 9–12). Scores on Form 1 and Form 2 are said to be "directly comparable," i.e., reported on the same scale. A technical report describes sketchily the development of the test, the converted score scales, the norming, and the standard characteristics, including reliability and a brief consideration of validity. The tests are said to be valid because well-qualified people have constructed them. In one study, the predictive validity of the test was measured by correlating test scores with scores on a composite of all regular English tests given in the first semester; the correlation obtained was .67.

The test appears to have been competently developed, although it would be difficult to justify the claim quoted at the beginning of this review. The manual for interpreting the scores is helpfully arranged. The norms (1960) and the conversion procedures are clearly explained. A classification of the mechanical error items in each form will help the teacher check the coverage. The technical manual adds certain facts for those interested in the techniques which have been followed.

Such a test, obviously, has limited value. As stated in the manual, such tests should "never discourage teachers from setting as many free-writing exercises for their students as possible," and neither should they be taken as measuring all of the necessary skills which are required for effective writing. However, when properly interpreted, these tests have the values described in the manual and can serve the classroom teacher well.

For reviews of the complete battery, see 256; for reviews of the earlier edition of the complete battery, see 4:155 and 3:120.

[259]

*English Language and Literature: National Teacher Examinations.** College seniors and teachers; 1940–62; for more complete information, see 700; 80(90) minutes; Educational Testing Service. *

HOLLAND ROBERTS, *Director, Academic Freedom Committee, P.O. Box 5503, San Francisco, California.* [Review of Form KNT.]

Secondary school supervisors of English, administrators, teacher education institutions, and organizations concerned with modern trends in the preparation and selection of high school teachers of English will find a unique, useful testing tool in this 1962 edition of the English Language and Literature test of the National Teacher Examinations. It is part of the program initiated by the American Council on Education in 1940 and since 1950 administered annually by Educational Testing Service in many centers throughout the United States.

Form KNT is an objective type examination of 105 items each offering five possible answers from which the examinee is asked to choose the one he thinks best. The testmakers have made an effort "to get at the quality of the test-taker's thinking and judgment—e.g., his ability to interpret, analyze, synthesize, evaluate," and to write items requiring "reasoning and application of principles rather than the recollection of specific facts." They have designed a systematic approach to the examination of *theoretical* preparation for the teaching of high school English as it is commonly practiced in the United States today, emphasizing in the main some of the newer progressive thinking of leaders in the National Council of Teachers of English. The test presents a variety of the problems that every English teacher faces in the classroom and in school staff meetings.

All the major areas of secondary English teaching are represented: poetry, prose, oral and written composition—including creative writing and listening—language usage and grammar, and film, but it would be interesting to know how the testmakers arrived at the emphases they have given to the various divisions. More than three fourths of the items deal with literature, with prose outweighing poetry. Written composition, oral composition, reading, and usage follow in this order. What are the assumptions and rationale back of these proportions? No authority is given and no studies are cited.

One of the special values of the test is the effective way in which modern thinking in current English usage and composition is brought into sharp focus in contrast with conventional and unscholarly procedures which center attention on formal grammar and rules. Everyday classroom situations in literature are presented, such as a class consideration of a poem by Robert Frost. The test taker is asked to choose one of five meanings, e.g., the main theme,

the mood, or prevailing emotion. Of course, a thoughtful teacher or student will not often find what he wants to say in the alternatives which even the best of objective tests impose. Those who refuse to accept a rigid mechanical framework are penalized and their thinking cannot be properly evaluated without some opportunity for commentary. No such opportunity is offered. There is the further serious limitation that the classroom situations described are presented scantily. The most capable, talented teacher could not tell from the brief descriptions given what to do without experience with the class or student. It is much like asking a physician to prescribe without seeing the patient. Medical ethics do not allow physicians to prescribe *in absentia,* and teachers should not be asked to make snap judgments about the education of students they know nothing about.

There is little indication that the testmakers are aware of the great social currents which are sweeping through America and over the mountains and plains of every continent. The new horizons are not visible here. There is a single reference to Chekhov and almost no other mention of the wide range of world literature. Latin America, Asia, Africa, and continental Europe are blank areas, with no hint of their literary heritage. Even the rich fields ploughed by English and American authors are poorly represented. There is no indication of the socially significant creative work of Mark Twain, Thoreau, Melville, Emerson, Jack London, and Whitman. Negro writers are conspicuously lacking. Apparently the American Revolution, the continuing struggle for the freedom of the Negro people from the Civil War down to the present, and the rising, urgent campaign for world peace are out of bounds in the English classroom as here conceived. There is no recognition of the principle that living content of major significance for our times is the core of literature and all communication. It is a central failure of this test as of many English classrooms that the subject matter is shallow and offers little challenging guidance to the student's and teacher's concern with language and literature in the swirling current of life outside the classroom doors. The form is here. The essence of the teaching of English—the unity of form and nascent content—is not grasped. There is a modernity in method but the principle that growth in ability to speak and write and know significant literature depends upon grappling with the basic and creative problems of the students' lives is lacking.

In short, in its basic conception this test falls short in covering the content with which American teachers of English must deal if they are to prepare their students to understand the meaning and uses of literature and composition in the era of the expanding world of the space ship. There is no evidence that the narrowly conceived content of this test reflects our richest literature or the new world currents which are deepening and widening the teaching of English. The authors of the coming revision have a major opportunity to enlarge the conception of what an English teacher can be.

Those who use the present examination form will be aware that it is far too brief to evaluate sufficiently the theoretical grasp of those who take it and that such a pencil and paper objective test makes no attempt to discover what the person who takes it would *do* in the English classroom. As a supplementary device it has its uses if the results are evaluated in relationship to more thorough efforts to plumb the qualities needed in the English classroom. The search for talent and creativity in the theory of the teaching of English and for applied knowledge as it functions in the schoolroom lie beyond it.

For reviews of the testing program, see 700, 5:538, and 4:802.

[260]
English Language and Literature: Teacher Education Examination Program. College seniors preparing to teach secondary school; 1957; inactive form of *English Language and Literature: National Teacher Examinations;* for more complete information, see 709; IBM; 80(95) minutes; Educational Testing Service. *

For a review of the testing program, see 5:543. For reviews of the National Teacher Examinations, *see 700, 5:538, and 4:802.*

[261]
*English Progress Tests. Various ages 7.5–14; 1952–63; 11 levels; 8*s.* per 12 tests; 9*d.* per single copy; 1*s.* per manual for any one level except *b, h, j,* and *k*; prices include purchase tax; postage extra; A. F. Watts (*a, e, g, i, k*), M. A. Brimer (*c, g, i*), S. M. Unwin (*j*), Betsy Barnard (*b*), Valerie Land (*f*), and Jennifer Henchman (*h*); published for the National Foundation for Educational Research in

England and Wales; Newnes Educational Publishing Co. Ltd. *
a) ENGLISH PROGRESS TEST A. Ages 8.0–9.0; 1952–60; 1 form ['52, 6 pages]; manual ['60, 8 pages]; 39(45) minutes.
b) ENGLISH PROGRESS TEST A2. Ages 7.5–9.0; 1962; 1 form ['62, 8 pages]; mimeographed directions ['63, 5 pages]; no data on reliability; no norms; directions free on special request from the National Foundation; (40–45) minutes.
c) ENGLISH PROGRESS TEST B. Ages 9.0–10.0; 1956–62; 1 form ['56, 7 pages]; manual ['62, 7 pages, identical with 1957 manual except for additional norms]; (40–45) minutes.
d) ENGLISH PROGRESS TEST B2. Ages 8.5–10.0; 1959–60; 1 form ['59, 7 pages]; manual ['60, 7 pages]; (40–45) minutes.
e) ENGLISH PROGRESS TEST C. Ages 10.0–11.0; 1952–60; formerly called *English Grading Test 3;* 1 form ['52, 8 pages]; revised manual ('60, 7 pages); (50–55) minutes.
f) ENGLISH PROGRESS TEST C2. Ages 9.5–11.0; 1961; 1 form ['61, 8 pages]; manual ['61, 7 pages]; (40–45) minutes.
g) ENGLISH PROGRESS TEST D. Ages 11.0–12.0; 1956; 1 form ['56, 7 pages]; manual ['56, 8 pages]; provisional norms; (40–45) minutes.
h) ENGLISH PROGRESS TEST D2. Ages 10.0–11.0; 1963; 1 form ['63, 8 pages]; mimeographed directions ['63, 6 pages]; no data on reliability; no norms; directions free on special request from the National Foundation; 45(50) minutes.
i) ENGLISH PROGRESS TEST E. Ages 12.0–13.0; 1956; 1 form ['56, 8 pages]; manual ['56, 8 pages]; provisional norms; (40–45) minutes.
j) ENGLISH PROGRESS TEST E2. Ages 11.0–13.0; 1962–63; 1 form ['62, 8 pages]; mimeographed directions ['63, 6 pages]; no data on reliability; no norms; directions free on special request from the National Foundation; 45(50) minutes.
k) ENGLISH PROGRESS TEST F. Ages 13.0–14.0; 1953; 1 form ['53, 8 pages]; manual ['53, 10 pages]; no data on reliability; 1*s.* 3*d.* per manual; (50–55) minutes.

For reviews by Neil Gourlay and Stanley Nisbet, see 5:187.

[262]
*English Test (Adv.). Ages 12–0 to 13–11; 1954–60; 4 tests; distribution restricted to directors of education; 10*s.* per 12 tests; 1*s.* per single copy; 1*s.* 3*d.* per manual for any one test; prices include purchase tax; postage extra; 50(55) minutes; G. A. V. Morgan (*a*); published for the National Foundation for Educational Research in England and Wales; Newnes Educational Publishing Co. Ltd. *
a) ENGLISH TEST (ADV.) 1. 1954–55; 1 form ['54, 11 pages]; manual ['55, 11 pages].
b) ENGLISH TEST (ADV.) 2. 1957; 1 form ['57, 12 pages]; manual ('57, 12 pages).
c) ENGLISH TEST (ADV.) 3. 1958; 1 form ['58, 12 pages]; manual ('58, 9 pages).
d) ENGLISH TEST (ADV.) 4. 1960; 1 form ['60, 12 pages]; manual ('60, 10 pages).

A. E. G. PILLINER, *Senior Lecturer in Education, University of Edinburgh, Edinburgh, Scotland.*

The authors give no specific indication of the purpose of these tests. From the title, the age range in the norms, and the description of the standardisation groups, the tests are apparently intended to discriminate levels of English attainment of children of age 12 to 14.

In all cases the time allowance is 50 minutes. There are 120 items in the first test, and 100 in each of the others. The measures obtained are standardised scores, normally distributed with mean 100 and standard deviation 15.

The norms for the first three tests are based on the performances of 1,500 to 2,000 children "in a chosen area." It is a pity that the test constructors do not give more information. If the "chosen area" is (as seems probable) a single Local Education Authority, the norms will be appropriate for the group of children tested on that occasion in that authority. The manuals do not tell us, however, how closely performance in that authority conforms to performance in a national sample.

A more serious matter is the manner in which reliability data are presented. The only coefficient reported is a KR-20 for each test based on a random sample of around 200 scripts. In the manual for Test 2, for example, it is stated that "the value was found to be .979. This leads to the value of 2.2 for the standard error (S.E.) of the tests. The Kuder-Richardson formula is accepted for comparison of tests, being associated with (although distinct from) the test-retest correlation." This statement is gravely misleading. Who accepts KR-20 for comparison of tests? What does it mean to say that KR-20 is "associated with (although distinct from) the test-retest correlation"? KR-20 does have its legitimate uses. It is a valuable measure of the internal consistency of a test. As Cronbach has illuminatingly shown, it is the mean of the boosted split-half coefficients obtained from every possible split of the test into halves. It is the lower bound of the coefficient of equivalence of the test. All these are valid and informative uses of KR-20. But to quote the numerical value of the standard error derived from KR-20 as "being associated with (although distinct from) the test-retest correlation" is, at best, vague, and, at worst, invalid and erroneous. Specifically, a standard error of 2.2 (based on KR-20 = .979) is the inferred upper bound to the variability of a child's standardised score from one test to another, when it is reasonable to assume that the content of each test is a stratified sample from a complex universe of items, and when the occasions of testing are identical; or (which amounts to the same thing) when one test, constructed according to this specification, is substituted for another, similarly constructed, on a single occasion of testing. However, the assumptions underlying the precise statement made in the previous sentence are not met in the actual testing situation. Firstly, inspection shows that the tests are *not* parallel in the sense defined above. Secondly, grounds of convenience, which fixed the date of testing, might have fixed another date; and it cannot be assumed that the actual occasion of testing, and the alternative occasion which *might* have been chosen, are identical in the sense demanded by the specification on which alone the precise interpretation of KR-20 and the corresponding standard error of measurement are valid estimates.

Apart from these statistical defects, the manuals are well done. The instructions for administration and directions for marking are clear and unambiguous; the tables of norms are easy to read; and the answers in the marking key are aligned with the questions in the test—a useful procedure increasingly employed by the better test agencies producing hand scored tests.

Judging by the norms, the tests are of appropriate difficulty and the raw score dispersion is adequate (the latter is reported specifically for the first test only). On all four tests the mean raw score of the girls in the reference groups was, as usual, significantly superior to that of the boys. The reported increases in score with age show no consistent pattern. For Test 2 the increase is reported, without comment, as equivalent (for boys) to 1.049 points of standardised score, and (for girls) to .048, the difference being highly significant. Accordingly, separate sets of norms have been constructed for the two sexes, and it must be admitted that those for girls present a surprising appearance. Can these figures be truly representative?

The forms of the items in the tests include multiple choice, open-ended with forced responses, and open-ended with unforced responses (the testee, in the latter, being required to complete a sentence of which part is presented, the marker having discretion to accept or reject). The printing of the tests is admirable, and the overall effect pleasing to the eye. The test material, however, is uneven in qual-

English Test (Adv.)

ity; some parts of each test fall below the generally high standard. There are two main points of criticism. Firstly, insufficient care has gone into the editing of the tests; and secondly, the final versions appear to have escaped scrutiny by a critical subject expert.

Of all tests, those of English attainment in particular should be impeccable in style and should display a sensitive awareness of how precise statement is dependent on the flexibility of language. Judged by these criteria, the tests fall short in some measure. Nevertheless, as one would expect with tests bearing the imprimatur of the National Foundation for Educational Research, they are competently constructed and basically well founded. Statistically, the tests are patently sound, and a not extensive though critical revision would transform them into models that others would do well to follow. Following such revision this reviewer would not hesitate to commend them to the most critical user.

[263]

★English Test (Four-Year Course): Affiliation Testing Program for Catholic Secondary Schools. Grade 12 and students who are candidates for the high school diploma issued by the Catholic University of America; 1949–63; administered annually in May at individual schools; IBM; new form issued annually; Form Z ('63, 15 pages) used in 1963 program; separate answer sheets must be used; 50¢ per test and IBM answer sheet; postpaid; specimen set of the complete battery free; fee includes purchase of test booklets, scoring, and other services; for more complete information, see 758; 90(100) minutes; Program of Affiliation, Catholic University of America. *

HENRY CHAUNCEY, *President, Educational Testing Service, Princeton, New Jersey.* [Review of Forms Y and Z.]

We are informed in the interpretive materials that the number of items used in each area of testing is proportioned to an index of emphasis in instruction. Consequently, we can conclude that the four-year course, for which the test serves as an achievement measure, is to be outlined somewhat as follows: spelling (10–13 per cent), grammar and usage (9–12), punctuation (9–10), capitalization (5), vocabulary (13), paragraph analysis (6–7), literary history (24–27), literary forms (7), identification of literary works (6), and analysis of a poem (5–7). The test is to be regarded as an objective or indirect measure of accomplishment in studies that have been described as follows:

The objectives of the four-year course in English are to provide the student with skill in the communicative arts of reading, writing, and speaking, and to lead him through close contact with masterpieces of literary art to a sense of artistic form and to some development of his own literary powers of concentration, interpretation, and discrimination.

The problem of the reviewer is to decide whether the test is adequate as a measure of these objectives. Since "skill" in the communicative arts and a "sense" of literary form, as well as some development of "literary powers," are major objectives, one would expect, at a minimum, a reading test on unfamiliar literary, or other, materials to put these skills to work. The outline of test content, however, runs heavily to rules and forms, and to facts and types and literary information.

An examination of test items confirms the preliminary judgment, for the emphasis is strongly upon "what have you been taught about _____?" rather than "what have you learned about _____, and what can you do with it?" The grammar and usage items are not applicatory but analytical (identifying "nominatives of address," for example), requiring knowledge of the term rather than careful use, or distinction in use, of the thing itself. (In Form Y, the illustration of this type, item 43, is itself an example of poor use and inadequate or improper punctuation.) In paragraph analysis, questions do not pertain to judgment of what is said, as content, or the effectiveness of the saying, but only to the formalized "topic sentence, means of transition, type of development" kind of analysis. Pages of the test are devoted to literature, but none to its comprehension or judgment—merely to its recall as type and identity, where memory is everything and "skill" or "sense of" are not even hinted. A careful student might, one should judge, do exceptionally well on the literature items without having read any of the works mentioned.

The problem of the reviewer has, therefore, changed focus: Is the test inadequate for the objectives stated, or are the objectives so colored, or even twisted, by a pedagogical concept that this kind of test is a faithful mirror of the instruction? There is some internal evidence that the latter is the case. We are informed that the test is validated against grades in English courses, and the figures [1] are high:

1 The publisher reports validity coefficients corrected for attenuation. The validity coefficients presented in this review were computed from data presented in the manual.

Form Y, .55; Form Z, .69. The conclusion would seem to be that the test is measuring the outcomes of instruction and, on its own terms, therefore, it is an excellent test. That it is testing outcomes of English instruction of what must be the most dismally traditional sort is beside the point. The kind of instruction is a matter of curriculum and pedagogical emphasis, beyond the scope of a test review.

For a review of the complete program, see 758.

[264]

*English Tests 1, 3–13. Ages 10 to 11–11; 1951–62; 12 tests (12 pages except for c–e); distribution restricted to directors of education; 10s. per 12 tests; 1s. per single copy; manual for any one test: 1s. for a and c, 1s. 3d. for b, d–l; prices include purchase tax; postage extra; 50(55) minutes except for a and c; G. A. V. Morgan (a–d), M. A. Brimer (e), and A. E. Davies (h); published for the National Foundation for Educational Research in England and Wales; Newnes Educational Publishing Co. Ltd. *
a) ENGLISH TEST 1. 1951–58; 1 form ['51]; manual ['58, 8 pages]; 45(50) minutes.
b) ENGLISH TEST 3. 1952–53; 1 form ['52]; manual ['53, 10 pages].
c) ENGLISH TEST 4. 1953–57; 1 form ['53, 10 pages]; manual ('57, 8 pages); 40(45) minutes.
d) ENGLISH TEST 5. 1954–55; 1 form ['54, 10 pages]; manual ('55, 10 pages); no norms for ages 11–6 to 11–11.
e) ENGLISH TEST 6. 1955–56; 1 form ['55, 11 pages]; manual ('56, 12 pages); no norms for ages 11–10 to 11–11.
f) ENGLISH TEST 7. 1956–59; 1 form ['56]; manual ('59, 12 pages, identical with 1957 manual).
g) ENGLISH TEST 8. 1957–58; 1 form ['57]; manual ('58, 12 pages).
h) ENGLISH TEST 9. 1958–59; 1 form ['58]; manual ('59, 12 pages).
i) ENGLISH TEST 10. 1959–60; 1 form ['59]; manual ('60, 12 pages).
j) ENGLISH TEST 11. 1960–61; 1 form ['60]; manual ('61, 12 pages); Welsh edition ['61] available.
k) ENGLISH TEST 12. 1961–62; 1 form ['61]; manual ('62, 11 pages).
l) ENGLISH TEST 13. 1962–63; forms 13A, 13B, ['62]; manual ('63, 12 pages) for each form.

REFERENCES

1. MORETON, C. ANNE, AND BUTCHER, H. J. "Are Rural Children Handicapped by the Use of Speeded Tests in Selection Procedures?" *Brit J Ed Psychol* 33:22–30 F '63. * (PA 38:684)

STANLEY NISBET, *Professor of Education, University of Glasgow, Glasgow, Scotland.*

These "closed" tests, obtainable only by directors of education, have been used extensively in England during the past 10 years, and are still used as part of the assessment batteries whereby pupils are allocated to types of secondary school. Since the main purpose of such batteries is to discriminate between the able minority (fit for a grammar school) and the rest, the tests are rather too difficult for the less able children in the age group, but they give plenty of headroom for the brightest.

The following comments are based on a study of the tests and manuals themselves, without supplementary data.

a) There are a few items in each test in which, if the marking key is strictly followed, injustice would seem to be done to some pupils (for example, items 10, 88, and 92 in Test 1; items 7, 12, and 110–113 in Test 3; and item 40 in Test 6).

b) There are numerous items to which exception could be taken on grounds of layout, correctness, or clarity (for example, items 13, 14, 23, 24 ff., 46, 65 ff., 73, and 78 in Test 1; and items 6 and 20 in Test 6).

c) The number of questionable items decreases as the series goes on. It is clear that lessons learned from the application of the earlier tests were applied in the construction of the later ones.

d) As the series proceeded, a deliberate policy was adopted of decreasing the number of totally objective items (for example, multiple choice) and increasing the number of "controlled completion" and "creative response" items. This is a defensible policy (the reviewer would go further and say it is desirable), but no evidence is given of the *amount* of objectivity actually achieved in these open-response items. The Kuder-Richardson reliability coefficient would appear to show merely the general interitem correlation when each script is marked by a single person: it offers no information about agreement between independent markers. If this is so, it is strange to read in some of the manuals, after the Kuder-Richardson coefficient has been quoted, that "the reliability of this test is very high despite the deliberate inclusion of some items requiring an element of subjectivity in the marking." [1]

e) Since this is a test of English it is perhaps surprising that so many items call for mental gymnastics of the type normally associated with intelligence tests and relatively fewer items call for the straightforward comprehension of English passages.

f) Much ingenuity has been shown in de-

[1] Since writing the above the reviewer has seen the next tests in this series (13A and 13B). Some of the criticisms made of the earlier tests no longer apply, and in particular the manuals give experimental evidence of agreement between different markers.

vising new types of items, especially those allowing a measure of freedom in the response. Some of these appear quite promising.

SUMMARY. In the light of these comments, it would be difficult to recommend the tests, though it is possible that some of the misgivings might be allayed by further data, especially on item analysis.

H. J. SANTS, *Lecturer in Education, University College of North Wales, Bangor, Wales.*

The manuals, with details about construction, standardisation, sex differences, reliability, and administration, conspicuously avoid comment about what the tests may be measuring. However, insofar as standardised objective tests of English and arithmetic are used together with intelligence tests in selection procedures at the end of primary schooling, it can be assumed that the items have been based on the common elements of the English syllabi in use in primary schools. In order to cope successfully with these tests a child would not in fact necessarily need to have had a formal teaching in English grammar, although this would probably be an advantage, but he would need a familiarity with the written word and some interest in the structure of language. For example, Test 12 begins with items requiring the child to substitute pronouns for proper names. This could be tackled intuitively from background reading or it could be negotiated from a conscious knowledge of syntax comparable to the test deviser's.

Considerable use is made throughout the series of the sentence completion test. Completing a sentence appears to call for some particular kind of verbal reasoning, and thus these English tests are not merely tests of attainment in the sense of being tests of knowledge about ways of classifying parts of language. Indeed, explicit mention is made in the series from 1956 onwards of a policy of increasing the number of controlled completion items and creative response items generally at the expense of selective response questions requiring a tick or underlining. The trend away from the testing of attainment based on the school syllabus towards a testing of the ability to use the basic constructions of primary school English in a general way has, perhaps, been responsible for the decrease in the number of items drawn from school subjects, like history and geography. In Test 1

there are references to Napoleon and his battles and to summers in Australia in November, whereas in Test 12 topics are much more akin to the topics of basic school reading books with reference to John at the football match and Mary and her holidays.

The subject matter of any book or document that a 10- or 11-year-old child reads is surely in part responsible for his attitudes towards the material; but there is not a word of explanation about choice of topics in the manuals. Nor indeed is there any evidence that the matter has been given much thought. Items for girls are sprinkled tentatively. Some alarming topics, such as disaster at sea, are used repeatedly throughout the series. The themes of objective tests have a monotonous oddity which may well be one of the many unfortunate consequences of the close familiarity which test designers have with the work of their predecessors.

In terms of currently accepted notions about test construction this series of tests has undoubtedly improved over the years with the backing of research carried out by the National Foundation's own workers as well as others. Great care has been taken over standardisation of administration, but just because of this the teachers and children using the tests must inevitably feel a great sense of their taking part in a very important occasion. The use of tests as a sole means of selecting children for secondary education is on the decrease in Great Britain. One of the widespread objections to using test results is that a child's ability is being sampled on a single decisive occasion with resultant anxiety. In considering the tests under review it is surprising that very little thought appears to have been given to reducing test situation strain by considering the impression that a child would get from the appearance of these publications. Publishers of other school material for children have been giving increasing care and skill to the improvement of layout.

The 1951 test booklet has the words ENGLISH TEST 1 in enormous block capitals with the Foundation's name boldly across the top. There are large underlined warnings about not wasting time and working carefully. The general impression is that of a government form. By 1961 the booklet is much improved in this respect, but even here the instructions to the child are presented like a public notice, num-

English Tests 1, 3–13

bered from 1 to 6, and end with the rigorous command ASK NO QUESTIONS AT ALL ONCE THE TEST HAS BEGUN. Greater efforts could surely be made to present tests to children in a manner more in keeping with normal classroom procedure without losing the necessary standard control of administration.

Emphasis has been given in this review to neglect of the child's view because this continued neglect in the field of group testing is in striking contrast to a prevailing child-centered approach to education. Nevertheless this series of standardised attainment tests in English has been thoughtfully improved from year to year and the tests under review are about as efficient as tests of their kind are likely to be within the framework of current test theory. The danger is that in so efficiently meeting the demands of selecting by examination, the skills which have been found to be the easiest to test will become those which will dominate both primers and teachers.

[265]

*English Usage: Every Pupil Test. Grades 3–4, 5–6, 7–9, 10–12; 1929–64; new form (4 pages) usually issued each December and April; forms from previous testing programs also available; 4 levels; general directions sheet ('63, 2 pages); no data on reliability; Ohio norms for new forms available following testing program; 5¢ per test; 3¢ per key; postpaid; 40(45) minutes; Ohio Scholarship Tests. *

REFERENCES

1. EDMINSTON, R. W., AND GINGERICH, C. N. "The Relation of Factors of English Usage to Composition." *J Ed Res* 36:269–71 D '42. * *(PA* 17:2169)
2. GROFF, PATRICK J. "Parts of Speech in Standardized English Tests." *Sch R* 69:457–60 w '61. *

For a review by J. R. Gerberich of the 1946 forms, see 3:127.

[266]

*Essentials of English Tests, Revised Edition. Grades 7–13; 1939–61; 6 scores: spelling, grammatical usage, word usage, sentence structure, punctuation and capitalization, total; Forms A, B, ('61, 8 pages, identical with forms copyrighted in 1939 and 1940 except for revisions in 12 items); manual ['61, 6 pages, essentially the same as 1944 manual except for wording changes]; no norms for grade 13; reliability data and norms the same as published in 1939–44; $2.50 per 25 tests, postage extra; 75¢ per specimen set of both forms, postpaid; 45(50) minutes; original edition by Dora V. Smith and Constance M. McCullough, revision by Carolyne Green; American Guidance Service, Inc. *

J. RAYMOND GERBERICH, *Visiting Professor of Education, University of Maryland, College Park, Maryland.*

The *Essentials of English Tests* include parts on spelling, grammatical usage, word usage,

sentence structure, and punctuation and capitalization. Supplementary materials consist of a six-page manual; of a folder including norms, a score tabulation form, and a class record; of strip scoring keys, plus optional transparent overlays for Part 5; and of four-page forms for use in analyzing errors. The test booklets carry both 1940 and 1961 copyright dates but neither a copyright date nor a printing date appears on the manual or any of the other materials.

In Parts 1, 2, and 3, the pupil is asked to discriminate between what is correct and what is incorrect in: (a) spellings of 25 words appearing in list form, (b) grammatical usages of 44 italicized words and phrases appearing in context in an essay of some 450 words, and (c) word usages in unspecified portions of 15 rather short sentences. Two patterns of pupil responses are asked for in these completion-type parts—a "C" for each item judged to be correct and a word or phrase designed to correct errors in all other items. In Part 3, the pupil is also asked to underline the word he judges to be incorrect in each "wrong" sentence.

Part 4 is composed of 20 four-option multiple choice items in each of which the same idea is expressed in four different ways. The pupil is asked to mark the sentence structure that best expresses the idea. Part 5 consists of a short narrative setting and a dependent business letter in which 57 underlined and numbered positions indicate points where errors in capitalization, errors or omissions in punctuation, or even combinations of a capitalization and punctuation error may exist. If the pupil thinks there is a mistake or an omission at any underlined point in the passage, he is asked to make an appropriate insertion. He is not asked to respond in any way, however, to those underlined positions where he thinks the usage is correct.

Although the format of the booklets and accompanying materials is in general quite good, several discrepancies that careful editing would have eliminated detract from the test in minor degree.

A more important consideration is that portions of Part 4, on sentence structure, seem not to come up to modern standards of item writing. For example, several items fail to include the same details in all four options (A-8; A-13; B-13) and others employ two sentences or sentence fragments in some options instead of the implied if not promised one sentence (A-1; A-9; B-1). Again, one item presents one good and three incredibly bad options (B-1), whereas another (B-4), to be more specific, offers three grammatically acceptable versions of opposition to drinking—one to drinking in general (option *a*) and two to drinking in the assembly (options *b* and *c*). Since face validity and empirical validity are not often contradictory for achievement test items, it is difficult to harmonize the structural limitations of these items, and perhaps of others, with desirable degrees of discriminative power.

Scoring problems may well arise for Part 3, on word usage, and Part 5, on capitalization and punctuation. The intent in Part 3 is apparently to provide for a maximum score of 15 by counting one point for each correct underlining and one point for each correct completion and dividing the total by two. However, there is no mention in the scoring key of how responses to the errorless sentences are to be scored or how the fractional values that will inevitably result when the total is divided by two are to be handled. Even more serious problems are likely to occur in Part 5, where points are awarded in such an array of patterns that scoring is unlikely to be handled objectively by most classroom teachers. One point is variously supposed to be awarded, for example, for no response, for one simple response, for two separate and separated responses, for a compound two-step response, for a simple triple response, and for a complex three-step response.

Three of the most important characteristics of a test—validity, reliability, and comparability of results—receive very sketchy attention in the manual and tables of norms. Validity is based, according to the manual, on studies of usage and of errors, content of English placement tests for college freshmen, opinions of English specialists, and "item experimentation" involving 1,416 high school pupils and 400 college students. Only the last of these four sources receives more than passing attention. Statements about reliability are even more deficient in comprehension of the technical problems involved, as evidenced by failure to mention range of talent or to present other important background information. In fact, the sole quantitative observation is that "the corre-

lation of score between comparable forms ran about as usual (.87 to .89)."

The tables of norms, designated as "Grade Profiles," show what the authors term "percentile readings" (the 5th, 25th, 50th, 75th, and 95th percentiles within grades) for the five part scores and total scores based on 36,480 pupils in grades 7 to 12 representing "all sections of the country." Separate tables appear for Forms A and B as well as for grades 7 to 12. No norms are given for grade 13, even though the booklets specify that the test is designed for use with college freshmen. It is true that the manual suggests at one point that major values occur when the teacher analyzes the errors of individual pupils on the special form provided and uses the results in remedial teaching. Elsewhere, however, the values of "percentile distributions" for making "intra-school comparisons" are stressed.

A comparison of the 1961 revision with the 1939–40 first edition discloses very few differences. About a dozen items in the two comparable Forms A and B vary in great or small degree. The revision is somewhat improved in printing and paper quality over the original, but the formats are almost identical. The accessory materials differ slightly in their organization and format but hardly at all in their content. The parallelism extends even to the percentile norms, identical in the two editions, which means that they must be based on the 36,480 pupils in grades 7 to 12 who were tested prior to 1940. The new manual, too, differs from its predecessor primarily in unimportant details of wording.

A revision of an achievement test, especially one that appears as much as two decades after its predecessor, should reflect improved understanding of the abilities it is designed to measure, refinement in techniques of item writing, progress in methods of establishing validity and reliability, and more insightful assistance to test users through the manual of directions and other supplementary materials.

The preface to the manual of this English test sets the stage for updating the instrument by indicating that a testing program in this area must keep pace with rapid changes in language usages and pedagogical methods as revealed through restudy and research. The disharmony between this modern stage setting and the 1940-style production is portended, however, by a succeeding comment that only "a very limited revision" seemed to be necessary at this time because of the foresight of the original "editors."

Since the 1961 revision and its 1939–40 predecessor differ insignificantly in content, and not at all in accompanying norms or evidence concerning reliability and validity, it must be concluded that the difference of 21 years in copyright dates reflects the chief distinction between the two editions. A book publisher is sometimes criticized for putting out a new "edition" that differs from its predecessor in such minor revisions on a small number of pages that only a careful scrutiny will reveal differences between what are more nearly two printings than two editions. The differences between the two editions under discussion here are so minor that a similar indictment of the *Essentials of English Tests* does not seem to be at all inappropriate.

It is reasonable to expect, moreover, that the 1961 revision of this test should reflect ideas presented in the three reviews of the first edition that appeared in the *Third Mental Measurements Yearbook* in 1949 and the recommendations for authors and publishers of achievement tests that were published in the middle 1950's by two national organizations concerned with measurement and evaluation. However, the preceding portions of this review indicate that the revisions were so minor that at best they can be looked upon as a patch-up job. Moreover, there is no evidence to indicate that the revision took any account of the Technical Recommendations. Of the 43 major recommendations in that source, in fact, most of them listed as essential for a well standardized test, the *Essentials of English Tests* met only five and distinctly failed to meet 25, or 58 per cent, whereas the remaining 13 were classified by this reviewer as doubtful or not applicable to this test. The greatest deficiencies occur for the sections on validity, reliability, and scales and norms, where the English test failed to conform to the recommendations respectively in 11 of 18, 5 of 7, and 4 of 8 instances. An inescapable conclusion is that the first edition was better according to 1940 understandings about the characteristics of good achievement tests than is the 1961 revision in terms of 1961 criteria.

For reviews by Charlotte Croon Davis and Gerald V. Lannholm, see 3:128 (1 excerpt).

Essentials of English Tests

[267]
*The Iowa Tests of Educational Development: Test 3, Correctness and Appropriateness of Expression. Grades 9–12; 1942–61; IBM; Forms X-3S, Y-3S, ('52, 9 pages); battery examiner's manual ('58, c1949–57, 23 pages); battery general manual ('59, 37 pages); student profile leaflet, sixth edition ('61, c1958, 2 pages); see the complete battery entry (14b) for other accessories; no data on reliability; separate answer sheets must be used; $2.40 per 20 tests; $5 per 100 IBM answer sheets; 50¢ per scoring stencil; $3 per specimen set of the complete battery; postage extra; 60(70) minutes for full length version, 40(50) minutes for class period version; prepared under the direction of E. F. Lindquist; Science Research Associates, Inc. *

REFERENCES
1. GROFF, PATRICK J. "Parts of Speech in Standardized English Tests." *Sch R* 69:457–60 w '61. *

For reviews of the complete battery, see 14 and 5:17; for reviews of earlier forms, see 4:17 and 3:12.

[268]
*Language Arts: Minnesota High School Achievement Examinations. Grades 7, 8, 9, 10, 11, 12; 1955–63; earlier forms called *English IX–XII; Midwest High School Achievement Examinations;* series formerly called *Midwest High School Achievement Examinations;* new form issued each May; norms available in June following release of new form; Form F ('63, 4–8 pages) used in 1963 testing; 6 levels; no specific manual; series manual ('63, 4 pages); series norms ['63, 4 pages]; series cumulative profile ('62, 2 pages); no data on reliability; no description of normative population; 12¢ per test; $2.50 per 100 profiles; postage extra; 20¢ per specimen set, postpaid; 60(65) minutes; American Guidance Service, Inc. *

MARVIN D. GLOCK, *Professor of Educational Psychology, Cornell University, Ithaca, New York.* [Review of Forms E and F.]

The manual states that "this battery of tests is designed primarily for the improvement of instruction." Examples of the use of the Minnesota High School Achievement Examinations to realize this aim are cited in the series manual as follows. (*a*) Each test is divided into a number of units and the number of questions in each unit reflects the relative importance of the unit in the course. Teachers can spot units on which their students did poorly and adjust the teaching program accordingly. (*b*) Teachers can compare performance on local teacher-made tests with performance on the Minnesota test. A discrepancy indicates that an evaluation of local procedures might be needed. (*c*) Similar to the first example, the average achievement levels on the various Minnesota tests can be compared to determine subject matter areas which need greater stress or better teaching methods.

Although the manual states that "the items.... were chosen because they measured the subject matter objectives of the curriculum," it does not state what these objectives are or how they were selected as curriculum objectives. This information is extremely important since the manual recommends close scrutiny of the local curricula when pupils deviate widely from the norms of the tests.

No information is given concerning the reliability of the tests.

Although the manual mentions the use of the tests to detect units which are poorly taught, no norms are supplied for individual units. Norms for the total scores are supplied, but there is no mention of the number of people or the specific schools from which the norms were compiled.

The tests are easy to administer since they can be given to large groups and since each test has a time limit of one hour. If the results of individual units are to be used by schools, it would have been advantageous, however, to have allotted a given amount of time per unit to assure appropriate attention to each unit.

The tests, with 109–150 items per exam, are designed to be hand scored. The entire test is of a multiple choice format and answer sheets which can be machine scored could be used, but are not supplied.

It is difficult to compare the content of the tests at various grade levels for several reasons. The tests are divided into units, but the number varies from 6 to 12 units per test, depending upon the grade level and form. Also, the descriptive title for a given unit is not uniform. For example, the questions in the unit titled "Language Study Skills," grade 7, are almost identical to those classified as the "Library" unit in grade 9.

In addition to the differences in labeling of like units, there are differences in the combinations which make up a unit. Questions similar to those which form the unit, "Sources of Information," grade 12, appear in the "Language Study Skills" and the "Library" units mentioned above, but the latter two units encompass a broader area. Some variability in units also occurs from Form E to Form F at the same grade level.

The reviewer grouped the units in Form F into 6 broad categories after examining the type of question in each unit. The following table shows the amount to which each category is stressed at the various grade levels by giving the percentage of the total questions which deal with each category.

Category	Grade					
	7	8	9	10	11	12
Literature	—	21	24	9	42	28
Spelling	23	10	11	28	18	9
Vocabulary	23	10	11	17	11	21
Grammar	44	59	37	37	24	12
Composition	—	—	7	9	5	21
Library	10	—	10	—	—	9

It is doubtful that each test has "a selected number of questions reflecting the importance of each unit in the course." From the distribution of questions, one would be forced to conclude that knowledge of literature is not one of the "subject matter objectives of the curriculum" in the language arts in grade 7, and that its importance in the curriculum varies greatly from year to year, being of little significance in grade 10, but extremely important in grade 11. The amount of emphasis in each category also varies with the form.

The manual states, in reference to all the tests in the series, "the ratio of concept questions to purely factual questions differs widely by tests because of the nature of the particular subject." Within the same subject area, however, the ratio also varies widely. For example, in the literature category, all of the questions at grade 9 are factual and many of the questions at grade 10 involve interpretation of literature selections.

EVALUATION. The manual gives insufficient information concerning test construction, validation, reliability, and composition of norms. The purpose of the test is to measure the subject matter objectives of the curriculum, but the nonuniform nature of the test content at the six grade levels and across forms, along with the lack of any apparent developmental trends in the stress placed upon subject areas (with the possible exception of a decrease of stress on grammar), introduces doubt as to the realization of the test purpose.

The suggested use of unit scores is not recommended, and the use of total scores should be preceded by a careful examination of the test content at each level. The tests are not recommended as an evaluative guide for school curricula.

For a review by Roger A. Richards of earlier forms, see 5:186.

Language Arts: Minnesota High School Achievement Examinations

[269]

★**Language Perception Test.** Business and industry; 1959–63; forms 1, 2, 3, ('59, 2 pages, form designations do not appear on tests); manual ['63, 5 unnumbered pages]; reliability data for 1 form (unspecified) only; norms for males only; $2 per 25 tests; 10¢ per key; $1 per manual; postage extra; $1 per specimen set, postpaid; 5(10) minutes; Richardson, Bellows, Henry & Co., Inc. *

[270]

★**Metropolitan Achievement Tests: High School Language Tests.** Grades 9–12; 1962–64; subtest of *Metropolitan Achievement Tests;* 4 scores: reading, spelling, language, language study skills; IBM and MRC; Forms AM ('62), BM ('63), (12 pages); manual ('64, c1962–64, 28 pages); content outline ['64, 4 pages]; revised interpretive manual for the battery ('64, c1962–64, 16 pages); separate answer sheets must be used; $6 per 35 tests; $2.25 per 35 IBM answer sheets; 40¢ per set of scoring stencils; $4 per 100 sets of Harbor answer cards (machine scoring service, by Measurement Research Center, Inc., may be arranged through the publisher); 40¢ per specimen set; postage extra; 95(112) minutes; Walter N. Durost, William H. Evans, James D. Leake, Howard A. Bowman, Clarke Cosgrove, and John G. Read; Harcourt, Brace & World, Inc. *

For reviews of the complete battery, see 15.

[271]

★**[Moray House English Tests.]** Ages 8.5–10.5, 10–12, 12–14; 1935–63; 3 levels; distribution restricted to education authorities; 56s. per 100 tests; 12d. per single copy; 1s. 9d. per manual for any one form of any one test; postpaid; purchase tax extra; 40(50) minutes; Department of Education, University of Edinburgh; University of London Press Ltd. *
a) MORAY HOUSE JUNIOR ENGLISH TEST. Ages 8.5–10.5; 1949–58; 2 forms: *Junior English Test* ['52], *Junior English Test 2* ['58], (11 pages); manual [dates same as for tests, 12 pages] for each form.
b) MORAY HOUSE ENGLISH TEST. Ages 10–12; 1935–63; 1–2 new forms issued annually; 11 forms (12 pages) currently available: forms 23 ['53], 24 ['54], 25 ['55], 27 ['57], 28 ['58], 30 ['59], 31 ['60], 32 ['60], 33 ['61], 34 ['62], 35 ['63]; manual (dates same as for tests, 11 pages) for each form.
c) MORAY HOUSE ENGLISH TEST (ADV.). Ages 12–14; 1947–58; forms 1 ['56], 2 ['58], (12 pages); manual [dates same as for tests, 12 pages] for each form.

REFERENCES

1. LAMBERT, CONSTANCE M. "Symposium on Selection of Pupils for Different Types of Secondary Schools: 7, A Survey of Ability and Interest at the Stage of Transfer." *Brit J Ed Psychol* 19:67–81 Je '49. *
2. PILLINER, A. E. G. "The Position and Size of the Border-Line Group in an Examination." *Brit J Ed Psychol* 20:133–6 Je '50. * *(PA* 25:1281)
3. EMMETT, W. G., AND WILMUT, F. S. "The Prediction of School Certificate Performance in Specific Subjects." *Brit J Ed Psychol* 22:52–62 F '52. * *(PA* 27:667)
4. EMMETT, W. G. "Secondary Modern and Grammar School Performance Predicted by Tests Given in Primary Schools." *Brit J Ed Psychol* 24:91–8 Je '54. * *(PA* 29:3036)
5. PEEL, E. A., AND ARMSTRONG, H. G. "Symposium: The Use of Essays in Selection at 11+; 2, The Predictive Power of the English Composition in the 11+ Examination." *Brit J Ed Psychol* 26:163–71 N '56. * *(PA* 31:8840)
6. MUKHERJEE, L. "An Analysis of the Degree of Relationship Between Comprehension Questions and Mechanical Aspects of English in Moray House English Tests." *Brit J Ed Psychol* 28:79 F '58. * *(PA* 33:6838)
7. NISBET, JOHN, AND BUCHAN, JIM. "The Long-Term Follow-Up of Assessments at Age Eleven." *Brit J Ed Psychol* 29:1–8 F '59. * *(PA* 34:3444)

M. ALAN BRIMER, *Senior Research Fellow in Education, University of Bristol, Bristol, England.*

FORMS 33, 34, AND 35. This test is designed exclusively for use in selective admission to secondary schools in Britain and its distribution is restricted to Directors of Education of Local Education Authorities. Each form is intended to be used as part of a battery, the complementary tests being measures of verbal reasoning and arithmetic. Since forms 33, 34, and 35 are to be used as the terminal tests of a six-year course of primary education, there is also a responsibility for them to produce favourable effects upon primary school syllabuses in the last two years.

The forms under review represent consecutive publications over the years 1961–1963; thus differences in content and presentation may represent progressive adjustments to syllabus. Each form is composed of 120 items grouped according to type of process, there being a cyclical arrangement of groups with progressive increase in difficulty. Throughout, there is a concern for objectivity, only one answer to each question being permissible, and a majority (66 to 75 per cent) of questions demanding selection of response from given alternatives. All three forms have a basically similar pattern; reading comprehension and vocabulary items are dominant features. Language usage, spelling, grammatical control, and punctuation are consistently appearing elements. Form 33 contains five items requiring matching of verse samples and four requiring identification of the style of prose passages which have no parallel in 34 and 35. Form 35 alone tackles the hoary problem of assessing parsing and attempts to avoid reference to formal grammatical categories by asking children to select, from the words in the second sentence of a pair, a word which "does the same work" as the word marked in the first sentence. In most cases this is achieved without ambiguity, but in the first item of the set, the adjective to be matched may be regarded as qualitative and attributive and the answer expected is qualitative and predicative. An alternative choice of answer would be the possessive, attributive adjective, which is not admitted in the scoring key. A similar objection could be lodged against item 94.

Despite occasional items evaluating understanding of metaphor, the emphasis throughout is on word knowledge and verbal reasoning. Since no evidence is presented on construct or content validity, the criteria against which these aspects of the tests are to be judged can only be presumed. It is fair to observe, however, that Moray House maintains a close relationship with the education authorities which cooperate in the standardisation, and receives back data bearing on construction. It may be presumed that care is taken to adjust test content to the syllabuses followed. The way in which such cooperation may act is suggested by the change in treatment of punctuation from form 33 to form 35. Form 33 contains five punctuation items which are the last items of the 120. Under the speeded conditions of testing, it is unlikely that many children will attempt them. In form 34 there is only one punctuation item, the 115th item of the test. This apparent depreciation of punctuation was perhaps unfavourably received, since in form 35 there are five punctuation items in the first quarter of the test.

Administration and scoring of Moray House tests have become standardised over many years and, for British teachers, represent the most familiar system of test handling. Preliminary instructions are read with the children and after testing has begun it is the child's responsibility to interpret the explanations of the various item types. The explanations require considerable reading comprehension in themselves and there is little consistency between forms in supplementing explanations with examples. Answers are often indirect, requiring the number of the correct response to be given, although no penalty is imposed for failure to conform with the required method of recording the answer.

The norms provided are in the form of normalised scores with mean 100 and standard deviation 15, and they incorporate adjustments for each month of age. The standardisation samples are large (between 22,778 and 38,265 children) and have been drawn from education authority areas in such a way as to form representative samples of children of this age in England. Reliabilities calculated by an internal consistency method do not fall below .98 and must be regarded as very high. It would have been helpful to the authorities using the test if standard errors of measurement had been quoted and if these had included the standard error of the age adjustment. Significant sex differences in mean scores in favour of girls are reported for each of the forms but separate norms are not provided.

No evidence of construct, content, or predictive validity is presented. Moray House tests are institutionalised in English education, and there is a temptation to regard this reticence as justified by the long exposure of previous tests in the series to scrupulous examination. However, the limited content of the tests and the restriction of the response by item form casts doubt on the construct and content validity. The independent predictive value of each form within its battery must be limited by its high correlation with the accompanying verbal reasoning test of each series. In each case at least 81 per cent of the variance of the English test is accounted for by verbal reasoning. Even the arithmetic test has over 70 per cent of its variance in common with the English test in each case. There would seem to be a need for more venturesome sampling of English language skills than these forms attempt.

The standard of technical competence in construction represented by the control of mean raw score, by the consistently high standard deviation of raw score, and by high reliability, needs to be matched by an equal concern for the range of functions evaluated. A new form of the *Moray House English Test* appears every year and has its effects upon the primary school English syllabus as well as upon the admission of children to secondary schools. Under these conditions, the responsibility of Moray House is clear; as yet this responsibility does not seem to have been faced with the same readiness to admit change as it has by its competitor, the National Foundation for Educational Research.

ADVANCED FORM 2. This test is designed specifically for use in selecting children for transfer between secondary schools in Great Britain. It is intended to be used in conjunction with a verbal reasoning test and an arithmetic test.

There is little diversity of content and process within the 120 items, which appear to be characterised by a preoccupation with objectivity. Over three quarters of the items require selective responses and no item requires continuous written English. Eighty-one items are devoted to reading comprehension and vocabulary, including 20 in paragraph completion tasks. Spelling and punctuation occupy 17 items; sentence structure and verb forms, 11;

Moray House English Tests

rhymes, 6; and literary knowledge, 6. The heavy weighting in favour of reading and vocabulary skills and the absence of opportunities for the children to use their own words is undoubtedly deliberate. Nevertheless, to teachers of English in secondary schools, the test must seem curiously restricted and biased and even retrogressive in its neglect of fluency and precision of expression.

No account is given of the methods of construction or the principles which guided it. For most users of the test, the reputation of Moray House is sufficient guarantee that care and skill have gone into the preparation, but even the most eminent of test construction agencies has a duty to give to its clients an account of the syllabus considerations that have led to the particular sampling of attainment represented by the test.

Administration and scoring procedures follow a pattern well known to British teachers. No difficulties are likely to arise in applying them. Raw scores are converted to normalised scores with mean 100 and standard deviation 15, with age adjustments at intervals of one month. The normalised scores and age adjustments are based on the performances of a sample of adequate size. However, the sample was drawn from only two education authority areas, two separate year-groups of children in one authority being combined with one from a second area to provide the standardisation data. Both authority areas are small and how representative the sample is of children of this age in England must be questioned. A warning is given in the manual that "norms on an attainment test must always be of a somewhat tentative nature" and that performance "will depend on the school syllabus and on the time devoted in schools to the subject." The manual also warns that the test is difficult and this is borne out in the norms, where mean raw score at median age is given as 44.

Reliability, evaluated by an internal consistency method, is high, but this is not surprising in a test of this length and of such relatively homogeneous content. No evidence of construct, content, or predictive validity is given in the manual and evidence of concomitant variation is restricted to correlations with performances on a verbal reasoning test and an arithmetic test.

Despite all the adverse comments offered above, it must be remembered that this test

follows a pattern well tried in England, and that the impoverishment of content and item form is probably explained by an attempt to assess only elements that can be regarded as common to diverse syllabuses. It is perhaps time that the conventions of the past were reexamined in the light of more recently defined syllabus objectives.

[272]
★Nationwide English Grammar Examination. Grades 4-12; 1959-63; new form issued each April; norms available following the testing program; 1 form ('63, 2 pages); no manual; mimeographed norms ('63, 1 page); no data on reliability; 10¢ per test, postage extra; (40-45) minutes; [Donald R. Honz]; Educational Stimuli. *

[273]
*Novelty Grammar Tests, Second Revision. High school; 1936-61; volume of 74 short-answer tests (1 page each) on specific areas of grammar; 1 form ('61, c1936-61, 170 pages); no data on reliability; no norms; $3 per test booklet (tests may be reproduced without permission), cash orders postpaid; administration time not reported; Clarine Coffin and Frank Connor; J. Weston Walch, Publisher. *

[274]
★The Pribble-Dallmann Diagnostic Tests in Elementary Language Skills. Grades 3-4, 5-6, 7-8; 1948-61; tests for grades 7-8 called *Pribble-Dallmann Diagnostic Tests in Basic English Skills;* 3 levels; all forms and manuals essentially the same as materials copyrighted in 1948-61; reliability data the same as reported in 1948-49; norms the same as those labeled tentative in 1948-49; specimen set not available; postage extra; Evalin Pribble and Martha Dallmann; Lyons & Carnahan. *
a) GRADES 3-4. 1949-61; 5 scores: sentences, punctuation, capitalization, choosing the right words, total; Forms A, B, ('61, 7 pages); manual ['61, 5 pages]; $2.20 per 25 tests; 26(36) minutes for grade 3, 23(33) minutes for grade 4.
b) GRADES 5-6. 1949-61; 6 scores: same as for grades 3-4 plus unnecessary words; Forms A, B, ('61, 8 pages); manual ['61, 5 pages]; $2.20 per 25 tests; 35(45) minutes.
c) GRADES 7-8. 1948-61; 8 scores: sentences, verbs, nouns, pronouns and modifiers, spelling, capitalization, punctuation, total; Forms A, B, ('61, 11 pages); manual ['61, 3 pages]; $3 per 25 tests; 46(51) minutes.

WILLIAM H. LUCIO, *Professor of Education, University of California, Los Angeles, California.*

Each of the three Pribble-Dallmann tests covers a two-grade sequence—3 and 4, 5 and 6, and 7 and 8. There are two forms at each level. The test entry above indicates the subsections and time requirements for the three tests. The test booklets are printed on an acceptable quality of paper with typography appropriately differentiated between the lower and the upper grade tests. Answers to test items are entered in the test booklets. Scores are the number of correct responses. No norms other than medians are provided. The manuals contain relatively clear and simple directions for test administration.

The manuals provide a minimum of information concerning the construction of the tests, the establishment of normative data, and the curriculum validity of the content. With regard to validity, further information concerning the universe of linguistic skills sampled, the explicit curriculum outcomes assessed, the kinds of item analyses performed, and the relationships among the three levels of the test should be provided.

Alternate form reliability coefficients—the decimal points are obviously misplaced—are reported as follows: 98.5 ($n = 26$, grade 4); 94.39 ($n = 27$, grade 6); and 91.6 ($n = 37$, grade 7). Even if the decimals were properly placed, these reliabilities are of little value considering the size and selection of samples and the absence of adequate population description. No information on the reliability of part scores is given—a serious omission in a diagnostic test.

Medians or "norms" are reported for each subsection of the tests by grade level, but no information is provided regarding the determination of these medians. If the medians are based on the same small samples used to calculate the test reliabilities, then little importance can be attached to them. The instructions on the use of the medians do not provide explicit enough directions for analyzing the tests for diagnostic purposes. For example, one section of the grades 7–8 manual states: "A comparison of each pupil's scores with the norms for each part will enable a teacher to discover each pupil's weaknesses in language usage. Such comparisons will materially aid in planning the individual remedial work." However, another section of the manual states: "Finding a pupil's score on a test and comparing it with the median for his grade is, after all, not a very important function of a diagnostic test. More important is the detailed study of a pupil's errors for suggestions in teaching." Users of the tests might be less confused in interpreting these comments if diagnostic indices of performance and explicit information on what is being tested and the significance thereof were presented in the manuals.

Though both forms of all three tests were examined, particular reference will be made to Form A. Most of the comments on Form A are also applicable to Form B. In general, study of the items in the tests revealed shortcomings of both a substantive and mechanical nature.

The test for grades 3–4 appears to test only for certain "common errors" in English usage. As with the other tests in the battery, the ability to understand vocabulary is not tested. The section on sentences contains a total of eight items. To what extent this section tests correct English is debatable. The section on the use of *and* contains no examples of the use of *and* in legitimately joining clauses. The practice examples for the section on punctuation, unlike examples in other sections, do not provide the examinee with the opportunity to demonstrate understanding by means of a written answer; instead, oral instructions and responses are employed. No purpose seems served by deviating from the general pattern of instructions for this particular subtest. The items in the punctuation section require that only one punctuation mark be added to each sentence, with the result that the responses may be too predictable.

The test for grades 5–6 contains a number of questionable items, judged by contemporary test writing standards. The subsection on sentences presents several items in which unrelated ideas are joined by the word *and,* requiring the examinee to determine which part of the total item is a sentence. Several of the sentences which are paired would hardly ever appear in the same paragraph. For children to join such disparate ideas as appear in these sentences by the word *and* would seem unlikely. As in the other tests, punctuation items require only one response to complete the item, so that the presence of one set of marks may signal the need for the other. Several items are unrealistic, e.g., "(Leave, Let) your wraps in the hall." It is doubtful that any child would use *let* in this particular sentence. In some items, keyed for a single correct answer, either choice would be acceptable, e.g., "The (Jones, Joneses) live next door." Some items seem out of place in a particular set.

The test for grades 7–8 reveals shortcomings in item writing similar to those discovered in the other tests. The section on sentences requires the examinee to determine which groups of words make complete sentences. However, of the total of 13 items in this section, at least 5 items lack proper punctuation which, if included, would change the responses entirely. Such items are confusing, since they well could be punctuated as sentences in writing and thus be acceptable. The items in the section on the use of *and, then,* and *so* seem unrealistic. Some of the sentences in this section, even with or without the use of the required insert choice words, would hardly ever follow one another. In the section on nouns several items seem overly simple for the intended grade level. Is it possible that any eighth grade student given the test items "How many (child) are in the group?" and "How many (man) are on the job?" does not know the forms *children* or *men?* The inclusion of non-discriminating items tends to decrease the value of the test.

Overall, these tests cover a small number of pet items and do not cover them economically. Apparently almost no improvement in certain skills, such as punctuation, is expected over the years covered by the tests. Each test involves the same very limited set of situations. Contemporary English language programs appear to be concerned with an order of linguistic skills differing in degree and kind from those which these tests purport to measure. Because these tests do not reflect a precise application of commonly accepted procedures for test development and standardization, lack adequate data on reliability and validity, display a number of shortcomings in item construction, and do not provide specific diagnostic indices for the user, they do not warrant serious consideration for use as diagnostic tests of English skills.

GEORGE D. SPACHE, *Professor of Education, and Head, Reading Laboratory and Clinic, University of Florida, Gainesville, Florida.*

These tests represent an attempt to provide diagnostic information which would lead directly to differentiated instruction in English mechanics. The tests for grades 3–4 and 5–6 are essentially similar in sampling the pupil's sentence sense, and knowledge of capitalization, punctuation, and usage. (The test for grades 5–6 also has a score for "unnecessary words.") That for grades 7–8 includes similar tests plus a brief spelling scale and separate scores for verbs, nouns, and pronouns and modifiers.

The separate tests have a degree of face validity in that they obviously sample the skills

they purport to measure. The question of the adequacy of the sampling of significant skills, or the content validity of the tests, is debatable. The authors suggest that the primary function of each subtest is to indicate the pupil's errors and thus reveal the difficulties that should be given attention in group or individual remedial work. Whether this suggestion can be implemented with the facts supplied by the authors is very doubtful.

No detailed lists of the skills tested in each subtest, nor of those facts which the average pupil should know, are given. The norms simply list the median number of correct answers found in each subtest for groups of what are presumably average pupils. For example, the capitalization test in grades 3–4 includes nine items and samples five types of capitalization. The norms indicate that, on the average, third graders answer three items correctly, while fourth graders achieve five items. There is no indication which three items third graders know, nor which of the five types of capitalization they should know.

Perhaps the authors intend for teachers to assume that the tests sample all significant skills and that remedial instruction should be given to correct any pupil errors. Following this assumption, teachers would provide sufficient instruction on all the types of items in each subtest until the pupils could perform in all types without error. Yet the norms show that such a procedure is impractical and literally impossible, for there is very little gain in the norms for subtest scores from year to year. The tests are also inconsistent in their identification of the fundamental language skills, for the skill of spelling appears only in the test for grades 7–8. Apparently spelling is not a significant language skill prior to this level.

For survey testing, the test-retest reliability coefficients quoted by the authors are certainly adequate. It would have been helpful, both in evaluating the tests and in interpreting class performance, if the authors had supplied some information regarding the size and nature of the normative population, the reliabilities of part scores, and standard errors of measurement for the various scores. Norms expressed in percentiles, stanines, or scaled scores would also have permitted more intelligent interpretation of the scores.

In summary, the tests fail to achieve their primary purpose of supplying diagnostic information to guide instruction by (*a*) not clarifying the true significance of the various skills tested; and (*b*) not indicating the expected performances of pupils in each subskill. At best, the tests can serve only a survey function in sampling pupil progress in the large areas of capitalization, punctuation, and usage.

[275]

★The Pribble-McCrory Diagnostic Tests in Practical English Grammar. Grades 9–10, 11–12; 1942–60; 8 scores: sentences, verbs, pronouns, adjectives and adverbs, nouns, redundancy, punctuation, total; Forms A, B, C, ['60, 8 pages]; 2 levels; manual ['60, 4 pages] for each level; all forms and manuals essentially the same as materials copyrighted in 1942–44; norms and reliability data the same as reported in 1942–44; $2 per 25 tests, postage extra; specimen set not available (sample copy of tests free); Evalin E. Pribble and John R. McCrory; Lyons & Carnahan. *
a) TEST 1. Grades 9–10; 1944–60; 44(49) minutes.
b) TEST 2. Grades 11–13; 1942–60; 45(50) minutes.

CLARENCE DERRICK, *Professor of English, and Chairman, Humanities Department, University of Florida, Gainesville, Florida.*

The title of this "test" raises three questions: Is it a test? Is it diagnostic? Is it concerned with "grammar"? This reviewer's answer to all three of these questions is no.

English teachers have available to them workbooks where the student fills in the blanks. This "test" uses the workbook format as illustrated in the following item: "4. (were, was) I heard that you . . . . . . ill." English tests in usage have a limited function, but even this limited function is further reduced when there is no provision for machine scoring. A good standardized objective test permits an evaluation of an individual's performance in comparison with the performance of a carefully selected and described normative population. This "test" gives only median scores for each of the subtests. What do these median scores mean? The three-page "manual" has this significant comment: "The medians given above are based on reports sent in by schools from widely separated parts of the country." One marvels at the unsophistication and ignorance of a test author who would write such a statement as explanation of normative data and procedures.

A good diagnostic test has parts sufficiently long that the part scores have stability. Test 1 in this series has parts with these numbers of items: 20, **77**, 22, 16, 20, 12, 10. There is no evidence of the reliabilities of any of these parts and it is extremely doubtful that, even if

they had been calculated, the publisher could afford to expose them to the light of day. Most modern English teachers draw a distinction between "grammar" and "usage." Neither in the "test" nor in the "manual" is there evidence of an awareness of this distinction.

Test 1, designed for grades 9 and 10, is similar to, but not identical with, Test 2, designed for grades 11 and 12 and the first year of college. In both forms the subtest "Verbs" has the largest number of items—77 in Test 1 and 68 in Test 2. The medians for Test 1 for the subtest "Verbs" for May testing is 64 in grade 9 and 65 in grade 10. For Form 2, the corresponding medians for grades 11 and 12 are 61 and 61. What do these figures indicate? First, that students in grade 9 do just about as well as those in grade 10 and that students in grade 11 do as well as those in grade 12. Secondly, that these tests are too easy, since the median score for Test 1 is 83 per cent of the total possible score and in Test 2 is 90 per cent of the total possible score.

As classroom exercises these materials would be useful to an English teacher, but to classify them as standardized "tests" is to be guilty of gross mislabeling. The disclaimer in the "manual" that "Comparison of a class or an individual with standards is not an important function of a diagnostic test" cannot be accepted. The *Pribble-McCrory Diagnostic Tests in Practical English Grammar* are not tests, they are not diagnostic, and in many situations they are not practical.

[276]

*The Purdue High School English Test. Grades 9–12; 1931–62; an abbreviated modification of *New Purdue Placement Test in English* (1931–55, see 5:199) which is also available; all items selected from the earlier test; 6 scores: grammar, punctuation, effective expression, vocabulary, spelling, total; IBM and MRC; Forms 1, 2, ('62, 7 pages); manual ('62, 22 pages); separate answer sheets or cards must be used; $4.20 per 35 tests; $2.49 per set of 35 self-marking answer sheets and manual; $3.15 per 100 IBM answer sheets; 42¢ per set of scoring stencils; $2.55 per 100 MRC answer cards (machine scoring service, by Measurement Research Center, Inc., may be arranged through the publisher); 42¢ per manual; 84¢ per specimen set; postage extra; 36(45) minutes; H. H. Remmers, R. D. Franklin, G. S. Wykoff, and J. H. McKee; Houghton Mifflin Co. *

CHARLOTTE CROON DAVIS, *Test Research Service, Bronxville, New York.*

What conclusion does the reader of this review draw from the following observations about this test?

a) Of the 20 items in Part 1 (Grammar), five in each form hinge on using the proper case of pronoun as the object of a preposition; five others in each form on agreement between subject and verb. To mention some of the omissions: no item in either form tests the distinction between *lie* and *lay*, *sit* and *set*, *leave* and *let*, *its* and *it's*, *their* and *they're*, *your* and *you're*, or *between* and *among*; or the common misuse of *real* to modify an adjective or an adverb, of *whom* where *who* is correct, or of an adverb in place of a predicate adjective ("he feels badly"). How *neither* should be construed rates two items in Form 2, but neither form contains an item touching on the singularity of *each* or *every*.

b) Of the 30 items in Part 2 (Punctuation), 12 in Form 1 and 13 in Form 2 concern the semicolon used correctly, or the semicolon used incorrectly, or some other mark used where a semicolon would be correct; only one item in each form deals with the punctuation to be used in a direct quotation; and no item deals with an incorrect use of the colon or of the question mark.

c) Item 4 in Part 4 (Vocabulary) of Form 1 requires the examinee to recognize that *ardent* means *fervent*; item 22 that *fervor* means *ardor*. Items 26 of Form 1 and 24 of Form 2 overlap similarly.

d) Nine of the 90 words covered in Part 5 (Spelling) of Form 1 recur in Form 2. One word, *apparatus*, occurs twice in the same form. One item includes the word *grammer*, despite its appearance, spelled correctly, as the title of a preceding part.

If the reader has concluded that these examples—and more could readily be cited—of duplication of content and inadequacy of coverage indicate that the test authors were careless, he would be mistaken. The manual makes it clear that the items were carefully, systematically chosen. They are the "best two thirds" of those in the corresponding parts of Forms D and E of the *New Purdue Placement Test in English*, published in 1955. "Best" appears to mean those items that turned out to have high discrimination (internal-consistency) indices and be of suitable difficulty when Forms D and E were given to 370 students in grades 9–12, chosen so as to "insure a wide range of knowledge in the areas to be measured by the test." Since the process of item selection also accomplished the equating of Forms 1 and 2 ("items with similar statistics were paired and one item from each pair was assigned to each form"), the authors apparently deemed it wise to let these statistics determine the content. The statistical matching of items to produce parallel forms, however, does not guarantee that raw scores on the forms will exactly correspond. Table 9 in the manual gives a difference of two points in mean total raw score between Forms 1 and 2, which is roughly equivalent to four percentile ranks on the norms tables provided.

Nevertheless, the norms are not differentiated by form, though they are by sex.

These illustrations of what can happen when statistics control item selection are stressed for two reasons: to demonstrate that the results are likely to aid and comfort those who make it their business to carp at objective tests and condemn their use; and to urge test authors to regard difficulty and discrimination indices as two considerations among many, and not as overriding determiners, in assembling tests.

Part 3 (Effective Expression) consists of 20 sentences, each of which is to be marked *r* if it is "clear and effective" or *w* if it is "not clear or if it is not effective." Most of those that are keyed *w* are seriously faulty in structure and consequently test the ability to recognize ineffective expression at a rather low level. These items present no problem to the able examinee; but how is he to mark a sentence that is not wrong, not unclear, but not particularly effective?

Consider this sentence: "The wall paper [*sic*] was of a pattern which was old-fashioned but which still pleased most people." Although purists would object to *which* in the restrictive clauses, there is nothing wrong with the sentence by currently accepted standards; and it is perfectly clear. But would it not be somewhat more effective—that is, less wordy and awkward—if expressed in any one of the following ways? (The reviewer prefers the third version.) (*a*) "The pattern of the wallpaper was old-fashioned but still pleasing to most people." (*b*) "Though old-fashioned, the pattern of the wallpaper pleased most people." (*c*) Most people liked the old-fashioned pattern of the wallpaper."

The truly discerning and critical examinee is likely to regard sentences like this one as ineffective and therefore to miss them, since they are keyed *r*. If he thereby obtains, say, a raw score of 14 instead of 19, his percentile rank on this part will be 72 rather than 99.

The trouble lies in using the right-wrong response dichotomy in this area. The examinee doesn't know among what ways of expressing the idea in a sentence the test author made his judgment. A better technique is to present two or more ways of expressing the idea and to ask the examinee to choose the more (or the most) effective.

The items in Parts 1 and 2, also, would be more direct and searching if the examinee had to *select* the right grammatical form and the right punctuation instead of merely marking each sentence "right" or "wrong" as a whole. The latter procedure is one step further away from what the student does when he is actually writing or speaking. Moreover, it is certain that these sentences are occasionally marked *r* or *w* for completely irrelevant reasons; examinees are sometimes unaware of what point a sentence is intended to test.

Now to call attention to some of the praiseworthy features of the test: the format is clear and pleasing; the time limit fits neatly into the average class period; the self-marking answer sheet is convenient to use and easy to score; the norms are based on a nationwide representative sample of students in a randomly selected group of high schools.

Perhaps more useful than the table of percentages of students in the norms group who responded in various ways to "opinion questions" (presented as evidence of "construct validity"), which occupies two pages in the manual, would be percentile tables for each part *by grade*. It would also be informative to have reliability coefficients based on *single-grade* samples (especially since the group on which the coefficients were computed represents the same nationwide range of ability as the norms group), as well as data supporting the statement that "the test is essentially a power test in that most students will have time to attempt all of the items." This statement appears inconsistent with one made earlier in the manual that "an error of a few seconds in the time allowed may mean a difference of several points in a score," which suggests that some parts, at least, are rather highly speeded for some examinees. Whether most examinees do actually have time to consider (not just hastily guess at) all the items is important; because over half of the items are two-choice, guessing (which the examinees are told to do, if necessary, in order to answer all the items) could play a substantial part in the scores of some examinees.

To sum up: the advantages of this test are convenience and economy in administration, scoring, and interpretation of scores; the faults lie in subject matter coverage, item content, and techniques of testing. Since excellence in the latter areas is basic to the construction of *good* achievement tests and no amount of subsequent statistical manipulation of the items or detailed analyses of the norms group can compensate for lacks in the fundamentals, the reviewer cannot recommend this test. In her opinion, it is inferior—in the ways that matter most—to many of the tests available in this field.

BENJAMIN ROSNER, *Director, Test Development Division, Educational Testing Service, Princeton, New Jersey.*

The *Purdue High School English Test* was designed to provide a less time consuming estimate of a student's knowledge of "good English" than the *New Purdue Placement Test in English* from which it was derived. The briefer version, which can be administered within a single class period, yields five subtest scores (Grammar, Punctuation, Effective Expression, Vocabulary, and Spelling) and a total test score. Total group norms are provided for subtest scores and separate sex and grade norms accompany the total test score. As the normative emphasis implies, total test performance is the more significant index. Overall, the total score yields an acceptable measure of what are essentially the mechanics of English usage confounded by a rather inadequate assessment of effective English expression.

From a test administrator's point of view, the manual is satisfactory. Instructions for administering and scoring are clear, although the organization of the test booklet may interfere with rigorous control over the exposure time of the subtests. Because each subtest occupies a single page, pairs of tests are exposed simultaneously. To avoid double exposure it is necessary for the student to fold back the pages of the test booklet. This procedure, however, is likely to reduce the life span of the booklet. An alternate assembly plan, which should not add significantly to production costs, would be to reverse the printing on successive pages.

Traditionally, the validity of achievement tests is supported by evidence of curricular relevance. Unfortunately no such information is available. Evidence of validity is based largely on correlations between total test score and self-reported grades in school. The reported correlation of .60 with English grades and "usual school grades" may indicate appreciable concurrent validity. On the other hand, correlations of similar magnitude are frequently reported for tests of mental ability generally, and verbal aptitude particularly. The same argument would tend to depreciate the reported contingencies between total test performance and a number of student characteristics. Although the total test score appears correlated—and in the expected direction—with student social class, grade level, curriculum track, career plans, study habits, and sex, similar associations are likely to be found with general measures of scholastic aptitude. The somewhat indirect evidence of concurrent and construct validity would be markedly enhanced by direct testimony of content validity.

Although the reliability of the total test score is acceptable (K-R 21 is .91), the reliabilities of several subtests are markedly inadequate. Particularly deficient is the reliability of Effective Expression. The reported K-R 21 estimates of .49 and .55 for Forms 1 and 2, respectively, suggest the need for major revisions or deletion. Similarly inadequate are the reported reliabilities of approximately .70 and .65 for Grammar and Punctuation. Only Vocabulary and Spelling approach respectability with K-R 21's of approximately .80. Moreover, the probable saturation of the entire test with a speed factor makes even these reliability estimates somewhat spurious. The use of subtest scores for diagnostic purposes is emphatically not recommended.

In part, the inadequate reliabilities of the part scores may be attributed to their minimum length (the subtests contain either 20 or 30 items), and, in part, to their item format. Except for Vocabulary and Spelling, the subtests rely on a "right-wrong" item type. Considering the two choice format and the rather restricted test length, the subtests have a markedly curtailed non-chance score range. Adopting a uniform four-option multiple choice format would probably improve test reliability, even though increasing test length would add to testing time. If the subtest scores were ignored, the present instrument would provide a reasonable assessment of student knowledge of "good English." But if the part scores are regarded as desirable or meaningful components of the test, efforts will have to be made to enhance their reliability.

On a more positive note, the distribution of communities participating in the norming operation seems fairly representative of a nationwide secondary school population. Care seems to have been taken to ensure adequate regional, rural-urban, sex, and grade level representation. Although the norm group seems a bit more representative of the Midwest than other areas of the country, the potential distortion is rather minor and should not interfere with the general utility of the percentile and stanine total score norms. Because of the restricted non-chance ranges of the subtest scores, norms for part scores should probably be ignored. On the grammar test, for example, a chance score of 10 has a percentile rank of 45. A score of 12, still within reasonable chance limits, has a percentile rank of 64. Until the reliabilities of the subtest scores are improved, subtest norms might properly be deleted from the manual. Their presence only serves to encourage unwarranted practice.

In summary, the *Purdue High School English Test* may provide an adequate global assessment of a student's familiarity with conventional English usage. Evidence of content validity would increase its general acceptance, and improvement in subtest reliability would increase its general utility.

For reviews by Gerald V. Lannholm and M. J. Wantman of the earlier test, see 5:199.

[277]
*SRA Achievement Series: Language Arts. Grades 2-4, 4-6, 6-9; 1954-64; subtest of *SRA Achievement Series;* title on tests for grades 2-6 is *How Should We Say This?;* 2 editions; battery teacher's handbook ['64, c1955, 47 pages] for both editions; 50¢ per teacher's handbook; postage extra; Louis P. Thorpe, D. Welty Lefever, and Robert A. Naslund; Science Research Associates, Inc. *
a) FORMS A AND B. Grades 2-4, 4-6, 6-9; 1954-64; 3 scores: capitalization-punctuation, grammatical usage, spelling; IBM for grades 4-9; 3 levels; battery school administrator's manual ('58, c1955-56, 32 pages); battery technical supplement, second edition ('57, 45 pages); battery pupil progress and profile charts ('59, c1955-59, 4 pages); separate answer sheets must be used in grades 4-9; 90¢ per 20 pupil progress and profile charts; 50¢ per school administrator's manual; $1 per technical supplement; $1.50 per specimen set of any one level of the complete battery.
1) *Grades 2-4.* Forms A ('55), B ('57), (14 pages); battery examiner's manual, third edition ('60, c1955-60, 27 pages); $2 per 20 tests; 50¢ per hand scoring stencil; 70(95) minutes in 2 sessions.
2) *Grades 4-6.* IBM; Forms A ('54), B ('56), (16 pages); battery examiner's manual, second edition ('56, c1954-56, revised '60, 39 pages); $2.15 per 20 tests; $5 per 100 IBM scorable answer sheets; $1 per set of machine scoring stencils; 50¢ per hand scoring stencil; 75(90) minutes.
3) *Grades 6-9.* IBM; Forms A ['55], B ('56), (14 pages); battery examiner's manual, second edition ('56, c1955-56, revised '60, 39 pages); $2 per 20 tests; $5 per 100 IBM scorable answer sheets; $1 per set of machine scoring stencils; 50¢ per hand scoring stencil; 60(75) minutes.

b) FORMS C AND D. Grades 2–4; 1955–64; 4 scores: capitalization and punctuation, grammatical usage, spelling, total; Forms C ('55, revised '63), D ('57, revised '63), (18 pages); tests are essentially the same as Forms A and B, published in 1955 and 1957, respectively, except for format; battery examiner's manual ('64, c1955–64, 43 pages) for each form; battery test coordinator's manual ('64, c1961–64, 64 pages); battery pupil progress and profile charts ('64, c1955–64, 4 pages); $2 per 20 tests; 90¢ per 20 pupil progress and profile charts; 50¢ per test coordinator's manual; $2 per specimen set of the complete battery and the complete battery for grades 1–2; 60(85) minutes in 2 sessions.

REFERENCES
1. GROFF, PATRICK J. "Parts of Speech in Standardized English Tests." *Sch R* 69:457–60 w '61. *

MIRIAM M. BRYAN, *Associate Director of Test Development, Educational Testing Service, Princeton, New Jersey.* [Review of Forms A and B.]

These tests were most competently reviewed both as individual tests and as part of the series in *The Fifth Mental Measurements Yearbook* (see 5:200 and 5:21). This review will, therefore, be concerned with the single modification which has been made in the tests since they were reviewed earlier—the addition of a recall-type spelling test to the battery for grades 2–4—and with a few comments regarding content and format not mentioned by previous reviewers.

The spelling test was added to the battery for grades 2–4 to permit the plotting of growth in spelling achievement in all the grades in which it is generally taught. The test was added at the time Form B was developed.

From a list of 100 words assembled from standard word lists for grades 2–4, two 25-word lists of equal difficulty and equal range of difficulty were assembled after pretesting. Grade equivalent and percentile norms were then developed by administering the test system-wide in a single school system in conjunction with the equating of Form B to Form A of the whole battery. The words seem to be quite sensibly chosen. As might be expected, the test is extremely difficult in the first semester of grade 2 and of middle difficulty in the first semester of grade 4.

With regard to the spelling test for grades 4–6, and, to a slightly more limited extent, to the spelling test for grades 6–9, the reviewer has reservations. In these two batteries the spelling items are presented in the context of a continuous narrative, and the pupil is required to indicate the correct spelling by choosing among different spellings presented in multiple choice form. While the presentation of the spelling words in context is to be commended, one wonders whether the use of a narrative of more than 400 words to present a 20-item test in the 4–6 battery is not taxing the time and reading ability of the pupil who has already read through several pages of context in the capitalization-punctuation and grammatical usage sections. Add to the pupil load the fact that limiting the spelling items to 20 results in grade equivalent increases of between one half year and one year and increases of as many as 15 and 20 percentile points for each additional spelling correctly chosen and the evidence is quite convincing that a larger number of spelling words presented in more limited context would be desirable. In the battery for grades 6–9, where 30 spelling words are presented in approximately 350 words of context, the grade equivalent values and percentile ranks are more palatable, but there is still a lot of reading to be done.

In both batteries the work for the pupil would be greatly simplified if in the multiple choices from which he chooses the correct spelling, the word as it appears in the narrative were always in the same position, probably first with the other choices following. As the choices are presented now, the word as it appears in the narrative may be found in any position among the choices.

This same comment applies, by the way, to the arrangement of the choices in the capitalization-punctuation and grammatical usage sections in all the batteries. The reviewer can see no justification for requiring the pupil to hunt for an expression about the correctness of which he has already made his decision in the reading of the context.

The coverage in the capitalization-punctuation and grammatical usage sections of the batteries at all levels is quite complete even though several of the items included in the 2–4 battery seem somewhat sophisticated for pupils of the primary grades. The most serious criticism that the reviewer has of the 2–4 battery is of the lack of precision of the underlining of the items in the narratives. In at least 17 items in the two forms, cutting the underline short where end punctuation is involved results in there being two correct answers that can be claimed by the quibbler, and in one item making the underline too long results in there being no right answer. The lack of precision in underlining is also a problem in the 4–6 and 6–9 batteries, but to a much lesser degree.

In the batteries at all levels there is an occasional inconsistency between the punctuation required in a particular item situation and punctuation used elsewhere in the test. The inconsistencies involve the proper punctuation of nonrestrictive adjective clauses and the separation of an introductory adverbial clause from the rest of the sentence. Yes, even in the 2–4 battery, there is a punctuation item involving an introductory adverbial clause! Among the punctuation items the reviewer would question the validity of items involving the use of the comma before "and" in a series since language experts are not in agreement on this.

The accessory materials supplied with the batteries are quite complete and convenient, both for reference and for use. This reviewer agrees with previous reviewers that the information presented attests to the care with which the tests were constructed and standardized. Just two comments here: In the Pupil Progress and Profile Chart there is some confusion in the use of the word "scores" for "percentile ranks," but the correction of this involves only a minor editorial change. In the Examiner's Manual this reviewer could find no suggestions to either the examiner or the examinees regarding the proper placing and manipulating of the rather complicated answer sheet criticized by a previous reviewer. Such suggestions should be included.

Most of the critical comments of this reviewer are relatively minor when one considers the generally high quality of the tests themselves and the adequacy of the accessory materials insofar as both content and format are concerned. Except for some modification in the presentation of the spelling section in the two higher level batteries, all changes implied by the criticisms could be met with some careful editing when the tests are reprinted. All in all, the reviewer would rank these tests high among existing tests in language arts for the grade levels for which they are designed.

For reviews by Constance M. McCullough and Winifred L. Post of Forms A and B, see 5:200. For reviews of Forms A and B of the complete battery, see 21 and 5:21.

SRA Achievement Series: Language Arts

[278]

*Scholastic Achievement Series: English-Spelling. Grades 2.5–3, 4–6, 7–9; 1954–59; various titles used by publisher; for Catholic schools; subtest of Scholastic Achievement Series; 4 scores: punctuation and capitalization, correct usage, English total, spelling; IBM for grades 4–9; 3 levels; $3 per 20 tests; separate answer sheets may be used in grades 4–9; $1 per 20 IBM scorable answer sheets; 24¢ per scoring stencil; 50¢ per specimen set of any one level; postage extra; (40–50) minutes; Oliver F. Anderhalter, R. Stephen Gawkoski, and John O'Brien; Scholastic Testing Service, Inc. *
a) PRIMARY TEST. Grades 2.5–3; Forms A ('54, identical with English-spelling tests of complete battery copyrighted in 1953), B ('55), (6 pages); battery manual ('59, 12 pages).
b) ELEMENTARY TEST. Grades 4–6; IBM; Forms A ('54), B ('55), (12 pages); battery manual ('58, 21 pages, technical data and norms same as in 1955 manual).
c) ADVANCED TEST. Grades 7–9; IBM; Forms A ('54), B ('55), (13 pages); battery manual ('59, 22 pages, technical data and norms same as in 1955 manual).

REFERENCES

1. GROFF, PATRICK J. "Parts of Speech in Standardized English Tests." Sch R 69:457–60 w '61. *

For reviews by Geraldine Spaulding and Ruth Strickland, see 5:201. For reviews of the complete battery, see 23 and 5:23.

[279]

*Stanford Achievement Test: Spelling and Language Tests. Grades 4–5.5, 5.5–6.9, 7–9; 1941–64, c1940–64; same as spelling and language subtests of Stanford Achievement Test, [1964 Revision]; 2 scores: spelling, language; IBM and MRC; Form W ('64, 8–9 pages); 3 levels; manual ('64, 8 pages) for each level; supplementary directions ['64, 1 page each] for use with IBM answer sheets, Harbor answer cards; separate answer sheets or cards may be used; $1.75 per 35 IBM answer sheets; 40¢ per set of scoring stencils; $4 per 100 sets of Harbor answer cards (machine scoring service, by Measurement Research Center, Inc., may be arranged through the publisher); 40¢ per specimen set of any one level; postage extra; Truman L. Kelley, Richard Madden, Eric F. Gardner, and Herbert C. Rudman; Harcourt, Brace & World, Inc. *
a) INTERMEDIATE 1. Grades 4–5.5; $6 per 35 tests; 56(65) minutes.
b) INTERMEDIATE 2. Grades 5.5–6.9; $6 per 35 tests; 63(70) minutes.
c) ADVANCED. Grades 7–9; $5 per 35 tests; 61(70) minutes.

For a review of the complete battery, see 26; for a review of the 1953 revision, see 5:25; for reviews of earlier editions, see 4:25 and 3:18.

[280]

★Survey of Language Achievement: California Survey Series. Grades 7–9, 9–12; 1959; all items from California Language Test, 1957 Edition; 2 scores: English, spelling; IBM; 2 levels; $2.45 per 35 tests; separate answer sheets may be used; 5¢ per IBM answer sheet; 20¢ per scoring stencil; 10¢ per series class record sheet; 2¢ per series individual

record sheet; postage extra; 50¢ per specimen set of either level, postpaid; Ernest W. Tiegs and Willis W. Clark; California Test Bureau. *
a) JUNIOR HIGH LEVEL. Grades 7–9; Forms 1, 2, (8 pages); no specific manual; combined manual (20 pages) for this test and the junior high levels of tests 638 and 815; 27–28(36) minutes.
b) ADVANCED. Grades 9–12; Forms 1, 2, (9 pages); no specific manual; combined manual (20 pages) for this test, test 591, and the advanced level of test 815; 30–31(36) minutes.

MIRIAM M. BRYAN, *Associate Director of Test Development, Educational Testing Service, Princeton, New Jersey.*

These tests have been adapted from longer tests in the 1957 edition of the *California Achievement Tests,* reviewed both in *The Fifth Mental Measurements Yearbook* and in this Yearbook. Form 1 of each test has been produced from items taken from Forms Y and Z, and Form 2 from items taken from Forms W and X of the parent tests, so that, by proper selection of forms to be used, the shorter survey tests and the longer achievement tests can be administered to the same class without any item duplication.

The survey tests are designed to measure mastery in basic language skills: good English usage; knowledge of tense, person, number, case, and parts of speech; capitalization and punctuation; and spelling. The tests are not recommended for use for diagnostic purposes, such use being reserved for the longer tests.

A manual for each level, designed to accompany the survey tests of reading and arithmetic as well as the tests under review, offers data regarding the reliability and validity of the tests and the equivalence of the two forms; makes suggestions concerning the use of the tests for individual and group appraisal; gives directions for administering and scoring; describes the norms population and the norming procedure; and presents percentile, grade placement, and age norms.

Reliability coefficients, computed by Kuder-Richardson formula 21, are reported for two grades, 8 and 11. These are .95 for English and .90 for spelling for one junior high level form and .88 for English and .74 for spelling for one advanced form. The standard errors of measurement, expressed both in raw score and in grade placement units, are given for the two grades.

The description of the care with which the original selection of items for the parent tests was made and of the procedure which was fol-

lowed for the selection from the larger pool of items for equivalent forms of the shorter tests is impressive. If the parent tests possess high validity, then the shorter tests should also. (Only the English tests, by the way, are presented in a shorter form; the words in the spelling tests have not been changed.) Convincing data are also presented from experimental testing conducted to ensure that the two forms at each level would be equivalent with regard both to item difficulty and item discrimination.

That the standardization samples were rigorously selected with regard to geographical location, size of community, grade assignment, chronological age, and mental age is borne out by the account of the selection of the samples given in the manuals. Each individual tested also took a mental maturity test. Normative data presented in the manual include for each raw score or set of raw scores at each grade level a standard score, a percentile score, a percentile interval, and a grade placement score, all derived from the standardization data, and chronological age equivalents to grade placement scores, derived from an independent survey. At all grade levels the English tests appear to be of somewhat less than middle difficulty; this is not surprising since a large number of the items present two choices only and there is no correction for guessing. The spelling tests are of approximately middle difficulty for the middle grades for which they are intended.

The tests are of the multiple choice type throughout. The grammar and usage section employs discrete two-choice items, and the capitalization and punctuation section presents four-choice items in continuous context. In the spelling test four different words, any one of which may be misspelled, are presented in each item, making a total of 120 words for the student to review.

This reviewer would question the devotion of such a large proportion of the grammar and usage section to rules or familiarity with grammar terminology, especially in the advanced form where 28 out of 44 items are of the latter type. A previous reviewer of the parent tests listed several important elements of language as not being covered—among them the dangling element, the misplaced word, phrase, or clause, the lack of parallel structure, faulty comparisons, illogical metaphors—and as these

Survey of Language Achievement

elements were missing from the parent tests so they are missing from the shorter tests. The usage items dwell heavily on number, tense, and case forms, the choices ranging from the illiterate to the literate without, however, too much opportunity, because of the small number of items of this type, to measure comprehensively the steady progression in language competence that one would expect from grade to grade.

This reviewer would also question the heavy stress on capitalization. While the student is given an opportunity to show his familiarity with most of the basic rules for capitalization, the attempt to offer three incorrect choices with the correct choice in a single line of context pads the section unnecessarily and frequently results in some rather far-fetched options. Here the number of options could be reduced without any compromise to the contribution of the section to total test score.

In spite of these critical comments regarding content, which should really be directed to the parent tests rather than the tests under review, the reviewer is of the opinion that the survey tests have much to offer the English teacher who wants a measure of basic language competence which can be administered conveniently during a single class period and who understands the limitations of tests of this length. The tests compare favorably with other available language achievement tests of the same type with which the reviewer is familiar.

[281]

*Survey Tests of English Usage. Grades 9–13; 1947–49; some forms entitled *Achievement Test of English Usage;* Forms E ('47), H ('48), S ('49), (2 pages, for use at the beginning of either semester); Forms G ('47), N ('48), T ('49), (2 pages, for use during the second semester); Forms J, K, ('49, 2 pages) based on the book *Self-Aid in English Usage;* directions sheet (no date, 2 pages) including 1950 normative data; teacher's remedial sheet ('47, 2 pages); no data on reliability; $2.50 per 100 tests of Forms J or K; 90¢ per 30 tests of other forms; 35¢ per specimen set; postage extra; (35–40) minutes; L. J. O'Rourke; Psychological Institute. *

REFERENCES
1. GROFF, PATRICK J. "Parts of Speech in Standardized English Tests." *Sch R* 69:457–60 w '61. *

HOLLAND ROBERTS, *Director, Academic Freedom Committee, P.O. Box 5503, San Francisco, California.*

The pattern proposed in these English usage tests was established in the 1930's and is familiar to all experienced teachers who began their work a generation ago. At the opening of the school year, or any term, an individual written survey test is given each member of the class and is then followed by a parallel achievement test at the end of the year or semester. Each test of 75 short, generally single sentence unrelated items is divided into three parts: (*a*) Essential Points of Usage, (*b*) Points of Secondary Importance, and (*c*) Finer Points. Each test focuses attention on parts of speech, punctuation, capitalization, and sentence structure. In the opinion of the test builder, "The scores will enable teachers to determine their students' mastery in these classifications."

The approach the tests make to the problems of the English classroom shows unawareness of modern conceptions of language usage and many developments of the last decade in English teaching embodied in the publications of the National Council of Teachers of English. The tests concentrate on the mechanics of language and in so doing place student and teacher in an educational strait jacket that inhibits the free flow of thought and feeling basic to growth and significant communication. As Professor Robert C. Pooley wrote more than thirty years ago in the forward to the second printing of a National Council of Teachers of English monograph, Leonard's *Current English Usage:* [1] "Good usage is that form of speech which is appropriate to the purpose of the speaker, true to the language as it is, and comfortable to the speaker and listener. It is the product of custom, neither cramped by rule, nor freed from all restraint; it is never fixed, but changes with the organic life of the language." These usage tests violate the letter and the spirit of this established view of language usage.

A correlative basic limitation in the tests is the confusion resulting from the identification of usage with the mechanics of language. Mechanics as they are conceived here cease to be a means and become an end. As the philologist, Professor Arthur G. Kennedy of Stanford University, wrote in his monograph, *English Usage,* [2] "usage is the art of speaking

1 LEONARD, STERLING A. *Current English Usage.* National Council of Teachers of English, English Monographs, No. 1. Chicago, Ill.: the Council, 1935. Pp. xxii, 232.
2 KENNEDY, ARTHUR G. *English Usage: A Study in Policy and Procedure.* National Council of Teachers of English, English Monographs, No. 15. New York: D. Appleton-Century Co., 1942. Pp. 166.

and writing....[and] is broader than....grammar ....choice of words....punctuation."

There is nothing in these tests or the classroom drills for which they set the teaching pattern that bears any relationship to anything students think or want to say. That they are instead a Procrustean bed for teacher and students alike, a glance at the accompanying Teachers Remedial Sheet will quickly show. Rule 71 postulates that "The pronoun following *to be* is in the objective case when the infinitive *to be* links the pronoun to a noun or another pronoun in the objective case." It requires ingenuity and a tortuous approach to education to so obfuscate and belabor English usage.

Along with such examples of English jargon, numerous awkward and distorted sentences appear. The following un-English sentence is given as an example in the instructions in Form H of the test and marked "correct": "Carl and she went with us." Students are warned not to rewrite this and similar "models" of English usage.

The failure to grasp the meaning of English usage has led the test builder into other central difficulties. Language usage is a creative art. These are proofreading tests and there is no evidence offered that a high score correlates with ability to use customary usage in letters, reports, or imaginative literature, or in conversations or talks to groups. Even as tests of proofreading ability, they are formal classroom exercises with scant resemblance to life situations outside rigid school doors. If there is even any evidence that scores on these tests correlate positively with student ability to proofread their own writing or recognize usage problems and revise the written work of others in daily life situations, there is no hint of it in the test material.

Reference is made in the descriptive literature accompanying the tests to 1930 and 1947-50 studies from which "A new index of mastery of points of usage in each high school year and in college freshman classes was obtained," but there is no description of these studies or references to authoritative work done in the field of English. There is no support given for the statement, "The items are representative of the common types of errors." Whose errors? In what *social* situations?

Certain assumptions on which the tests are based need examination:

a) It is assumed that there is *one* unchanging standard of correct usage for all occasions. There is no distinction made between formal and informal English nor indication of their changing patterns.

b) The three categories into which each test is divided (Essential Points of Usage, Points of Secondary Importance, and Finer Points) have no scholarly or established educational basis and are purely arbitrary divisions that have no existence outside these tests.

c) Each item in the test is assumed to be of equal value and is given equal weight in arriving at a final score. Consortiums of things like cabbages and kings are added and subtracted, but no rationale is offered to give meaning to the total.

d) It is assumed that 75 items are sufficient to test a student's use of the infinite complexities of the English language.

Teachers and school authorities who wish to strengthen their students in the functional command of the English language will do well to look beyond early conventional tests of this character. Instead they should use the informal tests which emphasize constant varied practice in every day language, formal and informal usage. The first and final tests of language usage are to be found in every day speech and writing in social situations that encourage students to say something that has meaning to them. There are no mechanical shortcuts to testing and teaching the complexities of English usage. The Evaluating Scales developed by the National Council of Teachers of English are the most thoughtful and useful aids.

[282]

★T.C. English Test. Teachers college entrants; 1955-58; most items selected or adapted from *Cooperative English Test: Lower and Higher Levels,* Lower Level Tests A and C1; 5 scores: grammatical usage, spelling, punctuation and capitalization, comprehension, total; 1 form ['56, 6 pages]; mimeographed manual ['58, 6 pages]; no data on reliability; no norms for subscores; distribution restricted to teacher training institutions; separate answer sheets must be used; 6s. per 10 tests; 2s. per 10 answer sheets; 4s. per key; 2s. 6d. per manual; 7s. 6d. per specimen set; postpaid within Australia; 35(40) minutes; Australian Council for Educational Research. *

[283]

Test of English Usage. High school and college; 1950; 4 scores: mechanics of writing, accurate use of words, building sentences and paragraphs, total; IBM; Forms A, B, (9 pages); manual (15 pages); individual diagnostic record (4 pages); $3.50 per 35 tests; separate answer sheets may be used; 9¢ per Scoreze answer sheet; 5¢ per IBM answer sheet;

Test of English Usage

$1.05 per set of machine scoring stencils; 20¢ per hand scoring stencil; postage extra; 50¢ per specimen set, postpaid; 100(110) minutes; Henry D. Rinsland, Raymond W. Pence, Betty S. Beck, and Roland L. Beck; California Test Bureau. *

JOHN C. SHERWOOD, *Professor of English, University of Oregon, Eugene, Oregon.*

It would seem advisable at the very beginning to mention two characteristics of the test which might well be crucial in determining whether it would be suitable for a given testing situation. First of all, it should be understood that the test is regarded by its authors as "primarily diagnostic"; it must serve as a tool of instruction as well as for placement, must detect particular strengths and weaknesses in addition to giving a general rating of the student's competence in "usage." The manual makes specific suggestions for the use of the test in detecting and curing the linguistic maladies both of whole classes and of individual students. The choice of items for testing was determined in part by an actual check of the errors in 3,800 high school English papers. The diagnostic emphasis does not, of course, exclude the use of the test for placement purposes: percentile norms for grades 10–13 are provided, based on a reasonably large sampling from schools and colleges of various types in different parts of the country. The test seems somewhat long (100 minutes) to be used solely for placement; if no use is to be made of individual items for diagnosis, a shorter test, such as the 1960 revision of the Cooperative English expression test, would seem to be equally useful and more economical.

A second distinctive characteristic of the test is that the student is required not merely to recognize correct and incorrect forms, as with some tests, but also to make conscious application of specific rules and to know traditional grammatical terminology. In the punctuation section, for instance, a series of rules is printed, followed by a series of sentences to which the rules might be applicable: the student must match sentence to rule. Likewise in the verb forms section the student must name the form of the verb (past tense, past participle, etc.) to be used, and here the difficulty is increased by the use of terms such as "root infinitive" and "gerundive" (for present participle), a knowledge of which cannot be assumed even among students well grounded in traditional grammar. (It is true that they might

be able to guess the meaning of the terms from the examples given.) Possibly a student ought to be penalized for ignorance of the theory of grammar, regardless of whether he makes mistakes in practice; if so, we should frankly admit what we are doing and not pretend that we are testing skill in writing. Under present conditions, when various competing grammars (traditional, structural, and transformational) are in use, it seems more equitable to avoid as far as possible the use of terminology in testing students from varying backgrounds.

The terminology used suggests a rather conservative attitude toward grammar, an attitude which is also visible in the choice of items, which tend to distinguish between the correct and incorrect, standard and substandard rather than between degrees of rhetorical effectiveness. In this respect the section titles are somewhat deceptive. The section titled "Words in Action" proves to be concerned not with precise diction but with gross errors in such matters as agreement. "Building Sentences and Paragraphs" sounds rhetorical, but even here about half the sentence items involve the avoidance of error rather than the exercise of skill. It is only in the section on paragraphing that we find something which requires an active exercise of taste and judgment.

This rather interesting section is intended to test unity and coherence, the first by requiring the student to arrange specific details under the proper subheadings in a proposed theme, the second by requiring him to put the scrambled sentences of paragraphs back in their logical order. The exercises, especially the second, are rather cleverly done. This section might well be given special weight in selecting students for honors sections, since the rest of the test is largely concerned with mechanical matters which industrious but mediocre students often handle as well as their betters.

If this final section is the most interesting and artful of the exercises, still the general quality of the items seems very satisfactory—providing, of course, that one accepts the conservative views of the authors. Many constructions which have received the blessing of *College English* (not to mention *Webster's Third New International Dictionary!*) will still cost the student points on this test.

To conclude, this would appear to be a good test for certain situations. It is best suited for

Test of English Usage

diagnostic use, or for diagnosis and placement together; for placement alone it seems unnecessarily long. It would presumably work best with students who have had a rather conservative training and might discriminate against others, however competent they might be in actual composition. For testers who understand its character and want what it has to offer, it should give satisfactory service.

For a review by Charlotte Croon Davis, see 4:175.

[284]

★A Test of English Usage [Manasayan]. English-speaking high school and college students and adults; 1963–64; 1 form ('63, 9 pages); mimeographed manual ['64, 12 pages]; no norms (authors recommend use of local norms); separate answer sheets must be used; Rs. 12.50 per 25 tests; Rs. 2.50 per 25 answer sheets; Rs. 0.50 per set of scoring stencils; Rs. 2.50 per manual; postage extra; 35(45) minutes; A. Edwin Harper, Jr., and Rhea S. Das; Manasayan. *

[285]

★Test of Language Skill. Business and industry; 1949–63; 1 form ('49, 5 pages); manual ['63, 6 unnumbered pages]; $3.50 per 25 tests; 10¢ per key; $1 per manual; postage extra; $1 per specimen set, postpaid; 25(30) minutes; Richardson, Bellows, Henry & Co., Inc. *

[286]

Tressler English Minimum Essentials Tests, Revised Edition. Grades 8–12; 1932–56; 8 scores: grammatical correctness, vocabulary, punctuation and capitalization, the sentence and its parts, sentence sense, inflection and accent, spelling, total; IBM; Forms A ('54, 8 pages, identical with test copyrighted in 1941 except for changes in 4 items), AM ('56, 8 pages, machine scorable edition of Form A), B ('41, 8 pages), C ('41, 8 pages); manual ['55, 5 pages, identical with sheet copyrighted in 1941 except for minor changes]; no data on reliability; separate answer sheets must be used with Form AM; $2.90 per 35 tests; 7¢ per IBM answer sheet; 40¢ per machine scoring stencil; 50¢ per specimen set; postage extra; (40–50) minutes; J. C. Tressler; Bobbs-Merrill Co., Inc. *

REFERENCES
1. Groff, Patrick J. "Parts of Speech in Standardized English Tests." *Sch R* 69:457–60 w '61. *

Osmond E. Palmer, *Professor, Office of Evaluation Services, Michigan State University, East Lansing, Michigan.*

The various forms of this test were worked out rather carefully, except that the answer sheet and the scoring stencil for Form AM—even those recently received from the publisher for review—are mislabeled Form A and the keying of Test 3, items 34–35 in AM, disagrees with that of the same items in Form A, Test 3, sentence 9. The forms are fairly comparable, though not exactly so. Subtest 1,

Grammatical Correctness, contains a fairly good range of defensible points to test for, even though it requires the student to choose only between two responses. Subtest 2, Vocabulary, has a wide range of words and is generally well done. So also is subtest 7, Spelling. One would guess that the total score on this test would reflect fairly well students' abilities. But, for the reasons discussed below, the test would not be as useful as others in telling teachers about their students' competence in English essentials.

The data given in the pamphlet Directions for Administering and Scoring are not very adequate. The directions to the student are too brief. He is not warned, for example, that subtest 1 will be scored on the basis of rights minus wrongs. Further, in the spelling subtest of the machine scorable Form AM, the student is told to mark the number of the misspelled word and to spell it correctly in the space provided on the answer sheet. Nowhere, however, in the directions for scoring or on the scoring stencil for this form is there any indication that this part of the test must be hand scored; nor is the scorer told whether he is to give any credit for recognition of the misspelled word if the student does not spell it correctly.

The norms (based on "more than twenty thousand scores") look valid enough, but these are the same norms that were provided in the directions published in 1941. One suspects that, particularly at the upper end, the norms do not reflect too accurately the performance of the current generation of students. Norms are given only by grade and not by sex, but on a test in this area girls regularly perform better than boys. The grade-equivalent scores given for each of the subtests are meaningless because the subtests are short and in some cases ambiguous.

The value of subtest 3, Punctuation and Capitalization, is dubious. In the three hand scored forms, this subtest consists of 10 sentences in which all capitalization and internal and terminal punctuation have been removed. In these forms the student has to insert in the test booklet all necessary capitalization and punctuation, the required number of insertions ranging from 2 to 13 per sentence. He can, however, score only 10 points, one for each sentence which is punctuated exactly as the key demands. There is no ambiguity in the key; nevertheless, a student could make a correct decision in 70 out of 75 cases in Form B and still score very poorly on the subtest. (I had to look very sharply to see whether a final period had been omitted.) Besides this, one can question the significance of asking a student to capitalize George, Chicago, and August; it seems to me that most students by ninth grade capitalize such words automatically. Similarly, one may question the likelihood of error when the terminal punctuation of a sentence is simply a period.

The author seems to have recognized these last two points when he came to make out subtest 3 of Form AM, the machine scorable form. He supplied most of the capitals omitted from Form A and inserted terminal punctuation in all but one of the sentences (8 out of 10) which end in a period. He then put numbers at various points below the sentences to come up with a total of 40 items (compared to the 55 corrections required in the 10 sentences in Form A and the 75 required in Form B). To keep the same number of points for punctuation (10) in all forms of the test, he decided that the score for this section in Form AM would be one fourth of the number of right responses. The validity of requiring students to make several correct judgments in order to earn one point on the hand scored forms is dubious.

Subtests 1–3 and 7 simply require the student to recognize or supply an acceptable grammatical form, mark of punctuation, or correct spelling. The other three subtests, however, expect him to understand grammatical terminology and to apply it. The terminology is not very extensive or complicated, but so few items are involved that one would not be able to be sure whether the student did not have the information asked for or whether he simply did not understand the term involved. Three items ask the student to identify a sentence as simple, complex, or compound. Four ask him to identify the "subject word" and the "verb" in a sentence. In three others he is asked to supply the correct form of a verb, such as, "past perfect active of *bite,*" "past passive of *tear.*"

More indefensible yet are the four items in each form devoted to pronunciation. Not only is this an inadequate sample and its relationship to minimum essentials dubious, but in most cases the words chosen are those with an unusual, and consequently ambiguous, accent.

For three of the four words in Form C— "orchestra," "municipal," and "hospitable"— *Webster's Third New International Dictionary* shows two more or less acceptable pronunciations. One may quarrel with Merriam-Webster, but their book is recent and their pronunciations are based upon transcripts of the current speech practices of educated people.

There are also a few items in each form which are not well done. One would prefer another synonym for "frankly" than "freely" (Form A), and something other than "mistaken" for "fallacious" (Form C). One can also object to the range of style in the tests. Some sentences, taken, apparently, from student papers, are barely acceptable; others are highly literary and formal. The range is from extremely colloquial sentences (for examples, "The boy who was called on to recite said that uriah's hair which was red was cropped close to his head" in Form A, "In reply to your advertisement in the Sunday *Journal* for a nurse with hospital training I am applying for the place" in Form C, and "Lord Bridgewater's family took part in the play his sister taking the part of a lady" in Form C) to extremely literary ones (for examples, "Of thy unspoken word thou art master; thy spoken word is master of thee" in Form B and "The applause of listening senates to command.... [and three more lines of suspension before the main part of the sentence] Their lot forbade" in Form C).

This test would not do as good a job for the teacher as the SRA *Writing Skills Test,* which is much more recent, has, consequently, more meaningful norms, covers much of the same ground, and is not open to the objections raised against various parts of this test.

ROGER A. RICHARDS, *Assistant Professor of English, Jersey City State College, Jersey City, New Jersey.*

Among many English teachers, the name of Tressler is nearly a charmed word. Even those who are not enthusiasts of the Tressler series of textbooks regard the author with respect. It is to be hoped that the confidence inspired by the Tressler name will not be automatically transferred to this test. There is no reason to believe that the tests are in any way correlated, in content or in quality, with the textbook series.

Despite the changes in the teaching of English over the past quarter century, the tests currently marketed are substantially the same as those produced in 1941. The only real revision, in fact, involved the adaptation of Form A to machine scorable format. In the testing of capitalization and punctuation, the modification increased validity, though in other sections the new (1956) Form AM appears less valid than its counterpart of the old fashioned variety.

It is almost a mistake to consider these as standardized tests; they might more accurately be regarded as simply printed exercises available nationally. Instructions for administration are indefinite, the following excerpt being typical: "Give every pupil time to complete the tests. If necessary, hurry along the especially slow ones."

There is no information concerning reliability or validity, nor does the author state what the purposes of the test are. Although there is a table of norms, these appear not to be very trustworthy. On Test 1, for example, a chance score (10 right out of 20 items) corresponds to a grade placement of 10.9. An eighth grader on a lucky day might very possibly earn a grade equivalent of 11.7 on this section even if he couldn't read English.

The content of the tests is not good enough to make one want to overlook the deficiencies of standardization. Sampling of the various skills and content areas covered by the test is so meager as to make the subscores meaningless. In many places the items are ambiguous. Consider, for example, the test on "Punctuation and Capitalization" in Forms A, B, and C, in which the student is told, "Do not divide one good sentence into two sentences." There is room for much legitimate debate over what constitutes a "good sentence," especially among students who understand how to use a semicolon. The same difficulty arises in Test 5, "Sentence Sense," in which the student must indicate "the number of complete sentences in each of the following." Moreover, the lack of context makes a few items unanswerable, notably those involving decisions concerning restrictive or non-restrictive clauses.

In short, one wonders how these tests could ever have been of substantial value. If they were, they long ago ceased to be. They should, therefore, be replaced by materials which are more sophisticated in measurement technique and which are in content more compatible with modern thinking concerning the nature of language and the determination of acceptable usage.

[Other Tests]

For tests not listed above, see the following entries in *Tests in Print*: 398, 403–4, 407–8, 410–1, 417–9, 420a, 421–2, 425–8, 432–3, 435–6, 440, 442, 444–6, 448, 455, 457, 459, 461–4, 467–8, 471–2, 475, 477, and 479–80; out of print: 399, 412, 415–6, 420, 430, 439, 441, 443, and 452–4.

COMPOSITION

[287]

*College Entrance Examination Board Achievement Test: English Composition. Candidates for college entrance; 1943–64; for more complete information, see 760; 60(80) minutes; program administered for the College Entrance Examination Board by Educational Testing Service. *

REFERENCES

1–6. See 4:178.
7–20. See 5:204.
21. BLACK, D. B. "A Comparison of the Performance on Selected Standardized Tests to That on the Alberta Grade XII Departmental Examination of a Select Group of University of Alberta Freshmen." *Alberta J Ed Res* 5:180–90 S '59. * (PA 34:6559)
22. PALMER, ORVILLE. "Sense or Nonsense? The Objective Testing of English Composition." *Engl J* 50:314–20 My '61. *
23. FARMER, PAUL. "Literature, Reading, and the College Board Exams." *Engl J* 51:9–13 Ja '62. *
24. FRENCH, JOHN W. "The Creativity Dimension in Student Writing." *West Reg Conf Testing Probl* 11:45–57 ['62]. *
25. *Manual of Freshman Class Profiles, 1963 Edition.* Princeton, N.J.: College Entrance Examination Board, 1963. Pp. 642. *
26. NOYES, EDWARD S. "Essay and Objective Tests in English." *Col Board R* 49:7–11 w '63. *

CHARLOTTE CROON DAVIS, *Test Research Service, Bronxville, New York.* [Review of Forms FBE1, KBE, and KBO3.]

Each of the forms sent for review consists of three parts, or subtests. In one form (KBE), internal time limits are enforced; in the other two forms, the amount of time to be spent on each part is merely suggested. The nine subtests represented by these three forms include seven different types of exercise, as follows: (*a*) recognizing which underlined part of a sentence, if any, contains an error in usage; (*b*) recognizing both the existence of an error and, if it exists, the best way to correct it; (*c*) recognizing whether a sentence is erroneous and, if so, identifying the error as poor diction, wordiness, use of clichés, or faulty grammar; (*d*) recognizing which one of four lines appropriately completes a stanza of poetry and deciding in what way each of the other three lines is inappropriate—whether in meaning, rhythm, or style; (*e*) rephrasing a sentence to accord with a given change in its structure (although in format this is a recognition exercise—and therefore objectively scorable—the examinee has actually to reconstruct the sentence in his mind); (*f*) arranging the sentences of a paragraph in logical order; and (*g*) correcting a badly written theme by adding or omitting words, shifting their position, or by rewriting whole phrases, clauses, or sentences.

Exercise type *g,* called the "interlinear," comes fairly close to free writing and is not objectively scorable. The CEEB examiners in English, all of whom have served as readers of the interlinear, are "convinced of its value" but concerned about its scoring cost. To find out how it compares with the objective types of exercise listed above as a measure of writing skill, the CEEB has conducted an interesting and important study.[1] Each of the (nearly) 650 participating students wrote five essays on assigned topics, each of which was rated by five different readers; the sum of these 25 ratings (by 25 different readers) became the criterion score, which appears to be about as pure a measure of writing ability as can be secured in an experimental setup and which turned out to have the high reliability coefficient of .92. This type of criterion, though troublesome and expensive to obtain, is certainly much better than the often used one of grades in English composition courses, which are influenced by many extraneous factors.

The correlations between the eight subtests (there were two interlinears—one dealing with a narrative, the other with exposition) and the criterion ranged from .71 (for type *a*) to .46 (type *f*); the interlinear coefficients were .67 and .64. When various combinations of three subtests were correlated with the criterion, the coefficients ranged from .78 to .72. The highest ones occurred when the combination included an interlinear, but the differences among the correlations, though statistically significant, are so small that whether this exercise is worth its extra cost is still debatable. (In the reviewer's opinion, another factor to be considered is the time required for each type of exercise; 30 minutes is allotted to, or suggested for, the interlinear whereas the examinee is expected

to do each of the objective subtests in 15 or 20 minutes. Perhaps some combination of *four* 15-minute objective subtests would predict the criterion better than any combination of *three* tests. The question of predictive efficiency per unit of time is not discussed in either of the brief preliminary reports of the study available to the reviewer.)

On the basis of this evidence, Edward S. Noyes, a CEEB vice-president and in years past a skeptical and severe critic of attempts to measure writing ability objectively,[2] concluded that "it seems impossible to justify any longer the criticism that the ECT—*whether it consists of objective items only* or includes an interlinear exercise—is not a sound measurement of the ability to write" [reviewer's italics].

After systematic inspection of the objective subtests included in these forms, the reviewer believes that their substantial correlations with the criterion are due partly to their high quality. The various testing techniques are well worked out and, with the possible exception of type *d,* suited to their purpose; some show ingenuity and originality. The range of usage errors covered is wide and the selection sensible. On the whole, the items seem natural and uncontrived (though doubtless they are not); many are thought provoking and even searching. In only a very few cases did the reviewer wonder what an item was driving at or think that an unkeyed response might be defensible. One minor objection is to penalizing the student who has been taught—perhaps by an old-fashioned, finicky parent (like the reviewer)—to prefer *that* to *which* in a restrictive clause. It would be better not to raise this issue at all.

The descriptive booklet furnished to prospective examinees is excellent. The instructions regarding whether and when to guess are explicit and fair, and the fact that the objective subtests are scored with a correction for chance success[3] should reduce the influence of certain personality factors and a certain kind of coaching. The illustrative ECT items in the booklet are well chosen, and enough of

1 Type *d* was not included in the study; instead an analogous prose exercise was used in which the examinee recognizes which one of four sentences appropriately completes a paragraph and classifies each of the other three sentences as lacking in sense, improper in tone or diction, or grammatically faulty. The latter exercise has more face validity since most students will need to express themselves far more often in prose than in verse. Type *d* seems more appropriate to a test of literary comprehension or appreciation.

2 In an earlier MMY (3:120), Noyes said that " 'effectiveness of expression'....can only be discovered by giving the student a blank page and a pencil and setting him to write." 3 The need for this correction is shown by the fact that only 44 per cent of the students who took Form KBO3 in May 1962 finished the third subtest. Obviously this form at least (percentages finishing were not given for the other forms) is speeded for most examinees.

them are unkeyed to provide a bona fide work sample. A key to these items is supplied at the end of the section on the ECT so that the student can score his responses, perhaps discover the source of any mistakes, and, most important, make sure that he understands exactly what he is to do in each type of exercise. Counselors and teachers should insist that all students who are to take the ECT follow this procedure since the examinee who is unacquainted with the various exercises may be handicapped.

Although the writer does not recall the specific content of the ECT forms reviewed in a previous MMY (4:178), it is her considered opinion that certain of the testing techniques in the present forms, the instructions about guessing, and the method of scoring the objective subtests are significantly better than those used by the CEEB thirteen years ago.

ROBERT C. POOLEY, *Professor of English, University of Wisconsin, Madison, Wisconsin.* [Review of Forms FBE1 and KBE.]

This test, designed to measure indirectly writing ability, is to be administered in 60 minutes. Two parts of each form are objective, with multiple choice answers recorded on an answer sheet for machine scoring. The third part is a free response exercise answered by interlinear changes and corrections on the test booklet.

FORM FBE1. Section 1 is designed to measure objectively the ability to organize written paragraphs and a poem. The student reads a paragraph as separate sentences out of order. He then indicates his rearrangement of the material by responding to such questions as "Which sentence did you put first?" and "Which sentence did you put after (a)?" In the poem the stanzas are disarranged units. There are four of these exercises.

Section 2 measures taste and sensitivity. The materials offered deal with figurative language, meaning, and tone in prose and poetry, and also rhythm in poetry. The student responds by using a four-letter key to indicate whether he considers each of four suggested completions for a missing line in a poem: appropriate, inappropriate in rhythm or meter, inappropriate in style or tone, or inappropriate in meaning. There are four of these exercises.

Section 3, the free response section, presents a poorly written passage to be revised. The student is instructed to locate anything he thinks defective and correct it, by changing the position of words, adding or deleting words, or rewriting whole clauses or sentences. He is cautioned not to attempt to rewrite the entire piece. Ordinary correction procedures are sanctioned as in marking proof. The authorized changes are furnished in an answer key which the examiner compares with the students' markings. Provision is made for alternate acceptable changes. This exercise presents about 50 items for correction, including punctuation, capitalization, word choice, word order, numbers agreement, and tense agreement.

This test is notable for its omission of the oft-repeated usage items: no "who-whom" situations, no "reason is....because," no "everybody brought their books." It is indeed gratifying to note that composition ability can be measured without resort to these chestnuts. Confusions of number and tense and other problems of concord are dealt with in Part 3.

FORM KBE. Closely parallel to Form FBE1, this test is printed in two separate booklets to permit the interlinear exercise to be scored separately from the machine scored portion. In this form Section 1 is the interlinear exercise, clearly printed and widely spaced for effective correction. The text of the exercise contains infelicities and awkwardnesses of expression, together with specific faults of number of agreement, tense sequence, and mechanics. This is a proofreading exercise at its best, affording every opportunity to the student to reveal his sensitivity to concord and apt phrasing. Thirty minutes' time is allowed.

Section 2 comprises sentences with underlined lettered words and phrases some of which present errors in word choice, usage, grammar, and idiom. Some of the underlined items are correct. The student marks a separate answer sheet to indicate his judgment on each sentence. This section contains such usage items as "couldn't hardly," "who-whom," "lay-laid," "one" followed by "they," "our," etc., "data were," and many others. There are 30 of these sentences to be dealt with in 15 minutes.

Section 3 contains 60 sentences representing examples of poor diction, verbosity and redundancy, clichés and abused metaphors, and faulty grammar and sentence structure. Not more than one such error occurs in a sentence, and some are without error. The student uses a key to indicate which, if any, of these errors is present in each sentence. Fifteen minutes' time is allowed.

While the interlinear portion of this form is very good indeed, the two following sections are weak in presenting too much of the same thing in both parts, and in relying too heavily upon infelicities of usage.

CONCLUSION. One may ask, "this is all very interesting, but does the test measure the ability to write expository prose?" Can a test that requires no writing measure the ability to write? The answer, based upon an exhaustive study recently completed (26), seems a convincing affirmative. Six hundred and fifty students from eleventh and twelfth grades of 24 different schools each wrote five essays, each of which was read and evaluated by five trained readers. The total of the five readers' ratings of the five essays was used as the criterion of writing ability. Each of the students also took eight subtests (two interlinear exercises and eight objective sections) from forms of the ECT. The correlations between theme ratings and various combinations of the subtests are high ranging from .72 to .78. It appears that the ECT measures quality of writing at least as well as five readers of five compositions by the same subject; since most themes are read by one reader only, it may be assumed that the reliability of ECT is greater than the reliability of any one reader.

The great advance of Form FBE1 over previous tests is its avoidance of details of usage and its emphasis upon organization of thought and the felicitous flow of good prose. Evidence is not available as to which of these forms is more highly predictive of success in college composition, but intuition at least would favor the form which seems to strike closer to the foundations of good writing. Sensitivity to usage is undoubtedly a factor in the prediction of writing success, but it should not become, as it does in Form KBE, the principal criterion. Form FBE1 might be improved by a little more attention to the more subtle ·aspects of usage. Form KBE could profit from the addition of tests of organization and the flow of prose.

HOLLAND ROBERTS, *Director, Academic Freedom Committee, P.O. Box 5503, San Francisco, California.* [Review of Forms FBE1, KBE, and KBO3.]

The rapid nationwide increase in the use of the College Board entrance examinations centers attention on the English composition test. It is administered to at least 70 per cent more students than the number taking any of the 14 other CEEB achievement tests. Like the others, it is "developed to reflect, as far as possible, what is being taught in secondary schools, and at the same time, to show whether students are prepared for the work they will be expected to do as freshmen in college." Within this broad area the ECT is specifically designed "to measure, however indirectly, only the ability to write" (26). The testmakers assert, "it is abundantly clear that, although the English Composition Test is not a direct measure of writing ability, it does measure the underlying abilities which are necessary to good writing * correctness and effectiveness of expression, organizational ability, and taste and sensitivity in the use of language." The time allowed to reach these sweeping objectives is one hour and the instrument generally has been an objective multiple choice group test which includes six types of items: (*a*) sentence structure correction; (*b*) recognition of faulty usage—grammar, diction, and minimal attention to basic structure and mechanics; (*c*) correcting sentence errors such as mistakes in grammar, diction, verbosity, clichés, and bad metaphors; (*d*) reorganizing sentences in a scrambled paragraph; (*e*) filling in a missing sentence in a paragraph from four choices in which the selection tests the student's knowledge of grammar, diction, construction, and good sense; and (*f*) shifting the parts of a sentence to improve construction.

Form KBO3 is made up of 100 items based in the main upon the correction and rephrasing of single sentences or the rearrangement of scrambled paragraphs. Form FBE1 offers 41 scrambled sentences and poetry completion items and a purposely poorly written brief prose passage to be revised; the 1962 Form KBE consists of a 275–300 word prose passage arranged for interlinear correction and 60 objective items. Maximum time allowed for consideration of the 60 individual items averages one half minute. The basic assumption appears to be that ability in English composition can be measured by testing the mechanics of writing.

How well do these composition tests accomplish their purpose? Can they predict academic success in college? Speaking of all tests in the Admissions Testing Program, the testmakers indicate that the findings of studies provide evidence that a combination of the test scores with high school records will "provide greater accuracy of prediction of college grades than is provided by high school records alone." However, "the College Board recommends that colleges planning to require the tests for admission conduct validity studies designed to evaluate the efficacy of the tests for their own local groups and conditions." For the composition test a Kuder-Richardson formula 20 reliability of .85 and a standard error of measurement of 39 is reported, indicating satisfactory discrimination among the members of the test group.

But do these hour long tests measure writing ability? Here the question is still moot. It is difficult to say what the tests measure. The publishers have given no definition of this complex of thought and personal and social action called "writing ability," nor of the underlying abilities they state the test measures: "correctness and effectiveness of expression, organizational ability, and taste and sensitivity in the use of the language." They report that in their search for a "pure" criterion they studied eleventh and twelfth grade students in 24 varied College Board secondary schools from all major geographic regions. They asked each student to write five essays on five given topics, two of 40 minutes with an expository-argumentative topic and three of 20 minutes each—one expository, one descriptive, and one narrative. When the research workers found agreement among the essay readers on each piece of student writing and a positive correlation between the scores on each subtest and the total essay scores, they concluded that "the ECT objective items do an amazingly effective job of ranking students' writing ability in the same way that a trained group of readers would rank them on a sizeable sample of their actual writing."

Can we now conclude with the *College Board Review* (26) that the test is a sound measure of the ability to write? However interesting and useful these studies may be, they have not yet grappled with the problem outside the limited bounds of the restricted schoolroom situation in which students are working against the pressure of time on set imposed topics. For those teachers who think that writing ability is the capacity to communicate in a normal life situation, convincing evidence on the value of what these tests measure is not yet in. To evaluate a piece of writing we need to know to whom it was addressed, why it was created, and under what conditions. What purpose did it serve for writer and recipient? If a high school student has nothing he wants to say on a topic imposed on him, can we then judge his ability to write by what he produces in brief, rigid periods under compulsion? Writing worth reading comes out of a person who has something he wants to communicate. The conditions set up should help him do it.

The College Board's Committee on Examinations apparently is concerned to overcome weaknesses in these objective, machine scored composition tests, as it has now authorized the examiners in English to use a theme as one of the subtests. This is an important step toward reality and away from the pedagogical stereotype that fritters away millions of valuable student hours by concentrating as these tests have upon form and skill to the exclusion of content. Perhaps the next move will be to insure that the writing is communication under normal life conditions.

This key question of subject matter applies to all sections of the tests in their present form—to both the single sentence items and the paragraphs and verses to which the student is asked to respond. From the fragments of which the test sentences, paragraphs, and verses are made, a student cannot know much about what the authors wanted to say. The first part of many of the test items is a puzzle in guessing at the meaning. When the student is formulating or revising his own written work he *knows* what he wants to say. That is the test of sanity and a basic principle in composition teaching which many testmakers, and some teachers, have yet to bring into their work. Form and content are a unity in viable composition as in all rational thought and daily activity. There can be no divorcement. The danger in using tests such as these is that teachers will organize the work of the English classroom so that their students can pass them and so distort the curriculum.

In the 1962 Guide for Admissions Officers, the College Board, in commenting on the error of measurement, recognizes two other omnipresent test problems: "All tests are limited by the number of questions they can ask and the time available to answer them. Thus, even the best test can do no more than provide an incomplete sampling of the student's capabilities. It follows that a series of tests, even if made as comparable as possible and taken by the same student, will yield varying scores." Further, the *College Board Review* (*26*) cautions that "there will always be students whose performances in class belie their test scores." It is useful to keep these balanced statements in mind in using tests and in working on the improvement of composition tests in English in the days ahead.

For a review by Charlotte Croon Davis of earlier forms, see 4:178. For reviews of the testing program, see 760.

[288]
★College Entrance Examination Board Placement Tests: English Composition Test. Entering college freshmen; 1962–63, c1958–63; tests are reprints of inactive forms of *College Entrance Examination Board Achievement Test: English Composition;* IBM; Forms KPL1, KPL2, in a single booklet (c1958–62, 30 pages); for more complete information, see 759; 60(70) minutes; program administered for the College Entrance Examination Board by Educational Testing Service. *

For reviews of the College Entrance Examination Board Achievement Test: English Composition, *see 287 and 4:178.*

[289]
★College Entrance Examination Board Writing Sample. Candidates for college entrance; 1960–63; tests are not scored but are sent ungraded to the student's secondary school and 1–3 colleges or scholarship programs designated at time of application; for more complete information, see 760; 60(75) minutes; program administered for the College Entrance Examination Board by Educational Testing Service. *

REFERENCES
1. BLAU, HAROLD. *How to Write the College Entrance Examination "Writing Sample."* Philadelphia, Pa.: Chilton Co., 1961. Pp. xi, 100. *
2. VALENTINE, JOHN A. "The First Year of the Writing Sample." *Col Board R* 46:22–6 w '62. *

ROBERT C. POOLEY, *Professor of English, University of Wisconsin, Madison, Wisconsin.* [Review of Forms KWS3 and LWS1 through LWS6.]

This test, designed to be used alone or to supplement the *College Entrance Examination Board Achievement Test: English Composition,* is on one sheet printed on both sides. The face contains the instructions, including information to the student that he is writing an original and four carbons at the same time. Fifteen minutes time is allowed to read the

instructions, to supply necessary information on the forms, and to plan the essay. When the supervisor gives the instruction *Begin Work* the student has a full hour for the writing and correcting of his essay.

The reverse of the sheet is labeled "Assignment Sheet" and contains a brief statement or quotation, ranging from two to nine lines in length, which the student is to use for his subject. He is asked to write a well planned essay of from 300 to 500 words, arranged into several paragraphs. When the essay is completed, the student is instructed to underline the sentence which he thinks comes closest to summarizing his central idea.

The Writing Sample is not scored by the CEEB but only by the institution receiving it. Although it is not a standardized test, it is in wide use, 126,280 students having written Samples in 1961–1962. The reasons given for its use are (*a*) to provide samples of a student's writing under controlled conditions, and (*b*) to emphasize the significance of written compositions to encourage schools to lay more stress on writing. There is no evidence to date concerning the effectiveness of this second reason.

Most schools using the Writing Sample employ it as a supplement to the English composition test (ECT). The topics for writing were chosen by a panel of college English teachers, who sponsored a trial run of 10 topics. From this trial run the best four were chosen for the four different forms of the Writing Sample in its first year of use. The results of the trial run have set criteria for the continuing selection of topics.

For so subjective a test the evaluation must necessarily be subjective. To begin with, the device of a quotation is probably as fair and challenging a motivation of writing as any can be. While the difficulty of the quotation itself may vary from year to year, as indeed it does vary in length, every student who writes from a certain quotation is compared only with other students using the same stimulus, and furthermore is judged only in his own institution by the same judges. Judges may be influenced by memories of previous years to consider one set of papers superior to another, but the relative standing of any particular student in any one year is not jeopardized. The quotation as the source of an essay is obviously superior in fairness to any list of specific subjects, no matter how wisely chosen. It is inconceivable that a national test of essay writing could be based on one specific subject only.

In a broader sense, the true evaluation of the Writing Sample lies in the demand for it. All present evidence points to it as currently filling a need or meeting an objective of value to admissions officers and committees. If the opinion often expressed is true, that a person writes from what he is as a result of the totality of his experience, then the composition written as an honest reaction to a thought provoking quotation comes as close as anything can to revealing the kind of person who is applying for admission to the college. The wide use of the Writing Sample would seem to be evidence that many college officials believe that the free essay reveals information of value in the appraisal of applicants beyond what objective tests can furnish. While this belief has not yet been incontrovertibly established, it appears valid enough to justify the expenditure of money and professional time in acting on it. As a device for securing non-objective data about college entrance candidates, the Writing Sample is convenient, efficient, and apparently rewarding.

For reviews of the testing program, see 760.

[290]

★**Nationwide English Composition Examination.** Grades 4-12; 1959-63; new form issued each April; norms available following the testing program; 1 form ('63, 2 pages); no manual; mimeographed norms ('63, 1 page); no data on reliability; 10¢ per test, postage extra; (40-45) minutes; [Donald R. Honz]; Educational Stimuli. *

[291]

*****Sequential Tests of Educational Progress: Essay Test.** Grades 4-6, 7-9, 10-12, 13-14; 1957-62; Forms A, B, C, D, ('57, 7 pages); 4 levels; handbook ('57, 34 pages) for each level; battery technical report ('57, 58 pages); 1958 SCAT-STEP supplement ('58, 32 pages); 1962 SCAT-STEP supplement ('62, 49 pages); battery profile ('57, 1 page); battery student report ('58, 4 pages); $1 per 20 tests; 50¢ per 20 profiles; 50¢ per 20 student reports; $1 per handbook; $1 per technical report and supplement; postage extra; $1.25 per specimen set (includes sample handbook but not technical report; $1 per supplement); cash orders postpaid; 35(40) minutes; Cooperative Test Division. *

a) LEVEL 4. Grades 4-6; Forms 4A, 4B, 4C, 4D.
b) LEVEL 3. Grades 7-9; Forms 3A, 3B, 3C, 3D.
c) LEVEL 2. Grades 10-12; Forms 2A, 2B, 2C, 2D.
d) LEVEL 1. Grades 13-14; Forms 1A, 1B, 1C, 1D.

REFERENCES

1. BLACK, DONALD B. "A Note on the Use in Alberta of the Sequential Tests of Educational Progress: Essay Test." *Alberta J Ed Res* 4:172-80 S '58. *
2. ANDERSON, C. C. "The New Step Essay Test as a

Measure of Composition Ability." *Ed & Psychol Meas* 20:95-102 sp '60. * (*PA* 34:8329)
3. FINDLEY, WARREN G. "Improvement of Writing Ability in the Elementary Grades." *Yearb Nat Council Meas Ed* 20:149-52 '63. * (*PA* 38:9260)

For reviews by John S. Diekhoff, John M. Stalnaker, and Louis C. Zahner, see 5:206. For reviews of the complete battery, see 25 and 5:24.

[292]

*****Sequential Tests of Educational Progress: Writing.** Grades 4-6, 7-9, 10-12, 13-14; 1956-63; IBM and Grade-O-Mat; Forms A, B, ('57, c1956-57, 11-20 pages); 4 levels; battery directions ('57, 12 pages); interpretive manual ('57, 32 pages); battery technical report ('57, 58 pages); 1958 SCAT-STEP supplement ('58, 32 pages); 1962 SCAT-STEP supplement ('62, 49 pages); 1963 SCAT-STEP supplement of urban norms ('63, 16 pages); battery teacher's guide ('59, 85 pages); battery profile ('57, 1 page); battery student report ('58, 4 pages); no data on reliability of Form B; separate answer sheets must be used; $4 per 20 tests; $1 per 20 IBM scorable answer sheets; 25¢ per scoring stencil; see 666 for prices of Grade-O-Mat cards; $1 per 20 profiles; $1 per 20 student reports; $1 per interpretive manual; $1 per technical report; $1 per supplement; $1 per teacher's guide; postage extra; $2 per specimen set, cash orders postpaid; 70(90-100) minutes; Cooperative Test Division. *

a) LEVEL 4. Grades 4-6; Forms 4A, 4B.
b) LEVEL 3. Grades 7-9; Forms 3A, 3B.
c) LEVEL 2. Grades 10-12; Forms 2A, 2B.
d) LEVEL 1. Grades 12-13; Forms 1A, 1B.

REFERENCES

1. GROFF, PATRICK J. "Parts of Speech in Standardized English Tests." *Sch R* 69:457-60 w '61. *
2. ENDLER, NORMAN S., AND STEINBERG, DANNY. "Prediction of Academic Achievement at the University Level." *Personnel & Guid J* 41:694-9 Ap '63. * (*PA* 39:2888)
3. MICHAEL, WILLIAM B.; CATHCART, ROBERT; ZIMMERMAN, WAYNE S.; AND MILFS, MILO. "Gains in Various Measures of Communication Skills Relative to Three Curricular Patterns in College." *Ed & Psychol Meas* 23:365-74 su '63. * (*PA* 38:1384)

HILLEL BLACK, *Senior Editor, Saturday Evening Post, New York, New York.*

To anyone concerned with the paucity of good writing among students, the STEP writing tests can only be described as performing a grave disservice to the teaching of English composition. This review will attempt to show why this is so.

STEP Writing, according to the Manual for Interpreting Scores, contains items which fall into five categories. They are: organization, conventions, critical thinking, effectiveness, and appropriateness.

While the aims are inclusive, these tests fail in all but the second category. In this category, they only partially succeed in measuring "conventions" when the mental process is an act of memory involving such mechanical tasks as spelling and punctuation. Let us examine "organization" as an illustration of failure.

It is certainly apparent to every reviewer in the MMY that there are a multiplicity of ways in which he could have ordered his ideas and facts in writing his critique. The choice he eventually makes is an individual choice which cannot be made for him. He must weed out the trivial, discard the irrelevant, and organize his material in such a way that he makes sense effectively. The creation and selection of ideas and the ordering of facts are his. Yet the STEP writing tests leave the student without this choice. What choice he does make consists largely of taking facts and ideas already organized for him and then performing what may be called minor editing, such as rearranging or deleting sentences. The skills required for writing anything are infinitely more difficult and creative than making minor editorial revisions. To equate the two, as the authors do, is misleading and presumptuous. Moreover, it has yet to be shown that creativity can be measured or even identified through the multiple choice format. Yet this in effect is what the STEP writing tests claim they can do.

But let us be more precise. According to one of the authors' selection criteria, "The materials [in the writing tests] should represent *typical writing needs* and desires of the student through careful selection of situations and forms of writing" [italics added]. It is for this reason that the examples on which the questions are based were written by students themselves.

One of the most distressing aspects of the tests is that only rarely does this student material rise to the level of mediocrity. Indeed, it would appear that the "typical writing needs" of our students are so great that we are in imminent danger of seeing the collapse of the English language. To take one example, in Form 1B, eight questions are based on a 248-word student editorial with the heading, "Treat Us Like Adults." This illustrates the kind of material employed to measure college freshmen and sophomores. In introducing the material to the students the authors note, perhaps wryly, "This article, submitted by a freshman applicant for a position on the staff of a college weekly, was returned to the writer for revision." Part of the material follows:

1 It is time this college woke up and started treating we, the students, like grown-ups and not like a bunch of high school kids. **2** Why should there be compulsory class attendance? **3** We graduated high school and now we should be allowed to grow up **4** We all learned how to study in high school so we should be allowed to do it on our own here. **5** Most of us students would go to class anyway. * **14** Our parents would like us to have these things and they pay the bills. **15** We need to grow in other ways, not just intelectual. **16** Only four years until we are out in the world. **17** That doesnt give us much time in order to be responsible and take care of ourselves. **18** Socializing and recreation are just as worthwhile as much knowledge and high marks later on.

It is not possible to see how such material—and many other examples could be given—can form the basis for measuring four of the five categories which the tests' authors rightly suggest go into making good writing. For instance, item 8 corrects the first sentence to read as follows: "It is time this college woke up and started treating us students like grown-ups...." What is disturbing about this "correct" choice is that it abounds in clichés. Selecting the correctly worded clichés cannot be a test of writing skills. The only sensible alternative, an alternative which is not offered, is to eliminate the sentence and write one that is entirely new and different.

In item 13, the student is asked to select the simplest and most accurate revision of sentence 17. Again recall the problems involved in writing. Certainly a key to good writing is rewriting. But a writer must know what to revise. Once someone else has picked out the sentence or phrase that needs correction, the creative aspect of writing markedly diminishes. In short, this kind of question, which occurs repeatedly, measures only a peripheral aspect of the craft.

Question 15 asks: "Of the following possible weaknesses of this paper as an editorial, which is most serious?" The student is then given the following choices: "A Its misspelled words B Its poorly constructed sentences C Immature phrasing D Its unsupported generalizations."

Let us put aside the question's obvious weakness. While the correct answer is supposedly D, excellent arguments can be made to support C and possibly B. But the most apparent alternative is not even offered and that is the editorial's superficiality of thought, which truly is its essential weakness. In addition to subjecting a student to impoverished ideas atrociously expressed—a dubious educational device—the tests with their inherent limitations prevent him from offering any original concepts composed in an original manner. To contend, as the authors do, that "The STEP Writing tests seek to measure comprehensively the full range of skills involved in the process of good writing" must put a strain on any writer's credulity. Hopefully any educator who wishes to measure "the full range of skills involved in the process of good writing" will resort to writing itself, despite what he has been told about his frailty to make an intelligent, sensitive, and reliable judgment.

ALBERT N. HIERONYMUS, *Professor of Education and Psychology, State University of Iowa, Iowa City, Iowa.*

This is a series of highly ingenious and well constructed tests in an area in which objective measurement has always been extremely difficult. They are excellent tests of what might be termed the power of writing: organization, clarity, effectiveness, and appropriateness of expression. They call for the application of higher level mental processes of reasoning and judgment.

The tests require a relatively advanced level of reading comprehension, not so much in the original passages as in the items. In understanding the passages, considerable emphasis is placed upon ascertaining the meaning of poorly (atrociously!) written materials in order to substitute more precise or elegant versions of the same ideas. Most of the material is interesting and cleverly adapted to the purposes of the tests.

It is not entirely clear whether the skills specifications for the tests were determined before or after the tests were constructed. There is considerable disparity between the statement of relative emphasis in the Manual for Interpreting and the classifications presented in the Teacher's Guide. For example, for the five skills categories (organization, conventions, critical thinking, effectiveness, and appropriateness) at Level 4, the relative emphasis is listed as 30, 20, 15, 20, and 15 per cent, respectively. When the total number of items in the two forms (120) is used as a base, the relative emphasis is 27, 67, 16, 43, and 25 per cent, respectively. When the total number of item classifications (213) is used as a base, the relative emphasis is 15, 38, 9, 24, and 14 per cent. Similar discrepancies are to be found at other levels. There are also marked differences between forms.

As tests of the mechanics of writing, these leave much to be desired; they are inefficient and incomplete. This is largely the result of the general philosophy underlying the whole STEP venture: to achieve continuity of measurement throughout grades 4–14. The fact that the commonly accepted objectives of the writing program differ radically at the extremes of this grade range makes compromise inevitable. These tests appear to be better suited to the objectives at higher grade levels than to those at lower levels. Of the 60 items in Level 4, Form A (grades 4–6), for example, only 1 item is concerned primarily with spelling; 1 with capitalization; 6 with punctuation; and 4 with correctness of word usage. Only two uses of the comma are tested as error situations —one with the salutation and the other with the complimentary close of a friendly letter. This would appear to under-represent the place of mechanics in the language skills program through grade 6.

Apparently it has been necessary to compromise also with the ideal in item difficulty distributions, especially at the lower levels. In grade 4, the median difficulty index (per cent right) was 32 in Form A and 35 in Form B. Seventeen items in Form A and 11 items in Form B were at or below chance (25 per cent). In Level 4, the raw score medians were 35, 46, and 57 per cent of the total number of items for grades 4, 5, and 6, respectively, instead of the 62.5 per cent which was stated as a goal. In Level 3, these were 43, 48, and 57 per cent, respectively, for grades 7, 8, and 9.

A "show-of-hands" method of item analysis is recommended as one of the principal follow-up techniques. Methods of evaluating the statistical significance of differences between class performance and the item analysis norm are provided. Unfortunately, this appears to be such a "scientific" procedure for locating areas in need of concentrated attention that users are likely to forget the differences between norms and standards and the role that sound judgment plays in setting expectation.

Issues relating to SCAT and to the STEP battery as a whole are treated elsewhere. However, on the issue of the use of percentile bands, data on the reliabilities of differences for college freshmen presented in the 1958 SCAT-STEP Supplement reflect upon the uniqueness of the writing test. Of particular interest are the reliabilities of differences between STEP Reading and STEP Writing

(.04), and between STEP Writing and SCAT Verbal (.27). These low reliabilities make the rule-of-thumb procedures for interpreting profile differences for an individual student highly suspect. This is pointed out in the Supplement but one wonders what changes in procedures for profile comparisons would be necessary if similar data were available for Reading, Listening, and Writing for the other levels.

SUMMARY. The tests measure very effectively higher-order writing skills, particularly those of effectiveness and appropriateness which tend to be slighted in other batteries. There is more operational and statistical overlap with reading than is desirable. The tests should be supplemented with better measures of the mechanical writing skills, particularly in the elementary and junior high schools.

Personnel & Guid J 42:298–303 N '63. Dean A. Allen. The Fifth Mental Measurements Yearbook....contains three reviews of the full STEP series of achievement tests and three of STEP-Writing; all six deserve the close attention of test users and test publishers. Many of the present reviewer's observations derive from the discussions in Buros, but in addition to study of the original STEP-W materials, the published literature related to STEP-W has been searched in an effort to bring this evaluation of the test up to date. * The student-written passages that comprise STEP-W are almost unvarying in their poor quality and trivial content. Not only are they shot through with errors, misconstructions, and infelicities of every sort, of which only a few are singled out for revision, but the choice of topics is altogether disappointing. The use of such inferior material not only renders the reading of the tests, as Stalnaker (in Buros, p. 362) puts it, "an ordeal....for the student who is sensitive to the written word," but all too often makes the student's choice of *best answer* hinge on the relative importance he assigns to consistency of style vs. good English. In some items a clearly superior revision is so out of keeping with the rest of the passage that to mark it as *best* or *most effective* means virtually to disregard the context from which it was drawn. There are a few instances (an average of one or two per 30-item part) of items with no acceptable good answer, with two or more equally good answers, or with a clearly wrong answer keyed as correct. For the most part, the keyed answers appear to be defensible; careful editing would have avoided the mistakes noted. * There is evidence that STEP-W has a heavy loading of a general factor. * Comparable data for college freshmen —correlations between STEP-W and the other STEP and SCAT tests (1958, *Supplement,* p. 28)—confirm the impression that, in avoiding subject matter dealt with in specific courses, STEP-W may be measuring general scholastic aptitude rather than writing skills as such. * The use of bands rather than single scores sets an example which other test publishers are urged to consider following. * Surprisingly lacking are correlations between alternate forms, data one would assume to be almost obligatory evidence of careful test construction. * Converted scores are in fact not comparable in terms of percentile ranks. Consider comparisons across fields. A college freshman who earned a converted score of 286 on all Level 1 STEP tests would fall at mid-percentile ranks of 11 in reading, 15 in listening, 25 in writing, 34 in social studies, 57 in science, and 63 in mathematics. Such variations in percentile equivalents would be understandable in the case of raw scores—it would mean only that the tests were not equally difficult—but the concept of "a common continuous score scale" seems to imply a parallelism within the STEP battery which does not exist, at least in terms of percentile equivalents. If we consider scores earned within a single field in successive grades, we find a similar lack of comparability, though the publishers state that converted scores "represent a statistical derivation and are more meaningful (than raw scores) because through their use scores from form to form of STEP-Writing are comparable" * While there is a rough relation between converted scores and median achievement level in that converted scores get higher as one goes up the grades, there is no regular pace or pattern of increments with "growth" or normal progress through the grades. Moreover, these grade-by-grade converted score increments vary from test to test; the median student gains one point on STEP-Writing between grades 6 and 7 but gains 10 points on STEP-Reading. As it turns out, converted scores are never really useful for comparisons between different students' scores on the same test, or between a single student's scores on two tests in different fields or two tests at different levels in the same field. The publishers, while insisting on the use of converted scores, actually make all comparisons between tests, levels, students, and fields on the basis of percentiles (which could as easily be obtained from raw scores), and they instruct test users to do the same. The interpolated operation of translating raw scores to converted scores is apparently unnecessary. * Despite promises in the various STEP materials that additional data would be forthcoming, and despite the critical comment of the reviewers in Buros directed against the lack of appropriate statistical evidence, almost five years after its birth, STEP-W is still without the obvious sorts of reliability information, information which should accompany distribution of a test battery. * The absence of data accompanying publication of STEP-W and the meager evidence at hand five years later make it impossible either to endorse or to discount any statement of the test's validity beyond the original assertion of content validity. The correlations may be simply reflections of the fact that any test of general intellectual aptitude will bear some relationship to school performance. The 1958 *Supplement* reports briefly on one study, and the 1962 *Supplement* on three studies, comparing STEP-W scores with school grades. All are unpublished. This situation caused the author to undertake a further investigation of STEP-W. * Entering freshmen at Bowdoin College were tested on STEP-W in the fall of 1961. The split-half (odd-even) reliability coefficient was found to be 0.43, which corrected by the Spearman-Brown formula, becomes 0.60, obviously too low to afford confidence in the stability of individual students' scores. The poor reliability is partly the result of the homogeneity of Bowdoin students with regard to writing skills, but then, homogeneity greater than that of the nationwide norming group would characterize almost any single school or college sample. Freshmen at Bowdoin take a required course, English 1–2, in which success is largely dependent on writing skills. The correlation between final grades and STEP-W raw scores was 0.39. The correlation between STEP-W and SAT-V scores was found to be 0.46. Moreover, the r between SAT-V and grades in English 1–2 was 0.49. In spite of the fact that students are admitted to Bowdoin in part on the basis of SAT-V scores, SAT-V appears to be a somewhat better predictor of grades in the freshman

writing course than does STEP-Writing. *Conclusions.* No over-all grade can be awarded the STEP publishers for their aims and their accomplishments. Individual test users will have to make the judgment about the worth of STEP-W in their own schools. But some final comments may serve as guidelines. A. STEP-W has been ambitiously conceived, carefully planned, and attractively printed. B. Detailed presentation of technical information regarding development, norming, statistical methods, and the like accompanies the test. C. A very large variety of accessory materials and interpretive literature is available and necessary for full use of STEP-W. D. In their effort to avoid dependence on local course content, the publishers may have produced a measure more of general scholastic aptitude than of writing skills. E. Statistical evidence of validity and reliability is inadequate. F. The test content is largely trivial, tedious, and unnecessarily, though deliberately, fraught with errors; so much so that the intelligent student's task in selecting suitable revisions may come down to pitting his desire to preserve consistency of (poor) style against his feeling for literate writing. G. Presentation of scores as percentile bands rather than as single numbers is a commendably cautious tactic in guarding against the appearance of precision where it does not exist. H. Converted scores, a feature of which the publishers are unaccountably proud, seem to be needless or even misleading. I. Finally, and perhaps most important, is the question of whether STEP-W (or any multiple-choice test, for that matter) can accurately assess writing ability. Although the arguments against the inefficiency, the unreliability of grading, and the limited sampling of content typical of essay tests are persuasive, traditionalists will doubtless persist in their belief that the best way to judge writing skills is to examine specimens of students' writing. They will ask: Does STEP-W really measure what it claims to measure? If we take at face value the publishers' statement that content validity is a criterion by which to judge STEP-W, then Zahner's description seems reasonable: that STEP-W is not a test of writing at all but "somewhere between a test of proofreading and one of editing" (Buros, p. 362). The burden of demonstrating usefulness falls on the publishers. So it is remarkable that, among all the statistics relating to the test, none can be found comparing STEP-W scores with any other measure of writing, including even the companion STEP essay writing test. Five years after publication, STEP-Writing is still an attractive test of uncertain worth.

For reviews by Charlotte Croon Davis, John M. Stalnaker, and Louis C. Zahner, see 5:207. For reviews of the complete battery, see 25 and 5:24.

[293]
★**Writing Skills Test.** Grades 9–12; 1961, c1960–61; IBM; Form A ('61, c1960, 8 pages); manual ('61, 31 pages); separate answer sheets must be used; $3 per 20 tests; $4 per 100 IBM answer sheets; 25¢ per scoring stencil; 75¢ per specimen set; postage extra; 40(50) minutes; Macklin Thomas; Science Research Associates, Inc. *

WILLIAM E. COFFMAN, *Director of Research and Development, College Board Programs Division, Educational Testing Service, Princeton, New Jersey.*

The *Writing Skills Test,* according to the manual, is offered for use "as a measure of English course achievement" in grades 9–12, "in the differential assignment of students to English sections," and "as a teaching aid." The test itself is described as "an easily administered, forty-minute examination of some of the basic skills used in composition."

The potential user will agree with the description. He may wonder, however, at the recommended uses, for of all the sample data presented in the manual, the most appropriate in the reviewer's opinion are based on "college freshmen students attending....a large urban junior college....in Illinois." He may suspect that a test originally constructed for use in the placement of college freshmen has been "adapted" to secondary school use because of the larger market. In such a case, the appropriateness of the "adaptation" becomes of crucial significance.

The test is unusually difficult for unselected students in grades 9–12. There are 70 four-choice and five-choice questions and the score is number of right answers. Thus, the mean chance score is 15.5 and the standard deviation of chance scores is 3.5. From the norms table, it is possible to determine that if a boy in the ninth grade sample had marked his paper at random, he would have had one chance in six of scoring above the 50th percentile for ninth grade boys. A twelfth grade boy adopting the same strategy would have one chance in six of scoring above the 23rd percentile. From the data regarding item difficulty, it can be determined that there are 29 five-choice items which were answered correctly by 62 per cent or fewer of the sample from the twelfth grade norms population and 24 four-choice items which were answered correctly by 60 per cent or fewer of the sample. This means that, if the possibility of correct guesses is taken into account for each item, fewer than half of the samples from the norms population of twelfth graders know the answer to 53 of the 70 questions. Of course, since most students do not mark at random, this difficult test turns out to have validity even for ninth grade groups. However, the user must realize that there is always the danger that in individual cases scores well up in the distribution may represent only random responses. Since similar tests are available which contain easier questions covering essentially the same content, it is difficult to justify the use of this particular test for typical high school groups.

In view of the difficulty of the test for the high school samples, it is surprising to read in the manual, "The test apparently does not possess enough ceiling to discriminate between students at colleges that have selective admissions policies." This statement is based on the fact that at a small liberal arts college and a large private university in Illinois, the mean scores were, respectively, 49.86 and 53.01. But these scores are only 7.11 and 10.26 points above the ideal mean of 42.75; they are fully 20.14 and 16.99 points below the ceiling of 70. In contrast, the mean scores for the national samples of ninth and tenth graders were 23.90 and 28.04. These scores are 18.85 and 14.71 points below the ideal mean and only 8.40 and 12.54 points above the chance score of 15.50. If there is a problem with the test, it is that it has too high a floor for ordinary secondary school classes, not too low a ceiling for classes of college freshmen.

The test will have limited usefulness for measuring English course achievement at any level because there are no parallel forms. The manual contains data indicating high stability in measurement over an academic year (test-retest correlations range from .87 to .91) but there is no information regarding how much of the mean difference is due to growth and how much is due to practice effect. Certainly, if the teacher adopts the advice in the manual to use the test as a basis for class discussion, its usefulness as a measuring instrument will be destroyed for the students in that class. With only one form available, one may doubt the usefulness of class discussion of results. The sample of 70 questions is quite small in comparison with the hundreds of exercises to be found in the typical textbook. As a method of demonstrating the need for concentrated effort in preparation for taking a parallel test, class discussion of results might have some value; as a means of teaching basic principles of writing, it is of doubtful value.

The recommendation that the test be used in combination with essay ratings to place students in sections needs to be examined critically. It is proposed in the manual that high scoring students and low scoring students be placed on the basis of the test score alone and that essay papers be read for those scoring in the middle of the distribution. Such a plan is highly attractive because it reduces the number of essays to be read; however, it has the effect of basing the final decision on the less reliable measure—a procedure exactly the opposite of what is desirable.

Research studies have demonstrated that a combination of essay rating and objective test scores provides the optimum measurement of composition skill per unit of testing time; on the other hand, the combination does not result in "greatly improved" accuracy as claimed by the author of the *Writing Skills Test*. The improvement is only slight when all essays are rated and included in the combination; if essay scores are used as a second stage in a sequence, the results may actually be less accurate. Unreliable essay scores are a poor basis for deciding the fate of borderline cases; in combination with scores from good objective tests, they can be expected to increase validity a little.

The *Writing Skills Test* appears to be appropriate for use in differential assignment of college freshmen or students in above average classes in grades 9–12. The national norms data provided in the manual are appropriate primarily for showing how inadequate is the preparation of the typical secondary school student for a test of this sort. Without parallel forms, the test is of limited value in evaluating learning. While considerable ingenuity has been exercised in developing the questions for the test, the item pool from which the questions

were chosen appears to have been limited; otherwise there would be no excuse for publishing a single form only and including in it such extremely difficult items. The prospective user would do well to examine the test booklet carefully and arrive at his own conclusions regarding the adequacy of the sampling for purposes other than differential assignment.

OSMOND E. PALMER, *Professor, Office of Evaluation Services, Michigan State University, East Lansing, Michigan.*

This test is nearly a model, so far as it goes, of what a good objective test can be. It is carefully worked out. There is a 31-page manual giving directions for administering the test and for using the test results, showing the difficulty of each item at each grade level, and giving a lengthy discussion of the norming of the test and correlation data with grades in English, with other English tests, and with reading and psychological tests. In addition, the sections on grammar and punctuation contain a statement of the rule involved for each item and how that rule applies specifically.

The front of the answer sheet shows percentile norms at each grade level for boys and girls combined; the back gives percentiles for boys and girls separately. Since there is a mean difference of approximately five points in favor of girls this distinction is well worth making.

The test itself is attractively printed and each section is preceded by a statement of purpose and by directions as extensive as necessary. For instance, the spelling section which uses a common set of responses for all items reprints the set in abbreviated form for each item. And the last section, Sentence Building, which contains a type of item the student probably has never seen, is preceded by two examples.

The test consists of six parts. In the vocabulary section a single word is followed by four foils. In Sentence Recognition a group of unpunctuated sentences is written as a block and the student is to decide how many sentences there are in each block (none to four or more). In the grammar part, one continuous sentence is split into five responses in one of which an error has been introduced. In Punctuation and Mechanics an error has been made at one of five lettered points in a sentence. Each spelling item consists of seven words one of which is misspelled. The student is to find that word and then decide whether he would correct it by changing one letter to another, by taking out one or more letters, by putting in one or more letters, or by switching letters around. One cannot tell from this whether the correction a student selects is meant to apply to the misspelled word or to some other word which he thinks is misspelled.

Sentence Building, the last section, contains an ingenious type of item. The attempt is to see how well a student can handle the structure of the language by giving him a good sentence and then asking him to rewrite it (mentally) with a different construction involved. For instance, given the sentence, "He is compelled by circumstances to earn his own living," the student has to decide which of five words or expressions would appear in the sentence if it were recast to begin with "Circumstances." The options are "made," "he," "him," "compelled," and "compelling." This type of item has two virtues. It moves from a good English sentence to a good English sentence and does not require the student to recognize an error which possibly he does not make; and, it is hoped, it gives some measure of the student's ability to handle a variety of sentence patterns in his own writing.

One finds little to quarrel with in the test. The vocabulary words are well chosen and the answer marked right is clearly best. The spelling section has a judicious selection of words illustrating the rules and the spelling demons. The section on grammar avoids testing for tricky points, and cleverly introduces a couple of simple who-whom situations in the foils but does not directly test for them. When, however, there are only 10 items on grammar one wishes that 2 of them had not been devoted to the omission of "d" in "he is suppose to" and to the use of the possessive with a gerund. Some of the sentences in the grammar section were selected, seemingly, from student papers and strike one as being a bit too colloquial. A student might be tempted to mark as an error "I really grew hot [angry]."

The main question one has to raise about the test, and the author is aware of it, is how does it relate to English as taught? One can well ask whether in a writing skills test one can justify devoting 23 of 70 items to vocabulary. This reviewer would like to see more items devoted to grammar and punctuation; he would

like to see some items on capitalization (proper adjectives, words like "the North," use of capitals in titles); he would like to see some attempt to measure a student's sense of organization and his ability to choose in a specific context the word that best fits that context.

This test, however, may be used with a great deal of confidence to measure reliably what it does measure.

[Other Tests]

For tests not listed above, see the following entry in *Tests in Print:* 484 (out of print).

LITERATURE

[294]

*American Literature: Every Pupil Test. High school; 1934–64; new form (4 pages) usually issued each April; forms from previous testing programs also available; general directions sheet ('63, 2 pages); no data on reliability; Ohio norms for new forms available following testing program; 5¢ per test; 3¢ per key; postpaid; 40(45) minutes; Ohio Scholarship Tests. *

[295]

★Book Review Tests. High school; 1950–63; 1 form; 195 tests (4 pages) on specific books: *Abe Lincoln in Illinois* ['60], *Abe Lincoln Grows Up* ['57], Drinkwater's *Abraham Lincoln* ['60], *Adam Bede* ['58], *Age of Innocence* ['63], *Aku Aku* ['63], *Alice Adams* ['58], *All the King's Men* ['59], *An American Tragedy* ['63], *Animal Farm* ['60], *Anna and the King of Siam* ['61], *Anna Karenina* ['63], *Anne Frank: The Diary of a Young Girl* ['59], *Around the World in Eighty Days* ['63], *Arms and the Man* ['63], *The Autobiography of Benjamin Franklin* ['57], *Autocrat of the Breakfast Table* ['63], *Babbitt* ['58], *The Babe Ruth Story* ['57], *The Barretts of Wimpole Street* ['59], *Beau Geste* ['58], *Bell for Adano* ['62], *Ben Hur* ['58], *Beowulf* ['59], *The Black Arrow* ['53], *Black Beauty* ['63], *The Black Rose* ['63], *Brave New World* ['61], *Brideshead Revisited* ['63], *The Bridge of San Luis Rey* ['58], *Brothers Karamazov* ['59], *The Caine Mutiny* ['58], *The Call of the Wild* ['53], *The Canterbury Tales* ['53], *Captains Courageous* ['57], *The Child Buyer* ['63], *A Christmas Carol* ['53], *The Citadel* ['50], *The Count of Monte Cristo* ['58], *The Courtship of Miles Standish* ['58], *The Covered Wagon* ['57], *The Cricket on the Hearth* ['63], *The Crisis* ['58], *Cry, the Beloved Country* ['60], *Cyrano de Bergerac* ['58], *Day of Infamy* ['63], *Death Be Not Proud* ['61], *The Deerslayer* ['58], *A Descent Into the Maelstrom* ['59], *The Devil and Daniel Webster* ['63], *Dragon Seed* ['58], *Dr. Jekyll and Mr. Hyde* ['59], *Drums* ['59], *Drums Along the Mohawk* ['59], *The Egg and I* ['63], *The Enemy Within* ['63], *Enoch Arden* ['57, identical—except for title and format—with the out of print 1947 form of the test on this book in the series *Objective Tests in English*], *George Washington Carver* ['63], *Giants in the Earth* ['58], *Gone With the Wind* ['58], *Goodbye, Mr. Chips* ['59], *The Good Earth* ['53], *Good Morning, Miss Dove* ['58], *The Grapes of Wrath* ['61], *The Great Stone Face* ['59], *Green Mansions* ['59], *Green Pastures* ['62], *Gulliver's*

Travels ['58], *Heidi* ['59], *Hie to the Hunters* ['62],
The History of Henry Esmond ['60], *Hiroshima*
['60], *The Hoosier Schoolmaster* ['58], *The Hound
of the Baskervilles* ['63], *How Green Was My Valley*
['58], *The Hurricane* ['63], *The Iliad* ['58], *The In-
nocents Abroad* ['63], *Intruder in the Dust* ['63],
Jane Eyre ['58], *John Brown's Body* ['60], *Jude the
Obscure* ['63], *The Jungle* ['63], *The Jungle Books*
['63], *The Keys of the Kingdom* ['63], *Kon Tiki* ['59],
A Lantern in Her Hand ['53], *The Last of the
Mohicans* ['58], *The Last of the Plainsmen* ['57], *The
Late George Apley* ['63], *Leaves of Grass* ['63], *The
Legend of Sleepy Hollow* ['59], *Les Miserables* ['58],
Let the Hurricane Roar ['63], *Life on the Mississippi*
['63], *Life With Father* ['63], *The Light in the Forest*
['62], *The Light That Failed* ['58], *The Little Foxes*
['62], *The Little Minister* ['58], *Little Women* ['57],
The Lively Lady ['61], *Lord Jim* ['58], *Lord of the
Flies* ['63], *Lorna Doone* ['58], *Lost Horizon* ['60],
Love Is Eternal ['60], *The Loved One* ['63], *Madame
Curie* ['63], *The Magnificent Ambersons* ['53], *Mag-
nificent Obsession* ['60], *Main Street* ['58], *Maria
Chapdelaine* ['58], *The Master of Ballantrae* ['58],
Masters of Deceit ['63], *The Mayor of Casterbridge*
['57], *Men Against the Sea* ['63], *Men of Iron* ['58],
The Mill on the Floss ['58], *Milton* ['60], *Monsieur
Beaucaire* ['58], *The Moonstone* ['63], *Mutiny on the
Bounty* ['58], *My Antonia* ['57], *My Friend Flicka*
['59], *My Name Is Aram* ['60], *A Nation of Sheep*
['63], *The Night They Burned the Mountain* ['63],
Northwest Passage ['60], *O Pioneers!* ['60], *The Old
Man and the Sea* ['58], *Old Yeller* ['63], *On the
Beach* ['63], *The Oregon Trail* ['57], *Our Town* ['53],
The Ox Bow Incident ['60], *Paradise Lost* ['53], *The
Pathfinder* ['63], *The Pearl* ['62], *The Pearl Lagoon*
['58], *Penrod* ['60], *The Perfect Tribute* ['59], *The
Pilgrim's Progress* ['53], *Pitcairn's Island* ['63], *Point
of No Return* ['63], *Pride and Prejudice* ['58], *The
Prince and the Pauper* ['57], *The Prisoner of Chillon*
['60], *Profiles in Courage* ['63], *Pygmalion* ['62],
Quentin Durward ['58], *Quo Vadis* ['62], *Ramona*
['58], *Random Harvest* ['63], *The Red Badge of
Courage* ['53], *The Red Pony* ['61], *Richard Carvel*
['63], *Rip Van Winkle* ['59], *The Robe* ['60], *Robinson Crusoe* ['53], *Saratoga Trunk* ['60], *Scaramouche*
['62], *School for Scandal* ['61], *Sea Wolf* ['59], *The
Secret Garden* ['63], *A Separate Peace* ['61], *Seven-
teen* ['59], *Show Boat* ['60], *A Single Pebble* ['63],
Sink the Bismarck ['63], *The Story of My Life* ['62],
Swiss Family Robinson ['63], *Tales From Shakespeare* ['60], *Tess of the D'Urbervilles* ['58], *The
Three Musketeers* ['63], *To Have and to Hold* ['58],
To Kill a Mockingbird ['61], *Tom Sawyer* ['53], *The
Turn of the Screw* ['63], *Twice Told Tales* ['63],
Two Years Before the Mast ['62], *Uncle Tom's Cabin*
['59], *The Unknown Lincoln* ['57], *Up From Slavery*
['60], *Vanity Fair* ['53], *Victory* ['62], *The Virginian*
['57], *The Voice of Bugle Ann* ['63], *The Wall* ['63],
Washington Square ['63], *The Way West* ['57], *Witness* ['63], *Wuthering Heights* ['57], *Yankee From
Olympus* ['63], *You Can't Go Home Again* ['63]; no
manual; no data on reliability; no norms; 1–4 copies
of any one test, 15¢ each; 5 or more copies, 10¢ each;
$14.95 per complete set; cash orders postpaid; [25–
30] minutes per test; Joseph Bamberger (5 tests),
F. S. Belcher, Jr. (25 tests), Frances Chastain (4
tests), M. Dorothy (27 tests), Nellie F. Falk (47
tests), Eugene W. Graham (4 tests), Robert J. Jones
(31 tests), Carl H. Larson (20 tests), Margaret
Leeney (1 test), Donald Racky, Jr. (24 tests), and
Robert Ruby (5 tests); Perfection Form Co.*

[296]

★**Catholic Book Tests.** Grades 7–10, 10–12, 1954; 2
levels; at each level, 2 series of 30 tests (1 page) on
specific Catholic literary works; directions (2 sheets);
no data on reliability; no norms; $1.25 per series,
postage extra; (3–5) minutes per test; teachers and
librarians of the U.S. Province Brothers of Holy
Cross; Bruce Publishing Co.*

a) FIRST SERIES. Grades 10–12; 30 tests: *And Spare
Me Not in the Making, The Art of Courageous Liv-
ing, Burnt Out Incense, The Deer Cry, Fire in the
Rain, God Goes to Murderer's Row, God's Under-
ground, The Great Mantle, I Had to Know, Karen,
Late Have I Loved Thee, A Life of Mary, Co-Re-
demptrix, The Mark, Miracle at Carville, More Mur-
der in a Nunnery, Murder at St. Dennis, Mystic in
Motley, And Nora Said "Yes," Nun in Red China, Our
Lady of Light, Our Lady's Fool, Pacific Hopscotch,
St. Angela of the Ursulines, Saints Westward, Shep-
herd's Tartan, The Story of Therese Neumann, Tar
Heel Apostle, Tomorrow's Memories, Where There
Is Love, Yankee Priest.*

b) SECOND SERIES. Grades 10–12; 30 tests: *At the End
of the Santa Fe Trail, Brother Andre of Mount Royal,
Brother Petroc's Return, Calvary in China, Cardinal
Mindszenty, Chaminade: Apostle of Mary, The
Chosen, Color Ebony, Damien the Leper, The Early
Days of Maryknoll, Father Paul of Graymoor, Gates
of Dannemora, Giant in the Wilderness, The Happi-
ness of Father Happé, The House on Humility Street,
The Mass of Brother Michel, The Mouse Hunter, My
Hay Ain't In, My Russian Yesterdays, The Next
Thing, The Quiet Light, Reproachfully Yours, The
Road to Damascus, St. John Baptist de La Salle, Six
O'Clock Mass, Springs of Silence, Star Inn, The
Stranger, Tumbleweed, The Vatican.*

c) THIRD SERIES. Grades 7–10; 30 tests: *Accent on
Laughter, The Boy Jesus, Captain Johnny Ford, City
on a Mountain, Dark Was the Wilderness, The Glow-
ing Lily, The Good Bad Boy, Larger Than the Sky,
Louis Braille, The Man Who Sold Christmas, Man-
gled Hands, The Maryknoll Story, Mississippi Black-
robe, Nothing Ever Happens to Me!, Pattern for
Tomorrow, The Pirate's Prisoner, Polish Folk Tales,
Queen of Heaven, The Red Flame of Sound, Roman
Collar Detective, Royal Banners Fly, Running Waters,
Saint Maria Goretti, Save Us a Seat, Timmy, A
Shepherd and a King, Strong Men South, That Boy!,
These Two Hands, Three Cheers for Tomorrow,
Tom Playfair.*

d) FOURTH SERIES. Grades 7–10: 30 tests; *The Ad-
ventures of Ramon of Bolivia, Arrows of Iron, Blood
on the Mountain, Children of Fatima, The Children of
La Salette, Eskimo Parish, Flying Priest Over the
Arctic, God and the General's Daughter, Hero of the
Hills, Little Queen, Man of Molokai, Master of Mis-
chief Makers, The Medal, Mickey O'Brien, Ned
Haskins, Nicholas the Boy King, The Oldest Story,
The Parish Priest of Ars, Patrick O'Neal: Dona
Maria, Paul of St. Peter's, Pennies for Pauline, Plot
at Nicaragua, Pope Pius XII, Quest of Don Bosco,
Scott and His Men, Sketch Me, Berta Hummel!,
Spirit of Joques Prep, The Story of Mary, The Mother
of Jesus, The Yang Brothers, A Year to Grow.*

[297]

*****Davis-Roahen-Schrammel American Literature
Test.** High school and college; 1938–58: Forms A
Revised ('58), B ('39), (4 pages); manual ('38, 4
pages); Form A Revised norms ['58]; no data on reliability of Form A Revised; $1.20 per 25 tests, postage
extra; 25¢ per specimen set, postpaid; 60(65) min-

utes; V. A. Davis, R. L. Roahen, and H. E. Schrammel; Bureau of Educational Measurements. *

For reviews by Paul B. Diederich and Violet Hughes, see 40:1300.

[298]
*English Literature: Every Pupil Test. High school; 1934–64; new form (4 pages) usually issued each April; forms from previous testing programs also available; general directions sheet ('63, 2 pages); no data on reliability; Ohio norms for new forms available following testing program; 5¢ per test; 3¢ per key; postpaid; 40(45) minutes; Ohio Scholarship Tests. *

[299]
*The Graduate Record Examinations Advanced Tests: Literature. Grades 16–17; 1939–63; for more complete information, see 762; 180(200) minutes; Educational Testing Service. *

For a review by Robert C. Pooley of an earlier form, see 5:215. For a review of the testing program, see 5:601.

[300]
*The Iowa Tests of Educational Development: Test 7, Ability to Interpret Literary Materials. Grades 9–12; 1942–61; IBM; Forms X-3S, Y-3S, ('52, 7 pages); battery examiner's manual ('58, c1949–57, 23 pages); battery general manual ('59, 37 pages); student profile leaflet, sixth edition ('61, c1958, 2 pages); see the complete battery entry (14b) for other accessories; no data on reliability; separate answer sheets must be used; $2.40 per 20 tests; $5 per 100 IBM answer sheets; 50¢ per scoring stencil; $3 per specimen set of the complete battery; postage extra; 50(60) minutes for full length version, 40(50) minutes for class period version; prepared under the direction of E. F. Lindquist; Science Research Associates, Inc. *

REFERENCES
1. TRELA, THADDEUS MICHAEL. *A Comparison of Ninth Grade Achievement on Selected Measures of General Reading Comprehension, Critical Thinking, and General Educational Development.* Doctor's thesis, University of Missouri (Columbia, Mo.), 1962. (DA 23:2382)

For reviews of the complete battery, see 5:17; for reviews of earlier forms, see 4:17 and 3:12.

[301]
*Literature: Every Pupil Scholarship Test. Grades 7–8, 9–12; 1928–64; some test booklet titles for grades 7–8 are *Elementary Literature;* new form (4 pages) usually issued each January and April; forms from previous testing programs also available; 2 levels; general directions sheet ['63, 2 pages]; no data on reliability; norms for new forms available following testing program; 4¢ per test; 4¢ per key; postage extra; 40(45) minutes; Bureau of Educational Measurements. *

[302]
★Objective Tests in American Anthology. High school; 1959–61; 1 form; 6 tests: 5 tests ('59, 4 pages) on specific periods and a final examination ('61, 6 pages); no manual; no data on reliability; no norms;

5 or more tests with answer sheet, 10¢ each; 15¢ per key (free with 24 or more copies of any one test); $1.55 per specimen set; cash orders postpaid; [60] minutes per test; Carl H. Larson; Perfection Form Co. *

[303]
★Objective Tests in English Anthology. High school; 1959; 1 form; 8 tests: 7 tests (4 pages) on specific periods and a final examination (6 pages); no manual; no data on reliability; no norms; 5 or more tests with answer sheet, 10¢ each; 15¢ per key (free with 24 or more copies of any one test); $2.15 per specimen set; cash orders postpaid; [60] minutes per test; Carl H. Larson; Perfection Form Co. *

[304]
*Objective Tests in English. High school; 1929–63; 1 form (except where otherwise indicated); 102 tests (4 pages unless otherwise indicated) on specific books: *Abe Lincoln Grows Up* ('61), *Anthony and Cleopatra* ('52), *Arrowsmith* ('55), *As You Like It* ('47), *Bleak House* ('63), *The Bridge of San Luis Rey* ('63), *The Call of the Wild* ('57), *A Christmas Carol* ('56), *Cimarron* ('57), *Come Rack! Come Rope!* ('54), *A Connecticut Yankee in King Arthur's Court* ('54), *Crime and Punishment* ('60, 5 pages), *The Crisis* ('54), *David Copperfield* ('31–48), *Death Comes for the Archbishop* ('54), *Doctor Zhivago* ['61], *Dombey and Son* ('63), *Don Quixote* ('54), *Enoch Arden* ('47–57), *Ethan Frome* ('55), *Evangeline* ('29–57), *Giants in the Earth* ('54), *Gods, Heroes and Men of Ancient Greece* ('63), *Great Expectations* ('53), *The Great Gatsby* ('63), *Hamlet* ('31–48), *Henry IV* ('63, in 2 parts), *Henry V* ('31), *The House of Seven Gables* ('47–56), *Huckleberry Finn* ('50), *The Human Comedy* ('56, 3 pages), *The Idylls of the King* ('29–47), *Ivanhoe* ('48), *Jane Eyre* ('54), *Johnny Tremain* ('50), *Julius Caesar* (2 forms: '48, '57), *Kenilworth* ('32), *Kidnapped* ('48), *Kim* ('57), *King Lear* ('29), *King Richard II* ('63), *King Richard III* ('63), *The Lady of the Lake* ('29–48), *The Last of the Mohicans* ('56), *Les Miserables* ('63), *Little Dorrit* ('63), *Lorna Doone* ('52), *Lost Endeavor* ('56), *Macbeth* (2 forms: '48, '57), *The Man Without a Country* ('32), *Martin Chuzzlewit* ('63), *The Merchant of Venice* ('29–49), *A Midsummer Night's Dream* ('31–48), *The Mill on the Floss* ('56), *Moby Dick* ('49), *Much Ado About Nothing* ('60), *Nicholas Nickleby* ('63), *The Odyssey* ('55), *Of Human Bondage* ('59), *The Old Curiosity Shop* ('63), *The Old Man and the Sea* ('63), *Oliver Twist* ('50), *Othello* ('29, 3 pages), *Our Town* ('56, 3 pages), *Pickwick Papers* ('60), *Prester John* ('55), *Pride and Prejudice* ('54), *The Red Badge of Courage* ('56), *The Return of the Native* ('51), *The Rime of the Ancient Mariner* (2 forms: '47, 3 pages; '63), *The Rise of Silas Lapham* ('52), *Romeo and Juliet* ('29–49), *Ruggles of Red Gap* ('57), *The Scarlet Letter* ('32), *The Scarlet Pimpernel* ('54), *Shadows on the Rock* ('54, 3 pages), *She Stoops to Conquer* ('49), *Silas Marner* (2 forms: '48, 3 pages; '57), *Sir Roger de Coverlay Papers* ('31), *The Sketch Book* ('37), *Snow-Bound* ('31–48), *So Big* ('57), *Sohrab and Rustum* ('29–57), *The Spy* ('31), *A Tale of Two Cities* (2 forms: '48, '57), *The Talisman* ('54), *The Taming of the Shrew* ('59), *The Tempest* ('48), *The Thread That Runs So True* ('63), *To Have and to Hold* ('57), *Treasure Island* ('47), *The Turmoil* ('56), *Twelfth Night* ('50), *Twenty Thousand Leagues Under the Sea* ('56), *The Vicar of Wakefield* ('47), *The Virginian* ('54), *The Vision of Sir Launfal* ('48), *War and Peace* ('63), *The White Company* ('60), *White Fang* ('58),

Wuthering Heights ('56), *The Yearling* ('50); no manual; no data on reliability; no norms; 1–4 copies of any one test with key, 30¢ each; 5 or more copies, 10¢ each; 15¢ per key (free with 24 or more copies of any one test); $19.95 per complete set; cash orders postpaid; (20–40) minutes per test; F. S. Belcher, Jr. (25 tests), Frances Chastain (6 tests), Alpha Hobbs Darlington (7 tests), Sarah E. Dorn (3 tests), M. Dorothy (2 tests), Nellie F. Falk (26 tests), Robert J. Jones (2 tests), Alta H. Kibler (1 test), Carl H. Larson (1 test), Margaret Leeney (1 test), Dorothy A. Mason (1 test), Claude E. Stephenson (4 tests), Garland Miller Taylor (15 tests), M. Teresa (5 tests), Augusta Kibler Turpin (2 tests), Hannah Van Nostrand (1 test), Paul E. White (1 test), Maye Alexander Wilson (2 tests), and LaDuskie Wood (2 tests); Perfection Form Co. *

[305]

★**Outside Reading Tests for Freshmen and Sophomores.** Grades 9–10; 1956; volume of short tests on 500 specific books; 1 form (165 pages); key booklet (19 pages); no data on reliability; no norms; $2.50 per set of test book and key booklet (tests may be reproduced without permission), cash orders postpaid; [10] minutes per test; Christobel M. Cordell; J. Weston Walch, Publisher. *

[306]

★**Outside Reading Tests for Juniors and Seniors, Third Edition.** Grades 11–12; 1950–63; volume of short tests on 600 specific books; 1 form ('63, c1958–63, 228 pages); key booklet ('63, c1958–63, 35 pages); no data on reliability; no norms; $3 per set of test book and key booklet (tests may be reproduced without permission), cash orders postpaid; [10] minutes per test; Christobel M. Cordell; J. Weston Walch, Publisher. *

[307]

★**Outside Reading Tests for Junior High Schools.** Grades 7–9; 1959; volume of short tests on 350 specific books; 1 form (164 pages); key booklet ['59, 29 pages]; no data on reliability; no norms; $2.50 per set of test book and key booklet (tests may be reproduced without permission), cash orders postpaid; [10] minutes per test; Christobel M. Cordell; J. Weston Walch, Publisher. *

[Other Tests]

For tests not listed above, see the following entries in *Tests in Print:* 487, 495–6, 501, 505, 507, 509, 512–3, 515, 517–9, and 521; out of print: 485, 488, 490, 492–3, and 520.

SPEECH

[307a]

★**The Arizona Articulation Proficiency Scale.** Mental ages 2–14; 1963; individual; 1 form (67 cards); may also be administered as a short form using only 44 cards; manual (11 pages plus sample copies of record booklet and survey test form); record booklet (4 pages); survey test form (1 page); no data on reliability; no description of normative population; $20 per set of cards, 25 record booklets, 25 survey test forms, and manual; $6.50 per 25 record booklets; $3.50 per 25 survey test forms; $3.50 per manual; postpaid; [20–30] minutes; Janet Barker; Western Psychological Services. *

REFERENCES
1. BARKER, JANET O. "A Numerical Measure of Articulation." *J Speech & Hearing Disorders* 25:79–88 F '60. (PA 35:264)
2. BARKER, JANET, AND ENGLAND, GENE. "A Numerical Measure of Articulation: Further Developments." *J Speech & Hearing Disorders* 27:23–7 F '62. * (PA 36:5GH23B)

[308]

★**Forms From Diagnostic Methods in Speech Pathology.** Children and adults with speech problems; 1952–63; 20 forms consisting of coordination forms, rating scales, attitude surveys, and biographical questionnaires (1–6 pages, each reprinted separately from *1* below); manual (see *1* below); no data on reliability; 5¢ per copy of Forms 1–2, 9–14, 17–20; 8¢ per copy of Forms 3–4, 6–8, 16; 10¢ per copy of Forms 5, 15; $7.50 per manual (available from publisher, Harper & Row, Publishers, Inc.); postage extra; Wendell Johnson, Frederic L. Darley, and D. C. Spriestersbach; Interstate Printers and Publishers, Inc. *

a) FORM 1, CHART OF SIGNIFICANT VARIATIONS IN SEVERITY OF THE STUTTERING PROBLEM SINCE ONSET.
b) FORM 2, GENERAL SPEECH BEHAVIOR RATING.
c) FORM 3, ARTICULATION TEST. Special printing of combined record and analysis sheets of *Templin-Darley Screening and Diagnostic Tests of Articulation.*
d) FORM 4, SPEECH MECHANISM EXAMINATION.
e) FORM 5, GENERAL VOICE QUALITY EXAMINATION.
f) FORM 6, SUPPLEMENTARY EXAMINATION FOR BREATHINESS.
g) FORM 7, SUPPLEMENTARY EXAMINATION FOR HARSHNESS.
h) FORM 8, SUPPLEMENTARY EXAMINATION FOR NASALITY.
i) FORM 9, MEASURES OF SPEECH AND LANGUAGE DEVELOPMENT.
j) FORM 10, MEASURES OF RATE OF SPEAKING AND ORAL READING.
k) FORM 11, MEASURES OF DISFLUENCY OF SPEAKING AND ORAL READING.
l) FORM 12, SPEAKING-TIME LOG.
m) FORM 13, CHECK LIST OF STUTTERING REACTIONS.
n) FORM 14, SCALE FOR RATING SEVERITY OF STUTTERING.
o) FORM 15, IOWA SCALE OF ATTITUDE TOWARD STUTTERING.
p) FORM 16, STUTTERER'S SELF-RATINGS OF REACTIONS TO SPEECH SITUATIONS.
q) FORM 17, MEASURES OF ADAPTATION OF STUTTERING AND ORAL READING RATE.
r) FORM 18, MEASURES OF STUTTERING CONSISTENCY.
s) FORM 19, IOWA UNIMANUAL HAND USAGE QUESTIONNAIRE.
t) FORM 20, IOWA PERFORMANCE TEST OF SELECTED MANUAL ACTIVITIES.

REFERENCES
1. JOHNSON, WENDELL; DARLEY, FREDERIC L.; AND SPRIESTERSBACH, D. C. *Diagnostic Methods in Speech Pathology.* New York: Harper & Row, Publishers, Inc., 1963. Pp. xvii, 347. *

For excerpts from reviews of the manual, see B281.

[309]

The Graduate Record Examinations Advanced Tests: Speech. Grades 16–17; 1953; available only in the Institutional Testing Program; for more complete information, see 762; 180(200) minutes; Educational Testing Service. *

REFERENCES

1. CROCKER, LIONEL. "The Graduate Record Examination and the Small College." *Speech Teach* 8:246–50 S '59. *

For a review of the testing program, see 5:601.

[310]

★**The Houston Test for Language Development.** Ages 6 months to 3 years, 3–6 years; 1958–63; individual; 1 form; 2 levels; $20 per complete kit of both levels; postpaid; (30) minutes; Margaret Crabtree; Houston Test Co. *

a) [PART 1.] Ages 6 months to 3 years; 1958; mimeographed manual ('58, 26 pages); scoring sheet ['58, 2 pages]; $7.50 per examiner's kit of manual, set of 20 vocabulary cards, and 25 scoring sheets; $3.50 per manual.

b) PART 2. Ages 3–6; 1963; manual ('63, 38 pages); record form ('63, 4 pages); no data on reliability; $15 per examiner's kit of manual, set of 38 vocabulary cards (20 of which are the same as those used with part 1), set of test objects, and 20 record forms; $3 per manual.

REFERENCES

1. CRABTREE, MARGARET COOPER. *The Construction and Trial Study of a Language Development Test for Children Up to Three Years of Age.* Doctor's thesis, University of Houston (Houston, Tex.), 1957. (*DA* 17:1713)

[311]

★**An Integrated Articulation Test for Use With Children With Cerebral Palsy.** Ages 3–16; 1961; individual; orally administered; 2 forms; manual (24 pages, including copies of 5 record sheets for each form); 50¢ per manual, postpaid; [75–100] minutes in 2 sessions; Orvis C. Irwin; Cerebral Palsy Review. *

REFERENCES

1. IRWIN, ORVIS C. "A Short Test for Use With Cerebral Palsy Children." *J Speech & Hearing Disorders* 21:446–9 S '56. * (*PA* 31:5028)
2. IRWIN, ORVIS C. "A Second Short Test for Use With Children Who Have Cerebral Palsy." *Cerebral Palsy R* 18:18–9 Jl–Ag '57. * (*PA* 33:1990)
3. IRWIN, ORVIS C. "Validation of Short Consonant Articulation Tests for Use With Children Who Have Cerebral Palsy." *Cerebral Palsy R* 18:12 Mr–Ap '57. * (*PA* 32:5806)
4. IRWIN, ORVIS C. "A Fourth Short Consonant Test for Use With Children With Cerebral Palsy." *Cerebral Palsy R* 19:12–4 Mr–Ap '58. * (*PA* 33:8881)
5. IRWIN, ORVIS C. "A Third Short Consonant Test for Use With Children With Cerebral Palsy." *Cerebral Palsy R* 19:8–10 Ja–F '58. * (*PA* 33:6597)
6. IRWIN, ORVIS C. "A Short Vowel Test for Use With Children With Cerebral Palsy." *Cerebral Palsy R* 21:3–4 Jl–Ag '60. * (*PA* 35:2516)
7. IRWIN, ORVIS C. "A Manual of Articulation Testing for Use With Children With Cerebral Palsy." *Cerebral Palsy R* 22:1–24 My–Je '61. * (*PA* 36:2JH01I)
8. IRWIN, ORVIS C. "Verification of Results Obtained With an Integrated Articulation Test for Use With Children With Cerebral Palsy." *Cerebral Palsy R* 22:8–13 S–O '61. * (*PA* 36:4JH08I)
9. IRWIN, ORVIS C. "The Applicability of an Articulation Test With Mentally Retarded Children." *Cerebral Palsy R* 24:3–8 Ja–F '63. * (*PA* 37:8158)

[312]

★**Language Modalities Test for Aphasia.** Adults; 1961; individual; Forms 1, 2, (26 pages); manual (91 pages); instruction manual (15 pages, reprinted from manual); record booklet (21 pages) for each form; medical history-scoring summary (4 pages); $35 per examiner's kit of 20 response booklets, 10 record booklets for each form, filmstrip for each form, 20 medical history-scoring summary forms, manual, and 4 instruction manuals; $3 per 10 response booklets; $4 per 10 record booklets; $7 per filmstrip; $3.50 per 10 medical history-scoring summary forms; $3 per man-

ual; $1 per 4 instruction manuals; postage extra; 35 mm. filmstrip viewer or projector necessary for administration; a filmstrip viewer (DuKane Corporation Model 576-48A) may also be purchased through the publisher: $74.50 plus postage; (60–90) minutes in 1–3 sessions; Joseph M. Wepman and Lyle V. Jones; Education-Industry Service. *

REFERENCES

1. JONES, LYLE V., AND WEPMAN, JOSEPH M. "Dimensions of Language Performance in Aphasia." *J Speech & Hearing Res* 4:220–32 S '61. * (*PA* 36:2JE20J) Comments by Hildred Schuell and James J. Jenkins. 4:295–9 S '61. *

T. R. MILES, *Professor of Psychology, University College of North Wales, Bangor, Wales.*

This test is the result of collaboration between a psychometric laboratory and a speech and language clinic. Its purpose is to make possible the collection of meaningful information about aphasic patients in a standardised form, with a view to both therapy and research. Both visual and auditory stimuli are used, and the subject is set many varieties of tasks, such as naming pictures, repeating words, copying geometric forms, matching them from a choice of visually presented alternatives, and so on.

A theoretical distinction is drawn between aphasia in the strict sense on the one hand—a failure to comprehend verbal symbols—and agnosia and apraxia on the other. Aphasia is regarded as a disorder of integration, agnosia and apraxia as disorders of transmission. The former involves failure to match incoming stimuli to existing concepts; the latter two involve failure of the motor or "output" processes. In earlier work, according to the authors, this distinction is not made as clear as it should have been.

The authors, in the reviewer's opinion, have done an excellent job. Their theoretical approach seems promising and is backed by careful and well documented evidence; the test items are well chosen, and the instructions are clearly set out. In addition they have shown how effective inter-disciplinary collaboration can sometimes be; indeed it is one of the interesting things about the study of aphasia that a large number of different disciplines can all contribute to our understanding of it.

There are a few minor points of criticism. The statement in the manual that "Unimpaired children about ten years of age are known to be able to respond to every item without difficulty" is put forward without supporting evidence; and in the section on research findings it is somewhat tantalising to be given the conclusions and even the level of statistical significance without being given the statistics! Also, since the authors' classification of aphasias includes "semantic" and "syntactical," which are terms also used in Head's somewhat different classification, some comparison between the authors' views and those of Head would perhaps have been interesting. Finally, there may be potential users for whom expense is a highly relevant consideration. It is not entirely clear what is gained by the use of filmstrip in place of printed cards for the presentation of visual material, and one must point out that the subjects' response booklet, though admittedly inexpensive, consists for the most part of almost blank sheets! Possibly the publishers could consider putting a cheaper version of the test on the market.

These, however, are only minor criticisms; the whole publication is an important addition to the literature on aphasia, of interest not only to psychologists working in the clinical field but also to those who are concerned with more theoretical issues.

[313]

★Nationwide Speech Examination. Grades 4-12; 1959-63; new form issued each April; norms available following the testing program; 1 form ('63, 2 pages); no manual; mimeographed norms ('63, 1 page); no data on reliability; 10¢ per test, postage extra; (40–45) minutes; [Donald R. Honz]; Educational Stimuli. *

[313a]

★The Orzeck Aphasia Evaluation. Mental and brain damaged patients; 1964; individual; 1 form; manual (9 pages plus sample copy of record booklet); record booklet (4 pages); no data on reliability and validity; no norms; $8 per set of 25 record booklets and manual; $6.50 per 25 record booklets; $2 per manual; postpaid; (30–40) minutes; Arthur Z. Orzeck; Western Psychological Services. *

[314]

★Speech Articulation Test for Young Children (Revised Edition). Ages 3.5-8.5; 1955; individual; 1 form; manual (30 pages, including test materials and record form); no data on reliability; $1.10 per manual, postage extra; [30] minutes; Merlin J. Mecham; [University Press, Brigham Young University]. *

[315]

★Templin-Darley Screening and Diagnostic Tests of Articulation. Ages 3-8; 1960; individual; 1 form (4 pages); 2 tests: screening test, total diagnostic test; manual (157 pages); no data on reliability of diagnostic test; $1.50 per manual including test materials; 75¢ per 25 record forms; postage extra; $1.70 per specimen set, postpaid; [10–20] minutes for screening test, [30–60] minutes for total diagnostic test; Mildred C. Templin and Frederic L. Darley; Bureau of Educational Research and Service. *

REFERENCES

1. TEMPLIN, MILDRED C. "A Non-Diagnostic Articulation Test." J Speech Disorders 12:392–6 D '47. * (PA 22:4206)
2. TEMPLIN, MILDRED C. "Spontaneous Versus Imitated Verbalization in Testing Articulation in Preschool Children." J Speech Disorders 12:293–300 S '47. *
3. TEMPLIN, MILDRED C. "Norms on a Screening Test of Articulation for Ages Three Through Eight." J Speech & Hearing Disorders 18:323–31 D '53. * (PA 28:6284)
4. SPRIESTERSBACH, DUANE C.; DARLEY, FREDERIC L.; AND ROUSE, VERNA. "Articulation of a Group of Children With Cleft Lips and Palates." J Speech & Hearing Disorders 21:436–45 S '56. * (PA 31:4910)
5. TEMPLIN, MILDRED C. Certain Language Skills in Children. University of Minnesota, Institute of Child Welfare Monograph Series, No. 26. Minneapolis, Minn.: University of Minnesota Press, 1957. Pp. xviii, 183. * (PA 31:7556)
6. JORDAN, EVAN P. "Articulation Test Measures and Listener Ratings of Articulation Defectiveness." J Speech & Hearing Res 3:303–19 D '60. * (PA 35:2534)
7. MORRIS, HUGHLETT L.; SPRIESTERSBACH, D. C.; AND DARLEY, FREDERIC L. "An Articulation Test for Assessing Competency of Velopharyngeal Closure." J Speech & Hearing Res 4:48–55 Mr '61. * (PA 35:6795)
8. SIEGEL, GERALD M. "Experienced and Inexperienced Articulation Examiners." J Speech & Hearing Disorders 27:28–35 F '62. * (PA 36:5GH28S)
9. BETTS, CARL EUGENE. Communication Skills of Mentally Retarded Children Aged 7, 9, and 11. Doctor's thesis, State University of Iowa (Iowa City, Iowa), 1963. (DA 24:888)

J Speech & Hearing Disorders 28:97–8 F '63. Harry Hollien. * Happily, the authors have been very precise and thorough in developing these tests; regrettably, such thoroughness is often lacking for test construction in the area of speech pathology and audiology. Moreover, they have demonstrated not only the ability to carry out the basic research necessary for the development of a sound test, but also the ability to keep clearly in mind the very real needs of the speech clinician and client while doing so. In addition, the clear, precise presentation of both the research results and administration procedures allows the user to gather the necessary information concerning articulation skills while remaining cognizant of the interrelationships of clients' performance with the provided normative data. The Templin-Darley manual provides the clinician with a complete articulation testing kit which consists of (1) a diagnostic test of articulation with associated descriptions, (2) similar materials for a shorter screening test of articulation, (3) sentences for testing older subjects, (4) a set of 57 black and white test cards to stimulate spontaneous speech of young children, and (5) a copy of the test form. All materials, except the test forms, are bound into a single volume of modest size. * The speech clinician may encounter some difficulty with client fatigue when the diagnostic test is administered. The number of items (176) included would seem excessive and might lead to this problem especially when the test is given to young children. * this difficulty may be circumvented....by administering parts of the test at successive meetings. * The

Templin-Darley screening test of articulation consists of 50 items which are drawn from the larger diagnostic test. * Included in the manual are a set of 57 cards containing 176 black and white drawings. These cards are arranged in such a way that the first 16 constitute the 50-item screening test and the total set, the diagnostic test. * the 176 drawings are not among the strong features of these tests. The quality of the drawings is somewhat uneven— some are small, others ambiguous, and yet others suffer from lack of skill of the artist. On the other hand, they present reasonably and simply the appropriate stimuli and, with the assistance of the starter phrases, it should be easy to elicit the desired responses. Having the picture articulation cards bound into the manual would seem to be a real advantage in the testing situation and clinicians report that this feature allows smooth test administration. * designed basically to test those individuals who exhibit inadequate articulation of speech sounds as a primary problem. Undoubtedly, the tests also can be used to assess the articulation of individuals whose speech problem is secondary, such as those with cleft palate or cerebral palsy. Better yet, the Templin-Darley tests could be used as the basic tool supplemented by special articulation tests, such as O. C. Irwin's articulation test for children with cerebral palsy. In any event, the Templin-Darley tests are a very welcome addition to the available tools in speech pathology. * they should be included among every speech clinician's materials.

Speech Teach 11:175 Mr '62. Al Knox. This test requires skill in speech science, phonetics, and speech pathology, and sophistication in testing. It should not be attempted by anyone other than a qualified speech pathologist. The manual....should be studied by every student of speech pathology.

[316]

★Verbal Language Development Scale. Birth to age 15; 1958–59; extension of the communication section of *Vineland Social Maturity Scale* (see 5:120); behavior checklist for use in interviewing adult informants; 1 form ('59, 4 pages); manual ('58, 10 pages); no data on reliability; $1.30 per 25 score sheets; 50¢ per manual; postage extra; 55¢ per specimen set, postpaid; [30] minutes; Merlin J. Mecham; Educational Test Bureau. *

REFERENCES
1. MECHAM, MERLIN J. "The Development and Application of Procedures for Measuring Speech Improvement in Mentally Defective Children." *Am J Mental Def* 60:301–6 O '55. * (PA 30:6096)
2. MECHAM, MERLIN J. "A Scale for Screening Level of

Verbal Communication Behavior in Cerebral Palsy." *Cerebral Palsy R* 18:22–3 Jl–Ag '57. * (PA 33:1994)
3. WILLIAMS, W. G. *An Appraisal of the Adequacy and Usefulness of an Objective Language Scale When Administered to Elementary School Children.* Master's thesis, Brigham Young University (Provo, Utah), 1958.
4. BARNARD, L. W. *The Validation of a Scale for Measuring Level of Verbal Communication Behavior in Children.* Master's thesis, Brigham Young University (Provo, Utah), 1959.
5. MECHAM, MERLIN J. "Measurement of Verbal Language Development in Cerebral Palsy." *Cerebral Palsy R* 21:3–4 My–Je '60. * (PA 35:2520)
6. WILLIAMS, WILLIAM G. "The Adequacy and Usefulness of an Objective Language Scale When Administered to Elementary School Children." *J Ed Res* 54:30–3 S '60. *
7. BOWN, JESSE CLINTON, JR., AND MECHAM, MERLIN J. "The Assessment of Verbal Language Development in Deaf Children." *Volta R* 63:228–30 My '61. *

[Other Tests]
For tests not listed above, see the following entries in *Tests in Print*: 526–8 and 530; out of print: 522.

SPELLING

[317]

Ayer Standardized Spelling Test. Grades 9–12; 1950; Forms 1, 2, ('50, 1 page); directions ('50, 4 pages) for each form; no data on reliability; $1 per 40 tests; 25¢ per specimen set; cash orders postpaid; (30) minutes; Fred C. Ayer; Steck Co.*

GUS P. PLESSAS, *Associate Professor of Education, Sacramento State College, Sacramento, California.*

The *Ayer Standardized Spelling Test* is designed to measure general spelling achievement among students in high school. The test includes two comparable forms having 30 test words each.

The procedures for administering the test are simple and easy. Each test word is pronounced, read in a prepared sentence, and pronounced again; thus, the meaning of each word to be spelled is illustrated adequately. The students, in turn, write the spelling words in blanks in the test sentences printed on individual test sheets. Sufficient space is provided in each sentence to allow for writing in the blanks.

Technical sources and procedures for selecting the test words are not stated in the manual, nor is the validity of the test reported. However, in a separately published bulletin,[1] Ayer implies that these words are usually taught in elementary school and are commonly found in the writings of high school students. A careful analysis of these words does indicate that the test has a measure of curricular validity, even though the selection of words is questionable in some respects on the basis of utility. For

1 AYER, FRED C. *The Evaluation and Measurement of High School Spelling.* Austin, Tex.: Steck Co., 1950. Pp. 6. *

instance, 27 per cent of the words in Form 1 and 43 per cent of the words in Form 2 are not included among the most frequently written words by children and adults in Fitzgerald's *A Basic Life Spelling Vocabulary.*[2]

The standardization of the test is based on scores of 35,000 high school students in 48 states. Unfortunately, however, reliability data are not presented in the manual. Since the spelling test includes only 30 words, reliability information concerning the instrument assumes greater importance, and, undoubtedly, 10 or 20 additional words would insure a higher degree of reliability.

The normative data include the standard scores for each word in terms of per cent correct in grades 9 through 12 in addition to average per cent scores for the total test at each high school grade. Since the test was published in 1950, recent evidence suggests that the standardized scores need revision in order to provide a basis for comparison against current standards. For example, according to the *New Iowa Spelling Scale,* at the eighth grade level, the per cent correct is higher than the per cent indicated in the manual at the ninth grade level in spelling four words in Form 1 and six words in Form 2, or 17 per cent of the total words.

The individual test sheets or summary forms that accompany the test facilitate the comparison of the spelling status of an individual, class, or school with national norms in such a way that above average, average, or below average performances are identified. The test, however, does not adequately satisfy the claims advanced by its author. First, it does not have sufficient level of difficulty to satisfactorily discriminate spelling ability among average or above average groups of high school students, particularly those in the junior or senior year. The mean per cent of correct spelling of the Form 2 words, for instance, is 81 and 85 for grades 11 and 12, respectively, for the average high school. Second, the test does not reveal specific strengths or weaknesses, because it does not have any diagnostic features to determine a student's strong and weak areas in spelling. Third, the test does not point out a specific level—such as a grade level score or percentile rank—at which an individual performs in spelling. Fourth, in no way will the

results of this test indicate specific approaches in teaching spelling, since the knowledge of individual errors is not sufficient to reveal detailed weakness other than a general level of high, average, or low spelling performance. At best, this instrument serves as a general measure of spelling ability among high school students, particularly at the freshman level.

For a review by Harold H. Bixler, see 4:198.

[318]

*Gates-Russell Spelling Diagnostic Tests. Grades 2–6; 1937–40; 9 scores: spelling words orally, word pronunciation, giving letters for letter sounds, spelling one syllable, spelling two syllables, word reversals, spelling attack, auditory discrimination, visual-auditory-kinaesthetic and combined study methods; individual; 1 form ('37, 4 pages); revised manual ('40, 53 pages); no description of normative population; $2.25 per 35 tests; $1 per specimen set (must be purchased to obtain manual); postpaid; Arthur I. Gates and David H. Russell; Bureau of Publications. *

For a review by George Spache, see 4:200; for reviews by John C. Almack and Thomas G. Foran, see 38:1159.

[319]

★Group Diagnostic Spelling Test. Grades 9–13; 1958; Forms A, B, ['58, 3 mimeographed pages]; hectographed manual ['58, 7 pages]; separate answer sheets must be used; 5¢ per test; 1¢ per mimeographed answer sheet; 25¢ per manual; 35¢ per specimen set; postpaid; (20–30) minutes; Thomas G. Kemp; Reading Laboratory and Clinic. *

[320]

*Lincoln Diagnostic Spelling Tests. Grades 2–4 or 2–5, 4–8 or 5–8, 8–12 or 9–12; 1941–62; 2 editions; A. L. Lincoln.

a) [EDUCATIONAL RECORDS BUREAU EDITION.] Grades 2–4 or 2–5, 4–8, 8–12; 1941–62; 3 levels; norms for independent school students only; 8¢ per test, postage extra; Educational Records Bureau. *

1) *Lincoln Primary Spelling Test.* Grades 2–4 in independent schools or 2–5 in public schools; 1960–62; Forms W and X for fall testing, Y and Z for spring testing; response booklet ('60, 4 pages) for all forms; dictation lists (6 pages): Forms W ['61], X ['60], Y ['61], Z ['62]; mimeographed manual ('60, 7 pages); norms (1 page): Forms W ('61), X ('60), Y ('62), Z ('62); no data on reliability; norms for grades 2 and 3 only; [60] minutes.

2) *Lincoln Intermediate Spelling Test.* Grades 4–8; 1941–62; Forms A, B, C, ('49, 4 pages, identical with tests published in 1947 and 1948), D ('49, 4 pages); Forms A and C for fall testing, B and D for spring testing; dictation list (1 page) for each form; combined manual ('51, 10 pages) for this test and 3) below; revised norms (1 page): Forms A ('61), B ('62), C ('60), D ('61); (30–40) minutes.

3) *Lincoln Diagnostic Spelling Test* [Advanced]. Grades 8–12; 1941–62; Forms 1 ('49, identical with test copyrighted in 1941), 2 ['42], 3 ['43], 4 ['44], (4 pages); dictation list (1 page) for each form; combined manual ('51, 10 pages) for this test and 2) above; revised fall norms (1 page): Forms 1

2 FITZGERALD, JAMES A. *A Basic Life Spelling Vocabulary.* Milwaukee, Wis.: Bruce Publishing Co., 1951. Pp. 161. *

Lincoln Diagnostic Spelling Tests

('62), 2 ('61), 3 ('59), 4 ('57); revised spring
norms (1 page): Forms 1 ('58), 2 ('60), 3 ('62),
4 ('61); (30–40) minutes.
b) [BOBBS-MERRILL COMPANY EDITION.] Grades 5–8,
9–12; 1949–56; Forms A (for fall testing), B (for
spring testing); 2 levels; manual ('56, 16 pages);
tentative norms; $3.15 per 35 tests; 50¢ per specimen
set; postage extra; (30–40) minutes; Bobbs-Merrill
Co., Inc. *
  1) *Intermediate.* Grades 5–8; Forms A, B, ('56,
  4 pages, same as Forms A, B of the *Lincoln Intermediate Spelling Test* published in 1947 and 1948).
  2) *Advanced.* Grades 9–12; Forms A, B, ('56, 4
  pages, same as Forms 1, 2 of *Lincoln Diagnostic
  Spelling Test* published in 1941 and 1942).

REFERENCES
  1. TOWNSEND, AGATHA. "A Study of the Lincoln Diagnostic
Spelling Test." *Ed Rec B* 38:49–53 Je '43. *
  2. TOWNSEND, AGATHA. "A Report on the Use of the Lincoln Intermediate Spelling Test." *Ed Rec B* 49:40–8 F '48. *
(PA 22:3648)
  3. LUNTZ, LESTER. "A Comparison of Results Obtained
With Dictation and Multiple-Choice Spelling Tests." *Ed
Rec B* 65:76–84 F '55. * (PA 29:7866)
  4. WALDMAN, JOHN, AND TRIGGS, FRANCES ORALIND. "Measurement of Word Attack Skills." *El Engl* 35:450–63 N '58. *
  5. TRAXLER, ARTHUR E. "Some Data on the Difficulty, Reliability, and Validity of a New Spelling Test for the Primary
Grades." *Ed Rec B* 77:67–73 Jl '60. *
  6. VECCHIONE, NICHOLAS. "Sex Differences in Spelling
Skills of Independent Secondary School Pupils." *Ed Rec B*
76:65–8 F '60. *

GUS P. PLESSAS, *Associate Professor of Education, Sacramento State College, Sacramento,
California.* [Review of the Educational Records Bureau Edition.]

PRIMARY TEST. The *Lincoln Primary Spelling
Test* is constructed to include three distinct but
overlapping levels of spelling words so that the
same test with different words can be used with
children of independent schools (in grades 2–
4) and those (in grades 3–5) of public schools.

The spelling words, selected from Gates' *A
List of Spelling Difficulties in 3876 Words,*
total 144, only 72 of which are used in any one
testing situation. Since the appropriate words
are identified according to grade level, type of
school, and time of testing (fall or spring),
the starting and stopping points are different
for each grade level and for the independent
and public schools.

According to the manual, the words are
arranged in ascending order of difficulty, covering a grade placement of from 1.1 to 7.1.
Included is the median grade placement value
of each level of spelling words. Although not
stating so explicitly in the manual, the author
apparently assigned a grade value to each word
on the basis of its average grade placement as
reported by Gates. These reported grade placement values can be misleading if they are
equated with difficulty levels. For instance, the
author advances the notion that the words to
be spelled are ranked according to their spell-

ing difficulty. Perhaps the words are in the
order of difficulty, but this arrangement cannot
be defended solely on the basis of their grade
placement, particularly as identified by Gates.
In the first place, grade placement of spelling
words is determined mainly by their frequency
of use, permanent value, and difficulty. In the
second place, Gates' work, which began in 1928
and was published in 1937, included the average grade placement of words in various textbooks and courses of study that are now at
least 30 years old. As a consequence, for example, Gates' placement of the spelling word
rolled is 2.55, but according to the *New Iowa
Spelling Scale,* only 28 per cent of third grade
children can correctly spell it. In contrast,
Gates' average grade placement for the word
maybe is 4.55, but 49 per cent of children in
third grade classes can spell this word correctly.
Therefore, to say that the words in the test are
arranged according to their difficulty is not
entirely accurate.

In the manual, the author states, "The Primary Level of the Lincoln Spelling Test series
is designed to pinpoint a selected number of
strengths and weaknesses in word attack or
phonics." Although the test is organized to
provide diagnostic information in terms of the
pupils' spelling performances, no evidence or
validity studies are presented to support the
major aim of the test. This point is discussed
in more detail in the next section of this review
(*Lincoln Intermediate Spelling Test*).

Percentile ratings and grade score equivalents accompany the test. The percentile norms,
however, are based on grossly inadequate numbers. Illustrative of the situation is Form X,
for which percentile ranks are based on 98
pupils in grade 2 and 92 pupils in grade 3.
Furthermore, the percentile scale was extended
only to grades 2 and 3. In addition, there is no
evidence to indicate the basis upon which the
grade score equivalents were determined. It
seems that the grade scores were arbitrarily
derived by statistical extrapolation.

Satisfactory directions for administering and
scoring the test are provided in the manual.
The pupils write the spelling words in a specially prepared booklet which has adequate
space for writing the words and which is also
organized to facilitate correcting.

Perhaps the best use of this spelling test is
as a general measure of spelling achievement
among children in the primary grades, despite

the fact that no data concerning validity and reliability are provided.

INTERMEDIATE TEST. The *Lincoln Intermediate Spelling Test,* for grades 5–8, is designed to measure spelling achievement with particular attention to the evaluation of specific disabilities. It includes four reasonably equivalent forms, each consisting of 100 words arranged generally in ascending order of difficulty as indicated by their average grade placement according to Gates, Betts, and the New York State List, which are the sources of the words.

The words are also arranged so that words representing a common phonetic element or a particular spelling generalization bear a common final digit. Each word can easily be identified by category to facilitate the diagnosis of spelling performances when spelling errors are recorded by categories, which include erroneous pronunciation in terms of number of syllables, the *ie-ei* rule, the *y* to *i* rule, final *e* before a suffix, double consonant, spelling demons, prefixes and suffixes, erroneous pronunciation in terms of quality of syllables, homonyms, and possessives and contractions.

Students write the words in a thoughtfully prepared booklet. Beside each blank is an illustrative sentence with the spelling word omitted so that the students can check the meaning of the word as it is pronounced. Thus, since the examiner does not need to use the words in sentences, the time for testing is reduced to approximately 40 minutes. Most sentences which illustrate the meanings of the words are carefully written.

Despite a reported total score correlation of .90 between performances of seventh graders on the *Lincoln Intermediate Spelling Test* and on the spelling section of the *Stanford Achievement Test,* there is serious question regarding the validity of the diagnostic features and of the part scores. The fact that a student misspells several words that have been classified in the same way does not necessarily indicate a related weakness. For example, in spelling words having affixes a pupil can easily misspell the base word rather than the affix, in which case his problem may be unrelated to the spelling of suffixes. Similarly, what does it mean when a student misspells demons among other misspelled words? Is this a case of general or specific disability? Furthermore, since each category is represented by only 10 words, the

usefulness of the diagnostic aspects of the test is sharply limited, especially since the words are listed in ascending order of difficulty and many students will not spell correctly many words at the upper levels of the test. It seems important to stress, therefore, that the diagnosis of spelling disabilities is an individual matter and that the use of this test for such a purpose involves much more than simply categorizing misspelled words; it involves the judicious interpretation of each misspelled word.

Reliabilities for the total test and for the part scores of the intermediate test are reported to have a median coefficient of .93 for the five grades from 4 through 8.

Median and quartile scores and percentile ratings for independent schools accompany the test. Norms for public schools are available only upon request from the publisher.

In short, this test is perhaps best used as a measure of general spelling achievement of students in grades 4 through 8 in independent schools.

ADVANCED TEST. The chief purpose of the *Lincoln Diagnostic Spelling Test* is to evaluate certain areas in the spelling performances of students in grades 8–12. This test purports to examine the effect of pronunciation, enunciation, and use of rules on spelling.

The words in the test are not arranged in order of difficulty, but follow the classification system outlined above for the intermediate test, except that at this level the erroneous pronunciation (quality of syllables) category is replaced by one dealing with Latin endings. The criticism of the lower level is equally applicable to this test. Similarly the method of administration is identical.

Validity and reliability studies are cited in the manual. As evidence for statistical validity, Townsend (*1*) reports a .93 correlation with Mechanics of Expression of the *Cooperative English Test,* Form T, which included a spelling section. Correlation of .85 was found by Spaulding [1] in a comparison of the Lincoln test and the *Progressive Achievement Tests.* This finding perhaps indicates the validity of the test as a measure of spelling achievement; however, its curricular validity as a diagnostic instrument is questionable, particularly in light of some areas purportedly tested in spelling.

1 SPAULDING, GERALDINE. "The Use of the Progressive Achievement Test at the Ninth-Grade Level in Independent Schools." *Ed Rec B* 56:73–7 Ja '51. •

Lincoln Diagnostic Spelling Tests

Townsend and Spaulding also reported total score reliability coefficients (Spearman-Brown) of .93 and .89, respectively; however, the Spearman-Brown reliabilities of the part scores were considerably lower. Among 118 independent school pupils in grade 10, Townsend found a range of .47 to .80 with a median of .69.

As a standardized test for national use, this test has normative data in terms of percentile ranks for independent schools, but the number of cases used to standardize the measure is low for certain grades and forms. For example, the standardization of Form 1, fall 1962, involved only 514 students at Grade 8.

In summary, the *Lincoln Diagnostic Spelling Test* is best used as a general measure of spelling performance with some analytical features to assess deficiencies in the use of certain spelling rules among students at the high school level of independent schools.

For reviews by Walter Scribner Guiler and George Spache of the intermediate and advanced tests, see 4:202–3.

[321]

★**Nationwide Spelling Examination.** Grades 4–12; 1959–63; new form issued each April; norms available following the testing program; 1 form ('63, 2 pages); no manual; mimeographed norms ('63, 1 page); no data on reliability; 10¢ per test, postage extra; (40–45) minutes; [Donald R. Honz]; Educational Stimuli. *

[322]

★**The New Iowa Spelling Scale.** Grades 2–8; 1954; master word list with difficulty values by grades from which teacher may compile tests; manual ('54, 180 pages including word list); no data on reliability; 65¢ per manual, postage extra; Harry A. Greene; Bureau of Educational Research and Service. *

REFERENCES

1. GROFF, PATRICK J. "The New Iowa Spelling Scale: How Phonetic Is It?" *El Sch J* 62:46–9 O '61. *

[323]

*****Spelling and Vocabulary: Every Pupil Test.** Grades 3–4, 5–6, 7–9, 10–12; 1948–64; new form (4 pages) usually issued each December and April; forms from previous testing programs also available; 4 levels; general directions sheet ('63, 2 pages); no data on reliability; Ohio norms for new forms available following testing program; 5¢ per test; 3¢ per key; postpaid; 40(45) minutes; Ohio Scholarship Tests. *

[324]

★**[Spelling and Word Meaning Tests.]** Business and industry; 1957–62; 1 form ('57, 5 pages); 2 tests in a single booklet; manual ['63, 9 unnumbered pages]; no data on reliability; $3.50 per 25 tests; 10¢ per key; 75¢ per manual; postage extra; $1 per specimen set, postpaid; 10(20) minutes; Richardson, Bellows, Henry & Co., Inc. *

[325]

*****Spelling: Every Pupil Scholarship Test.** Grades 3, 4–6, 7–8, 9–12; 1928–64; new form (2 pages) usually issued each January and April; forms from previous testing programs also available; 4 levels; general directions sheet ['63, 2 pages]; no data on reliability; norms for new forms available following testing program; 4¢ per test; 4¢ per key; postage extra; 15(20) minutes for grades 3–8, 30(35) minutes for grades 9–12; Bureau of Educational Measurements. *

[326]

Traxler High School Spelling Test. Grades 9–12; 1937–55; Forms 1, 2, 3, ('55, 2 pages, same as tests published in 1937–40); manual ('55, 4 pages); no data on reliability of Form 3; norms based upon testing in private schools in 1937–40; $2.80 per 35 tests; 50¢ per specimen set; postage extra; administration time not reported; Arthur E. Traxler; Bobbs-Merrill Co., Inc. *

GUS P. PLESSAS, *Associate Professor of Education, Sacramento State College, Sacramento, California.*

Although the purpose is not stated, the *Traxler High School Spelling Test* appears designed to measure general spelling ability among students in grades 9 through 12.

Unlike typical test procedures for presenting words to be spelled by saying the word, using it in a sentence, and repeating it, the procedures for presenting the spelling words in this test are simplified. The test words are pronounced by the examiner and the students write them on the form provided. For each word there is a sentence in which the dictated word is replaced by dots. Illustrative sentences, without the spelling words, are printed beside the appropriate blanks that are at the right side of the page. Consequently, this organization has the favorable result of reducing the testing time and of facilitating the correction of the test.

According to the directions, the illustrative sentences are given to help the student understand the spelling words; however, a careful examination of these sentences suggests that many are inadequate to illustrate satisfactorily the meanings of the words to be spelled. Consider the following examples. In Form 1, *miscellaneous* is illustrated by the sentence "That is a....group," and *sovereign* is represented by "He is the....of the entire nation." Likewise, in Form 2, *occurrence* is illustrated by the sentence "This is a rare....in our city," and *appropriate* is demonstrated by "This is the....page." Obviously, students who are unfamiliar with *miscellaneous, occurrence, sovereign,* and *appropriate* are not particularly aided by these illustrative sentences in trying to infer the meanings of these spelling words.

This spelling test has three 50-word forms, of which Forms 1 and 2 are judged equivalent. The test words in these two forms were selected from the *Buckingham Extension of the Ayers Spelling Scale* and checked against Horn's *A Basic Writing Vocabulary.* Although selected on the same basis, the spelling words in Form 3 are more difficult in order that a higher level of spelling achievement can be measured, particularly among exceptional students. Thus, Form 3 is not comparable to Forms 1 and 2, and it should not be used as an equated form to measure spelling progress.

The test manual reports that no statistical study was conducted to determine the validity of the spelling instrument but states that the test has face validity because the words to be spelled represent a sample of high school students' active spelling vocabulary, since most of the words are found in the more common 5,000 words of the Horn list. However, according to Fitzgerald's list of 2,650 most commonly written words by children and adults, Forms 1, 2, and 3 have 32, 24, and 2 per cents, respectively, of their words among the most common. This finding suggests that there is a higher degree of curricular validity for Forms 1 and 2 than for Form 3 and that many spelling words in Form 3 are questionable on the basis of utility. For example, such spelling words as *hippopotamus, maneuver, chandelier,* and *distillery* are not likely to be part of the "active" writing vocabulary of high school students.

Reliability coefficients are reported above .90 for correlations between scores on Form 1 and scores on Form 2 made by students in one public high school. Unfortunately, however, the number of cases upon which the reliability data were determined seems indeed small and inadequate for a standardized instrument that is for high school use in all states; moreover, no information is given regarding the reliability of Form 3. Similarly, percentile norms are based on scores of less than 500 students for any particular test form at a specific grade with a range from 191 to 471. A typical example is the standardization data of Form 2 at the ninth grade, in which the percentile norms are based on only 388 pupils. This unsatisfac-

tory number has certainly weakened the dependability of the test, especially the norms.

For a review by Henry D. Rinsland, see 4:212.

[Other Tests]

For tests not listed above, see the following entries in *Tests in Print*: 531–2, 534, 538–40, 542, 545, 547, 552, 555–7, and 559; out of print: 535–6, 541, 550, and 554.

VOCABULARY

[327]

A.C.E.R. Word Knowledge Test—Adult Form B. Ages 18 and over; 1933–60; Form B ['54, 4 pages, identical with part 1 of *A.C.E.R. Silent Reading Tests,* Form B for grades 3–8 except for directions]; mimeographed manual ('60, 11 pages); 3s. 6d. per 10 tests; 3s. per key; 3s. per manual; 6s. 6d. per specimen set; postpaid within Australia; 8(10) minutes; T. M. Whitford (manual) and the Australian Council for Educational Research; the Council. *

REFERENCES
1. BUCKLOW, MAXINE, AND DOUGHTY, PATRICIA. "The Use of Aptitude Tests in Clerical Employment: The Selection of Accounting Machinists." *Personnel Pract B* 13:35–44 S '57. * (PA 33:2256)

For a review by Fred J. Schonell of the reading test, see 5:616.

[328]

★*American Literacy Test.* Adults; 1962; vocabulary; 1 form (3 pages); manual (2 pages); norms for "university seniors," "technical trade candidates," and "illiterates"; normative groups not otherwise described; $3 per 25 tests; $1 per specimen set of 5 tests (must be purchased to obtain manual); cash orders postpaid; 4(10) minutes; John J. McCarty; Psychometric Affiliates. *

VICTOR H. NOLL, *Professor of Education, Michigan State University, East Lansing, Michigan.*

This test consists of 50 four-response multiple choice vocabulary items which require the subject to select the choice which "means the same or about the same" as the stimulus word. Answers are marked on the test blank, although standard machine scorable answer sheets could be used with a slight modification in directions. The time allowed is four minutes. Test-retest reliability based on 59 subjects, six weeks intervening, is reported as .82. Scores on the test for 43 students in English at Southern Illinois University yielded a correlation of .49 with scores on a test of English fundamentals. A point biserial coefficient contrasting the performance on the test of 263 associate degree candidates with that of 102 senior engineers was found to be .82. Scores of 16 illiterates were all below 10, which is below a chance score for anyone attempting all items. Percentile norms are given for university seniors, technical trade candidates, and illiterates. Since these norms are not otherwise described, one may infer that they are based on the 102 engineers, 263 associate degree candidates, and 16 illiterates mentioned above.

The test purports to be a "highly useful test of literacy," "economical of time, efficient in design and reliability of construction, and well-spiralled or graduated in item difficulty so as to yield reliable spread of respondents according to degree of literacy." It also purports to "bear some reasonable relation to knowledge of the grammar and mechanics of the English language."

The test seems misnamed in the generally accepted use of the term literacy, that is, the ability to read and write. It is not a test of reading (except in the very limited sense that many reading tests contain tests of word knowledge as part of the total) and it is obviously not a test of ability to write. The claim that it is economical of time is substantiated by the fact that it requires only four minutes of working time plus possibly five minutes for instructions. If being printed on a four page folder and having one page left over means "efficient in design" the claim is justified. Since the reviewer does not know what is meant by the latter part of the statement that a highly useful test of literacy should be "efficient in design and *reliability of construction,*" and since no information on this point is given, no judgment as to how well this purpose was achieved can be rendered. No information is provided on the basis for selection of words to be included or on results of item analysis. That items vary in percentage of correct responses between 20 and 92 for 300 adults hardly constitutes an adequate criterion for selection for the final form.

Information on reliability and validity is difficult to interpret because of (*a*) small numbers of subjects involved in most instances, (*b*) lack of information regarding the nature of these subjects, and (*c*) questionable statistical technique.

Lacking information as noted, the test must be regarded as simply a collection of 50 vocabulary items little different from, or better

than, what any teacher might put together over a quiet weekend. It appears to have no unusual qualities or superior merit though the implications of the statements by the author and publisher lead one to expect them. Few of the recommendations of the committees on test standards appear to have been met. At 12¢ per copy it seems like no bargain at all.

[329]

★**Bruce Vocabulary Inventory.** Business and industry; 1959; IBM; 1 form (4 pages); manual (4 pages); $5 per 25 tests; 25¢ per hand scoring key; separate answer sheets may be used; $2.75 per 25 IBM answer sheets; 50¢ per set of scoring stencils; 75¢ per manual; $1 per specimen set; cash orders postpaid; (15–25) minutes; Martin M. Bruce; the Author. *

[330]

Durost-Center Word Mastery Test: Evaluation and Adjustment Series. Grades 9–13; 1951–52, c1950–52; 3 scores: vocabulary, vocabulary in context, use of context; IBM; Form AM ('51, 7 pages); manual ('52, 15 pages); separate answer sheets must be used; $4.70 per 35 tests; $1.75 per 35 IBM answer sheets; 40¢ per specimen set; postage extra; 60(80) minutes in 2 sessions 2–7 days apart; Walter N. Durost and Stella S. Center; [Harcourt, Brace & World, Inc.]. *

GEORGE P. WINSHIP, JR., *Professor of English, King College, Bristol, Tennessee.*

The distinctive feature of the *Durost-Center Word Mastery Test* is the score representing the use of context in determining the meaning of a word. The student is examined twice on the same 100 words, once in a conventional multiple response test presenting the basic word alone with four choices, and a second time including a sentence using each word in a meaningful way. If the two parts of the test are administered several days apart, there should be a marked improvement when the words are encountered the second time in context. This improvement is held to be a measure of the student's ability to make use of contextual clues as a means of building his own vocabulary: a score representing the difference is expressed as a percentile rank; separate scores on the two parts may also be expressed as percentile ranks.

No information is given in the manual about the effect of giving the first part of the test (the isolated words) twice to the same students. It would seem that for certain students, at least, there might be a measurable improvement after a week even without context.

In many vocabulary tests employing context, the sentences are by intention sometimes ambiguous; they give no help. The authors of this test have tried to make the sentences meaningful. The range of helpfulness may be indicated by these examples: "The law says we should not molest that which belongs to others. To *molest* means to: (1) desire, (2) copy, (3) harm, (4) alter." Here each of the suggested synonyms fits fairly well in the sentence. The context gives little aid. This is an unusual example; more characteristic is this: "A child resents being scolded for something which he did not do. To *resent* is to: (1) store up, (2) deny, (3) feel angry, (4) admit." Here the context is helpful. Although the third alternative should be "feel angry at," a person totally unfamiliar with the word *resent* can still solve the item by a very careful examination of the context. From the inspection of Form AM, I should judge that no contexts are misleading, that nearly half of them give substantial help (narrowing the choice to about two alternatives), and about half of the contexts give the tested word away entirely. That is, they would do so to a very intelligent student entirely unacquainted with the word. This student is somewhat imaginary. Those who are skilful in determining meanings from context have already learned most of the words, which are well distributed through the first 20,000 words in frequency in the Thorndike-Lorge lists. Those who are unfamiliar with such words obviously lack skills in reading. The most obvious exceptions would be those whose native tongue is not English.

Certainly the skill tested is one of the most important to any student interested in reading more effectively. The Use of Context score would seem to tell the teacher very little she would not already know from other sources. But it might tell the student a good deal. His failures, and particularly his successes, in determining the meaning of a word from its use in a sentence on this test will tell him more about how to read than a great deal of exhortation.

The Durost-Center test seems best adapted to the lower secondary grades or to classes not above average in reading ability. For teachers working with students who lack skill in determining meanings from context, it can be a valuable tool.

For a review by A. N. Hieronymus, see 5:233.

[331]

★**Gulick Vocabulary Survey.** College and superior high school seniors; 1961, c1954–61; IBM; Forms A1, A2, B1, B2, ('61, c1954–57, 6 pages); manual ('61, c1957–61, 17 pages); student report ('61, c1957–61, 1 page); data card ('61, c1957–61, 1 page); norms for college freshmen only; separate answer sheets must be used; 15¢ per test; 50¢ per set of scoring stencils (available only with 25 or more tests); 3¢ per student report; 3¢ per data card; 50¢ per manual (free with 25 or more tests); postage extra; specimen set free; IBM answer sheets must be purchased elsewhere; (35–40) minutes; Sidney L. Gulick and Darrell Holmes (manual); Chandler Publishing Co. *

REFERENCES
1. GULICK, SIDNEY L., AND HOLMES, DARRELL. "A Vocabulary Tool for the English Teacher." *Col Engl* 19:214–7 F '58. *

GEORGE P. WINSHIP, JR., *Professor of English, King College, Bristol, Tennessee.*

The four forms of the *Gulick Vocabulary Survey* are multiple choice tests of 100 items each. In Forms A1 and A2 the words to be identified appear alone; in Forms B1 and B2 they are given in short phrases of context which sometimes identify the general area of meaning; in other instances they give no information but possibly build confidence in the student. Occasionally the context serves only to confuse: consider *"Intersperse* your answer with examples." This should, of course, have been *"Intersperse* examples in your answer," and if it had been so phrased, an able student could have selected *scatter,* the "correct" answer. As it stands, a student sensitive to English will be drawn toward two wrong answers, *enliven* and *fill up.* "Scatter your answer with examples" is clearly impossible.

This item raises a question of fundamental importance, that of what kind of skill in diction is being examined. To be sure, most of the 400 items offer clear cut choices to students familiar with the words. So do numerous other carefully constructed vocabulary tests now on the market. What is distinctive about this Survey? Each form comprises a random selection from the Thorndike-Lorge list of 30,000 words (omitting the most frequent 10,000); thus each word correctly identified on one of the tests should indicate a probable "knowledge" of 200 words from among the 20,000 most important for a high school or college student to study. Or such is the assumption expressed in the manual and implied on the tests themselves and in the accompanying report form. For example, a raw score of 60 out of the 100 items is said to mean that the student knows 60 times 200 or 12,000 words, in addition to nearly all of the 10,000 commonest words in printed English, or a total of 22,000 words. Such a score would place him at the 80th percentile of college freshmen. A total of 24,000, or about 10 more right answers, is a basis for prediction of success in graduate school. A total vocabulary of 18,000 or less presages grave difficulty in college.

These observations are of great interest and, if true, of great importance to guidance counselors and teachers. The test may be used, of course, for the placement or comparative rating of students whether or not it accurately estimates the size of their total vocabularies. But the total estimate is the special feature of the Gulick Survey. It is for this reason that the author has adhered strictly to a sampling procedure to select his words. Many of these which he has been obliged to use are easy and obvious, even though they fall beyond the first 10,000 of the Thorndike-Lorge list. There seems to be little point in testing the knowledge of tomcat, overgrown, brainless, and snow-white. But since these words have to be in the test, the test writer is impelled to construct reasonably difficult items by searching out obscure synonyms or distractors, and not infrequently the item is as tricky as the casket scene in *The Merchant of Venice*.

Apparently no clear definition exists of a student's "knowledge" of a word. In our schools we define this knowledge as the student's ability to match a word with one of four other words, which may vary widely in their familiarity and their ability to confuse him. He may recognize the word in one context or several but not in the sense selected for the test. To take a simple example, on this test a city boy must show he knows *newt* (and 199 other words) by matching it with *salamander*. He has never seen the little lizard, but he has met "eye of newt" in *Macbeth* and supposes it to be some small animal, probably disgusting. To him, however, a salamander is an oil heater used by builders to dry plaster in wet weather, or possibly a mythical being in *The Rape of the Lock*. He can't match it with *newt*. There go his 200 words, though he is reasonably knowledgeable. On the other hand, he may "correctly" identify *devourer* as *glutton* without recognizing the difference in connotation and even denotation between the words. He may identify *unfelt* as *being not aware of* without recognizing that these ex-

pressions are grammatically opposite and cannot possibly be interchanged.

The claim is made that the four forms are "comparable" and that "a student taking two forms of the test usually obtains scores within five points of equality." A very small scale test by the reviewer indicates that A1 is considerably more difficult than the others and B2 considerably easier. However strict the mathematical procedure for the random selection of words, there apparently is no uniformity of difficulty of the distractors.

In short, the four forms of the *Gulick Vocabulary Survey* are fairly well constructed multiple choice tests of a conventional sort. The special feature, which is the estimate of the total size of the student's vocabulary, is of doubtful value since no clear concept of "knowledge" of a word is implied. As a teaching tool, these tests are somewhat inefficient since so many of the words present no important difficulty.

[332]

*The Iowa Tests of Educational Development: Test 8, General Vocabulary. Grades 9–12; 1942–61; IBM; Forms X-3S, Y-3S, ('52, 3 pages); battery examiner's manual ('58, c1949–57, 23 pages); battery general manual ('59, 37 pages); student profile leaflet, sixth edition ('61, c1958, 2 pages); see the complete battery entry (14b) for other accessories; no data on reliability; separate answer sheets must be used; $2.40 per 20 tests; $5 per 100 IBM answer sheets; 50¢ per scoring stencil; $3 per specimen set of the complete battery; postage extra; 22(30) minutes; prepared under the direction of E. F. Lindquist; Science Research Associates, Inc. *

For reviews of the complete battery, see 14 and 5:17; for reviews of earlier forms, see 4:17 and 3:12.

[333]

*Johnson O'Connor English Vocabulary Worksamples. Ages 9–14, 15 and over, "high vocabulary students and adults"; 1934–62; 3 levels; mimeographed manual ('60, 37 pages); no data on reliability; $5 per set of manual and any 2 forms, postpaid; specimen set not available; [30] minutes; Johnson O'Connor and others; Human Engineering Laboratory Inc. *
a) INTERMEDIATE FORM WORKSAMPLE 176. Ages 9–14; form AD ('56, c1944–56, 4 pages); also available on tape for use with ages 7–10 and persons with reading difficulty.
b) WORKSAMPLE 95. Ages 15 and over; all but 3–7 items of Forms AD, BC, and CC are revisions of items from *The Inglis Tests of English Vocabulary* (see 5:234); Forms AD ('39), BC ('41), CC ('41), DB ('36), EB ('41), IA ('47), JB ('62), (4 pages except Form IA, 10 mimeographed pages); Form JB, titled *Intermediate Worksample 95*, is an easier form and may also be used with ages 9–14; Form

IA is a more difficult form; norms for Form JB based on an earlier edition.

c) ADVANCED FORM WORKSAMPLE 180. "High vocabulary students and adults"; Form 180 AD ('55, c1949–55, 4 pages).

REFERENCES

1. O'CONNOR, JOHNSON, AND FILLEY, MARY E. "A Junior English Vocabulary Test." *Personnel J* 12:204–12 D '33. * (*PA* 8:2783)
2. ACHARD, F. H., AND CLARKE, FLORENCE H. "You *Can* Measure the Probability of Success as a Supervisor." *Personnel* 21:353–73 My '45. *
3. GELMAN, BABETTE. *A Preliminary Comparison of Vocabulary Levels With Choice of Reading Material.* Human Engineering Laboratory, Inc., Technical Report No. 176. Boston, Mass.: the Laboratory, October 1945. Pp. 24. *
4. FISHER, FRANCES. *Scenario on Word Straggled 95 A D Word Number 83.* Human Engineering Laboratory, Inc., Technical Report No. 208. Boston, Mass.: the Laboratory, January 1946. Pp. 4. *
5. UHRBROCK, RICHARD STEPHEN. "Construction of a Selection Test for College Graduates." *J General Psychol* 41:153–93 O '49. * (*PA* 24:4874)

[334]

★Johnson O'Connor Vocabulary Tests. Professionals; 1937–58; 6 tests; no manual; no data on reliability; no norms; $1 per test, postpaid; [10–30] minutes; [Johnson O'Connor and staff]; Human Engineering Laboratory Inc. *

a) JOHNSON O'CONNOR VOCABULARY OF MATHEMATICS. 1945–56; Forms 280 AA, 280 BB, 280 CB, ('56, 4 pages).
b) JOHNSON O'CONNOR VOCABULARY OF ARCHITECTURE. 1946–56; Form 250 AB ('56, 4 pages).
c) JOHNSON O'CONNOR VOCABULARY OF MUSIC. 1945–56; Form 295 AC ('56, 4 pages).
d) JOHNSON O'CONNOR VOCABULARY OF PHYSICS. 1937–58; Forms 181 CC ('56), 181 DC ('56), 181 EB ('58), (4 pages).
e) JOHNSON O'CONNOR VOCABULARY OF RADIO AND PHYSICS. 1952–56; Form 370 AC ('56, 4 pages).
f) JOHNSON O'CONNOR VOCABULARY OF SPORTS. 1953–56; Form 375 AD ('56, 4 pages).

[335]

★Nationwide English Vocabulary Examination. Grades 4–12; 1959–63; new form issued each April; norms available following the testing program; 1 form ('63, 2 pages); no manual; mimeographed norms ('63, 1 page); no data on reliability; 10¢ per test, postage extra; (40–45) minutes; [Donald R. Honz]; Educational Stimuli. *

[336]

*New Standard Vocabulary Test. Grades 7–12; 1955–63; reprinted from the Educational Edition of *Reader's Digest;* IBM; Forms A ('61), C ('62), and E ('63) for fall testing, B ('62), D ('63), and F ('61) for spring testing, (12 pages, Forms A, B, and C identical with tests copyrighted 1955, 1956, and 1956, respectively, except for slight modification in 1 sentence of directions; Forms D, E, and F identical with tests copyrighted 1957, 1957, and' 1958, respectively); manual ('59, 23 pages); $2.50 per 35 tests; separate answer sheets may be used; $3 per 100 IBM answer sheets; postpaid; answer sheet scoring stencils must be constructed locally; 30(35) minutes; Miriam M. Bryan, Janet G. Afflerbach, and Herbert A. Landry; Educational Division, Reader's Digest Services, Inc. *

For reviews by Richard A. Meade and Osmond E. Palmer, see 5:236.

[337]

Quick-Scoring Vocabulary Test: Dominion Tests. Grades 9–13; 1958; Forms A, B, (2 pages); preliminary manual (4 pages); $1 per 25 test-answer sheets; 20¢ per scoring stencil; 75¢ per specimen set; postage extra; 20(30) minutes; Department of Educational Research, Ontario College of Education, University of Toronto; distributed by Guidance Centre. *

STEPHEN HUNKA, *Assistant Professor of Educational Psychology, University of Alberta, Edmonton, Alberta, Canada.*

The *Quick-Scoring Vocabulary Test* consists of two forms, each containing 90 multiple choice items. Each item presents the stimulus word followed by five words, one of which the student is to select as being the same or nearly the same as the stimulus word. Each question is contained within an enclosed rectangle and responses are marked directly within this area, by blackening a small rectangular space. Plastic scoring stencils are supplied. The scoring sheet appears similar to an IBM sheet, but the manual makes no reference to the possibility of electronic scoring. A single raw score is obtained for each paper and conversion of this score to a percentile is recommended.

Although the manual appears adequate with respect to the details of test administration and scoring, it leaves much to be desired when recommendations of the American Psychological Association are considered. Parallel form reliability coefficients are given for each of five grade levels, and tend to vary between .90 and .93. However, evidence that in fact Forms A and B are comparable is lacking. No means or standard deviations based upon both forms are reported. No measures of item difficulty or internal consistency are reported.

Estimates of the validity of the tests, either predictive, content, or construct, are also lacking; in fact, the user is given no indication as to the type of decisions for which the test may be helpful. The percentile norms are based upon sample sizes ranging from 1,133 to 2,639 at each grade level selected in Ontario during 1956. Characteristics of the norming group other than grade level are lacking, thus making it difficult to determine whether a user's sample is similar to the norming population. No emphasis has been placed upon collection of local norms.

The universe of content from which the words were selected is not defined. An analysis of the frequency of occurrence of stimulus and answer words was made by the reviewer

Quick-Scoring Vocabulary Test

using Thorndike and Lorge's *Teacher's Word Book of 30,000 Words.* In Form A 70 per cent and in Form B 80 per cent of the stimulus words fall into the category 1 to 8 per million. In most instances the correct word in the alternatives appears with considerably greater frequency than the stimulus word.

The most serious deficiency in the test rests in the failure of the authors to describe adequately: (a) the universe of content, (b) the characteristics of the norming group, and (c) how the test score can assist the user in making better decisions about the testee. For the present time it is recommended that the *Durost-Center Word Mastery Test* be used. Although this test may be considered deficient to some extent according to criteria b and c, the psychometric characteristics have been much more carefully explored and reported.

[338]

★**A Test of Active Vocabulary.** Grades 9-12; 1961; Forms A, B, (8 pages); no manual; no data on reliability; no norms; 2 or more tests, 15¢ each; 20¢ per single copy; postpaid; 30(35) minutes; Paul W. Lehmann; Educational Publications. *

[339]

*Vocabulary: Every Pupil Scholarship Test. High school; 1935-64; new form (2 pages) usually issued each January and April; forms from previous testing programs also available; general directions sheet ['63, 2 pages]; no data on reliability; norms for new forms available following testing program; 4¢ per test; 4¢ per key; postage extra; 40(45) minutes; Bureau of Educational Measurements. *

[340]

★**Vocabulary Test** [Management Service Co.]. Employee applicants; 1949; 1 form (1 page); mimeographed instructions (1 page); no data on reliability; no description of normative population; $3 per 10 tests, cash orders postpaid; specimen set not available; (10) minutes; Eugene J. Benge; [Management Service Co.]. *

[341]

★**Vocabulary Test** [Richardson, Bellows, Henry & Co.]. Applicants for clerical and stenographic positions; 1948-63; 1 form ('48, 2 pages); manual ['63, 7 unnumbered pages]; no data on reliability; $2 per 25 tests; 10¢ per key; 75¢ per manual; postage extra; 75¢ per specimen set, postpaid; 5(10) minutes; Richardson, Bellows, Henry & Co., Inc. *

[342]

★**Vocabulary Test—GT.** Ages 21 and over; 1957-60; based on items standardized for *I.E.R. Intelligence Scale CAVD;* Forms 1 ('57), 2 ('57), 3 ('58), 4 ('58), 5 ('60), (1 page); mimeographed directions-norms ('60, 6 pages); no data on reliability; 5¢ per test; $1 per specimen set of all forms (must be purchased to obtain directions-norms); postpaid; (5-10) minutes; Robert L. Thorndike (1,2) and Irving Lorge (3,4,5); Institute of Psychological Research. *

Quick-Scoring Vocabulary Test

REFERENCES

1. THORNDIKE, ROBERT L. "Two Screening Tests of Verbal Intelligence." *J Appl Psychol* 26:128-35 Ap '42. * (PA 16:4205)
2. THORNDIKE, ROBERT L., AND GALLUP, GEORGE H. "Verbal Intelligence of the American Adult." *J General Psychol* 30:75-85 Ja '44. * (PA 18:2290)
3. THORNDIKE, ROBERT L. "An Evaluation of the Adult Intellectual Status of Terman's Gifted Children." *J Genetic Psychol* 72:17-27 Mr '48. * (PA 22:4836)
4. MINER, JOHN B. *Intelligence in the United States.* New York: Springer Publishing Co., Inc., 1957. Pp. xii, 180. * (PA 32:1344)
5. MINER, JOHN B. "On the Use of a Short Vocabulary Test to Measure General Intelligence." *J Ed Psychol* 52:157-60 Je '61. *
6. GRANICK, SAMUEL. "Comparative Analysis of Psychotic Depressives With Matched Normals on Some Untimed Verbal Intelligence Tests." *J Consult Psychol* 27:439-43 O '63. * (PA 38:4628)

ROBERT E. STAKE, *Associate Director, Office of Educational Testing, University of Illinois, Urbana, Illinois.*

Intelligence is not simply verbal ability. A vocabulary test exposes but one facet of intellect. Furthermore, not enough behavior can be sampled in a five-minute testing period (in this decade) to provide a valid index of any important intellectual trait. Yet we find continuing efforts to develop a quick vocabulary test for the measurement of intelligence. A person interested in describing individual human beings should ignore these efforts. But a person interested in comparisons, even crude comparisons, of groups of human beings may find these efforts useful.

Verbal ability is an important dimension of intellect, and vocabulary items have gained general acceptance for the estimation of verbal ability. For these reasons, and because vocabulary items are easily and quickly administered, the vocabulary test continues to be utilized to measure intellect by those persons who are investigating something other than intellect.

With the *Vocabulary Test—GT,* the authors have provided such investigators with five "equivalent" forms of a 20-item, multiple choice, verbal ability test. The items can be completed by most adults in less than 10 minutes. One can infer from the manual that just about any directions that suit the investigator will do. Thorndike and Gallup (2), for example, told respondents that the words were being screened for a quiz show; Miner (4) administered the items orally when it seemed that the respondent had difficulty reading them.

The vocabulary words were selected by E. L. Thorndike before 1925. No basis of selection, either of words or of alternative responses, has been indicated in the manual or literature. (An examinee cramming for this test would be wise to study words beginning with a, b, and c because over half of these vocabulary words do.) An updated study of word usage would probably eliminate such archaisms as *flying machine* and *beshrew* and locate words more indicative of intellectual effectiveness than *bray, chirrup,* and *abattoir.*

Some alternative responses appear to be more difficult words than the stem word. Many distractors are synonyms of approximate homonyms, such as *tool* with *AWE.* Some pairs of distractors are related, probably leading naïve examinees to guess between them. With such deliberate distraction less than 20 per cent will respond correctly to some of the difficult items, and discrimination thereby is enhanced.

Although test reliability is not reported in the manual, R. L. Thorndike (*1*) estimated it at .83 for parallel forms used with an adult population. This is commendable reliability for five minutes of testing. The manual includes approximate score equivalences with the *Otis Self-Administering Tests of Mental Ability, American Council on Education Psychological Examination,* and *Army General Classification Test.* Norms are based on large and reasonably well defined groups.

Much of the vocabulary used in this test is over four hundred years old, and many of the items are over forty years old. Still, the test is a new one, needing more refinement and revision if it is to be even an auxiliary tool for the educator, sociologist, and industrial psychologist. Because it is a five-minute test, it is relatively unreliable. It is easy to administer, but the chances of examinees misinterpreting instructions are relatively high. Because the investigator usually doesn't worry much about administering such a simple test, the chances are higher that he will forget that intelligence is not simply verbal ability. As a final word of caution, perhaps neither the *Vocabulary Test—GT* nor any other five-minute vocabulary test should be used by anyone not capable of building a better test himself.

[342a]
★Vocabulary Test for High School Students and College Freshmen. Grades 9–13; 1964; IBM; Forms A, B, (2 pages); manual (9 pages); provisional norms; $3.30 per 35 IBM 1230 test-answer sheets; 25¢ per scoring stencil; 50¢ per specimen set; postage extra; 15(20) minutes; Arthur E. Traxler; Bobbs-Merrill Co., Inc. *

[343]
★Word Clue Test. Grades 5 and over; 1962; functional vocabulary; Forms A, B, AA, (15 pages); test booklet title of Form AA is *Word Clue Appraisal;* manual (6 pages); no data on reliability; no norms; distribution of Forms A and B restricted to schools; separate answer sheets must be used; 25¢ per test; $2 per 100 answer sheets; 20¢ per scoring stencil; 60¢ per specimen set of Forms A and B; postage extra; (40–45) minutes; Stanford E. Taylor, Helen Frackenpohl, and Arthur S. McDonald; Educational Developmental Laboratories, Inc. *

[Other Tests]
For tests not listed above, see the following entries in *Tests in Print:* 562–3, 566–7, 570–2, 574, 578, and 582–3; out of print: 565 and 576–7; status unknown: 584.

ENGLISH — SEVENTH MMY

REVIEWS BY *Nicholas Anastasiow, Fred H. Borgen, M. A. Brimer, Nancy W. Burton, John B. Carroll, William E. Coffman, Clarence Derrick, Paul B. Diederich, Vincent R. D'Oyley, Ralph D. Dutch, Leonard S. Feldt, Robert Fitzpatrick, R. Gulliford, David P. Harris, Thomas D. Horn, Joan J. Michael, Walter J. Moore, Stanley Nisbet, Ellis Batten Page, Osmond E. Palmer, William H. Perkins, Robert C. Pooley, Alan C. Purves, Carleton B. Shay, John C. Sherwood, David A. Walker, George P. Winship, Jr., Blaine R. Worthen, and Albert H. Yee.*

[184]

*Advanced Placement Examination in English.
High school students desiring credit for college level courses or admission to advanced courses; 1954-70; Forms RBP ('69, 10 pages), SBP ('70, 14 pages) in 2 booklets (objective, essay); for more complete information, see 662; 180(200) minutes; program administered for the College Entrance Examination Board by Educational Testing Service. *

REFERENCE

1. SMITH, EUGENE H. "English Composition in the Advanced Placement Program." *Engl J* 54:495-501 S '65. *

For a review of the testing program, see 662.

[185]

★Bristol Achievement Tests: English Language.
Ages 8-0 to 9-11, 9-0 to 10-11, 10-0 to 11-11, 11-0 to 12-11, 12-0 to 13-11; 1969; 6 scores; word meaning, paragraph meaning, sentence organisation, organisation of ideas, spelling and punctuation, total; Forms A, B, ['69, 7-8 pages]; 5 levels; administrative manual ['69, 8 pages] for each level; battery interpretive manual (78 pages); battery profile ['69, 2 pages] for each form; £1.90 per 25 tests; £1 per 25 profiles; 60p per teacher's set (without interpretive manual) of any one level (must be purchased to obtain administrative manual and keys); 75p per interpretive manual; postage extra; 50(55) minutes for levels 1-3, 40(45) minutes for levels 4-5; Alan Brimer and Herbert Gross; Thomas Nelson & Sons Ltd. *

RALPH D. DUTCH, *Principal Lecturer in Educational Psychology, Aberdeen College of Education, Aberdeen, Scotland.*

Many of the attainment tests commonly used by British teachers and educational researchers are pitifully inadequate, and at this time of major changes in curricula and methods, teachers especially are desperately in need of well standardised tests, tailored to modern behavioural objectives, to rescue them from a fog of uncertainty and anxiety as to what results all these changes are producing. Fortunately, most adult teachers have now outgrown the fashion of regarding any form of evaluation as a symbol of reaction and academic fettering, and the *Bristol Achievement Tests* are consequently coming on the market at an opportune time.

From the start, this reviewer wishes to emphasise that, whatever shortcomings in detail these tests have, it is his opinion that as a complete battery they represent, both in sophistication of design and comprehensiveness of range if not yet in subject matter, a considerable advance in testing practice in Britain. Although this review will be concerned with the English tests, the aim of the whole battery is to provide a profile of a child's cognitive skills in the basic areas of numeracy and literacy, together with the basic concepts and understandings underlying performance in the social and scientific areas. Sets of Mathematics and Study Skills tests are therefore provided, equivalent in range and standardisation to the English tests described below.

The English tests cover five overlapping age ranges, from second year junior to second year secondary, the norms for each test being designed to cover a whole school year group (called level). This means that each child will have his scores compared with children of the same age and amount of school experience rather than with age peers who may have had a very different time of exposure to teaching. There are parallel forms at each of the five levels so that progress during a school year can always be evaluated against performance on a fresh but equivalently difficult test.

The standardisation of the tests was carried out on large samples of children selected with the intention of forming a nationally representative sample, and the interpretive manual contains an unusually full and open account of how this was done. The interpretation of raw scores offers several novel features. First, the raw scores are converted to standardised scores, then each subtest score is changed to the decile or percentile equivalent for that level and age group. Then, for each of the other subtests, the score is found that might have been expected from the child's reading ability as shown on one subtest, and finally the error limits of each score are calculated and shown on a profile, along with the actual score and the expected score. Reliability coefficients are based, not on internal consistency measures, but on correlations between scores on Form A and Form B. Standard errors of measurement are given and form an important consideration in interpreting test scores. The authors hope to counteract the tendency of teachers to read too much meaning into a single score or difference between scores by using the standard errors of the subscores to show the range within which a true score is likely to be. Unfortunately, some of the reliability measures, especially on the Organisation of Ideas subtests, are low (down to .59), and the range of error is so wide that educational decisions would be very hard for teachers to make on the basis of such variability. The authors are aware of this danger and suggest using 95 percent confidence limits where decisions to the possible detriment of a child are concerned and 68 percent where positive remedial action might be taken. This seems an unrealistic distinction and one beyond the patience or expertise of most teachers. In fact, to get the most out of these tests demands a degree of statistical understanding sadly lacking in most of the teachers who might use them; the Profile Sheet instructions could usefully be expanded and simplified.

After all this sophistication, the actual test contents are somewhat disappointing. The authors realise the need to test underlying principles and strategies rather than specific attainments and they have largely just played their hunches as to what these principles and strategies are where skill at English is concerned. At each level there are five subtests, covering the same areas at each level, though the more advanced levels have more items on expressive skills and fewer on reading comprehension. In Part 1 (Word Meaning), the child has to underline the word in a sentence that corresponds to the word underlined for him in a preceding sentence. The second sentence contains ingenious decoy words. For Part 2 (Paragraph Meaning), the child completes gaps in a continuous narrative, the missing words being either simple or previously mentioned, so that vocabulary by itself matters little. Part 3 (Sentence Organisation) consists of items in which the child has to complete, modify, or unscram-

ble the words of a sentence. In Part 4 (Organisation of Ideas), the child has in one section to put a series of ideas in the best order to produce a story and in the other to rearrange a sentence to give as many different meanings as possible. Part 5 (Spelling and Punctuation) means what it says and the authors are unnecessarily apologetic about including these measures in their test.

Now, in the absence of any factorial analysis of the contents or any attempt at even a concurrent validity measure, it is impossible to say whether the authors have caught the important English skills or not. Nor is it possible to use some of these tests diagnostically in the sense that they clearly indicate a course of generalisable remedial action. In these respects the tests are promising but still at an early stage in their development.

In general, then, these tests represent an honest and thorough attempt at an updated coverage of English language skills; in some respects they need working up and supplementing, and evidence on validity is urgently required, but for teachers who are prepared to make the effort to get the maximum use from them, they form part of a battery with distinct advantages over similar British productions in this field. The excellent interpretive manual is a must.

For a review of the complete battery, see 4.

[186]

★**CLEP Subject Examination in English Composition.** 1 year or equivalent; 1965-70; for college accreditation of nontraditional study, advanced placement, or assessment of educational achievement; tests administered monthly at regional centers throughout the United States; tests also available for institutional testing at any time; Form NCT ('65, 20 pages); optional essay supplement: Form NCT-A ('65, 3 pages); for program accessories, see 664; rental and scoring fee, $5 per student; postpaid; essay supplement scored by the college; 90(95) minutes, same for essay supplement; program administered for the College Entrance Examination Board by Educational Testing Service. *

DAVID P. HARRIS, *Professor of Linguistics, and Director, The American Language Institute, Georgetown University, Washington, D.C.* [Review of Form NCT.]

This is a 90-minute objective test consisting of 120 five-choice items; it may be supplemented with a 90-minute optional essay section, which requires the student first to paraphrase a given passage and then to organize two sets of information into separate paragraphs, using specified methods of development. (No advice on scoring the essay section is provided.) The purpose of the test, in the words of the publisher, is "to measure....knowledge of the theoretical aspects of writing usually taught in a beginning two-semester college course in composition and....ability to put into practice the principles of good writing." Thus, the test aims at measuring not only writing skill as such but also "a knowledge of the fundamental principles of rhetoric and of such elements of language facts, grammar, and logic as may be useful for the improvement of writing skill." In the objective portion, on which this review will concentrate, three types of problems account for about three-fourths of the test content.

Error-recognition items are used to measure the student's ability to write sentences that are grammatically, stylistically, and mechanically acceptable. Each item consists of a sentence with four underlined segments, one of which may contain an "error" according to the "requirements of standard written English"; otherwise, the student selects the fifth—"no error"—option. Though some of the sentences contain blatant "errors," those that do are mixed in with others which, in the reviewer's opinion, test recognition of stylistic faults of too subtle a nature to be useful discriminators. Moreover, a couple of the "no-error" items are written so infelicitously that it seems criminal to allow them to pass as acceptable. (Three English professors, given this 21-item section by the reviewer, each made at least two "mistakes.")

Sentence-conversion items test the student's sentence-writing dexterity. Here, sentences are to be rewritten according to specific directions (e.g., "Change the first verb to a noun used as the subject of the sentence"). The student does the rephrasing in his head or in the margins of his test book, then selects the one option containing a word or phrase that occurs in his revised version. If none of the options fits his sentence, he is advised to "rephrase the sentence again so that it includes a word or phrase that is listed." The revised sentences are seldom superior to the originals; the purpose of these items is to have the student demonstrate his ability to construct various sentence types upon demand. For the most part, the terminology of the instructions is fairly basic, though there are instances where a reasonably competent writer might not understand the technical description of sentences he is quite capable of creating on

his own: e.g., "Substitute an infinitive for the first gerund." A rather elaborate set of directions is required for this kind of exercise, filling nearly a full page in the test book.

Paragraph-analysis items consist of sets of questions, each of which is based on a given paragraph, designed to test the student's understanding of the author's overall strategy, method of organization, use of stylistic devices, and the like. In some cases the student is asked to identify faults in the writing or to select the best rewriting of a specific sentence. The analytic questions set the widest possible range of tasks, from explaining an author's choice of punctuation to giving technical names for literary devices. There are six such paragraph-analysis sets, which, very wisely, are spaced throughout the test to avoid monotony.

The remaining quarter of the test items probe the student's knowledge of the history of the English language and of modern English grammar, his understanding of the principles of coherence and logic in writing, and his ability to use bibliographical tools and the conventions of the documented paper. Most of this miscellaneous matter seems appropriate in terms of the stated test objectives, though as always one might quarrel with isolated items. Should we expect our freshman composition students to know Greek prefixes on sight, to know the chief foreign source of the technical vocabulary of hairdressers, or to know the function of *Baird's Manual* (luckily, only a distractor)? Fortunately, relatively few such questionable items appear.

In the test as a whole, the quality of the item writing is high. The reviewer puzzled over only two or three problems and found only one item (item 47) where there are definitely multiple right answers, due to a careless wording of the question. Except for the necessarily lengthy explanation for the sentence-conversion items, the test directions are brief but unequivocal. Particularly welcome are the very explicit instructions about guessing.

Test results are reported as scaled scores ranging from 20 to 80 with a mean of 50 and a standard deviation of 10. Norms were obtained in May-June 1965 by administering the test to full-time undergraduate students near the end of freshman composition courses. The test analysis of September 1965 indicates that the norms group found the test rather difficult and slightly speeded. The K-R 20 reliability was .87. Two related criteria were used for one study of validation: course grades estimated by instructors before the final examination ($r = .50$) and final course grades ($r = .57$). The publisher's attractive Score Interpretation Guide also includes normative data in the form of percentile ranks and graphs comparing distributions of scores with grades received in appropriate courses.

The matter of test validity leads the reviewer to voice one cautionary note. As may be observed from the summary of test content, the test designers clearly had in mind a very traditional kind of composition course, one that gives almost equal attention to writing and *talk about* writing, with the discussion couched in fairly technical language. (A rough tally indicates that about one item in five requires an understanding of one or more specialized terms: "compound verb," "analysis by partition," "synecdoche," "epigrammatic," etc.) For institutions where composition is still taught in this manner, the test could be expected to prove reasonably valid and useful. Where composition classes are less terminology-oriented, the test might be considerably less appropriate. Thus, for some of the recommended academic uses, such as the evaluation of "nontraditional college-level education....[and] the placement, accreditation, and admission of transfer students," the test requires cautious use. For the same reason there is a danger that the test will be misapplied by the nonacademic types of users whom the publisher has (secondarily) in mind: "business and industrial educators, and individuals responsible for certification and licensing programs." It is hoped that they, and all other potential users, will read with care the publisher's admirably thorough descriptive material.

For reviews of the testing program, see 664 (3 reviews).

[187]

*California Achievement Tests: Language, 1970 Edition. Grades 1.5–2, 2–4, 4–6, 6–9, 9–12; 1933–70; previous edition (see 6:251) still available; 4 or 5 scores: auding (level 1 only), mechanics, usage and structure, total, spelling; 1 form; 5 levels; for battery manuals and accessories, see 5; separate answer sheets (CompuScan [NCS], Digitek, IBM 1230) may be used in grades 4–12; postage extra; original edition by Ernest W. Tiegs and Willis W. Clark; CTB/McGraw-Hill. *

a) LEVEL 1. Grades 1.5–2; Form A ('70, 6 pages); $5 per 35 tests; $2.45 per specimen set, postpaid; 37(65) minutes.

b) LEVEL 2. Grades 2–4; Form A ('70, 6 pages); prices same as for level 1; 35(60) minutes.
c) LEVEL 3. Grades 4–6; Form A ('70, 15 pages); $6 per 35 tests; $2.50 per 50 CompuScan or Digitek answer sheets; $3 per 50 IBM answer sheets; $1 per IBM hand scoring stencil; $2 per specimen set, postpaid; CompuScan scoring service, 22¢ and over per test; 43(70) minutes.
d) LEVEL 4. Grades 6–9; Form A ('70, 15 pages); prices same as for level 3; 43(70) minutes.
e) LEVEL 5. Grades 9–12; Form A ('70, 15 pages); prices same as for level 3; 47(75) minutes.

REFERENCES

1–3. See 5:177.
4. See 6:251.
5. TURNER, DANIEL. *A Study of Speech Effectiveness and Personal and Social Adjustment Among Ninth Grade Pupils.* Doctor's thesis, Boston University (Boston, Mass.), 1957. (*DA* 17:2902)
6. PALATE, E. L. "The Measurement of Sentence Structure of Deaf Children." *Alberta J Ed Res* 8:39–44 Mr '62. * (*PA* 37:3492)

For a review by Richard E. Schutz of an earlier edition, see 6:251; for reviews by Constance M. McCullough and Winifred L. Post, see 5:177; for reviews by Gerald V. Lannholm and Robert C. Pooley, see 4:151; for reviews by Harry A. Greene and J. Paul Leonard, see 2:1292. For reviews of earlier editions of the complete battery, see 6:3 (2 reviews), 5:2 (1 review), 4:2 (3 reviews), 3:15 (1 review), 2:1193 (2 reviews), and 1:876 (1 review, 1 excerpt).

[188]

*College Board Achievement Test in English Composition. Candidates for college entrance; 1943–71; test administered each January, March, May, July, and December at centers established by the publisher; for more complete information, see 663; 60(80) minutes; program administered for the College Entrance Examination Board by Educational Testing Service. *

REFERENCES

1–6. See 4:178.
7–20. See 5:204.
21–26. See 6:287.
27. CLARK, EUGENE WARREN. *An Evaluation of Predictive Criteria for a Group of High Ability College Freshmen.* Doctor's thesis, University of Denver (Denver, Colo.), 1963. (*DA* 25:957)
28. COLLEGE ENTRANCE EXAMINATION BOARD. *Manual of Freshman Class Profiles, 1964 Edition.* Princeton, N.J.: the Board, 1964. Pp. xiv, 584. * (Earlier editions published in 1961, 1962, and 1963.)
29. FRENCH, JOHN W. "New Tests for Predicting the Performance of College Students With High-Level Aptitude." *J Ed Psychol* 55:185–94 Ag '64. * (*PA* 39:5979)
30. IVANOFF, JOHN M.; MALLOY, JOHN P.; AND ROSE, JANET R. "Achievement, Aptitude, and Biographical Measures as Predictors of Success in Nursing Training." *Ed & Psychol Meas* 24:389–91 su '64. * (*PA* 39:5972)
31. SHOSTAK, JEROME. *How to Prepare for College Board Achievement Tests: English Composition and the Writing Sample.* Great Neck, N.Y.: Barron's Educational Series, Inc., 1964. Pp. vi, 116. *
32. BARTH, CARL A. "Kinds of Language Knowledge Required by College Entrance Examinations." *Engl J* 54:824–9 D '65. *
33. HALLADAY, ROY ELDON. *The Effect of Certain Subcultural Background Factors on the Prediction of Grades at the University of Michigan.* Doctor's thesis, Michigan State University (East Lansing, Mich.), 1966. (*DA* 27:2780A)
34. MARSHALL, JOSEPH JEMERSON. *Non-Cognitive Variables as a Predictor of Academic Achievement Among Freshmen, Sophomores, and Juniors at Abilene Christian College.* Doctor's thesis, Baylor University (Waco, Tex.), 1968. (*DA* 29:3833A)
35. ELLEDGE, SCOTT. "For the Board's English Tests: As

an Old Era Ends, What Lies Ahead?" *Col Board R* 71:22–7 sp '69. *

36. PUGH, RICHARD C.; MORGAN, JAMES M.; AND LUDLOW, H. GLENN. *Predicting Success for Indiana University Freshmen Using the CEEB Achievement Tests, the CEEB Scholastic Aptitude Test, and High School Rank.* Indiana Studies in Prediction, No. 13. Bloomington, Ind.: Bureau of Educational Studies and Testing, Indiana University, April 1970. Pp. xi, 39. *

For reviews by Charlotte Croon Davis, Robert C. Pooley, and Holland Roberts of earlier forms, see 6:287; for a review by Charlotte Croon Davis (with Frederick B. Davis), see 4:178. For reviews of the testing program, see 6:760 (2 reviews).

[189]

★**College English Placement Test.** College entrants; 1969; CEPT; 1 form (12 pages); Part 2 consists of 2 optional essay questions; manual (16 pages); no information on marking, reliability, or norms presented for Part 2; separate answer sheets (IBM 1230, MRC, self-marking) must be used; $7.50 per 50 tests; $5.70 per 100 IBM 1230 answer sheets; $4.95 per 50 self-marking answer sheets; $3 per 100 MRC answer cards; 60¢ per IBM 1230 scoring stencil; 45¢ per manual; 90¢ per specimen set; postage extra; MRC scoring service, 18¢ per test; 45(55) minutes for Part 1; Oscar M. Haugh and James I. Brown; Houghton Mifflin Co. *

CLARENCE DERRICK, *Professor of Humanities, University of Florida, Gainesville, Florida.*

The stated purpose of this test is to give "an objective guide for the placement of college freshmen in English composition classes." The basic assumption is that the "usual steps in writing a composition" can be analyzed and reformulated into groups of objective test items. Even if one accepts the principle that most measurement is indirect, not everyone will accept the assumption and the actualization of the assumption of this test. As one takes the test, one wonders if the test is *really* the kind of mental activity that is involved when one *really* writes a composition. In Part 1, the objective part of the test, there are 13 different sets of items to be answered in 45 minutes. An unstated skill being tested is the ability to change gears; there is plenty of opportunity for gear shifting in this test. It does not help when two of the three sample exercises presented to "familiarize yourself with the kinds of items in the test" are not in the test in that form.

Earlier tests of "mechanics of expression" and "usage" designed to be used in sectioning freshmen emphasized spelling, punctuation, capitalization, usage, etc. The CEPT gives little emphasis to these categories. The various sections of the test include judgments relating to the selection of a subject for a composition; identification of dominant, subordinate, and irrelevant topics from unorganized data; grouping related and unrelated topics; judging which transitional connectives are best; distinguishing which sentence in a group is most effectively expressed; verbal analogies; an artificial language exercise; and finally a set of 21 usage items.

The manual contains this statement: "The 106 items in Part One of CEPT are all objective and *thus only one answer is correct for each question* [italics added]." An objective test has been defined as a test which can be *scored* by someone who has no knowledge of the subject matter. There is subjectivity in objective tests and room for some variation of opinion. Not always is there only one correct answer. Item 73, for example, is in a group of items that requires a decision whether a given sentence creates an unfavorable impression or a favorable impression. Would everyone agree that *He's frugal* creates a favorable rather than an unfavorable impression? Would frugality be recognized as a cardinal virtue by all college freshmen, particularly when they write home for funds at the end of the month? Item 51 requires a student to select Sentence B as more effective than Sentence C.

B. Some loose boards laid on the railroad ties provided a footing for the man and his executioners.

C. Some loose boards laid on the ties supporting the rails provided a footing for the man and his executioners.

The only difference is between "railroad ties" and "ties supporting the rails." Conceivably there could be a context when "ties supporting the rails" fits the writer's intention.

Part 2 of CEPT is an optional essay section. Its inclusion is based on the theory that a combination of objective items with an essay is more valid than either type of item alone. In the first of two essays, within a 25-minute time limit the student writes on one of two propositions. In the second essay, with a time limit of 35 minutes, the student attacks or defends a single proposition. The essay topics are well chosen, and most college freshmen should be able to write on them. The evaluation of these essays has to be done locally without the kind of assistance the STEP Essay Tests provide with their samples of student essays.

The CEPT has been carefully constructed and standardized. The manual contains the right amount of information that can be understood by a teacher with some familiarity with norms, validity, reliability, and standard errors of measurement. One lack is any information about the speededness of the test. With so many different item types in one test, the student will use a certain amount of time figuring out just what he is expected to do. Most test constructors want a test to be relatively unspeeded and use as a criterion that at least 75 percent of the students finish the test within the time limits. The fact that the directions for the CEPT call for students to begin item 40 after 21 minutes is a hint that students may not have time to complete all parts of the test.

The manual states that additional validity studies are being planned but are not yet available. The most important correlation that should be sought is a correlation between CEPT and a measure of verbal aptitude. This reviewer suspects that what CEPT measures is verbal aptitude, which is, of course, reasonably well correlated with ability to write. However, if a good measure of verbal aptitude is already available for all freshmen, the usefulness of CEPT is reduced.

In summary, CEPT is a recent test that differs from most screening tests used to evaluate freshmen competence in writing. The test authors have a point of view and a plan which they have carried out at a high level of competence.

OSMOND E. PALMER, *Professor, Office of Evaluation Services, Michigan State University, East Lansing, Michigan.*

This is an original, exciting, and extremely well prepared test. The authors decided to examine systematically all the things involved in composition. They devote only 27 of 106 items to matters of grammar and mechanics. The rest of the test involves items on limiting a topic, organizing materials in narrative and expository paragraphs, securing continuity within paragraphs, and making logical connections between the various parts of a sentence. There is a vocabulary section involving both like and unlike words and there are items getting at the connotation rather than the denotation of words.

Probably one of the things which gives this test its unique quality is its flexibility. The authors are not committed to any one form of item or to any set number of foils. In multiple choice

items they use five responses when the responses are short, but when responses are long, as in the items on effective sentence structure, they use four. Often they use key-list items, and the keys contain from two to five responses. For the section on connotation the key is simply favorable-unfavorable. For some organization items they do not go beyond the logical three-part choice: a main topic, a subtopic, irrelevant. The items on mechanics refer to underlined portions of an essay, and the student uses a five-point key to indicate what, if anything, is wrong: capitalization, form, punctuation, spelling, no error. The test on vocabulary increases its range and simplifies directions by using the proportion technique: "Conspicuous is to hidden as PROXIMITY is to" or "Genuine is to authentic as EXOTIC is to."

The format of the test is also good. The items on the page are well spaced and the pages are usually not crowded.

The most interesting innovation is the creation of a nonsense verb and its principal parts and the requirement that the student supply the proper part in a series of sentences. It seems to me this is an economical way to get at a student's understanding of the English verbal system.

I take exception to only four items in the test. Item 37 asks the student to pick out a sentence in which there is no transitional word. I think that all of the sentences contain a transitional word: the *first* in sentence 3 locates an event in time as well as the *after* in sentence 2. Item 40 is tricky. Foil B introduces a sentence pattern which occurs in handbooks as the proper way to handle the construction, but then by omitting the word *other*, it is made illogical. Several of my colleagues and I missed this omission. Item 94 is supposed to illustrate the use of the wrong form of a word; but the choice is between *in* and *into*, and I do not consider *into* a morphological change of *in*. The one really ambiguous item is item 76. The student has to decide "Which underlined word has the widest range of application?" and he has to choose among *lie, falsehood, untruth, fib, misrepresentation.* I think that this depends too much on the authors' interpretation of "widest." I chose *untruth.* The authors want *misrepresentation* as the right response; to me this word suggests a specific, though unnamed, object with which I can compare a given statement. But when we say *untrue* we are simply putting a thing in a class with all other false things.

I also quarrel with this test on the basis of an omission. The authors suggest the need to have an essay in addition to the objective test and they present two essay topics at the end of the test booklet which the colleges can use if they wish. But they do not suggest that the topics have been tried out to see if they work well, and they have no advice to give the reader about grading the essays. The authors missed a golden opportunity, as part of the standardization, to have essays written. If they had given them the multiple readings involved in a recent College Board study [1] and correlated the essay scores with the part and total scores of their objective test, they could have assured prospective users of their test that the objective test did, in fact, correlate highly with students' ability to write. For the first time on a national scale it could have been pointed out that well-prepared and well-balanced objective tests do measure something very close to students' ability to write. A more immediate and practical benefit could have followed. Annotated samples of inferior, average, and superior papers could have been printed in the manual to serve as a guide to those colleges using the essays as part of the test.

[190]

*College Placement Test in English Composition. Entering college freshmen; 1962-70, c1958-70; CPTEC; irregularly scheduled reprintings of inactive forms of *College Board Achievement Test in English Composition;* Forms RPL1, RPL2, ['69, reprint of 1966 tests] in a single booklet (25 pages); for more complete information, see 665; 60(70) minutes; program administered for the College Entrance Examination Board by Educational Testing Service. *

REFERENCES

1. JACOBS, PAUL I. "Effects of Coaching on the College Board English Composition Test." *Ed & Psychol Meas* 26:55-67 sp '66. * (*PA* 40:9225)
2. HILTON, THOMAS L., AND MYERS, ALBERT E. "Personal Background, Experience and School Achievement: An Investigation of the Contribution of Questionnaire Data to Academic Prediction." *J Ed Meas* 4:69-80 su '67. * (*PA* 42:4570)
3. BURGESS, THOMAS C. "Estimating Average Freshman Class Ability From Preliminary Information." *J Col Stud Personnel* 10(3):161-3 My '69. *

JOHN C. SHERWOOD, *Professor of English, University of Oregon, Eugene, Oregon.*

The College Placement Test Program, of which this test forms a part, is intended "to place students at the appropriate level of study in college" through "the sensitive matching of student and course"; the individual college is

1 GODSHALK, FRED I.; SWINEFORD, FRANCES; AND COFFMAN, WILLIAM. *The Measurement of Writing Ability.* New York: College Entrance Examination Board, 1966. Pp. viii, 84.

advised not to use any of the tests without a preliminary validity survey to determine local applicability and to establish local norms for actual placement—full instructions for both validation and placement are provided in the manual.

The composition test is specifically "designed to measure the ability to write clear, effective English." This statement can be accepted only with some qualification. In the first place, as everyone knows, such tests are not tests of writing but of certain critical skills thought to have some correlation with writing skill; as far as the exercise resembles any part of the creative process, it resembles the stage of revision and proofreading—except that it is not his own ideas which the student is revising. Second, whatever the test measures, it measures only in one-sentence units; there is no demand to criticize, much less produce, larger units of composition and more extended patterns of thought. Thirdly, "clear, effective" might be better translated as "following the traditional conventions of standard written English as expounded by conservative handbooks"; clarity is seldom an issue, since even the faulty examples are not really obscure, and if effectiveness means rising above mere mechanical correctness in the direction of eloquence, that issue arises in only one section and then in a limited form. (There may, of course, be an unexpressed assumption that correctness is ipso facto effective.) Finally, of the problems relevant to the issues of clarity and effectiveness, some are heavily emphasized and others slighted; punctuation is hardly covered at all.

The test booklet contains not one but two tests, exactly parallel in structure and with very similar items. In either case, the first section contains 35 one-sentence exercises, in each of which four words or phrases are underlined; one or none may be faulty, and the student must pick out (but not diagnose) the one error or pronounce the sentence faultless. The faulty items are chiefly offenses against balance, symmetry, and consistency; they are of the each-of-us-brought-their-book, to-run-sing-and-to-dance sort of thing, and liberals might doubt whether some of them are really errors. The items seem generally unambiguous if one accepts the conventions of the test-makers.

In the second section the student faces another 35 possibly faulty sentences; each must be either pronounced correct or identified as exhibiting one of four errors: faulty diction (words which are not exact, not idiomatic, or not acceptable in standard written English); wordiness; clichés and inappropriate metaphors; faulty grammar and sentence structure (a category which has roughly the same emphasis as Part A of the test). Again the items seem generally unambiguous (especially the wordiness and cliché items!), though there might be some hesitation in ruling whether certain structural flaws offend against idiom (hence diction) or against grammar; the distinction may often be more semantic than real. The wordiness and cliché categories do genuinely raise the issue of rhetorical effectiveness as distinguished from mechanical correctness; it might, however, be wondered whether these particular problems of effectiveness deserve to be stressed and so many others passed over. The last section is the most ingenious and creative; here the student must actually construct sentences, if only in his mind. What we have is a series of single-sentence items, not necessarily faulty; in each case a change in the structure of one part of the sentence is suggested, and the student must determine what effects the change will have on other parts of the sentence —a process which requires him to rephrase the whole sentence and thus to approximate the creative process. For instance, offered the sentence "Poetry, like all the other arts, is to a very large degree a mode of imitation," he could be asked to consider the effect of beginning with the words "Poetry and all the other arts" (the example comes from a descriptive booklet rather than the test itself and is more obvious and mechanical than most). Many of the items could be answered only by someone who has both a quick, sharp mind and a well-developed sense of English syntax.

What are we to conclude about the usefulness of the test—or, to put the matter in more practical terms, can we conclude that it is promising enough to justify the "validity test" which the publishers honestly suggest as preliminary to any local use? Probably yes, if a comparison with comparable tests seems to suggest that it best fits the local need or emphasis. On the one hand, its use does involve an act of faith: one must assume a correlation between the skills tested and such untested skills as organization and punctuation, and between critical ability and actual writing performance. On the other hand, the test is carefully done,

generally unambiguous, sometimes ingenious. Success on the test would certainly indicate a clarity of mind and feeling for style which ought to enable the possessor to produce good expository prose, though the contrary might not be true—failure to solve some of the test's puzzles need not indicate incompetence in simple expression. The test need be viewed with no more suspicion than is appropriate to any objective test of writing.

For reviews by Charlotte Croon Davis, Robert C. Pooley, and Holland Roberts of earlier forms, see 6:287; for a review by Charlotte Croon Davis (with Frederick B. Davis), see 4:178. For a review of the testing program, see 665.

[191]

★Comprehensive Tests of Basic Skills: Language. Grades 2.5-4, 4-6, 6-8, 8-12; 1968-70; 4 scores: mechanics, expression, spelling, total; 2 forms; 4 levels; for battery manuals and accessories, see 9; separate answer sheets (CompuScan [NCS], Digitek, IBM 1230, Scoreze) must be used for levels 2-4; postage extra; $1.75 per specimen set of any one level, postpaid; CTB/McGraw-Hill. *
a) LEVEL 1. Grades 2.5-4; Forms Q ('68, 8 pages), R ('69, 8 pages); $5.35 per 35 tests; 35(55) minutes.
b) LEVEL 2. Grades 4-6; Forms Q ('68, 10 pages), R ('69, 10 pages); $5.75 per 35 tests; $2.50 per 50 Digitek or IBM answer sheets; $3 per 50 CompuScan answer sheets; $2.75 per 25 Scoreze answer sheets; $1 per IBM hand scoring stencil; CompuScan scoring service, 17¢ and over per test; 38(58) minutes.
c) LEVEL 3. Grades 6-8; Forms Q ('68, 13 pages), R ('69, 13 pages); prices same as for level 2; 37(57) minutes.
d) LEVEL 4. Grades 8-12; Forms Q ('68, 13 pages), R ('69, 13 pages); prices same as for level 2; 35(55) minutes.

For reviews of the complete battery, see 9 (2 reviews, 3 excerpts).

[192]

English Progress Tests. Various ages 7-3 to 15-6; 1952-70; 17 levels; 5p per test; 7p per manual for any one level except f (no manuals for g and l-q, mimeographed directions free on request from NFER); postpaid within U.K.; published for the National Foundation for Educational Research in England and Wales; Ginn & Co. Ltd.
a) ENGLISH PROGRESS TEST A. Ages 8-0 to 9-0; 1952-60; 1 form ['52, 6 pages]; manual ['60, 8 pages]; (40-45) minutes; A. F. Watts.
b) ENGLISH PROGRESS TEST B. Ages 9-0 to 10-6; 1956-62; 1 form ['56, 7 pages]; manual ['62, 7 pages]; norms for ages 8-6 to 10-0 only; (40-45) minutes; M. A. Brimer.
c) ENGLISH PROGRESS TEST C. Ages 10-0 to 11-0; 1952-60; formerly called *English Grading Test 3*; 1 form ['52, 8 pages]; revised manual ('60, 7 pages); (45-50) minutes; A. F. Watts.
d) ENGLISH PROGRESS TEST D. Ages 11-0 to 12-0; 1956; 1 form ['56, 7 pages]; manual ['56, 8 pages]; pro-

visional norms; (40–45) minutes; M. A. Brimer and A. F. Watts.

e) ENGLISH PROGRESS TEST E. Ages 12-0 to 13-0; 1956; 1 form ['56, 8 pages]; manual ['56, 8 pages]; provisional norms; (40–45) minutes; M. A. Brimer and A. F. Watts.

f) ENGLISH PROGRESS TEST F. Ages 13-0 to 14-0; 1953; 1 form ['53, 8 pages]; manual ['53, 10 pages]; no data on reliability; 8p per manual; (40–50) minutes; A. F. Watts.

g) ENGLISH PROGRESS TEST G. Ages 13-0 to 15-6; 1962; 1 form ['62, 8 pages]; mimeographed directions ['62, 4 pages]; no data on reliability; no norms; (35–45) minutes; S. M. Unwin.

h) ENGLISH PROGRESS TEST A2. Ages 7-3 to 8-11; 1962–66; 1 form ['62, 8 pages]; manual ['66, 8 pages]; (40–50) minutes; Betsy Barnard.

i) ENGLISH PROGRESS TEST B2. Ages 8-6 to 10-0; 1959–60; 1 form ['59, 7 pages]; manual ['60, 7 pages]; (40–45) minutes.

j) ENGLISH PROGRESS TEST C2. Ages 9-6 to 11-0; 1961; 1 form ['61, 8 pages]; manual ['61, 7 pages]; (40–45) minutes; Valerie Land.

k) ENGLISH PROGRESS TEST D2. Ages 10-6 to 12-0; 1963–64; 1 form ['63, 8 pages]; manual ['64, 7 pages]; (40–45) minutes; Jennifer Henchman.

l) ENGLISH PROGRESS TEST E2. Ages 11-0 to 12-6; 1962–63; 1 form ['62, 8 pages]; mimeographed directions ['63, 6 pages]; no data on reliability; no norms; 45(50) minutes; S. M. Unwin.

m) ENGLISH PROGRESS TEST F2. Ages 12-0 to 13-6; 1963; 1 form ['63, 8 pages]; mimeographed directions ['63, 6 pages]; no data on reliability; no norms; 45(50) minutes; Jennifer Henchman and Elsa Hendry.

n) ENGLISH PROGRESS TEST B3. Ages 8-0 to 9-6; 1970; 1 form ['70, 8 pages]; mimeographed directions ['70, 4 pages]; no data on reliability; no norms; (45–50) minutes.

o) ENGLISH PROGRESS TEST C3. Ages 9-0 to 10-6; 1970; 1 form ['70, 6 pages]; mimeographed directions ['70, 5 pages]; no data on reliability; no norms; (45–50) minutes.

p) ENGLISH PROGRESS TEST D3. Ages 10-0 to 11-6; 1970; 1 form ['70, 6 pages]; mimeographed directions ['70, 4 pages]; no data on reliability; no norms; (45–50) minutes.

q) ENGLISH PROGRESS TEST F3. Ages 12-0 to 13-6; 1969; 1 form ['69, 8 pages]; mimeographed directions ['69, 6 pages]; provisional norms ('69, 1 page); no data on reliability; no norms for ages 12-0 to 12-8; norms free on request from NFER; (40–45) minutes.

For reviews by Neil Gourlay and Stanley Nisbet of Tests A–F, see 5:187.

[193]

*English Tests (Adv.). Ages 12-0 to 13-11; 1954–67; 4 tests; distribution restricted to directors of education; 7p per test; 8p per manual for any one test except *d;* postpaid in U.K.; 50(55) minutes; published for the National Foundation for Educational Research in England and Wales; Ginn & Co. Ltd. *

a) ENGLISH TEST (ADV.) 1. 1954–55; 1 form ['54, 11 pages]; manual ('55, 11 pages); G. A. V. Morgan.

b) ENGLISH TEST (ADV.) 3. 1958; 1 form ['58, 12 pages]; manual (9 pages).

c) ENGLISH TEST (ADV.) 4. 1960; 1 form ['60, 12 pages]; manual (10 pages).

d) ENGLISH TEST (ADV.) 5. 1962–67; 1 form ['62, 12 pages]; mimeographed directions for administration ['62, 10 pages]; provisional norms ['67, 1 page]; directions and norms free on request from NFER.

STANLEY NISBET, *Professor of Education, University of Glasgow, Glasgow, Scotland.*

This series for the 12–14 age group was produced between 1954 and 1962. In general design and standardization procedure it follows the pattern of the well-known Moray House tests (which also include a series for this age range). The tests are almost wholly objective in form, though each test includes a few open-ended items which involve a slight degree of subjectivity in scoring. The usual fields are covered—comprehension, vocabulary, usage, word formation, sentence structure, spelling, and the like. The tables of norms enable test scores to be translated into standardized scores with a mean of 100 and an SD of 15. No indication is given as to the purposes for which the tests should be used, but one may assume, from their character and from certain comments in the handbooks, that they were designed as instruments of selection.

The construction and standardization of the tests would seem to be sound and the handbooks are reasonably informative. A few features of the norms, however, make one wonder if the standardizing groups (usually containing between 1,500 and 2,000 boys and girls) were truly representative. For instance, the conversion tables for Tests 1 and 3 show a steep increase of score with age, that for Test 4 shows a very small increase, and that for Test 2,[1] where separate norms for boys and girls are given, shows a steep increase for boys and hardly any for girls. When we come to Test 5, we are told that the age increment is so small that age has been ignored in the table altogether.

Coming to the content of the tests, we find that the items vary considerably in validity, or at least in face validity. (*a*) Some items strike one as being very good indicators of ability in English, such as those which require the selection of the best word to fill the blank in a sentence (e.g., items 68–74, Test 1) or the creative completion of a sentence beginning and/or ending with given words (e.g., 55–61, Test 1; 41–5, Test 2). (*b*) Some items, good enough in themselves as items, appear to be testing general intelligence more than ability in English, e.g., the reconstruction of a long sentence by rearranging eight groups of words (45–61, Test 5). Other examples are 14–20, Test 1; 18–22 and 31–40, Test 2; 12–21, Test

1 Test 2, published in 1957, is out of print.

3; 54–61 and 68–73, Test 5. (c) Other items are just faulty items—awkward wording, puzzling instructions, omission of necessary punctuation, items penalizing children whose dialect deviates slightly from standard English pronunciation, and even an apparent misprint (94, Test 3) and a misspelling (99, Test 2). The reviewer has reason to find fault at least with the following: 31–2, 43–9, and 98, Test 1; 14, 46, 49, 52, 85, 87–90, and 92, Test 2; 24, 35, 50, 60, 67–8, and 75, Test 3; 36, 38, 50, 52, and 92, Test 4; and 8–9, 20, and 27, Test 5.

The most disquieting feature of these English tests, however, is nothing less than the uneven quality of the English which they themselves contain. One comes across poor English everywhere—in items, in instructions, in passages for comprehension. To take a single example, the bottom third of page 5 and most of page 6 in Test 2 are hardly likely to inspire confidence in the test as an instrument claiming to appraise mastery of written English.

The reviewer would therefore hesitate to recommend the tests as tests of English, though they would probably be effective as tests of verbal intelligence.

For a review by A. E. G. Pilliner of Tests 1–4, see 6:262.

[194]

English Tests 13–20. Ages 10-0 to 11-11; 1951–70; 8 tests (12 pages for *a–d*, 8 pages for *e–h*); new test published annually except for 1970; distribution restricted to directors of education; 7p per test (*a–d*); 5p per test (*e–h*); 8p per manual; postpaid within U.K.; 50(55) minutes for *a–e*, 45(50) minutes for *f–h*; published for the National Foundation for Educational Research in England and Wales; Ginn & Co. Ltd. *

a) ENGLISH TEST 13. 1962–63; forms 13A, 13B, ['62]; manual ('63, 12 pages) for each form.
b) ENGLISH TEST 14. 1963–64; 1 form ['63]; manual ('64, 12 pages).
c) ENGLISH TEST 15. 1964–65; 1 form ['64]; manual ('65, 12 pages).
d) ENGLISH TEST 16. 1965–66; 1 form ['65]; manual ('66, 12 pages).
e) ENGLISH TEST 17. 1966–67; 1 form ['66]; manual ('67, 12 pages).
f) ENGLISH TEST 18. 1967–68; 1 form ['67]; manual ('68, 12 pages).
g) ENGLISH TEST 19. 1968–69; 1 form ['68]; manual ('69, 12 pages).
h) ENGLISH TEST 20. 1969–70; 1 form ['69]; manual ('70, 12 pages).

REFERENCE

1. See 6:264.

R. GULLIFORD, *Senior Lecturer in Education, The University of Birmingham, Birmingham, England.*

These well constructed tests were prepared for use in selection procedures for secondary education in England. Interest in this review centres on how the test constructors, with considerable experience behind them, have modified their procedures through the eight tests in response to recent developments in the teaching of English and to the increased influence of linguistics.

The test constructors' awareness of the need for change is obvious from the variety of items which have been tried and from statements in the test manuals such as, "new types of item have been introduced to test the appropriate use of words and the appreciation of well-written English" and "the [test] marks a further stage in the development of tests of the mainly creative response type in which the emphasis on formal grammar is kept to a minimum."

A comparison of the earlier and later tests in the series from 13 to 20 does not show as much change as one might hope for in the direction of more open-ended, truly creative responses. Nevertheless, the trend is in the right direction. Examination of the marking keys for the later tests shows a much greater range of acceptable alternative answers and greater discretion left to the marker.

There is a discernible change in the test content. Whereas Test 13, for example, includes many questions on word structure (making plural and tense changes, substituting pronouns for nouns), Test 19 places the emphasis on sentences (rewriting jumbled sentences, sequencing sentences, selecting or producing words or phrases indicated by the syntax and meaning of a continuous passage) and greater weight is given to the ability to read and comprehend a continuous passage. Reduction by half in the number of items in Test 17 onwards but with the same time allowed is further evidence of the greater degree of judgment and thought required instead of an immediate response.

Tests of the ability to manipulate sentence structures are attempted in several ways: sequencing phrases, rewriting jumbled sentences, and rewriting sentences using the passive transformation. The latter prompts the question whether items involving other transformations could not have been devised and whether sentence completion from a supplied beginning would not have been feasible—presumably problems of ensuring optimum pupil response and of marking may have proved limiting factors.

In general, the more recent tests show a marked development towards testing language in more adequate contexts so that they leave one with less of the feeling of having skipped arbitrarily through innumerable situations and artificial sentences.

A technique which is included in two tests— identifying the meaning of a nonsense word from several sentence contents—is not used in the last two tests, though, strangely, an item based on homophones continues to be used. One wonders what the rationale of this is since it might prompt teachers to give attention to a rather insignificant aspect of teaching English.

While there are certain consistencies of content in these eight tests (all contain passages for comprehension, some punctuation tasks, and vocabulary items), there are also variations from test to test and one wonders what are the underlying assumptions about attainment in English. This is not adequately discussed in any of the manuals and since test content is likely to influence teaching, it might be useful to state explicitly the range of language skills which the testers are trying directly or indirectly to sample. Such a statement might help schools to avoid the danger of assuming that test techniques devised to probe certain kinds of linguistic skills are necessarily desirable and profitable as teaching procedures.

For reviews by Stanley Nisbet and H. J. Sants of earlier tests, see 6:264.

[195]
★Grammar, Usage, and Structure Test and Vocabulary Test. College entrants; 1963–68; 2 tests in one booklet; 1 form ('63, 9 pages); combined manual ('68, 43 pages) for this test and R:57; separate answer sheets must be used; $4 per 20 tests; $1 per manual; 50¢ per specimen set; postpaid; answer sheets must be obtained locally; 60(65) minutes for both tests; William A. McCartney; the Author. *

[196]
*Hoyum-Sanders English Tests. 1, 2 semesters in grades 2–4, 5–6, 7–8; 1962–64; first published 1962–63 in the Every Pupil Scholarship Test series; 3 tests; Forms A, B, ('64, 4 pages); 2 levels labeled Tests 1, 2; manual ('64, 5 pages); $1.75 per 25 tests, postage extra; 75¢ per specimen set of any one test, postpaid; 40(45) minutes; Vera Davis Hoyum and M. W. Sanders; Data Processing and Educational Measurement Center. *
a) HOYUM-SANDERS ELEMENTARY ENGLISH TEST. 1, 2 semesters in grades 2–4.
b) HOYUM-SANDERS INTERMEDIATE ENGLISH TEST. 1, 2 semesters in grades 5–6.

c) HOYUM-SANDERS JUNIOR HIGH SCHOOL ENGLISH TEST. 1, 2 semesters in grades 7–8.

PAUL B. DIEDERICH, *Senior Research Associate, Educational Testing Service, Princeton, New Jersey.*

Although this publisher is not noted for care or sophistication in test construction, these English tests for grades 2–8 seem to be good, useful measures of knowledge of rules governing correctness in writing and ability to apply the rules to the kinds of sentences that students write. The points covered are those that are stressed in composition textbooks for the grades for which these tests are intended, and they correspond pretty well to the types of errors in student writing. There are very few items about which even the most permissive of linguists would argue that the alternatives are equally acceptable, and there are almost none that concern fine points, disputed usages, or problems that do not arise in ordinary student writing. The sentences that present these problems deal with matters that students in these grades often write about themselves. They are easy to understand, and they do not sound like the artificial sentences that grammarians so often concoct. Grammatical terminology is avoided almost entirely up to the tests for grades 7–8, and then it is limited to terms needed to explain why the option chosen is correct. There is one final section in each test of 10 items on alphabetization, included for obvious reasons, but apart from that, everything included in these tests contributes to the impression that a student has or has not mastered the ordinary conventions of writing. If a teacher does not expect these tests to reveal anything more than this, he ought to find them quite useful as measures of status and growth and, to a limited extent, as pointers toward areas in which a class needs to improve.

For the last-mentioned purpose of class diagnosis, it is unfortunate that some sections of these tests have different numbers of items in Forms A and B. For example, it would be hard to tell whether a class had improved in usage when there are 50 items of this sort in Form A of the intermediate tests and 40 items in Form B. Teachers would have to change raw scores to percent correct, and many would forget or not take the trouble to do so. It is so easy to produce large numbers of items like these and to make sure that those selected for published forms are equal in difficulty that there is no apparent reason for inequality in numbers of items in sections of forms intended to be equivalent.

All 12 forms of these tests have six sections: Sentence Recognition, Capitalization, Punctuation, Contractions and Possessives, Usage, and Alphabetization. The manual gives the impression that the intermediate and junior high tests do not have the section Contractions and Possessives and substitute a section on "reference materials, such as guide words and index" for Alphabetization, but this is inaccurate; the same six sections appear throughout. The section "Contractions, Possessives" has "Plurals" included in some forms and "Spelling" in others, usually because one or two items (out of 10 or 15)—like "monkeys, monkies" or "sheep, sheeps"—might be classified either way. These items might better be eliminated, since the label should not give the impression that these tests include spelling.

The main objection I would have to these tests is that they must be highly speeded. With a uniform time limit of 40 minutes, there are 95 items in the elementary tests, either 115 or 120 in the intermediate tests, and 135 in the junior high tests. The test of this sort that I admire most, the *Writing Skills Test* (for grades 9–12) by Macklin Thomas, published by SRA, has 70 items with the same time limit, and I doubt that the operations involved (except in one final section of 10 items) take more time than those of the Hoyum-Sanders tests. The norms tables for the latter, however, seem to indicate that the norms population was almost incredibly fast. In Test 1, Form A, for example, the average student got 69 out of 95 items right in grade 4, 92 out of 120 right in grade 6, and 93 out of 135 right in grade 8. The 90th percentile student got about four-fifths right in these grades. If this is representative, the use of the split-half method is not seriously questionable in computing reliabilities, which range from .86 to .93.

The same manual of four pages is used for the tests at all three levels—elementary, intermediate, and junior high. As usual, it does not give enough information about the development, tryout, and validation of the tests to satisfy the sophisticated, but the one serious error occurs in a paragraph explaining the norms. There are four tables of raw scores corresponding to percentiles (at intervals of 5) for Tests 1-A, 1-B,

2-A, and 2-B, and each table has columns for grades 2 through 8. These tables would be easier to interpret if headings were added to indicate that the columns for grades 2, 3, and 4 are based on the elementary tests, columns for grades 5 and 6 on the intermediate tests, and columns for grades 7 and 8 on the junior high tests. In the catalogue it is stated that Test 1 at each level is for the first semester and Test 2 for the second; Forms A and B of each test are equivalent. In the manual, however, one is directed to use Form A norms for all scores made in the first half of the school year, Form B norms for the second—apparently for both Test 1 and Test 2. This must be wrong, since the Form B norms show no consistent advance over Form A norms; instead, they bear out the catalogue statement that these forms are equivalent. The Test 2 norms, however, are slightly but consistently higher than the Test 1 norms, bearing out the catalogue statement that Test 1 is for the first semester and Test 2 for the second. This paragraph in the manual concludes, "Be sure to use the correct Table with reference Mid-year and End of Year and test form." No spik English?

The manual also says that raw scores may be converted into grade equivalent scores by using these norms tables but fortunately does not tell how. Only a mathematician could do it, and if he had a conscience, he would refuse, since there are different numbers of items and differences in content at successive levels and no administrations to justify placing all three levels on the same scale.

[197]

*Language Arts: Minnesota High School Achievement Examinations. Grades 7, 8, 9, 10, 11, 12; 1955–70; new form issued each May; Form GJ Rev. ('70, 6–7 pages); 6 levels; no specific manual; series manual ('70, 16 pages); no data on reliability; 12¢ per test, postage extra; $1.10 per specimen set, postpaid; 60(65) minutes; edited by V. L. Lohmann; American Guidance Service, Inc. *

For a review by Marvin D. Glock of earlier forms, see 6:268; for a review by Roger A. Richards, see 5:186.

[198]

★Language Arts Tests: Content Evaluation Series. Grades 7–9; 1969; Form 1; 3 tests in 1 booklet (33 pages); manual (24 pages); series technical manual (21 pages); separate answer sheets (MRC) must be used; $15 per 35 tests; $4.20 per 35 answer sheets; $1.05 per set of hand scoring stencils; 60¢ per manual; 90¢ per technical manual; $1.35 per specimen set of series; postage extra; scoring service, 27¢ per test booklet; 40(50) minutes per test; Elsa Graser (*a*), Leonard Freyman (*b*), Ruth Reeves (*c*); Houghton Mifflin Co. *

a) LANGUAGE ABILITY TEST: CONTENT EVALUATION SERIES.

b) COMPOSITION TEST: CONTENT EVALUATION SERIES.

c) LITERATURE TEST: CONTENT EVALUATION SERIES.

JOAN J. MICHAEL, *Associate Professor of Educational Psychology, California State College at Long Beach, Long Beach, California.*

The *Language Arts Tests* measure achievement in three general areas: language ability, composition, and literature. To the great credit of this set of tests, the authors have taken considerable pains in the construction of a detailed outline of the major and specific objectives for each of the three tests. To assist the reader in evaluating the content, the authors have prepared item classifications which indicate how each item is related to the particular outline. Thus, a prospective user is provided with an effective means of deciding upon content validity for any particular curriculum. Kudos, for this feature!

In the Language Ability Test the two major objectives stated are "to assess the student's understanding of the basic structure of the English language" and "to assess the student's ability to use sentence elements effectively in standard patterns." Of the 58 items comprising this test, only 14 are devoted to "basic structure," and the remaining 44 are devoted to the use of sentence elements. Appropriate selection of language usage problems from both the traditional and the newer patterns of English instruction have been included. Before using, however, a teacher has to decide whether the balance of items between traditional and new patterns is appropriate for a given curriculum. This reviewer raises some question about the variety of the format of items. In 40 minutes of testing time the examinee is required to read, understand, and implement eight different sets of instructions for answering the questions. Especially for lower ability students, this task in itself would appear to be formidable.

Of course, the continued challenge by teachers of English to the use of multiple choice items to evaluate students' composition skills remains. If the reader can accept the premise that this type of test offers a useful complement but not a substitute for actual samples of writing, then the Composition Test may be judged upon its merits as one form of assessment. The major objectives as set forth in the outline of the Composition Test are those of invention, arrangement, and style. Of the 60 items in this test, 31 were devoted to arrangement, 24 to style, and 5 to invention. As would be expected for this type of test, the choosing and restricting of the subject and stating of the purpose receive less emphasis than do the problems of organization and style. The content of this test appears to be based upon a rather thorough analysis of student errors; however, for the 7th, 8th, and 9th grade levels, this test seems to be a rather difficult undertaking. Moreover, in 40 minutes of testing time, the examinee is required to read and understand over 60 items, and to implement some 13 different sets of instructions.

The Literature Test is directed not toward factual content, but rather toward the significance and understanding of literary works. The teacher's manual outlines the three major objectives of this test as "overall comprehension," "response to techniques common to imaginative literature," and "literary interpretations." Of the 45 items, 16 are devoted to comprehension; 18 to techniques such as figurative language, contrast, emphasis, or implications; and 11 to literary interpretations of fiction, poetry, essay, and drama. The subject matter of the selections appears quite appropriate for the junior high level; however, the amount of reading required in a 40-minute time span to answer the 45 items is rather sizable. Students with poor reading skills might possibly be overwhelmed with the task involved.

The teacher's manual provides the user with administration and scoring directions, an explanation of the various types of scores suggested, conversion tables, bibliography, as well as the aforementioned outlines of the three tests. With respect to the various types of scores provided, the percentile ranks and stanines seem appropriate; however, the manner in which the standard scores were derived from a normalized curve seems so unusual as to lessen their usability. These standard scores were derived from the *total* weighted distribution of students in grades 7, 8, and 9. This weighted distribution interferes with ease of interpretation at any given grade level on a given test.

Split-half reliability estimates for the subtests range from .84 to .95. The high intercorrelations among the subtests (.69 to .75) are possibly a result of the sizable reading factor involved in the tests. No validity coefficients are shown; however, the outlines of specifications for the tests do serve this purpose. Finally, as an indication of criterion-related validity, an expectancy table pitting Language Ability Test scores against final English grades is shown.

In summary, the *Language Arts Tests* seem to this reviewer to be thoughtfully conceived and implemented but difficult and quite possibly inappropriate for lower ability students.

BLAINE R. WORTHEN, *Co-director, Laboratory of Educational Research, University of Colorado, Boulder, Colorado.*

Specific purposes of these three tests are to assess student progress in the three subject areas over the three junior-high years and to diagnose areas of strength and weakness for individual students.

TEST CONTENT. The teacher's manual contains a rationale and content outline for each of the tests and a classification of the items according to that outline. Each item number is listed with a numerical indicator of the point in the outline that the item is designed to measure. Attempting to use these two lists to determine how a content classification is represented by test items is laborious and the lists should be combined with items listed under each point in the outline.

The Language Ability Test is concentrated on areas which research seems to indicate are of greatest importance in language development—the structure of basic English and use of sentence elements in standard sentence patterns. Although the rationale states that no particular grammatical method is tested and no traditional grammatical terms are used, the student who has been exposed to structural grammar may have an advantage. The student must know what "sentence patterns" or "standard patterns of usage" are for 19 of the 58 items; 16 items use nonsense sentences that might be most readily deciphered by students familiar with structural grammar.

The Composition Test is designed to assess student ability to manipulate his language effectively; three principles of classical rhetoric—invention, organization, and style—are proposed as vehicles for this assessment. Inspection of the test shows that 21 of the 60 items cover choosing the main headings and subheadings of an outline. Twenty-three other items involve choosing among sentences embodying such considerations as "judicious infinitive splitting," "faulty reference," or "use of subordinate clauses." Two sets of items are interdependent;

one set includes 16 items which require arranging topics in an outline and another includes 6 items which require arranging sentences in a paragraph. Within each set, responding to one item influences the responses to the remaining items. This means that only 38 of the items on the test are independent. More seriously, a student could conceivably miss over one-third of the items by making only two wrong choices.

The Literature Test is intended to measure ability to identify important types of literature and "feeling for literature." Questions refer to five passages: one story, one essay, two poems, and one play. The questions stress analysis; 20 of the 45 items deal with "the central thought," "tone," or "implications." Although the level of reading difficulty appears to be appropriate for the other two tests, the required reading level in this test may be too high for a number of students in grades 7–9. Leaving the literary passages aside, some questions are unnecessarily complex and may penalize students who have considerable "feeling for literature" but have not been introduced to specific technical terms. Several questions require knowledge of terms such as "alliteration," "stanza," "simile," "metaphor," "rhyme scheme," and "unaccented syllables."

All three tests were difficult for seventh graders in the standardization group. The average seventh grade score for each was less than half the items. The median score for seventh graders on two of the tests—Composition and Literature—is not significantly different from chance; i.e., for half the seventh graders, one cannot be confident that the student did not achieve his score by random guessing.

TEST USE. The test format is excellent for all three tests. Directions for preparing for the test period and administering the test are quite explicit and will likely prove especially helpful to the beginner. Directions for scoring and reporting results are also clear and complete.

Scores for each test can be reported in four ways: raw scores, within-grade percentiles, within-grade stanines, and across-grade standard scores (normalized T scores). The latter "is provided so that scores from different subject areas and grade levels can be compared." One infers that such scores would be used to construct profiles, but no further discussion is given. Conversion tables are supplied in both the technical and teacher's manuals.

It is indicated in the manuals that the test

results might be used diagnostically with individual students. This seems unwarranted, since there are far too few items in most content areas to permit any reliable diagnoses. These tests should be viewed as group tests and appropriate for diagnostic use at that level only.

ITEM ANALYSIS. It is stated in the technical manual that item analyses were performed on preliminary forms of the test. The criteria were "a suitable range of difficulty" and "discrimination powers." Unfortunately, these criteria are not specified and item analysis data are not reported. It is also unfortunate that in the age of computers, discrimination indices were computed using the upper and lower 27 percent method rather than point-biserial coefficients or other indices of discrimination.

NORMS. Three factors were considered in drawing the sample for test standardization: community size, community location, and grade. Within these categories, the sampling plan used in the Project Talent survey was adopted and schools were selected randomly from the "community size by location" categories. Rates of noncooperation, mortality, and unusable results were not reported. "In all, 50,336 tests were administered in 27 schools from 21 districts representing 17 states." However, this selection of schools did not fully meet the specified sample requirements. There was marked overrepresentation of rural Northeast communities and underrepresentation of rural West and urban Southeast communities. Overall, rural communities were overrepresented and urban communities underrepresented. A weighting system was employed. "Actual returns were reported in 112 cells....these cells were then weighted to more closely meet the requirements of the sample." Unfortunately, the weighting system is inadequately described and test users are left to wonder how closely the weighted results meet the sample requirements. Given this ambiguity, one must also wonder how useful norms from this sample will be for interpreting test results in metropolitan schools. A further description of the sample (by sex, school and district size, race, socioeconomic status, etc.) would better enable users to determine the applicability of the norms to their schools.

RELIABILITY. Means, standard deviations, and standard errors of measurement for both raw and standard scores, and split-half correlations are reported for all three tests. These statistics were computed from "a systematic sample of 400 tests per grade per test." The system for selecting this sample is not reported.

Split-half reliabilities range from .84 to .95. These reliability coefficients are described as representing "the degree to which the performance of the student remains stable." However, the split-half method is a measure of internal consistency, not stability. Since the tests are to be used three times (at grades 7, 8, and 9) for assessing progress, the manual should give a reliability coefficient that does indicate stability over time. Particularly, one needs data on potential practice effects, since the same test, same form, could be used three times.

A more serious drawback of the split-half method, however, is the effect of speededness on the coefficient. Precisely 40 minutes are allotted for each test and instructions stress enforcing this time limit. There is no evidence that this period allows most students to finish the test. It may be that the high number of seventh grade scores which are not significantly different from chance reflects the effect of speed rather than test difficulty.

Although standard errors of measurement are listed for both raw and standard scores, useful information on the interpretation of these data are not included.

VALIDITY. Validity data on the *Language Arts Tests* are limited. Content validity is based on (a) an analysis of leading textbooks and courses of study for content and weighting of test specifications, and (b) examination of the specifications by curriculum experts to confirm appropriateness and coverage of content. However, no description of the specifications or experts' reactions to them are provided; agreement of experts with the final selection of items is implied, but no supporting data are offered.

Criterion-related validity is limited to a single study; the expectancy tables presented show positive relationships between scores on each of the tests and final eighth-grade English grades. Although correlation coefficients would have given more information about validity, the failure to use an independent criterion is a more serious deficiency. No mention is made of possible criterion contamination—any effect of the test scores on the final grades is ignored. In short, one can have confidence only in claims for content validity, and even there considerable appeal to faith is necessary.

summary. In spite of the criticisms noted above, the *Language Arts Tests* are appropriate for assessing end-of-year achievement in the three specified language areas, especially in grades 8 and 9. They are interesting tests with a blend of traditional and innovative content. Content validity for the tests appears acceptable, but an explicit description of content validation processes is needed before one can be confident about such validity. Inclusion of a stability reliability index is a must, especially in view of the use of the same tests across three grade levels. Users should be provided better descriptions of norm groups and criteria used in the item analyses. Item interdependencies should be reduced or eliminated in the Literature Test and item difficulties and time limits should be reconsidered on all three tests. If these inadequacies can be corrected, these tests should prove very useful in assessing proficiency in the three language areas. In the meantime, interpretation of test results will be most difficult and the tests should be used only by those who understand the limitations involved.

[199]

*Mechanics of Written English. High school; 1940–66; 6 scores: punctuation, recognition of non-standard usage, capitalization, vocabulary, spelling, total; 1 form ('66, 11 pages, identical with Form 59B published in 1959 except for title page); mimeographed scoring directions [no date, 3 pages, identical with directions for Form 59B except for omission of norms]; no data on reliability; no norms; $1 per 10 tests, postpaid; 25¢ per single copy, cash orders only; 50(55) minutes; R. S. Hunting; High School Testing Service, Purdue University. *

[200]

*Metropolitan Achievement Tests: High School Language Tests. Grades 9–13; 1962–64; catalog uses the title *Metropolitan High School Language Tests*; 4 scores: reading, spelling, language, language study skills; Forms Am ('62, 12 pages), Bm ('63, 12 pages); manual ('64, 28 pages); for battery accessories, see 15; separate answer sheets (Digitek, Harbor, IBM 805, IBM 1230) must be used; $8.50 per 35 tests; $2.80 per 35 Digitek answer sheets; $2.90 per 35 IBM 805 answer sheets; $3.30 per 35 IBM 1230 answer sheets; $6 per 100 sets of Harbor answer cards; 70¢ per Digitek scoring stencil; $1.40 per set of IBM scoring stencils; $1.50 per specimen set; postage extra; Harbor scoring service, 19¢ and over per test; IBM scoring service, 33¢ and over per test; 95(112) minutes; Walter N. Durost, William H. Evans, James D. Leake, Howard A. Bowman, Clarke Cosgrove, and John G. Read; Harcourt Brace Jovanovich, Inc. *

Leonard S. Feldt, *Professor of Education, The University of Iowa, Iowa City, Iowa.*

The original edition of the *Metropolitan Achievement Tests* was published approximately 40 years ago. Its long history is rivaled by only one or two competing batteries, including the *Stanford Achievement Tests,* distributed by the same publisher. The high school battery is a relatively new addition to the testing scene, however, having first appeared in 1962. The forms under review bear copyright dates of 1962 and 1963. Thus, they appear to be the original extensions of the Metropolitan battery to grades 9–13.

The first three passages of the reading test follow the traditional pattern of such instruments. Each selection is approximately 400–500 words in length and is followed by a series of seven or eight questions. The final passage presents an innovation at the high school level. A fairly long selection (about 800 words) is presented to the examinee for 10 minutes of preliminary study. At the end of this period, he turns the page and must answer a series of questions without opportunity to reread the material. This is apparently an attempt to reflect in the test the kind of recall situation commonly encountered in school work. However, there is no evidence in the manual to indicate that this approach reveals a unique aspect of the reading process. If there is a new recall element introduced, do we want to see the student with a facile memory receive a higher reading score than a classmate not similarly blessed? This may be an academic question, since the variance associated with differences in memory may be insignificant. The recall period is, after all, very short.

The authors state that the questions bear on four aspects of the selections: main idea or purpose of the passage, inferences from the passage, perception of details, and deduction of the meanings of words from the context. The manual does not indicate the category to which each item belongs. This reviewer found few items which he would consider very penetrating or which require a high level of critical insight. Perhaps this follows from the fact that the passages themselves, while quite interesting, do not include any that seem very meaty or demanding. In their daily work, high school juniors and seniors are confronted with more sophisticated material than these tests offer. Competing reading tests, such as those found in the STEP and ITED batteries, pose more of a challenge, with questions that probe more deeply than do the materials represented here.

The spelling and language exercises include a response that may be unique to this battery.

It is "don't know." This option may provide relief from the frustration some examinees feel when forced to choose one answer from several equally attractive possibilities. But surely most students and practically all teachers will realize that no credit can be earned by selecting this response. If any students are tempted to mark it (there are no data in the manual on this point), the scores become unnecessarily and undesirably sensitive to the test-taking skills and naiveté of the examinee.

The spelling test, involving 55 items of the "right-wrong-don't know" variety, and one of the language usage subtests introduce another novelty: a worksheet on which the examinee records the correct spelling or the correct grammatical form of words that are incorrect in the test exercises. The teacher uses these worksheets for diagnosis if he wishes, but they are ignored in the scoring of the tests. They would seem to open the way to some interesting research possibilities. They could be used, for example, to document the contention that those who recognize an error do know the correct language forms. No such studies are reported in the test manual.

The capitalization and punctuation subtest proved somewhat confusing to this reviewer when he used the IBM 1230 answer sheet. The item responses are printed on the sheet, and one must constantly bear in mind that the response space which applies to an option *follows* rather than *precedes* it. This can be forgotten. Also, the text material in this subtest includes obvious errors which the student must ignore. The directions might have noted this fact.

In general, the language tests represent a compromise between identifying errors and specifying the reasons why a usage is unacceptable. Some teachers may consider the reasons important and be happy that the test demands this knowledge. But others might have preferred some items devoted to effectiveness of phrasing, organization of ideas, and so on. The entire test deals exclusively with issues of right and wrong, rather than better or worse.

The test scores can be interpreted via norms based on "age-controlled" samples (pupils who have been regularly promoted) or the scores of students enrolled in college preparatory curriculums. The former have been used for many years in conjunction with the lower levels of this battery. As a previous reviewer has pointed out (6:15), the specifications for the national

standardization may have been well formulated, but the execution of the plan probably fell short of the publisher's hopes. Fewer than 30 school systems are represented in the norms.

The manual describes the developmental program quite well, but validity rests solely on the efforts of the authors to build tests consistent with "expert pronouncements," "current research," "representative courses of study," and "widely used textbooks." How well they succeeded, each teacher must decide for himself. The reliability data must be considered with caution. K-R 20 coefficients were computed from the same data and samples used to make the final item selection—a procedure which leads to biased coefficients. Split-half estimates are based on two school systems and, more crucially, on scores from grades 10 and 11 combined. Such pooling of grade data is not a sound procedure. Why samples from the national standardization were not used for reliability estimation is not explained.

In summary, this reviewer finds both the reading and the language tests less penetrating and narrower in scope than multiple choice tests can be. Where the decision on their use is not tied to adoption of the battery as a whole, he would strongly suggest consideration of competing instruments.

DAVID P. HARRIS, *Professor of Linguistics and Director, The American Language Institute, Georgetown University, Washington, D.C.*

These tests are comprised of four separate measures which can be used independently. Test 1, Reading, consists of 40 four-choice items based on four selections. The first three passages in Form Am range roughly between 450 and 500 words in length; those in Form Bm are all slightly shorter. These passages are followed by seven or eight items each. The fourth selection is about twice as long as the others, and students are to answer the 17 questions without referring back to the passage. Test selections are interesting and varied in content, and the items are soundly written. Factual questions are interspersed with inferential problems and questions about the author's purpose, as well as with a few pure vocabulary items. The inclusion of one section testing recall is appropriate, though the choice of subject for the Am passage seems questionable: it is for the most part a conventional discussion of reading techniques, and the student who has been taught anything about intensive and extensive reading and skimming ought to be able to answer seven or eight items on the basis of prior knowledge alone.

Test 2, Spelling, presents the 55 test words in one-sentence contexts. The student marks each word R (right), W (wrong), or DK (don't know). Words he considers misspelled are then to be spelled correctly on a work sheet. These spellings are not counted in the scoring; they are intended to provide additional information for the teacher. Unfortunately, no advice is given the student as to whether it is better to guess or to mark the DK option (which is also used in Tests 3 and 4), and one supposes that the test-wise student will gain an advantage by limiting himself to R and W choices. Most of the test words are reasonably appropriate for high school students, though a handful of words in each form seem to have been chosen primarily for their spelling peculiarities, not for their probable utility value: *lacquer, silhouette, exhilaration,* etc.

Test 3, Language, is divided into three parts: punctuation and capitalization (25 items based on a passage in which most punctuation and capitalization have been omitted); correct usage (35 sentences with underlined words); and sentence style and structure (13 sentences which either are acceptable or contain one of several designated types of "errors"). Though this should be one of the strongest tests in the battery, it is, alas, the weakest. It is hard to believe that, after so many years of emphasis on descriptive grammar and levels of usage, we should still find tests demanding that the "rules" of formal written English be applied to highly colloquial contexts. Can we still reasonably insist that our students mark as incorrect "I wish today *was* Saturday"? Does anyone still find it appropriate to drill "This is *he* speaking"? This test puts far too much emphasis on the traditional shibboleths: e.g., *"these* kind of apples," "taller than *me,"* "it was *him,"* "all the farther I read." And surely if such matters of divided usage are worthy of any attention at all, it is only when they appear in formal or semiformal writing and spoil the general tone. To drill or test them in contexts that suggest conversation between friends is to set back our understanding of the language by several decades.

Of far greater potential value is the section on sentence style and structure, where faulty sentences of various kinds are presented to the student for analysis. But this part of the test has only 13 problems (compared with 25 for punctuation and capitalization), and the student has only to select an appropriate description of the sentence faults: "Modifier is misplaced," "Sentence is incomplete," etc. The reviewer would strongly urge, first, that this part of the test be considerably expanded and, second, that at least some items require the student to choose the best of alternative ways of expressing the same idea, so that his task would be more than simply attaching labels.

Test 4, Language Study Skills (only 32 items), is concerned with the student's ability to interpret dictionary entries and to utilize various reference sources (tables of contents, card catalogue, *Readers' Guide,* etc.). The test measures some useful learnings, though the 12 dictionary items, based on three highly simplified dictionary entries, seem repetitive and rather easy. High school students should certainly be able to handle the standard "college" dictionaries, and a more valid and challenging test could be constructed around a reproduced page from such a dictionary, as was done in the old *Cooperative Dictionary Test.*

The publisher provides a wide range of clear and helpful information on the tests. Results are expressed in terms of a normalized standard score scale having a mean of 50 and a standard deviation of 15. Tables are given for converting standard scores to percentile ranks and stanines, with separate norms for age-controlled and college-preparatory groups. Separate test data on both test forms are provided for the 9th through 12th grades. Reliability has been estimated by three methods: K-R 20, split-half, and alternate forms. K-R 20 coefficients for Form Bm of Test 1 and for both forms of Test 4 are below .85, suggesting cautious use of these tests as measures of individual performance. Unfortunately, no data are offered on combinations of the tests, nor is there any information on degree of speededness, which would be particularly helpful in the case of Test 1, Reading.

The manual proposes four specific uses for the tests: (*a*) appraisal of student progress, (*b*) educational and vocational guidance, (*c*) evaluation of instructional programs "as a basis for curriculum revision," and (*d*) evaluation of instructional material. Certain of the tests, and particularly Test 1, Reading, might be of some use as diagnostic or achievement instruments. On the other hand, the extremely old-fashioned character of Test 3, Language, renders it inappropriate for most diagnostic or achievement testing, and to use it as a basis for curriculum reform or as a measure of the adequacy of modern instructional materials could prove downright destructive.

For reviews of the complete battery, see 15 (2 reviews) and 6:15 (3 reviews).

[201]

★**Missouri College English Test.** Grades 12–13; 1964–65; MCET; Forms B, C, ('64, 8 pages) ; Form C is restricted to colleges; manual ('65, 16 pages) ; supplementary grade 12 norms available on request; separate answer sheets (Digitek, IBM 805, IBM 1230) must be used; $7 per 35 tests; $2.30 per 35 IBM 805 answer sheets; $2.80 per 35 Digitek or IBM 1230 answer sheets; 70¢ per scoring stencil; $1.50 per specimen set; postage extra; IBM scoring service, 19¢ and over per test; 40(50) minutes; Robert Callis and Willoughby Johnson; Harcourt Brace Jovanovich, Inc. * (Form A is out of print.)

REFERENCE

1. WILLIS, CARL G., AND NICHOLSON, JAMES. "Series II SCAT as a College Aptitude Measure." *Ed & Psychol Meas* 30(4):971–5 w '70. *

JOHN B. CARROLL, *Senior Research Psychologist, Educational Testing Service, Princeton, New Jersey.*

This is a competently constructed, well standardized test which is, as the manual puts it, "generally concerned with the mechanics and the effectiveness of written expression." One is impressed with the amount of effort that apparently went into the drawing up of specifications, the writing of items, the obtaining of comments and suggestions from subject-matter specialists, the updating of the test in 1962–63 after it was discovered that entering college freshmen were increasingly better prepared, and the final norming.

Each of the three equivalent forms has three parts. Part 1 requires the examinee to register whether each of 60 underlined segments in a group of themes contains an error in the mechanics of expression and, if so, whether the error is one of capitalization, "grammar," punctuation, or spelling. Most of the errors are of the rather elementary sort that continually plague teachers of English composition, and the segments that are keyed as having no error contain expressions that will often tempt the unsure student to believe there is an error. Throughout, the emphasis is on standards of formal correctness; occasionally the student is expected to recognize such a standard even though it may be somewhat unrealistic, as when

he must identify a "grammatical" error in the phrase "who we are sure we can trust," even though the phrase in question occurs in a quoted, informal conversation.

Part 2 has 10 items requiring the student to decide which one of four sentences best expresses an idea; the distractors are awkward, ungainly sentences that would never be approved by a good editor, yet item difficulty data included in the manual reveal that significant proportions of students do not recognize the keyed choices. Occasionally, however, even a good editor might disagree with the key (e.g., items 65 and 70 in Form A), and sometimes the keyed choices are of dubious excellence stylistically (e.g., item 69, Form A). The difficulty and discrimination indices tend to confirm these judgments.

Part 3 asks the student to indicate the order in which sentences should be arranged in four 5-sentence paragraphs, for a total of 20 items.

The user of this test should note that by far the largest portion of the test is concerned with elementary mechanics of expression. Apparently this is what English instructors are most worried about. (Incidentally, the test authors should attend to their own mechanics: in Table 10 of the manual, we find a mention of the "principle [sic] parts" of verbs.)

The authors claim this is a power test because "it was determined that a 90-item test could be completed in 40 minutes by the vast majority of college freshmen." Nevertheless, they make the common mistake of reporting split-half reliability coefficients without pointing out that they may be inflated because of possible speededness.

The norms for the test appear to be highly adequate, based on data obtained from freshmen enrolled at 81 two- and four-year public and private colleges. Supplementary data available from the publisher give norms for 968 students completing 12th grade English in five comprehensive high schools in New York State. It is somewhat saddening to note the relatively poor showing of all these students; the median score for all college freshmen is about 51 right out of 90, and the distribution extends down to the level of chance scores.

On the basis of the technical excellence of its standardization and the trouble the authors took to insure its content validity, this test can be recommended to high school and college English teachers who want a global measure of knowledge of the ordinary mechanics of English expression at the 12th grade or college freshman level. Its usefulness as a diagnostic test, however, would be limited both by the fact that relatively small numbers of items pertain to each category of error and by the fact that obtaining diagnostic information from the answer sheets would entail considerable effort. Its main use would be for placement in college freshman writing courses or for the identification of students needing remedial teaching.

CLARENCE DERRICK, *Professor of Humanities, University of Florida, Gainesville, Florida.*

The item types used to evaluate objectively what the test constructor hopes is related to writing proficiency are of two general types— "mechanics" items and "effectiveness" items. Since 60 of the 90 items in this test are "mechanics" items, the *Missouri College English Test* will serve best in those situations where punctuation, capitalization, spelling, and grammar are emphasized. (The writers of this test do not make the distinction between the terms *grammar* and *usage*.)

The mechanics items are presented in "selections....adapted from essays written by college students" with certain underlined parts to be examined for errors in capitalization, "grammar," punctuation, and spelling. The fifth possibility is that the underlined portion contains no error. Supposedly the use of student essays presents a natural situation. Although this item type has been used frequently in other tests, this reviewer has never liked it. The test taker is put in a proofreading situation, and how many of us are good proof readers? Too much depends on visual acuity. The person who would not misspell a particular word may fail to detect that a letter is missing. Another limitation is that the underlined portion may not present a situation where all the categories are live options. For example, an item in Form B: "Considering the *remarkable facility of the minature camera as....*" Is capitalization a possibility? Is punctuation? Is "grammar"? Essentially this item is a two-choice item—spelling or no error.

In Part 2, the examinee selects from four sentences the one that expresses the idea best. Of the three item types in the test, this item type seems to have the most "face validity" for evaluating proficiency in writing. To state that one item type is preferable to another type is

not to say that all items using that format are equally good. The trick in the item type in Part 2 is to have as the keyed answer a sentence that most people would regard as better expressing the idea in the sentence and still not have the choice too obvious—not an easy trick.

Part 3 uses another familiar item type. The examinee is presented with five sentences in scrambled order and then responds to a series of questions: "Which sentence should be placed *first?* Which *second?*" etc. This reviewer has never been sure exactly what is being measured by this item type, but he doubts that it has much to do with the ability to organize one's own sentences, which is presumably the rationale for it. Furthermore, the experienced test taker knows that his performance on this item type is facilitated if he writes a number by each sentence in what he considers the proper sequence and then answers the questions. However, the directions for the *Missouri College English Test* do not permit him to write in the test booklet.

The *Missouri College English Test* is a device to separate sheep from goats in the traditional freshman composition course and to urge students to follow the path of "correctness." Those who want a test that gives less emphasis to mechanics and more emphasis to stylistic matters and diction should examine such tests as the *Cooperative English Tests* and the *College English Placement Test*.

[202]

*Moray House English Tests.** Ages 8.5–10.5, 10–12, 12–14; 1935–70; 3 levels; distribution restricted to education authorities; £1 per 20 tests; 5p per single copy; 12½p per manual for any one form of any one test; postage extra; 40(50) minutes; Godfrey Thomson Unit, University of Edinburgh; University of London Press Ltd. *

a) MORAY HOUSE JUNIOR ENGLISH TEST. Ages 8.5–10.5; 1952–70; 4 forms: *Junior English Test 1* ['52], *Junior English Test 3* ('64), 5 ('70), 6 ('70), (11–12 pages); manual [dates same as for tests, 12 pages] for each form.

b) MORAY HOUSE ENGLISH TEST. Ages 10–12; 1935–69; 1–2 new forms issued annually; 10 forms (12 pages) currently available: forms 33 ['61], 34 ['62], 35 ['63], 36 ('64), 37 ('65), 38 ('65), 39 ('66), 40 ('67), 41 ('68), 42 ('69); manual (dates same as for tests, 11–12 pages) for each form.

c) MORAY HOUSE ENGLISH TEST (ADV.). Ages 12–14; 1947–58; forms 1 ['56], 2 ['58], (12 pages); manual [dates same as for tests, 12 pages] for each form.

REFERENCES

1–7. See 6:271.
8. MACNAMARA, JOHN. "Zero Error and Practice Effects in Moray House English Quotients." *Brit J Ed Psychol* 34:315–20 N '64. * (PA 39:8704)

For a review by M. Alan Brimer, see 6:271.

[203]

*National Teacher Examinations: English Language and Literature. College seniors and teachers; 1940–70; Forms RNT1 ('69, 23 pages), RNT2 ('69, 21 pages), SNT ('70, 23 pages) ; descriptive booklet ('70, 8 pages) ; for more complete information, see 582; 120(165) minutes; Educational Testing Service. *

REFERENCE

1. MEDLIN, YANCEY LEONARD. *An Analysis of Some Aspects of the English Proficiency of White Secondary School Teacher Candidates in North Carolina, 1959–1961.* Doctor's thesis, University of North Carolina (Chapel Hill, N.C.), 1962. (*DA* 24: 1495)

For a review by Holland Roberts of an earlier form, see 6:259. For reviews of the testing program, see 582 (2 reviews), 6:700 (1 review), 5:538 (3 reviews), and 4:802 (1 review).

[204]

★Pacific Tests of English Attainment and Skills: Pacific Test Series. Job applicants in Papua and New Guinea; 1933–68; PTEAS; 3 tests; manual ('68, 31 pages) ; Aus $2.50 per manual; $3 per specimen set; postpaid within Australia; I. G. Ord; Australian Council for Educational Research. *
a) PACIFIC READING COMPREHENSION TEST. 1933–68; PRCT ; adaptation of Part 3 of *A.C.E.R. Silent Reading Test,* Forms A and B (see 5:616) ; Forms A, B, ('68, 3 pages, each form consists of 12 items from Form L plus 4 more difficult items), L ('68, 4 pages) ; Aus 75¢ per 10 tests; 10(15) minutes for Forms A and B, 12(17) minutes for Form L.
b) PACIFIC WORD KNOWLEDGE TEST. 1933–68; PWKT ; 1 form ('68, 2 pages) ; Aus 50¢ per 10 tests; 12(17) minutes.
c) PACIFIC WORD FORMATION TEST. 1968; PWFT ; 1 form (4 pages) ; Aus $1 per 10 tests; 19(24) minutes.

[205]

★Picture Story Language Test. Ages 7–17; 1965; PSLT ; a developmental scale for written language; 5 scores: productivity (total words, total sentences, words per sentence), syntax, abstract-concrete; record form (4 pages) ; test picture (1 card) ; manual ('65, 292 pages) title is *Development and Disorders of Written Language: Vol. 1, Picture Story Language Test;* $7.50 per 100 record forms; $4.75 per picture; $8.50 per manual; postage extra; (20–30) minutes; Helmer R. Myklebust; Grune & Stratton, Inc. *

REFERENCES

1. MYKLEBUST, HELMER R. *Development and Disorders of Written Language: Vol. 1, Picture Story Language Test.* New York: Grune & Stratton, Inc., 1965. Pp. xiii, 278. *
2. MASON, CHARLES WILBURN. *An Analysis of the Interrelationships of Variables in Selected Language Skills of Intermediate and Upper Elementary School Students.* Doctor's thesis, Southern Illinois University (Carbondale, Ill.), 1968. (*DA* 29:3043A)
3. MOORE, ANTHONY BRYAN. *Reasoning Ability and Verbal Proficiency in Deaf and Hearing Children.* Doctor's thesis, University of Massachusetts (Amherst, Mass.), 1968. (*DA* 29:4381B)
4. O'TOOLE, THOMAS JAMES. *The Effect of a Long-Term Functional Articulation Problem on the Language Skills of Seventh Grade Boys.* Doctor's thesis, University of Maryland (College Park, Md.), 1968. (*DAI* 30:3424B)
5. LEWIS, FRANKLIN D.; BELL, D. BRUCE; AND ANDERSON, ROBERT P. "Reading Retardation: A Bi-Racial Comparison." *J Read* 13(6):433–6, 474–8 Mr '70. *

NICHOLAS ANASTASIOW, *Director, Institute for Child Study, Indiana University, Bloomington, Indiana.*

This test is a relatively new diagnostic, clinical instrument for assessing the writing development of children. The test manual is a clothbound book in which the author discusses his rationale for how children's writing skills develop. He maintains that deficits in writing ability are related to abnormalities in the peripheral and central nervous system, caused by psychogenic disturbances and psycho-social deprivation. A major purpose of the test is to serve "as a diagnostic instrument for the study of children with language disorders and other types of learning disabilities." The child is presented with a picture about which he is asked to write a story. From these written stories, scales are developed to measure length (productivity), correctness of expression (syntax), and to attempt to measure content or meaning of the sentence (abstract-concrete). Thus, number of words, number of sentences, and words per sentence are counted; accuracy of word usage, of word endings, and of pronunciation is rated; and errors of additions, omissions, substitutions, and word order are counted.

The norming sample is described as consisting of three types of public school populations from one Midwestern state. A group of educators chose the schools as being representative but what they are representative of is not clear. Only odd years from ages 7 to 17 were sampled. The described norming procedures are very inadequate.

The means and standard deviations are presented by age and sex. Some growth curves are not linear. There is a large overlapping across ages in the range of scores for each scale but the author fails to comment upon these findings. For example, for total words a mean of 90.4 with a standard deviation of 51.5 was obtained at age 9 and a mean of 116.0 and standard deviation 56.0 at age 11. All scales were determined on the same sample; the description of how these data were obtained is inadequate. The author states that the instrument appears to be a valid test. However, validity is not adequately described. The author refers to studies with handicapped children, which are to be reported in a second volume. However, at this time, five years after the publication of the first volume, the second volume has not been published.

Reliability is based on test-retest and split-half data. The author reports that the test-retest correlations were statistically significant but does not present the data for the reader to determine what the statement means. This could be very misleading, as these correlations may be beyond chance, but as reported in his book the odd-even reliabilities range from .38 to .84 for words per sentence and from .52 to .92 on the syntax scale. Thus, most of the reliabilities are below adequate levels of test standards. Inter-rater reliabilities are below .90 on some of the scales. For the syntax scale, for example, the ranges are from .34 to .95 for individual ratings by three trained examiners.

In summary, the data as presented do not provide sufficient confidence that the test is either a reliable or valid measure of a child's writing skills. In addition, the author interpolates scores for ages not sampled. This is a dubious practice, considering the large standard deviation for the ages sampled. The *Picture Story Language Test* is a relatively untried projective technique with inadequate psychometric data presented to support the supposition the author maintains.

WILLIAM H. PERKINS, *Professor in Communicative Disorders, University of Southern California, Los Angeles, California.*

The *Picture Story Language Test* is intended as a diagnostic instrument for appraising normal and abnormal development of written language. This test evolved from several theoretical constructs: (*a*) that language is more than a signalling device; it is a system for attaching meaning to abstract symbols for expression of ideas; (*b*) that writing follows reading, which follows speech; (*c*) that whereas speech depends on integrity of the auditory system for learning, reading also depends on the visual system, and writing on coordination of these sensory processes with the motor system. Written language is therefore viewed as man's highest verbal achievement, and disorders of writing can reflect inability to learn auditorally, visually, tactually, or motorically.

The PSLT is a landmark test of written language. Not only is it based on a defensible theoretical foundation, but it has also been developed as a standardized test of facility with the written word and as an instrument for differential diagnosis of learning disabilities. The normal sample of 747 children from one Midwestern state was drawn from three school populations: metropolitan, rural, and suburban. Both sexes were represented about equally at

six age levels from 7 to 17, and a wide range of socioeconomic levels and cultural backgrounds was included. Although these norms probably apply to all children with average school experience, no evidence is yet available on geographic differences in written language development. The handicapped were studied separately and the data on those with learning disabilities, mental retardation, speech defects, social-emotional disturbance, and reading disabilities were to be reported separately in a second volume which, unfortunately, never was published.

Such evidence as is available indicates that the PSLT is a valid test of facility with the written word. Although the various tests have not been factor analyzed to determine the extent to which they test separate functions, they do have face validity. As normal children mature, their scores on the productivity, syntax, and abstract-concrete scales tend to improve. Too, handicapped children for whom language impairment would be expected reflect linguistic limitations in PSLT results. By comparison with such other tests as purport to measure the same functions, the PSLT appears to be a valid measure of written language.

For reliability, test-retest and odd-even methods have been used. The syntax and words-per-sentence scores meet acceptable standards of reliability, although reliability coefficients are lowest at age levels 11 and 13, suggesting greater performance variability at these ages. Using trained and untrained groups to determine interscorer reliability, the productivity and abstract-concrete scales emerge as scales that can be reliably administered irrespective of training. Training in use of the syntax scale, however, is critical for its use.

The PSLT is a valuable instrument for assessing facility with written language. Although it could also be used to evaluate spoken language, this is not a purpose for which it was designed, nor would it be particularly useful. The assumption underlying the test is that the spoken form is basic to the written form, an assumption supported by evidence that acquisition of reading and writing correlates highly with intelligence, whereas acquisition of speech requires only minimal intellectual capacity. For its purpose, this test stands apart as a valid reliable instrument for which normative data are available.

Cont Psychol 11:458 S '66. Joseph M. Wepman. * a manual for a new and relatively untried test for the development of written language in children. It has little theoretical substance and perhaps is better described as a statement of position rather than one of theory. Its greatest virtue lies in the care in which the author has elaborated the presentation and scoring principles for the new test. For the psychologist interested in a written projective test, the "picture story language test" might well provide the basis for a good psychological analysis. At the present time it is used as a study of the development of syntax more than anything else.

Percept & Motor Skills 22:667 Ap '66. C. H. Ammons. * The manual contains tables of normative data, illustrations of stories, and some specific information concerning reliability and validity. Several indices reflecting consistency suggest that reliability is reasonable. However, assessment of validity will require considerable ingenuity and further work. On this basis then, the interpretation of test protocols should be tentative at best.

[206]

*SRA Achievement Series: Language Arts. Grades 2–4, 4–9; 1954–69; 4 scores: capitalization and punctuation, grammatical usage, spelling, total; 2 forms; 4 levels in 2 booklets; no specific manuals; for series manuals and accessories, see 18; postage extra; Louis P. Thorpe, D. Welty Lefever, and Robert A. Naslund; Science Research Associates, Inc. *
a) HAND SCORED EDITION. Grades 2–4; 1955–68; test booklet title is *How Should We Say This?*; Forms C, D, ('63, 18 pages); $3.75 per 25 tests; 60(85) minutes in 2 sessions.
b) MULTILEVEL EDITION. Grades 4–9; 1963–69; Forms C, D, ('63, 27 pages); 3 levels: blue (grades 4.5–6.5), green (grades 6.5–8.5), and red (grades 8.5–9) in a single booklet; separate series answer sheets (Digitek, DocuTran, IBM 805, IBM 1230) must be used; $8.70 per 25 tests; $9.30 per 100 DocuTran answer sheets; 70(85) minutes.

REFERENCE

1. See 6:277.

For a review by Miriam M. Bryan of earlier forms, see 6:277; for reviews by Constance M. McCullough and Winifred L. Post, see 5:200. For reviews of the complete battery, see 18 (2 reviews), 6:21 (1 review), and 5:21 (2 reviews).

[207]

★Senior English Test. Technical college entrants; 1963–64; 1 form ['63, 8 pages]; mimeographed manual ('64, 8 pages); provisional norms ['63]; 5p per test, postpaid within U.K.; manual and norms free on request from NFER; 60(65) minutes; published for the

National Foundation for Educational Research in England and Wales; Ginn & Co. Ltd. *

M. A. BRIMER, *Head of Research Unit, School of Education, University of Bristol, Bristol, England.*

The *Senior English Test* has been constructed with the cooperation of teachers to meet a particular need in England and Wales to measure general skills in the comprehension and use of English amongst entrants to technical college courses. Since the test is still in a developmental stage, despite its first introduction in 1963–64, the administrative manual (dated 1964) and a set of tentative norms are issued in duplicated form. No data on construction, reliability, or validity are reported.

Nineteen of the 56 items elicit a free response from the student and 13 require the construction of complete sentences. Vocabulary is tested through a "cross-word" item type, though independence of items is largely retained. Reading comprehension, sentence construction, the organisation of ideas in continuous prose, competence in syntactical usage, spelling, and insertion of periods are also represented, though with too few items to yield part scores.

Scoring is not entirely objective. Judgement of the quality of the response in relation to criteria given in the marking key is demanded in the case of 19 items. Moreover, in other items, where misspellings are not penalised, the marker must judge whether or not the subject's intention was to write the correct word, however it is spelled. Inevitably this must lead to increase in between-marker variation and to reduced reliability. Yet the loss in reliability may be compensated by improved construct validity.

Provisional t-score norms are offered for age groups 15–0 to 15–11 and 16–0 to 16–11, based, respectively, on 206 and 271 engineering student entrants to technical colleges. The absence of further data on the constitution of the sample, on construction, reliability, or validity precludes the possibility of a full assessment of the test. Only the reputation of the NFER would inspire confidence in an instrument which is so lacking in relevant data.

DAVID A. WALKER, *Formerly Director, The Scottish Council for Research in Education, Edinburgh, Scotland.*

This test was designed to assess the basic

knowledge of English possessed by entrants to courses in technical colleges. It contains 51 items, in 5 of which the candidate can earn two marks, the remainder carrying one mark each. The test begins with an easy crossword puzzle and continues with exercises in reading comprehension, word completion, punctuation, rearrangement of parts of a paragraph, completion of a paragraph using given phrases, and sentence construction. The manual gives clear instructions on the administration of the test and a marking key. Provisional conversion tables for 15-year-olds and 16-year-olds enable the test user to convert raw scores for these age-groups to T scores with mean at 50 and standard deviation of 10.

While the intention behind the test is praiseworthy, the execution unfortunately falls much below the standard expected from the National Foundation for Educational Research in England and Wales. The first reading comprehension passage, which is characterised by figurative language, is more appropriate to the material handled by able pupils following an academic course. The second passage contains vocabulary which is quite inappropriate for students of the type entering technical courses. The weight given to correctness of spelling seems unduly great; a candidate who knows that lines which meet at infinity are parallel, but misspells "parallel" scores zero. The test of punctuation is a satisfactory one, but the marking scheme makes nonsense of the section in that a candidate who supplies a sufficiently large number of strokes between words is certain to collect full marks but is not penalised for the surplus and incorrect strokes he has inserted. Nineteen of the responses are open-ended; although instructions for allocating marks are given in the manual, it is doubtful whether they are sufficiently precise to obviate differences between markers.

The provisional norms which are supplied are based on relatively small numbers of students. The manual, which was prepared in 1964, expresses the hope that standardisation data to be obtained for the period 1963-65 would enable more widely based conversion tables to be produced. An inquiry at the Foundation in August 1970 revealed that no further information had been made available and that there was none at that date on the reliability and validity of the test.

On the whole, it would appear to be wise to regard this test as an experiment in a difficult field.

[208]

★Stanford Achievement Test: High School English and Spelling Tests. Grades 9-12; 1965-66; catalog uses the title Stanford High School English and Spelling Tests; subtest of Stanford Achievement Test: High School Basic Battery; Forms W, X, ('65, 9 pages); no specific manual; battery manual ('65, 48 pages); supplementary directions ('66, 4 pages) for each type of answer sheet; separate answer sheets (IBM 805, IBM 1230) must be used; $8.20 per 35 tests; $2.30 per 35 IBM 805 answer sheets; $2.80 per 35 IBM 1230 answer sheets; $1.40 per set of scoring stencils; $1.20 per battery manual; $2 per specimen set; postage extra; scoring service, 19¢ and over per test; 60(65) minutes; Eric F. Gardner, Jack C. Merwin, Robert Callis, and Richard Madden; Harcourt Brace Jovanovich, Inc. *

VINCENT R. D'OYLEY, Professor of Education, The Ontario Institute for Studies in Education, The University of Toronto, Toronto, Ontario, Canada.[1]

These tests form part of a new comprehensive battery, designed as an extension of the Stanford Achievement Test series for grades 1-9. The English test consists of 85 items spread over three sections, mechanics, style, and paragraph organization; the spelling test has 60 items, each consisting of four unrelated words, one of which is misspelled.

There is much evidence of careful planning, imaginative writing, and thorough analysis in every phase of the development of these tests. The manual is clearly organized and comprehensive. It is readable, even by the unsophisticated teacher; its content is neatly outlined in such a way as to assist local administrators in test selection. The norming procedures are difficult to fault, and the norms themselves, presented in stanines and percentiles for each of grades 9-12, are easy to determine from the charts. The acceptable and unacceptable uses of the tests are spelled out in simple though very general terms. For the teacher, item statistics and charts denoting standard errors of differences for the whole battery are rendered more helpful by the use of illustrative examples of their use.

The directions for administering the test are clear and not too verbose; the illustrative examples appear suitable and adequate. On the basis of these factors, the high school test selector should be well pleased with this instrument.

1 The reviewer wishes to acknowledge with thanks the assistance of Dr. Warrick Elley in the preparation of this review.

Turning to the content of the tests themselves, however, he may wish to ponder some of the following points: The English test consists of 85 objective items designed to measure "as many of the important objectives of a modern comprehensive high school as possible." While it is recognized that essay writing cannot be sampled in an objective test, it is somewhat unfortunate that only 10 of the 85 items are devoted to writing style, an important objective. Items on paragraph arrangement have a superficial appeal in this respect, but the evidence concerning this type of item obtained in the ETS study on the measurement of writing ability [2] is scarcely promising enough to warrant 25 items. In this study, paragraph arrangement items proved the least valid of seven item types. One suspects that such questions simulate rather imperfectly the task faced by children in composing their own thoughts.

The heavy emphasis on mechanics (59 percent of the items) may reflect what is currently found in "appropriate courses of study and textbooks." Whether such emphases correspond to actual teaching time and whether these routine skills are predictive of success in writing ability, the "important objective," are debatable points, however. It is disappointing to see as many as 11 spelling items in the mechanics section, when it is realized that spelling is adequately tested elsewhere. And if the test is not to be used diagnostically, then the inclusion of 13 items on capitalization seems excessive. Some of this testing time could have been devoted to more basic writing skills, which are objectively assessable with reasonable validity through such items as the sentence completion, construction shift, and sentence combining. Then the "backwash" effects on instruction could well be healthier than that of a test which calls for superficial skills.

The test constructors have shown considerable ingenuity in placing their mechanics items within continuous, interesting paragraphs. The classification of errors according to type (capitalization, grammar, punctuation, spelling, and no error) is an interesting departure, presumably designed to pinpoint more precisely the student's ability to recognize the nature of the error involved. This approach runs into difficulty only when an item requires a change in

2 GODSHALK, FRED I.; SWINEFORD, FRANCES; AND COFFMAN, WILLIAM E. *The Measurement of Writing Ability.* New York: College Entrance Examination Board, 1966. Pp. viii, 84.

punctuation or capitalization, as in "So when the local newspaper announced her engagement, we were shocked, it was, to say the least, quite a surprise" and "He had been at all the famous battles, he had fought good." Many of these items are not really five-choice, since some of the underlined sections could not contain spelling or capitalization errors plausible enough to attract high school students. Since the reliability of the test is high, however, it is likely that this feature has been carefully watched in item selection. Nevertheless, the utility of some of these items should be studied carefully over the next few years.

The 10 items on style are well constructed and unambiguous, a feature not easy to ensure when the student's task is to choose amongst four expressions of the same ideas. One wonders only about the efficiency of such items in terms of time. Students must read 60 to 80 words, usually with some repetition, in order to score one point. It is likely that sentence completion and sentence correction items could achieve the same end in considerably less testing time.

The spelling test requires the student to identify 60 misspelt words from groups of four. Most of the 240 words included are definitely common errors or potential errors in students' writing. A few, however, seem implausibly misspelt (e.g., "costomers," "slepped") and such distractors as "favorable" and "oftener" are not wisely chosen. Some critics may question the use of isolated words as a valid test of spelling, but the authors do report that a correlation of .87 was found between this kind of spelling item and a dictated test at grade 8 level. One might have wished for further information on this point. The face validity of most of the words chosen and the reliability coefficients of .87 to .94 make for considerable confidence in the value of this test for those who like a comprehensive measure of spelling ability.

The authors went to considerable pains to describe the procedures adopted for establishing equivalence of forms, but they failed to report equivalent forms reliability, so that the high coefficients presented for single form administrations could well be misleading. The extent of speededness is not reported and with 85 items to complete in 40 minutes, time may well have been a problem. And since the internal reliability coefficients were calculated on the total

Stanford Achievement Test: High School English and Spelling Tests

standardization sample, they would, then, be spuriously high. Some reassurance on these matters is surely to be expected.

It is unfortunate that no validity statistics are presented in this manual. True, the subtest intercorrelations are helpful, but the high correlations between English and Otis IQ's (around .80) raise some doubts which are not completely settled by an inspection for content validity. Some correlations with other measures of important objectives in English would have been an asset.

One further matter bothered this reviewer. The fact that the norms are midyear should have been reported either in the introduction or with the norms table. Teachers wishing to use the tests in the fall for placement and planning, or in the spring for end-of-year evaluation, will need to adjust the norms for their purposes, and guidance on this matter might have been helpful.

Leonard S. Feldt, *Professor of Education, The University of Iowa, Iowa City, Iowa.*

In *The Sixth Mental Measurements Yearbook* the reviewer of a widely used English test offered this judgment: "The test undoubtedly serves some use in measuring a student's ability to criticize writing, but the only adequate test of effectiveness is to give the student a subject, a blank sheet of paper, and a pen, and ask him to write" (6:256). The very large number of English teachers who share this skepticism for multiple choice exercises are likely to find their views reinforced by the Stanford Achievement Test in English. Even those more favorably disposed may have several reservations about it.

To live within the restrictions of the multiple choice format, English test authors generally require the examinee to perform one or two editorial tasks: (*a*) indicate the errors they find in a composition, or (*b*) select the best of several suggested revisions which remedy possible defects in a composition. Neither of these, as the quoted reviewer so succinctly puts it, is equivalent to producing either the original version or its revision. But if a choice must be made between these approaches, most teachers would probably prefer the second—recognition of error coupled with awareness of a satisfactory revision. Part A of the Stanford test, which includes 50 of the 85 items, requires only the correct categorization of the error as one

of capitalization, grammar, punctuation, or spelling. Correction of the error—even by a recognition process—is not demanded.

The potential weakness of this approach may be illustrated by an item taken from a paragraph on the flags of the Confederacy. It begins as follows:

> There <u>were three confederate flags.</u> The first of
> <u>41</u>
> these was called the <u>"Stars and bars."</u>
> <u>42</u>

In exercise 41 there is obviously an error in capitalization, and it is so keyed. But the student is not asked about, or permitted to challenge, this uninspired opening sentence. Were various revisions presented for his consideration, he could be required both to diagnose the error in capitalization and to show sensitivity to this lackluster beginning. In exercise 42, the wayward student who feels the quotation marks should be omitted will incorrectly categorize the error as one of punctuation. But what of the student who feels no initial upper case letters are called for and hence classifies the error as one of capitalization? He would get the item correct—unfortunately.

It may be that the great majority of high school students who choose the proper error classification for any item do so for the right reasons. Perhaps appropriate categorization of an error can be taken as a trustworthy sign that the examinee could correct the error. However, the manual presents no evidence on these points.

It is worth noting with respect to this first portion of the language test that 9 or 10 items actually contain spelling errors. Moreover, the "error in spelling" option is available in every exercise, and hence it exerts additional influence as a distractor. Since the battery includes a 60-item spelling test bound in the same booklet as the English test, one wonders why spelling was given this additional emphasis.

Parts B and C of the test pose somewhat different tasks for the student. Each exercise of Part B presents four variations of a single sentence, and the examinee selects the best phrasing. Unlike items in Part A, these *do* require more than categorization of errors. There are only 10 such exercises, however.

In Part C, the student must indicate the optimal order of the five sentences of a paragraph. This is an attempt to measure sensitivity to logical sequence in the development of ideas. The item format is ingenious, but many students may respond on the basis of grammatical clues. For example, in a paragraph summarizing the stages of a man's career, one sentence begins : "The next period includes." Another starts : "Then, the years from about 60 or 65." The introductory phrases suggest immediately that these could not be the opening sentences of the paragraph. This reviewer found that he paid about as much attention to the construction of the sentences as to their content. In several of the paragraphs two or three different sequences could be justified if one considered only the ideas conveyed by the sentences. The presence of telltale words and phrases, rather than an inherent organizational logic, often seems to dictate which order conforms to the key.

The spelling exercises are of the "find-the-misspelled-word" variety, with four words per item. All of the most prevalent types of error seem to be represented, but the authors appear to have given the social utility principle little weight on occasion. Such words as *pestiferous, mnemonic, impious, cuneiform,* and *archipelago* seem more appropriate for a spelling bee.

The manual for the Stanford battery is unusually complete and, in general, a model of good reporting practices. Though short on information relating the scores to data external to the tests, the manual does contain a wealth of information : the developmental steps leading to publication, raw and standard score means and standard deviations, the results of a factor analysis, correlations among subtests, individual item classifications, item difficulty values by grade. Normative data are reported for several different populations : total grade groups, college preparatory students of each grade, groups which have taken a continuous sequence of courses in such areas as mathematics or science, and groups at different levels of Otis intelligence. In view of the normative data provided, one regrettable omission is information on the reliability of the scores *within IQ levels*.

This reviewer would take issue with the authors' interpretations of the standard scores, which are based on the distributions of combined samples from grades 9 through 12. The usual claim is made that any standard score value, like 57, "has the same meaning for all forms and tests in the battery." Yet if one takes the authors' illustrative value and checks it through the various norms tables, the data tend to contradict this contention. In grade 9, for example, the percentile rank of standard score

57 varies between 82 and 92. In grade 12 it varies between 46 and 66. These inconsistencies, while not surprising, raise questions regarding the soundness of the suggested test-to-test comparisons of standard scores.

To sum up, this reviewer is very favorably impressed by the test manual but less so by the test itself. Because it is so complete, the manual could be used effectively to supplement the textbook in a course in educational measurement. But English teachers may find other instruments better designed to measure effectiveness of written expression.

For reviews of the complete battery, see 27 (2 reviews).

[209]

*Stanford Achievement Test: Spelling and Language Tests.** Grades 4.0–5.4, 5.5–6.9, 7.0–9.9; 1940–68; catalog uses the title *Stanford Language Tests;* same as spelling and language subtests of *Stanford Achievement Test;* 2 scores: spelling, language; 2 forms; 3 levels; battery technical supplement ('66, 55 pages) ; expected grade score tables ('68, 10 pages) based on *Otis-Lennon Mental Ability Test* available on request; battery teachers guide ('65, 8 pages) for each level; supplementary directions ['64–66, 1–2 pages] for each type of answer sheet; $7.50 per 35 tests; 60¢ per key; separate answer sheets (Digitek, Harbor, IBM 805, IBM 1230) may be used; $2.30 per 35 IBM 805 answer sheets; $2.80 per 35 Digitek or IBM 1230 answer sheets; $6 per 100 sets of Harbor answer cards; $1.40 per set of Digitek or IBM scoring stencils; $2 per technical supplement; 50¢ per teachers guide; $1.75 per specimen set of any one level; postage extra; Harbor or IBM scoring service, 19¢ and over per spelling or language subtest; Braille and large type editions available from American Printing House for the Blind; Truman L. Kelley, Richard Madden, Eric F. Gardner, and Herbert C. Rudman; Harcourt Brace Jovanovich, Inc. *
a) INTERMEDIATE 1. Grades 4.0–5.4; Forms W, X, ('64, 8 pages) ; manual ('64, 11 pages) ; 56(70) minutes in 2 sessions.
b) INTERMEDIATE 2. Grades 5.5–6.9; Forms W, X, ('64, 9 pages) ; manual ('64, 12 pages) ; 63(75) minutes in 2 sessions.
c) ADVANCED. Grades 7.0–9.9; Forms W, X, ('64, 9 pages) ; manual ('64, 12 pages) ; 61(75) minutes in 2 sessions.

WILLIAM E. COFFMAN, *E. F. Lindquist Professor of Educational Measurement, The University of Iowa, Iowa City, Iowa.*

The purposes of the authors of the *Stanford Achievement Test* are set forth in the manuals that accompany the three levels. The test battery was

developed to measure the important knowledges, skills, and understandings commonly accepted as desirable outcomes of the major branches of the elementary curriculum. The tests are intended to provide dependable measures of these outcomes, comparable from subject to subject and grade to grade, for use in connection with improvement of instruction, pupil guidance, and evaluation of progress. The tests have been planned with a view toward simplicity of administration, scoring, and interpretation, so that they may be used effectively by persons with little or no formal training in the use of standard tests.

With respect to validity, the manual states:

The validity of *Stanford Achievement Test* is best thought of as the extent to which the content of the test constitutes a representative sample of the skills and knowledges which are the goals of instruction. This *content*, or *curricular*, validity must be assessed through a careful analysis of the actual content of each subtest in relation to the objectives of instruction in the various fields.

Since the authors rest their case for validity on the nature of the content, it seems appropriate to begin the evaluation of the tests by examining the content in some detail. Since they have aimed at simplicity of administration, scoring, and interpretation, it seems appropriate to ask how well they have achieved their purposes and at the same time to inquire concerning possible unintended effects.

Each level of the tests provides two scores, a score for spelling and a score for language. The language score is based on five separately timed sections containing questions in usage, punctuation, capitalization, dictionary skills, and sentence sense. No attempt is made to measure effectiveness of expression, in contrast to correctness of expression.

Although there are slight differences in format from level to level, the Intermediate 2 level illustrates the essential elements of the format and content. Each of the 56 items in this level of the spelling test consists of four words, one of which is spelled incorrectly.

The usage section of the language test consists of sentences, each with two alternate options for a word or phrase in the sentence. The examinee marks one of three responses: only option 1 makes the sentence correct, only option 2 makes the sentence correct, or neither option is correct. The punctuation and the capitalization sections consist of passages printed without either punctuation or capitalization. Certain words are underlined and numbered. In the punctuation section, two marks of punctuation are suggested to follow each numbered word, the student indicating which of the marks is correct or that neither is appropriate. Some of the words that should be followed by punctuation are not underlined. In the capitalization section, the examinee is to select one of two choices, C (capital letter) or s (small

letter), for each of the underlined words and mark the appropriate answer space. Some of the words that should be capitalized in a corrected passage are not underlined. The dictionary skills section consists of four-choice questions based on simulated dictionary entries. Some require that the examinee read a sentence and decide which of four definitions in a simulated dictionary entry corresponds to the use of the word in a sentence given in the item. Finally, the sentence sense subtest consists of word groupings to be placed in one of three categories: can be correctly punctuated as one sentence, could be punctuated as two sentences, or not a complete sentence. Altogether, eight different coding operations are involved in making responses when marking answers in the test booklet.

Only a single set of conversions from raw scores to grade scores is provided, but no evidence is cited to support the assumption that scores are equivalent regardless of whether answers are marked in the test booklet, on IBM 805, IBM 1230, Harbor, or Digitek answer sheets. The impression one gets in working through the test is that a considerable amount of clerical aptitude is involved. One might also wonder whether or not this form of testing is likely to encourage teachers to drill their pupils using exercises like those in the test in preference to giving them exercises providing practice in writing and editing connected discourse.

In general, sound test development procedures were followed in building the test package. The test items were written and coded according to a detailed content outline, test items were pretested on carefully chosen samples prior to the assembly of the final forms, national norms were established on the basis of sound sampling techniques, special norms by IQ level are reported, item difficulty values based on the norms sample are provided, and tables relating scores on these tests to scores on corresponding tests in earlier editions of both the *Stanford Achievement Test* and the *Metropolitan Achievement Test* are included in the technical supplement. There are, however, no regional norms for individuals and no norms for schools, even at the national level. The user is cautioned not to interpret subscores for individuals, but the normative data that are provided—the 25th, 50th, and 75th percentiles for individuals in the national sample—are hardly

Stanford Achievement Test: Spelling and Language Tests

the proper norms for interpreting group performance.

Reliability coefficients and standard errors of measurement are reported for each test at half-grade intervals over the range of grades for which each form is intended. These data are sufficient for users trained in technical aspects of testing. However, "persons with little or no formal training in the use of standard tests" will need additional guidance if they are to avoid misinterpretation. Unfortunately, no further assistance is provided in the manual regarding interpretation of errors of measurement. Furthermore, grade scores clearly in the chance range are generated without any clear indication that they are suspect.

In summary, the spelling and language tests of the Stanford battery provide scores on certain aspects of correctness of expression in writing. The normative data, as far as they go, do permit comparisons of scores from subject to subject and grade to grade. It is doubtful, however, that teachers who lack training in technical aspects of measurement can develop sound interpretations without guidance beyond that provided in the manual. Finally, a detailed examination of the content of the test does not support the claim that it constitutes a representative sample of the skills and knowledges which are the goals of instruction in language and spelling. Rather, it constitutes a highly artificial and indirect approach to the measurement of certain of those knowledges and skills. Whenever such indirect measurement is proposed, it is necessary to show that the advantages of such an approach outweigh the disadvantages. Teachers who view the goal of language instruction as skill in communicating in correct and effective written discourse will have serious reservations about the appropriateness of the types of items included in these tests. They will seek other tests containing objective items that simulate more closely the activity of the pupil as he writes and edits his own manuscript.

Unfortunately, the greater the departure of the test item from the direct task it is attempting to simulate, the greater the temptation to drill pupils directly on items like those in the test— or even on the test items themselves. Good teachers have always resisted the temptation, knowing that the validity of indirect measurement depends on its remaining indirect. Recently, however, there has developed an interest in "accountability" and school systems in vari-

ous parts of the country, according to newspaper accounts, have contracted with private corporations to bring the students' achievement scores up to or above national grade-level norms. It is to be devoutly hoped that the *Stanford Achievement Test: Spelling and Language Tests* will not become the criterion measures for any of these performance contracts. As models of what should be taught in the schools, they fall quite short.

As indirect measures of certain of the skills teachers attempt to develop in the elementary school years, and in the hands of teachers adequately trained in the interpretation of standardized tests, these particular tests may have value. The value will be greater if the tests are used as part of the Stanford battery so that scores in spelling and language may be related to scores in other areas, particularly reading and vocabulary. The value will be enhanced if the tests are being used in the context of a continuing testing program with local norms and longitudinal data. The value will be enhanced if scores on the test are related to measures of other aspects of language instruction, particularly "effectiveness of expression" in contrast to "correctness of expression." The value will be enhanced if teachers resist vigorously the temptation to teach for the test. For the school with a long history of use of these tests, their continued use may be justified. For schools looking for a separate test of spelling and language, competing tests should be examined carefully.

CARLETON B. SHAY, *Professor of Education and Associate Dean, School of Education, California State College, Los Angeles, California.*

The Spelling and Language Tests comprise two of the six to ten subtests (according to level) of the *Stanford Achievement Test* battery. Available in booklets separate from the battery at only the upper three levels, they share battery answer sheets, norms, teacher's guides for interpretation, and technical data. Color coding is used as a convenient means of distinguishing materials at each level. At successive levels, the 15-minute spelling test consists of 50, 56, and 58 items of the one-misspelled-of-four multiple choice variety. The language portion consists of five separately timed tests: usage, punctuation, capitalization, dictionary skills, and sentence sense, yielding a single overall score. With the exception of a portion of the dictionary skills items, the language test deals only with aspects of grammar.

The only information upon which to evaluate content validity consists of general descriptions of test content and, for language only, item content outlines. According to the authors, content validation "demands a systematic comparison of the test's contents with the curriculum used by the school." This is certainly true, and the authors are to be commended for insisting on this comparison and resisting any claim of satisfactory content validity. At the same time, more information could have been given to help in making this evaluation, such as clearer definitions of the content universe sampled and identification of textbook series, courses of study, word lists, and other material used. Correlations between the scores on the 1953 and 1964 editions (.79 to .87) are presented as additional evidence of validity. This is important information, but of dubious value in the context of validity, since an edition which is being replaced is considered an adequate criterion. Other validity-related data, of use primarily to the test specialist, are tables which show that "mean scores on the test increase for successively higher grades" and within-grades correlation coefficients between the Stanford and the *Otis Quick-Scoring Mental Ability Test,* which range from .55 to .65 for spelling and .70 to .75 for language.

Split-half reliability coefficients and K-R 20 reliability coefficients are given for each grade for each test. These coefficients are high, as might be expected: .91 to .94. The technical supplement discusses the effect of speededness on reliability (it spuriously inflates reliability coefficients), and concludes that for the Stanford, "speededness is a negligible factor." This conclusion is based on a study of the influence of speed on scores, which used the 1953 edition and was assumed valid for the 1964 edition. As a result of this study, ratios of items to time were reduced for five battery subtests; unfortunately, these subtests are not identified. Since the serial position of items is only roughly in order of increasing difficulty, and there are marked exceptions, particularly on the subtests of capitalization and dictionary skills, it is hoped that the language test was among those whose ratios of items to time were reduced. Comprehensive tables of other reliability data are given, including standard errors of measurement and language part-score reliability coefficients. No

equivalent-forms reliability coefficients are given, however—a serious omission which invalidates the contention that alternate forms of the test are interchangeable. In lieu of these vital data, only a general description of the equating program is given. There are no test-retest reliability data either, although we are assured that "as this type of reliability data becomes available, it will be duly reported."

The standardization group is not a representative sample of the country as a whole, and, technically, it is not claimed to be. Nevertheless, a technicality does not absolve the publisher from the responsibility of providing such a norm group, since users will treat the norms as representative whether they are or not. The consequences of decisions based on nonrepresentative norms can be extreme. Test users should also heed this advice: applicability of norms demands a systematic comparison of the standardization sample with the pupils tested by the school. If the groups are not alike, the results are not interpretable with respect to the norms. Corrections may be applied but should be avoided, as they imply a false accuracy easily overinterpreted. Selection of another test with suitable norms, or the establishment of local norms are desirable alternatives.

The standardization group warrants closer scrutiny. Otis IQ medians for grades 4 through 9 are 109, 109, 109, 108, 108, and 106. Not only are these IQ's high, but they decrease with grade level, contrary to the increase found in most studies. No children less than nine years of age at grade 4, ten years at grade 5, eleven years at grade 6, etc., were included in the standardization sample. At the same time, students up to two years and eleven months more than this minimum were included. It would appear, at first glance, that the standardization sample is simply overage and over-intelligent, but the bias is even more serious when it is realized that the IQ level is high despite the exclusion of the youngest, and generally brightest, students from the standardization group. We are informed that integrated, segregated, and private sectarian and nonsectarian schools were included and that median family income and number of years of schooling were in "essential agreement" with census figures. This is reassuring, but no data are given; the only other demographic data are a distribution of school systems by region and a list of standardization communities, which shows an un-

Stanford Achievement Test: Spelling and Language Tests

derrepresentation of data from large city school systems. It is clear from the data, for example, that the Stanford is not appropriate for a large urban school system with a significant minority population. To reiterate: the norm group is *not* representative.

Norms include grade scores (grade equivalents without decimal points), percentile ranks, and stanines. Tables provided allow correction of grade scores as a function of Otis IQ stanines, or alternately, a comparison with grade scores corresponding to quartile points for Otis stanines. Directions for interpretation of scores with each type of norm are clear and fairly complete, though hazards of overinterpretation could be emphasized more in the technical supplement. The tests should be easy to give and score with all types of answer sheets; directions are clear and concise.

The teachers' guides are, in some respects, useful and innovative and, in other respects, disappointing. A review of test content is followed by a section on interpretation which includes samples of individual cases and an explanation of the use of class analysis chart. The basic thesis of "Diagnose, Evaluate, Plan" is well conceived, clearly explained, and, when used with the battery, realistically useful to teachers. Data are limited to stanines and are presented so as to provide a conscientious but unsophisticated teacher the minimum opportunity to overinterpret. Suggestions for interpretation are of less use to spelling and language test users than for users of the whole battery, since relative strengths and weaknesses are an important component of the diagnostic scheme. The suggestions given for remedial instruction are disappointing. Remediation must be based on careful diagnosis, and the tests are not intended to perform this function. Some suggestions imply that the teacher should construct his own diagnostic instruments based on skills presumably tested but not specifically related to test content, rather than using available tests designed for that purpose. Others describe general observations or methods which should already be in the teacher's repertoire.

In short, the content of the *Stanford Achievement Tests: Spelling and Language Tests* has been carefully prepared, and the tests should be easy to use. Technical information reported is accurate. The efforts thus far named are impressive, but the standardization group is not representative, some vital technical informa-

tion is not reported, and the attempts to educate those who would benefit most by such information are insufficient for the 1970's. In these days of guaranteed performance contracts, or the equivalent politically, tests must be better, users more enlightened, and data more complete. Specifically, the user must assure himself that the test content matches his curriculum and the norm group matches his pupils. The test should be renormed on a nationally representative sample if any inferences are to be made with regard to "national norms." The publisher should provide more technical and interpretive information, especially that dealing with the standardization group, retesting and alternate forms. And, finally, the number of items per grade level should be increased if grade norms continue to be used. If the test user is unwilling to apply the above comparisons and the publisher unable to supply the necessary data, use of the Stanford language and spelling tests is ill-advised.

For reviews of the complete battery, see 25 (1 excerpt), 6:26 (1 review, 1 excerpt), 5:25 (1 review), 4:25 (2 reviews), and 3:18 (2 reviews).

[210]

★**Tests of Academic Progress: Composition.** Grades 9–12; 1964–66; Form 1 ('64, 15 pages); 4 levels (grades 9, 10, 11, 12) in a single booklet; no specific manual; battery teacher's manual ('64, 62 pages); battery manual for administrators, supervisors, and counselors ('65, 45 pages); battery norms booklet for IQ levels ('66, 26 pages); separate answer cards (MRC) must be used; 30¢ per test; $3 per 100 MRC answer cards; $1.20 per battery teacher's manual; 96¢ per battery administrator's manual; 60¢ per battery norms booklet; $3 per specimen set of the complete battery; postage extra; scoring service, 27¢ per test; 60(70) minutes; Dale P. Scannell and Oscar M. Haugh; Houghton Mifflin Co. *

REFERENCE

1. GOOLSBY, THOMAS M., JR. "The Appropriateness of the Tests of Academic Progress for an Experimental School." *Ed & Psychol Meas* 30(4):967–70 w '70. *

ELLIS BATTEN PAGE, *Professor of Educational Psychology, University of Connecticut, Storrs, Connecticut.*

CONTENT. For each grade, the test content consists of some sample printed documents (letters or parts of essays such as a high school student might write) which contain unmarked errors. The lines of each document are numbered for reference; each document is followed by 10 to 13 questions. Each question contains some stem, such as "Which is the best way to write line 1?" or "How should lines 1, 2, and 3 be punctuated?" or "Which is the correct way to write the first three words in line 14?" or even "Which, if any, is the correct way to divide the last word that is hyphenated on line 16?" Then each stem is followed by four provided alternatives, only one of which is "correct."

Often these questions center on particular problems, such as how a verb should be formed or how a quotation should be punctuated. At other times, the question asks what kind of change, if any, might be necessary in a line. Some items are quite independent of the passage, such as identifying first-order spelling errors (misspellings in any context, like *thier*). Other items require study of the entire sample document: picking a paragraph's topic sentence from among all the sentences, or deciding how the document should be paragraphed.

This reviewer (a former teacher of English) took the test to study face validity and was not very satisfied. In some cases, the prose was so poorly constructed that the specific questions seemed a playing at the fringe. And since some fundamental errors are uncorrected, taking the test will not be wholly constructive as a learning experience. Also, at times there is an extrinsic logical tip-off (as in the common "all-of-the-above" construction). And some solutions themselves seem, at best, highly debatable (for example, sympathised, a commonplace British spelling, is keyed as flatly "wrong").

FORMAT. But the most serious criticism of the test's face validity concerns its format. The usual multiple choice item, in the usual test, calls upon the student to keep track of *two* sequences: the questions in the booklet, and the responses on the answer sheet. This composition test calls upon the student to keep track of at least *three* sequences, since it is necessary to consult the passage itself, as well as the question and the answer card. And for some items (for example, where one is asked to choose the "transitional word" from among four possible alternatives), the student has to keep track of six different locations! And all of these are indexed by different numbers, not letters. There may be four competing locations in four different line numbers (or even combinations of lines), and then there may be the inhibition created by the question number (in both booklet and card) and alternative choices (in both booklet and card). The student's final choice, then, may be doggedly encoded as "lines 22–23, which are alternative 3, for question 17." The

necessary intensive, clerical concentration must indicate something, but its relevance to composition is surely unproved. It is urged that test builders stay away from this format. To lessen confusion, alternatives and questions should all be incorporated with the test passage.

INSTRUCTION ABOUT GUESSING. One of the standing dilemmas in honest test administration is what to say about guessing (see Page, 6:14). The student instructions for the TAP battery include the admonition: "If you have *no* idea *whatsoever* about the answer, omit the exercise on the answer sheet." In other words, the student should leave it blank. Yet no penalty is levied for wrong answers, and the student who follows this instruction will lower his score compared with the next student who, wisely or cynically, disregards it. Furthermore, in applying the suggested rule, a student will often be too self-critical. He may not "think" he knows the answer, but he *might* be able to eliminate one or two competing alternatives, in which case his chance of raising his score would be even better than chance.

A study of the norms reveals just how much guessing can accomplish. Let us assume a student "knows" enough answers to reach the 48th percentile on the 9th grade norms and then "blindly" guesses the rest. He will, by disregarding the instruction and by guessing only with average luck, raise his performance to the 90th percentile—a gain of 42 percentile points! If the 11th grade student at the 46th percentile does the same, he will jump to the 88th. And if a student at the 75th percentile does it, he will jump to the 98th percentile—from above average, to very superior. By their instruction, then, the test publishers seem to be penalizing students for obedience. Instructions not to guess should be abolished, and all students should be encouraged to try all items, even where a "correction" is applied.

INFORMATION ABOUT THE TEST. The battery is accompanied by a fairly flossy package of manuals and auxiliary services. In the Manual for Administrators, Supervisors, and Counselors, a chapter on interpretation leaves much to be desired. The "standard score" (SS) is discussed as if it were a great improvement over the raw score in "meaning." But for most grades, since there is no easy significance of the SS *except in terms of the 11th grade norms,* the improvement is not clear. The grade-adjusted percentile rank (PR) is of course more mean-

Tests of Academic Progress: Composition

ingful, but to obtain it we must make a double transformation, first to the SS, *then* to the PR. Where such conversion is done by hand, new tables would have to be derived for efficiency, since they are not supplied by the publisher. When one *does* compare the raw score with the PR, one realizes just how fragile, or unstable, many PR differences will inevitably be.

This instability is not recognized clearly in the manual. Where profiles are discussed, only standard scores are compared, and not always wisely. A sample profile treats a student tested in his 10th and 11th grades. (As we have seen, if the same form were used, this would result in exactly the *same* items over about two-thirds of the test.) In discussing the profile, the manual states that, where gains of three or four SS points have been made (about the same number of raw score points), these are regarded as "normal" growth. Where one subtest has only *one* point change, this is regarded as "growth.... less than one would expect." And where six points of change occur, this is regarded as "progress....greater than average." The manual suggests that "Reasons for such growth should be sought." Given the stated levels of reliability, especially interform agreement, all such conjectures would be based upon trivial observed differences. Pursuing "the reasons" for such differences is probably a waste of time and should not be encouraged.

RELIABILITY. Such skepticism is supported by evidence from the same manual, where the standard errors of measurement for the Composition Test are shown to range *about 3.6 raw score points*. And these standard errors, as is customary for commercial tests, are based upon split-half reliabilities (averaging about .90), rather than the always lower coefficients which would be derived from test-retest experiments over time, or from inter-form agreement.

VALIDITY. A still more damaging consideration, however, concerns statistical validity. The user who searches for persuasive evidence of such validity will simply search in vain. In the manual, printed in 1965, it is stated that "At the time of this printing, the authors have not had an opportunity to collect comprehensive evidence of concurrent or predictive validity." This is puzzling, since some of the norm schools could easily have reported student grades. In any case, when the present reviewer contacted the test company five years later, he was not reassured. There are some unpublished tables

from a small local study in Billings, Montana. These show correlations for 380 students between the various subtests and *overall* grade-point average (*r*'s in the high .60's). There were other unpublished results from Billings for correlations of the subtests with Otis IQ (also in the high .60's). There was nothing more.

In other words, even after five years, there was *no statistical evidence for specific validity of any subtest*. Particularly for composition, this negligence seems inexcusable, since natural compositions are easy to obtain and can be reliably appraised by judge panels.

SUMMARY. The *Test of Academic Progress: Composition* seems questionable in some of its contents and unnecessarily confusing in student procedure. It lacks any evidence of statistical validity, even after five years of sale. There are some good aspects to the test but, on balance, these negative criticisms seem central and severe. They suggest that school testers search elsewhere before selecting this test.

OSMOND E. PALMER, *Professor, Office of Evaluation Services, Michigan State University, East Lansing, Michigan.*

This test, unlike most, consists of 142 items only some of which are answered at each grade level. Ninth graders start with item 1 and work through 70; tenth do items 23–92; eleventh, 47–117; and twelfth, 71–142. Thus there is a 40-odd item overlap between successive grades. Only the ninth and twelfth graders take totally different tests. The justification for this is that it permits testing more specifically for those things covered in a given year and that it provides a more accurate measure of progress.

In the case of English, there is probably less need to make a distinction among grades than elsewhere, because in English classes the same things are reviewed from year to year and it is not likely that the same things are covered in a given year in different school systems. For instance, this test measures the use of footnoting only at the twelfth-grade level; but footnoting is probably not taught in some schools at all—the National Council of Teachers of English recommends against it—and in some schools it is taught as early as the ninth grade.

It might be enlightening to know exactly how much improvement tenth graders show on the items taken by ninth graders, and so forth, but the data presented in the manuals do not tell us this. In the norms sample, eleventh graders

Tests of Academic Progress: Composition

scored somewhat better than ninth graders. But since the tables report in terms of standard scores, one does not know exactly what this means in terms of improvement in number of items right. One can tease something out from the last table given in the teacher's manual, which shows the raw score necessary to achieve a certain standard score. The ninth grade test is somewhat easier for ninth graders than the twelfth grade test is for twelfth graders. The tenth and eleventh grade results fall between these two. If it is true that the tests become increasingly difficult, then the mean raw scores might drop slightly. Is this the reason why raw scores were suppressed in the manuals? For the teacher, it is probably best to look at the tests themselves, to see what they cover and how well they cover it.

The test attempts to involve all aspects of the writing situation: mechanics, including spelling; sentence structure; word choice; and organization. The attempt to be so comprehensive involves rigorous decisions on inclusion and exclusion, but the test does not seem to show this, as my comments on several aspects of it will illustrate.

Only about a dozen items deal with verbs, verbals, or tense sequence. Two of these (7 and 39) deal with *should of* and *must of,* which have more to do with the transcription of the spoken language and careful proofreading than with showing (as the manual states) that the student is "having difficulty with his verbs." Three (52, 55, 56) have to do with the agreement of subject and verb, none at the twelfth grade level; and three (43, 67, 94) with tense sequence, one at the twelfth grade level. Beyond these, item 68 involves a dangling participle and item 133 a split infinitive, the latter having two acceptable answers in addition to the split itself, which is not a bad one. Only one item tests for the problem involved in verbs frequently confused (lie-lay) and one (item 39) suggests that *forgotten* may be the only past participle of *forget.* One obviously cannot do much curriculum revision or reteaching from this smattering of information about how the student handles verbs and tense sequences.

One can also quarrel with the items testing capitalization. There is no item which invites the student to capitalize a point of the compass or a season of the year; there is none on proper adjectives or geographical places; in titles, only the capitalization of short adjectives is involved.

And about half of these items are dubious. The girl who capitalizes Recipe Book (61) (probably a substitute title for her mother's) and Burnt Sugar Cake (63) should have the option of doing so. A student who looked up C(?)opperhead (a Southern sympathizer in the 1860's) in the current series of Merriam-Webster dictionaries would pick 2 (rather than 3) as the right answer for item 111.

In the light of the failure to measure certain things adequately, one is annoyed to find some things that *are* tested for. Item 64 insists that Sam must use an apostrophe in his store title, Sam's Superette, but Consumers Power (of Michigan) does not. One of the few items on agreement between subject and verb, item 52, involves the combination of *neither-nor* with a change of number—sufficiently rare to be passed over. With only six to nine spelling items in each grade level of the test, one wishes the authors had skipped words like "sympathise" and "karmelize." The applicant for a job as errand boy must write "advertisement" rather than "ad," according to item 72.

Several of the questions on matters of style are, it seems to me, matters of personal taste. The letter of application seemingly suffers from overuse of the word I, but since one of the revisions (78) eliminates two uses, I find no good answer for item 79. Similarly, item 104 calls for making a fourth paragraph in an essay of about 160 words; I look for a response which would reduce the paragraphing. The review of the movie *David Copperfield* uses (several times) "pals," which various dictionaries list as slang or colloquial. Item 50 asks how the student would write a particular expression in this essay in formal English; but to introduce the sentence keyed as right is to do violence to the tone of the essay. Response 2 would not be bad and response 1 is not taboo on the basis of the current Merriam-Webster dictionaries.

Item 121 in the second scrambled paragraph exercise demands a special comment. One has to decide which sentence should follow Sentence B and he is supposed to pick Sentence D. The sentences are these: "B. His books, *Alice In Wonderland* and *Through The Looking Glass,* are known the world over; and have been translated into many languages. D. These books also contained many humerous [*sic*] poems such as *Jabberwocky,* a poem containing words that had never been used before." To me, the *also*

Tests of Academic Progress: Composition

of Sentence D suggests that the previous sentence had been detailing the major content and that this sentence is going on to talk about content. But obviously Sentence B is not about content: it simply mentions the titles of Carroll's two children's books and talks about their popularity. Since the topic of this essay is to show that Lewis Carroll is famous for his children's books and not for his teaching or his books on logic and mathematics, one suspects that this sentence was intended to be irrelevant and marked for omission, like one in the previous exercise. But *humerous* (a spelling item) crept into it and since it contained the only occasion to test for the use of quotation marks for the title of a poem, somebody forgot the original intention. (One also wonders why the second capital T was left in *Through The,* since it is not tested for, and whether at one stage it was planned to have a question on the tense of *contained.*)

A lot of thought seems to have gone into the conception of this test, but the child which was produced was not nourished properly.

For a review of the complete battery, see 31.

[211]

★**Tests of Basic Experiences: Language.** Prekgn-kgn, kgn-grade 1; 1970–71; 1 form; Levels K ('70, 34 pages), L ('70, 18 pages); for battery manual and accessories, see 33; $9 per 30 tests, postage extra; scoring service, $1.20 per test; (25) minutes; Margaret H. Moss; CTB/McGraw-Hill. *

REFERENCE

1. Moss, MARGARET H. *Performance of Disadvantaged and Middle-Class Preschool Children on a Language Coding Test of Space and Location.* Doctor's thesis, George Washington University (Washington, D.C.), 1968.

For a review of the complete battery, see 33.

[212]

*****Walton-Sanders English Test.** 1, 2 semesters in grades 9–13; 1962–64; first published 1962–63 in the Every Pupil Scholarship Test series; Forms A, B, ('64, 8 pages); 2 levels labeled Tests 1, 2; manual ('64, 6 pages); no norms for college freshmen; $1.75 per 25 tests, postage extra; 75¢ per specimen set, postpaid; 50(55) minutes; Charles E. Walton and M. W. Sanders; Data Processing and Educational Measurement Center. *

[213]

★**Watson English Usage and Appreciation Test, Fourth Edition.** Grades 4–8; 1966; 1 form (8 pages); manual (8 pages); no data on reliability; Can $2.75 per 25 tests; 25¢ per manual; 40¢ per specimen set; postage extra; 30(40) minutes; G. Milton Watson; Book Society of Canada Ltd. *

VINCENT R. D'OYLEY, *Professor of Education, The Ontario Institute for Studies in Education, The University of Toronto, Toronto, Ontario, Canada.*[1]

This test sets out to measure a variety of English skills in order to assist teachers in grade placement and diagnosis. It is designed for pupils in grades 4 to 8, but it reports grade equivalent scores ranging from grades 1.1 to 12.0 and age equivalents from 6–11 to 17–1.

Apart from the laudable aims of the test constructor, it is difficult to make positive statements about the test. Clearly, it has been produced by a well-meaning educator but with little concern for the APA Standards. The manual contains no information on reliability coefficients or standard errors of measurement. There is only a hint of validity-consciousness in the statement that "there is a significantly positive correlation between scores on this test and the ability to write and speak correct, lucid English." No technical supplement has been planned, although at least four to five thousand students write the test annually in one Ontario city alone.

The norming sample is described most inadequately: "about 1,300 pupils from grades 4 to 8" representing "a wide cross-section of social background, and [ranging] in I.Q. from 70 to 140." The only graph presented refers to results from two schools only. The misconceptions evident in the section relating to interpretation of scores must be seen as unfortunate. The determination of achievement level as a function of the test is played down at the seventh and eighth grade levels because the scores in the standardization sample departed slightly from normality, the apparent ideal of the test constructor. The extraordinary generalization is made that pupils scoring 12 percent below their grade median should be retested or retaught. A cursory inspection of the chart from which this conclusion was drawn is sufficient to show that the raw scores which are 12 percent below the median lie between the 25th and 75th percentiles in grades 4–7 and below the 25th percentile in grade 8. The blindness to such other interpretative factors as the background of children and suitability of the test in relation to curricular objectives makes this generalization a dangerous one. For the percentage-oriented teacher, formulae are presented to convert raw score (out of 200) to a percentage appropriate

1 The reviewer wishes to acknowledge with thanks the assistance of Dr. Warrick Elley in the preparation of this review.

Tests of Academic Progress: Composition

for each grade level. The application of this formula results in more than one quarter of the grades 6–7 standardization sample receiving percentages above 100.

No information is given about the calculations or extrapolations required for the grade and age equivalents presented, in very awkward format, in the manual. We are told only that the extreme norms "have been established by exterpolation [*sic*] and comparison with standardized *reading* tests giving grade levels." The meaningfulness of a grade equivalent of 1.1 on a test designed primarily for children around grade 6 is puzzling. But how such refinement of scale could be attained from a sample of 1,300, providing equivalent norms for 12 grade levels, is positively perplexing. It is unlikely that 10 students scored below grade 2 level, yet grade equivalents are given for every month from 1.1 upwards. We sincerely hope that teachers do not use these test results for grade placement, as the manual recommends.

The test itself leaves much to be desired. There is no explanation of how the skills to be tested and the weightings for each topic were arrived at, but the lack of correspondence between subtest title and item content suggests that such a blueprint would not have contributed helpfully to content validity. For instance, the Organization subtest contains items requiring the selection of descriptive adjectives and verbs, the Word Meanings subtest calls for homonyms, and the Appreciation subtest for general knowledge about trees.

The instructions intended for pupils are inadequate in content and confused in style. They give no directions about guessing or changing answers, no practice exercises, and no statements about how to mark correct answers in multiple choice questions. The diversity of question types must present a bewildering task for the pupil: the first eight questions require him to answer in no less than six different ways.

Matching questions typically contain the same number of items in each list, and many of these lists are so heterogeneous that pupils can score highly with only limited knowledge. Many completion items are sufficiently ambiguous to cast doubt on the claimed objective nature of the items—e.g., "I tiptoed into the room as _____ as possible."

The Word Usage subtest contains some original items on the expression of mood, spoilt only by the ambiguity involved in deciding which subject or person is supposed to experience the mood—the author, or one or more of the persons or animals referred to in the sentences.

The heavy emphasis on grammar and its technical terms make this test unsuitable for teachers who stress a more functional approach to language; the educational value of many other items is difficult to defend. Of what predictive or diagnostic utility, to grade 6 pupils, is knowledge of the word "lye," or information about when "a knell [is] rung"?

The test has been carelessly proofread. For instance, two items on page 7 have omitted the underlinings mentioned in the instructions; *then* is used incorrectly as a conjunction in the instructions at the top of page 8. The manual refers to nonexistant charts "on pages 5 and 6," and later it reports that "the intervals....*does not vary*." Many possible alternative answers could have been included in the answer key, but it should be pointed out that any further additions to this cumbersome key would make it virtually unusable. Teachers will be unenthusiastic about this aspect of the test.

In short, there is little to recommend in the *Watson English Usage and Appreciation Test*. Even the title is unfortunate. One noun used adjectivally is permissible; three are too many. Mention of usage and appreciation seems arbitrary in this hotchpotch of topics ranging over paragraph organization, reading comprehension, vocabulary knowledge, idiomatic expressions, sentence classification, plurals and possessives, parts of speech, and sentence structure. Of the 165 items, only 10 measure appropriate English usage, and 10 measure appreciation. The title of the test is as likely to mislead the teacher as much as the results it produces.

[214]

★**Writing Test: McGraw-Hill Basic Skills System.** Grades 11–14; 1970; also called *MHBSS Writing Test;* although designed for use with the MHBSS instructional program, the test may be used independently; 4 scores: language mechanics, sentence patterns, paragraph patterns, total; Forms A, B, (14 pages); manual (34 pages); separate answer sheets (Digitek, IBM 1230, Scoreze) must be used; $6 per 25 tests; $2.50 per 50 IBM or Digitek answer sheets; $3 per 25 Scoreze answer sheets; $1 per IBM or Digitek scoring stencil; postage extra; $1.25 per specimen set, postpaid; IBM scoring service, 25¢ and over per test ($20 minimum); 45(55) minutes; Alton L. Raygor; McGraw-Hill Book Co., Inc. *

LEONARD S. FELDT, *Professor of Education, The University of Iowa, Iowa City, Iowa.*

In reviewing standardized achievement tests, one occasionally encounters a curious phenomenon. An instrument may strike the reviewer as quite unattractive in terms of item quality, content, or skill coverage, but the test may be accompanied by an excellent manual. Normative data may have been conscientiously gathered, the technical information competently analyzed, and the facts fully reported. The effort appears to be wasted, however, on essentially a poor test. In other instances one encounters the opposite situation. The test itself may offer many interesting exercises and represent a commendable effort at measuring important skills, but it may be poorly documented in a technical sense. The norms may be so biased as to be useless, the validity data very limited, and the facts on reliability suspect. This latter description seems to fit the MHBSS *Writing Test*.

This instrument was developed primarily for use in conjunction with the instructional materials that comprise the McGraw-Hill Basic Skills System: Writing. The test is sold separately, however, and teachers may wish to consider it solely on its own merits. Whether or not the instructional materials from which the test stems can be successfully used to improve the user's language skills (and to raise the test scores) cannot be considered here. Composition teachers should evaluate these materials quite apart from the test. But it is worth noting that the test was developed to accompany the instructional materials and hence is closely coordinated with them.

Some of the introductory statements in the manuals make a fairly strong pitch for the diagnostic potential of the test. Its two forms constitute the initial and final phases of an instructional system involving diagnosis, prescription, instruction, and evaluation. Later statements back off a bit from any promise of highly detailed, individual diagnosis, claiming that the *Writing Test* is designed "to be diagnostic only in a general way." Determination of student weaknesses is officially sanctioned only through consideration of the three part scores, but there are hints that more detailed analysis of item responses may pay dividends.

The distribution of exercises and the three part scores suggest the skills of concern to the authors. The first score is derived from 30 items concerned with mechanics: capitalization, punctuation, and grammar (tense, pronoun forms, subject-verb agreement, and so forth).

The second score is based on 26 items which require classification of sentence types (complex, compound, etc.), choice of pronouns (who, which, etc.), detection of nonparallel constructions, and feel for appropriate transitional words and phrases to introduce or connect sentences. The final part presents 15 exercises bearing on the construction of paragraphs: identification of appropriate topic sentences, development sentences, and concluding sentences; awareness of the proper sequence of sentences; and judgment of the most appropriate division of sentences into paragraphs. Those familiar with objective tests in this area will probably recognize the unique emphasis given to paragraph construction. In summary, about 40 items deal with matters of right and wrong, 20 items concern issues of effectiveness or appropriateness, and 10 items involve classification of sentence types, including sentence fragments.

A few supplementary observations about the types of exercises used in the test may head off possible disappointment. First, the mechanics items of Part 1 do not yield separate scores for punctuation, capitalization, and usage. Also, they require that the examinee merely classify an error, not select a correct version of the offending words or phrases. Error detection, but not correction, is also characteristic of the pronoun and parallelism exercises of Part 2. Second, very few of the exercises require the student to choose the most effective, appropriate, precise, or colorful word or phrase to express an idea, rather than to detect an outright error. Part 3 deals largely with the appropriateness of the content of entire sentences, not with the phrasing of ideas in small segments of a composition. Finally, in attempting to assess the several aspects of writing in 45 minutes, the authors were forced to limit the number of exercises that deal with each. Despite these limitations, many teachers may find the test more attractive than competing instruments, particularly because of its concern for paragraph construction.

Turning now to the technical characteristics of the test, we find a number of serious limitations. Apparently the publishers could not fully convince themselves of the need to invest the effort in norming and validation that are now accepted as part of test publication. Three sets of norms are provided, corresponding to the three populations for which the instruction system is intended: (*a*) college-bound students in

Writing Test: McGraw-Hill Basic Skills System

grades 11 and 12, (b) two-year college students, and (c) freshmen in four-year colleges. The samples used to develop the norms were chosen by very casual procedures—so casual, in fact, that the manual frankly warns the user that no sample can be considered to represent the population implied by the norm-group designation. The extent of the differential biases in these samples may be suggested by the fact that the high school groups have a median of 48.5 and the four-year college freshmen a median of 43.5 on Form B. The user would be well advised to heed the publisher's advice about developing local norms.

Reliability and item data are based on all three samples combined, a procedure not considered appropriate even with the best of samples. Even within this artificially heterogeneous group, reliability of the part scores is relatively modest for individual diagnosis—below .70 for about half of the parts on the two forms. Though the test was developed for use before and after a specific course, no studies are available as to the impact of the course on the test scores. The publishers recommend this instrument for sectioning classes in English composition, a function it may be well designed to serve. But surprisingly, they disclaim responsibility for demonstrating its value for this purpose. Another fault is the absence of correlations among the part scores, data that are easily obtained and quite important for diagnostic tests. The manual is very frank in recognizing these shortcomings, but this sincerity—while refreshing—does not offset the handicaps that they impose on the user.

With reactions as mixed as these, one is hard pressed to arrive at a balanced summary statement. The test deserves consideration by those who agree with the authors' skill emphasis. But users should be prepared to develop their own norms and to invest more than the usual effort in the study of local reliability and validity.

LITERATURE

[215]

★CLEP Subject Examination in Analysis and Interpretation of Literature. 1 year or equivalent; 1964–70; for college accreditation of nontraditional study, advanced placement, or assessment of educational achievement; tests administered monthly at regional centers throughout the United States; tests also

available for institutional testing at any time; Form MCT ('64, 16 pages); optional essay supplement: Form MCT-A ('64, 2 pages); for program accessories, see 664; rental and scoring fee, $5 per student; postpaid; essay supplement scored by the college; 90(95) minutes, same for essay supplement; program administered for the College Entrance Examination Board by Educational Testing Service. *

For reviews of the testing program, see 664 (3 reviews).

[216]

★CLEP Subject Examination in English Literature. 1 year or equivalent; 1970; for college accreditation of nontraditional study, advanced placement, or assessment of educational achievement; tests administered monthly at regional centers throughout the United States; tests also available for institutional testing at any time; Forms SCT1, SCT2, (17 pages); optional essay supplement: Form SCT1A (3 pages); for program accessories, see 664; rental and scoring fee, $5 per student; postpaid; essay supplement scored by the college; 90(95) minutes, same for essay supplement; program administered for the College Entrance Examination Board by Educational Testing Service. *

For reviews of the testing program, see 664 (3 reviews).

[217]

★College Board Achievement Test in Literature. Candidates for college entrance; 1968–71; test administered each January and May at centers established by the publisher; for more complete information, see 663; 60(80) minutes; program administered for the College Entrance Examination Board by Educational Testing Service. *

REFERENCES

1. PURVES, ALAN C. "Designing the Board's New Literature Achievement Test." *Col Board R* 67:16–20 sp '68. *
2. ELLEDGE, SCOTT. "For the Board's English Tests: As an Old Era Ends, What Lies Ahead?" *Col Board R* 71:22–7 sp '69. *

[218]

★College Placement Test in Literature. Entering college freshmen; 1968–70; CPTL; irregularly scheduled reprintings of inactive forms of *College Board Achievement Test in Literature;* Form SPL ['70, reprint of 1968 test, 12 pages]; for more complete information, see 665; 60(70) minutes; program administered for the College Entrance Examination Board by Educational Testing Service. *

For a review of the testing program, see 665.

[219]

*The Graduate Record Examinations Advanced Literature in English Test. Graduate school candidates; 1939–70; 4 current forms ('67–70, 32–40 pages); descriptive booklet ('70, 10 pages); for more complete information, see 667; 180(200) minutes; Educational Testing Service. *

REFERENCE

1. LANNHOLM, GERALD V.; MARCO, GARY L.; AND SCHRADER, WILLIAM B. *Cooperative Studies of Predicting Graduate School Success,* pp. 34–45. Graduate Record Examinations Special Report No. 68-3. Princeton, N.J.: Educational Testing Service, August 1968. Pp. 92. *

For a review by Robert C. Pooley of an earlier form, see 5:215. For reviews of the testing program, see 667 (1 review) and 5:601 (1 review).

[220]

*Hollingsworth-Sanders Junior High School Literature Test. 1, 2 semesters in grades 7–8; 1962–64; first published 1962–63 in the Every Pupil Scholarship Test series; Forms A, B, ('64, 4 pages); 2 levels labeled Tests 1, 2; manual ('64, 2 pages); $1.75 per 25 tests, postage extra; 75¢ per specimen set, postpaid; 40(50) minutes; Leon Hollingsworth and M. W. Sanders; Data Processing and Educational Measurement Center. *

PAUL B. DIEDERICH, *Senior Research Associate, Educational Testing Service, Princeton, New Jersey.*

These literature tests must have been based on a particular anthology, not named in the manual or catalogue, since they consist mainly of factual items on a large number of selections that can hardly be common to all anthologies used in grades 7–8. Test 1, Form A, for example, has 90 factual items based on 52 selections, 31 represented by one item apiece, 15 by two items, 4 by three items, and one each by four and five items, together with eight items unconnected with particular selections.

Most of the factual items would be easy if a student had read the selection and remembered anything at all about it. They are fairly represented by such stems as "Selection A is about" (in which the responses are the names of five sports) and "Selection B is a" (poem, short story, play, etc.). More difficult items ask which of five authors wrote the selection or which of five names was the name of a principal character. A small number of items test recall of details that hardly seem worth remembering. For example, one of the few selections that may be remembered by teachers who have not used this anthology is the story of "The Cat and the Pain Killer" from *The Adventures of Tom Sawyer*. One would expect an item on what was the point of this episode, or what Aunt Polly learned from it. Not so; the question asks for the name of the cat.

An item unconnected with a particular selection is, "One of Mark Twain's early jobs was" (soldier, cub pilot, minstrel singer, organ player, printer). The keyed answer is "cub pilot," but Mark Twain had been a printer for nine years (1847–56) before he took up piloting and became a soldier immediately afterwards (1861). This mistake is important mainly because it reveals the lack of an independent critical review and pretesting before publication.

"Factual" items on literary works need not be trivial. For example, in one tryout form of a test on *Huckleberry Finn,* one item asks, "In which direction do Huck and Jim travel on the Mississippi River?" (north, south, east, west). I included this item reluctantly, thinking that no one could possibly get it wrong, but in a large tryout population only 56 percent got it right; 34 percent thought the characters were going north! How one could float north on a raft on a river that runs south is beyond my power to imagine, and the mistake reveals serious confusion and unawareness of the setting. The factual items in the tests under review, however, are not of this order. Once you know what, in general, a selection is about, who wrote it, the names of the principal characters, and whether it is a short story, poem, play, etc., you are likely to get a high score. On the average over the four forms, there are also 14 quotations with a choice of five titles of selections from which they were taken, and 17 words (not necessarily literary terms) with a choice of five brief definitions. The objectives of the study of literature at this stage of development are hardly represented at all.

The only manual, called Manual of Directions, is printed on both sides of a small sheet. The stated objective is "to measure understanding and knowledge of literature," and the items are said to have undergone numerous revisions based on statistical studies of test results and the criticism of teachers and test construction specialists. There is a table of percentiles for grades 7 and 8, said to be based on January and April administrations in the Nation-Wide Every Pupil Scholarship Testing Programs of 1962 and 1963, and the number of cases ranges from 1,494 to 1,743. Split-half reliabilities of .88 to .93 are reported for each form in grades 7 and 8. Since the tests could hardly be used unless one happened to be using the anthology on which they are based and since they test only memory of salient points in or about these selections, there is no point in commenting on the weaknesses of the manual.

[221]

*Hoskins-Sanders Literature Test. 1, 2 semesters grades 9–13; 1962–64; first published 1962–63 in the Every Pupil Scholarship Test series; Forms A, B, ('64, 4 pages); 2 levels labeled Tests 1, 2; manual ('64, 3 pages); no norms for college freshmen; $1.75

per 25 tests, postage extra; 75¢ per specimen set, postpaid; 40(45) minutes; Thomas Hoskins and M. W. Sanders; Data Processing and Educational Measurement Center. *

ALAN C. PURVES, *Professor of English, University of Illinois, Urbana, Illinois.*

The *Hoskins-Sanders Literature Test* consists of four forms of 150 four-choice items each. Almost all of the items call for recall of authors, titles, characters, incidents, lines, or tropes from English and American literature (with a few questions on world literature). Each form has about four items dealing with literary terms, but most items are of the type, "He was a famous after-dinner speaker, conversationalist, and poet: 1. Thoreau 2. Emerson 3. Whittier 4. Holmes" or "This novel is really an allegorical presentation of man's struggle with nature and with evil: 1. Chance 2. The Man of Property 3. The Scarlet Letter 4. Moby Dick." Needless to say, many of the other items are as unanswerable as these two.

Accompanying the tests is a manual indicating that the items deal with "35 classical selections"; I count 35 in the first third of each form and wonder whether Saki's "The Interlopers" (as good a short short story as it may be) is even a neglected classic. There are several items on such untaught authors as Louis Bromfield, Albert Bigelow Paine, and Helen Hunt Jackson, and no items dealing with black literature. There are norms—purportedly national—of 1962-63, which are revealing. Even then, before the great curriculum reforms had fully taken hold, the 99th percentile at grade 12 averages 91 out of 150 and the 75th percentile averages 59. Evidently, few students even then read the handbooks of literature that Hoskins and Sanders are testing.

These tests are, then, picayune, invalid, and unrepresentative of the secondary school English curriculum. They are also poorly edited. Representing, as they do, all that education in literature and testing in literature have been moving away from in the past twenty years, they should be avoided by all.

[222]

★A Look at Literature: The NCTE Cooperative Test of Critical Reading and Appreciation. Grades 4-6; 1968-69; 3 scores: Parts 1 (selections read aloud by examiner while read silently by examinee), 2 (selections read silently by examinee), total; Forms A ('68, 16 pages), B ('68, 19 pages); manual ('69, 38 pages); use of the unnamed part scores not discussed; norms for highly selected fifth graders only; $7 per 20 tests; separate answer sheets (Digitek-IBM

805) may be used; $4 per 100 answer sheets; $2 per manual; $2.50 per specimen set; cash orders postpaid; (60-70) minutes; developed and sponsored jointly by Research Foundation of the National Council of Teachers of English and Educational Testing Service; Cooperative Tests and Services. *

NANCY W. BURTON, *Fellow, Laboratory of Educational Research, University of Colorado, Boulder, Colorado.*

A Look at Literature, developed jointly by an NCTE committee and ETS, reflects well on both—the literature selections and questions are good and the construction and statistical procedures were sound.

The authors clearly wish to encourage the inclusion of literature in the elementary curriculum. By constructing a test they seem to be using the old saw, tests limit curriculum, backhand. To further their commendable design, more than half of the three pages of suggestions for using the test covers ways to use the test to teach literature. The other uses discussed are research, evaluation, and instructional planning. General use is restricted because the test has not been standardized or normed. Furthermore, for an unnormed test, it is expensive.

Each form contains 14 short literary selections and 50 four-option multiple choice questions. The first half of the test is to be read aloud by the administrator, partially to decrease the effect of students' reading ability. This interesting notion enhances the instrument's research value and, in one sense, content validity, although the oral reading factor would restrict standardization procedures. The test booklets are attractive and well laid out.

The literary selections are of high quality—diverse, appealing, and generally up-to-date. Excerpting from longer selections was very well done. The vocabulary level is not high—most difficult words are to be read aloud. Many questions, however, call for sophistication of interpretation; the rationale underlying the keyed responses was not always obvious to the reviewer.

The test development was competently done and completely reported. A couple of aspects deserve special mention: (*a*) The selection of passages and editing of items appear to have been done entirely by the test developers. No outside experts, beyond the NCTE committee, or literature search are mentioned. (*b*) An apparently successful effort was made to statistically equate the two forms by using a common equating test. The equating procedure is, however, not described adequately for most test users.

The authors have been most conscientious in explaining methods and limitations. Means, standard deviations, standard errors of measurement, K-R 20 reliabilities, correlations with STEP Reading, and average biserial discriminations and average difficulties are reported.

No content validity is insured beyond that provided by the NCTE committee's expertise. As might be expected, correlations of .78 and .79 between total LAL scores and STEP Reading "suggest that whatever is being measured is not distinct from reading in general." The K-R 20 reliabilities are only moderately good, ranging from .68 to .76 for part scores and .83 for total scores.

The mean item difficulties for Forms A and B are reported as .53 and .56, respectively, somewhat lower than optimum .625. This would not in itself be serious, but the sample was a high-ability group of fifth graders whose mean STEP reading score was at the 89th percentile. One should therefore be very cautious in giving the test to average and low-ability students in fifth or sixth grade, or to *any* fourth graders.

SUMMARY. The advantage of *A Look at Literature* is its freshness. The test is the only one of its kind, the literary selections are not tired or shopworn, the idea of reading part of the test aloud is interesting, and the conscientious reporting in the manual is refreshing. Its disadvantages are in interpretation. Without norms or validity data, its use is pretty much limited to criterion referenced testing or to districts that wish to develop local norms.

WALTER J. MOORE, *Professor of Elementary Education, University of Illinois, Urbana, Illinois.*

This test is described in the manual as a research instrument, designed to measure "the ability to respond critically to specific literary selections." According to the authors, "Responding to *A Look at Literature* calls for such operations as interpreting, valuing, comparing, inferring, appreciating, restating, attending to, relating, identifying with, and understanding." Selections were chosen to represent as many as possible of the modes of literary expression found in imaginative prose and poetry deemed suitable for children. Thus, under the general heading of prose are found such categories as

description, fanciful dialogue, realistic dialogue, fable, myth, fanciful narrative, realistic narrative, and the tall tale. Under poetry are found humorous and lyric subdivisions.

Certain "response modes were defined prior to the development of the test and item writers tried to write questions that would fit into one of three categories": translation, extension, and awareness. Translation involves "low-level inferences, comprehension of meanings, definition, restatement, recognition of elements." Extension includes "interpretation, prediction, comparison, higher-level inferences, use of the givens to go beyond the givens." Awareness is said to be exhibited by "perception of styles and their relationships, recognition of points of view and of the author's craft and its effects." The categories are not mutually exclusive.

The manual frankly discusses the limitations of the test. The test contains a few questions and their associated selections that have succeeded in discriminating between those students who score high on each part of the test and those who score low. As one reviews the test, certain concerns are felt, and one of these is the statistical validity of the test. The manual confesses that "only face validity is considered" and that before statistical validity can be established, further research is required. A real limitation on the generalizability of the results of the use of the tests resides in an absence of "norms on which to base interpretations of the test scores. The students whose test results are reported....are a select, not a random, group. By and large, they are middle-class urban and suburban pupils of average or above-average general ability, and they are above-average readers."

"*A Look at Literature* will need to be supplemented by other tests and data-gathering procedures. * [Its sponsors hope that] it will give rise to the development of companion instruments aimed also at the measurement of response and sensitivity." They rightly recognize the necessity for the establishment of the statistical validity of the test. The NCTE committee of teachers, librarians, and specialists in literature for children had as their goal the development of a research instrument—this they now have and it is a good one. It is suggested in the manual that the test may be used "informally as an aid in instruction" and as "a useful resource in teacher education, both pre-service and in-service." This reviewer feels

Look at Literature

that these ends may well be served by the test in its present state and recommends its use in these areas.

[223]

*Objective Tests in American Anthology. High school; 1959–64; 2 forms; no manual; no data on reliability; no norms; $3.45 per complete specimen set; postage extra; [60] minutes per test; Perfection Form Co. *

a) FIRST SERIES. 1959–61; 6 tests: 5 tests ('59, 4 pages) on specific periods and a final examination ('61, 6 pages); 10 or more tests same title, 15¢ each; $1.75 per specimen set; Carl H. Larson.

b) ALTERNATE SERIES. 1964; series title is Alternate Objective Tests in American Anthology; 7 tests: 6 tests (4 pages) on specific periods and a final examination (4 pages); separate answer sheets (IBM 805) must be used; 10 or more tests same title, with answer sheets, 15¢ each; 25 or more answer sheets, 3¢ each; $2.15 per specimen set; Dorothy A. Mason.

[224]

*Objective Tests in English Anthology. High school; 1959–64; 2 forms; no manual; no data on reliability; no norms; $4.75 per complete specimen set; postage extra; [60] minutes per test; Perfection Form Co. *

a) FIRST SERIES. 1959; 8 tests: 7 tests (4 pages) on specific periods and a final examination (6 pages); 10 or more tests same title, 15¢ each; $2.45 per specimen set; Carl H. Larson.

b) ALTERNATE SERIES. 1964; series title is Alternate Objective Tests in English Anthology; 9 tests: 7 tests (4 pages) on specific periods, a final examination (5 pages), and a test entitled The English Novel (4 pages); separate answer sheets (IBM 805) must be used; 10 or more tests same title with answer sheets, 15¢ each; 25 or more answer sheets, 3¢ each; $2.75 per specimen set; Dorothy A. Mason.

[225]

★Tests of Academic Progress: Literature. Grades 9–12; 1964–66; Form 1 ('64, 15 pages); 4 levels (grades 9, 10, 11, 12) in a single booklet; no specific manual; battery teacher's manual ('64, 62 pages); battery manual for administrators, supervisors, and counselors ('65, 45 pages); battery norms booklet for IQ levels ('66, 26 pages); separate answer cards (MRC) must be used; 30¢ per test; $3 per 100 MRC answer cards; $1.20 per battery teacher's manual; 96¢ per battery administrator's manual; 60¢ per battery norms booklet; $3 per specimen set of the complete battery; postage extra; scoring service, 27¢ per test; 50(60) minutes; Dale P. Scannell and Oscar M. Haugh; Houghton Mifflin Co. *

REFERENCE

1. GOOLSBY, THOMAS M., JR. "The Appropriateness of the Tests of Academic Progress for an Experimental School." Ed & Psychol Meas 30(4):967–70 w '70. *

ROBERT C. POOLEY, Professor Emeritus of English, University of Wisconsin, Madison, Wisconsin.

Part of a battery entitled Tests of Academic Progress, this literature test undertakes to measure the success of students in grades 9 through 12 in reading and interpreting six types of literature: the short story, novel, essay, narrative poem, lyric poem, and drama. Responses are made by choosing one of four options in multiple choice questions. To keep the test within bounds of space and time (50 minutes) the selections are necessarily very brief; for example, the sample of the whole field of drama offered a ninth grade student is a quotation of 22 lines. The two longest selections consist of 47 lines each.

To cover the four years of high school in one test, the exercises are overlapping. Of the total of 126 test items, the first 60 are performed by ninth grade students; tenth grade students begin at item 21 and continue through item 82, and so on. The ninth grade performs 60 items, the tenth grade 62 items, the eleventh grade 64 items, and the twelfth grade 66 items. If the test were repeated annually, more than half of the items for grades 10 through 12 would be repeated by the same students.

The selections of literature are well chosen to provide unfamiliar but typical quotations from standard authors. In Form 1 the authors total 12 and include Harte, Frost, Crane, Hawthorne, Thoreau, Byron, Keats, and Shakespeare. Each grade level is tested by items including the six types of literature. The test items, which are questions or statements based on the reading of the sample quotations, are classified into four general categories: understanding meaning in context; understanding the content of a literary selection; understanding literary devices; and using literary background. The last category includes exercises in identifying literary types, identifying authors by textual evidence or simple elimination, and identifying characteristics and styles of writing. A table on page 40 of the teacher's manual classifies each item for Forms 1 and 2 (only Form 1 is available), providing not only an analysis of the content of the tests, but also the means to a diagnostic analysis of individual pupil performance as a method of determining areas of competence and insufficiency.

The test items are ingeniously devised. For example, the words picked out for identification of meaning in the ninth grade test can all be determined by the context, requiring no previous knowledge of the word but exercising the skill of recognizing meaning in context. I find no objection to the questions calling for recognition of figures of speech, nor for such literary devices as alliteration, assonance, simile, and onomatopoeia, which appear for the first time in the tenth grade portion of the test. In a test

of this nature I seriously question the significance of identifying terms of prosody such as
iambic pentameter, trochaic tetrameter, iambic
tetrameter, and trochaic pentameter, or, more
erudite, the identification of such stanza forms
as Chaucerian, Spenserian, ottava rima, and
terza rima. I doubt whether the majority of
high school English teachers could make these
identifications correctly. Too many of the items
for grades 11 and 12 contain these gratuitous
technicalities. On the other hand, a large portion
of the items require inferences from the content
and context; these are well done and are, in
my opinion, the most valuable part of the test.

The manual for administrators presents
within-grade reliability coefficients ranging from
.85 to .90. These coefficients are high enough
to warrant confidence in the measuring worth
of the test in its own narrow sphere, but they
point to caution in the interpretation of the
score of any particular student, especially at
the midpoint of the range.

The authors state in the same manual that
the Literature test measures four general categories of literary knowledge (listed above)
"which reflect the major goals of the teaching
of literature." This is a considerable overstate-
ment. Few teachers of English would agree
that the four categories employed by the authors
constitute "the major goals" of teaching literature. More accurate is this statement in the
teacher's manual: "The purpose of *Test 6:
Literature* is to determine how well a student
can apply what he has learned in his English
classes to the reading and interpretation of the
following six types of literature: the short
story, novel, essay, narrative poem, lyric poem,
and drama." This is a true description which
emphasizes that this is a reading test for a
specific field; it measures with some degree of
accuracy the success of students in reading
pieces of literature for meaning, for the detection of literary devices, and for the application
of past literary experience to a present reading.
These skills are valuable in achieving the goals
of literature in the curriculum, but they are not
in themselves the major goals.

In a report which has influenced the teaching
of English for over 50 years [1] these excerpts
are among the listed goals for teaching literature in high schools: (*a*) "broaden, deepen, and

enrich the imaginative and emotional life of the
student," (*b*) "arouse in the minds of pupils
an admiration for great personalities," (*c*)
"raise the plane of enjoyment in reading to
progressively higher levels," (*d*) "give to the
student....a sense of [the] abundance of interesting material, and a trained ability and desire
to find for himself such intellectual and spiritual
food as he may need," and (*e*) "feel more
sensitively and deeply, and to imagine more
vividly, but to think more accurately and intelligently."

If these are the fundamental goals for the
teaching of literature in high schools, and I
believe the majority of English teachers would
accept them as such, then the materials measured in this test bear very slight relationship
to these goals. The test is not at fault; it is the
title that is wrong. The test in its present form
measures specific skills; these skills undoubtedly
assist in achieving the goals for teaching literature, but these skills are not the goals. It must
be admitted that the accepted goals are very
difficult, if not impossible, of quantitative measurement. This problem has plagued the makers
of tests of literature since objective testing
began. Practically all teachers of English recognize the present impossibility of testing for
gains in achieving the true goals of literature
instruction. The authors of this test are at fault
only in labelling the test "Literature" without
qualification and for the statement that the four
categories of the test items "reflect the major
goals of the teaching of literature."

The potential harm of this claim lies in the
assumption that a teacher who teaches exclusively the skills measured in this test is a
superior teacher of literature and that a teacher
whose students do not do so well on this test
is thereby an inferior teacher. School administrators and an uninformed public sometimes
make such assumptions. The end result might
be the neglect of the true goals of literature
instruction in favor of skills which can be
measured. The test itself is a satisfactory instrument for the measurement of specific contribu-
tory skills to the reading of literature, as an
index of progress in these skills. It should be
titled not "Literature," but "A Test of Basic
Skills in the Reading of Literature."

ALAN C. PURVES, *Professor of English, University of Illinois, Urbana, Illinois.*

The literature test consists of 12 passages of

1 HOSIC, JAMES FLEMING, COMPILER. *Reorganization of English in Secondary Schools,* pp. 63–4. Bulletin, 1917, No. 2,
Bureau of Education. Washington, D.C.: United States Government Printing Office, 1917. Pp. 181. *

Tests of Academic Progress: Literature

prose, verse, and drama, each with 9 to 12 four-choice items related to it. The test is so arranged that ninth grade students do passages 1–6; tenth grade students, 3–8; eleventh grade students, 5–10; and twelfth grade students, 7–12. The tests have a median reliability for the four levels of .88 and have norms based on good national samples. There is an item classification consisting of 13 subcategories grouped into four categories (understanding meanings in context, understanding content, understanding literary devices, and using literary background).

The test package has a statistical and marketing sheen that would lead the careless user to accept the test as a measure of literary understanding. Underneath this sheen, however, is a trivial test of reading comprehension (interestingly, the test has a .83 correlation with the reading test in the same series).

To take the items and the item classification first, one sees that the items measuring an understanding of literary devices simply ask the student to identify the devices. Calling something a simile is not understanding it. Of the items dealing with understanding main ideas, a good number ask the student to give a title to the work; others ask him to indicate the author's purpose, e.g., to narrate, describe, persuade, or explain. Neither of these kinds of items measures the understanding of main ideas save indirectly (and often ambiguously).

Beyond the problem of the classificatory terms is the balance of the test. Seventy-six of the items measure understanding meanings and understanding content, in other words, comprehension of the substance of the passages; of these, 21 are vocabulary items. There is nothing wrong with testing literal comprehension in a literature test, but the dominance of this kind of item leads a student to think that this is all there is to literary understanding. No items appear dealing with the relationships of part to part, part to whole, style to thought, or language to tone, dealing with the structure, the tone, or the attitude of the writer, or dealing with the justification of interpretation of the passage; surely these are major aspects of literary study. Further, the items connected with a passage seem to have no functional relationship to the passage; there seems to be no reason for asking those particular questions. As a whole, then, the test borders on the trivial.

So much of the test also seems to be measuring test wiseness. Specific determiners abound, as in these four options: expository, descriptive, narrative, narrative and descriptive. There are many "none of the above" and "all of the above" items, including one on a passage from Thoreau (in which there is reference to the author by name): "Who wrote this selection? (1) Thackeray (2) Tolstoy (3) There is no way of telling who wrote this selection (4) None of the above." Another item asks for the best title for a selection; a sharp student would see that the title is printed in the acknowledgments.

The selections chosen are generally adequate, but not "advanced and challenging" as the manual claims. One of the selections, from Hawthorne's *The Scarlet Letter* should have been avoided, since the work is so widespread in the curriculum and since two of the items test more the student's knowledge of the work than his ability to read the passage with literary acumen.

There are so many flaws in the content of this test that it is hard to summarize one's judgment of it, but one suspects that the definition of literary ability that produced the specifications and the items was reinterpreted by the psychometric editors and not carried through by those knowledgeable about literary study. It would seem, too, that all of the effort went into the norming process and not enough into the validation process. Validity in a literature test is based less on the pedigree of the passages chosen than on the behaviors measured by the items. By that definition of validity these tests are invalid and certainly inferior to the publisher's other literature test, that in the Content Evaluation series. Prospective users of the *Tests of Academic Progress: Literature* should be very careful not to use the literature portion of the tests to make judgments about a student's literary ability.

JOHN C. SHERWOOD, *Professor of English, University of Oregon, Eugene, Oregon.*

The battery of *Tests of Academic Progress* is intended "to provide an efficient and comprehensive appraisal of student progress toward the most widely accepted academic goals of secondary education"; the tests provide, in other words, a mechanism by which a local school or system can rate individuals or classes for purposes of placement, course planning, and the like. Each test consists of four different but overlapping grade level tests (e.g., grade 9 will answer exercises 1–60; grade 10, exercises 21–82), so that it can serve for all four grades. There is a considerable mass of statistical material, including not only norms for various levels and even times of the year but also "Special Percentile Norms for IQ Levels" directed to educators rash enough to attempt to identify over- and under-achievement (to be honest, the accompanying instructions clearly warn against any hasty judgments in such matters). The literature test is designed to find out how well the student "can interpret selections taken from many different kinds of literature" (actually "the short story, novel, essay, narrative poem, lyric poem, and drama") or, more specifically, to test "the ability to understand the meaning of words, phrases, and sentences in context; the ability to understand the content of literary selections; the ability to understand the use of literary devices." If such phrases as "ability to understand the content" seem on the vague side, an analysis of the test may help to define more sharply what is actually being tested: (a) Ordinary unspecialized reading comprehension, the ability to understand the text, sometimes taking the form of mere attentiveness (e.g., the ability to identify a selection as from "a play of more than one act" from the fact that it is plainly labeled "Act One"). (b) A type of reading comprehension more specifically literary, such as the ability to estimate a character from clues in the dialogue. (c) Knowledge of certain formal and technical matters, such as genre, meter, and figures of speech. (d) Finally, command of some odds and ends of literary history, as evidenced by the ability to identify authors and periods from clues in style and content.

In considering the usefulness of the test, we might first ask whether the inclusion of items from literary history is expedient in a test ostensibly intended to measure interpretation. It certainly muddles the issue, for although interpretation might be thought of as a kind of unity, history is a large and amorphous realm, which really ought to be tested in terms of identified areas such as English, continental, or classical. Of the authors actually quoted, all are English or American, mostly of the nineteenth century. An idea of the kind of traditional curriculum the editors had in mind is suggested by their defensive statement that the answer to one item would be obvious to "any-

one who knows that Frost was a poet, that Stevenson did not write of incidents concerning broncos and Mexican dialect, and that the language is unlike anything written by Joel Chandler Harris." Even assuming that it is important to know what Stevenson did *not* write, we are getting a rather provincial view of literary history; a student could be widely read in the masterpieces of Western culture and still come to grief with the items on this test. It would seem better to test literary history separately and more systematically, unless, to be sure, the group tested had exactly the background the editors had in mind, in which case the questions might seem rather easy.

Turning to the genuinely interpretive items, we note little of subtlety, little of that sense of the complexity and ambiguity of literature which the formalist school has taught us so much about. There is likewise no attempt to assess literary taste or value judgments; and perhaps for these reasons the questions tend to be unambiguous, with answers which the experienced reader can easily spot. Some seem to be little more than exercises in labeling. The student may be asked to determine whether a passage is "vivid," "wordy," "exact," or "colorful," to decide whether an author's purpose was "to tell a story," "to describe a scene," "to criticize a way of life," or "to entertain the reader with an amusing situation." Such categories are crude and vague and ambiguities are not lacking; pity the student who must choose between the labels "autobiographical" and "humorous" with reference to a passage which has elements of both categories. Much of the questioning involves matters of fact—what is going on? where is the scene? who are the persons involved?—or involves defining the obvious prose significance. Problems of tone and attitude, much less the more elusive shades of meaning, do not get much beyond asking whether the author "approved" or "disapproved" of the events or whether a passage shows a "humorous vein" or an "ironic sense."

We might conclude by asking what progress a student would have made if his performance on the test did in fact improve over the years. We should expect that he had extended somewhat his knowledge of literary history, especially of the nineteenth century; that he had extended his vocabulary; that he had acquired a good command of the formal mechanics of literature—meter, rhyme schemes, figures, and the

Tests of Academic Progress: Literature

like—though this command might not go beyond the ability to identify, and need not involve the ability to show how such devices function in context. He would have maintained or increased his ability to read a text closely and attentively with a strong sense of detail, especially factual detail, but not necessarily with a sense of literary meaning as that has been understood since the new critics burst on the scene; as for the recently revived concern with the social and political bearings of literature, this simply belongs to a different world from the one assumed by the editors. Admittedly the skills emphasized are important to literary study; probably a student who did well on this test would have no great trouble in adjusting to college literature courses. But the fact remains that for the twelfth grade at least the test operates at a more pedestrian level than is appropriate to much secondary study today.

For a review of the complete battery, see 31.

[226]
★**The Undergraduate Record Examinations: Literature Tests.** College; 1969–70; 2 tests: field, modular; descriptive booklet ('70, 12 pages); for more complete information, see 671; Educational Testing Service. *
a) LITERATURE TEST. Forms RUR ('69, 28 pages), SUR ('70, 27 pages); 120(140) minutes.
b) EUROPEAN AND AMERICAN LITERATURE TEST: A MODULAR TEST DESIGNED TO COMPLEMENT THE TWO-HOUR LITERATURE TEST. Form SUR ('70, 13 pages); 45(55) minutes.

For reviews of the testing program, see 671 (2 reviews).

SPELLING

[227]
*****Kansas Spelling Tests.** 1, 2 semesters in grades 3, 4–6, 7–8; 1962–64; first published 1962–63 in the Every Pupil Scholarship Test series; 3 tests; Forms A, B, ('64, 4 pages); 2 levels labeled Tests 1, 2; manual ('64, 5 pages); $1.75 per 25 tests, postage extra; 75¢ per specimen set of any one test, postpaid; 15(20) minutes; Connie Moritz, Alice Robinson, Mary T. Williams, and M. W. Sanders; Data Processing and Educational Measurement Center. *
a) KANSAS ELEMENTARY SPELLING TEST. 1, 2 semesters in grade 3.
b) KANSAS INTERMEDIATE SPELLING TEST. 1, 2 semesters in grades 4–6.
c) KANSAS JUNIOR HIGH SCHOOL SPELLING TEST. 1, 2 semesters in grades 7–8.

[228]
★**N.B. Spelling Tests.** Standards 1–3, 3–5, 6–8, 8–10 for English pupils and 3–5, 6–8, 8–10 for Afrikaans pupils; [1964]; Forms A, B, (2 pages); 4 levels labeled Series 2, 3, 4, 5; Series 5 for English pupils

only; preliminary manual (18 pages); 20c per 10 tests; 30c per scoring key; 40c per manual; postpaid within South Africa; specimen set not available; Afrikaans edition available; (45) minutes; Human Sciences Research Council. *

[229]
*****Sanders-Fletcher Spelling Test.** 1, 2 semesters in grades 9–13; 1962–64; first published 1962–63 in the Every Pupil Scholarship Test series; Forms A, B, ('64, 4 pages); 2 levels labeled Tests 1, 2; manual ('64, 4 pages); no norms for college freshmen; $1.75 per 25 tests, postage extra; 75¢ per specimen set, postpaid; 30(35) minutes; Gwen Fletcher and M. W. Sanders; Data Processing and Educational Measurement Center. *

THOMAS D. HORN, *Professor of Curriculum and Instruction and Chairman of the Department, The University of Texas, Austin, Texas.*

Four forms are available for grades 9–12 and college freshmen. 1A and 1B are described as equivalent for the first semester of instruction; 2A and 2B are equivalent for the second semester. However, the manual refers to 4 equivalent forms. Each contains 150 items requiring a total of 315 word judgments. Part 1 of each form requires the testee to mark correct spellings with a plus, misspellings with a minus; Part 2 of each form requires the selection of the correct word from a choice of two within sentences (some foils are misspelled; however, some are homonyms, e.g., *cereal, serial,* and some are correctly spelled but do not fit in the sentence, e.g., *desert, dessert,* which adds a vocabulary dimension to the test); Part 3 of each form requires the testee to select the misspelled word from five possibilities (no *none* response). No information is given concerning the number of words used more than once in the four tests.

Directions for giving the test are printed on the test blanks which require the testee to read the directions and answer the items as directed. The extent to which scores for pupils with reading difficulties would be affected by no assistance in test orientation is not known. This reviewer found the small print size used on the tests increased the likelihood of error.

Although the test manual states that the words were selected on the "basis of functional significance, frequency of usage, and incidence of misspellings" by using "the Buckingham Extension of the Ayres Spelling Scale, the New Standard High School Spelling Scale, the Thorndike word list, and a number of recognized spelling tests," no criteria for selection are identified. In checking the test words against

Ernest Horn's list of 10,000 words most commonly used in writing, the number of words found in Horn were: (*a*) Test 1A, 163 words of 315 judgments (some used more than once); (*b*) Test 1B, 117 of 315; (*c*) Test 2A, 175 of 315; and (*d*) Test 2B, 135 of 315. This appears to reflect an overabundance of spelling "demons" and/or infrequently written words in the tests. Geographic bias in the selection of words is represented in the use of *Wichita* and *Manhattan*. Words never seen or heard by a testee, e.g., *rhapsody, tiara,* represent special problems for disadvantaged populations. Words with more than one pronunciation, e.g., *variegate,* which may be pronounced with either three or four syllables, add to the spelling difficulty of a particular word. Nevertheless, these examples would provide "top" to a high school test.

Concurrent with the issue of word-selection validity is the use of words with more than one correct spelling, e.g., *acknowledgment* and *acknowledgement; saleable* and *salable; obligato* and *obbligato; eerie* and *eery; guerilla* and *guerrilla.* In some cases, the preferred spelling was not used, thus a student knowing a correct preferred spelling, but not alternative spellings, would receive no credit for what he did know. The trade name *Sanforized* appears, in form 2B, item 62, as *Sanforize* as a correct spelling, thereby requiring a wrong answer to receive credit. A key error occurs in Test 2B, item 80.

In addressing themselves to the issue of whether or not an objective spelling test is an adequate measure of spelling ability, the authors set up a pattern "so that each grade would have a fair distribution of easy, moderately difficult, and difficult words." The pattern is not described. As tentative lists were assembled, they were "administered to students both as objective tests and as pronounced lists and error studies made on each set." This procedure seems essential if incorrect spellings are to serve as challenging foils.

In some cases, an element of luck exists when the testee faces a relatively easy misspelling, e.g., *concurr,* followed by *chandelier, carrion, fabrikoid,* and *lustre* (for which the preferred spelling is *luster*) as foils. Also, the student's background and mental set on misspellings out of context may lead him to see *solder* as a misspelling of *soldier.*

Normative data "were computed from 20,423 high school student scores which were reported by cooperating schools in four nation-wide testing programs." However, this population is not described. It is obvious that linguistically different students in the inner city or in migrant populations would not have an easy time with words such as *iridescent, plagiarize* and *crystalline.* Percentile norms are provided for each of grades 9–12.

Test reliability was determined by the split-half method. Coefficients of reliability ranged from .79 to .90 among the various grade levels.

The authors suggest five ways the test results may be used:

a) "For determining student achievement": This is questionable since the measures on this test are norm-referenced. Information about general performance levels may be obtained, but the components of any given spelling program might differ widely from the measures used in the test. One can see that criterion-based measures, e.g., 100 percent mastery of a given corpus of words, would evoke different interpretations.

b) "For checking the efficiency of instruction": For much the same reasons as were indicated in *a*) above, using scores in this way has serious limitations. The greatest validity for instructional efficiency would hold for those teachers who "teach the test."

c) "For assigning school marks": In the light of current trends in high school English curricula, and because of the nature of norm-referenced measures, the authors' suggested practice of translating percentile scores into school marks seems rather dubious.

d) "For analyzing student and class weaknesses": The fact that this test is dealing with norm-referenced measures results in the weakness identified by Klein,[1] that of "failing to provide specific information about particular skill development and needs." Also, no means for the analysis of spelling difficulties is provided in the manual, other than admonishing the user that "after the specific weaknesses and handicaps are located, remedial measures may be applied intelligently." Problems of phonetic misspellings, homonyms, or misspellings due to mispronunciation are examples of problem clusters which could have been provided for teacher and student analysis. With individual and class error information for the foregoing problem areas, instructional prescriptions could then be intelligently made.

1 KLEIN, STEPHEN. "Evaluating Tests in Terms of the Information They Provide." *Eval Comment* 2(2):1–6 Je '70. *

e) "For motivating student effort": While it is true that some students rise to the occasion when undertaking a test and some actually enjoy the competitiveness of test taking or regard the experience as something of a game, there are significant numbers of other students who face a testing session with fear, resentment, or a "couldn't care less" attitude. Here again, we are facing the issue of norm-referenced versus criterion-referenced measures in terms of relevant instructional objectives in spelling.

In summary, this reviewer has some doubts concerning the validity of word selection for this test. The lack of test orientation for testees and the overly small print size would appear to handicap unsophisticated test takers. Most importantly, the suggested uses of the test do not appear to be appropriate.

[230]

★Spelling Test: McGraw-Hill Basic Skills System. Grades 11–14; 1970; also called *MHBSS Spelling Test;* although designed for use with the MHBSS instructional program, the test may be used independently; Forms A, B, (7 pages); manual (31 pages); separate answer sheets (Digitek, IBM 1230, Scoreze) must be used; $4.90 per 25 tests; $2.50 per 50 Digitek or IBM answer sheets; $3 per 25 Scoreze answer sheets; $1 per Digitek or IBM scoring stencil; postage extra; $1.25 per specimen set, postpaid; IBM scoring service, 25¢ and over per test ($20 minimum); 20(30) minutes; Alton L. Raygor; McGraw-Hill Book Co., Inc. *

THOMAS D. HORN, *Professor of Curriculum and Instruction and Chairman of the Department, The University of Texas, Austin, Texas.*

Each form of this test consists of 50 items; Form A requires 215 word judgments and Form B requires 219 word judgments, the difference caused by the number of paired homonyms or easily confused words selected. Each test item appears as one or two sentences. The student determines "which one, if any, of the four underlined words in each item is misspelled; a 'none wrong' response is provided for each item." Homonyms and easily confused words are forced into context by the sentence in which they appear. The manual states that no word or derivative of that word about which the testee must make a judgment appears more than once in the same form; "it recurs neither as an answer choice in another item nor in the context of another sentence." However, five exceptions to this were found as shown below. The manual provides extremely useful tables of: (*a*) misspellings; (*b*) the word list for each form in alphabetical order with the item num- ber for each word; and (*c*) words repeated, but not in the same form (i.e., ninth and ninety), are listed alphabetically with the form and item number indicated. Unfortunately, the confusing actual title of this last table, "Words Not Repeated in the Same Form," apparently confused the table compiler. A check of the tests reveals that five words are actually in the same form in both Form A and Form B, i.e., secretary, seized, subtle, superintendent and tremendous. Also, the word *attempting* indicated as being included in item 38, Form B, does not appear there; *governors,* identified as being included in item 18, Form A, does not appear; *ninety,* identified as item 56, Form B, should be item 46. Gremlins also got into the word list for Form B, with *benefit* and *obvious* being misspelled.

Complete and detailed directions for administering the test are provided in the manual. Testee directions are clear and each form provides a practice item.

The words selected for these tests were drawn from Pollack's study of misspellings and seven other lists of words commonly misspelled by high school and college students. The "spelling demons" of these lists were combined by computer in a collated list which included the frequency with which each word appeared on the eight lists. Again, the computer was used to select, "first the most frequently misspelled word on the Pollack list, and then, using a table of random numbers, it selected randomly three other words from the collated list. These four words together [plus a 'none' response], were used to create a test item. The second test item's words were selected in a similar manner. The second most frequently misspelled word on the Pollack list was grouped with three other randomly selected words" plus the "none" response. This was continued until enough items were secured for a try-out edition. Using the words and sentences, an "experimental version of the test was then tried out on other populations [not identified] for the purpose of gathering item analysis data. Items were selected from these try-outs on the basis of their difficulty and discrimination indices." This reviewer checked the words finally selected for the published tests against Horn's *Basic Writing Vocabulary.* Form A contains 170 words (79 percent) which are also in Horn; Form B contains 172 words (79 percent). This appears to reflect significantly higher validity when compared with the

Sanders-Fletcher Spelling Test and probably also reflects the intended population for which the MHBSS test was designed, i.e., "high school juniors or seniors who are planning to attend college....two-year college students, and ....students in the early years of four-year colleges and universities." Students found to be poor spellers may be guided by test results "toward remedial or developmental instruction in spelling." In addition, the authors are careful to point out that criterion-related validity must be determined by test users in terms of instructional objectives.

K-R 20 reliabilities of .89 and .90 are reported for the two forms. No claim is made that any of the normative populations represent a random sample. Tables are provided to convert raw scores to percentile ranks, stanines, and standard scores. The section describing norming procedures is written in quite an informative and readable way, particularly for the nonspecialist administrator.

The section describing scoring, reporting, and interpreting test results is, likewise, informative and readable. Although the list of words used in developing this test was the same as that used in developing the McGraw-Hill Basic Skills System Instructional Materials in spelling, the manual manages to maintain low-key suggestions to use the latter materials. The desirability of building an atlas of norms, e.g., representing geographic and linguistic differences, is reflected by the author's comment concerning use of local norms. Use of the test scores for diagnostic interpretations is realistic in only a general way. The SCOREZE answer sheet does provide a useful, though limited, analysis of learning difficulties by identifying the items representing such errors as vowel substitution, double consonants, and homonyms. However, the incidence of items representing particular difficulties is not always proportional between forms, e.g., Form A has 8 double-consonant items, Form B contains 2; Form A contains 11 vowel-substitution items, Form B contains 15. The number of "none" responses is the same for both forms.

In short, this test is recommended for use, keeping in mind the issues involved in criterion-related validity. It is hoped that the discrepancies identified in the foregoing paragraphs may be eliminated in the next edition of the materials.

ALBERT H. YEE, *Professor of Curriculum and Instruction, University of Wisconsin, Madison, Wisconsin.*

The McGraw-Hill Basic Skills System (MHBSS) provides diagnosis and training for college-bound high school juniors and seniors and college freshmen and sophomores in six academic skill areas—reading, writing, spelling, vocabulary, study skills, and mathematics. Each area's materials contain a diagnostic test, a self-instructional, remedial program with workbook and audiotape, and a second test to evaluate the student's achievement after his training.

The MHBSS Spelling Test is not complex, and explicit directions in the manual make test administration quite clear and simple to follow. A raw score of total correct responses is easily converted to a standard T score, stanine, and percentile ranking. No subscales were developed for diagnosis of specific problems, because the test authors were not able to find reliable information on diagnostic schemes. Thus, the test authors suggest that on the basis of total score results, "A student's adviser must make a subjective judgment in selecting....an activity for the student."

Thus, such guidance leads to quite generalized interpretation of results. The high scorer is identified as being capable of spelling when he wants to do so and probably able to recognize situations when he needs aid. A low score indicates that a student does not recognize his spelling errors and may have a poor attitude toward improving his spelling proficiency. The test authors say those students scoring in the middle range are potentially the most willing and able to profit from remedial instruction, such as provided by the MHBSS worktext, *Basic Spelling Skills: A Program to Self-Instruction.*

The test items require the examinee to identify one or none of four underlined words in one or two sentences as being incorrectly spelled. The test words were selected from a frequency count of 4,482 different misspelled words and word-groups of students that Pollack [1] collected from 599 college English teachers in 1950. The passage of 20 years could make a difference in what words are misspelled and what problems students have. The English proficiency of high school graduates has steadily improved in the last two decades and has

[1] POLLACK, THOMAS CLARK. "Spelling Report." *Col Engl* 16:102–9 N '54. *

Spelling Test: McGraw-Hill Basic Skills System

reached the level where many universities, such as the University of Wisconsin, have abolished the traditionally required year of English for most freshmen. However, the respectable work done to standardize the test appears to make it up-to-date and provides norms relevant to modern students. The standardization sample included freshmen from five 4-year colleges or universities, first year students from 14 junior colleges, and college preparatory juniors and seniors from 13 high schools distributed in the four main geographic regions of the USA.

The basis of the MHBSS Spelling Test, therefore, is simply students' accuracy in recognizing correctly spelled and misspelled words. The test authors claim that spelling recognition items produce test scores that correlate positively with proficiency in spelling dictated words. To support such a claim, they report a correlation of .85 between an experimental version of the test and the spelling section of the *Cooperative English Test,* Form OM; but the manual does not report the sample size and is not completely clear concerning the details of the item analyses conducted with the responses of other samples. The discussion of test validity is brief and vague; it does not appear that adequate crossvalidation was accomplished. Since the spelling section of the *Cooperative English Test,* Form OM, is also comprised of recognition-type items, the empirical question remains open of whether the test predicts the criterion. Even if spelling recognition scores correlate as well as .85, there remains about 28 percent of the variance that is still unexplained.

The criterion of spelling behavior in this test follows the traditional definition of spelling that one envisions in school spelling lists and spelling "bees." Ability to reproduce spellings upon demand is a significant aspect of spelling achievement but there is more to spelling than that. Personke and Yee [2] have developed a theoretical model of spelling behavior that incorporates all pertinent behaviors involved in spelling and systematically structures them into five distinct yet complementary channels of processing spelling behavior. Based in part on modern communications and systems theories, the model specifies what decisions and operations follow

2 PERSONKE, CARL R., AND YEE, ALBERT H. "A Model for the Analysis of Spelling Behavior." *El Engl* 43:278–84 Mr '66. *
PERSONKE, CARL R., AND YEE, ALBERT H. "The Situational Choice and the Spelling Program." *El Engl* 45:32–7+ Ja '68. *

different spelling contingencies and their relative efficiency in achieving the desired outcome.

Pure rote spelling without conscious effort to reproduce the words as one writes his thoughts, is efficient, mature spelling. However, there are different levels of spelling response, such as occasions when spelling may be consciously produced through phonetic rules or with the aid of one or several external sources and/or verified in various ways. Students need to learn rote spelling, rules, situational choices, etc., through practice and instruction to develop comprehensive spelling behavior. Schools need to systematize their instructional programs accordingly. The traditional spelling programs for elementary and middle school students provide skills and exercises that may be viewed as steps toward comprehensive, if not systematic, instruction; but the criterion behavior all such programs focus upon is narrowly perceived, as can be found in the MHBSS Spelling Test. Thus, the test provides little diagnostic help beyond classifying scores as high, medium, and poor. Advisers are asked to make their own judgments of specific student needs and strengths. As with all other existing spelling tests, its construct validity leaves much to be desired.

From a technical point of view, the MHBSS Spelling Test appears to have been given adequate attention as to standardization, item discrimination, internal consistency, and intercorrelation with three of the other five MHBSS tests (with reading, .55; vocabulary, .47; and mathematics, .38). The test authors state that correlations with writing and study skills will be computed later when those tests are completed. Also, reliability will be estimated later with test-retest and Form A and B correlations to assess test stability and equivalence.

Although this reviewer finds serious fault with its construct validity and would like to see some crossvalidation done, the MHBSS Spelling Test compares well with other traditional spelling tests available.

VOCABULARY

[231]
*Bruce Vocabulary Inventory. Business and industry; 1959–67; 1 form ('59, 4 pages); manual ('59, 4 pages); supplementary norms ['63 and '67, 1 page]; reliability data for raw scores only; $6 per 20 tests; 35¢ per key; separate answer sheets (IBM 805) may

be used; $3.25 per 20 answer sheets; $1 per set of scoring stencils; $1.50 per manual; $2.25 per specimen set with hand scoring key, $2.50 with scoring stencils; cash orders postpaid, 10% extra on charge orders; (15–25) minutes; Martin M. Bruce; Martin M. Bruce, Ph.D., Publishers. *

FRED H. BORGEN, *Research Psychologist, National Merit Scholarship Corporation, Evanston, Illinois.*

The *Bruce Vocabulary Inventory* is presented as an aid for personnel decisions in industry and business, presumably throughout the range of white collar employees. The manual does not specify just what uses might be most appropriate for the test, but it implies that it might be used as a brief measure of intelligence, as well as a measure of verbal comprehension and usage. The test consists of 100 four-alternative multiple choice items, each with the correct alternative meaning the same or most nearly the same as the key word. The 100 key words, which were randomly selected from the *Oxford Universal Dictionary,* are roughly arranged in terms of increasing difficulty. There is no time limit, and "a person with a high school education will generally complete the form in about 15–20 minutes."

Few vocabulary tests specify how words were selected, and the author of this test is to be commended for using a precise method of compiling the sample of words. The nature of the particular vocabulary domain, however, may not be appropriate for many business uses and the user may prefer a vocabulary test containing words with more functional and pragmatic usage.

The selection of items and the wise use of distractors make for a wide range of difficulty among the items; hence, the instrument can be expected to make reliable discriminations over a wide variety of applicant groups, particularly those of average or higher ability. The distractors have been carefully selected to foil the respondent with incomplete knowledge of a word, and correct guessing is therefore minimized. Unfortunately, some of the distractors are more difficult than the key word; distractors for moderately difficult words include such stumpers as, rani, adiposity, virgule, nipa, and intaglio.

The manual appropriately warns that "too heavy reliance on this test as a vocabulary measure and as an indicator of intellectual level is discouraged. The test user should view test results as suggestive rather than as definitely diagnostically significant."

The manual claims that a special value of this particular vocabulary test is the availability of norms for industrial and business groups. This claim places a major burden on the adequacy of the norms the author provides, yet in several respects the norms appear deficient. The manual lists the job titles in the various norm groups but gives no evidence that the groups are representative of any naturally occurring population. For example, the white collar group contains such diverse workers as statisticians and switchboard operators, but one suspects, in the absence of evidence to the contrary, that the composition of the white collar group is ad hoc, rather than representative of the general population of white collar workers. The norm group for the "total employed population" is a simple composite of most of the available groups and is rather heavily weighted, to some unspecified extent, with persons of well above average education.

Further, there is a disturbing lack of agreement between the norms in the manual (1959) and the supplemental norms issued in 1963 and 1967. Median score for the "total employed population" is listed as 77 in the manual, while the supplementary norms for "countrywide evaluatees" give a median of 65. Similarly, for "white collar" personnel there is a major discrepancy between the 1959 norms and the supplementary norms: medians of 77 versus 67, respectively. These are discrepancies of nearly a full standard deviation, raising a red flag cautioning the user about the meaningfulness of the norms for his setting. The performance levels for many of the norm groups seem to be exceptionally high, particularly for executives and middle management. A raw score of 75 correct for the 100 items falls at the 2nd percentile for executives, 15th percentile for middle management, 50th percentile for engineers, and *also* at the 50th percentile for the total employed population. Some of these group differences suggest that the test administration or sampling conditions may have been quite different for the various norm groups. Finally, one's confidence in the technical adequacy of the norms is further shaken by the fact that in four out of nine cases the median score listed in the manual for a specific norm group does not correspond with the score falling at the 50th percentile in the norms! In view of these reservations about the accuracy and generalizability of the norms, the usual recommendations about the development of local norms need even greater emphasis for this test.

The manual gives the pretense of offering validity data, but, in fact, criterion-related validity information showing the utility of the instrument as a selection device is critically lacking. One looks in vain for a correlation between scores on this test and job performance. The "validity" section of the manual merely presents correlations between this test and other tests of vocabulary knowledge and general ability. The correlations with general ability tests range from .53 to .67, and despite the manual's claim that "vocabulary development is consistently highly correlated with intelligence," these values are not high enough to support the use of this test as an adequate substitute for a longer measure of general ability, particularly if decisions about individuals are required.

The APA Task Force on Employment Testing of Minority Groups[1] warns against the possibility of unfair personnel practices resulting from the use of a job-irrelevant or unduly difficult aptitude test to screen applicants or candidates for promotion. The difficulty level and apparent irrelevance of many of the words to business usage raise questions about the fairness of the instrument with disadvantaged populations. It is conceivable that one may get a good measure of social background with this test but not a measure of adequacy of word usage in any practical setting. The method of selection of the words, by sampling from a dictionary, tends to make some of the key words archaic and infrequently used in everyday communications. Such an emphasis is laudable for a test designed to predict skill at solving crossword puzzles, but if the task is to identify people with an adequate vocabulary for a particular employment role, it is *logically* difficult to justify the use of this test. It may be *empirically* quite defensible, but we are given no information to decide this issue. In the absence of empirical evidence for the validity of this test with culturally different groups, extreme caution is urged in the use of this test for selection purposes in any setting where applicants come from diverse social backgrounds.

In summary, the vocabulary domain repre-

sented by this test has been carefully specified and the items are well constructed. Although the manual fails to emphasize the value of locally developed norms, this need is particularly intense in this case because of the apparent deficiencies in the published norms. Insufficient validity information is given to justify the use of this instrument as a selection device. Ideally, the user of this test should be able to conduct validity studies within his own organization with special attention, where appropriate to the validity of the test, to specific jobs and specific groups of applicants.

ROBERT FITZPATRICK, *Principal Research Scientist, American Institutes for Research, Pittsburgh, Pennsylvania.*

In the brief manual for this test, the author justifies the development of still another vocabulary test on the grounds that no other such test has been standardized on employed groups. But he could have developed norms using employed groups for any of several other vocabulary tests, to essentially the same effect. The normative data he has provided, though useful and reasonably well described, are not so extensive or unusual as to outweigh the disadvantages of proliferating tests.

The 100 stimulus words for the test, according to the manual, "were chosen at random from the even numbered pages of the Oxford Universal Dictionary." This can scarcely have been the whole method, since all the words are nouns, verbs, or adjectives. Whatever the exact method, it resulted in a rather odd set of words. The greatest oddity is that two of the words are *applaud* and *applause.*

The *Oxford Universal Dictionary* is an abridgement of the *Oxford English Dictionary,* a classic work which is both relatively old and British. Thus, item 83, *defedation,* does not appear in the *Random House Dictionary of the English Language* (1967, hereafter abbreviated as RH) and is listed as archaic in *Webster's Third New International Dictionary* (1966, hereafter WT). For the stimulus word *hoyden,* the keyed synonym *clown* does not appear in RH and appears in WT only as part of a definition labeled obsolete: "a rude clownish youth." Similarly, *overflow* for *redound* is not given by RH and is labeled archaic by WT.

Some other questionable pairings: the key for *theory* is *hypothesis;* for *commissary, commissioner;* for *espy, spy;* for *treadle, lever;* for

1 APA TASK FORCE ON EMPLOYMENT TESTING OF MINORITY GROUPS. "Job Testing and the Disadvantaged." *Am Psychol* 24(7):637–50 Jl '69. *

Bruce Vocabulary Inventory

tangential, erratic (the last scarcely justified by one definition in WT: "deviating widely and sometimes erratically"). As a synonym for *jovial, happy* is keyed in preference to another choice, *pleasant;* for *substantiate, prove* is preferred to *bolster;* and for *pointless, meaningless* to *rounded.* (Some of these pairings might be suitable for examinees who speak the British version of the language. However, the norms appear to be based wholly on Americans and the test is marketed in the United States.)

Such difficulties are usually thought likely to lead to considerable guessing by examinees, to reduced reliability, and to poor validity. Other vocabulary tests have achieved useful results without such ambiguities, archaisms, and odd definitions. Even if some gain in validity of one kind or another resulted from these means, it might not be worth it. A test serves many functions, intended or not. It is, for example, a learning experience for the examinee. The examinee also judges the whole testing movement on the basis of his perceptions of the fairness and relevance of the tests he takes. Surely it is important on a number of grounds to be as accurate, fair, and relevant as we can in our tests.

The idea of sampling words for a vocabulary test from a dictionary is a superficially attractive one. But a dictionary is a repository of (not entirely obsolete) words and does not distinguish, other than by the length of the listings, the relative importance of the words. How should the items in a vocabulary test be chosen? Many would agree that the stimulus words should represent a sample from some population of words. But what is the best population? In a spelling test developed for the *Clerical Skills Series,* Bruce chose the stimulus words on the basis of his observations of common errors in business contexts. For the applications to industry intended by Bruce, it might be appropriate to sample from the *Wall Street Journal* or *Business Week.* Then, one could assess the degree to which the examinee has a relevant vocabulary. The basic difficulty is not the choice of an old British dictionary to sample from, but the choice of any dictionary.

The directions give the examinee no hint of whether he should guess if uncertain of the answer. Since the score is the number correct, the examinee who guesses has an advantage.

Reliability and validity are discussed only very briefly in the manual. Reliability is on the low side but is adequate as reported. Validity data consist entirely of correlations with other tests. More data are available on the vocabulary test of the *Clerical Skills Series,* consisting of the odd-numbered items of this test. The latter data are generally favorable and suggest that, if data are collected for the full version, they may be better than inspection of the test suggests.

It is possible that the *Bruce Vocabulary Inventory* may have some value in rather specialized applications, but its use at present, especially for persons who learned English in America, is not recommended.

[232]

RBH Vocabulary Test. Applicants for clerical and stenographic positions; 1948–63; 1 form ('48, 2 pages); manual ['63, 8 pages]; directions (no date, 2 pages); no data on reliability; $3.50 per 25 tests; 50¢ per key; $1.50 per manual; $1.50 per specimen set; postage extra; 5(10) minutes; Richardson, Bellows, Henry & Co., Inc. *

FRED H. BORGEN, *Research Psychologist, National Merit Scholarship Corporation, Evanston, Illinois.*

The *RBH Vocabulary Test* is designed as a brief measure of verbal skills for use in the "screening and selection of applicants of both sexes for a variety of clerical and stenographic positions." Sixty-four pairs of words are presented on a single page and the examinee is given a total of five minutes to decide whether the words in each pair mean the same thing, are opposite in meaning, or are neither the same nor opposite. Inspection of the items substantiates the manual's claim that the items are appropriate for a wide range of clerical applicants, with item-difficulties apparently suitable for all but the marginally literate and the exceptionally able.

Two pairs of words, which are synonyms in this reviewer's dictionary, are incorrectly keyed. The words *effrontery-temerity* are incorrectly keyed as opposites and *limpid-lucid* are incorrectly keyed as being neither synonyms nor antonyms. Such carelessness is a matter of concern on a test as brief as this where reliability is likely to be marginal even when the test is correctly scored.

Wisely, the normative and other data have been presented separately for men and women; the normative data for women, representing both applicant and employee groups, are somewhat more precise. However, this apparent preciseness of the norms is seductive, since the composition of the norm groups is neither well specified nor representative of any significant population. Cross-checking of the tables in the manual reveals that a single oil company was the source for *all* of the women in the employees' norm group and 91 percent of the men in the male norm group. Thus, the norms are not representative of any widely relevant reference group and, at best, will have only suggestive value in most settings. Users should take seriously the authors' injunction that "norms developed on local populations are always of most value."

For some unexplained reason, the authors present no reliability data to demonstrate either internal consistency or temporal stability for scores on this test. If one were evaluating a test for personnel decisions and were forced to have either reliability *or* validity data, he no doubt would choose validity data. The fact that the present validity data show some non-zero relationship of *Vocabulary Test* scores with job performance does indicate minimal reliability for this 64-item test. Moreover, the correlations for this test with other tests do at least give some lower-bound estimates of the reliability of this instrument. For example, scores on this test are shown to correlate .77 with scores on the *RBH Test of Language Skills*. But why must we perform such mental gymnastics to divine the reliability of this test when the authors could easily have calculated reliability coefficients? Such information should be considered mandatory, particularly for an instrument which consists of only a five-minute sample of behavior.

It is refreshing to see validity data reported with such candor. The manual presents eight small-scale validity studies in samples of clerical workers, usually with annual performance ratings as the criterion. Regrettably, the authors do not make clear whether the coefficients reflect concurrent or predictive validity. Five of the eight validity coefficients fall between .15 and .21, and—here the candor enters—two of the coefficients are embarrassingly negative at −.08 and −.14. Because of the very small size of most of the validation samples, the correlations are statistically significant for only two studies; however, if one is willing to pool the results over the several studies, he should be able to conclude confidently that there is a generally significant relationship between test score and clerical performance. For seven of the eight validity studies the manual explicitly reports that this vocabulary test was used, at least in part, for the selection of the employees in the validation samples. Consequently, there is some truncation of test score variance in these samples and the obtained correlations probably underestimate the actual validity of the test as a selection device. It seems fair to conclude that the test has a promising, though quite modest, capacity to predict performance in some clerical occupations.

The authors have made a good beginning in presenting validity data. Confidence in the instrument will be enhanced by continued development of more extensive and more precise validity information. Future studies should be based on larger samples, and some studies should include other predictive variables to indicate the incremental validity of this particular test. Such extended information should help the potential user identify the kinds of situations where this test is likely to be most appropriate as a selection device.

In summary, this is an attractively packaged test which *appears* to be a well-designed quick measure of the verbal skills of applicants for clerical and stenographic positions. The data presented in the manual partially confirm these expectations for the test, although the manual is distressingly brief and is particularly negligent in failing to report reliability data. No claims can be made for the generality of the norms; users will be better served by locally developed norms. Because of the sparseness of the information in the manual, the ideal user of this test should be qualified to judge the merit of this instrument for personnel decisions in his own setting. This effort would include: (*a*) modifying the present scoring key for the two items which are miskeyed; and (*b*) collecting local normative, reliability, and validity data. Potential users not prepared to undertake these steps should probably await appropriate revisions and clarification by the test publishers.

[233]

*Sanders-Fletcher Vocabulary Test. 1, 2 semesters in grades 9–13; 1938–64; first published 1938 in the Every Pupil Scholarship Test series; Forms A, B, ('64, 4 pages); 2 levels labeled Tests 1, 2; manual ('64, 3 pages); $1.75 per 25 tests, postage extra; 75¢ per specimen set, postpaid; 40(45) minutes; Gwen Fletcher and M. W. Sanders; Data Processing and Educational Measurement Center. *

Sanders-Fletcher Vocabulary Test

[234]
*Survey Test of Vocabulary. Grades 3–12; 1931–
65; Forms X₄ ('40, 4 pages, identical with Form X
copyrighted 1931), Z₄ ('65, 4 pages) ; no manual; key-
norms sheets (no dates) ; no data on reliability; $2.25
per 50 tests, postage extra; 25¢ per specimen set, postpaid; 20(25) minutes; L. J. O'Rourke; O'Rourke
Publications. *

REFERENCES

1. See 3:167.
2–4. See 5:239.

*For reviews by Verner M. Sims and Clifford
Woody, see 3:167.*

[235]
Vocabulary Test for High School Students and
College Freshmen. Grades 9–13; 1964; Forms A, B,
(2 pages) ; manual (9 pages) ; reliability data for
longer experimental form only; provisional norms;
$3.60 per 35 IBM 1230 test-answer sheets; $1 per set
of scoring stencils; 60¢ per specimen set; postage
extra; 15(20) minutes; Arthur E. Traxler; Bobbs-
Merrill Co., Inc. *

REFERENCE

1. TRAXLER, ARTHUR E. "Some Aspects of the Vocabulary
of Independent Secondary School Pupils." *Ed Rec B* 87:44–9
F '65. *

GEORGE P. WINSHIP, JR., *Professor of English
and Chairman of the Department, King College,
Bristol, Tennessee.*

Two neat little vocabulary tests, 50 words
apiece, not in booklets but printed directly on
IBM answer sheets, promise great usefulness.
They are simple to administer, take only 15
minutes of working time, and cost about a dime
a copy.

The tests were copyrighted in 1964, having
been constructed and tried out in the early
'60's. The words and definitions were chosen,
however, not on the basis of what students were
then reading and having trouble in understanding, but rather from the Thorndike-Lorge frequency list (published in 1944 but based upon
much earlier books) and from the *Thorndike
Century Senior Dictionary* of 1941. The impression given by the tests is strangely quaint,
like that of a reprinted Montgomery Ward
catalog or a McGuffey *Reader.*

The stem words are given in a sentence or
brief context, but the compiler appears to have
worked from his frequency list and his dictionary in isolation from the living language on
which students are to be tested. An item reads,
"Her dress has longitudinal stripes," although
that adjective is generally employed for a hori-
zontal dimension, and dresses are always described with the wearer standing. (Even the
Shorter Oxford Dictionary marks the vertical
use as obsolete.) *Combustible* is matched to
inflammable in spite of the confusion recently

created by the revival of *flammable* in this
sense. For "She has a *seductive* manner," the
correct answer is *captivating,* in spite of what
high school and college students have been reading the past few years. "He used the native
parlance" is to be equated with *language,* as if
parlance were normally used for Spanish,
French, Swahili, or the like. Any of these items
might have been produced with a dictionary by
a foreigner knowing a little English, or by a
computer. Few items do anything to teach or to
test a really sensitive command of idiomatic
English, and some of them actually penalize the
well-read student who has met the words in a
variety of literary contexts.

Mental measurements are not diagnostic tools
in isolation from the whole process of education; they are an element in education. A vocabulary test may render a young person more or
less aware of the meanings and use of words.
The student is a living being, and the cells of
his intellect ought not to be killed under the
microscope.

J Ed Meas 3:71–2 sp '66. Joan Bollenbacher.
* An unfortunate misprint in Table 4 should
be noted * "*ACT* Total Score" is listed in error,
instead of "*ACE* Total Score." While the ACE
Total Score is discussed in the text, the casual
reader who looks only at the statistical table
could misinterpret this statistic as relating to
the American College Test. * the manual....is
clearly written and should be understood even
by those who are scared of statistics * In the
view of English curriculum consultants whom
the writer consulted, the range of difficulty of
the items is such that it should make the test a
useful instrument to determine which pupils are
weak in vocabulary, which are proficient. The
instructions are clear and should cause no problem. The pale blue print of the IBM 1230
answer sheet, however, may be difficult for some
pupils to read. Perhaps a darker ink compatible
to the 1230 could be located for the next printing. The item choices are well done and contain
no clues that would give the word away. In
summary, the test is a good one to provide just
what the author said—"a simple, easily and
quickly administered test of general vocabulary
for use with high school students and freshmen
entering college."

[236]
★Vocabulary Test: McGraw-Hill Basic Skills
System. Grades 11–14; 1970; also called *MHBSS*

Vocabulary Test; although designed for use with the MHBSS instructional program, the test may be used independently; Forms A, B, (7 pages); manual (31 pages); separate answer sheets (Digitek, IBM 1230, Scoreze) must be used; $4.90 per 25 tests; $2.50 per 50 Digitek or IBM answer sheets; $3 per 25 Scoreze answer sheets; $1 per Digitek or IBM scoring stencil; postage extra; $1.25 per specimen set, postpaid; IBM scoring service, 25¢ and over per test ($20 minimum); 12(22) minutes; Alton L. Raygor; McGraw-Hill Book Co., Inc. *

GEORGE P. WINSHIP, JR., *Professor of English and Chairman of the Department, King College, Bristol, Tennessee.*

These tests are part of the extensive battery of tests, tapes, books, and cards comprising the McGraw-Hill's Basic Skills System. Though only the vocabulary test is discussed here, it should be considered in relation to all these materials.

They have been produced, according to the publisher, largely for the sake of ill-prepared students who are attempting the college experience under open admissions policies. Specifically, the materials begin at a tenth-grade level of difficulty with content from college subjects. There are tests to diagnose deficiencies in several distinct elements of intellectual skill (listening, skimming, taking notes, and the like)—more than a dozen skills grouped in six tests, of which vocabulary, at 12 minutes, is the shortest. There are instructional and practice materials for each of the skills, and a parallel form of each test to confirm after the practice that the skill has indeed been learned.

The purpose is worthy, for the sake of the millions who have the maturity, ambition, and intelligence to profit from college but who lack the techniques of study. These are not only the "disadvantaged"; recommended youngsters from good schools need some of this help.

The vocabulary tests are in two parts. First are 30 words to be identified by meaning (6 minutes), then 25 problems in interpreting roots and affixes (the rest of the student's 12 minutes); for an average score he should finish about half the items correctly. The words are drawn from fields studied in college (examples are, *morphology, anode, antecedent, primogeniture*); the items are carefully ordered by difficulty. This part is directly diagnostic of the deficiencies in vocabulary which will give a student trouble. The second part tests ability to use etymology to master hard words. It contains artificial combinations for which he must select plausible meanings (*neophobia* he should iden-

tify as "fear of newness," *reduct,* as "to lead again").

The part with artificial words will seem to most teachers the more interesting, I believe, and to most students the more bewildering. A highly qualified student who has been taught to notice etymology will be put off by some insensitively constructed nonce words: the unlikely *nonvoluta* and *satisverus* may make him pause (and lose points). For *malvert* he is required to select "a bad turn," but he ought to boggle at it for a moment, searching in vain for the proper equivalent, "to turn badly" ("a bad turn" might be a *malversion*). So the best student will be penalized. But this ideal student was not intended to use the MHBSS in the first place.

Much more likely is that the *average* student on the first, or diagnostic, test will be so confused by this unfamiliar way of gauging his knowledge that he will score deceptively low. Such has been my experience when a class meets a problem that is novel or original; and I have tried this kind of etymological exercise. There are wide differences in the students' ability to cope with the unfamiliar. This ability, of course, is important to success in college, but it is not the same as knowing words. The present test is supposed to diagnose a particular weakness and to measure the success of particular MHBSS materials. But it is certainly possible that the second test, after the instruction, will come as a more familiar and much less formidable task; would the second scores not be higher, for many students, whether the instruction had been effective or not? (Only trials in which students take both tests without intervening lessons in etymology can resolve this possible ambiguity of the test scores.)

In view of our sense of urgency to meet the needs of the ill-prepared and of the advent of schemes that promise quick and measurable gains for problem students, we must take great care that our measures are valid as well as reliable.

[237]

*Word Clue Tests. Grades 7–13 and adults; 1962–65; designed primarily for use with instructional booklets in the Word Clues series; 2 tests; manual ('65, 6 pages); no data on reliability; no norms; separate answer sheets must be used; 25¢ per test; $2 per 100 answer sheets; 20¢ per scoring stencil; 50¢ per manual (free with 25 or more tests); postage extra; (40–45) minutes; Stanford E. Taylor, Helen Frackenpohl, and Arthur S. McDonald; Educational Developmental Laboratories, Inc. *

a) WORD CLUE TEST. WCT; Forms A, B, ('62, 15 pages); 65¢ per specimen set.

b) WORD CLUE APPRAISAL. WCA; special edition available to nonprofessionals for self appraisal; Forms AA ('62, 15 pages), BB ('65, 15 pages).

[238]

★**Word Understanding.** Grades 6–12; 1969; WU; 1 form; 2 editions; manual ['69, 3 pages]; norms for junior high school only; $3.75 per 25 tests; 50¢ per manual; $1 per specimen set of either edition; postpaid; 8(10) minutes; R. Hoepfner, M. Hendricks, and R. H. Silverman; Monitor. *

a) REUSABLE EDITION. 1 form (3 pages); separate answer sheets (IBM 805) must be used; $1 per 25 answer sheets; 50¢ per scoring stencil.

b) CONSUMABLE EDITION. Form C (3 pages); 50¢ per key.

TIP II SCANNING INDEX

This classified index of all tests in *Tests in Print II* can be used to determine what tests are available in areas besides English. Citations are to test entry numbers in TIP II. The population for which a test is intended is included. Stars indicate tests not previously listed in an MMY; asterisks indicate tests revised or supplemented since last listed. The English portion of this index, the only part relevant to this monograph, is repeated at the end of this volume.

ACHIEVEMENT BATTERIES

Academic Proficiency Battery [South Africa], college entrants, see 1

Adult Basic Education Student Survey, poorly educated adults in basic education classes, see 2

Adult Basic Learning Examination, adults with achievement levels grades 1–12, see 3

American School Achievement Tests, grades 1–9, see 4

Bristol Achievement Tests [England], ages 8–13, see 5

*CLEP General Examinations: Humanities, 1–2 years of college or equivalent, see 6

*California Achievement Tests, grades 1–14, see 7

Canadian Tests of Basic Skills [Canada], grades 3–8, see 8

Classification and Placement Examination, grade 8 and high school entrants, see 9

*College-Level Examination Program General Examinations, 1–2 years of college or equivalent, see 10

*Comprehensive Tests of Basic Skills, grades kgn–12, see 11

Cooperative Primary Tests, grades 1.5–3, see 12

★*Educational Skills Tests: College Edition,* open-door college entrants, see 13

General Tests of Language and Arithmetic [South Africa], standards 5–7, see 14

Gray-Votaw-Rogers General Achievement Tests, grades 1–9, see 15

★*Guidance Test for Junior Secondary Bantu Pupils in Form 3* [South Africa], see 16

High School Fundamentals Evaluation Test, grades 9–12, see 17

Iowa High School Content Examination, grades 11–13, see 18

*Iowa Tests of Basic Skills, grades 1.7–9, see 19

*Iowa Tests of Educational Development, grades 9–12, see 20

Ligondé Equivalence Test [Canada], adults who left elementary or secondary school 15–20 years ago, see 21

*Metropolitan Achievement Tests, grades kgn–9, see 22

National Achievement Tests, grades 4–9, see 23

*National Educational Development Tests, grades 7–10, see 24

*National Teacher Examinations: Common Examinations, college seniors and teachers, see 25

Peabody Individual Achievement Test, grades kgn–12, see 26

★*Primary Survey Tests,* grades 2–3, see 27

Public School Achievement Tests, grades 3–8, see 28

*SRA Achievement Series, grades 1–9, see 29

*SRA Assessment Survey, grades 1–12, see 30

*SRA High School Placement Test, grade 9 entrants, see 31

*STS Closed High School Placement Test, grade 9 entrants, see 32

*STS Educational Development Series, grades 2–12, see 33

*Scholastic Proficiency Battery [South Africa], standards 8–10, see 34

*Sequential Tests of Educational Progress, grades 4–14, see 35

*Stanford Achievement Test, grades 1.5–9, see 36

Stanford Achievement Test: High School Basic Battery, grades 9–12, see 37

*Stanford Early School Achievement Test, grades kgn–1.5, see 38

★*Stanford Test of Academic Skills,* grades 8–12 and first year junior/community college, see 39

Survey of College Achievement, grades 13–14, see 40

*Teacher Education Examination Program: General Professional Examinations, college seniors preparing to teach, see 41

*Test for High School Entrants, high school entrants, see 42

Test of Reading and Number: Inter-American Series, grade 4 entrants, see 43

*Tests of Academic Progress, grades 9–12, see 44

ENGLISH

LITERATURE

SPELLING

VOCABULARY

FINE ARTS

ART

MUSIC

FOREIGN LANGUAGES

ARABIC

CHINESE

ENGLISH

FRENCH

GERMAN

GREEK

HEBREW

ITALIAN

LATIN

RUSSIAN

SPANISH

INTELLIGENCE

GROUP

INDIVIDUAL

SPECIFIC

MATHEMATICS

ALGEBRA

ERB Modern Elementary Algebra Test, grades 8–9, see 675

ERB Modern Second Year Algebra Test, high school, see 676

Elementary Algebra: Achievement Examinations for Secondary Schools, high school, see 677

Elementary Algebra: Minnesota High School Achievement Examinations, high school, see 678

First Year Algebra Test: National Achievement Tests, 1 year high school, see 679

Illinois Algebra Test, 1–2 semesters high school, see 680

Iowa Algebra Aptitude Test, grade 8, see 681

Kepner Mid-Year Algebra Achievement Tests, 1 semester high school, see 682

Lankton First-Year Algebra Test, grades 8–12, see 683

Lee Test of Algebraic Ability, grades 7–8, see 684

Mid-Year Algebra Test, high school, see 685

★Modern Algebra Test: Content Evaluation Series, 1 year high school, see 686

★Objective Tests in Mathematics: Algebra [England], ages 15 and over, see 687

Orleans-Hanna Algebra Prognosis Test, grades 7–11, see 688

Survey Test of Algebraic Aptitude, grade 8, see 689

ARITHMETIC

A.C.E.R. Arithmetic Tests: Standardized for Use in New Zealand [New Zealand], ages 9–12, see 690

A.C.E.R. Number Test [Australia], ages 13.5 and over, see 691

★Adston Diagnostic Instruments in Elementary School Mathematics: Whole Numbers, grades 4–8, see 692

American Numerical Test, adults in "that great middle and upper middle block of vocations which emphasize shop and white collar skills involving number competence," see 693

American School Achievement Tests: Arithmetic Readiness, grades kgn–1, see 694

American School Achievement Tests: Part 2, Arithmetic, grades 2–9, see 695

Analytical Survey Test in Computational Arithmetic, grades 7–12, see 696

Arithmetic Computation: Public School Achievement Tests, grades 3–8, see 697

Arithmetic Reasoning: Public School Achievement Tests, grades 3–8, see 698

Arithmetic Reasoning Test, clerical applicants and high school, see 699

Arithmetic Test (Fundamentals and Reasoning): Municipal Tests, grades 3–8, see 700

Arithmetic Test: National Achievement Tests, grades 3–8, see 701

*Arithmetic Tests EA2A and EA4 [England], ages 14.5 and over, see 702

*Arithmetical Problems: Test A/68 [South Africa], job applicants with at least 10 years of education, see 703

Basic Skills in Arithmetic Test, grades 6–12, see 704

Bobbs-Merrill Arithmetic Achievement Tests, grades 1–9, see 705

Brief Survey of Arithmetic Skills, grades 7–12, see 706

*Comprehensive Tests of Basic Skills: Arithmetic, grades 2.5–12, see 707

Computation Test A/67 [South Africa], job applicants with at least 6 years of education, see 708

Cooperative Mathematics Tests: Arithmetic, grades 7–9, see 709

*Cotswold Junior Arithmetic Ability Tests [Scotland], ages 8.5–10.5, see 710

*Cotswold Measurement of Ability: Arithmetic [Scotland], ages 10–12, see 711

*Diagnostic Arithmetic Tests [South Africa], standards 2–5 (ages 9–12), see 712

Diagnostic Chart for Fundamental Processes in Arithmetic, grades 2–8, see 713

★Diagnostic Decimal Tests 1–3 [Australia], ages 9–13, see 714

Diagnostic Fractions Test 3 [Australia], ages 7–11, see 715

Diagnostic Number Tests 1–2 [Australia], ages 8–12, see 716

Diagnostic Tests and Self-Helps in Arithmetic, grades 3–12, see 717

*ERB Modern Arithmetic Test, grades 5–6, see 718

Emporia Arithmetic Tests, grades 1–8, see 719

Kelvin Measurement of Ability in Arithmetic [Scotland], ages 7–12, see 720

★KeyMath Diagnostic Arithmetic Test, grades kgn–7, see 721

Moray House Arithmetic Test [England], ages 10–12, see 722

★Moreton Arithmetic Tests [Australia], grades 6–7, see 723

N.B. Arithmetic Tests [South Africa], standards 2–8 (ages 9–15), see 724

Number Test DE [England], ages 10.5–12.5, see 725

*Office Arithmetic Test, job applicants, see 726

RBH Arithmetic Fundamentals Test, business and industry, see 727

RBH Arithmetic Reasoning Test, business and industry, see 728

RBH Shop Arithmetic Test, industry, see 729

Revised Southend Attainment Test in Mechanical Arithmetic [England], ages 7–15, see 730

SRA Achievement Series: Arithmetic, grades 1–9, see 731

SRA Arithmetic Index, job applicants with poor educational backgrounds, see 732–3

Schonell Diagnostic Arithmetic Tests [Scotland], ages 7–13, see 734

*Seeing Through Arithmetic Tests, grades 1–6, see 735

Southend Attainment Test in Mechanical Arithmetic [England], ages 6–14, see 736

Staffordshire Arithmetic Test [England], ages 7–15, see 737

Stanford Diagnostic Arithmetic Test, grades 2.5–8.5, see 738

Survey Tests of Arithmetic Fundamentals [Canada], grades 3–8, see 739

Test A/8: Arithmetic [South Africa], technical college students and applicants for clerical and trade positions with 8–12 years of education, see 740

Watson Number-Readiness Test [Canada], grades kgn–1, see 741

CALCULUS

*Advanced Placement Examination in Mathematics: Calculus, high school students desiring credit for college level courses or admission to advanced courses, see 742

*CLEP Subject Examination in Introductory Calculus, 1 year or equivalent, see 743

Cooperative Mathematics Tests: Calculus, high school and college, see 744

GEOMETRY

Cooperative Mathematics Tests: Analytic Geometry, high school and college, see 745

SPECIAL FIELDS

TRIGONOMETRY

MISCELLANEOUS

AGRICULTURE

BLIND

BUSINESS EDUCATION

COMPUTATIONAL & TESTING DEVICES

★*Bowman Chronological Age Calculator,* see 802
Bowman M.A. and I.Q. Kalculator, see 803
**Chronological Age Computer,* ages 3-7 to 19-5, see 804
Dominion Table for Converting Mental Age to I.Q. [Canada], see 805
Grade Averaging Charts, see 806
I.Q. Calculator, see 807
★*Mental Age Calculator,* see 808
**Multiple Purpose Self Trainer,* high school and adults, see 809
Psychometric Research and Service Chart Showing the Davis Difficulty and Discrimination Indices for Item Analysis [India], see 810
Rapid-Rater, see 811
★*Ratio I.Q. Computer,* see 812

COURTSHIP & MARRIAGE

★*Albert Mate Selection Check List,* premarital counselees, see 813
California Marriage Readiness Evaluation, premarital counselees, see 814
Caring Relationship Inventory, marital counselees, see 815
Courtship Analysis, adults, see 816
Dating Problems Checklist, high school and college, see 817
El Senoussi Multiphasic Marital Inventory, premarital and marital counselees, see 818
★*I-Am Sentence Completion Test,* marital counselees, see 819
Individual and Family Developmental Review, counselees and therapy patients, see 820
★*Love Attitudes Inventory,* grades 12–16, see 821
Male Impotence Test, adult males, see 822
Marital Communication Inventory, adults, see 823
★*Marital Diagnostic Inventory,* marital counselees, see 824
Marital Roles Inventory, marital counselees, see 825
Marriage Adjustment Form, adults, see 826
Marriage Adjustment Inventory, marital counselees, see 827
Marriage Adjustment Sentence Completion Survey, marital counselees, see 828
Marriage Analysis, married couples in counseling, see 829
★*Marriage Expectation Inventories,* engaged and married couples, see 830
Marriage-Personality Inventory, individuals and couples, see 831
Marriage Prediction Schedule, adults, see 832
Marriage Role Expectation Inventory, adolescents and adults, see 833
**Marriage Scale (For Measuring Compatibility of Interests),* premarital or married counselees, see 834
★*Marriage Skills Analysis,* marital counselees, see 835
Otto Pre-Marital Counseling Schedules, adult couples, see 836
★*Pair Attraction Inventory,* college and adults, see 837
Sex Knowledge Inventory, sex education classes in high school and college and adults, see 838
Sexual Development Scale for Females, adult females, see 839
**Taylor-Johnson Temperament Analysis,* grades 7–16 and adults, see 840
Thorman Family Relations Conference Situation Questionnaire, families receiving therapy, see 841

DRIVING & SAFETY EDUCATION

**American Automobile Association Driver Testing Apparatus,* drivers, see 842
**Bicycle Safety—Performance and Skill Tests,* ages 10–16, see 843
Driver Attitude Survey, drivers, see 844
★*Driving Skill Exercises,* automobile drivers, see 845
General Test on Traffic and Driving Knowledge, drivers, see 846
Hannaford Industrial Safety Attitude Scales, industry, see 847
McGlade Road Test for Use in Driver Licensing, Education and Employment, prospective drivers, see 848
Road Test Check List for Passenger Car Drivers, passenger car drivers, see 849
Siebrecht Attitude Scale, grades 9–16 and adults, see 850
★*Simplified Road Test,* drivers, see 851

EDUCATION

Academic Freedom Survey, college students and faculty, see 852
**CLEP Subject Examination in History of American Education,* 1 semester or equivalent, see 853
**CLEP Subject Examination in Tests and Measurements,* 1 semester or equivalent, see 854
★*Classroom Atmosphere Questionnaire,* grades 4–9, see 855
★*Comprehensive Teaching and Training Evaluation,* college and training programs, see 856
★*Counseling Services Assessment Blank,* college and adult counseling clients, see 857
★*Course Evaluation Questionnaire,* high school and college, see 858
Diagnostic Teacher-Rating Scale, grades 4–12, see 859
★*Educational Values Assessment Questionnaire,* adults, see 860
Faculty Morale Scale for Institutional Improvement, college faculty, see 861
★*General Tests of Language and Arithmetic for Students* [South Africa], first and second year Bantu candidates for primary teacher's certificate, see 862
**Graduate Record Examinations Advanced Education Test,* graduate school candidates, see 863
**Illinois Course Evaluation Questionnaire,* college, see 864
Illinois Ratings of Teacher Effectiveness, grades 9–12, see 865
Illinois Teacher Evaluation Questionnaire, grades 7–12, see 866
**Junior Index of Motivation,* grades 7–12, see 867
Minnesota Teacher Attitude Inventory, elementary and secondary school teachers and students in grades 12–17, see 868
**National Teacher Examinations,* college seniors and teachers, see 869
**National Teacher Examinations: Early Childhood Education,* college seniors and teachers, see 870
**National Teacher Examinations: Education in an Urban Setting,* college seniors and teachers, see 871
**National Teacher Examinations: Education in the Elementary School,* college seniors and teachers, see 872
**National Teacher Examinations: Education of Mentally Retarded,* college seniors and teachers, see 873
★*National Teacher Examinations: Educational Administration and Supervision,* prospective principals, see 874
★*National Teacher Examinations: Guidance Counselor,* prospective guidance counselors, see 875

HANDWRITING

HEALTH & PHYSICAL EDUCATION

HOME ECONOMICS

Minnesota Check List for Food Preparation and Serving, grades 7–16 and adults, see 951
★*National Teacher Examinations: Home Economics Education,* college seniors and teachers, see 952
★*Nutrition Information Test,* grades 9–16 and adults, see 953
Scales for Appraising High School Homemaking Programs, pupils, teachers, community members, and administrators, see 954
★*Teacher Education Examination Program: Home Economics Education,* college seniors preparing to teach secondary school, see 955
★*Test of Family Life Knowledge and Attitudes,* grade 12 boys and girls seeking Betty Crocker college scholarships and awards, see 956–66

INDUSTRIAL ARTS

Drawing: Cooperative Industrial Arts Tests, 1 semester grades 7–9, see 967
Electricity/Electronics: Cooperative Industrial Arts Tests, 1 semester grades 7–9, see 968
Emporia Industrial Arts Test, high school, see 969
General Industrial Arts: Cooperative Industrial Arts Tests, 1 year grades 7–9, see 970
Metals: Cooperative Industrial Arts Tests, 1 semester grades 7–9, see 971
★*National Teacher Examinations: Industrial Arts Education,* college seniors and teachers, see 972
★*Teacher Education Examination Program: Industrial Arts,* college seniors preparing to teach secondary school, see 973
Technical and Scholastic Test: Dailey Vocational Tests, grades 8–12 and adults, see 974
Woods: Cooperative Industrial Arts Tests, 1 semester grades 7–9, see 975

LEARNING DISABILITIES

★*Automated Graphogestalt Technique,* grades 1–4, see 976
★*Basic Screening and Referral Form for Children With Suspected Learning and Behavioral Disabilities,* grades 1–12, see 977
★*Cutrona Child Study Profile of Psycho-Educational Abilities,* grades kgn–3, see 978
First Grade Screening Test, first grade entrants, see 979
★*Grassi Basic Cognitive Evaluation,* ages 3–9, see 980
Illinois Test of Psycholinguistic Abilities, ages 2–10, see 981; *Filmed Demonstration of the ITPA,* see 982
★*Individual Learning Disabilities Classroom Screening Instrument,* grades 1–3, see 983
Meeting Street School Screening Test, grades kgn–1, see 984
★*Psychoeducational Inventory of Basic Learning Abilities,* ages 5–12 with suspected learning disabilities, see 985
Psychoeducational Profile of Basic Learning Abilities, ages 2–14 with learning disabilities, see 986
★*Pupil Rating Scale: Screening for Learning Disabilities,* grades 3–4, see 987
Screening Test for the Assignment of Remedial Treatments, ages 4-6 to 6-5, see 988
Screening Tests for Identifying Children With Specific Language Disability, grades 1–4, see 989
Specific Language Disability Test, "average to high IQ" children in grades 6–8, see 990
Valett Developmental Survey of Basic Learning Abilities, ages 2–7, see 991

LISTENING COMPREHENSION

★*Assessment of Children's Language Comprehension,* ages 2–6, see 992
Brown-Carlsen Listening Comprehension Test, grades 9–16 and adults, see 993
Cooperative Primary Tests: Listening, grades 1.5–3, see 994
Orr-Graham Listening Test, junior high school boys, see 995
★*Progressive Achievement Tests of Listening Comprehension* [New Zealand], standards 1–4 and Forms I–IV (ages 7–14), see 996
Sequential Tests of Educational Progress: Listening, grades 4–14, see 997
★*Tests for Auditory Comprehension of Language,* ages 3–7, see 997A

PHILOSOPHY

Graduate Record Examinations Advanced Philosophy Test, graduate school candidates, see 998
Undergraduate Program Field Tests: Philosophy Test, college, see 999
Undergraduate Program Field Tests: Scholastic Philosophy Test, college, see 1000

PSYCHOLOGY

Aden-Crosthwait Adolescent Psychology Achievement Test, college, see 1001
CLEP Subject Examination in Educational Psychology, 1 semester or equivalent, see 1002
CLEP Subject Examination in General Psychology, 1 semester or equivalent, see 1003
Cass-Sanders Psychology Test, high school and college, see 1004
Graduate Record Examinations Advanced Psychology Test, graduate school candidates, see 1005
Undergraduate Program Field Tests: Psychology Test, college, see 1006

RECORD & REPORT FORMS

A/9 Cumulative Record Folder, grades kgn–12, see 1007
American Council on Education Cumulative Record Folders, grades 1–16, see 1008
California Cumulative Record and Health Insert, grades 1–12, see 1009
Cassel Developmental Record, birth to death, see 1010
Florida Cumulative Guidance Record, grades 1–12, see 1011
G.C. Anecdotal Record Form [Canada], teachers' recordings of student actions, see 1012
Guidance Cumulative Folder and Record Forms, grades kgn–12, see 1013
Height Weight Interpretation Folders, ages 4–17, see 1014
Junior High School Record, grades 7–10, see 1015
Ontario School Record System [Canada], grades kgn–13, see 1016
★*Permanent Record Folder,* exceptional children, see 1017
★*Psychodiagnostic Test Report Blank,* psychologists' test data on clients, see 1018
Secondary-School Record, grades 9–12, see 1019

RELIGIOUS EDUCATION

Achievement Test in Jewish History, junior high school, see 1020

★*Achievement Test—Jewish Life and Observances,* grades 5–7, see 1021

★*Achievement Test—The State of Israel,* "pupils who have completed an organized course of study on the State of Israel," see 1022

★*Bible and You,* ages 13 and over, see 1023

★*Biblical Survey Test,* college, see 1024

Concordia Bible Information Inventory, grades 4–8, see 1025

Inventory of Religious Activities and Interests, high school and college students considering church-related occupations and theological school students, see 1025A

Religious Attitudes Inventory, religious counselees, see 1026

Standardized Bible Content Tests, Bible college, see 1027

Theological School Inventory, incoming seminary students, see 1028

Youth Research Survey, ages 13–19, see 1029

SCORING MACHINES & SERVICES

Automata EDT 1200 Educational Data Terminal, see 1030

Hankes Scoring Service, see 1031

IBM 1230 Optical Mark Scoring Reader, see 1032

★*IBM 3881 Optical Mark Reader,* see 1033

MRC Scoring and Reporting Services, see 1034

NCS Scoring and Reporting Services, see 1035

NCS Sentry 70, see 1036

OpScan Test Scoring and Document Scanning System, see 1037

Psychological Resources, see 1038

SOCIOECONOMIC STATUS

American Home Scale, grades 8–16, see 1039

Environmental Participation Index, culturally disadvantaged ages 12 and over, see 1040

Home Index, grades 4–12, see 1040A

Socio-Economic Status Scales [India], urban students, adults, and rural families, see 1041

STATISTICS

CLEP Subject Examination in Statistics, 1 semester or equivalent, see 1042

★*Objective Tests in Mathematics: Statistics* [England], ages 15 and over, see 1043

TEST PROGRAMS

ACT Assessment, candidates for college entrance, see 1044

Advanced Placement Examinations, high school students desiring credit for college level courses or admission to advanced courses, see 1045

Canadian Test Battery, Grade 10 [Canada], see 1046

Canadian Test Battery, Grades 8–9 [Canada], grades 8.5–9.0, see 1047

College Board Admissions Testing Program, candidates for college entrance, see 1048

★*College Guidance Program,* grade 11, see 1049

College-Level Examination Program, 1–2 years of college or equivalent, see 1050

College Placement Tests, entering college freshmen, see 1051

Comparative Guidance and Placement Program, entrants to two-year colleges and vocational-technical institutes, see 1052

Graduate Record Examinations: National Program for Graduate School Selection, graduate school candidates, see 1053

Junior College Placement Program, junior college entrants, see 1054

National Guidance Testing Program, grades 1.5–14, see 1055

National Science Foundation Graduate Fellowship Testing Program, applicants for N.S.F. fellowships for graduate study in the sciences, see 1056

★*Ohio Survey Tests,* grades 4, 6, 8, and 10, see 1057

Project Talent Test Battery, grades 9–12, see 1058

Secondary School Admission Test, grades 5–10, see 1059

★*Service for Admission to College and University Testing Program* [Canada], candidates for college entrance, see 1060

★*Testing Academic Achievement,* high school students desiring credit for college level courses or advanced placement, entering college freshmen, and 1–2 years of college or equivalent, see 1061

Undergraduate Program for Counseling and Evaluation, college, see 1062

MULTI-APTITUDE BATTERIES

Academic Promise Tests, grades 6–9, see 1063

★*Academic-Technical Aptitude Tests* [South Africa], "coloured pupils" in standards 6–8, see 1064

★*Aptitude Test for Junior Secondary Pupils* [South Africa], Bantus in Form I, see 1065

Aptitude Tests for Occupations, grades 9–13 and adults, see 1066

★*Armed Services Vocational Aptitude Battery,* high school, see 1067

Detroit General Aptitudes Examination, grades 6–12, see 1068

Differential Aptitude Tests, grades 8–12 and adults, see 1069

Differential Test Battery [England], ages 7 to "top university level," see 1070

Employee Aptitude Survey, ages 16 and over, see 1071

Flanagan Aptitude Classification Tests, grades 9–12 and adults, see 1072

General Aptitude Test Battery, grades 9–12 and adults, see 1073

Guilford-Zimmerman Aptitude Survey, grades 9–16 and adults, see 1074

High Level Battery: Test A/75 [South Africa], adults with at least 12 years of education, see 1075

★*International Primary Factors Test Battery,* grades 5 and over, see 1076

Jastak Test of Potential Ability and Behavior Stability, ages 11.5–14.5, see 1077

Job-Tests Program, adults, see 1078

★*Junior Aptitude Tests for Indian South Africans* [South Africa], standards 6–8, see 1079

Measurement of Skill, adults, see 1080

PERSONALITY

NONPROJECTIVE

PROJECTIVE

READING

DIAGNOSTIC

MISCELLANEOUS

OC Diagnostic Syllabizing Test, grades 4–6, see 1668
Phonics Test for Teachers, reading methods courses, see 1669
Reader Rater With Self-Scoring Profile, ages 15 and over, see 1670
Reader's Inventory, entrants to a reading improvement course for secondary and college students and adults, see 1671
Reading Eye II, grades 1–16 and adults, see 1672
Reading Versatility Test, grades 5–16, see 1673
Roswell-Chall Auditory Blending Test, grades 1–4, see 1674
Word Discrimination Test, grades 1–8, see 1675
★*Word Recognition Test* [England], preschool to age 8.5, see 1676

ORAL

★*Concise Word Reading Tests* [Australia], ages 7–12, see 1677
Flash-X Sight Vocabulary Test, grades 1–2, see 1678
Gilmore Oral Reading Test, grades 1–8, see 1679
Graded Word Reading Test [England], ages 5 and over, see 1680
Gray Oral Reading Test, grades 1–16 and adults, see 1681
Holborn Reading Scale [England], ages 5.5–10, see 1682
Neale Analysis of Reading Ability [England], ages 6–13, see 1683
★*Oral Reading Criterion Test,* reading level grades 1–7, see 1684
Oral Word Reading Test [New Zealand], ages 7–11, see 1685
★*Reading Miscue Inventory,* grades 1–7, see 1686
★*St. Lucia Graded Word Reading Test* [Australia], grades 2–7, see 1687
Slosson Oral Reading Test, grades 1–8 and high school, see 1688
Standardized Oral Reading Check Tests, grades 1–8, see 1689
Standardized Oral Reading Paragraphs, grades 1–8, see 1690

READINESS

ABC Inventory to Determine Kindergarten and School Readiness, entrants to kgn and grade 1, see 1691
APELL Test, Assessment Program of Early Learning Levels, ages 4.5–7, see 1692
Academic Readiness and End of First Grade Progress Scales, grade 1, see 1693
American School Reading Readiness Test, first grade entrants, see 1694
★*Analysis of Readiness Skills: Reading and Mathematics,* grades kgn–1, see 1695
Anton Brenner Developmental Gestalt Test of School Readiness, ages 5–6, see 1696
Basic Concept Inventory, preschool and kgn, see 1697
Binion-Beck Reading Readiness Test for Kindergarten and First Grade, grades kgn–1, see 1698
Clymer-Barrett Prereading Battery, first grade entrants, see 1699
Contemporary School Readiness Test, first grade entrants, see 1700
★*Delco Readiness Test,* first grade entrants, see 1701
Gates-MacGinitie Reading Tests: Readiness Skills, grades kgn–1, see 1702
Gesell Developmental Tests, ages 5–10, see 1703
Group Test of Reading Readiness, grades kgn–1, see 1704
Harrison-Stroud Reading Readiness Profiles, grades kgn–1, see 1705

★*Initial Survey Test,* first grade entrants, see 1706
★*Inventory of Primary Skills,* grades kgn–1, see 1707
★*Kindergarten Behavioural Index* [Australia], grades kgn–1, see 1708
Kindergarten Evaluation of Learning Potential, kgn, see 1709
★*LRS Seriation Test,* ages 4–6, see 1710
Lee-Clark Reading Readiness Test, grades kgn–1, see 1711
Lippincott Reading Readiness Test, grades kgn–1, see 1712
McHugh-McParland Reading Readiness Test, grades kgn–1, see 1713
Macmillan Reading Readiness Test, first grade entrants, see 1714
Maturity Level for School Entrance and Reading Readiness, grades kgn–1, see 1715
Metropolitan Readiness Tests, grades kgn–1, see 1716
Murphy-Durrell Reading Readiness Analysis, first grade entrants, see 1717
Parent Readiness Evaluation of Preschoolers, ages 3–9 to 5–8, see 1718
★*Pre-Reading Assessment Kit* [Canada], grades kgn–1, see 1719
★*Prereading Expectancy Screening Scales,* first grade entrants, see 1720
Pre-Reading Screening Procedures, first grade entrants of average or superior intelligence, see 1721
★*Preschool and Kindergarten Performance Profile,* preschool and kgn, see 1722
Primary Academic Sentiment Scale, ages 4-4 to 7-3, see 1723
Reading Aptitude Tests, grades kgn–1, see 1724
★*Reading Inventory Probe 1,* grades 1–2, see 1725
Reversal Test [Sweden], grade 1 entrants, see 1726
Riley Preschool Developmental Screening Inventory, ages 3–5, see 1727
School Readiness Checklist, ages 5–6, see 1728
School Readiness Survey, ages 4–6, see 1729
Screening Test of Academic Readiness, ages 4-0 to 6-5, see 1730
Sprigle School Readiness Screening Test, ages 4–6 to 6–9, see 1731
Steinbach Test of Reading Readiness, grades kgn–1, see 1732
Van Wagenen Reading Readiness Scales, first grade entrants, see 1733
Watson Reading-Readiness Test [Canada], grades kgn–1, see 1734

SPECIAL FIELDS

ANPA Foundation Newspaper Test, grades 7–12, see 1735
Adult Basic Reading Inventory, functionally illiterate adolescents and adults, see 1736
Iowa Tests of Educational Development: Ability to Interpret Reading Materials in the Social Studies, grades 9–12, see 1737
Iowa Tests of Educational Development: Ability to Interpret Reading Materials in the Natural Sciences, grades 9–12, see 1738
Purdue Reading Test for Industrial Supervisors, supervisors, see 1739
RBH Scientific Reading Test, employees in technical companies, see 1740
Reading Adequacy "READ" Test: Individual Placement Series, adults in industry, see 1741
Reading: Adult Basic Education Student Survey, poorly educated adults, see 1742
Reading Comprehension Test for Personnel Selection [England], applicants for technical training programs with high verbal content, see 1743

★*Reading/Everyday Activities in Life,* high school and "adults at basic education levels," see 1744
Robinson-Hall Reading Tests, college, see 1745
SRA Reading Index, job applicants with poor educational backgrounds, see 1746
Understanding Communication (Verbal Comprehension), industrial employees at the skilled level or below, see 1747

SPEED

*Basic Reading Rate Scale, grades 3–12, see 1748
Minnesota Speed of Reading Test for College Students, grades 12–16, see 1749

STUDY SKILLS

Bristol Achievement Tests: Study Skills [England], ages 8–13, see 1750
College Adjustment and Study Skills Inventory, college, see 1751
*Comprehensive Tests of Basic Skills: Study Skills, grades 2.5–12, see 1752
★*Cornell Class-Reasoning Test,* grades 4–12, see 1753
★*Cornell Conditional-Reasoning Test,* grades 4–12, see 1754
Cornell Critical Thinking Test, grades 7–16, see 1755
★*Cornell Learning and Study Skills Inventory,* grades 7–16, see 1756
Evaluation Aptitude Test, candidates for college and graduate school entrance, see 1757

*Iowa Tests of Educational Development: Use of Sources of Information, grades 9–12, see 1758
Library Orientation Test for College Freshmen, grade 13, see 1759
★*Library Tests,* college, see 1760
Logical Reasoning, grades 9–16 and adults, see 1761
★*National Test of Library Skills,* grades 2–12, see 1762
Nationwide Library Skills Examination, grades 4–12, see 1763
OC Diagnostic Dictionary Test, grades 5–8, see 1764
SRA Achievement Series: Work-Study Skills, grades 4–9, see 1765
*Study Attitudes and Methods Survey, high school and college, see 1766
Study Habits Checklist, grades 9–14, see 1767
Study Habits Inventory, grades 12–16, see 1768
Study Performance Test, high school and college, see 1769
Study Skills Counseling Evaluation, high school and college, see 1770
Study Skills Test: McGraw-Hill Basic Skills System, grades 11–14, see 1771
Survey of Study Habits and Attitudes, grades 7–14, see 1772
Test on Use of the Dictionary, high school and college, see 1773
★*Uncritical Inference Test,* college, see 1774
Watson-Glaser Critical Thinking Appraisal, grades 9–16 and adults, see 1775
★*Wisconsin Tests of Reading Skill Development: Study Skills,* grades kgn–7, see 1776

SCIENCE

Adkins-McBride General Science Test, high school, see 1777
Borman-Sanders Elementary Science Test, grades 5–8, see 1778
*CLEP General Examinations: Natural Sciences, 1–2 years of college or equivalent, see 1779
Cooperative Science Tests: Advanced General Science, grades 8–9, see 1780
Cooperative Science Tests: General Science, grades 7–9, see 1781
Elementary Science Test: National Achievement Tests, grades 4–6, see 1782
Emporia General Science Test, 1–2 semesters high school, see 1783
★*General Science Test* [South Africa], matriculants and higher, see 1784
General Science Test: National Achievement Tests, grades 7–9, see 1785
General Science III: Achievement Examinations for Secondary Schools, high school, see 1786
*Iowa Tests of Educational Development: General Background in the Natural Sciences, grades 9–12, see 1787
*National Teacher Examinations: Biology and General Science, college seniors and teachers, see 1788
*National Teacher Examinations: Chemistry, Physics and General Science, college seniors and teachers, see 1789
SRA Achievement Series: Science, grades 4–9, see 1790
*Science: Minnesota High School Achievement Examinations, grades 7–9, see 1791
Science Tests: Content Evaluation Series, grades 8–9, see 1792

Scientific Knowledge and Aptitude Test [India], high school, see 1793
*Sequential Tests of Educational Progress: Science, grades 4–14, see 1794
Stanford Achievement Test: High School Science Test, grades 9–12, see 1795
Stanford Achievement Test: Science, grades 5.5–9.9, see 1796
*Teacher Education Examination Program: Biology and General Science, college seniors preparing to teach secondary school, see 1797
*Teacher Education Examination Program: Chemistry, Physics and General Science, college seniors preparing to teach secondary school, see 1798
Tests of Academic Progress: Science, grades 9–12, see 1799

BIOLOGY

*Advanced Placement Examination in Biology, high school students desiring credit for college level courses or admission to advanced courses, see 1800
*BSCS Achievement Tests, grade 10, see 1801
*Biological Science: Interaction of Experiments and Ideas, grades 10–12, see 1802
*Biology: Minnesota High School Achievement Examinations, high school, see 1803
*CLEP Subject Examination in Biology, 1 year or equivalent, see 1804
*College Board Achievement Test in Biology, candidates for college entrance, see 1805
*College Placement Test in Biology, entering college freshmen, see 1806

Cooperative Biology Test: Educational Records Bureau Edition, high school, see 1807

Cooperative Science Tests: Biology, grades 10–12, see 1808

Emporia Biology Test, 1–2 semesters high school, see 1809

General Biology Test: National Achievement Tests, high school, see 1810

Graduate Record Examinations Advanced Biology Test, graduate school candidates, see 1811

Nelson Biology Test, grades 9–13, see 1812

Undergraduate Program Field Tests: Biology Test, college, see 1813

CHEMISTRY

ACS Cooperative Examination Brief Course in Organic Chemistry, 1 semester college, see 1814

ACS Cooperative Examination in Analytical Chemistry, Graduate Level, entering graduate students, see 1815

ACS Cooperative Examination in Biochemistry, college, see 1816

ACS Cooperative Examination in Brief Physical Chemistry, 1 semester college, see 1817

ACS Cooperative Examination in Brief Qualitative Analysis, college, see 1818

ACS Cooperative Examination in General Chemistry, 1 year college, see 1819

ACS Cooperative Examination in Inorganic Chemistry, grades 15–16, see 1820

ACS Cooperative Examination in Inorganic Chemistry, Graduate Level, entering graduate students, see 1821

ACS Cooperative Examination in Inorganic-Organic-Biological Chemistry (for Paramedical Programs), 1–2 semesters of chemistry for nursing, home economics, and other paramedical students, see 1822

ACS Cooperative Examination in Instrumental Analysis, grades 15–16, see 1823

ACS Cooperative Examination in Organic Chemistry, 1 year college, see 1824

ACS Cooperative Examination in Organic Chemistry, Graduate Level, entering graduate students, see 1825

ACS Cooperative Examination in Physical Chemistry, 1 year college, see 1826

ACS Cooperative Examination in Physical Chemistry, Graduate Level, entering graduate students, see 1827

ACS Cooperative Examination in Qualitative Analysis, college, see 1828

ACS Cooperative Examination in Quantitative Analysis, college, see 1829

ACS-NSTA Cooperative Examination in High School Chemistry, 1 year high school, see 1830

ACS-NSTA Cooperative Examination in High School Chemistry: Advanced Level, advanced high school classes, see 1831

Advanced Placement Examination in Chemistry, high school students desiring credit for college level courses or admission to advanced courses, see 1832

CLEP Subject Examination in General Chemistry, 1 year or equivalent, see 1833

Chemistry: Achievement Examinations for Secondary Schools, high school, see 1834

Chemistry Achievement Test for CHEM Study or Equivalent, high school, see 1835

Chemistry: Minnesota High School Achievement Examinations, high school, see 1836

College Board Achievement Test in Chemistry, candidates for college entrance, see 1837

College Placement Test in Chemistry, entering college freshmen, see 1838

Cooperative Chemistry Test: Educational Records Bureau Edition, high school, see 1839

Cooperative Science Tests: Chemistry, grades 10–12, see 1840

Emporia Chemistry Test, 1–2 semesters high school, see 1841

General Chemistry Test: National Achievement Tests, grades 10–16, see 1842

Graduate Record Examinations Advanced Chemistry Test, graduate school candidates, see 1843

Iowa Placement Examinations: Chemistry Aptitude, grades 12–13, see 1844

Iowa Placement Examinations: Chemistry Training, grades 12–13, see 1845

RBH Test of Chemical Comprehension, employee applicants and applicants for nurses' training, see 1846

Toledo Chemistry Placement Examination, college entrants, see 1847

Undergraduate Program Field Tests: Chemistry Test, college, see 1848

GEOLOGY

CLEP Subject Examination in Geology, 1 year or equivalent, see 1849

Graduate Record Examinations Advanced Geology Test, graduate school candidates, see 1850

Undergraduate Program Field Tests: Geology Test, college, see 1851

MISCELLANEOUS

Butler Life Science Concept Test, grades 1–6, see 1852

Dubins Earth Science Test, grades 8–12, see 1853

★*NM Concepts of Ecology Test,* grades 6–8, see 1854

★*Science Attitude Questionnaire* [England], secondary school, see 1855

Test on Understanding Science, grades 9–12, see 1856

Tests of Basic Experiences: Science, prekgn–grade 1, see 1857

PHYSICS

Advanced Placement Examination in Physics, high school students desiring credit for college level courses or admission to advanced courses, see 1858

College Board Achievement Test in Physics, candidates for college entrance, see 1859

College Placement Test in Physics, entering college freshmen, see 1860

Cooperative Physics Test: Educational Records Bureau Edition, high school, see 1861

Cooperative Science Tests: Physics, grades 10–12, see 1862

Dunning-Abeles Physics Test, grades 10–13, see 1863

Emporia Physics Test, 1–2 semesters high school, see 1864

General Physics Test: National Achievement Tests, grades 10–16, see 1865

Graduate Record Examinations Advanced Physics Test, graduate school candidates, see 1866

Iowa Placement Examinations: Physics Aptitude, grades 12–13, see 1867

Iowa Placement Examinations: Physics Training, grades 12–13, see 1868

★*Objective Tests in Physics,* high school, see 1869

Physics: Achievement Examinations for Secondary Schools, high school, see 1870

Physics: Minnesota High School Achievement Examinations, high school, see 1871

Tests of the Physical Science Study Committee, high school, see 1872

Undergraduate Program Field Tests: Physics Test, college, see 1873

SENSORY-MOTOR

D-K Scale of Lateral Dominance, grades 2–6, see 1874
Developmental Test of Visual-Motor Integration, ages 2–15, see 1875
★*Frostig Movement Skills Test Battery,* ages 6–12, see 1876
Harris Tests of Lateral Dominance, ages 7 and over, see 1877
Leavell Hand-Eye Coordinator Tests, ages 8–14, see 1878
MKM Picture Arrangement Test, grades kgn–6, see 1879
Moore Eye-Hand Coordination and Color-Matching Test, ages 2 and over, see 1880
Perceptual Forms Test, ages 5–8, see 1881
Primary Visual Motor Test, ages 4–8, see 1882
Purdue Perceptual-Motor Survey, ages 6–10, see 1883
★*Rosner Perceptual Survey,* ages 5–12, see 1884
Southern California Kinesthesia and Tactile Perception Tests, ages 4–8, see 1885
Southern California Perceptual-Motor Tests, ages 4–8, see 1886
Southern California Sensory Integration Tests, ages 4–10 with learning problems, see 1887
Spatial Orientation Memory Test, ages 5–8, see 1888
★*Symbol Digit Modalities Test,* ages 8 and over, see 1889
Trankell's Laterality Tests [Sweden], left-handed children in grades 1–2, see 1890
★*Wold Digit-Symbol Test,* ages 6–16, see 1891
★*Wold Sentence Copying Test,* grades 2–8, see 1892
★*Wold Visuo-Motor Test,* ages 6–16, see 1893

MOTOR

★*Devereux Test of Extremity Coordination,* emotionally handicapped and neurologically impaired ages 4–10, see 1894
Lincoln-Oseretsky Motor Development Scale, ages 6–14, see 1895
★*Manual Accuracy and Speed Test,* ages 4 and over, see 1896
★*Motor Problems Inventory,* preschool–grade 5, see 1897
Oseretsky Tests of Motor Proficiency: A Translation From the Portuguese Adaptation, ages 4–16, see 1898
Perrin Motor Coordination Test, adults, see 1899
Rail-Walking Test, ages 5 and over, see 1900
Smedley Hand Dynamometer, ages 6–18, see 1901
Southern California Motor Accuracy Test, ages 4–7 with nervous system dysfunction, see 1902
★*Teaching Research Motor-Development Scale,* moderately and severely retarded (preschool–grade 12), see 1903
★*Test of Motor Impairment* [Canada], ages 5–14, see 1904

VISION

A-B-C Vision Test for Ocular Dominance, ages 5 and over, see 1905
AO Sight Screener, adults, see 1906
Atlantic City Eye Test, grades 1 and over, see 1907
Basic Screen Test—Vision: Measurement of Skill Test 12, job applicants, see 1908
Burnham-Clark-Munsell Color Memory Test, adults, see 1909
Dennis Visual Perception Scale, grades 1–6, see 1910
Dvorine Pseudo-Isochromatic Plates, ages 3 and over, see 1911
Farnsworth Dichotomous Test for Color Blindness: Panel D–15, ages 12 and over, see 1912
Farnsworth-Munsell 100-Hue Test for the Examination of Color Discrimination, mental ages 12 and over, see 1913
★*Guy's Colour Vision Test for Young Children* [England], ages 3–5 and handicapped, see 1914
Inter-Society Color Council Color Aptitude Test, adults, see 1915
Keystone Ready-to-Read Tests, school entrants, see 1916
Keystone Tests of Binocular Skill, grades 1 and over, see 1917
Keystone Visual Screening Tests, preschool and over, see 1918
MKM Binocular Preschool Test, preschool, see 1919
MKM Monocular and Binocular Reading Test, grades 1 and over, see 1920
Marianne Frostig Developmental Test of Visual Perception, ages 3–8, see 1921
★*Motor-Free Visual Perception Test,* ages 4–8, see 1922
Ortho-Rater, adults, see 1923
Pseudo-Isochromatic Plates for Testing Color Perception, ages 7 and over, see 1924
School Vision Tester, grades kgn and over, see 1925
★*Sheridan Gardiner Test of Visual Acuity* [England], ages 5 and over, see 1926
★*Sloan Achromatopsia Test,* individuals suspected of total color blindness, see 1927
Southern California Figure-Ground Visual Perception Test, ages 4–10, see 1928
Spache Binocular Reading Test, nonreaders and grades 1 and over, see 1929
★*Speed of Color Discrimination Test,* college, see 1930
Stycar Vision Tests [England], ages 6 months to 7 years, see 1931
Test for Colour-Blindness [Japan], ages 4 and over, see 1932
★*3-D Test of Visualization Skill,* ages 3–8, see 1933
Titmus Vision Tester, ages 3 and over. see 1934
★*Visualization Test of Three Dimensional Orthographic Shape,* high school and college, see 1935

SOCIAL STUDIES

American History—Government—Problems of Democracy: Acorn Achievement Tests, grades 9–16, see 1936
American School Achievement Tests: Social Studies and Science, grades 4–9, see 1937
CLEP General Examinations: Social Sciences and History, 1–2 years of college or equivalent, see 1938
College Board Achievement Test in American History and Social Studies, candidates for college entrance, see 1939
College Board Achievement Test in European History

CONTEMPORARY AFFAIRS

ECONOMICS

GEOGRAPHY

HISTORY

POLITICAL SCIENCE

SOCIOLOGY

SPEECH AND HEARING

HEARING

SPEECH

★*Edinburgh Articulation Test* [Scotland], ages 3–5, see 2070

Examining for Aphasia, adolescents and adults, see 2071

★*Fairview Language Evaluation Scale,* mentally retarded, see 2072

★*Fisher-Logemann Test of Articulation Competence,* preschool and over, see 2073

Forms From Diagnostic Methods in Speech Pathology, children and adults with speech problems, see 2074

*Goldman-Fristoe Test of Articulation, ages 2 and over, see 2075

Halstead Aphasia Test, adults, see 2076

Houston Test for Language Development, ages 6 months to 6 years, see 2077

Language Facility Test, ages 3 and over, see 2078

Language Modalities Test for Aphasia, adults, see 2079

*Minnesota Test for Differential Diagnosis of Aphasia, adults, see 2080

*National Teacher Examinations: Speech-Communication and Theatre, college seniors and teachers, see 2081

*National Teacher Examinations: Speech Pathology, college seniors and teachers, see 2082

Nationwide Speech Examination, grades 4–12, see 2083

★*Northwestern Syntax Screening Test,* ages 3–7, see 2084

Orzeck Aphasia Evaluation, mental and brain damaged patients, see 2085

Photo Articulation Test, ages 3–12, see 2086

*Porch Index of Communicative Ability, adults, see 2087

Predictive Screening Test of Articulation, grade 1, see 2088

*Riley Articulation and Language Test, grades kgn–2, see 2089

Screening Deep Test of Articulation, grades kgn and over, see 2090

*Screening Speech Articulation Test, ages 3.5–8.5, see 2091

*Sklar Aphasia Scale, brain damaged adults, see 2092

Speech Defect Questionnaire, ages 6 and over, see 2093

Speech Diagnostic Chart, grades 1–8, see 2094

Templin-Darley Tests of Articulation, ages 3 and over, see 2095

★*Undergraduate Program Field Tests: Drama and Theatre Test,* college, see 2096

Utah Test of Language Development, ages 1.5 to 14.5, see 2097

*Verbal Language Development Scale, birth to age 15, see 2098

Weidner-Fensch Speech Screening Test, grades 1–3, see 2099

VOCATIONS

★*ACT Assessment of Career Development,* grades 8–11, see 2100

★*ACT Career Planning Program,* entrants to postsecondary educational institutions, see 2101

*Aptitude Inventory, employee applicants, see 2102

★*Career Maturity Inventory,* grades 6–12, see 2103

★*Classification Test Battery* [South Africa], illiterate and semiliterate applicants for unskilled and semi-skilled mining jobs, see 2104

Dailey Vocational Tests, grades 8–12 and adults, see 2105

*ETSA Tests, job applicants, see 2106

*Flanagan Industrial Tests, business and industry, see 2107

Individual Placement Series, high school and adults, see 2108

★*New Mexico Career Education Test Series,* grades 9–12, see 2109

Personal History Index, job applicants, see 2110

Steward Basic Factors Inventory, applicants for sales and office positions, see 2111

Steward Personnel Tests, applicants for sales and office positions, see 2112

TAV Selection System, adults, see 2113

Vocational Planning Inventory, vocational students in grades 8–12 and grade 13 entrants, see 2114

WLW Employment Inventory, adults, see 2115

★*Wide Range Employment Sample Test,* ages 16–35 (normal and handicapped), see 2116

CLERICAL

ACER Short Clerical Test—Form C [Australia], ages 13 and over, see 2117

A.C.E.R. Speed and Accuracy Tests [Australia], ages 13.5 and over, see 2118

APT Dictation Test, stenographers, see 2119

★*Appraisal of Occupational Aptitudes,* high school and adults, see 2120

Clerical Skills Series, clerical workers and applicants, see 2121

Clerical Tests, applicants for clerical positions, see 2122

Clerical Tests, Series N, applicants for clerical positions not involving frequent use of typewriter or verbal skill, see 2123

Clerical Tests, Series V, applicants for typing and stenographic positions, see 2124

Clerical Worker Examination, clerical workers, see 2125

Cross Reference Test, clerical job applicants, see 2126

Curtis Verbal-Clerical Skills Tests, applicants for clerical positions, see 2127

*General Clerical Ability Test, job applicants, see 2128

*General Clerical Test, grades 9–16 and clerical job applicants, see 2129

*Group Test 20 [England], ages 15 and over, see 2130

*Group Tests 61A, 64, and 66A [England], clerical applicants, see 2131

*Hay Clerical Test Battery, applicants for clerical positions, see 2132

L & L Clerical Tests, applicants for office positions, see 2133

McCann Typing Tests, applicants for typing positions, see 2134

Minnesota Clerical Test, grades 8–12 and adults, see 2135

Office Skills Achievement Test, employees, see 2136

*Office Worker Test, office workers, see 2137

O'Rourke Clerical Aptitude Test, Junior Grade, applicants for clerical positions, see 2138

Personnel Institute Clerical Tests, clerical personnel and typists-stenographers-secretaries, see 2139

Personnel Research Institute Clerical Battery, applicants for clerical positions, see 2140

Personnel Research Institute Test of Shorthand Skills, stenographers, see 2141

Purdue Clerical Adaptability Test, applicants for clerical positions, see 2142

RBH Checking Test, applicants for clerical and stenographic positions, see 2143

RBH Classifying Test, business and industry, see 2144

RBH Number Checking Test, business and industry, see 2145

MANUAL DEXTERITY

APT Manual Dexterity Test, automobile and truck mechanics and mechanics' helpers, see **2222**

Crawford Small Parts Dexterity Test, high school and adults, see **2223**

Crissey Dexterity Test, job applicants, see **2224**

Hand-Tool Dexterity Test, adolescents and adults, see **2225**

Manipulative Aptitude Test, grades 9–16 and adults, see **2226**

Minnesota Rate of Manipulation Test, grade 7 to adults, see **2227**

O'Connor Finger Dexterity Test, ages 14 and over, see **2228**

O'Connor Tweezer Dexterity Test, ages 14 and over, see **2229**

★*One Hole Test,* job applicants, see **2230**

Pennsylvania Bi-Manual Worksample, ages 16 and over, see **2231**

Practical Dexterity Board, ages 8 and over, see **2232**

Purdue Hand Precision Test, ages 17 and over, see **2233**

Purdue Pegboard, grades 9–16 and adults, see **2234**

Stromberg Dexterity Test, trade school and adults, see **2235**

Yarn Dexterity Test, textile workers and applicants, see **2236**

MECHANICAL ABILITY

A.C.E.R. Mechanical Comprehension Test [Australia], ages 13.5 and over, see **2237**

A.C.E.R. Mechanical Reasoning Test [Australia], ages 13–9 and over, see **2238**

Bennett Mechanical Comprehension Test, grades 9–12 and adults, see **2239**

Chriswell Structural Dexterity Test, grades 7–9, see **2240**

College Placement Test in Spatial Relations, entering college freshmen, see **2241**

Cox Mechanical and Manual Tests [England], boys ages 10 and over, see **2242**

Curtis Object Completion and Space Form Tests, applicants for mechanical and technical jobs, see **2243**

Detroit Mechanical Aptitudes Examination, grades 7–16, see **2244**

Flags: A Test of Space Thinking, industrial employees, see **2245**

Form Perception Test [South Africa], illiterate and semiliterate adults, see **2246**

Form Relations Group Test [England], ages 14 and over, see **2247**

Group Test 80A [England], ages 15 and over, see **2248**

Group Test 81 [England], ages 14 and over, see **2249**

Group Test 82 [England], ages 14.5 and over, see **2250**

MacQuarrie Test for Mechanical Ability, grades 7 and over, see **2251**

Mechanical Aptitude Test: Acorn National Aptitude Tests, grades 7–16 and adults, see **2252**

Mechanical Comprehension Test [South Africa], male technical apprentices and trainee engineer applicants, see **2253**

Mechanical Information Test [England], ages 15 and over, see **2254**

Mechanical Movements: A Test of Mechanical Comprehension, industrial employees, see **2255**

Mechanical Reasoning: Differential Aptitude Tests, grades 8–12 and adults, see **2256**

Mellenbruch Mechanical Motivation Test, grades 6–16 and adults, see **2257**

Minnesota Spatial Relations Test, ages 11 and over, see **2258**

O'Connor Wiggly Block, ages 16 and over, see **2259**

O'Rourke Mechanical Aptitude Test, grades 7–12 and adults, see **2260**

Perceptual Battery [South Africa], job applicants with at least 10 years of education, see **2261**

Primary Mechanical Ability Tests, applicants for positions requiring mechanical ability, see **2262**

Purdue Mechanical Adaptability Test, males ages 15 and over, see **2263**

RBH Three-Dimensional Space Test, industrial workers in mechanical fields, see **2264**

RBH Two-Dimensional Space Test, business and industry, see **2265**

Revised Minnesota Paper Form Board Test, grades 9–16 and adults, see **2266**

SRA Mechanical Aptitudes, grades 9–12 and adults, see **2267**

Space Relations: Differential Aptitude Tests, grades 8–12 and adults, see **2268**

Spatial Tests EG, 2, and 3 [England], ages 10–13 and 15–17, see **2269**

Spatial Visualization Test: Dailey Vocational Tests, grades 8–12 and adults, see **2270**

Vincent Mechanical Diagrams Test [England], ages 15 and over, see **2271**

Weights and Pulleys: A Test of Intuitive Mechanics, engineering students and industrial employees, see **2272**

MISCELLANEOUS

Alpha Biographical Inventory, grades 9–12, see **2273**

Biographical Index, college and industry, see **2274**

Business Judgment Test, adults, see **2275**

Conference Evaluation, conference participants, see **2276**

Conference Meeting Rating Scale, conference leaders and participants, see **2277**

★*Continuous Letter Checking and Continuous Symbol Checking* [South Africa], ages 12 and over, see **2278–9**

Gullo Workshop and Seminar Evaluation, workshop and seminar participants, see **2280**

Job Attitude Analysis, production and clerical workers, see **2281**

Mathematical and Technical Test [England], ages 11 and over, see **2282**

Minnesota Importance Questionnaire, vocational counselees, see **2283**

★*Minnesota Job Description Questionnaire,* employees and supervisors, see **2284**

Minnesota Satisfaction Questionnaire, business and industry, see **2285**

Per-Flu-Dex Tests, college and industry, see **2286**

RBH Breadth of Information, business and industry, see **2287**

Self-Rating Scale for Leadership Qualifications, adults, see **2288**

Tear Ballot for Industry, employees in industry, see **2289**

Test Orientation Procedure, job applicants and trainees, see **2290**

Tests A/9 and A/10 [South Africa], applicants for technical and apprentice jobs, see **2291**

Whisler Strategy Test, business and industry, see **2292**

Work Information Inventory, employee groups in industry, see **2293**

SELECTION & RATING FORMS

SPECIFIC VOCATIONS

ACCOUNTING

BUSINESS

COMPUTER PROGRAMMING

DENTISTRY

ENGINEERING

LAW

MEDICINE

Colleges of Podiatry Admission Test, grades 14 and over, see 2354

Medical College Admission Test, applicants for admission to member colleges of the Association of American Medical Colleges, see 2355

Medical School Instructor Attitude Inventory, medical school faculty members, see 2356

★*Optometry College Admission Test,* optometry college applicants, see 2357

Veterinary Aptitude Test, veterinary school applicants, see 2358

MISCELLANEOUS

Architectural School Aptitude Test, architectural school applicants, see 2359

Chemical Operators Selection Test, chemical operators and applicants, see 2360

Fire Promotion Tests, prospective firemen promotees, see 2361

Firefighter Test, prospective firemen, see 2362

Fireman Examination, prospective firemen, see 2363

General Municipal Employees Performance (Efficiency) Rating System, municipal employees, see 2364

Journalism Test, high school, see 2365

★*Law Enforcement Perception Questionnaire,* law enforcement personnel, see 2366

Memory and Observation Tests for Policeman, prospective policemen, see 2367

Police Performance Rating System, policemen, see 2368

Police Promotion Tests, prospective policemen promotees, see 2369

Policeman Examination, prospective policemen, see 2370

Policeman Test, policemen and prospective policemen, see 2371

Potter-Nash Aptitude Test for Lumber Inspectors and Other General Personnel Who Handle Lumber, employees in woodworking industries, see 2372

★*Test for Firefighter B-1,* firemen and prospective firemen, see 2373

★*Test for Police Officer A-1,* policemen and prospective policemen, see 2374

Visual Comprehension Test for Detective, prospective police detectives, see 2375

NURSING

Achievement Tests in Nursing, students in schools of registered nursing, see 2376

Achievement Tests in Practical Nursing, practical nursing students, see 2377

Empathy Inventory, nursing instructors, see 2378

Entrance Examination for Schools of Nursing, nursing school applicants, see 2379

Entrance Examination for Schools of Practical Nursing, practical nursing school applicants, see 2380

George Washington University Series Nursing Tests, prospective nurses, see 2381

Luther Hospital Sentence Completions, prospective nursing students, see 2382

NLN Achievement Tests for Schools Preparing Registered Nurses, students in state-approved schools preparing registered nurses, see 2383

NLN Aide Selection Test, applicants for aide positions in hospitals and home health agencies, see 2384

NLN Practical Nursing Achievement Tests, students in state-approved schools of practical nursing, see 2385

NLN Pre-Admission and Classification Examination, practical nursing school entrants, see 2386

NLN Pre-Nursing and Guidance Examination, ap-

plicants for admission to state-approved schools preparing registered nurses, see 2387

Netherne Study Difficulties Battery for Student Nurses [England], student nurses, see 2388

Nurse Attitudes Inventory, prospective nursing students, see 2389

PSB-Aptitude for Practical Nursing Examination, applicants for admission to practical nursing schools, see 2390

RESEARCH

Research Personnel Review Form, research and engineering and scientific firms, see 2391

Supervisor's Evaluation of Research Personnel, research personnel, see 2392

Surveys of Research Administration and Environment, research and engineering and scientific firms, see 2393

Technical Personnel Recruiting Inventory, research and engineering and scientific firms, see 2394

SELLING

Aptitudes Associates Test of Sales Aptitude, applicants for sales positions, see 2395

Combination Inventory, Form 2, prospective debit life insurance salesmen, see 2396

Detroit Retail Selling Inventory, candidates for training in retail selling, see 2397

Evaluation Record, prospective life insurance agency managers, see 2398

Hall Salespower Inventory, salesmen, see 2399

Hanes Sales Selection Inventory, insurance and printing salesmen, see 2400

Information Index, life and health insurance agents, see 2401

LIAMA Inventory of Job Attitudes, life insurance field personnel, see 2402

Personnel Institute Hiring Kit, applicants for sales positions, see 2403

SRA Sales Attitudes Check List, applicants for sales positions, see 2404

Sales Aptitude Test, job applicants, see 2405

Sales Comprehension Test, applicants for sales positions, see 2406

Sales Method Index, life insurance agents, see 2407

Sales Motivation Inventory, applicants for sales positions, see 2408

Sales Sentence Completion Blank, applicants for sales positions, see 2409

Steward Life Insurance Knowledge Test, applicants for life insurance agent or supervisory positions, see 2410

Steward Occupational Objectives Inventory, applicants for supervisory positions in life insurance companies or agencies, see 2411

Steward Personal Background Inventory, applicants for sales positions, see 2412

Test for Ability to Sell: George Washington University Series, grades 7-16 and adults, see 2413

★*Test of Retail Sales Insight,* retail clerks and students, see 2414

SKILLED TRADES

Electrical Sophistication Test, job applicants, see 2415

Fiesenheiser Test of Ability to Read Drawings, trade school and adults, see 2416

Mechanical Familiarity Test, job applicants, see 2417

Mechanical Handyman Test, maintenance workers, see 2418

Mechanical Knowledge Test, job applicants, see 2419

SUPERVISION

TRANSPORTATION

PUBLISHERS DIRECTORY
AND INDEX

This directory and index gives the addresses and tests of all publishers represented in this volume. References are to entry numbers, not to page numbers. Stars indicate test publishers with test catalogs listing 10 or more tests.

★American Guidance Service, Inc., Publishers' Bldg., Circle Pines, Minn. 55014:
Essentials of English Tests, 81
Minnesota High School Achievement Examinations: Language Arts, 90

American Printing House for the Blind, Inc., 1839 Frankfort Ave., Louisville, Ky. 40206:
Sequential Tests of Educational Progress: Writing, 113
Stanford Achievement Test: Spelling and Language Tests, 115

American Testing Co., 6301 S.W. Fifth St., Fort Lauderdale, Fla. 33317:
Language Arts Diagnostic Probes, 89

★Australian Council for Educational Research, P.O. Box 210, Hawthorn, Vic. 3122, Australia:
A.C.E.R. Word Knowledge Test—Adult Form B, 163
Pacific Tests of English Attainment and Skills: Pacific Test Series, 102

Berry Language Tests, 4332 Pine Crest Road, Rockford, Ill. 61107:
Berry-Talbott Language Test, 55

★Bobbs-Merrill Co., Inc. (The), 4300 West 62nd St., Indianapolis, Ind. 46268:
Achievement Examinations for Secondary Schools: English IX–XII, 74
American School Achievement Tests: Language and Spelling, 52
Analytical Survey Test in English Fundamentals, 53
Buckingham Extension of the Ayres Spelling Scale, 146
Lincoln Diagnostic Spelling Tests, 152b
Pressey Diagnostic Tests in English Composition, 104
Traxler High School Spelling Test, 162
Tressler English Minimum Essentials Test, 121
Vocabulary Test for High School Students and College Freshmen, 176

Book Society of Canada Ltd. (The), 4386 Sheppard Ave., East, P.O. Box 200, Agincourt, Ont. M1S 3B6, Canada:
Watson English Usage and Appreciation Test, 123

★Bruce (Martin M.), Ph.D., Publishers, 340 Oxford Road, New Rochelle, N.Y. 10804:
Bruce Vocabulary Inventory, 165

★Bureau of Educational Measurements, Kansas State Teachers College, 1200 Commercial, Emporia, Kan. 66802:
Barrett-Ryan English Test, 54
Hollingsworth-Sanders Junior High School Literature Test, 136
Hoskins-Sanders Literature Test, 137
Hoyum-Sanders English Tests, 85
Kansas Spelling Tests, 150

Sanders-Fletcher Spelling Test, 156
Sanders-Fletcher Vocabulary Test, 172
Walton-Sanders English Test, 122

★Bureau of Educational Research and Service, University of Iowa, Iowa City, Iowa 52240:
Iowa Placement Examinations
English Aptitude, 86
English Training, 87
Iowa Spelling Scales, 149
New Iowa Spelling Scale, 155

★CTB/McGraw-Hill, Del Monte Research Park, Monterey, Calif. 93940:
California Achievement Tests: Language, 61
Comprehensive Tests of Basic Skills: Language, 68
Tests of Basic Experiences: Language, 120

Case Western Reserve University. See Personnel Research Institute.

College Entrance Examination Board, 888 Seventh Ave., New York, N.Y. 10019:
Advanced Placement Examinations: English, 51
CLEP General Examinations: English Composition, 58
CLEP Subject Examinations
American Literature, 127
Analysis and Interpretation of Literature, 128
English Composition, 59
English Literature, 129
Freshman English, 60
College Board Achievement Tests
English Composition, 64
Literature, 130
College Placement Tests
English Composition, 67
Literature, 131

★Cooperative Tests and Services, Educational Testing Service, Princeton, N.J. 08540:
Cooperative English Tests, 69
English Expression, 73
Cooperative Literature Tests, 132
Cooperative Primary Tests: Writing Skills, 70
Look at Literature, 141
Sequential Tests of Educational Progress
English Expression, 112
Writing, 113

Educational Developmental Laboratories, Inc., 1221 Avenue of the Americas, New York, N.Y. 10020:
Word Clue Tests, 180

Educational Publications, Dublin, N.H. 03444:
Test of Active Vocabulary, 174

Educational Records Bureau, Box 619, Princeton, N.J. 08540:
Lincoln Diagnostic Spelling Tests, 152

Educational Stimuli, Telegram Bldg., Superior, Wis. 54880:
Nationwide English Composition Examination, 97
Nationwide English Grammar Examination, 98
Nationwide English Vocabulary Examination, 169
Nationwide Spelling Examination, 154

★Educational Testing Service, Princeton, N.J. 08540 (*See also* College Entrance Examination Board, Cooperative Tests and Services, and Educational Records Bureau.):
Graduate Record Examinations Advanced Literature in English Test, 135
National Teacher Examinations: English Language and Literature, 96
Teacher Education Examination Program: English Language and Literature, 117
Undergraduate Program Field Tests: Literature Tests, 144

Gibson (Robert) & Sons, Glasgow, Ltd., 17 Fitzroy Place, Glasgow G37SF, Scotland:
Cotswold Junior English Ability Test, 71
Cotswold Measurement of Ability: English, 72
Kelvin Measurement of Spelling Ability, 151

★Ginn & Co. Ltd., Elsinore House, Buckingham St., Aylesbury, Bucks, England:
English Progress Tests, 75
English Test FG, 76
English Tests (Adv.), 79
English Tests 14–20 and 22, 80
Senior English Test, 111

Grune & Stratton, Inc., 111 Fifth Ave., New York, N.Y. 10003:
Picture Story Language Test, 103

★Guidance Centre, University of Toronto, 1000 Yonge St., Toronto, Ont. M4W 2K8, Canada:
Canadian Achievement Test in English, 62
Canadian English Achievement Test, 63

★Harcourt Brace Jovanovich, Inc., 757 Third Ave., New York, N.Y. 10017:
Stanford Achievement Test: High School English and Spelling Tests, 114
Stanford Achievement Test: Spelling and Language Tests, 115

★Houghton Mifflin Co., 110 Tremont St., Boston, Mass. 02107:
College English Placement Test, 65
Dailey Vocational Tests: Business English Test, 57
Language Arts Tests: Content Evaluation Series, 91
New Purdue Placement Test in English, 99
Purdue High School English Test, 105
Tests of Academic Progress
  Composition, 119
  Literature, 143

Human Engineering Laboratory Inc., 347 Beacon St., Boston, Mass. 02116:
Johnson O'Connor English Vocabulary Worksamples, 167
Johnson O'Connor Vocabulary Tests, 168

★Human Sciences Research Council, Private Bag 41, Pretoria, Republic of South Africa:
N.B. Spelling Tests, 153

Kansas State Teachers College. *See* Bureau of Educational Measurements.

McCartney (William A.), P.O. Box 507, Kaneohe, Hawaii 96744:
Grammar, Usage, and Structure Test and Vocabulary Test, 84

McGraw-Hill Book Co., Inc., 1221 Avenue of the Americas, New York, N.Y. 10020:
McGraw-Hill Basic Skills System
  Spelling Test, 160
  Vocabulary Test, 177
  Writing Test, 125

Manasayan, 32 Netaji Subhash Marg, Delhi 110006, India:
Test of English Usage, 118

★Monitor, P.O. Box 2337, Hollywood, Calif. 90028:
Word Understanding, 182

Nelson (Thomas) & Sons Ltd., Lincoln Way, Windmill Road, Sunbury-on-Thames, Middlesex TW16 7HP, England:
Bristol Achievement Tests: English Language, 56

Oliver & Boyd, Croythorn House, 23 Ravelston Terrace, Edinburgh EH4 3TJ, Scotland:
Schonell Diagnostic English Tests, 110

O'Rourke Publications, P.O. Box 1118, Lake Alfred, Fla. 33850:
Survey Test of Vocabulary, 173
Survey Tests of English Usage, 116

Perfection Form Co. (The), 214 West Eighth St., Logan, Iowa 51546:
American Literature Anthology Tests, 126
English Literature Anthology Tests, 133
Grammar and Usage Test Series, 83
Literature Tests/Objective, 140
Objective Tests in Constructive English, 100
Objective Tests in Punctuation, 101
Poetry Test/Objective, 142
World Literature Anthology Tests, 145

Personnel Research Institute, Case Western Reserve University, 1695 Magnolia Drive, Cleveland, Ohio 44106:
Spelling Test for Clerical Workers, 159

Peterson (Shailer), University of Texas Dental School at San Antonio, 7703 Floyd Curl Drive, San Antonio, Tex. 78284:
Word Dexterity Test, 181

★Psychological Corporation (The), 304 East 45th St., New York, N.Y. 10017:
Differential Aptitude Tests
  Language Usage, 93
  Spelling, 157
Wide Range Vocabulary Test, 179

★Psychometric Affiliates, Box 3167, Munster, Ind. 46321:
American Literacy Test, 164
Functional Grammar Test, 82
National Achievement Tests
  College English Test, 66
  English Test, 78
  English Test: Municipal Tests, 77
  Literature Test, 139
  Spelling Test, 161
  Vocabulary Test, 178

Reading Laboratory and Clinic, University of Florida, Gainesville, Fla. 32601:
Group Diagnostic Spelling Test, 148
Snelling Errors Test, 158

★Richardson, Bellows, Henry & Co., Inc., 1140 Connecticut Ave. N.W., Washington, D.C. 20036:
Language Perception Test, 92
RBH Spelling Test and Word Meaning Test, 106
RBH Test of Language Skills, 107
RBH Vocabulary Test, 171

★Science Research Associates, Inc., 259 East Erie St., Chicago, Ill. 60611:
Iowa Tests of Educational Development
  Ability to Interpret Literary Materials, 138
  Correctness and Appropriateness of Expression, 88
  General Vocabulary, 166
SRA Achievement Series: Language Arts, 108
Writing Skills Test, 124

Scott, Foresman & Co., 1900 East Lake Ave., Glenview, Ill. 60025:
Vocabulary Survey Test, 175

Service for Admission to College and University, 151 Slater St., Ottawa 4, Ont., Canada:
Canadian English Language Achievement Test, 63A

★Sheridan Psychological Services, Inc., P.O. Box 6101, Orange, Calif. 92667:
Correct Spelling, 147

Silliman (Henrietta), 404 North Washington, Toulon, Ill. 61483:
English Tests for Outside Reading, 134

★University Book Store, 360 State St., West Lafayette, Ind. 47906:
Purdue Industrial Supervisors Word-Meaning Test, 170

University of Iowa. *See* Bureau of Educational Research and Service.

★University of London Press Ltd., St. Paul's House, Warwick Lane, London EC4P 4AH, England:
Moray House English Tests, 95

University of Toronto. *See* Guidance Centre.

INDEX OF TITLES

This index lists (*a*) English tests in print as of February 1, 1974, and (*b*) English tests out of print, status unknown, or reclassified since last listed in the English section of a *Mental Measurements Yearbook* (MMY). Citations are to test entries, not to pages. Numbers without colons refer to in print tests listed in this volume; numbers with colons refer to tests out of print, status unknown, or reclassified. Unless preceded by the word *"consult,"* all numbers containing colons refer to tests in this volume. The guide numbers next to the outside margins in the running heads of the reprint sections should be used to locate a particular test. The first reprint section, from *Tests in Print II* (TIP II), has guide numbers ranging from 51 to 182; the second reprint section, from the 1st MMY, 1:957 to 1:1162; the third reprint section, from the 2nd MMY, 2:1267 to 2:1322; etc. To obtain the latest information on a test no longer classified with English tests, the reader must consult either TIP II (if the test is in print) or an MMY (if the test is out of print). For example, "Weidner-Fensch Speech Screening Test, 5:221; reclassified, *consult* T2:2099" indicates that this test, 221 in the 5th MMY, has since been reclassified and for the latest information, test 2099 in TIP II must be consulted. Superseded titles are listed with cross references to the current title. Tests which are part of a series are listed under their individual titles and also their series titles.

INDEX OF NAMES

This analytical index indicates whether a citation refers to authorship of a test, test review, excerpted review, or a reference for a specific test. Citations are to test numbers, not to page numbers. In the reprint sections, the numbers of the first and last tests on facing pages are given in the running heads next to the outside margins. Numbers without colons refer to in print tests presented in the section reprinted from TIP II. Interpret abbreviations and numbers for in print tests as follows: *"test, 55"* indicates authorship of test 55; *"rev, 91,"* authorship of a review of test 91; *"exc, 81,"* authorship of an excerpted review of test 81; and *"ref, 157,"* authorship of one or more references for test 157. (The Cumulative Name Index for that test must be consulted to locate the references.) Numbers with colons (e.g., 6:330, test 330 in the 6th MMY) refer to out of print tests included in the material reprinted from the MMY's, unless otherwise indicated. In the reprint sections, the yearbook digit preceding the colon is given in the running head only.

ABBOTT, A.: *test, 2:1270*
Abt, L. E.: *ref, 4:216(11)*
Achard, F. H.: *ref, 167*
Adams, M.: *ref, 87*
Adams, S.: *ref, 99*
Adams, W. M.: *ref, 87*
Afflerbach, J. G.: *rev, 5:232; test, 5:179, 6:336*
Akamine, T.: *ref, 69*
Alexander, W. P.: *test, 2:1279*
Allen, D. A.: *exc, 113*
Almack, J. C.: *rev, 1:1159, 2:1310, 2:1315*
Aloia, A. D.: *ref, 69*
Alper, T. G.: *test, 5:232; ref, 5:232(1)*
Alusow, F. T.: *ref, 3:150(4)*
Ammons, C. H.: *exc, 103*
Anastasiow, N.: *rev, 103*
Anderhalter, O. F.: *test, 6:278*
Anderson, A. W.: *ref, 69*
Anderson, C. C.: *ref, 6:291(2)*
Anderson, I. H.: *ref, 3:163(3)*
Anderson, K. E.: *ref, 6:255(12–3, 15)*
Anderson, M. R.: *ref, 54*
Anderson, R. E.: *ref, 69*
Anderson, R. P.: *ref, 103*
Anderson, S. B.: *ref, 69*
Anderson, W. A.: *test, 2:1315*
Andrew, D. C.: *ref, 69*
Angers, W. P.: *ref, 69*
Annen, I.: *ref, 3:161(4)*
Armstrong, C.: *test, 4:168*
Armstrong, H. G.: *ref, 95*
Arsenian, S.: *ref, 69*
Artley, A. S.: *ref, 69*
Ashbaugh, E. J.: *test, 149; ref, 149, 2:1271(3)*
Asher, E. J.: *test, 3:132; ref, 2:1284(1)*
Atwell, C. R.: *test, 179; ref, 179*
Australian Council for Educational

Research: *test, 2:1309, 5:173, 5:222, 6:282*
Averill, L. A.: *ref, 69*
Ayer, F. C.: *test, 6:317; ref, 4:198(1)*
Ayers, J. D.: *rev, 63*

BABBOTT, E. F.: *ref, 69, 152*
Badal, A. W.: *ref, 113*
Bailey, R. B.: *ref, 69*
Baker, P. C.: *ref, 99*
Ballantyne, R. H.: *ref, 69*
Ballenger, H. L.: *test, 4:165*
Bannochie, M. N.: *ref, 103*
Barnard, B.: *test, 75*
Barnes, W.: *rev, 1:969A*
Barnett, T. M.: *ref, 69*
Barnette, W. L.: *ref, 87*
Barnhart, E. L.: *ref, 6:255(15)*
Barrett, D. M.: *ref, 69*
Barrett, E. R.: *test, 54, 3:139, 5:176*
Barrett, R. S.: *ref, 69*
Barth, C. A.: *ref, 64*
Bashaw, W. L.: *ref, 69*
Bates, C. O.: *ref, 105*
Bechtel, J.: *test, 3:127*
Beck, B. S.: *test, 6:283*
Beck, R. L.: *rev, 2:1272, 2:1278; test, 2:1293, 6:283; ref, 2:1271(4–5), 2:1293(1–3)*
Beers, F. S.: *test, 1:970, 4:213, 6:255*
Belai, L.: *ref, 69*
Bell, D. B.: *ref, 103*
Bell, J. C.: *ref, 104*
Belman, H. S.: *ref, 99*
Benge, E. J.: *test, 6:340*
Bennett, G. K.: *test, 93, 157; ref, 3:159(2)*
Benson, D.: *ref, 170*
Berdie, R. F.: *ref, 69*
Berg, I. A.: *ref, 69*
Berg, J. C.: *test, 1:964*

Bergeron, W. L.: *ref, 69*
Bernard, H. W.: *ref, 3:163(5)*
Berner, W.: *ref, 69*
Berry, C. A.: *ref, 69*
Berry, M. F.: *test, 55*
Bessent, E. W.: *ref, 69*
Bixler, H. H.: *rev, 159, 3:158, 3:162, 3:164, 4:198, 4:204; test, 2:1312, 2:1313.1, 4:206; ref, 2:1312(2)*
Black, D. B.: *ref, 64, 69, 6:291(1)*
Black, H.: *rev, 113*
Black, H. P.: *ref, 105*
Blau, H.: *ref, 6:289(1)*
Bobbitt, J. M.: *ref, 64*
Boe, E. E.: *ref, 69*
Bollenbacher, J.: *exc, 176*
Bolton, E. B.: *ref, 69*
Bonk, E. C.: *ref, 69*
Bonner, L. W.: *ref, 99, 105*
Book-A-Day Series: *test, 4:189*
Borgen, F. H.: *rev, 165, 171*
Bou, I. R.: *ref, 4:176(1)*
Bourne, R. K.: *ref, 93*
Bowers, E. V.: *test, 104*
Bowman, A. E.: *ref, 69*
Bowman, H. A.: *test, 7:200*
Boyd, J. D.: *ref, 69*
Bradford, J. M.: *test, 5:179*
Bretnall, D.: *ref, 69*
Brimer, A.: *test, 56*
Brimer, M. A.: *rev, 52, 71–2, 95, 111; test, 75*
Broom, M. E.: *rev, 2:1310*
Brothers, W. L.: *ref, 69*
Brown, F. G.: *ref, 69*
Brown, J. I.: *test, 65; ref, 99*
Brown, L.: *ref, 69*
Brown, T. O.: *ref, 69*
Bruce, M. M.: *test, 165*
Bryan, A. I.: *test, 2:1308*
Bryan, M. M.: *rev, 108, 6:280; test, 5:179, 6:336*
Buchan, J.: *ref, 95*

Sopchak, A. L.: *ref,* 61
Southworth, J. A.: *ref,* 69
Space, M. N.: *ref,* 69
Spache, G.: *rev,* 152, 4:200; *test,* 158
Spache, G. D.: *rev,* 6:274
Spahr, B. J. W.: *ref,* 99
Spaulding, G.: *rev,* 5:201; *test,* 2:1276, 2:1286, 5:179, 6:255; *ref,* 69
Speer, R. K.: *rev,* 2:1295; *test,* 77–8, 139, 161, 178, 4:191
Spitzer, H. F.: *test,* 4:150
Spoerl, D. T.: *ref,* 99
Spohrer, M. A.: *ref,* 69
Spolsky, B.: *rev,* 62–3
Stacey, C. L.: *ref,* 4:216(15)
Stack, S. E.: *ref,* 69
Stahmann, R. F.: *ref,* 69
Stake, R. E.: *rev,* 6:342
Stallings, W. M.: *ref,* 69
Stalnaker, J. M.: *rev,* 73, 113, 1:961, 2:1293, 4:187, 5:206, 6:255; *ref,* 86–7
Staples, J. D.: *ref,* 159
Stapleton, M. R.: *ref,* 69
Stapp, H. I.: *test,* 5:195
Stead, W. H.: *ref,* 173
Steeves, H. R.: *test,* 2:1270
Stegman, E. J.: *ref,* 54
Steinberg, D.: *ref,* 113
Stephans, P.: *ref,* 69
Stinson, P. J.: *ref,* 69
Stoddard, G. D.: *test,* 86–7; *ref,* 86–7
Stoke, S. M.: *ref,* 64
Stolper, B. J. R.: *test,* 2:1294
Stone, D. B.: *ref,* 69
Stovall, E. L.: *test,* 4:190
Strabel, E.: *ref,* 69
Stratton, C.: *test,* 2:1269
Strickland, R.: *rev,* 5:196, 5:201
Stucky, M. O.: *ref,* 6:255(12–3)
Stuit, D. B.: *test,* 87; *ref,* 87, 2:1271(8)
Super, D. E.: *ref,* 4:216(13)
Swanson, E. O.: *ref,* 69
Sweeney, M. R.: *ref,* 69
Swineford, F.: *ref,* 64
Symonds, P. M.: *ref,* 146

TALBOTT, R.: *test,* 55
Tate, D. J.: *test,* 3:164
Taulbee, G. C.: *ref,* 69, 6:255(16)
Taylor, D.: *test,* 4:156
Taylor, J.: *ref,* 69
Taylor, S. E.: *test,* 180
Teachers College Personnel Association: *test,* 2:1280
Tenney, E. A.: *rev,* 2:1299
Tenopyr, M. L.: *ref,* 113
Terman, L. M.: *test,* 4:174, 4:195
Thibault, P.: *test,* 5:179
Thomas, C. A.: *rev,* 76, 5:176; *ref,* 51
Thomas, C. S.: *rev,* 1:961, 1:971, 2:1267, 2:1293; *test,* 2:1271
Thomas, M.: *test,* 124
Thompson, A.: *rev,* 4:199, 4:205
Thompson, C. E.: *ref,* 3:166(8)
Thompson, J. H.: *rev,* 1:961, 1:970–1
Thompson, W. R.: *test,* 4:177

Thorndike, E. L.: *ref,* 2:1271(1)
Thorndike, R. L.: *test,* 6:342; *ref,* 6:342(1–3)
Thorpe, L. P.: *test,* 108
Thouless, R. H.: *rev,* 110, 3:124
Thurstone, L. L.: *ref,* 69
Tidyman, W. F.: *ref,* 149
Tiegs, E. W.: *test,* 61, 6:280
Tiffin, J.: *test,* 170
Topetzes, N. J.: *ref,* 69, 86
Torgerson, T. L.: *test,* 3:138
Torres, L.: *ref,* 69
Towley, C.: *test,* 74
Townsend, A.: *ref,* 152
Trabue, M. R.: *ref,* 146
Travers, R. M. W.: *ref,* 69
Traxler, A.: *ref,* 69
Traxler, A. E.: *rev,* 2:1321; *test,* 162, 176; *ref,* 69, 152, 176, 2:1299(2)
Trela, T. M.: *ref,* 138
Tressler, J. C.: *test,* 121
Triggs, F. O.: *ref,* 152
Troy, E. M.: *ref,* 69
Troyer, M. E.: *test,* 3:125
Tucker, H.: *ref,* 69
Turner, D.: *ref,* 61

UHRBROCK, R. S.: *ref,* 86–7, 167, 5:234(10)
Ullman, B. L.: *test,* 4:197
United States Armed Forces Institute, Examinations Staff: *test,* 3:129–30, 5:181, 5:216
U.S. Province Brothers of Holy Cross: *test,* 6:296
University of Edinburgh, Godfrey Thomson Unit: *test,* 95
University of Toronto, Ontario College of Education, Department of Educational Research: *test,* 6:337
University of Wisconsin, School of Education, Bureau of Guidance and Records: *test,* 3:138
Unwin, S. M.: *test,* 75

VALENTINE, J. A.: *ref,* 6:289(2)
Van Derslice, J. F.: *ref,* 69
Van Wagenen, M. J.: *test,* 2:1295
Varnado, G. R.: *ref,* 99
Vaughan, A. T.: *ref,* 69
Vecchione, N.: *ref,* 152
Vick, M. C.: *ref,* 69
Victor, G. C.: *ref,* 3:116(2)
Vineyard, E. E.: *ref,* 69, 157
Vordenberg, W.: *ref,* 69
Votaw, D. F.: *ref,* 69

WAGNER, M. E.: *ref,* 69
Waldman, J.: *ref,* 152
Walker, B.: *test,* 69, 73
Walker, D. A.: *rev,* 111
Wallace, W. L.: *ref,* 69
Walston, R. L.: *test,* 3:141
Walter, R. W.: *test,* 5:234
Walters, N. R.: *ref,* 69
Walton, C. E.: *test,* 122
Wantman, M. J.: *rev,* 99
Waples, D.: *test,* 2:1294
War Manpower Commission, Division of Occupational Analysis, Staff: *ref,* 173

Ward, G.: *ref,* 69
Warner, S. B.: *test,* 89
Watson, G. M.: *test,* 123
Watts, A. F.: *test,* 75, 4:215; *ref,* 4:215(1)
Weaver, L. J.: *ref,* 64
Webb, S. C.: *ref,* 64, 69
Weisgerber, C. A.: *ref,* 138
Welch, W. B.: *ref,* 69
Wells, F. L.: *test,* 179; *ref,* 179
Welsh, M. L.: *ref,* 69
Wenberg, B. G.: *ref,* 69
Wepman, J. M.: *test,* 175; *exc,* 103
Werner, O. H.: *ref,* 104
Wershow, I. R.: *ref,* 69
Wesman, A. G.: *test,* 93, 157
Whaley, E. R.: *ref,* 69
Wharton, L. P.: *test,* 2:1321
Wheeler, D. K.: *rev,* 5:222
Wheeler, F.: *ref,* 113
White, V.: *ref,* 3:130(1–4)
Whitford, T. M.: *test,* 163
Wiggins, N. W.: *ref,* 69
Wilke, W. H.: *test,* 2:1308
Wilkins, T. B.: *ref,* 69
Williams, A. J.: *test,* 2:1310
Williams, J. E.: *ref,* 69
Williams, M. T.: *test,* 150
Williams, R. A.: *ref,* 69
Williams, V.: *ref,* 69
Williamson, E. G.: *ref,* 2:1271(9)
Willing, M. H.: *test,* 2:1271; *ref,* 104, 115, 4:179(1)
Willis, C. G.: *ref,* 7:201(1)
Willis, M.: *test,* 4:184, 4:213, 5:179
Wilmut, F. S.: *ref,* 95
Wilson, A. V.: *ref,* 69, 113
Wilson, E. C.: *test,* 1:969A
Wilson, G. M.: *rev,* 2:1315, 3:153, 3:157
Winship, G. P.: *rev,* 176–7, 6:330–1
Winston, W. E.: *ref,* 61
Wittenborn, J. R.: *ref,* 86–7
Wolins, L.: *ref,* 69
Wood, B. D.: *test,* 2:1270
Wood, E. R.: *test,* 54
Wood, S.: *ref,* 54, 61, 69, 81, 93, 105, 108, 113
Wood, W. R.: *test,* 1:975
Woody, C.: *rev,* 173, 178, 3:159
Worthen, B. R.: *rev,* 91
Wright, M. M.: *test,* 2:1307
Wrightstone, J. W.: *rev,* 2:1306; *exc,* 2:1291, 2:1293
Wrinn, M. J. J.: *test,* 4:190
Wyeth, E. R.: *ref,* 69
Wykoff, G. S.: *test,* 99, 105, 3:143, 4:169

YARBOROUGH, O. J.: *ref,* 3:146(1)
Yee, A. H.: *rev,* 160
Young, R. V.: *test,* 52, 3:117

ZABEL, R. L.: *ref,* 69
Zahner, L. C.: *rev,* 113, 2:1270–1, 3:130, 3:146, 5:206
Zektick, I. N.: *ref,* 167
Zimmerer, A. M.: *ref,* 69
Zimmerman, W. G.: *ref,* 69
Zimmerman, W. S.: *ref,* 113
Zwilling, V. T.: *ref,* 69

ENGLISH
SCANNING INDEX

This scanning index is an expanded table of contents listing all tests in this volume. Foreign tests are identified by listing the country of origin in brackets immediately after the title. The population for which a test is intended is presented to facilitate the search for tests for use with a particular group. Stars indicate tests not previously listed in a *Mental Measurements Yearbook*; asterisks indicate tests revised or supplemented since last listed. Numbers refer to test entries, not to pages.

ENGLISH

LITERATURE

SPELLING

VOCABULARY